Strategic Management Theory

An Integrated Approach

EIGHTH EDITION

Charles W. L. Hill
UNIVERSITY OF WASHINGTON

Gareth R. Jones
TEXAS A&M UNIVERSITY

Houghton Mifflin Company   Boston   New York

For my children, Elizabeth, Charlotte, and Michelle
Charles W. L. Hill

For Nicholas and Julia and Morgan and Nia
Gareth R. Jones

Executive Publisher: George Hoffman
Executive Editor: Lisé Johnson
Senior Marketing Manager: Nicole Hamm
Development Editor: Suzanna Smith
Senior Project Editor: Carol Merrigan
Art and Design Manager: Jill Haber
Cover Design Director: Tony Saizon
Senior Photo Editor: Jennifer Meyer Dare
Senior Composition Buyer: Chuck Dutton
New Title Project Manager: James Lonergan
Editorial Assistant: Kathryn White
Marketing Assistant: Tom DiGiano

Cover image: Jason Hawkes, www.jasonhawkes.com

Printed in the U.S.A.

Library of Congress Control Number: 2007934815

Instructor's examination copy:
ISBN-10: 0-547-00490-7
ISBN-13: 978-0-547-00490-7

For orders, use student text ISBNs:
ISBN-10: 0-618-89476-4
ISBN-13: 978-0-618-89476-5

2 3 4 5 6 7 8 9–DOW–11 10 09 08

Contents

2   External Analysis: The Identification of Opportunities and Threats   41

Part 2   The Nature of Competitive Advantage

3   Internal Analysis: Distinctive Competencies, Competitive Advantage, and Profitability   75

4   Building Competitive Advantage Through Functional-Level Strategy   109

Part 3   Strategies

5   Building Competitive Advantage Through Business-Level Strategy   149

6   Business-Level Strategy and the Industry Environment   186

7 Strategy and Technology 228

10 Corporate-Level Strategy: Formulating and Implementing Related and Unrelated Diversification 331

Part 4   Implementing Strategy

11   Corporate Performance, Governance, and Business Ethics   366

12   Implementing Strategy in Companies That Compete in a Single Industry   401

13 Implementing Strategy in Companies That Compete Across Industries and Countries

442

xii Contents

Appendix: Analyzing a Case Study and Writing a Case Study Analysis   C1

Preface

Since the seventh edition was published, this book has strengthened its position as the most widely used strategic management textbook on the market. This tells us that we continue to meet the expectations of existing users and attract many new users to our book. It is clear that most strategy instructors share with us a concern for currency in the text and its examples to ensure that cutting-edge issues and new developments in strategic management are continually addressed.

Just as in the last edition, our objective in writing the eighth edition has been to maintain all that was good about prior editions, while refining our approach to discussing established strategic management issues and adding new material to the text to present a more complete, clear, and current account of strategic management as we move steadily into the twenty-first century. We believe that the result is a book that is more closely aligned with the needs of today's professors and students and with the realities of competition in the new global environment.

Comprehensive and Up-to-Date Coverage

We have updated many of the features running throughout the chapters, including all new Opening Cases and Running Cases. For the Running Cases, Dell has replaced Wal-Mart as the focus company. In this edition, we have made no changes to the number or sequencing of our chapters. However, we have made many significant changes inside each chapter to refine and update our presentation of strategic management. Continuing real-world changes in strategic management practices such as the increased use of cost reduction strategies like global outsourcing, ethical issues, and lean production, and a continued emphasis on the business model as the driver of differentiation and competitive advantage, have led to many changes in our approach. To emphasize the importance of ethical decision making in strategic management, we have included a new feature in the end matter of every chapter that introduces concept-specific ethical dilemmas that could develop in a real-world business setting.

Throughout the revision process, we have been careful to preserve the *balanced and integrated* nature of our account of strategic management. As we have continued to add new material, we have also shortened or deleted coverage of out-of-date or less important models and concepts to help students identify and focus on the core concepts and issues in the field. We have also paid close attention to retaining the book's readability.

Practicing Strategic Management: An Interactive Approach

We have received a lot of positive feedback about the usefulness of the end-of-chapter exercises and assignments in the Practicing Strategic Management sections in our book. They offer a wide range of hands-on learning experiences for students. Following the Chapter Summary and Discussion Questions, each chapter contains the following exercises and assignments:

- *Small Group Exercise.* This short (20-minute) experiential exercise asks students to divide into groups and discuss a scenario concerning some aspect of strategic management. For example, the scenario in Chapter 11 asks students to identify the stakeholders of their educational institution and evaluate how stakeholders' claims are being and should be met.

- *Ethics Exercise.* The ethics exercise has replaced the Exploring the Web feature (now online). This feature has been developed to highlight the importance of ethical decision making in today's business environment. With today's current examples of poor decision making (as seen in Enron, Tyco, and WorldCom, to name a few), we hope to equip students with the tools they need to be strong ethical leaders.

- *Article File.* As in the last edition, this exercise requires students to search business magazines to identify a company that is facing a particular strategic management problem. For instance, students are asked to locate and research a company pursuing a low-cost or a differentiation strategy, and to describe this company's strategy, its advantages and disadvantages, and the core competencies required to pursue it. Students' presentations of their findings lead to lively class discussions.

- *Strategic Management Project.* In small groups, students choose a company to study for the whole semester and then analyze the company using the series of questions provided at the end of every chapter. For example, students might select Ford Motor Co. and, using the series of chapter questions, collect information on Ford's top managers, mission, ethical position, domestic and global strategy and structure, and so on. Students write a case study of their company and present it to the class at the end of the semester. In the past, we also had students present one or more of the cases in the book early in the semester, but now in our classes, we treat the students' own projects as the major class assignment and their case presentations as the climax of the semester's learning experience.

- *Closing Case Study.* A short closing case provides an opportunity for a short class discussion of a chapter-related theme.

In creating these exercises, it is not our intention to suggest that they should *all* be used for *every* chapter. For example, over a semester, an instructor might combine a group Strategic Management Project with five to six Article File assignments and five to six Exploring the Web exercises, while doing eight to ten Small Group Exercises in class.

We have found that our interactive approach to teaching strategic management appeals to students. It also greatly improves the quality of their learning experience. Our approach is more fully discussed in the *Instructor's Resource Manual*.

Teaching and Learning Aids

Taken together, the teaching and learning features of Strategic Management provide a package that is unsurpassed in its coverage and that supports the integrated approach that we have taken throughout the book.

For the Instructor

- The **Instructor's Resource Manual: Theory** has been completely revised. For each chapter, we provide a clearly focused synopsis, a list of teaching objectives, a comprehensive lecture outline, suggested answers to discussion questions, and comments on the end-of-chapter activities. Each chapter-opening case, Strategy in Action boxed feature, and chapter-closing case has a synopsis and a corresponding teaching note to help guide class discussion.

- The **HMTesting CD** has been revised and offers a set of comprehensive true/false and multiple-choice questions, and new essay questions for each chapter in the book. The mix of questions has been adjusted to provide fewer fact-based or simple memorization items and to provide more items that rely on synthesis or application. Also, more items now reflect real or hypothetical situations in organizations. Every question is keyed to the teaching objectives in the *Instructor's Resource Manual* and includes an answer and page reference to the textbook.

- The **video program** highlights many issues of interest and can be used to spark class discussion. It offers a compilation of footage from the Videos for Humanities series.

- An extensive **website** contains many features to aid instructors, including downloadable files for the text and case materials from the *Instructor's Resource Manuals*, the downloadable Premium and Basic PowerPoint slides, the Video Guide, and sample syllabi. Additional materials on the student website may also be of use to instructors.

- **Eduspace®**, powered by Blackboard®, is a course management tool that includes chapter outlines, chapter summaries, audio chapter summaries and quizzes, all questions from the textbook with suggested answers, Debate Issues, ACE self-test questions, auto-graded quizzes, Premium and Basic PowerPoint slides, Classroom Response System content, links to content on the websites, video activities, and test pools. A Course Materials Guide is available to help instructor organization.

- **Blackboard®/Web CT®** includes course material, chapter outlines, chapter summaries, audio chapter summaries and quizzes, all questions from the textbook with suggested answers, Premium and Basic PowerPoint slides, Classroom Response System content, links to content on the websites, video activities, and Test Bank content.

For the Student

- The student **website** includes chapter overviews, Internet exercises, ACE self-tests, audio summaries and quizzes, case discussion questions to help guide student case analysis, glossaries, flashcards for studying the key terms, a section with guidelines on how to do case study analysis, and much more.

Acknowledgments

This book is the product of far more than two authors. We are grateful to Lisé Johnson, our sponsor; Suzanna Smith, our editor; and Nicole Hamm, our marketing manager, for their help in promoting and developing the book and for providing us with timely feedback and information from professors and reviewers, which allowed us to shape the book to meet the needs of its intended market. We are also grateful to Carol Merrigan and Kristen Truncellito, project editors, for their adept handling of production. We are also grateful to the case authors for allowing us to use their materials. We also want to thank the departments of management at the University of Washington and Texas A&M University for providing the setting and atmosphere in which the book could be written, and the students of these universities who reacted to and provided input for many of our ideas. In addition, the following reviewers of this and earlier editions gave us valuable suggestions for improving the manuscript from its original version to its current form:

Ken Armstrong, *Anderson University*
Richard Babcock, *University of San Francisco*
Kunal Banerji, *West Virginia University*
Kevin Banning, *Auburn University – Montgomery*
Glenn Bassett, *University of Bridgeport*
Thomas H. Berliner, *The University of Texas at Dallas*
Bonnie Bollinger, *Ivy Technical Community College*
Richard G. Brandenburg, *University of Vermont*
Steven Braund, *University of Hull*
Philip Bromiley, *University of Minnesota*
Geoffrey Brooks, *Western Oregon State College*
Amanda Budde, *University of Hawaii*
Lowell Busenitz, *University of Houston*
Charles J. Capps III, *Sam Houston State University*
Don Caruth, *Texas A&M Commerce*
Gene R. Conaster, *Golden State University*
Steven W. Congden, *University of Hartford*
Catherine M. Daily, *Ohio State University*
Robert DeFillippi, *Suffolk University Sawyer School of Management*
Helen Deresky, *SUNY – Plattsburgh*
Gerald E. Evans, *The University of Montana*
John Fahy, *Trinity College, Dublin*
Patricia Feltes, *Southwest Missouri State University*
Bruce Fern, *New York University*
Mark Fiegener, *Oregon State University*
Chuck Foley, *Columbus State Community College*
Isaac Fox, *Washington State University*
Craig Galbraith, *University of North Carolina at Wilmington*
Scott R. Gallagher, *Rutgers University*
Eliezer Geisler, *Northeastern Illinois University*
Gretchen Gemeinhardt, *University of Houston*
Lynn Godkin, *Lamar University*
Sanjay Goel, *University of Minnesota – Duluth*
Robert L. Goldberg, *Northeastern University*
James Grinnell, *Merrimack College*
Russ Hagberg, *Northern Illinois University*
Allen Harmon, *University of Minnesota – Duluth*
David Hoopes, *California State University – Dominguez Hills*
Todd Hostager, *University of Wisconsin – Eau Claire*
Graham L. Hubbard, *University of Minnesota*
Tammy G. Hunt, *University of North Carolina at Wilmington*
James Gaius Ibe, *Morris College*
W. Grahm Irwin, *Miami University*
Homer Johnson, *Loyola University – Chicago*
Jonathan L. Johnson, *University of Arkansas – Walton College of Business Administration*
Marios Katsioloudes, *St. Joseph's University*

Robert Keating, *University of North Carolina at Wilmington*
Geoffrey King, *California State University – Fullerton*
John Kraft, *University of Florida*
Rico Lam, *University of Oregon*
Robert J. Litschert, *Virginia Polytechnic Institute and State University*
Franz T. Lohrke, *Louisiana State University*
Paul Mallette, *Colorado State University*
Daniel Marrone, *SUNY Farmingdale*
Lance A. Masters, *California State University – San Bernardino*
Robert N. McGrath, *Embry-Riddle Aeronautical University*
Charles Mercer, *Drury College*
Van Miller, *University of Dayton*
Tom Morris, *University of San Diego*
Joanna Mulholland, *West Chester University of Pennsylvania*
John Nebeck, *Viterbo University*
Richard Neubert, *University of Tennessee – Knoxville*
Francine Newth, *Providence College*
Don Okhomina, *Fayetteville State University*
Phaedon P. Papadopoulos, *Houston Baptist University*
John Pappalardo, *Keene State College*
Paul R. Reed, *Sam Houston State University*
Rhonda K. Reger, *Arizona State University*
Malika Richards, *Indiana University*
Simon Rodan, *San Jose State*
Stuart Rosenberg, *Dowling College*
Douglas Ross, *Towson University*
Ronald Sanchez, *University of Illinois*
Joseph A. Schenk, *University of Dayton*
Brian Shaffer, *University of Kentucky*
Leonard Sholtis, *Eastern Michigan University*
Pradip K. Shukla, *Chapman University*
Mel Sillmon, *University of Michigan – Dearborn*
Dennis L. Smart, *University of Nebraska at Omaha*
Barbara Spencer, *Clemson University*
Lawrence Steenberg, *University of Evansville*
Kim A. Stewart, *University of Denver*
Ted Takamura, *Warner Pacific College*
Scott Taylor, *Florida Metropolitan University*
Bobby Vaught, *Southwest Missouri State*
Robert P. Vichas, *Florida Atlantic University*
Edward Ward, *St. Cloud State University*
Kenneth Wendeln, *Indiana University*
Daniel L. White, *Drexel University*
Edgar L. Williams, Jr., *Norfolk State University*
Jun Zhao, *Governors State University*

Charles W. L. Hill
Gareth R. Jones

Strategic Leadership: Managing the Strategy-Making Process for Competitive Advantage

OPENING CASE

Dell Computer

Dell Computer has enjoyed a decade of very high profitability. Between 1998 and 2006, its average return on invested capital (ROIC) was a staggering 48.3%, far ahead of the profitability of competing manufacturers of personal computers (see Figure 1.1). Moreover, while the profitability of its competitors fell sharply during 2001–2004, reflecting a tough selling environment in the personal computer industry, Dell managed to maintain a very high ROIC. Clearly, Dell has had a sustained competitive advantage over its rivals. Where did this come from?

An answer can be found in Dell's business model: selling directly to retail customers. Michael Dell reasoned that by cutting out wholesalers and retailers, he would obtain the profit they would otherwise receive and could give part of the profit back to customers in the form of lower prices. Initially, Dell did its direct selling through mailings and telephone contacts, but since the mid-1990s, much of its sales have been made through its website. Dell's sophisticated website allows customers to mix and match product features such as microprocessors, memory, monitors, internal hard drives, CD and DVD drives, keyboard and mouse format, and so on, to customize their own computer systems. The ability to customize orders kept retail customers coming back to Dell and helped to drive sales to a record $55.9 billion in 2004.

Another reason for Dell's high performance is the way it manages its supply chain to minimize the costs of holding inventory. Dell has about 200 suppliers, over half of them located outside the United States. Dell uses the Internet to feed real-time information about order flow to its suppliers so they have up-to-the-minute information about demand trends for the components they produce, along with volume expectations for the upcoming four to twelve weeks. Dell's suppliers use this information to adjust their own production schedules, manufacturing just enough components for Dell's needs and shipping them by the most appropriate mode so that they arrive just in time for production. This tight coordination is pushed back even further down the supply chain because Dell shares this information with its suppliers' biggest suppliers.

Dell's goal is to coordinate its supply chain to such an extent that it drives all inventories out of the supply chain, apart from those actually in transit between suppliers and Dell, effectively replacing inventory with information. Dell has succeeded in driving down inventory to the lowest

Profitability of U.S. Personal Computer Makers

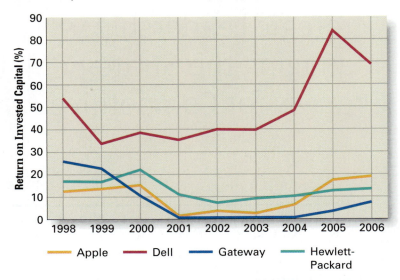

Source: Value Line Calculations. Data for 2006 are estimates based on three quarters.

level in the industry. In mid-2006, it was turning its inventory over every five days, compared to an average of forty-one days at key competitor Hewlett-Packard. This is a major source of competitive advantage in the computer industry, where component costs account for 75% of revenues and typically fall by 1% per week due to rapid obsolescence.

Despite its high profitability, between mid-2005 and mid-2006, Dell's stock lost half its market value, sliding from $42 a share to $22. There were several reasons for this. First, after years of trying, three of Dell's competitors, Acer, Hewlett-Packard, and Lenovo, had reduced their cost structure and become more competitive with Dell, enabling them to match Dell on prices and still make profits. Second, by 2005, the consumer market for PCs in developed nations had become mature. To keep growing, Dell tried to expand its share of the business market—but here it faces tough competition from Hewlett-Packard, which can offer business users a wider range of products, and extensive consulting services and

after-sales service and support, all things that business users value highly. Third, Dell's growth had been hurt by poor customer service. Dell had outsourced customer service to India in an attempt to reduce costs, only to find that poor service alienated its customers. Even though Dell moved customer service for business users back to the United States, some damage had already been done, and this only served to emphasize the difference between Dell and HP in the minds of business customers. Fourth, in an attempt to gain market share from competitors, Dell cut prices in 2005 and 2006, but it gained little in sales volume, made less profit per computer, and experienced only sluggish profit growth for 2006.

Many investors, deciding that Dell's years of rapid profit growth might be over, sold the stock. Looking forward, analysts think that Dell's profitability, as measured by ROIC, will decline from over 60% in 2006 to 30% by 2009 as competitors like Acer, Lenovo, and Hewlett-Packard start to match Dell's cost structure, and differentiate themselves from Dell in ways that users value.[1]

OVERVIEW

Why do some companies succeed while others fail? Why has Dell Computer been able to do so well in the fiercely competitive personal computer industry, while competitors like Gateway have struggled to make money? In the airline industry, how is it that Southwest Airlines has managed to keep increasing its revenues and profits through both good times and bad, while rivals such as US Airways and United Airlines have had to seek bankruptcy protection? What explains the persistent growth and profitability of Nucor Steel, now the largest steel maker in America, during a period when many of its once larger rivals disappeared into bankruptcy?

In this book, we argue that the strategies that a company's managers pursue have a major impact on its performance relative to its competitors. A **strategy** is a set of related actions that managers take to increase their company's performance. For most, if not all, companies, achieving superior performance relative to rivals is the ultimate challenge. If a company's strategies result in superior performance, it is said to have a competitive advantage. Dell Computer's strategies produced superior performance during the late 1990s and first half of the 2000s; as a result, Dell enjoyed a competitive advantage over its rivals. How did Dell achieve this competitive advantage? As explained in the Opening Case, it was due to the successful pursuit of a number of strategies by Dell's managers. These strategies enabled the company to lower its cost structure, charge low prices, gain market share, and become more profitable than its rivals. We will return to the example of Dell several times throughout this book in a Running Case that examines various aspects of Dell strategy and performance.

This book identifies and describes the strategies that managers can pursue to achieve superior performance and provide their company with a competitive advantage. One of its central aims is to give you a thorough understanding of the analytical techniques and skills necessary to identify and implement strategies successfully. The first step toward achieving this objective is to describe in more detail what superior performance and competitive advantage mean and to explain the pivotal role that managers play in leading the strategy-making process.

Strategic leadership is about how to most effectively manage a company's strategy-making process to create competitive advantage. The strategy-making process is the process by which managers select and then implement a set of strategies that aim to achieve a competitive advantage. **Strategy formulation** is the task of selecting strategies, whereas **strategy implementation** is the task of putting strategies into action, which includes designing, delivering, and supporting products; improving the efficiency and effectiveness of operations; and designing a company's organization structure, control systems, and culture. Paraphrasing the well-known saying that "success is 10% inspiration and 90% perspiration," in the strategic management arena we might say that "success is 10% formulation and 90% implementation." The task of selecting strategies is relatively easy (but requires good analysis and some inspiration); the hard part is putting those strategies into effect.

By the end of this chapter, you will understand how strategic leaders can manage the strategy-making process by formulating and implementing strategies that enable a company to achieve a competitive advantage and superior performance. Moreover, you will learn how the strategy-making process can go wrong and what managers can do to make this process more effective.

Strategic Leadership, Competitive Advantage, and Superior Performance

Strategic leadership is concerned with managing the strategy-making process to increase the performance of a company, thereby increasing the value of the enterprise to its owners, its shareholders. As shown in Figure 1.2, to increase shareholder value, managers must pursue strategies that increase the profitability of the company and ensure that profits grow (for more details, see the Appendix to this chapter). To do this, a company must be able to outperform its rivals; it must have a competitive advantage.

● **Superior Performance**

Maximizing shareholder value is the ultimate goal of profit-making companies, for two reasons. First, shareholders provide a company with the risk capital that enables managers to buy the resources needed to produce and sell goods and services. **Risk capital** is capital that cannot be recovered if a company fails and goes bankrupt. In the case of Dell, for example, shareholders provided the company with capital to build its assembly plants, invest in information systems, build its order taking and customer support system, and so on. Had Dell failed, its shareholders would have lost their money; their shares would have been worthless. Thus, shareholders will not provide risk capital unless they believe that managers are committed to pursuing strategies that give them a good return on their capital investment. Second, shareholders are the legal owners of a corporation, and their shares therefore represent a claim on the profits generated by a company. Thus, managers have an obligation to invest those profits in ways that maximize shareholder value. Of course, as explained later in this book, managers must behave in a legal, ethical, and socially responsible manner while working to maximize shareholder value.

By **shareholder value**, we mean the returns that shareholders earn from purchasing shares in a company. These returns come from two sources: (a) capital appreciation in the value of a company's shares and (b) dividend payments. For example, between January 2 and December 31, 2003, the value of one share in the bank JPMorgan increased from $23.96 to $35.78, which represents a capital appreciation of $11.82. In addition, JPMorgan paid out a dividend of $1.30 a share during 2003. Thus, if an investor had bought one share of JPMorgan on January 2 and held on to it for the entire year, her return would have been $13.12 ($11.82 + $1.30), an impressive 54.8% return on her investment. One reason JPMorgan's shareholders did so well during 2003 was that investors came to believe that managers were pursuing strategies that would both increase the long-term profitability of the company and significantly grow its profits in the future.

FIGURE 1.2

Determinants of Shareholder Value

One way of measuring the **profitability** of a company is by the return that it makes on the capital invested in the enterprise.[2] The return on invested capital (ROIC) that a company earns is defined as its net profit over the capital invested in the firm (profit/capital invested). By net profit, we mean net income after tax. By capital, we mean the sum of money invested in the company: that is, stockholders' equity plus debt owed to creditors. So defined, profitability is the result of how efficiently and effectively managers use the capital at their disposal to produce goods and services that satisfy customer needs. A company that uses its capital efficiently and effectively makes a positive return on invested capital.

The **profit growth** of a company can be measured by the increase in net profit over time. A company can grow its profits if it sells products in markets that are growing rapidly, gains market share from rivals, increases the amount it sells to existing customers, expands overseas, or diversifies profitably into new lines of business. For example, between 1996 and 2005, Dell increased its net profit from $531 million to $3.825 billion. It was able to do this because the company had a low cost structure, which enabled it to take market share from rivals such as Gateway, Hewlett-Packard, and IBM. In addition, the entire PC industry was growing at a healthy pace during this period, further boosting Dell's profits.

Together, profitability and profit growth are the principal drivers of shareholder value (see the Appendix to this chapter for details). To both boost profitability and grow profits over time, managers must formulate and implement strategies that give their company a competitive advantage over rivals. Dell's strategies achieved this until 2005. As a result, investors who purchased Dell stock on January 1, 1996, at $1.11 a share, and held that position until December 30, 2005, when the stock was worth $29.95, would have made a 2,700% return on their investment! However, as noted in the Opening Case, now Dell is finding it increasingly difficult to achieve profit growth and high profitability. Indeed, Dell's net profits shrank between 2005 and 2006. As a result, the shares traded as low as $18.95 in 2006, even though the company remained very profitable. To get the share price up, managers at Dell need to pursue strategies that reignite profit growth while maintaining the company's historically high profitability.

One of the key challenges managers face is to simultaneously generate high profitability and increase the profits of the company. As Dell's managers have discovered since 2005, companies that have high profitability but whose profits are not growing will not be as highly valued by shareholders as a company that has both high profitability and rapid profit growth (see the Appendix for details). At the same time, managers need to be aware that if they grow profits but profitability declines, that too will not be as highly valued by shareholders. What shareholders want to see, and what managers must try to deliver through strategic leadership, is *profitable growth*: that is, high profitability and sustainable profit growth. This is not easy, but some of the most successful enterprises of our era have achieved it—companies such as Microsoft, Intel, and Wal-Mart, and until 2005 at least, Dell.

● **Competitive Advantage and a Company's Business Model**

Managers do not make strategic decisions in a competitive vacuum. Their company is competing against other companies for customers. Competition is a rough-and-tumble process in which only the most efficient and effective companies win out. It is a race without end. To maximize shareholder value, managers must formulate and implement strategies that enable their company to outperform rivals—that give it a competitive advantage. A company is said to have a **competitive advantage** over its rivals when its profitability is greater than the average profitability and profit growth of other companies competing for the same set of customers. The higher its profitability relative to rivals, the greater its competitive advantage will be. A company has a **sustained competitive advantage** when its strategies enable it to maintain above-average profitability for a number of years. As discussed in the Opening Case, Dell had a significant and sustained competitive advantage over rivals such as Gateway and Hewlett-Packard between 1996 and 2004. That competitive advantage may now be starting to dissipate.

If a company has a sustained competitive advantage, it is likely to gain market share from its rivals and thus grow its profits more rapidly than those of rivals. In turn, competitive advantage will also lead to higher profit growth than that shown by rivals.

The key to understanding competitive advantage is appreciating how the different strategies managers pursue over time can create activities that fit together to make a company unique or different from its rivals and able to consistently outperform them. A **business model** is managers' conception of how the set of strategies their company pursues should mesh together into a congruent whole, enabling the company to gain a competitive advantage and achieve superior profitability and profit growth. In essence, a business model is a kind of mental model, or gestalt, of how the various strategies and capital investments made by a company should fit together to generate above-average profitability and profit growth. A business model encompasses the totality of how a company will:

- Select its customers
- Define and differentiate its product offerings
- Create value for its customers
- Acquire and keep customers
- Produce goods or services
- Lower costs
- Deliver those goods and services to the market
- Organize activities within the company
- Configure its resources
- Achieve and sustain a high level of profitability
- Grow the business over time

The business model at Dell Computer, for example, is based on the idea that costs can be lowered by selling directly to consumers and avoiding using a distribution channel (see the Opening Case). The cost savings that are attained as a result of this model are passed to consumers in the form of lower prices, which has enabled Dell to gain market share from rivals. Over time, this business model proved superior to the established business model in the industry, which involved selling computers through retailers.

Dell outperformed close rivals, like Gateway, who adopted the same basic direct-selling business model because Dell implemented its business model more effectively. Most important, Dell did a much better job of using the Internet to coordinate its supply chain and to match orders for computers to the delivery of inventory from suppliers, so that it increased its inventory turnover and reduced its costs.

The business model that managers develop may not only lead to higher profitability and thus competitive advantage at a certain point in time, but it may also help the firm to grow its profits over time, thereby maximizing shareholder value while maintaining or even increasing profitability. Dell's business model was so efficient and effective that it enabled the company to take market share from rivals and thereby increase its profits over time.

● **Industry Differences in Performance**

It is important to recognize that in addition to its business model and associated strategies, a company's performance is also determined by the characteristics of the industry in which it competes. Different industries are characterized by different competitive conditions. In some, demand is growing rapidly, and in others it is contracting. Some might be beset by excess capacity and persistent price wars, others by excess demand and rising prices. In some, technological change might be revolutionizing competition. Others might be characterized by a lack of technological change. In some industries, high profitability among incumbent companies might induce new companies to enter the industry, and these new entrants might depress prices and profits in the industry. In other industries, new entry might be difficult, and periods of high profitability might persist for a considerable time. Thus, the different competitive conditions prevailing in different industries might lead to differences in profitability and profit growth. For example, average profitability might be higher in some industries and lower in other industries because competitive conditions vary from industry to industry.

Figure 1.3 shows the average profitability, measured by ROIC, among companies in several different industries between 2002 and 2006. The drug industry had a favorable competitive environment: demand for drugs was high and competition was generally not based on price. Just the opposite was the case in the air transport industry, which was extremely price competitive. Exactly how industries differ is discussed in detail in Chapter 2. For now, the important point to remember is that the profitability and profit growth of a company are determined by two main factors: its relative success in its industry and the overall performance of its industry relative to other industries.[3]

● **Performance in Nonprofit Enterprises**

A final point concerns the concept of superior performance in the nonprofit sector. By definition, nonprofit enterprises such as government agencies, universities, and charities are not in "business" to make profits. Nevertheless, they are expected to use their resources efficiently and operate effectively, and their managers set goals to measure their performance. The performance goal for a business school might be to

FIGURE 1.3

Return on Invested Capital in Selected Industries, 2002–2006

Source: Value Line Investment Survey.

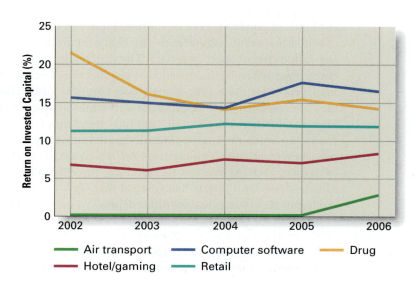

get its programs ranked among the best in the nation. The performance goal for a charity might be to prevent childhood illnesses in poor countries. The performance goal for a government agency might be to improve its services while not exceeding its budget. The managers of nonprofits need to map out strategies to attain these goals. They also need to understand that nonprofits compete with each other for scarce resources, just as businesses do. For example, charities compete for scarce donations, and their managers must plan and develop strategies that lead to high performance and demonstrate a track record of meeting performance goals. A successful strategy gives potential donors a compelling message about why they should contribute additional donations. Thus, planning and thinking strategically are as important for managers in the nonprofit sector as they are for managers in profit-seeking firms.

Strategic Managers

Managers are the linchpin in the strategy-making process. It is individual managers who must take responsibility for formulating strategies to attain a competitive advantage and for putting those strategies into effect. They must lead the strategy-making process. The strategies that made Dell Computer so successful were not chosen by some abstract entity known as the company; they were chosen by the company's founder, Michael Dell, and the managers he hired. Dell's success, like the success of any company, was based in large part on how well the company's managers performed their strategic roles. In this section, we look at the strategic roles of different managers. Later in the chapter, we discuss strategic leadership, which is how managers can effectively lead the strategy-making process.

In most companies, there are two main types of managers: **general managers**, who bear responsibility for the overall performance of the company or for one of its major self-contained subunits or divisions, and **functional managers**, who are responsible for supervising a particular function, that is, a task, activity, or operation, such as accounting, marketing, research and development (R&D), information technology, or logistics.

A company is a collection of functions or departments that work together to bring a particular good or service to the market. If a company provides several different kinds of goods or services, it often duplicates these functions and creates a series of self-contained divisions (each of which contains its own set of functions) to manage each different good or service. The general managers of these divisions then become responsible for their particular product line. The overriding concern of general managers is for the health of the whole company or division under their direction; they are responsible for deciding how to create a competitive advantage and achieve high profitability with the resources and capital they have at their disposal. Figure 1.4 shows the organization of a **multidivisional company**, that is, a company that competes in several different businesses and has created a separate self-contained division to manage each. As you can see, there are three main levels of management: corporate, business, and functional. General managers are found at the first two of these levels, but their strategic roles differ depending on their sphere of responsibility.

● **Corporate-Level Managers**   The corporate level of management consists of the chief executive officer (CEO), other senior executives, and corporate staff. These individuals occupy the apex of decision making within the organization. The CEO is the principal general manager. In

FIGURE 1.4

Levels of Strategic
Management

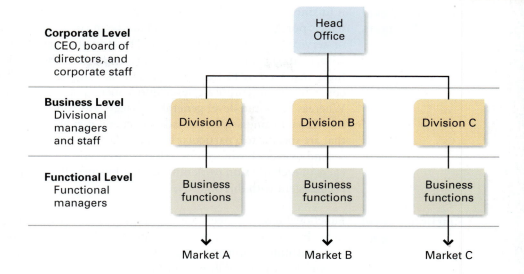

consultation with other senior executives, the role of corporate-level managers is to oversee the development of strategies for the whole organization. This role includes defining the goals of the organization, determining what businesses it should be in, allocating resources among the different businesses, formulating and implementing strategies that span individual businesses, and providing leadership for the entire organization.

Consider General Electric as an example. GE is active in a wide range of businesses, including lighting equipment, major appliances, motor and transportation equipment, turbine generators, construction and engineering services, industrial electronics, medical systems, aerospace, aircraft engines, and financial services. The main strategic responsibilities of its CEO, Jeffrey Immelt, are setting overall strategic goals, allocating resources among the different business areas, deciding whether the firm should divest itself of any of its businesses, and determining whether it should acquire any new ones. In other words, it is up to Immelt to develop strategies that span individual businesses; his concern is with building and managing the corporate portfolio of businesses to maximize corporate profitability.

It is not his specific responsibility to develop strategies for competing in the individual business areas, such as financial services. The development of such strategies is the responsibility of the general managers in these different businesses, or business-level managers. However, it is Immelt's responsibility to probe the strategic thinking of business-level managers to make sure that they are pursuing robust business models and strategies that will contribute toward the maximization of GE's long-run profitability, to coach and motivate those managers, to reward them for attaining or exceeding goals, and to hold them accountable for poor performance.

Corporate-level managers also provide a link between the people who oversee the strategic development of a firm and those who own it (the shareholders). Corporate-level managers, and particularly the CEO, can be viewed as the agents of shareholders.[4] It is their responsibility to ensure that the corporate and business strategies that the company pursues are consistent with maximizing profitability and profit growth. If they are not, then ultimately the CEO is likely to be called to account by the shareholders.

● **Business-Level Managers**

A **business unit** is a self-contained division (with its own functions—for example, finance, purchasing, production, and marketing departments) that provides a product or service for a particular market. The principal general manager at the business level, or the business-level manager, is the head of the division. The strategic role of these managers is to translate the general statements of direction and intent that come from the corporate level into concrete strategies for individual businesses. Whereas corporate-level general managers are concerned with strategies that span individual businesses, business-level general managers are concerned with strategies that are specific to a particular business. At GE, a major corporate goal is to be first or second in every business in which the corporation competes. Then the general managers in each division work out for their business the details of a business model that is consistent with this objective.

● **Functional-Level Managers**

Functional-level managers are responsible for the specific business functions or operations (human resources, purchasing, product development, customer service, and so on) that constitute a company or one of its divisions. Thus, a functional manager's sphere of responsibility is generally confined to one organizational activity, whereas general managers oversee the operation of a whole company or division. Although they are not responsible for the overall performance of the organization, functional managers nevertheless have a major strategic role: to develop functional strategies in their area that help fulfill the strategic objectives set by business- and corporate-level general managers.

In GE's aerospace business, for instance, manufacturing managers are responsible for developing manufacturing strategies consistent with corporate objectives. Moreover, functional managers provide most of the information that makes it possible for business- and corporate-level general managers to formulate realistic and attainable strategies. Indeed, because they are closer to the customer than is the typical general manager, functional managers themselves may generate important ideas that subsequently become major strategies for the company. Thus, it is important for general managers to listen closely to the ideas of their functional managers. An equally great responsibility for managers at the operational level is strategy implementation: the execution of corporate- and business-level plans.

The Strategy-Making Process

We can now turn our attention to the process by which managers formulate and implement strategies. Many writers have emphasized that strategy is the outcome of a formal planning process and that top management plays the most important role in this process.[5] Although this view has some basis in reality, it is not the whole story. As we shall see later in the chapter, valuable strategies often emerge from deep within the organization without prior planning. Nevertheless, a consideration of formal, rational planning is a useful starting point for our journey into the world of strategy. Accordingly, we consider what might be described as a typical formal strategic planning model for making strategy.

● **A Model of the Strategic Planning Process**

The formal strategic planning process has five main steps:

1. Select the corporate mission and major corporate goals.

2. Analyze the organization's external competitive environment to identify opportunities and threats.

3. Analyze the organization's internal operating environment to identify the organization's strengths and weaknesses.

4. Select strategies that build on the organization's strengths and correct its weaknesses in order to take advantage of external opportunities and counter external threats. These strategies should be consistent with the mission and major goals of the organization. They should be congruent and constitute a viable business model.

5. Implement the strategies.

The task of analyzing the organization's external and internal environments and then selecting appropriate strategies constitutes strategy formulation. In contrast, as noted earlier, strategy implementation involves putting the strategies (or plan) into action. This includes taking actions consistent with the selected strategies of the company at the corporate, business, and functional levels; allocating roles and responsibilities among managers (typically through the design of organization structure); allocating resources (including capital and money); setting short-term objectives; and designing the organization's control and reward systems. These steps are illustrated in Figure 1.5 (which can also be viewed as a plan for the rest of this book).

Each step in Figure 1.5 constitutes a sequential step in the strategic planning process. At step 1, each round or cycle of the planning process begins with a statement of the corporate mission and major corporate goals. This statement is shaped by the existing business model of the company. The mission statement is followed by the foundation of strategic thinking: external analysis, internal analysis, and strategic choice. The strategy-making process ends with the design of the organizational structure and the culture and control systems necessary to implement the organization's chosen strategy. This chapter discusses how to select a corporate mission and choose major goals. Other parts of strategic planning are reserved for later chapters, as indicated in Figure 1.5.

Some organizations go through a new cycle of the strategic planning process every year. This does not necessarily mean that managers choose a new strategy each year. In many instances, the result is simply to modify and reaffirm a strategy and structure already in place. The strategic plans generated by the planning process generally look out over a period of one to five years, with the plan being updated, or rolled forward, every year. In most organizations, the results of the annual strategic planning process are used as input into the budgetary process for the coming year so that strategic planning is used to shape resource allocation within the organization.

● Mission Statement

The first component of the strategic management process is crafting the organization's mission statement, which provides the framework or context within which strategies are formulated. A mission statement has four main components: a statement of the raison d'être of a company or organization—its reason for existence—which is normally referred to as the mission; a statement of some desired future state, usually referred to as the vision; a statement of the key values that the organization is committed to; and a statement of major goals.

THE MISSION A company's **mission** describes what the company does. For example, the mission of Kodak is to provide "customers with the solutions they need to capture, store, process, output, and communicate images—anywhere, anytime."[6] In other words, Kodak exists to provide imaging solutions to consumers. In its mission statement, Ford Motor Company describes itself as a company that is "passionately committed

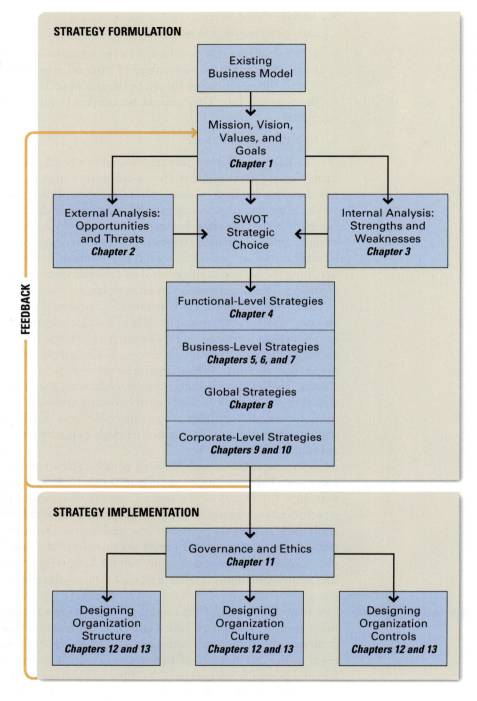

to providing personal mobility for people around the world. . . . We anticipate consumer need and deliver outstanding products and services that improve people's lives."[7] In short, Ford is a company that exists to satisfy consumer needs for personal mobility; that is its mission. Both of these missions focus on the customer needs that the company is trying to satisfy rather than on particular products (imaging and personal

FIGURE 1.6

Defining the Business

Source: D. F. Abell, *Defining the Business: The Starting Point of Strategic Planning* (Englewood Cliffs, N.J.: Prentice-Hall, 1980), p. 7.

Who is being satisfied?

Customer groups

What is being satisfied?

Customer needs

Business Definition

How are customer needs being satisfied?

Distinctive competencies

mobility rather than conventional film or cameras and automobiles). These are customer-oriented rather than product-oriented missions.

An important first step in the process of formulating a mission is to come up with a definition of the organization's business. Essentially, the definition answers these questions: "What is our business? What will it be? What should it be?"[8] The responses guide the formulation of the mission. To answer the question, "What is our business?" a company should define its business in terms of three dimensions: who is being satisfied (what customer groups), what is being satisfied (what customer needs), and how customers' needs are being satisfied (by what skills, knowledge, or distinctive competencies).[9] Figure 1.6 illustrates these dimensions.

This approach stresses the need for a *customer-oriented* rather than a *product-oriented* business definition. A product-oriented business definition focuses on the characteristics of the products sold and the markets served, not on which kinds of customer needs the products are satisfying. Such an approach obscures the company's true mission because a product is only the physical manifestation of applying a particular skill to satisfy a particular need for a particular customer group. In practice, that need may be served in many different ways, and a broad customer-oriented business definition that identifies these ways can safeguard companies from being caught unaware by major shifts in demand.

By helping anticipate demand shifts, a customer-oriented mission statement can also assist companies in capitalizing on changes in their environment. It can help answer the question, "What will our business be?" Kodak's mission statement—to provide "customers with the solutions they need to capture, store, process, output, and communicate images"—is a customer-oriented statement that focuses on customer needs rather than a particular product (or solution) for satisfying those needs, such as chemical film processing. For this reason, it is helping to drive Kodak's current investments in digital imaging technologies, which are now fast replacing its traditional business based on chemical film processing.

The need to take a customer-oriented view of a company's business has often been ignored. History is littered with the wreckage of once-great corporations that did not define their business or defined it incorrectly so that ultimately they declined. In the 1950s and 1960s, many office equipment companies such as Smith Corona and Underwood defined their businesses as being the production of typewriters. This product-oriented definition ignored the fact that they were really in the business of satisfying customers' information-processing needs. Unfortunately for those companies, when a new technology came along that better served customer needs for information processing (computers), demand for typewriters plummeted. The last great typewriter company, Smith Corona, went bankrupt in 1996, a victim of the success of computer-based word-processing technology.

In contrast, IBM correctly foresaw what its business would be. In the 1950s, IBM was a leader in the manufacture of typewriters and mechanical tabulating equipment using punch-card technology. However, unlike many of its competitors, IBM defined its business as providing a means for *information processing and storage*, rather than just supplying mechanical tabulating equipment and typewriters.[10] Given this definition, the company's subsequent moves into computers, software systems, office systems, and printers seem logical.

VISION The vision of a company lays out some desired future state; it articulates, often in bold terms, what the company would like to achieve. Nokia, the world's largest manufacturer of mobile (wireless) phones, operates with a very simple but powerful vision: "If it can go mobile, it will!" This vision implies that not only will voice telephony go mobile (it already has), but so will a host of other services based on data, such as imaging and Internet browsing. This vision has led Nokia to develop multimedia mobile handsets that not only can be used for voice communication but that also take pictures, browse the Internet, play games, and manipulate personal and corporate information.

VALUES The values of a company state how managers and employees should conduct themselves, how they should do business, and what kind of organization they should build to help a company achieve its mission. Insofar as they help drive and shape behavior within a company, values are commonly seen as the bedrock of a company's organizational culture: the set of values, norms, and standards that control how employees work to achieve an organization's mission and goals. An organization's culture is commonly seen as an important source of its competitive advantage.[11] (We discuss the issue of organization culture in depth in Chapter 12.) For example, Nucor Steel is one of the most productive and profitable steel firms in the world. Its competitive advantage is based in part on the extremely high productivity of its work force, which the company maintains is a direct result of its cultural values, which in turn determine how it treats its employees. These values are as follow:

- "Management is obligated to manage Nucor in such a way that employees will have the opportunity to earn according to their productivity."
- "Employees should be able to feel confident that if they do their jobs properly, they will have a job tomorrow."
- "Employees have the right to be treated fairly and must believe that they will be."
- "Employees must have an avenue of appeal when they believe they are being treated unfairly."[12]

At Nucor, values emphasizing pay for performance, job security, and fair treatment for employees help to create an atmosphere within the company that leads to high employee productivity. In turn, this has helped to give Nucor one of the lowest cost structures in its industry, which helps to explain the company's profitability in a very price-competitive business.

In one study of organizational values, researchers identified a set of values associated with high-performing organizations that help companies achieve superior financial performance through their impact on employee behavior.[13] These values included respect for the interests of key organizational stakeholders: individuals or groups that have an interest, claim, or stake in the company, in what it does, and in how well it performs.[14] They include stockholders, bondholders, employees, customers, the communities in which the company does business, and the general public. One study found that deep respect for the interests of customers, employees, suppliers, and shareholders was associated with high performance.[15] The study also noted that the encouragement of leadership and entrepreneurial behavior by mid- and lower-level managers and a willingness to support change efforts within the organization contributed to high performance. Companies that emphasize such values consistently throughout their organization include Hewlett-Packard, Wal-Mart, and PepsiCo. The same study identified the values of poorly performing companies— values that, as might be expected, are not articulated in company mission statements: (1) arrogance, particularly to ideas from outside the company; (2) a lack of respect for key stakeholders; and (3) a history of resisting change efforts and "punishing" mid- and lower-level managers who showed "too much leadership." General Motors was held up as an example of one such organization. According to the authors of this study, a mid- or lower-level manager who showed too much leadership and initiative there was not promoted!

MAJOR GOALS   Having stated the mission, vision, and key values, strategic managers can take the next step in the formulation of a mission statement: establishing major goals. A goal is a precise and measurable desired future state that a company attempts to realize. In this context, the purpose of goals is to specify with precision what must be done if the company is to attain its mission or vision.

Well-constructed goals have four main characteristics:[16]

- They are precise and measurable. Measurable goals give managers a yardstick or standard against which they can judge their performance.

- They address crucial issues. To maintain focus, managers should select a limited number of major goals to assess the performance of the company. The goals that are selected should be crucial or important ones.

- They are challenging but realistic. They give all employees an incentive to look for ways of improving the operations of an organization. If a goal is unrealistic in the challenges it poses, employees may give up; a goal that is too easy may fail to motivate managers and other employees.[17]

- They specify a time period in which the goals should be achieved, when that is appropriate. Time constraints tell employees that success requires a goal to be attained by a given date, not after that date. Deadlines can inject a sense of urgency into goal attainment and act as a motivator. However, not all goals require time constraints.

Well-constructed goals also provide a means by which the performance of managers can be evaluated.

As noted earlier, although most companies operate with a variety of goals, the central goal of most corporations is to maximize shareholder returns, and doing this requires both high profitability and sustained profit growth. Thus, most companies operate with goals for profitability and profit growth. However, it is important that top managers do not make the mistake of overemphasizing current profitability to the detriment of long-term profitability and profit growth.[18] The overzealous pursuit of current profitability to maximize short-term ROIC can encourage such misguided managerial actions as cutting expenditures judged to be nonessential in the short run—for instance, expenditures for research and development, marketing, and new capital investments. Although cutting current expenditure increases current profitability, the resulting underinvestment, lack of innovation, and diminished marketing can jeopardize long-run profitability and profit growth. These expenditures are vital if a company is to pursue its long-term mission and sustain its competitive advantage and profitability over time. Despite these negative consequences, managers may make such decisions because the adverse effects of a short-run orientation may not materialize and become apparent to shareholders for several years, or because they are under extreme pressure to hit short-term profitability goals.[19] It is also worth noting that pressures to maximize short-term profitability may drive managers to act unethically. This apparently occurred during the late 1990s at Enron Corporation, Tyco, WorldCom, and Computer Associates, where managers systematically inflated profits by manipulating financial accounts in a manner that misrepresented the true performance of the firm to shareholders. (Chapter 11 provides a detailed discussion of the issues.)

To guard against short-run behavior, managers need to ensure that they adopt goals whose attainment will increase the long-run performance and competitiveness of their enterprise. Long-term goals are related to such issues as product development, customer satisfaction, and efficiency, and they emphasize specific objectives or targets concerning such details as employee and capital productivity, product quality, innovation, customer satisfaction and customer service. At Dell Computer, for example, the goal of replacing inventory with information is to focus management attention on what can be done to increase inventory turnover and thus reduce costs.

● External Analysis

The second component of the strategic management process is an analysis of the organization's external operating environment. The essential purpose of the external analysis is to identify strategic opportunities and threats in the organization's operating environment that will affect how it pursues its mission. Strategy in Action 1.1 describes how an analysis of opportunities and threats in the external environment led to a strategic shift at Time Inc.

Three interrelated environments should be examined when undertaking an external analysis: the industry environment in which the company operates, the country or national environment, and the wider socioeconomic or macroenvironment. Analyzing the industry environment requires an assessment of the competitive structure of the company's industry, including the competitive position of the company and its major rivals. It also requires analysis of the nature, stage, dynamics, and history of the industry. Because many markets are now global markets, analyzing the industry environment also means assessing the impact of globalization on competition within an industry. Such an analysis may reveal that a company should move some production facilities to another nation, that it should aggressively expand in emerging markets such as China, or that it should beware of new competition from emerging nations. Analyzing the macroenvironment consists of examining macroeconomic, social, government, legal, international, and technological factors that may affect the company and its industry. We look at external analysis in Chapter 2.

Strategy in Action 1.1

Strategic Analysis at Time Inc.

Time Inc., the magazine publishing division of media conglomerate Time Warner, has a venerable history. Its magazine titles include *Time, Fortune, Sports Illustrated*, and *People*, all long-time leaders in their respective categories. By the mid 2000s, however, Time Inc. recognized that it needed to change its strategy. In 2005, circulation at *Time* was off by 12%; *Fortune*, by 10%; and *Sports Illustrated*, by 17%.

An external analysis revealed what was going on. The readership of Time's magazines was aging. Increasingly, younger readers were getting what they wanted from the Web. This was both a *threat* for Time Inc., since its Web offerings were not strong, and an *opportunity*, since with the right offerings Time Inc. could capture this audience. Time also realized that advertising dollars were migrating rapidly to the Web, and if the company was going to hold onto its share, its Web offerings had to be every bit as good as its print offerings.

An internal analysis revealed why, despite multiple attempts, Time had failed to capitalize on the opportunities offered by the emergence of the Web. Although Time had tremendous *strengths*, including powerful brands and strong reporting, development of its Web offerings had been hindered by a serious *weakness*—an editorial culture that regarded Web publishing as a backwater. At *People*, for example, the online operation used to be "like a distant moon" according to managing editor Martha Nelson. Managers at Time Inc. had also been worried that Web offerings would cannibalize print offerings and help to accelerate the decline in the circulation of magazines, with dire financial consequences for the company. As a result of this culture, efforts to move publications onto the Web were underfunded or were stymied by a lack of management attention and commitment.

It was Martha Nelson at *People* who in 2003 showed the way forward for the company. Her *strategy* for overcoming the *weakness* at Time Inc., and better exploiting *opportunities* on the Web, started with merging the print and online newsrooms at *People*, removing the distinction between them. Then she relaunched the magazine's online site, made major editorial commitments to Web publishing, stated that original content should appear on the Web, and emphasized the importance of driving traffic to the site and earning advertising revenues. Over the next two years, page views at People.com increased fivefold.

Ann Moore, the CEO at Time Inc., formalized this strategy in 2005, mandating that all print offerings should follow the lead of People.com, integrating print and online newsrooms and investing significantly more resources in Web publishing. To drive this home, Time hired several well-known bloggers to write for its online publications. The goal of Moore's strategy was to neutralize the cultural *weakness* that had hindered online efforts in the past at Time Inc. and to direct resources toward Web publishing.

In 2006, Time made another strategic move designed to exploit the opportunities associated with the Web when it started a partnership with the twenty-four-hour news channel, CNN, putting all of its financial magazines onto a site that is jointly owned, CNNMoney.com. The site, which offers free access to *Fortune, Money*, and *Business 2.0*, quickly took the third spot in online financial websites behind Yahoo finance and MSN. This was followed with a redesigned website for *Sports Illustrated* that has rolled out video downloads for iPods and mobile phones.

To drive home the shift to Web-centric publishing, in late 2006, Time announced another change in strategy—it would sell off eighteen magazine titles that, while good performers, did not appear to have much traction on the Web. Ann Moore stated that going forward Time would be focusing its energy, resources, and investments on the company's largest and most profitable brands, brands that have demonstrated an ability to draw large audiences in digital form.[a]

● **Internal Analysis**

Internal analysis, the third component of the strategic planning process, focuses on reviewing the resources, capabilities, and competencies of a company. The goal is to identify the strengths and weaknesses of the company. For example, as described in Strategy in Action 1.1, an internal analysis at Time Inc. revealed that while the company had strong well-known brands such as *Fortune*, *Money*, *Sports Illustrated*, and *People* (a strength), and a strong reporting capabilities (another strength), it suffered from a lack of editorial commitment to online publishing (a weakness). We consider internal analysis in Chapter 3.

● **SWOT Analysis and the Business Model**

The next component of strategic thinking requires the generation of a series of strategic alternatives, or choices of future strategies to pursue, given the company's internal strengths and weaknesses and its external opportunities and threats. The comparison of **s**trengths, **w**eaknesses, **o**pportunities, and **t**hreats is normally referred to as a **SWOT analysis**.[20] The central purpose is to identify the strategies to exploit external opportunities, counter threats, build on and protect company strengths, and eradicate weaknesses.

At Time Inc., managers saw the move of readership to the Web as both an *opportunity* that they must exploit and a *threat* to Time's established print magazines. They recognized that Time's well-known brands and strong reporting capabilities were *strengths* that would serve it well online, but that an editorial culture that marginalized online publishing was a *weakness* that had to be fixed. The *strategies* that managers at Time Inc. came up with included merging the print and online newsrooms to remove distinctions between them; investing significant financial resources in online sites; and entering into a partnership with CNN, which already had a strong online presence.

More generally, the goal of a SWOT analysis is to create, affirm, or fine-tune a company-specific business model that will best align, fit, or match a company's resources and capabilities to the demands of the environment in which it operates. Managers compare and contrast the various alternative possible strategies against each other and then identify the set of strategies that will create and sustain a competitive advantage. These strategies can be divided into four main categories:

- *Functional-level strategies*, directed at improving the effectiveness of operations within a company, such as manufacturing, marketing, materials management, product development, and customer service. We review functional-level strategies in Chapter 4.

- *Business-level strategies*, which encompasses the business's overall competitive theme, the way it positions itself in the marketplace to gain a competitive advantage, and the different positioning strategies that can be used in different industry settings—for example, cost leadership, differentiation, focusing on a particular niche or segment of the industry, or some combination of these. We review business-level strategies in Chapters 5, 6 and 7.

- *Global strategies*, which addresses how to expand operations outside the home country to grow and prosper in a world where competitive advantage is determined at a global level. We review global strategies in Chapter 8.

- *Corporate-level strategies*, which answer the primary questions: What business or businesses should we be in to maximize the long-run profitability and profit growth of the organization, and how should we enter and increase our presence in these businesses to gain a competitive advantage? We review corporate-level strategies in Chapters 9 and 10.

The strategies identified through a SWOT analysis should be congruent with each other. Thus, functional-level strategies should be consistent with, or support, the company's business-level strategy and global strategy. Moreover, as we explain later in this book, corporate-level strategies should support business-level strategies. When taken together, the various strategies pursued by a company constitute a viable business model. In essence, a SWOT analysis is a methodology for choosing between competing business models and for fine-tuning the business model that managers choose. For example, when Microsoft entered the videogame market with its Xbox offering, it had to settle on the best business model for competing in this market. Microsoft used a SWOT type of analysis to compare alternatives and settled on a "razor and razor blades" business model in which the Xbox console is priced below cost to build sales (the "razor"), while profits are made from royalties on the sale of games for the Xbox (the "blades").

Strategy Implementation

Having chosen a set of congruent strategies to achieve a competitive advantage and increase performance, managers must put those strategies into action: strategy has to be implemented. Strategy implementation involves taking actions at the functional, business, and corporate levels to execute a strategic plan. Implementation can include, for example, putting quality improvement programs into place, changing the way a product is designed, positioning the product differently in the marketplace, segmenting the marketing and offering different versions of the product to different consumer groups, implementing price increases or decreases, expanding through mergers and acquisitions, or downsizing the company by closing down or selling off parts of the company. These and other topics are discussed in detail in Chapters 4 through 10.

Strategy implementation also entails designing the best organization structure and the best culture and control systems to put a chosen strategy into action. In addition, senior managers need to put a governance system in place to make sure that all within the organization act in a manner that is not only consistent with maximizing profitability and profit growth but also legal and ethical. In this book, we look at the topic of governance and ethics in Chapter 11; we discuss the organization structure, culture, and controls required to implement business-level strategies in Chapter 12; and the structure, culture, and controls required to implement corporate-level strategies in Chapter 13.

The Feedback Loop

The feedback loop in Figure 1.5 indicates that strategic planning is ongoing; it never ends. Once a strategy has been implemented, its execution must be monitored to determine the extent to which strategic goals and objectives are actually being achieved and to what degree competitive advantage is being created and sustained. This information and knowledge pass back to the corporate level through feedback loops and become the input for the next round of strategy formulation and implementation. Top managers can then decide whether to reaffirm the existing business model and the existing strategies and goals or suggest changes for the future. For example, if a strategic goal proves too optimistic, the next time, a more conservative goal is set. Or feedback may reveal that the business model is not working, so managers may seek ways to change it. In essence, this is what happened at Time Inc. (see Strategy in Action 1.1). This may also be what is now happening at Dell Computer (see the Opening Case). Dell's business model, which worked so well for so long, now seems to be faltering, and to reestablish its competitive advantage in the personal computer industry, Dell's managers may well have to make strategic changes.

Strategy as an Emergent Process

The basic planning model suggests that a company's strategies are the result of a plan, that the strategic planning process itself is rational and highly structured, and that the process is orchestrated by top management. Several scholars have criticized the formal planning model for three main reasons: the unpredictability of the real world, the role that lower-level managers can play in the strategic management process, and the fact that many successful strategies are often the result of serendipity, not rational strategizing. They have advocated an alternative view of strategy making.[21]

Strategy Making in an Unpredictable World

Critics of formal planning systems argue that we live in a world in which uncertainty, complexity, and ambiguity dominate, and in which small chance events can have a large and unpredictable impact on outcomes.[22] In such circumstances, they claim, even the most carefully thought-out strategic plans are prone to being rendered useless by rapid and unforeseen change. In an unpredictable world, there is a premium on being able to respond quickly to changing circumstances and to alter the strategies of the organization accordingly. The dramatic rise of Google, for example, with its business model based revenues earned from advertising links associated with search results (the so-called pay-per-click business model), disrupted the online advertising industry in 2003–2004. Nobody foresaw this development or planned for it, but they had to respond to it, and rapidly. Companies with a strong online advertising presence, including Yahoo.com and Microsoft's MSN network, rapidly changed their strategies to adapt to the threat posed by Google. Specifically, both developed their own search engines and copied Google's pay-per-click business model. According to critics of formal systems, such a flexible approach to strategy making is not possible within the framework of a traditional strategic planning process, with its implicit assumption that an organization's strategies need to be reviewed only during the annual strategic planning exercise.

Autonomous Action: Strategy Making by Lower-Level Managers

Another criticism leveled at the rational planning model of strategy is that too much importance is attached to the role of top management, particularly the CEO.[23] An alternative view now gaining wide acceptance is that individual managers deep within an organization can and often do exert a profound influence over the strategic direction of the firm.[24] Writing with Robert Burgelman of Stanford University, Andy Grove, the former CEO of Intel, noted that many important strategic decisions at Intel were initiated not by top managers but by the autonomous action of lower-level managers deep within Intel who, on their own initiative, formulated new strategies and worked to persuade top-level managers to alter the strategic priorities of the firm.[25] These strategic decisions included the decision to exit an important market (the DRAM memory chip market) and to develop a certain class of microprocessors (RISC-based microprocessors) in direct contrast to the stated strategy of Intel's top managers. Similarly, the original prototype for Microsoft's first Xbox videogame system was developed by four lower-level engineering employees on their own initiative. They then successfully lobbied top managers to dedicate resources toward commercializing their prototype. Another example of autonomous action, this one at Starbucks, is given in Strategy in Action 1.2.

Autonomous action may be particularly important in helping established companies deal with the uncertainty created by the arrival of a radical new technology that changes the dominant paradigm in an industry.[26] Top managers usually rise to

Strategy in Action   1.2

Starbucks's Music Business

Anyone who has walked into a Starbucks cannot help but notice that, in addition to various coffee beverages and food, the company also sells music CDs. Most Starbucks stores now have racks displaying about twenty CDs. Reports suggest that when Starbucks decides to carry a CD, it typically ranks among the top four retailers selling it. The interesting thing about Starbucks's entry into music retailing is that it was not the result of a formal planning process. The company's journey into music retailing started in the late 1980s when Tim Jones, then the manager of a Starbucks in Seattle's University Village, started to bring his own tapes of music compilations into the store to play. Soon Jones was getting requests for copies from customers. Jones told this to Starbucks's CEO, Howard Schultz, and suggested that Starbucks start to sell its own music. At first, Schultz was skeptical but after repeated lobbying efforts by Jones, he eventually took up the suggestion. Today, Starbucks not only sells CDs, it is also moving into music downloading with its "Hear Music" Starbucks stores, where customers can listen to music from Starbucks's 200,000-song online music library while sipping their coffee and can burn their own CDs.[b]

preeminence by successfully executing the established strategy of the firm. Therefore, they may have an emotional commitment to the status quo and are often unable to see things from a different perspective. In this sense, they are a conservative force that promotes inertia. Lower-level managers, however, are less likely to have the same commitment to the status quo and have more to gain from promoting new technologies and strategies. They may be the first ones to recognize new strategic opportunities and lobby for strategic change. As described in Strategy in Action 1.3, this seems to have been the case at discount stockbroker, Charles Schwab, which had to adjust to the arrival of the Web in the 1990s.

• Serendipity and Strategy

Business history is replete with examples of accidental events that help to push companies in new and profitable directions. What these examples suggest is that many successful strategies are not the result of well-thought-out plans but of serendipity, that is, of stumbling across good things unexpectedly. One such example occurred at 3M during the 1960s. At that time, 3M was producing fluorocarbons for sale as coolant liquid in air conditioning equipment. One day, a researcher working with fluorocarbons in a 3M lab spilled some of the liquid on her shoes. Later that day when she spilled coffee over her shoes, she watched with interest as the coffee formed into little beads of liquid and then ran off her shoes without leaving a stain. Reflecting on this phenomenon, she realized that a fluorocarbon-based liquid might turn out to be useful for protecting fabrics from liquid stains, and so the idea for Scotch Guard was born. Subsequently, Scotch Guard became one of 3M's most profitable products and took the company into the fabric protection business, an area it had never planned to participate in.[27]

Serendipitous discoveries and events can open all sorts of profitable avenues for a company. But some companies have missed profitable opportunities because serendipitous discoveries or events were inconsistent with their prior (planned) conception of what their strategy should be. In one of the classic examples of such myopia, a century ago, the telegraph company Western Union turned down an opportunity to purchase

Strategy in Action

A Strategic Shift at Charles Schwab

In the mid-1990s, Charles Schwab was the most successful discount stockbroker in the world. Over twenty years, it had gained share from full-service brokers like Merrill Lynch by offering deep discounts on the commissions charged for stock trades. Although Schwab had a nationwide network of branches, most customers executed their trades through a telephone system called Telebroker. Others used online proprietary software, Street Smart, which had to be purchased from Schwab. It was a business model that worked well—then along came E*Trade.

E*Trade was a discount broker started in 1994 by Bill Porter, a physicist and inventor, to take advantage of the opportunity created by the rapid emergence of the World Wide Web. E*Trade launched the first dedicated website for online trading. E*Trade had no branches, no brokers, and no telephone system for taking orders, and thus it had a very low-cost structure. Customers traded stocks over the company's website. Due to its low-cost structure, E*Trade was able to announce a flat $14.95 commission on stock trades, a figure significantly below Schwab's average commission, which at the time was $65. It was clear from the outset that E*Trade and other online brokers, such as Ameritrade, who soon followed, offered a direct threat to Schwab. Not only were their cost structures and commission rates considerably below Schwab's, but the ease, speed, and flexibility of trading stocks over the Web suddenly made Schwab's Street Smart trading software seem limited and its telephone system antiquated.

Deep within Schwab, William Pearson, a young software specialist who had worked on the development of Street Smart, immediately saw the transformational power of the Web. Pearson believed that Schwab needed to develop its own Web-based software, and quickly. Try as he might, though, Pearson could not get the attention of his supervisor. He tried a number of other executives but found support hard to come by. Eventually he approached Anne Hennegar, a former Schwab manager who now worked as a consultant to the company. Hennegar suggest that Pearson meet with Tom Seip, an executive vice president at Schwab who was known for his ability to think outside the box. Hennegar approached Seip on Pearson's behalf, and Seip responded positively, asking her to set up a meeting. Hennegar and Pearson turned up expecting to meet just Seip, but to their surprise in walked Charles Schwab; his chief operating officer, David Pottruck; and the vice presidents in charge of strategic planning and the electronic brokerage arena.

As the group watched Pearson's demo of how a Web-based system would look and work, they became increasingly excited. It was clear to those in the room that a Web-based system using real-time information, personalization, customization, and interactivity all advanced Schwab's commitment to empowering customers. By the end of the meeting, Pearson had received a green light to start work on the project. A year later, Schwab launched its own Web-based offering, eSchwab, which enabled Schwab clients to execute stock trades for a low flat-rate commission. eSchwab went on to become the core of the company's offering, enabling it to stave off competition from deep discount brokers like E*Trade.[c]

the rights to an invention made by Alexander Graham Bell. The invention was the telephone, a technology that subsequently made the telegraph obsolete.

● **Intended and Emergent Strategies**

Henry Mintzberg's model of strategy development provides a more encompassing view of what strategy actually is. According to this model, illustrated in Figure 1.7, a company's realized strategy is the product of whatever planned strategies are actually put into action (the company's deliberate strategies) and of any unplanned, or emergent, strategies. In Mintzberg's view, many planned strategies are not implemented because of unpredicted changes in the environment (they are unrealized). Emergent strategies are the unplanned responses to unforeseen circumstances. They arise from

FIGURE 1.7

Emergent and
Deliberate Strategies

Data Source: Adapted from
H. Mintzberg and A. McGugh,
*Administrative Science
Quarterly*, Vol. 30. No. 2,
June 1985.

autonomous action by individual managers deep within the organization, from serendipitous discoveries or events, or from an unplanned strategic shift by top-level managers in response to changed circumstances. They are not the product of formal top-down planning mechanisms.

Mintzberg maintains that emergent strategies are often successful and may be more appropriate than intended strategies. In the classic description of this process, Richard Pascale described how this was the case for the entry of Honda Motor Co. into the U.S. motorcycle market.[28] When a number of Honda executives arrived in Los Angeles from Japan in 1959 to establish a U.S. operation, their original aim (intended strategy) was to focus on selling 250-cc and 350-cc machines to confirmed motorcycle enthusiasts rather than 50-cc Honda Cubs, which were a big hit in Japan. Their instinct told them that the Honda 50s were not suitable for the U.S. market, where everything was bigger and more luxurious than in Japan.

However, sales of the 250-cc and 350-cc bikes were sluggish, and the bikes themselves were plagued by mechanical failure. It looked as if Honda's strategy was going to fail. At the same time, the Japanese executives who were using the Honda 50s to run errands around Los Angeles were attracting a lot of attention. One day, they got a call from a Sears, Roebuck buyer who wanted to sell the 50-cc bikes to a broad market of Americans who were not necessarily motorcycle enthusiasts. The Honda executives were hesitant to sell the small bikes for fear of alienating serious bikers, who might then associate Honda with "wimpy" machines. In the end, however, they were pushed into doing so by the failure of the 250-cc and 350-cc models.

Honda had stumbled onto a previously untouched market segment that was to prove huge: the average American who had never owned a motorbike. Honda had also found an untried channel of distribution: general retailers rather than specialty motorbike stores. By 1964, nearly one out of every two motorcycles sold in the United States was a Honda.

The conventional explanation for Honda's success is that the company redefined the U.S. motorcycle industry with a brilliantly conceived intended strategy. The fact was that Honda's intended strategy was a near-disaster. The strategy that emerged did so not through planning but through unplanned action in response to unforeseen circumstances. Nevertheless, credit should be given to the Japanese management for recognizing the strength of the emergent strategy and for pursuing it with vigor.

The critical point demonstrated by the Honda example is that successful strategies can often emerge within an organization without prior planning and in response to unforeseen circumstances. As Mintzberg has noted, strategies can take root wherever people have the capacity to learn and the resources to support that capacity.

In practice, the strategies of most organizations are probably a combination of the intended (planned) and the emergent. The message for management is that it needs to recognize the process of emergence and to intervene when appropriate, killing off bad emergent strategies but nurturing potentially good ones.[29] To make such decisions, managers must be able to judge the worth of emergent strategies. They must be able to think strategically. Although emergent strategies arise from within the organization without prior planning—that is, without going through the steps illustrated in Figure 1.5 in a sequential fashion—top management still has to evaluate emergent strategies. Such evaluation involves comparing each emergent strategy with the organization's goals, external environmental opportunities and threats, and internal strengths and weaknesses. The objective is to assess whether the emergent strategy fits the company's needs and capabilities. In addition, Mintzberg stresses that an organization's capability to produce emergent strategies is a function of the kind of corporate culture that the organization's structure and control systems foster. In other words, the different components of the strategic management process are just as important from the perspective of emergent strategies as they are from the perspective of intended strategies.

Strategic Planning in Practice

Despite criticisms, research suggests that formal planning systems do help managers make better strategic decisions. A study that analyzed the results of twenty-six previously published studies came to the conclusion that, on average, strategic planning has a positive impact on company performance.[30] Another study of strategic planning in 656 firms found that formal planning methodologies and emergent strategies both form part of a good strategy formulation process, particularly in an unstable environment.[31] For strategic planning to work, it is important that top-level managers plan not just in the context of the current competitive environment but also in the context of the future competitive environment. To try to forecast what that future will look like, managers can use scenario planning techniques to plan for different possible futures. They can also involve operating managers in the planning process and seek to shape the future competitive environment by emphasizing strategic intent.

● **Scenario Planning**   One reason that strategic planning may fail over the long run is that strategic managers, in their initial enthusiasm for planning techniques, may forget that the future is inherently unpredictable. Even the best-laid plans can fall apart if unforeseen contingencies occur, and that happens all the time in the real world. The recognition that uncertainty makes it difficult to forecast the future accurately led planners at Royal Dutch Shell to pioneer the scenario approach to planning.[32] **Scenario planning** involves formulating plans that are based upon what-if scenarios about the future. In the typical scenario planning exercise, some scenarios are optimistic and some are pessimistic. Teams of managers are asked to develop specific strategies to cope with each scenario. A set of indicators is chosen to be used as signposts to track trends and identify the probability that any particular scenario is coming to pass. The idea is to get managers to understand the dynamic and complex nature of their environment, to think through problems in a strategic fashion, and to generate a range of strategic options that might be pursued under different circumstances.[33] The scenario approach to planning has spread rapidly among large companies. One survey found that over 50 percent of the *Fortune 500* companies use some form of scenario-planning methods.[34]

The oil company Royal Dutch Shell has perhaps done more than most to pioneer the concept of scenario planning, and its experience demonstrates the power of the approach.[35] Shell has been using scenario planning since the 1980s. Today, it uses two main scenarios to refine its strategic planning. The scenarios relate to future demand for oil. One, called "Dynamics as Usual," sees a gradual shift from carbon fuels such as oil to natural gas and eventually to renewable energy. The second scenario, "The Spirit of the Coming Age," looks at the possibility that a technological revolution will lead to a rapid shift to new energy sources.[36] Shell is making investments that will ensure the profitability of the company whichever scenario comes to pass, and it is carefully tracking technological and market trends for signs of which scenario is becoming more likely over time.

The great virtue of the scenario approach to planning is that it can push managers to think outside the box, to anticipate what they might have to do in different situations, and to learn that the world is a complex and unpredictable place that places a premium on flexibility rather than on inflexible plans based on assumptions about the future that may turn out to be incorrect. As a result of scenario planning, organizations might pursue one dominant strategy related to the scenario that is judged to be most likely, but they make some investments that will pay off if other scenarios come to the fore (see Figure 1.8). Thus, the current strategy of Shell is based on the assumption that the world will only gradually shift way from carbon-based fuels (its "Dynamics as Usual" scenario), but the company is also hedging its bets by investing in new energy technologies and mapping out a strategy to pursue should its second scenario come to pass.

● **Decentralized Planning**   A mistake that some companies have made in constructing their strategic planning process has been to treat planning as an exclusively top management responsibility. This ivory tower approach can result in strategic plans formulated in a vacuum by top managers who have little understanding or appreciation of current operating realities. Consequently, top managers may formulate strategies that do more harm than good.

FIGURE 1.8

Scenario Planning

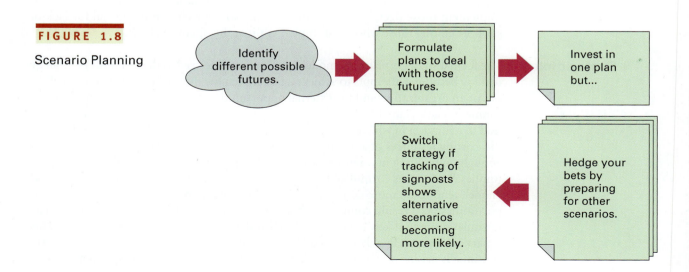

For example, when demographic data indicated that houses and families were shrinking, planners at GE's appliance group concluded that smaller appliances were the wave of the future. Because they had little contact with home builders and retailers, they did not realize that kitchens and bathrooms were the two rooms that were not shrinking. Nor did they appreciate that working women wanted big refrigerators to cut down on trips to the supermarket. GE ended up wasting a lot of time designing small appliances with limited demand.

The ivory tower concept of planning can also lead to tensions between corporate-, business-, and functional-level managers. The experience of GE's appliance group is again illuminating. Many of the corporate managers in the planning group were recruited from consulting firms or top-flight business schools. Many of the functional managers took this pattern of recruitment to mean that corporate managers did not think they were smart enough to think through strategic problems for themselves. They felt shut out of the decision-making process, which they believed to be unfairly constituted. Out of this perceived lack of procedural justice grew an us-versus-them mindset that quickly escalated into hostility. As a result, even when the planners were right, operating managers would not listen to them. For example, the planners correctly recognized the importance of the globalization of the appliance market and the emerging Japanese threat. However, operating managers, who then saw Sears, Roebuck as the competition, paid them little heed. Finally, ivory tower planning ignores the important strategic role of autonomous action by lower-level managers and serendipity.

Correcting the ivory tower approach to planning requires recognizing that successful strategic planning encompasses managers at all levels of the corporation. Much of the best planning can and should be done by business and functional managers who are closest to the facts; in other words, planning should be decentralized. The role of corporate-level planners should be that of facilitators who help business and functional managers do the planning by setting the broad strategic goals of the organization and providing the resources required to identify the strategies that might be required to attain those goals.

It is not enough to involve lower-level managers in the strategic planning process, however; they also need to perceive that the decision-making process is fair, a concept that Chan Kim and Renée Mauborgne refer to as procedural justice.[37] If people perceive the decision-making process to be unjust, they are less likely to be committed to any resulting decisions and to cooperate voluntarily in activities designed to implement those decisions. Consequently, the strategy chosen might fail for lack of support among those who must implement it at the operating level.

Strategic Intent

The formal strategic planning model has been characterized as the fit model of strategy making because it attempts to achieve a fit between the internal resources and capabilities of an organization and the external opportunities and threats in the industry environment. Gary Hamel and C. K. Prahalad have criticized the fit model because it can lead to a mindset in which management focuses too much on the degree of fit between the existing resources of a company and current environmental opportunities, and not enough on building new resources and capabilities to create and exploit future opportunities.[38] Strategies formulated with only the present in mind, argue Prahalad and Hamel, tend to be more concerned with today's problems than with tomorrow's opportunities. As a result, companies that rely exclusively on the fit approach to strategy formulation are unlikely to be able to build and maintain a competitive advantage. This is particularly true in a dynamic competitive environment, where new competitors are continually arising and new ways of doing business are constantly being invented.

As Prahalad and Hamel note, again and again, companies using the fit approach have been surprised by the ascent of competitors that initially seemed to lack the resources and capabilities needed to make them a real threat. This happened to Xerox, which ignored the rise of Canon and Ricoh in the photocopier market until they had become serious global competitors; to General Motors, which initially overlooked the threat posed by Toyota and Honda in the 1970s; and to Caterpillar, which ignored the danger Komatsu posed to its heavy earthmoving business until it was almost too late to respond.

The secret of the success of companies like Toyota, Canon, and Komatsu, according to Prahalad and Hamel, is that they all had bold ambitions that outstripped their existing resources and capabilities. All wanted to achieve global leadership, and they set out to build the resources and capabilities that would enable them to attain this goal. Consequently, top management created an obsession with winning at all levels of the organization that they sustained over a ten- to twenty-year quest for global leadership. Prahalad and Hamel refer to this type of obsession as **strategic intent**. They stress that strategic intent is more than simply unfettered ambition. It encompasses an active management process that includes "focusing the organization's attention on the essence of winning; motivating people by communicating the value of the target; leaving room for individual and team contributions; sustaining enthusiasm by providing new operational definitions as circumstances change; and using intent consistently to guide resource allocations."[39]

Thus, underlying the concept of strategic intent is the notion that strategic planning should be based on setting an ambitious vision and ambitious goals that stretch a company and then finding ways to build the resources and capabilities necessary to attain that vision and those goals. As Prahalad and Hamel note, in practice, the two approaches to strategy formulation are not mutually exclusive. All the components of the strategic planning process that we discussed earlier (see Figure 1.5) are important.

In addition, say Prahalad and Hamel, the strategic management process should begin with a challenging vision, such as attaining global leadership, that stretches the organization. Throughout the subsequent process, the emphasis should be on finding ways (strategies) to develop the resources and capabilities necessary to achieve these goals rather than on exploiting existing strengths to take advantage of existing opportunities. The difference between strategic fit and strategic intent, therefore, may just be one of emphasis. Strategic intent is more internally focused and is concerned with building new resources and capabilities. Strategic fit focuses more on matching existing resources and capabilities to the external environment.

Strategic Decision Making

Even the best-designed strategic planning systems will fail to produce the desired results if managers do not use the information at their disposal effectively. Consequently, it is important that strategic managers learn to make better use of the information they have and understand why they sometimes make poor decisions. One important way in which managers can make better use of their knowledge and information is to understand how common cognitive biases can result in good managers making bad decisions.[40]

● **Cognitive Biases and Strategic Decision Making**

The rationality of human decisionmakers is bounded by our own cognitive capabilities.[41] We are not supercomputers, and it is difficult for us to absorb and process large amounts of information effectively. As a result, when making decisions, we tend to fall back on certain rules of thumb, or heuristics, that help us to make sense out of a complex and uncertain world. However, sometimes these rules lead to severe and systematic errors in the decision-making process.[42] Systematic errors are those that appear time and time again. They seem to arise from a series of **cognitive biases** in the way that human decisionmakers process information and reach decisions. Because of cognitive biases, many managers end up making poor strategic decisions.

A number of biases have been verified repeatedly in laboratory settings, so we can be reasonably sure that they exist and that we are all prone to them.[43] The **prior hypothesis bias** refers to the fact that decisionmakers who have strong prior beliefs about the relationship between two variables tend to make decisions on the basis of these beliefs, even when presented with evidence that their beliefs are wrong. Moreover, they tend to seek and use information that is consistent with their prior beliefs while ignoring information that contradicts these beliefs. To put this bias in a strategic context, it suggests that a CEO who has a strong prior belief that a certain strategy makes sense might continue to pursue that strategy, despite evidence that it is inappropriate or failing.

Another well-known cognitive bias, **escalating commitment**, occurs when decisionmakers, having already committed significant resources to a project, commit even more resources even if they receive feedback that the project is failing.[44] This may be an irrational response; a more logical response would be to abandon the project and move on (that is, to cut your losses and run), rather than escalate commitment. Feelings of personal responsibility for a project apparently induce decisionmakers to stick with a project despite evidence that it is failing.

A third bias, **reasoning by analogy**, involves the use of simple analogies to make sense out of complex problems. The problem with this heuristic is that the analogy may not be valid. A fourth bias, **representativeness**, is rooted in the tendency to generalize from a small sample or even a single vivid anecdote. This bias violates the statistical law of large numbers, which says that it is inappropriate to generalize from a small sample, let alone from a single case. In many respects, the dot-com boom of the late 1990s was based on reasoning by analogy and representativeness. Prospective entrepreneurs saw some of the early dot-com companies such Amazon and Yahoo! achieve rapid success, at least judged by some metrics. Reasoning by analogy from a very small sample, they assumed that any dot-com could achieve similar success. Many investors reached similar conclusions. The result was a massive wave of start-ups that jumped into the Internet space in an attempt to capitalize on the perceived opportunities. That the vast majority of these companies subsequently went bankrupt is testament to the fact that the analogy was wrong and that the success of the small sample of early entrants was no guarantee that all dot-coms would succeed.

A fifth cognitive bias is referred to as **the illusion of control**: the tendency to overestimate one's ability to control events. General or top managers seem to be particularly prone to this bias: having risen to the top of an organization, they tend to be overconfident about their ability to succeed. According to Richard Roll, such overconfidence leads to what he has termed the hubris hypothesis of takeovers.[45] Roll argues that top managers are typically overconfident about their ability to create value by acquiring another company. Hence, they end up making poor acquisition decisions, often paying far too much for the companies they acquire. Subsequently, servicing the debt taken on to finance such an acquisition makes it all but impossible to make money from the acquisition.

The **availability error** is yet another common bias. The availability error arises from our predisposition to estimate the probability of an outcome based on how easy the outcome is to imagine. For example, more people seem to fear a plane crash than a car accident, and yet statistically one is far more likely to be killed in a car on the way to the airport than in a plane crash. They overweigh the probability of a plane crash because the outcome is easier to imagine, and because plane crashes are more vivid events than car crashes, which affect only small numbers of people at a time. As a result of the availability error, managers might allocate resources to a project whose outcome is easier to imagine rather than to one that might have the highest return.

● **Groupthink and Strategic Decisions**
Because most strategic decisions are made by groups, the group context within which decisions are made is clearly an important variable in determining whether cognitive biases will operate to adversely affect the strategic decision-making process. The psychologist Irvin Janis has argued that many groups are characterized by a process known as groupthink and, as a result, make poor strategic decisions.[46] Groupthink occurs when a group of decisionmakers embarks on a course of action without questioning underlying assumptions. Typically, a group coalesces around a person or policy. It ignores or filters out information that can be used to question the policy and develops after-the-fact rationalizations for its decision. Commitment to the mission or goals becomes based on an emotional rather than an objective assessment of the "correct" course of action. The consequences can be poor decisions.

The phenomenon of groupthink may explain, at least in part, why companies often make poor strategic decisions in spite of sophisticated strategic management. Janis traced many historical fiascoes to defective policymaking by government leaders who received social support from their in-group of advisers. For example, he suggested that President John F. Kennedy's inner circle suffered from groupthink when the members of this group supported the decision to launch the Bay of Pigs invasion of Cuba in 1961, even though available information showed that it would be an unsuccessful venture and would damage U.S. relations with other countries. Janis has observed that groupthink-dominated groups are characterized by strong pressures toward uniformity, which make their members avoid raising controversial issues, questioning weak arguments, or calling a halt to soft-headed thinking. As discussed in Strategy in Action 1.4, the Senate Intelligence Committee believed that groupthink biased CIA and other reports on Iraq's weapons of mass destruction that the Bush administration subsequently used to justify the 2003 invasion of that nation.

● **Techniques for Improving Decision Making**
The existence of cognitive biases and groupthink raises the issue of how to bring critical information to bear on the decision-making mechanism so that a company's strategic decisions are realistic and based on thorough evaluation. Two techniques known to enhance strategic thinking and counteract groupthink and cognitive biases are devil's advocacy and dialectic inquiry.[47]

Devil's advocacy requires the generation of both a plan and a critical analysis of the plan. One member of the decision-making group acts as the devil's advocate, bringing out all the reasons that might make the proposal unacceptable. In this way, decisionmakers can become aware of the possible perils of recommended courses of action.

Dialectic inquiry is more complex because it requires the generation of a plan (a thesis) and a counterplan (an antithesis) that reflect plausible but conflicting courses of action.[48] Strategic managers listen to a debate between advocates of the plan and counterplan and then decide which plan will lead to the higher performance. The purpose of the debate is to reveal the problems with definitions, recommended courses of action, and assumptions of both plans. As a result of this exercise, strategic managers are able to form a new and more encompassing conceptualization of the problem,

Strategy in Action

Was Intelligence on Iraq Biased by Groupthink?

In October 2002, intelligence agencies in the United States issued a national intelligence estimate on Iraq's efforts to procure and build weapons of mass destruction (WMDs). The report concluded that there was good evidence that Iraq was actively pursuing a nuclear weapons program and, furthermore, had tried to procure uranium for its bomb-making efforts from the African nation of Niger. In addition, the report claimed that Iraq was stockpiling chemical weapons, including mustard, saran, and nerve gas, and was actively pursuing a research program to produce biological weapons, including anthrax and smallpox viruses. The report was used by the Bush administration to help justify the 2003 invasion of Iraq, which culminated in the removal of Saddam Hussein's regime. The report also helped convince the U.S. Senate that Iraq was violating United Nations conditions imposed after the first Gulf War in 1991. On the basis of this intelligence, seventy-five senators voted to authorize the 2003 war.

By late 2003, however, it was becoming increasingly apparent that if there were WMDs in Iraq, they were very few in number and extremely well hidden. Had the prewar intelligence been wrong? In mid-2004, the Senate Intelligence Committee published a report evaluating the information contained in the October 2002 national intelligence estimate. The findings of the Senate report were endorsed by all seventeen members of the committee, nine Republicans and eight Democrats. In total, they constituted a damning indictment of the prewar intelligence provided by the CIA and others to the Bush administration and Congress.

The Senate report concluded that a groupthink dynamic inside American intelligence agencies generated a "collective presumption that Iraq had an active and growing weapons program." This internal bias, according to the senators, prompted analysts, collectors, and managers in the CIA and other agencies to "interpret ambiguous evidence as being conclusively indicative of a WMD program as well as ignore or minimize evidence that Iraq did not have active or expanding weapons of mass destruction programs." As a consequence, most of the key judgments in the October 2002 national intelligence estimate were "either overstated, or were not supported by the underlying intelligence reporting."

One of the most critical parts of the Senate report dealt with the prewar assessment of Iraq's nuclear weapons program. The report stated that the 2002 national intelligence estimate represented a sharp break from previous assessments, which had concluded that Iraq had not reconstituted its nuclear weapons program. The Senate report stated that the CIA made a significant shift in its assessment shortly after Vice President Dick Cheney began stating publicly that Iraq had actively reconstituted its nuclear weapons program. The implication was that the CIA gave the administration the information it thought it wanted rather than accurate information. Moreover, the Senate report claimed that the CIA's leading advocate of the Iraqi nuclear weapons threat withheld evidence from analysts who disagreed with him, misstated the analysis and information produced by others, and distributed misleading information both inside and outside the agency. The committee also concluded that the CIA overstated what it knew about Iraq's attempts to procure uranium from Niger and that it delayed for months examining documents pertaining to those attempts that would later prove to be forgeries.

On the topic of biological weapons, the Senate report concluded that none of the claims about Iraq's biological weapons or capabilities was supported by intelligence and that claims that Iraq had restarted its chemical weapons program were the results of "analytical judgments" and not based on hard evidence. The intelligence on biological weapons came from a single Iraqi defector code-named Curve Ball who was apparently an alcoholic and, in the opinion of the one person who had interviewed him, a Pentagon analyst, "utterly useless as a source." When the same analyst saw information provided by Curve Ball included in a speech that Colin Powell made to the United Nations to justify war with Iraq, he contacted the CIA to express his concerns. A CIA official quickly responded in an email: "Let's keep in mind the fact that this war's going to happen regardless of what Curve Ball said or didn't say. The powers that be probably aren't terribly interested in whether Curve Ball knows what he is talking about."

In sum, the Senate report painted a picture of intelligence institutions that selectively interpreted information to support what they thought administration policy was, while ignoring or dismissing contradictory information—sure signs of groupthink. At the same time, the report concluded that there was no evidence of undue political pressure by policymakers in the administration or Congress. Instead, the committee blamed intelligence leaders "who did not encourage analysts to challenge their assumptions, fully consider alternative arguments, accurately characterize the intelligence reporting, or counsel analysts who lost their objectivity." Be this as it may, an objective observer might also wonder why neither the Senate nor the administration asked hard questions about the quality and source of the intelligence information in the run-up to the war.[d]

which then becomes the final plan (a synthesis). Dialectic inquiry can promote strategic thinking.

Another technique for countering cognitive biases is the outside view, which has been championed by Nobel Prize winner Daniel Kahneman and his associates.[49] The **outside view** requires planners to identify a reference class of analogous past strategic initiatives, determine whether those initiatives succeeded or failed, and evaluate the project at hand against those prior initiatives. According to Kahneman, this technique is particularly useful for countering biases such as the illusion of control (hubris), reasoning by analogy, and representativeness. For example, when considering a potential acquisition, planners should look at the track record of acquisitions made by other enterprises (the reference class), determine if they succeeded or failed, and objectively evaluate the potential acquisition against that reference class. Kahneman argues that such a reality check against a large sample of prior events tends to constrain the inherent optimism of planners and produce more realistic assessments and plans.

Strategic Leadership

One of the key strategic roles of both general and functional managers is to use all their knowledge, energy, and enthusiasm to provide strategic leadership for their subordinates and develop a high-performing organization. Several authors have identified a few key characteristics of good strategic leaders that do lead to high performance: (1) vision, eloquence, and consistency; (2) articulation of a business model; (3) commitment; (4) being well informed; (5) willingness to delegate and empower; (6) astute use of power; and (7) emotional intelligence.[50]

● **Vision, Eloquence, and Consistency**

One of the key tasks of leadership is to give an organization a sense of direction. Strong leaders seem to have a clear and compelling vision of where the organization should go, are eloquent enough to communicate this vision to others within the organization in terms that energize people, and consistently articulate their vision until it becomes part of the organization's culture.[51]

In the political arena, John F. Kennedy, Winston Churchill, Martin Luther King, Jr., and Margaret Thatcher have all been held up as examples of visionary leaders. Think of the impact of Kennedy's sentence, "Ask not what your country can do for you, ask what you can do for your country," of King's "I have a dream" speech, and of Churchill's "we will never surrender." Kennedy and Thatcher were able to use their political office to push for governmental actions that were consistent with their vision.

Churchill's speech galvanized a nation to defend itself against an aggressor, and King was able to pressure the government from outside to make changes in society.

Examples of strong business leaders include Microsoft's Bill Gates; Jack Welch, the former CEO of General Electric; and Sam Walton, Wal-Mart's founder. For years, Bill Gates's vision of a world in which there would be a Windows-based personal computer on every desk was a driving force at Microsoft. More recently, the vision has evolved into one of a world in which Windows-based software can be found on any computing device, from PCs and servers to videogame consoles (Xbox), cell phones, and hand-held computers. At GE, Jack Welch was responsible for articulating the simple but powerful vision that GE should be first or second in every business in which it competed, or it should exit from that business. Similarly, it was Wal-Mart founder Sam Walton who established and articulated the vision that has been central to Wal-Mart's success: passing on cost savings from suppliers and operating efficiencies to customers in the form of everyday low prices.

Articulation of the Business Model

Another key characteristic of good strategic leaders is their ability to identify and articulate the business model the company will use to attain its vision. A business model is managers' conception of how the various strategies that the company pursues fit together into a congruent whole. At Dell Computer, for example, it was Michael Dell who identified and articulated the basic business model of the company: the direct sales business model. The various strategies that Dell has pursued over the years have refined this basic model, creating one that is very robust in terms of its efficiency and effectiveness. Although individual strategies can take root in many different places in an organization, and although their identification is not the exclusive preserve of top management, only strategic leaders have the perspective required to make sure that the various strategies fit together into a congruent whole and form a valid and compelling business model. If strategic leaders lack a clear conception of what the business model of the company is or should be, it is likely that the strategies the firm pursues will not fit together, and the result will be lack of focus and poor performance.

Commitment

Strong leaders demonstrate their commitment to their vision and business model by actions and words, and they often lead by example. Consider Nucor's former CEO, Ken Iverson. Nucor is a very efficient steel maker with perhaps the lowest cost structure in the steel industry. It has turned in thirty years of profitable performance in an industry where most other companies have lost money because of a relentless focus on cost minimization. In his tenure as CEO, Iverson set the example: he answered his own phone, employed only one secretary, drove an old car, flew coach class, and was proud of the fact that his base salary was the lowest of the *Fortune 500* CEOs (Iverson made most of his money from performance-based pay bonuses). This commitment was a powerful signal to employees that Iverson was serious about doing everything possible to minimize costs. It earned him the respect of Nucor employees and made them more willing to work hard. Although Iverson has retired, his legacy lives on in the cost-conscious organization culture that has been built at Nucor, and like all other great leaders, his impact will last beyond his tenure.

Being Well Informed

Effective strategic leaders develop a network of formal and informal sources who keep them well informed about what is going on within their company. At Starbucks for example, the first thing that CEO Jim Donald does every morning is call five to ten stores to talk to the managers and other employees there and get a sense for how their stores are performing. Donald also stops at a local Starbucks every morning on the way to work to buy his morning coffee. This has allowed him to get to know individual employees there very well. Donald finds these informal contacts to be a very useful source of information about how the company is performing.[52]

Similarly, Herb Kelleher at Southwest Airlines was able to find out much about the health of his company by dropping in unannounced on aircraft maintenance facilities and helping workers perform their tasks. Herb Kelleher would also often help airline attendants on Southwest flights, distributing refreshments and talking to customers. One frequent flyer on Southwest Airlines reported sitting next to Kelleher three times in ten years. Each time Kelleher asked him and others sitting nearby how Southwest Airlines was doing in a number of areas, looking for trends and spotting inconsistencies.[53]

Using informal and unconventional ways to gather information is wise because formal channels can be captured by special interests within the organization or by gatekeepers, managers who may misrepresent the true state of affairs to the leader. People like Donald and Kelleher who constantly interact with employees at all levels are better able to build informal information networks than leaders who closet themselves and never interact with lower-level employees.

● **Willingness to Delegate and Empower**

High-performance leaders are skilled at delegation. They recognize that unless they learn how to delegate effectively, they can quickly become overloaded with responsibilities. They also recognize that empowering subordinates to make decisions is a good motivation tool and often results in decisions being made by those who must implement them. At the same time, astute leaders recognize that they need to maintain control over certain key decisions. Thus, although they will delegate many important decisions to lower-level employees, they will not delegate those that they judge to be of critical importance to the future success of the organization, such as articulating the company's vision and business model.

● **The Astute Use of Power**

In a now classic article on leadership, Edward Wrapp noted that effective leaders tend to be very astute in their use of power.[54] He argued that strategic leaders must often play the power game with skill and attempt to build consensus for their ideas rather than use their authority to force ideas through; they must act as members of a coalition or its democratic leaders rather than as dictators. Jeffery Pfeffer has articulated a similar vision of the politically astute manager who gets things done in organizations through the intelligent use of power.[55] In Pfeffer's view, power comes from control over resources that are important to the organization: budgets, capital, positions, information, and knowledge. Politically astute managers use these resources to acquire another critical resource: critically placed allies who can help them attain their strategic objectives. Pfeffer stresses that one does not need to be a CEO to assemble power in an organization. Sometimes junior functional managers can build a surprisingly effective power base and use it to influence organizational outcomes.

● **Emotional Intelligence**

Emotional intelligence is a term that Daniel Goldman coined to describe a bundle of psychological attributes that many strong and effective leaders exhibit:[56]

● Self-awareness—the ability to understand one's own moods, emotions, and drives, as well as their effect on others.

● Self-regulation—the ability to control or redirect disruptive impulses or moods, that is, to think before acting.

- Motivation—a passion for work that goes beyond money or status and a propensity to pursue goals with energy and persistence.
- Empathy—the ability to understand the feelings and viewpoints of subordinates and to take those into account when making decisions.
- Social skills—friendliness with a purpose.

According to Goldman, leaders who possess these attributes—who exhibit a high degree of emotional intelligence—tend to be more effective than those who lack these attributes. Their self-awareness and self-regulation help to elicit the trust and confidence of subordinates. In Goldman's view, people respect leaders who, because they are self-aware, recognize their own limitations and, because they are self-regulating, consider decisions carefully. Goldman also argues that self-aware and self-regulating individuals tend to be more self-confident and therefore better able to cope with ambiguity and more open to change. A strong motivation exhibited in a passion for work can also be infectious, helping to persuade others to join together in pursuit of a common goal or organizational mission. Finally, strong empathy and social skills can help leaders earn the loyalty of subordinates. Empathetic and socially adept individuals tend to be skilled at managing disputes between managers, better able to find common ground and purpose among diverse constituencies, and better able to move people in a desired direction compared to leaders who lack these skills. In short, Goldman argues that the psychological makeup of a leader matters.

Summary of Chapter

1. A strategy is a set of related actions that managers take to increase their company's performance goals.
2. The major goal of companies is to maximize the returns that shareholders get from holding shares in the company. To maximize shareholder value, managers must pursue strategies that result in high and sustained profitability and also in profit growth.
3. The profitability of a company can be measured by the return that it makes on the capital invested in the enterprise. The profit growth of a company can be measured by the growth in earnings per share. Profitability and profit growth are determined by the strategies managers adopt.
4. A company has a competitive advantage over its rivals when it is more profitable than the average for all firms in its industry. It has a sustained competitive advantage when it is able to maintain above-average profitability over a number of years. In general, a company with a competitive advantage will grow its profits more rapidly than its rivals will.
5. General managers are responsible for the overall performance of the organization or for one of its major self-contained divisions. Their overriding strategic concern is for the health of the total organization under their direction.
6. Functional managers are responsible for a particular business function or operation. Although they lack general management responsibilities, they play a very important strategic role.
7. Formal strategic planning models stress that an organization's strategy is the outcome of a rational planning process.
8. The major components of the strategic management process are defining the mission, vision, and major goals of the organization; analyzing the external and internal environments of the organization; choosing a business model and strategies that align an organization's strengths and weaknesses with external environmental opportunities and threats; and adopting organizational structures and control systems to implement the organization's chosen strategies.
9. Strategy can emerge from deep within an organization in the absence of formal plans as lower-level managers respond to unpredicted situations.
10. Strategic planning often fails because executives do not plan for uncertainty and because ivory tower planners lose touch with operating realities.
11. The fit approach to strategic planning has been criticized for focusing too much on the degree of fit between existing resources and current opportunities,

and not enough on building new resources and capabilities to create and exploit future opportunities.

12. Strategic intent refers to an obsession with achieving an objective that stretches the company and requires it to build new resources and capabilities.

13. In spite of systematic planning, companies may adopt poor strategies if their decision-making processes are vulnerable to groupthink and if individual cognitive biases are allowed to intrude into the decision-making process.

14. Devil's advocacy, dialectic inquiry, and the outside view are techniques for enhancing the effectiveness of strategic decision making.

15. Good leaders of the strategy-making process have a number of key attributes: vision, eloquence, and consistency; ability to craft a business model; commitment; being well informed; a willingness to delegate and empower; political astuteness; and emotional intelligence.

Discussion Questions

1. What do we mean by strategy? How is a business model different from a strategy?

2. What do you think are the sources of sustained superior profitability?

3. Between 1997 and 2004, Microsoft's ROIC fell from 32% to 17.5%. Over the same period, Microsoft's profits grew from $3.45 billion to $11.33 billion. How can a company have declining profitability (as measured by ROIC) but growing profits? What do you think explains this situation at Microsoft? For 2004, analysts predicted that Microsoft's ROIC would jump to 35%. Why do you think this was the case? Was it due to any change in the company's strategy?

4. What are the strengths of formal strategic planning? What are its weaknesses?

5. Discuss the accuracy of the following statement: Formal strategic planning systems are irrelevant for firms competing in high-technology industries where the pace of change is so rapid that plans are routinely made obsolete by unforeseen events.

6. Pick the current or a past president of the United States and evaluate his performance against the leadership characteristics discussed in the text. On the basis of this comparison, do you think that the president was/is a good strategic leader? Why?

Practicing Strategic Management

SMALL-GROUP EXERCISE
Designing a Planning System

Break up into groups of three to five each and discuss the following scenario. Appoint one group member as a spokesperson who will communicate the group's findings to the class when called on to do so by the instructor.

You are a group of senior managers working for a fast-growing computer software company. Your product allows users to play interactive role-playing games over the Internet. In the past three years, your company has gone from being a start-up enterprise with ten employees and no revenues to a company with 250 employees and revenues of $60 million. It has been growing so rapidly that you have not had time to create a strategic plan, but now your board of directors is telling you that they want to see a plan, and they want it to drive decision making and resource allocation at the company. They want you

to design a planning process that will have the following attributes:

1. It will be democratic, involving as many key employees as possible in the process.

2. It will help to build a sense of shared vision within the company about how to continue to grow rapidly.

3. It will lead to the generation of three to five key strategies for the company.

4. It will drive the formulation of detailed action plans, and these plans will be subsequently linked to the company's annual operating budget.

Design a planning process to present to your board of directors. Think carefully about who should be included in this process. Be sure to outline the strengths and weaknesses of the approach you choose, and be prepared to justify why your approach might be superior to alternative approaches.

ARTICLE FILE 1

At the end of every chapter in this book is an article file task. The task requires you to search newspapers or magazines in the library for an example of a real company that satisfies the task question or issue.

Your first article file task is to find an example of a company that has recently changed its strategy. Identify whether this change was the outcome of a formal planning process or whether it was an emergent response to unforeseen events occurring in the company's environment.

STRATEGIC MANAGEMENT PROJECT
Module 1

To give you practical insight into the strategic management process, we provide a series of strategic modules; one is at the end of every chapter in this book. Each module asks you to collect and analyze information relating to the material discussed in that chapter. By completing these strategic modules, you will gain a clearer idea of the overall strategic management process.

The first step in this project is to pick a company to study. We recommend that you focus on the same company throughout the book. Remember also that we will be asking you for information about the corporate and international strategy of your company as well as its structure. We strongly recommend that you pick a company for which such information is likely to be available.

There are two approaches that can be used to select a company to study, and your instructor will tell you which one to follow. The first approach is to pick a well-known company that has a lot of information written about it. For example, large publicly held companies such as IBM, Microsoft, and Southwest Airlines are routinely covered in the business and financial press. By going to the library at your university, you should be able to track down a great deal of information on such companies. Many libraries now have comprehensive web-based electronic data search facilities such as *ABI/Inform*, the *Wall Street Journal Index*, the *F&S Index*, and the *Nexis-Lexis* databases. These enable you to identify any article that has been written in the business press on the company of your choice within the past few years. A number of nonelectronic data sources are also available and useful. For example, *F&S Predicasts* publishes an annual list of articles relating to major companies that appeared in the national and international business press. *S&P Industry Surveys* is also a great source for basic industry data, and *Value Line Ratings and Reports* contain good summaries of a firm's financial position and future prospects. Collect full financial information on the company that you pick. This information can be accessed from web-based electronic databases such as the *Edgar* database, which archives all forms that publicly quoted companies have to file with the Securities and Exchange Commission (SEC); for example, 10-K filings can be accessed from the SEC's *Edgar* database. Most SEC forms for public companies can now be accessed from Internet-based financial sites, such as Yahoo!'s finance site (www.finance.yahoo.com/).

A second approach is to pick a smaller company in your city or town to study. Although small companies are not routinely covered in the national business press, they may be covered in the local press. More importantly, this approach can work well if the management of the company will agree to talk to you at length about the strategy and structure of the company. If you happen to know somebody in such a company or if you have worked there at some point, this approach can be very worthwhile. However, we do not recommend this approach unless you can get a substantial amount of guaranteed access to the company of your choice. If in doubt, ask your instructor before making a decision. The key issue is to make sure that you have access to enough interesting information to complete a detailed and comprehensive analysis.

Your assignment for Module 1 is to choose a company to study and to obtain enough information about it to carry out the following instructions and answer the questions:

1. Give a short account of the history of the company, and trace the evolution of its strategy. Try to determine whether the strategic evolution of your company is the product of intended strategies, emergent strategies, or some combination of the two.
2. Identify the mission and major goals of the company.
3. Do a preliminary analysis of the internal strengths and weaknesses of the company and the opportunities and threats that it faces in its environment. On the basis of this analysis, identify the strategies that you think the company should pursue. (You will need to perform a much more detailed analysis later in the book.)
4. Who is the CEO of the company? Evaluate the CEO's leadership capabilities.

ETHICS EXERCISE

Sarah has recently been hired as an assistant manager by Smith & Sons, a midsize retail company located in her small town. Previously, Sarah worked for a smaller retail company that always seemed to be trailing along in Smith & Sons' wake, struggling to make ends meet. Both companies sell commonly used items such as greeting cards, stationery, party decorations, and more. Hoping to open her own retail store someday, Sarah was intrigued by the idea of working for a company that appeared to hold competitive advantage in the area.

John, Smith & Sons' manager and Sarah's superior, put Sarah out on the floor immediately. There she began to meet Smith & Sons' employees—the frontline who was expected to provide customer satisfaction and product information. During her second week on the job, Sarah met Molly, a single mother of two. Being a mother herself, Sarah found she had a lot in common with Molly and the two began to talk. Over the course of their talk, Molly revealed that she was being paid $6 an hour and could barely make ends meet. Sarah knew that her previous employer had been struggling, in part, due to the fact that she

was determined to pay her employees a fair wage. With jobs in short supply in the small town, Sarah resolved to talk with John to find out if something could be done.

That afternoon, Sarah brought the issue to John's attention. "John, I happen to know that some of the other retail firms in the area are raising pay rates in order to be fair to their employees. Don't you think that we should do the same to make certain that we retain our employees and their loyalty?"

John's response shocked Sarah. "How do you think we got to be successful, Sarah—by coddling our employees—by running business into the ground in order to focus on their best interests? No, we pay our employees as little as possible! They're a dime a dozen—if one leaves, another takes her place! Those other retail firms—they'll be going out of business sooner than they realize, and we'll still be here thriving."

1. Identify the ethical dilemma addressed in this case.
2. Do you think that paying low wages really contributes to Smith & Sons' competitive advantage?
3. How might the other companies offering higher wages gain competitive advantage over Smith & Sons?

CLOSING CASE

The Best-Laid Plans—Chrysler Hits the Wall

In 1998, after Germany's Daimler-Benz acquired Chrysler, the third largest U.S. automobile manufacturer, to form DaimlerChrysler, many observers thought that Chrysler would break away from its troubled U.S. brethren, Ford and General Motors, and join ranks with the Japanese automobile makers. The strategic plan was to emphasize bold design, better product quality, and higher productivity by sharing designs and parts between the two companies. Jurgen Schrempp, the CEO of the combined companies, told shareholders to "expect the extraordinary"

and went on to say that DaimlerChrysler "has the size, profitability and reach to take on everyone."

Eight years later, the grand scheme has proved extraordinary, but for all of the wrong reasons. In 2006, Chrysler saw its market share fall to 10.6%, and the company announced that it would lose $1.26 billion in 2006. This shocked shareholders, who had been told a few months earlier that the Chrysler unit would break even in 2006.

What went wrong? First, Schrempp and his planners may have overestimated Chrysler's competitiveness prior to the merger. Chrysler was the most profitable of the three U.S. auto companies in the late 1990s, but the U.S. economy was very strong and the company's core offering of pickup trucks, sport utility vehicles (SUVs), and minivans were the right product for a time of low gas prices. After the merger, the Germans discovered that Chrysler's factories were in worse shape than they had thought, and product quality was poor. Second, sharing design and engineering resources, and parts, between Daimler's Mercedez-Benz models and Chrysler proved to be very difficult. Mercedez was a luxury car maker, Chrysler a mass-market manufacturer, and it would take years to redesign Chrysler cars so that they could use Daimler parts and benefit from Daimler engineering. Nor did Daimler's engineers and managers seem enthusiastic about helping Chrysler, which many saw as a black hole into which a profitable Mercedes-Benz line would pour billions of euros.

To be fair, the new cars that Chrysler did produce, including the 300C sedan and the PT Cruiser, garnered good reviews. Sales of the 300C were strong, but not strong enough to shift the balance of Chrysler's business away from the small-truck segment.

Despite several years of financial struggle, by 2004, it looked as if things might finally be turning round at Chrysler. In 2004 and then again in 2005, the company made good money. The company actually gained market share in 2005. Dieter Zetsche, Chrysler's German CEO, hoped to capitalize on this with the introduction of a new SUV, the seven-seat Jeep Commander. Launched in mid-2005, the timing of the Commander could not have been worse. In 2005, the price of oil surged dramatically as strong demand from developed nations and China combined with tight supplies (which were made worse by supply disruptions caused by Hurricane Katrina). By mid-2006 oil had reached $70 a barrel, up from half that just eighteen months earlier, and gas prices hit $3 a gallon.

To make matters worse, Ford and General Motors, who themselves were hemorrhaging red ink, were engaged in an aggressive price war, offering deep incentives to move their own excess inventory, and Chrysler was forced to match prices or lose much share. Meanwhile, Japanese manufacturers, particularly Toyota and Honda, who had been expanding their U.S. production facilities for fifteen years, were gaining share with their smaller fuel-efficient offerings and popular hybrids.

In September 2006, Chrysler announced that due to a buildup of inventory on dealers' lots, it would cut production by 16%, double the planned figure announced in June 2006. In addition to slumping sales, Thomas LaSorda revealed that the company was facing sharply higher costs for its raw materials and parts, some of which were up as much as 60%. Chrysler was also suffering from high health care costs and pension liabilities to its unionized work force.

Scrambling to fill the gap in its product line, Chrysler announced that it might enter into a partnership with China's Chery Motors to produce small fuel-efficient cars in China, which would then be imported into the United States.[57]

Case Discussion Questions

1. What was the planned strategy at Daimler-Benz for Chrysler in 1988?

2. In retrospect, Daimler-Benz's plans for Chrysler seemed overoptimistic. What decision-making errors might Daimler-Benz have made in its evaluation of Chrysler? How might those errors have been avoided?

3. What opportunities and threats was Chrysler facing in 2005 and 2006? What were Chrysler's strengths and weaknesses? Did its product strategy make sense given these considerations?

4. Why did Chrysler get its forecasts for product sales and earnings so wrong in 2006? What does this teach you about the nature of planning?

5. What must Chrysler do now if it is to regain its footing in this industry?

Appendix to Chapter 1

Enterprise Valuation, ROIC, and Growth

The ultimate goal of strategy is to maximize the value of a company to its shareholders (subject to the important constraints that this is done in a legal, ethical, and socially responsible manner). The two main drivers of enterprise valuation are return on invested capital (ROIC) and the growth rate of profits, g.[58]

ROIC is defined as net operating profits less adjusted taxes (NOPLAT) over the invested capital of the enterprise (IC), where IC is the sum of the company's equity and debt (the method for calculating adjusted taxes need not concern us here). That is:

$$ROIC = NOPLAT/IC$$

where:

$$NOPLAT = \text{revenues} - \text{cost of goods sold}$$
$$- \text{operating expenses}$$
$$- \text{depreciation charges}$$
$$- \text{adjusted taxes}$$

$$IC = \text{value of shareholders' equity} + \text{value of debt}$$

The growth rate of profits, g, can be defined as the percentage increase in net operating profits (NOPLAT) over a given time period. More precisely:

$$g = [(NOPLAT_{t+1} - NOPLAT_t)/NOPLAT_t] \times 100$$

Note that if NOPLAT is increasing over time, earnings per share will also increase so long as (a) the number of shares stays constant, or (b) the number of shares outstanding increases more slowly than NOPLAT.

The valuation of a company can be calculated using discounted cash flow analysis and applying it to future expected free cash flows (free cash flow in a period is defined as NOPLAT − net investments). It can be shown that the valuation of a company so calculated is related to the company's weighted average cost of capital (WACC), which is the cost of the equity and debt that the firm uses to finance its business, and the company's ROIC. Specifically:

- If ROIC > WACC, the company is earning more than its cost of capital and it is creating value.
- If ROIC = WACC, the company is earning its cost of capital and its valuation will be stable.
- If ROIC < WACC, the company is earning less than its cost of capital and it is therefore destroying value.

A company that earns more than its cost of capital is even more valuable if it can grow its net operating profits less adjusted taxes (NOPLAT) over time. Conversely, a firm that is not earning its cost of capital destroys value if it grows its NOPLAT. This critical relationship between ROIC, g, and value is shown in Table A1.

In Table A1, the figures in the cells of the matrix represent the discounted present values of future free cash flows for a company that has a starting NOPLAT of $100, invested capital of $1,000, a cost of capital of 10%, and a twenty-five-year time horizon after which ROIC = cost of capital.

TABLE A1

ROIC, Growth, and Valuation

NOPLAT Growth g	ROIC 7.5%	ROIC 10.0%	ROIC 12.5%	ROIC 15%	ROIC 20%
3%	887	1,000	1,058	1,113	1,170
6%	708	1,000	1,117	1,295	1,442
9%	410	1,000	1,354	1,591	1,886

The important points revealed by this exercise are as follows:

1. A company with an already high ROIC can create more value by increasing its profit growth rate rather than pushing for an even higher ROIC. Thus, a company with an ROIC of 15% and a 3% growth rate can create more value by increasing its profit growth rate from 3% to 9% than it can by increasing ROIC to 20%.

2. A company with a low ROIC destroys value if it grows. Thus, if ROIC = 7.5%, a 9% growth rate for twenty-five years will produce less value than a 3% growth rate. This is because unprofitable growth requires capital investments, the cost of which cannot be covered. Unprofitable growth destroys value.

3. The best of both worlds is high ROIC and high growth.

Very few companies are able to maintain an ROIC > WACC and grow NOPLAT over time, but there are some notable examples, including Dell, Microsoft, and Wal-Mart. Because these companies have generally been able to fund their capital investment needs from internally generated cash flows, they have not had to issue more shares to raise capital. Thus, growth in NOPLAT has translated directly into higher earnings per share for these companies, making their shares more attractive to investors and leading to substantial share-price appreciation. By successfully pursuing strategies that result in a high ROIC and growing NOPLAT, these firms have maximized shareholder value.

External Analysis: The Identification of Opportunities and Threats

The United States Beer Industry

Over the last few decades, the United States beer industry has been characterized by a very clear trend toward an increase in the concentration of the market. Today, some 80% of all the beer consumed in the United States is produced by just three companies: Anheuser-Busch, SAB-Miller, and Molson Coors, up from 57% of the market in 1980. Anheuser-Busch had almost 50% of the market in 2006, up from just 28.2% in 1980. SAB-Miller (formed in 2002 when South African Breweries merged with Miller Beer) had around 19% of the market, and Molson Coors (formed in 2005 when Canada's Molson merged with Coors) had 11% of the market.

Anheuser Busch, SAB-Miller, and Molson Coors dominate the *mass-market* segment of the industry, where competition revolves around aggressive pricing, brand loyalty, wide distribution, and national advertising spending. In contrast, another segment in the industry, the *premium beer* segment, is served by a large number of microbrewers and importers, the majority of which have a market share of less than 1%. The premium segment focuses on discerning buyers. Producers are engaged in the art of craft brewing. They build their brands around taste and cover higher product costs by charging much higher prices—roughly twice as much for a six-pack as the mass-market brewers. The microbrewers and importers have been gaining share and currently account for around 11% of the total market.

The increase in concentration among mass-market brewers reflects a number of factors. First, consumption of beer in the United States has been gradually declining (even though consumption of premium beer has been increasing). Per-capita consumption of beer peaked at 34 gallons in 1980, fell to a low of 29.1 gallons in 2003, and crept back up to 30 gallons per capita in 2005. The decline in consumption was partly due to the growing popularity of substitutes, particularly wine and spirits. In 1994, Americans consumed 1.75 gallons of wine per capita. By 2005, the figure had risen 2.16 gallons. Consumption of spirits increased from 1.27 gallons per capita in 1994 to 1.34 gallons per capita over the same period.

Second, advertising spending has steadily increased, putting smaller mass-market brewers at a distinct disadvantage. In 1975, the industry was spending $0.18 a case on advertising; by 2002, it was spending $0.40 a case (these figures are in inflation-adjusted or constant dollars). Smaller mass-market brewers couldn't afford the expensive national television advertising campaigns required to match the spending of the largest firms in the industry, and they saw their market share shrink as a result.

Third, due to a combination of technological change in canning and distribution, and increased advertising expenditures, the size that a mass-market brewer has to attain in order to reap all economies of scale—called the *minimum efficient scale* of production—has steadily increased. In 1970, the minimum efficient scale of production was estimated to be 8 million barrels of beer a year, suggesting that a market share of 6.4% was required to reap significant economies of scale. By the early 2000s, the minimum efficient scale had increased to 23 million barrels, implying that a market share of 13.06% was required to reap significant scale economies.

In sum, the combination of declining demand, increasing advertising spending, and an increase in the minimum efficient scale of production put smaller mass-market brewers at a competitive disadvantage. Many sold out to the larger brewers or, in some cases, simply shut down. By the early 2000s, there were only twenty-four mass-market brewers left in the United States, down from eighty-two in 1970. Among the remaining mass-market brewers, Anheuser Busch is the most consistent performer due to its superior economies of scale. The company's return on invested capital (ROIC) has been high, fluctuating in the 17% to 23% range between 1996 and 2006, while net profits grew from $1.1 billion in 1996 to $2 billion in 2006. In contrast, both Coors and Miller, along with most other mass-market brewers, have had mediocre financial performance at best. Coors and Miller merged with Molson and SAB, respectively, in an attempt to gain scale economies.[1]

OVERVIEW

Strategy formulation begins with an analysis of the forces that shape competition in the industry in which a company is based. The goal is to understand the opportunities and threats confronting the firm and to use this understanding to identify strategies that will enable the company to outperform its rivals. **Opportunities** arise when a company can take advantage of conditions in its environment to formulate and implement strategies that enable it to become more profitable. For example, as discussed in the Opening Case, the growth in consumption of premium beer represents an *opportunity* for brewers to expand their sales volume by creating products for the premium segment. **Threats** arise when conditions in the external environment endanger the integrity and profitability of the company's business. Declining beer consumption and the rise in the minimum efficient scale of production have been *threats* to the profitability of all but the very largest mass-market brewers in the beer industry (see the Opening Case).

This chapter begins with an analysis of the industry environment. First, it examines concepts and tools for analyzing the competitive structure of an industry and identifying industry opportunities and threats. Second, it analyzes the competitive implications that arise when groups of companies within an industry pursue similar and different kinds of competitive strategies. Third, it explores the way an industry evolves over time and the accompanying changes in competitive conditions. Fourth, it looks at the way in which forces in the macroenvironment affect industry structure and influence opportunities and threats. By the end of the chapter, you will understand that to succeed, a company must either fit its strategy to the external environment in which it operates or be able to reshape the environment to its advantage through its chosen strategy.

Defining an Industry

An industry can be defined as a group of companies offering products or services that are close substitutes for each other—that is, products or services that satisfy the same basic customer needs. A company's closest competitors, its rivals, are those that serve the same basic customer needs. For example, carbonated drinks, fruit punches, and bottled water can be viewed as close substitutes for each other because they serve the same basic customer needs for refreshing and cold nonalcoholic beverages. Thus, we can talk about the soft drink industry, whose major players are Coca-Cola, PepsiCo, and Cadbury Schweppes. Similarly, desktop computers and notebook computers satisfy the same basic need that customers have for computer hardware on which to run personal productivity software; browse the Internet; send email; play games; and store, display, and manipulate digital images. Thus, we can talk about the personal computer industry, whose major players are Dell, Hewlett-Packard, Lenovo (the Chinese company that purchased IBM's personal computer business), Gateway, and Apple Computer.

The starting point of external analysis is to identify the industry that a company competes in. To do this, managers must begin by looking at the basic customer needs their company is serving—that is, they must take a customer-oriented view of their business as opposed to a product-oriented view (see Chapter 1). An industry is the supply side of a market, and companies in the industry are the suppliers. Customers are the demand side of a market and are the buyers of the industry's products. The basic customer needs that are served by a market define an industry's boundary. It is very important for managers to realize this, for if they define industry boundaries incorrectly, they may be caught flat-footed by the rise of competitors that serve the same basic customer needs with different product offerings. For example, Coca-Cola long saw itself as being in the soda industry—meaning carbonated soft drinks— whereas in fact, it was in the soft drink industry, which includes noncarbonated soft drinks. In the mid-1990s, Coca-Cola was caught by surprise by the rise of customer demand for bottled water and fruit drinks, which began to cut into the demand for sodas. Coca-Cola moved quickly to respond to these threats, introducing its own brand of water, Dasani, and acquiring orange-juice-maker Minute Maid. By defining its industry boundaries too narrowly, Coca-Cola almost missed the rapid rise of the noncarbonated soft drinks segment of the soft drinks market.

● **Industry and Sector**   An important distinction that needs to be made is between an industry and a sector. A sector is a group of closely related industries. For example, as illustrated in Figure 2.1, the computer sector comprises several related industries: the computer component industries (for example, the disk drive industry, the semiconductor industry, and the modem industry), the computer hardware industries (for example, the personal computer industry, the hand-held computer industry, and the mainframe computer industry), and the computer software industry. Industries within a sector may be involved with each other in many different ways. Companies in the computer component industries are the suppliers of firms in the computer hardware industries. Companies in the computer software industry provide important complements to computer hardware: the software programs that customers purchase to run on their hardware. And companies in the personal, hand-held, and mainframe industries are in indirect competition with each other because all provide products that are, to a degree, substitutes for each other.

FIGURE 2.1

The Computer Sector: Industries and Segments

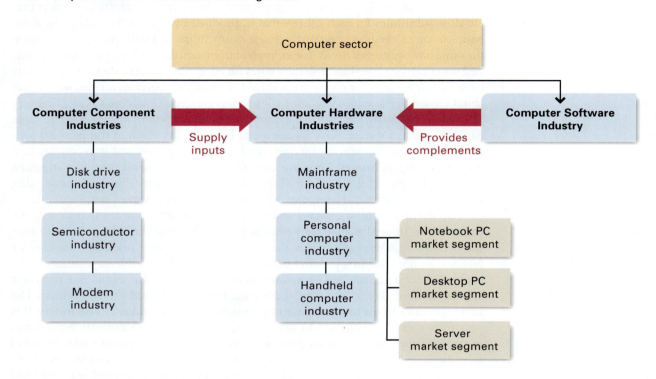

● **Industry and Market Segments**

It is also important to recognize the difference between an industry and the market segments within that industry. Market segments are distinct groups of customers within a market that can be differentiated from each other on the basis of their distinct attributes and specific demands. In the beer industry, for example, there are three main segments—consumers who drink long-established mass-market brands (for example, Budweiser), weight-conscious consumers who drink less filling, low-calorie mass-market brands (for example, Coors Light), and consumers who prefer premium-priced craft beer offered by microbreweries and many importers (see the Opening Case). Similarly, in the personal computer industry, there are different segments where customers desire desktop machines, lightweight portable machines, and servers that sit at the center of a network of personal computers (see Figure 2.1). Personal computer makers recognize the existence of these different segments by producing a range of product offerings that appeal to customers in different segments. Customers in all of these different segments, however, share a common need for PCs on which to run personal software applications.

● **Changing Industry Boundaries**

Industry boundaries may change over time as customer needs evolve or new technologies emerge that enable companies in hitherto unrelated industries to satisfy established customer needs in new ways. We have noted that during the 1990s, as consumers of soft drinks began to develop a taste for bottled water and noncarbonated fruit-based drinks, Coca-Cola found itself in direct competition with the manufacturers of bottled water and fruit-based soft drinks: all were in the same industry.

For an example of how technological change can alter industry boundaries, consider the convergence that is currently taking place between the computer and telecommunications industries. Historically, the telecommunications equipment industry has been considered a distinct entity from the computer hardware industry. However, as telecommunications equipment has moved from traditional analog technology to digital technology, so telecommunications equipment has increasingly come to resemble computers. The result is that the boundaries between these different industries are blurring. A digital wireless phone, for example, is nothing more than a small hand-held computer with a wireless connection, and small hand-held computers often now come with wireless capabilities, transforming them into phones. Thus, Nokia and Motorola, which manufacture wireless phones, are now finding themselves competing directly with Palm, which manufactures hand-held computers.

Industry competitive analysis begins by focusing on the overall industry in which a firm competes before market segments or sector-level issues are considered. Tools that managers can use to perform such industry analysis—Porter's five forces model, strategic group analysis, and industry life cycle analysis—are discussed in the following sections.

Porter's Five Forces Model

Once the boundaries of an industry have been identified, the task facing managers is to analyze competitive forces in the industry environment to identify opportunities and threats. Michael E. Porter's well-known framework, known as the five forces model, helps managers with this analysis.[2] His model, shown in Figure 2.2, focuses on five forces that shape competition within an industry: (1) the risk of entry by potential competitors, (2) the intensity of rivalry among established companies within an industry, (3) the bargaining power of buyers, (4) the bargaining power of suppliers, and (5) the closeness of substitutes to an industry's products.

Porter argues that the stronger each of these forces is, the more limited is the ability of established companies to raise prices and earn greater profits. Within Porter's framework, a strong competitive force can be regarded as a threat because it depresses profits. A weak competitive force can be viewed as an opportunity because it allows a company to earn greater profits. The strength of the five forces may change through

FIGURE 2.2

Porter's Five Forces Model

Source: Adapted and reprinted by permission of Harvard Business Review. From "How Competitive Forces Shape Strategy," by Michael E. Porter, *Harvard Business Review*, March/April 1979, copyright © 1979 by the President and Fellows of Harvard College. All rights reserved.

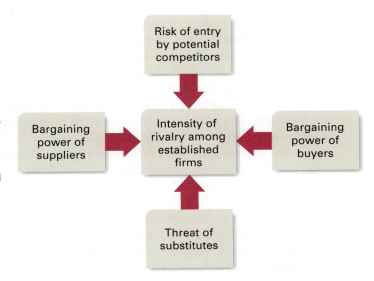

time as industry conditions change. The task facing managers is to recognize how changes in the five forces give rise to new opportunities and threats and to formulate appropriate strategic responses. In addition, it is possible for a company, through its choice of strategy, to alter the strength of one or more of the five forces to its advantage. This is discussed in the following chapters.

● **Risk of Entry by Potential Competitors**

Potential competitors are companies that are not currently competing in an industry but have the capability to do so if they choose. For example, cable television companies have recently emerged as potential competitors to traditional phone companies. New digital technologies have allowed cable companies to offer telephone service over the same cables that transmit television shows.

Established companies already operating in an industry often attempt to discourage potential competitors from entering the industry because the more companies that enter, the more difficult it becomes for established companies to protect their share of the market and generate profits. A high risk of entry by potential competitors represents a threat to the profitability of established companies. But if the risk of new entry is low, established companies can take advantage of this opportunity to raise prices and earn greater returns.

The risk of entry by potential competitors is a function of the height of barriers to entry, that is, factors that make it costly for companies to enter an industry. The greater the costs that potential competitors must bear to enter an industry, the greater are the barriers to entry and the weaker this competitive force. High entry barriers may keep potential competitors out of an industry even when industry profits are high. Important barriers to entry include economies of scale, brand loyalty, absolute cost advantages, customer switching costs, and government regulation.[3] An important strategy is building barriers to entry (in the case of incumbent firms) or finding ways to circumvent those barriers (in the case of new entrants). We shall discuss this topic in more detail in subsequent chapters.

ECONOMIES OF SCALE **Economies of scale** arise when unit costs fall as a firm expands its output. Sources of scale economies include (1) cost reductions gained through mass-producing a standardized output, (2) discounts on bulk purchases of raw material inputs and component parts, (3) the advantages gained by spreading fixed production costs over a large production volume, and (4) the cost savings associated with spreading marketing and advertising costs over a large volume of output. In the beer industry, for example, Anheuser Busch has been able to reap substantial scale economies by spreading the fixed costs associated with national advertising over its industry-leading sales volume (see the Opening case). If the cost advantages from economies of scale are significant, a new company that enters the industry and produces on a small scale suffers a significant cost disadvantage relative to established companies. If the new company decides to enter on a large scale in an attempt to obtain these economies of scale, it has to raise the capital required to build large-scale production facilities and bear the high risks associated with such an investment. A further risk of large-scale entry is that the increased supply of products will depress prices and result in vigorous retaliation by established companies. For these reasons, the threat of entry is reduced when established companies have economies of scale.

BRAND LOYALTY **Brand loyalty** exists when consumers have a preference for the products of established companies. A company can create brand loyalty through continuous advertising of its brand-name products and company name, patent protection of products, product innovation achieved through company research and development

(R&D) programs, an emphasis on high product quality, and good after-sales service. Significant brand loyalty makes it difficult for new entrants to take market share away from established companies. Thus, it reduces the threat of entry by potential competitors since they may see the task of breaking down well-established customer preferences as too costly. In the mass-market segments of the beer industry, for example, the brand loyalty enjoyed by Anheuser Busch (Budweiser), Molson Coors (Coors), and SAB-Miller (Miller) is such that new entry into these segments of the industry is very difficult. Hence, most new entrants have focused on the premium segment of the industry, where established brands have less of a hold. (For an example of how a company circumvented brand-based barriers to entry in the market for carbonated soft drinks, see Strategy in Action 2.1).

Strategy in Action   2.1

Circumventing Entry Barriers into the Soft Drink Industry

The soft drink industry has long been dominated by two companies, Coca-Cola and PepsiCo. By spending large sums of money on advertising and promotion, both companies have created significant brand loyalty and made it very difficult for new competitors to enter the industry and take market share away from these two giants. When new competitors do try to enter, both companies have responded by cutting prices and thus forcing the new entrant to curtail expansion plans.

However, in the early 1990s, the Cott Corporation, then a small Canadian bottling company, worked out a strategy for entering the soft drink market. Cott's strategy was deceptively simple. The company initially focused on the cola segment of the soft drink market. Cott signed a deal with Royal Crown Cola for exclusive global rights to its cola concentrate. RC Cola was a small player in the U.S. cola market. Its products were recognized as high quality, but RC Cola had never been able to effectively challenge Coke or Pepsi. Next, Cott signed a deal with a Canadian grocery retailer, Loblaw, to provide the retailer with its own private-label brand of cola. Priced low, the Loblaw private-label brand, known as President's Choice, was very successful and took share from both Coke and Pepsi.

Emboldened by this success, Cott decided to try to convince other retailers to carry private-label cola. To retailers, the value proposition was simple because, unlike its major rivals, Cott spent almost nothing on advertising and promotion. This constituted a major source of cost savings, which Cott passed on to retailers in the form of lower prices. For their part, the retailers found that they could significantly undercut the price of Coke and Pepsi colas and still make better profit margins on private-label brands than on branded colas.

Despite this compelling value proposition, few retailers were willing to sell private-label colas for fear of alienating Coca-Cola and Pepsi, whose products were a major draw of grocery store traffic. Cott's breakthrough came in 1992 when it signed a deal with Wal-Mart to supply the retailing giant with a private-label cola, called Sam's Choice (named after Wal-Mart founder Sam Walton). Wal-Mart proved to be the perfect distribution channel for Cott. The retailer was just starting to get into the grocery business, and consumers went to Wal-Mart not to buy branded merchandise but to get low prices.

As Wal-Mart's grocery business grew, so did Cott's sales. Cott soon added other flavors to its offering, such as lemon-lime soda, which would compete with Seven Up and Sprite. Moreover, pressured by Wal-Mart, other U.S. grocers had also started to introduce private-label sodas by the late 1990s, often turning to Cott to supply their needs.

By 2006, Cott had grown to become a $1.8 billion company. Its volume growth in an otherwise stagnant U.S. market for sodas has averaged around 12.5% between 2001 and 2006. Cott captured over 5% of the U.S. soda market in 2005, up from almost nothing a decade earlier, and held onto a 16% share of sodas in grocery stores, its core channel. The losers in this process have been Coca-Cola and PepsiCo, who are now facing the steady erosion of their brand loyalty and market share as consumers increasingly came to recognize the high quality and low price of private-label sodas.[a]

ABSOLUTE COST ADVANTAGES Sometimes established companies have an **absolute cost advantage** relative to potential entrants, meaning that entrants cannot expect to match the established companies' lower cost structure. Absolute cost advantages arise from three main sources: (1) superior production operations and processes due to accumulated experience, patents, or secret processes; (2) control of particular inputs required for production, such as labor, materials, equipment, or management skills, that are limited in their supply; and (3) access to cheaper funds because existing companies represent lower risks than new entrants. If established companies have an absolute cost advantage, the threat of entry as a competitive force is weaker.

CUSTOMER SWITCHING COSTS **Switching costs** arise when it costs a customer time, energy, and money to switch from the products offered by one established company to the products offered by a new entrant. When switching costs are high, customers can be locked in to the product offerings of established companies, even if new entrants offer better products.[4] A familiar example of switching costs concerns the costs associated with switching from one computer operating system to another. If a person currently uses Microsoft's Windows operating system and has a library of related software applications (for example, word-processing software, spreadsheet, games) and document files, it is expensive for that person to switch to another computer operating system. To effect the change, this person would have to buy a new set of software applications and convert all existing document files to run with the new system. Faced with such an expense of money and time, most people are unwilling to make the switch unless the competing operating system offers a substantial leap forward in performance. Thus, the higher the switching costs are, the higher is the barrier to entry for a company attempting to promote a new computer operating system.

GOVERNMENT REGULATION Historically, government regulation has constituted a major entry barrier into many industries. For example, until the mid-1990s, U.S. government regulation prohibited providers of long-distance telephone service from competing for local telephone service, and vice versa. Other potential providers of telephone service, including cable television service companies such as Time Warner and Comcast (which could, in theory, use their cables to carry telephone traffic as well as television signals), were prohibited from entering the market altogether. These regulatory barriers to entry significantly reduced the level of competition in both the local and long-distance telephone markets, enabling telephone companies to earn higher profits than might otherwise have been the case. All this changed in 1996 when the government deregulated the industry significantly. In the months that followed this announcement, local, long-distance, and cable television companies all announced their intention to enter each other's markets, and a host of new players emerged. The five forces model predicts that falling entry barriers due to government deregulation will result in significant new entry, an increase in the intensity of industry competition, and lower industry profit rates, and indeed, that is what occurred.

In summary, if established companies have built brand loyalty for their products, have an absolute cost advantage with respect to potential competitors, have significant scale economies, are the beneficiaries of high switching costs, or enjoy regulatory protection, the risk of entry by potential competitors is greatly diminished; it is a weak competitive force. Consequently, established companies can charge higher prices, and industry profits are higher. Evidence from academic research suggests that the height of barriers to entry is one of the most important determinants of profit rates in an industry.[5] Clearly, it is in the interest of established companies to pursue strategies consistent with raising entry barriers to secure these profits. By the same token, potential new entrants have to find strategies that allow them to circumvent barriers to entry.

LIMITS OF ENTRY BARRIERS Even when entry barriers are very high, new firms may still enter an industry if they perceive that the benefits outweigh the substantial costs of entry. This is what appears to have occurred in the telecommunications industry following deregulation in 1996. Deregulation led to a flood of new entrants such as Level 3 Communications, 360networks, and Global Crossing, who built fiber-optic networks to serve what they perceived as explosive growth in the amount of Internet traffic. These entrants had to undertake billions of dollars in capital expenditure to build their networks and match the scale advantages of established companies such as WorldCom. However, the new entrants were able to raise the capital to do so from investors who shared management's euphoric vision of future demand in the industry (Level 3 alone raised $13 billion). As it turned out, the euphoric vision of demand growth was based on the erroneous assumption that Internet traffic was growing at 1,000 percent a year when in fact it was growing at only 100 percent a year. When the euphoric vision proved to be false, many of the new entrants went bankrupt, but not before their investments had created excess capacity in the industry and sparked intense price competition that depressed the returns for all players, new entrants and established companies alike.

Rivalry Among Established Companies

The second of Porter's five competitive forces is the intensity of rivalry among established companies within an industry. Rivalry refers to the competitive struggle between companies in an industry to gain market share from each other. The competitive struggle can be fought using price, product design, advertising and promotion spending, direct selling efforts, and after-sales service and support. More intense rivalry implies lower prices or more spending on non-price-competitive weapons, or both. Because intense rivalry lowers prices and raises costs, it squeezes profits out of an industry. Thus, intense rivalry among established companies constitutes a strong threat to profitability. Alternatively, if rivalry is less intense, companies may have the opportunity to raise prices or reduce spending on non-price-competitive weapons, which leads to a higher level of industry profits. The intensity of rivalry among established companies within an industry is largely a function of four factors: (1) industry competitive structure, (2) demand conditions, (3) cost conditions, and (4) the height of exit barriers in the industry.

INDUSTRY COMPETITIVE STRUCTURE The competitive structure of an industry refers to the number and size distribution of companies in it, something that strategic managers determine at the beginning of an industry analysis. Industry structures vary, and different structures have different implications for the intensity of rivalry. A fragmented industry consists of a large number of small or medium-sized companies, none of which is in a position to determine industry price. A consolidated industry is dominated by a small number of large companies (an oligopoly) or, in extreme cases, by just one company (a monopoly), and companies often are in a position to determine industry prices. Examples of fragmented industries are agriculture, dry cleaning, video rental, health clubs, real estate brokerage, and sun tanning parlors. Consolidated industries include the aerospace, soft drink, automobile, pharmaceutical, stockbrokerage and beer industries. In the beer industry, for example, the top three firms account for 80% of industry sales (see the Opening Case).

Many fragmented industries are characterized by low entry barriers and commodity-type products that are hard to differentiate. The combination of these traits tends to result in boom-and-bust cycles as industry profits rise and fall. Low entry barriers imply that whenever demand is strong and profits are high, new entrants will flood the market, hoping to profit from the boom. The explosion in the number of video stores, health clubs, and sun tanning parlors during the 1980s and 1990s exemplifies this situation.

Often the flood of new entrants into a booming fragmented industry creates excess capacity, so companies start to cut prices in order to use their spare capacity. The difficulty companies face when trying to differentiate their products from those of competitors can exacerbate this tendency. The result is a price war, which depresses industry profits, forces some companies out of business, and deters potential new entrants. For example, after a decade of expansion and booming profits, many health clubs are now finding that they have to offer large discounts in order to hold on to their membership. In general, the more commodity-like an industry's product is, the more vicious will be the price war. This bust part of the cycle continues until overall industry capacity is brought into line with demand (through bankruptcies), at which point prices may stabilize again.

A fragmented industry structure, then, constitutes a threat rather than an opportunity. Most booms are relatively short-lived because of the ease of new entry and will be followed by price wars and bankruptcies. Because it is often difficult to differentiate products in these industries, the best strategy for a company is to try to minimize its costs so it will be profitable in a boom and survive any subsequent bust. Alternatively, companies might try to adopt strategies that change the underlying structure of fragmented industries and lead to a consolidated industry structure in which the level of industry profitability is increased. Exactly how companies can do this is something we shall consider in later chapters.

In consolidated industries, companies are interdependent because one company's competitive actions or moves (with regard to price, quality, and so on) directly affect the market share of its rivals and thus their profitability. When one company makes a move, this generally forces a response from its rivals, and the consequence of such competitive interdependence can be a dangerous competitive spiral. Rivalry increases as companies attempt to undercut each other's prices or offer customers more value in their products, pushing industry profits down in the process. The fare wars that have periodically created havoc in the airline industry provide a good illustration of this process.

Companies in consolidated industries sometimes seek to reduce this threat by following the prices set by the dominant company in the industry.[6] However, companies must be careful, for explicit face-to-face price-fixing agreements are illegal. (Tacit, indirect agreements, arrived at without direct or intentional communication, are legal.) Instead, companies set prices by watching, interpreting, anticipating, and responding to each other's behavior (something discussed in detail in Chapter 5 when the competitive dynamics of game theory is examined). However, tacit price-leadership agreements often break down under adverse economic conditions, as has occurred in the breakfast cereal industry, profiled in Strategy in Action 2.2.

Strategy in Action

2.2

Price Wars in the Breakfast Cereal Industry

For decades, the breakfast cereal industry was one of the most profitable in the United States. The industry has a consolidated structure dominated by Kellogg, General Mills, and Kraft Foods with its Post brand. Strong brand loyalty, coupled with control over the allocation of super-market shelf space, helped to limit the potential for new entry. Meanwhile, steady demand growth of around 3% per annum kept industry revenues expanding. Kellogg, which accounted for over 40% of the market share, acted as the price leader in the industry. Every year, Kellogg increased cereal prices, its rivals followed, and industry profits remained high.

This favorable industry structure started to change in the early 1990s when growth in demand slowed and then stagnated as a latte and bagel or muffin replaced cereal as the morning fare for many American adults. Then came the rise of powerful discounters such as Wal-Mart, which entered the grocery industry in the early 1990s and began to promote aggressively its own brand of cereal, priced significantly below the brand-name cereals. As the decade progressed, other grocery chains such as Kroger's started to follow suit, and brand loyalty in the industry began to decline as customers realized that a $2.50 bag of wheat flakes from Wal-Mart tasted about the same as a $3.50 box of Cornflakes from Kellogg. As sales of cheaper store-brand cereals began to take off, supermarkets were no longer as dependent on brand names to bring traffic into their stores and began to demand lower prices from the branded cereal manufacturers.

For several years, the manufacturers of brand cereals tried to hold out against these adverse trends, but in the mid-1990s the dam broke. In 1996, Kraft (then owned by Philip Morris) aggressively cut prices by 20% for its Post brand in an attempt to gain market share. Kellogg soon followed with a 19% price cut on two-thirds of its brands, and General Mills quickly did the same. The decades of tacit price collusion were officially over.

If the breakfast cereal companies were hoping that the price cuts would stimulate demand, they were wrong. Instead, demand remained flat while revenues and margins followed prices down, and Kellogg's operating margins dropped from 18% in 1995 to 10.2% in 1996, a trend experienced by the other brand cereal manufacturers.

By 2000, conditions had only worsened. Private-label sales continued to make inroads, gaining over 10% of the market. Moreover, sales of breakfast cereals started to contract at 1% per annum. To cap it off, an aggressive General Mills continued to launch expensive price and promotion campaigns in an attempt to take share away from the market leader. Kellogg saw its market share slip to just over 30% in 2001, behind the 31% now held by General Mills. For the first time since 1906, Kellogg no longer led the market. Moreover, profits at all three major producers remained weak in the face of continued price discounting.

In mid-2001, General Mills finally blinked and raised prices a modest 2% in response to its own rising costs. Competitors followed, signaling perhaps that after a decade of costly price warfare, pricing discipline might once more emerge in the industry. Both Kellogg and General Mills tried to move further away from price competition by focusing on brand extensions, such as Special K containing berries and new varieties of Cheerios. Kellogg's efforts with Special K helped the company recapture market leadership from General Mills. More important, the renewed emphasis on nonprice competition halted years of damaging price warfare, at least for the time being.[b]

● Industry Demand The level of industry demand is a second determinant of the intensity of rivalry among established companies. Growing demand from new customers or additional purchases by existing customers tend to moderate competition by providing greater scope for companies to compete for customers. Growing demand tends to reduce rivalry because all companies can sell more without taking market share away from other companies. High industry profits are often the result. Conversely, declining demand results in more rivalry as companies fight to maintain market share and revenues (as in the breakfast cereal industry). Demand declines when customers are leaving the marketplace or each customer is buying less. Now a company can grow only by taking market share away from other companies. Thus, declining demand constitutes a major threat because it increases the extent of rivalry between established companies.

● **Cost Conditions**   The cost structure of firms in an industry is a third determinant of rivalry. In industries where fixed costs are high, profitability tends to be highly leveraged to sales volume, and the desire to grow volume can spark intense rivalry. Fixed costs are the costs that must be borne before the firm makes a single sale. For example, before they can offer service, cable television companies have to lay cable in the ground; the cost of doing so is a fixed cost. Similarly, to offer air express service, a company like FedEx must invest in planes, package-sorting facilities, and delivery trucks—all fixed costs that require significant capital investments. In industries where the fixed costs of production are high, if sales volume is low, firms cannot cover their fixed costs and will not be profitable. Thus, they have an incentive to cut their prices and/or increase promotion spending to drive up sales volume so that they can cover their fixed costs. In situations where demand is not growing fast enough and too many companies are engaged in the same actions (cutting prices and/or raising promotion spending in an attempt to cover fixed costs), the result can be intense rivalry and lower profits. Research suggests that it is often the weakest firms in an industry that initiate such actions precisely because they are the ones struggling to cover their fixed costs.[7]

● **Exit Barriers**   Exit barriers are economic, strategic, and emotional factors that prevent companies from leaving an industry.[8] If exit barriers are high, companies become locked into an unprofitable industry where overall demand is static or declining. The result is often excess productive capacity, which leads to even more intense rivalry and price competition as companies cut prices in the attempt to obtain the customer orders needed to use their idle capacity and cover their fixed costs.[9] Common exit barriers include the following:

- Investments in assets such as specific machines, equipment, and operating facilities that are of little or no value in alternative uses or cannot be sold off. If the company wishes to leave the industry, it has to write off the book value of these assets.

- High fixed costs of exit, such as the severance pay, health benefits, and pensions that have to be paid to workers who are being made redundant when a company ceases to operate.

- Emotional attachments to an industry, as when a company's owners or employees are unwilling to exit from an industry for sentimental reasons or because of pride.

- Economic dependence on the industry because a company relies on a single industry for its revenue and profit.

- The need to maintain an expensive collection of assets at or above some minimum level in order to participate effectively in the industry.

- Bankruptcy regulations, particularly in the United States, where Chapter 11 bankruptcy provisions allow insolvent enterprises to continue operating and reorganize themselves under bankruptcy protection. These regulations can keep unprofitable assets in the industry, result in persistent excess capacity, and lengthen the time required to bring industry supply in line with demand.

As an example of the effect of exit barriers in practice, consider the express mail and parcel delivery industry. The key players in this industry, such as Federal Express and UPS, rely on the delivery business entirely for their revenues and profits. They have to be able to guarantee their customers that they will deliver packages to all major localities in the United States, and much of their investment is specific to this purpose. To meet this guarantee, they need a nationwide network of air routes and ground routes, an asset that is required in order to participate in the industry. If excess capacity develops in this industry, as it does from time to time, Federal Express cannot incrementally reduce or minimize its excess capacity by deciding not to fly to and deliver packages in, say, Miami because that proportion of its network is underused. If it did that, it would no longer be able to guarantee to its customers that it would be able to deliver packages to all major locations in the United States, and its customers would switch to some other carrier. Thus, the need to maintain a nationwide network is an exit barrier that can result in persistent excess capacity in the air express industry during periods of weak demand. Finally, both UPS and Federal Express managers and employees are emotionally tied to this industry because they both were first movers, in the ground and air segments of the industry, respectively, and because their employees are also major owners of their companies' stock and they are dependent financially on the fortunes of the delivery business.

● The Bargaining Power of Buyers

The third of Porter's five competitive forces is the bargaining power of buyers. An industry's buyers may be the individual customers who ultimately consume its products (its end-users) or the companies that distribute an industry's products to end-users, such as retailers and wholesalers. For example, while soap powder made by Procter & Gamble and Unilever is consumed by end-users, the principal buyers of soap powder are supermarket chains and discount stores, which resell the product to end-users. The bargaining power of buyers refers to the ability of buyers to bargain down prices charged by companies in the industry or to raise the costs of companies in the industry by demanding better product quality and service. By lowering prices and raising costs, powerful buyers can squeeze profits out of an industry. Thus, powerful buyers should be viewed as a threat. Alternatively, when buyers are in a weak bargaining position, companies in an industry can raise prices and perhaps reduce their costs by lowering product quality and service, thus increasing the level of industry profits. Buyers are most powerful in the following circumstances:

- When the industry that is supplying a particular product or service is composed of many small companies and the buyers are large and few in number. These circumstances allow the buyers to dominate supplying companies.

- When the buyers purchase in large quantities. In such circumstances, buyers can use their purchasing power as leverage to bargain for price reductions.

- When the supply industry depends on the buyers for a large percentage of its total orders.

- When switching costs are low so that buyers can play the supplying companies against each other to force down prices.

- When it is economically feasible for buyers to purchase an input from several companies at once so that buyers can play one company in the industry against another.

- When buyers can threaten to enter the industry and produce the product themselves and thus supply their own needs, also a tactic for forcing down industry prices.

The auto component supply industry, whose buyers are large automobile manufacturers such as GM, Ford, and DaimlerChrysler, is a good example of an industry in which buyers have strong bargaining power and thus a strong competitive threat. Why? The suppliers of auto components are numerous and typically small in scale; their buyers, the auto manufacturers, are large in size and few in number. DaimlerChrysler, for example, does business with nearly two thousand different component suppliers in the United States and normally contracts with a number of different companies to supply the same part. Additionally, to keep component prices down, both Ford and GM have used the threat of manufacturing a component themselves rather than buying it from auto component suppliers. The automakers have used their powerful position to play suppliers against each other, forcing down the price they have to pay for component parts and demanding better quality. If a component supplier objects, the automakers use the threat of switching to another supplier as a bargaining tool.

Another issue is that the relative power of buyers and suppliers tends to change in response to changing industry conditions. For example, because of changes now taking place in the pharmaceutical and health care industries, major buyers of pharmaceuticals (hospitals and health maintenance organizations) are gaining power over the suppliers of pharmaceuticals and have been able to demand lower prices. Strategy in Action 2.3 discusses how Wal-Mart's buying power has changed over the years as the company has become larger.

● The Bargaining Power of Suppliers

The fourth of Porter's five competitive forces is the bargaining power of suppliers—the organizations that provide inputs into the industry, such as materials, services, and labor (which may be individuals, organizations such as labor unions, or companies that supply contract labor). The bargaining power of suppliers refers to the ability of suppliers to raise input prices or to raise the costs of the industry in other ways—for example, by providing poor-quality inputs or poor service. Powerful suppliers squeeze profits out of an industry by raising the costs of companies in the industry. Thus, powerful suppliers are a threat. Alternatively, if suppliers are weak, companies in the industry have the opportunity to force down input prices and demand higher-quality inputs (such as more productive labor). As with buyers, the ability of suppliers to make demands on a company depends on their power relative to that of the company. Suppliers are most powerful in these situations:

- The product that suppliers sell has few substitutes and is vital to the companies in an industry.

- The profitability of suppliers is not significantly affected by the purchases of companies in a particular industry, in other words, when the industry is not an important customer to the suppliers.

- Companies in an industry would experience significant switching costs if they moved to the product of a different supplier because a particular supplier's products are unique or different. In such cases, the company depends on a particular supplier and cannot play suppliers against each other to reduce price.

- Suppliers can threaten to enter their customers' industry and use their inputs to produce products that would compete directly with those of companies already in the industry.

- Companies in the industry cannot threaten to enter their suppliers' industry and make their own inputs as a tactic for lowering the price of inputs.

Strategy in Action

2.3

Wal-Mart's Bargaining Power over Suppliers

When Wal-Mart and other discount retailers began in the 1960s, they were small operations with little purchasing power. To generate store traffic, they depended in large part on stocking nationally branded merchandise from well-known companies such as Procter & Gamble and Rubbermaid. Since the discounters did not have high sales volume, the nationally branded companies set the price. This meant that the discounters had to look for other ways to cut costs, which they typically did by emphasizing self-service in stripped-down stores located in the suburbs where land was cheaper (in the 1960s, the main competitors for discounters were full-service department stores like Sears that were often located in downtown shopping areas).

Discounters such as Kmart purchased their merchandise through wholesalers, who in turn bought from manufacturers. The wholesaler would come into a store and write an order, and when the merchandise arrived, the wholesaler would come in and stock the shelves, saving the retailer labor costs. However, Wal-Mart was located in Arkansas and placed its stores in small towns. Wholesalers were not particularly interested in serving a company that built its stores in such out-of-the-way places. They would do it only if Wal-Mart paid higher prices.

Wal-Mart's Sam Walton refused to pay higher prices. Instead he took his fledgling company public and used the capital raised to build a distribution center to stock merchandise. The distribution center would serve all stores within a 300-mile radius, with trucks leaving the distribution center daily to restock the stores. Because the distribution center was serving a collection of stores and thus buying in larger volumes, Walton found that he was able to cut the wholesalers out of the equation and order directly from manufacturers. The cost savings generated by not having to pay profits to wholesalers were then passed on to consumers in the form of lower prices, which helped Wal-Mart continue growing. This growth increased its buying power and thus its ability to demand deeper discounts from manufacturers.

Today Wal-Mart has turned its buying process into an art form. Since 8% of all retail sales in the United States are made in a Wal-Mart store, the company has enormous bargaining power over its suppliers. Suppliers of nationally branded products, such as Procter & Gamble, are no longer in a position to demand high prices. Rather, Wal-Mart is now so important to Procter & Gamble that it is able to demand deep discounts on its purchases. Moreover, Wal-Mart has itself become a brand that is more powerful than the brands of manufacturers. People don't go to Wal-Mart to buy branded goods; they go to Wal-Mart for the low prices. This simple fact has enabled Wal-Mart to bargain down the prices it pays, always passing on cost savings to consumers in the form of lower prices.

Since 1991, Wal-Mart has provided suppliers with real-time information on store sales through the use of individual stock keeping units (SKUs). These have allowed suppliers to optimize their own production processes, matching output to Wal-Mart's demands and avoiding under- or overproduction and the need to store inventory. The efficiencies that manufacturers gain from such information are passed on to Wal-Mart in the form of lower prices, and Wal-Mart then passes on those cost savings to consumers.[c]

An example of an industry in which companies are dependent on a powerful supplier is the personal computer industry. Personal computer firms are heavily dependent on Intel, the world's largest supplier of microprocessors for PCs. The industry standard for personal computers runs on Intel's microprocessor chips. Intel's competitors, such as Advanced Micro Devices (AMD), must develop and supply chips that are compatible with Intel's standard. Although AMD has developed competing chips, Pentium still supplies about 85% of the chips used in PCs primarily because only Intel has the manufacturing capacity required to serve a large share of the market. It is beyond the financial resources of Intel's competitors, such as AMD, to match the scale and efficiency of Intel's manufacturing systems. Thus, while PC manufacturers can buy some microprocessors from Intel's rivals, most notably AMD, they still have to turn to Intel for the bulk of their supply. Because Intel is in a powerful bargaining position, it can charge higher prices for its microprocessors than would be the case if its competitors were more numerous and stronger (that is, if the microprocessor industry were fragmented).

● Substitute Products

The final force in Porter's model is the threat of substitute products: the products of different businesses or industries that can satisfy similar customer needs. For example, companies in the coffee industry compete indirectly with those in the tea and soft drink industries because all three serve customer needs for nonalcoholic drinks. The existence of close substitutes is a strong competitive threat because this limits the price that companies in one industry can charge for their product, and thus industry profitability. If the price of coffee rises too much relative to that of tea or soft drinks, coffee drinkers may switch to those substitutes.

If an industry's products have few close substitutes, so that substitutes are a weak competitive force, then, other things being equal, companies in the industry have the opportunity to raise prices and earn additional profits. Thus, there is no close substitute for microprocessors, which gives companies like Intel and AMD the ability to charge higher prices than would be the case if there were a substitute for microprocessors.

● A Sixth Force: Complementors

Andrew Grove, the former CEO of Intel, has argued that Porter's five forces model ignores a sixth force: the power, vigor, and competence of complementors.[10] **Complementors** are companies that sell products that add value to (complement) the products of companies in an industry because when used together, the products better satisfy customer demands. For example, the complementors to the personal computer industry are the companies that make software applications to run on those machines. The greater the supply of high-quality software applications to run on personal computers, the greater is the value of personal computers to customers, the greater the demand for PCs, and the greater the profitability of the personal computer industry.

Grove's argument has a strong foundation in economic theory, which has long argued that both substitutes and complements influence demand in an industry.[11] Moreover, recent research has emphasized the importance of complementary products in determining demand and profitability in many high-technology industries, such as the computer industry in which Grove made his mark.[12] The issue, therefore, is that when complements are an important determinant of demand for an industry's products, industry profits depend critically on there being an adequate supply of complementary products. When the number of complementors is increasing and they produce attractive complementary products, this boosts demand and profits in the industry and can open up many new opportunities for creating value. Conversely, if complementors are weak and are not producing attractive complementary products, this can be a threat that slows industry growth and limits profitability.

● Porter's Model
Summarized

The systematic analysis of forces in the industry environment using the Porter framework is a powerful tool that helps managers to think strategically. It is important to recognize that one competitive force often affects the others, so that all forces need to be considered when performing industry analysis. Indeed, industry analysis leads managers to think systematically about how their strategic choices will be affected by the forces of industry competition and also about how their choices will affect the five forces and change conditions in the industry. For an example of industry analysis using Porter's framework, see the Running Case.

RUNNING CASE

Dell Computer and the Personal Computer Industry

The global personal computer industry is very competitive. On a global basis, Dell was the worldwide market share leader in 2005 with 18.1%, followed by Hewlett-Packard (15.6%), Lenovo (6.2%), Acer (4.7%), Fujitsu (4.1%), and Apple (2.2%). The remaining 49% of the market is accounted for by a long list of small companies, some of which focus on local markets and make unbranded so-called white box computers.

The long list of small companies reflects relatively low barriers to entry. The open architecture of the personal computer means that key components, such as an Intel compatible microprocessor, a Windows operating system, memory chips, a hard drive, and so on, can be purchased easily on the open market. Assembly is easy, requiring very little capital equipment or technical skills, and economies of scale in production are not particularly significant. Although small entrants lack the brand-name recognition of the market share leaders, they survive in the industry by pricing their machines a few hundred dollars below those of the market leaders and capturing the demand of price-sensitive consumers. This puts constant pressure on the prices that brand-name companies can charge.

Moreover, most buyers view the product offerings of different branded companies as very close substitutes for each other, so competition between them often defaults to price. Consequently, the average selling price of a PC has fallen from around $1,700 in 1999 to under $1,000 in 2006, and projections are that it may continue to fall, fueled in part by aggressive competition between Dell Computer and Hewlett-Packard.

The constant downward pressure on prices makes it hard for personal computer companies to have big gross margins, and this factor results in lower profitability. The downward pressure on prices has been exacerbated by slowing demand growth in many developed nations, including the world's largest market, the United States, where the market is now mature and demand is limited to replacement demand plus an expansion in the overall population.

To make matters worse, personal computer companies have long had to deal with two very powerful suppliers: Microsoft, which supplies the industry standard operating system, Windows, and Intel, which supplies the industry standard microprocessor. Microsoft and Intel have been able to charge high prices for their products, which has raised input costs for personal computer manufacturers and thus reduced their profitability.

In sum, the personal computer industry is not particularly attractive. The combination of low entry barriers, intense rivalry among established companies, slowing demand growth, buyers who are indifferent to the offerings of various companies and often look at price before anything else, and powerful suppliers who have raised the prices for key inputs all come together to make it difficult for established companies to earn decent profits. Against this background, the performance of Dell Computer over the last decade is nothing short of remarkable and illustrates just how strong the company's business model and competitive advantage had been.[d]

Strategic Groups Within Industries

Companies in an industry often differ significantly from each other with respect to the way they strategically position their products in the market in terms of such factors as the distribution channels they use, the market segments they serve, the quality of their products, technological leadership, customer service, pricing policy, advertising policy, and promotions. As a result of these differences, within most industries, it is possible to observe groups of companies in which each company follows a business model that is similar to that pursued by other companies in the group but is different from the business model followed by companies in other groups. These different groups of companies are known as strategic groups.[13]

Normally, the basic differences between the business models that companies in different strategic groups use can be captured by a relatively small number of strategic factors. For example, in the pharmaceutical industry, two main strategic groups stand out (see Figure 2.3).[14] One group, which includes such companies as Merck, Eli Lilly, and Pfizer, is characterized by a business model based on heavy R&D spending and a focus on developing new, proprietary, blockbuster drugs. The companies in this proprietary strategic group are pursuing a high-risk, high-return strategy. It is a high-risk strategy because basic drug research is difficult and expensive. Bringing a new drug to market can cost up to $800 million in R&D money and a decade of research and clinical trials. The risks are high because the failure rate in new drug development is very high: only one out of every five drugs entering clinical trials is ultimately approved by the U.S. Food and Drug Administration. However, the strategy is also a high-return one because a single successful drug can be patented, giving the innovator a twenty-year monopoly on its production and sale. This lets these proprietary companies charge a high price for the patented drug, allowing them to earn millions, if not billions, of dollars over the lifetime of the patent.

The second strategic group might be characterized as the generic drug strategic group. This group of companies, which includes Forest Labs, Mylan Labs, and Watson Pharmaceuticals, focuses on the manufacture of generic drugs: low-cost copies of

FIGURE 2.3

Strategic Groups in the Pharmaceutical Industry

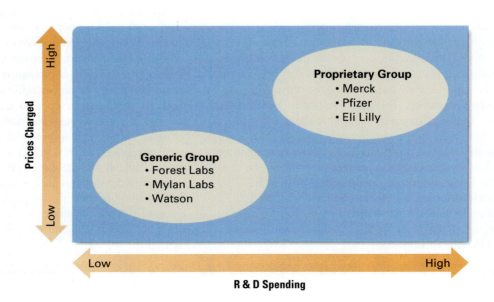

drugs that were developed by companies in the proprietary group whose patents have now expired. Low R&D spending, production efficiency, and an emphasis on low prices characterize the business models of companies in this strategic group. They are pursuing a low-risk, low-return strategy. It is low risk because they are not investing millions of dollars in R&D. It is low return because they cannot charge high prices.

● Implications of Strategic Groups

The concept of strategic groups has a number of implications for the identification of opportunities and threats within an industry. First, because all the companies in a strategic group are pursuing a similar business model, customers tend to view the products of such enterprises as direct substitutes for each other. Thus, a company's closest competitors are those in its strategic group, not those in other strategic groups in the industry. The most immediate threat to a company's profitability comes from rivals within its own strategic group. For example, a group of companies in the retail industry might be characterized as discounters. Included in this group are Wal-Mart, Kmart, Target, and Fred Meyer. These companies compete most vigorously with each other rather than with other retailers in different groups, such as Nordstrom or The Gap. Kmart, for example, was driven into bankruptcy in late 2001 not because Nordstrom or The Gap took business from it but because Wal-Mart and Target gained share in the discounting group by virtue of their superior strategic execution of the discounting business model.

A second competitive implication is that different strategic groups can have a different standing with respect to each of the competitive forces; thus, each strategic group may face a different set of opportunities and threats. The risk of new entry by potential competitors, the degree of rivalry among companies within a group, the bargaining power of buyers, the bargaining power of suppliers, and the competitive force of substitute and complementary products can each be a relatively strong or weak competitive force depending on the competitive positioning approach adopted by each strategic group in the industry. For example, in the pharmaceutical industry, companies in the proprietary group have historically been in a very powerful position in relation to buyers because their products are patented and there are no substitutes. Also, rivalry based on price competition within this group has been low because competition in the industry revolves around being the first to patent a new drug (so-called patent races), not around drug prices. Thus, companies in this group have been able to charge high prices and earn high profits. In contrast, companies in the generic group have been in a much weaker position because many companies are able to produce different versions of the same generic drug after patents expire. Thus, in this strategic group, products are close substitutes, rivalry has been high, and price competition has led to lower profits for this group compared to companies in the proprietary group.

● The Role of Mobility Barriers

It follows from the two issues discussed above that some strategic groups are more desirable than others because competitive forces open up greater opportunities and present fewer threats for those groups. Managers, after having analyzed their industry, might identify a strategic group where competitive forces are weaker and higher profits can be made. Sensing an opportunity, they might contemplate changing their business model and move to compete in that strategic group. However, taking advantage of this opportunity may be difficult because of mobility barriers between strategic groups.

Mobility barriers are within-industry factors that inhibit the movement of companies between strategic groups. They include the barriers to entry into a group and the barriers to exit from a company's existing group. For example, Forest Labs would encounter mobility barriers if it attempted to enter the proprietary group in the pharmaceutical industry because it lacks R&D skills, and building these skills would be an expensive proposition. Essentially, over time, companies in different groups develop different cost structures and skills and competencies that give them different pricing options and choices. A company contemplating entry into another strategic group must evaluate whether it has the ability to imitate, and indeed outperform, its potential competitors in that strategic group. Managers must determine if it is cost-effective to overcome mobility barriers before deciding whether the move is worthwhile.

In summary, an important task of industry analysis is to determine the sources of the similarities and differences among companies in an industry and to work out the broad themes that underlie competition in an industry. This analysis often reveals new opportunities to compete in an industry by developing new kinds of products to meet the needs of customers better. It can also reveal emerging threats that can be countered effectively by changing competitive strategy. This issue is taken up in Chapters 5, 6, and 7, which examine crafting competitive strategy in different kinds of markets to build a competitive advantage over rivals and best satisfy customer needs.

Industry Life Cycle Analysis

An important determinant of the strength of the competitive forces in an industry (and thus of the nature of opportunities and threats) is the changes that take place in it over time. The similarities and differences between companies in an industry often become more pronounced over time, and its strategic group structure frequently changes. The strength and nature of each of the competitive forces also change as an industry evolves, particularly the two forces of risk of entry by potential competitors and rivalry among existing firms.[15]

A useful tool for analyzing the effects of industry evolution on competitive forces is the **industry life cycle** model, which identifies five sequential stages in the evolution of an industry that lead to five distinct kinds of industry environment: embryonic industry, growth, shakeout, mature industry, and decline (see Figure 2.4). The task facing managers is to anticipate how the strength of competitive forces will

FIGURE 2.4

Stages in the Industry Life Cycle

change as the industry environment evolves and to formulate strategies that take advantage of opportunities as they arise and that counter emerging threats.

● Embryonic Industries

An embryonic industry is just beginning to develop (for example, personal computers and biotechnology in the 1970s, wireless communications in the 1980s, Internet retailing in the early 1990s, and nanotechnology today). Growth at this stage is slow because of such factors as buyers' unfamiliarity with the industry's product, high prices due to the inability of companies to reap any significant scale economies, and poorly developed distribution channels. Barriers to entry tend to be based on access to key technological know-how rather than cost economies or brand loyalty. If the core know-how required to compete in the industry is complex and difficult to grasp, barriers to entry can be quite high, and established companies will be protected from potential competitors. Rivalry in embryonic industries is based not so much on price as on educating customers, opening up distribution channels, and perfecting the design of the product. Such rivalry can be intense, and the company that is the first to solve design problems often has the opportunity to develop a significant market position. An embryonic industry may also be the creation of one company's innovative efforts, as happened with microprocessors (Intel), vacuum cleaners (Hoover), photocopiers (Xerox), and small package express delivery (FedEx). In such circumstances, the company has a major opportunity to capitalize on the lack of rivalry and build a strong hold on the market.

● Growth Industries

Once demand for the industry's product begins to take off, the industry develops the characteristics of a growth industry. In a growth industry, first-time demand is expanding rapidly as many new customers enter the market. Typically, an industry grows when customers become familiar with the product, prices fall because experience and scale economies have been attained, and distribution channels develop. The U.S. wireless telephone industry was in the growth stage for most of the 1990s. In 1990, there were only 5 million cellular subscribers in the nation. By 2006, this figure had increased to around 220 million, and overall demand was still growing.

Normally, the importance of control over technological knowledge as a barrier to entry has diminished by the time an industry enters its growth stage. Because few companies have yet achieved significant scale economies or built brand loyalty, other entry barriers tend to be relatively low as well, particularly early in the growth stage. Thus, the threat from potential competitors generally is highest at this point. Paradoxically, however, high growth usually means that new entrants can be absorbed into an industry without a marked increase in the intensity of rivalry. Thus, rivalry tends to be relatively low. Rapid growth in demand enables companies to expand their revenues and profits without taking market share away from competitors. A strategically aware company takes advantage of the relatively benign environment of the growth stage to prepare itself for the intense competition of the coming industry shakeout.

● Industry Shakeout

Explosive growth cannot be maintained indefinitely. Sooner or later, the rate of growth slows, and the industry enters the shakeout stage. In the shakeout stage, demand approaches saturation levels: most of the demand is limited to replacement because there are few potential first-time buyers left.

As an industry enters the shakeout stage, rivalry between companies becomes intense. Typically, companies that have become accustomed to rapid growth continue to add capacity at rates consistent with past growth. However, demand is no longer

FIGURE 2.5

Growth in Demand
and Capacity

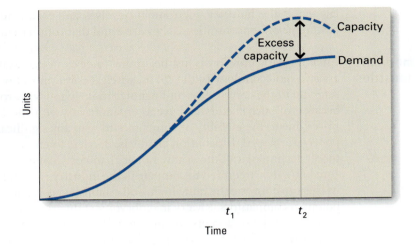

growing at historic rates, and the consequence is the emergence of excess productive capacity. This condition is illustrated in Figure 2.5, where the solid curve indicates the growth in demand over time and the broken curve indicates the growth in productive capacity over time. As you can see, past point t_1, demand growth becomes slower as the industry becomes mature. However, capacity continues to grow until time t_2. The gap between the solid and broken lines signifies excess capacity. In an attempt to use this capacity, companies often cut prices. The result can be a price war, which drives many of the most inefficient companies into bankruptcy and is enough to deter any new entry.

● **Mature Industries**   The shakeout stage ends when the industry enters its mature stage: the market is totally saturated, demand is limited to replacement demand, and growth is low or zero. What growth there is comes from population expansion that brings new customers into the market or an increase in replacement demand.

As an industry enters maturity, barriers to entry increase, and the threat of entry from potential competitors decreases. As growth slows during the shakeout, companies can no longer maintain historic growth rates merely by holding on to their market share. Competition for market share develops, driving down prices and often producing a price war, as has happened in the airline and personal computer industry. To survive the shakeout, companies begin to focus on minimizing costs and building brand loyalty. The airlines, for example, tried to cut operating costs by hiring nonunion labor and to build brand loyalty by introducing frequent-flyer programs. Personal computer companies have sought to build brand loyalty by providing excellent after-sales service and working to lower their cost structures. By the time an industry matures, the surviving companies are those that have brand loyalty and efficient low-cost operations. Because both these factors constitute a significant barrier to entry, the threat of entry by potential competitors is often greatly diminished. High entry barriers in mature industries can give companies the opportunity to increase prices and profits, although this does not always occur.

As a result of the shakeout, most industries in the maturity stage have consolidated and become oligopolies. Examples include the beer industry (see the Opening Case), breakfast cereal industry, and pharmaceutical industry. In mature industries, companies tend to recognize their interdependence and try to avoid price wars. Stable demand gives them the opportunity to enter into price-leadership agreements. The net effect is to reduce the threat of intense rivalry among established companies, thereby allowing greater profitability. Nevertheless, the stability of a mature industry is always threatened by further price wars. A general slump in economic activity can depress industry demand. As companies fight to maintain their revenues in the face of declining demand, price-leadership agreements break down, rivalry increases, and prices and profits fall. The periodic price wars that occur in the airline industry seem to follow this pattern.

● **Declining Industries**

Eventually, most industries enter a decline stage: growth becomes negative for a variety of reasons, including technological substitution (for example, air travel for rail travel), social changes (greater health consciousness hitting tobacco sales), demographics (the declining birthrate hurting the market for baby and child products), and international competition (low-cost foreign competition pushing the U.S. steel industry into decline). Within a declining industry, the degree of rivalry among established companies usually increases. Depending on the speed of the decline and the height of exit barriers, competitive pressures can become as fierce as in the shakeout stage.[16] The main problem in a declining industry is that falling demand leads to the emergence of excess capacity. In trying to use this capacity, companies begin to cut prices, thus sparking a price war. The U.S. steel industry experienced these problems because steel companies tried to use their excess capacity despite falling demand. The same problem occurred in the airline industry in the 1990–1992 period and again in 2001–2003, as companies cut prices to ensure that they would not be flying with half-empty planes (that is, that they would not be operating with substantial excess capacity). Exit barriers play a part in adjusting excess capacity. The greater the exit barriers, the harder it is for companies to reduce capacity and the greater is the threat of severe price competition.

● **Industry Life Cycle**

In summary, a third task of industry analysis is to identify the opportunities and threats that are characteristic of different kinds of industry environments in order to develop an effective business model and competitive strategy. Managers have to tailor their strategies to changing industry conditions. And they have to learn to recognize the crucial points in an industry's development so that they can forecast when the shakeout stage of an industry might begin or when an industry might be moving into decline. This is also true at the level of strategic groups because new embryonic groups may emerge as a result of shifts in customer needs and tastes, or some groups may grow rapidly because of changes in technology and others will decline as their customers defect.

Limitations of Models for Industry Analysis

The competitive forces, strategic groups, and life cycle models provide useful ways of thinking about and analyzing the nature of competition within an industry to identify opportunities and threats. However, each has its limitations, and managers need to be aware of their shortcomings.

● **Life Cycle Issues**

It is important to remember that the industry life cycle model is a generalization. In practice, industry life cycles do not always follow the pattern illustrated in Figure 2.4. In some cases, growth is so rapid that the embryonic stage is skipped altogether. In others, industries fail to get past the embryonic stage. Industry growth can be revitalized after long periods of decline through innovation or social change. For example, the health boom brought the bicycle industry back to life after a long period of decline.

The time span of the stages can also vary significantly from industry to industry. Some industries can stay in maturity almost indefinitely if their products become basic necessities of life, as is the case for the car industry. Other industries skip the mature stage and go straight into decline, as in the case of the vacuum tube industry. Transistors replaced vacuum tubes as a major component in electronic products even though the vacuum tube industry was still in its growth stage. Still other industries may go through several shakeouts before they enter full maturity, as appears to be happening in the telecommunications industry.

Innovation and Change

Over any reasonable length of time, in many industries competition can be viewed as a process driven by innovation.[17] Indeed, innovation is frequently the major factor in industry evolution and causes the movement through the industry life cycle. Innovation is attractive because companies that pioneer new products, processes, or strategies can often earn enormous profits. Consider the explosive growth of Toys "R" Us, Dell Computer, and Wal-Mart. In a variety of different ways, all of these companies were innovators. Toys "R" Us pioneered a new way of selling toys (through large discount warehouse-type stores), Dell pioneered a whole new way of selling personal computers (directly via telephone and then the Web), and Wal-Mart pioneered the low-price discount superstore concept.

Successful innovation can transform the nature of industry competition. In recent decades, one frequent consequence of innovation has been to lower the fixed costs of production, thereby reducing barriers to entry and allowing new and smaller enterprises to compete with large established organizations. For example, two decades ago, large integrated steel companies such as US Steel, LTV, and Bethlehem Steel dominated the steel industry. The industry was a typical oligopoly, dominated by a small number of large producers, in which tacit price collusion was practiced. Then along came a series of efficient mini-mill producers such as Nucor and Chaparral Steel, which used a new technology: electric arc furnaces. Over the past twenty years, they have revolutionized the structure of the industry. What was once a consolidated industry is now much more fragmented and price competitive. The successor company to US Steel, USX, now has only a 12% market share, down from 55% in the mid-1960s, and both Bethlehem and LTV went bankrupt. In contrast, the mini-mills as a group now hold over 40% of the market, up from 5% twenty years ago.[18] Thus, the mini-mill innovation has reshaped the nature of competition in the steel industry.[19] A competitive forces model applied to the industry in 1970 would look very different from a competitive forces model applied in 2004.

Michael Porter, the originator of the competitive forces and strategic group concepts, has explicitly recognized the role of innovation in revolutionizing industry structure. Porter now talks of innovations as "unfreezing" and "reshaping" industry structure. He argues that after a period of turbulence triggered by innovation, the structure of an industry once more settles down into a fairly stable pattern, and the five forces and strategic group concepts can once more be applied.[20] This view of the evolution of industry structure is often referred to as punctuated equilibrium.[21] The punctuated equilibrium view holds that long periods of equilibrium, when an industry's structure is stable, are punctuated by periods of rapid change when industry structure is revolutionized by innovation; there is an unfreezing and refreezing process.

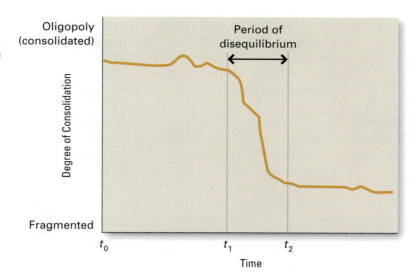

FIGURE 2.6

Punctuated Equilibrium
and Competitive
Structure

Figure 2.6 shows what punctuated equilibrium might look like for one key dimension of industry structure: competitive structure. From time t_0 to t_1, the competitive structure of the industry is a stable oligopoly, with a few companies sharing the market. At time t_1, a major new innovation is pioneered by either an existing company or a new entrant. The result is a period of turbulence between t_1 and t_2. After a while, the industry settles down into a new state of equilibrium, but now the competitive structure is far more fragmented. Note that the opposite could have happened: the industry could have become more consolidated, although this seems to be less common. In general, innovations seem to lower barriers to entry, allow more companies into the industry, and as a result lead to fragmentation rather than consolidation.

During a period of rapid change when industry structure is being revolutionized by innovation, value typically migrates to business models based on new positioning strategies.[22] In the stockbrokerage industry, value migrated away from the full-service broker model to the online trading model. In the steel industry, the introduction of electric arc technology led to a migration of value away from large, integrated enterprises and toward small mini-mills. In the book-selling industry, value has migrated away from small boutique bricks-and-mortar booksellers toward large bookstore chains like Barnes & Noble and online bookstores such as Amazon.com.

Because the competitive forces and strategic group models are static, they cannot adequately capture what occurs during periods of rapid change in the industry environment when value is migrating. Similarly, a simple view of the industry life cycle does not allow for an industry to repeat a stage or even jump stages that technological upheavals can lead to. Nevertheless, they are useful tools for analyzing industry structure during periods of stability.

Some scholars question the validity of the punctuated equilibrium approach. Richard D'Avani has argued that many industries are hypercompetitive, meaning that they are characterized by permanent and ongoing innovation and competitive change (the computer industry is often cited as an example of a hypercompetitive industry).[23] The structure of such industries is constantly being revolutionized by innovation, so there are no periods of equilibrium or stability. When this is the case, some might argue that the competitive forces and strategic group models are of limited value because they represent no more than snapshots of a constantly changing situation. Thus, managers must constantly repeat industry analysis and pay attention to changes in the forces of competition. Moreover, D'Avani and others claim that markets have become more hypercompetitive in the modern era, although recent research evidence seems to suggest that this is not the case, and many industries are characterized by long periods of relative stability.[24]

● **Company Differences**   Another criticism of industry models is that they overemphasize the importance of industry structure as a determinant of company performance and underemphasize the importance of variations or differences among companies within an industry or a strategic group.[25] As we discuss in the next chapter, there can be enormous variance in the profit rates of individual companies within an industry. Research by Richard Rumelt and his associates, for example, suggests that industry structure explains only about 10% of the variance in profit rates across companies.[26] The implication is that individual company differences explain much of the remainder. Other studies have put the explained variance closer to 20%, which is still not a large figure.[27] Similarly, a growing number of studies have found only weak evidence of a link between strategic group membership and company profit rates, despite the fact that the strategic group model predicts a strong link.[28] Collectively, these studies suggest that the individual resources and capabilities of a company are far more important determinants of its profitability than is the industry or strategic group of which the company is a member. Put differently, there are strong companies in tough industries where average profitability is low (for example, Anheuser-Busch in the beer industry and Dell in the personal computer industry), and weak companies in industries where average profitability is high.

Although these findings do not invalidate the five forces and strategic group models, they do imply that the models are only imperfect predictors of enterprise profitability. A company will not be profitable just because it is based in an attractive industry or strategic group. As we discuss in Chapters 3 and 4, more is required.

The Macroenvironment

Just as the decisions and actions of strategic managers can often change an industry's competitive structure, so too can changing conditions or forces in the wider macroenvironment, that is, the broader economic, global, technological, demographic, social, and political context in which companies and industries are embedded (see Figure 2.7). Changes in the forces in the macroenvironment can have a direct impact on any or all of the forces in Porter's model, thereby altering the relative strength of these forces and, with it, the attractiveness of an industry.

● **Macroeconomic Forces**   Macroeconomic forces affect the general health and well-being of a nation or the regional economy of an organization, which in turn affect companies' and industries' ability to earn an adequate rate of return. The four most important macroeconomic forces are the growth rate of the economy, interest rates, currency exchange rates, and inflation (or deflation) rates. Economic growth, because it leads to an expansion in customer expenditures, tends to produce a general easing of competitive pressures within an industry. This gives companies the opportunity to expand their operations and earn higher profits. Because economic decline (a recession) leads to a reduction in customer expenditures, it increases competitive pressures. Economic decline frequently causes price wars in mature industries.

FIGURE 2.7

The Role of the
Macroenvironment

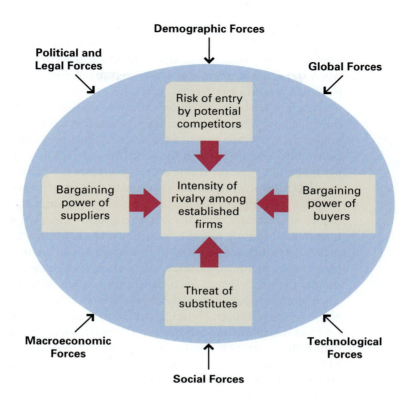

The level of interest rates can determine the demand for a company's products. Interest rates are important whenever customers routinely borrow money to finance their purchase of these products. The most obvious example is the housing market, where mortgage rates directly affect demand. Interest rates also have an impact on the sale of autos, appliances, and capital equipment, to give just a few examples. For companies in such industries, rising interest rates are a threat and falling rates an opportunity.

Interest rates are also important insofar as they influence a company's cost of capital and therefore its ability to raise funds and invest in new assets. The lower interest rates are, the lower will be the cost of capital for companies and the more investment there will be. This is not always a good thing. In the late 1990s, the very low cost of capital allowed dot-com and telecommunications companies with questionable business plans to raise large amounts of money and invest those funds in computers and telecommunications gear (the low cost of capital lowered barriers to entry by enabling start-ups to raise the capital required to circumvent entry barriers). This was initially good for the manufacturers of telecommunications equipment and computers, but the demand signal that was being sent was not sustainable: many of the dot-com and telecommunications start-ups of the 1990s went bankrupt between 2000 and 2002. Secondhand computers and telecommunications equipment from these bankrupt companies flooded the market, depressing first-time demand for that equipment and helping to plunge the computer and telecommunications equipment businesses into a deep slowdown. (For example, in January 2002, Internet auction house eBay listed more than three thousand Cisco products that were being auctioned for much less than their initial prices.)

Currency exchange rates define the value of different national currencies in relation to each other. Movement in currency exchange rates has a direct impact on the competitiveness of a company's products in the global marketplace. For example, when the value of the dollar is low compared with the value of other currencies, products made in the United States are relatively inexpensive and products made overseas are relatively expensive. A low or declining dollar reduces the threat from foreign competitors while creating opportunities for increased sales overseas. For example, the fall in the value of the dollar against the Japanese yen that occurred between 1985 and 1995, when the dollar-to-yen exchange rate declined from 240 yen per dollar to 85 yen per dollar, sharply increased the price of imported Japanese cars, giving U.S. car manufacturers some protection against those imports.

Price inflation can destabilize the economy, producing slower economic growth, higher interest rates, and volatile currency movements. If inflation keeps increasing, investment planning becomes hazardous. The key characteristic of inflation is that it makes the future less predictable. In an inflationary environment, it may be impossible to predict with any accuracy the real value of returns that can be earned from a project five years hence. Such uncertainty makes companies less willing to invest. Their holding back in turn depresses economic activity and ultimately pushes the economy into a slump. Thus, high inflation is a threat to companies.

Price deflation also has a destabilizing effect on economic activity. If prices are deflating, the real price of fixed payments goes up. This is particularly damaging for companies and individuals with a high level of debt who must make regular fixed payments on that debt. In a deflationary environment, the increase in the real value of debt consumes more of household and corporate cash flows, leaving less for other purchases and depressing the overall level of economic activity. Although significant deflation has not been seen since the 1930s, in the 1990s it started to take hold in Japan.

● **Global Forces**

Enormous changes in the world economic system have occurred over the last half-century. We review these changes in some detail in Chapter 8 when we discuss global strategy. For now, the important points to note are that barriers to international trade and investment have tumbled, and more and more countries are enjoying sustained economic growth. Economic growth in places like Brazil, China, and India is creating large new markets for companies' goods and services and is giving companies an opportunity to grow their profits faster by entering these nations. Falling barriers to international trade and investment have made it much easier to enter foreign nations. For example, twenty years ago, it was almost impossible for a western company to set up operations in China. Today, western and Japanese companies are investing over $50 billion a year in China. By the same token, however, falling barriers to international trade and investment have made it easier for foreign enterprises to enter the domestic markets of many companies (by lowering barriers to entry), thereby increasing the intensity of competition and lowering profitability. Because of these changes, many formerly isolated domestic markets have now become part of a much larger, and more competitive, global marketplace, creating myriad threats and opportunities for companies. We shall return to this topic and discuss it in more detail in Chapter 8.

● **Technological Forces**

Since World War II, the pace of technological change has accelerated.[29] This has unleashed a process that has been called a "perennial gale of creative destruction."[30] Technological change can make established products obsolete overnight and simultaneously create a host of new product possibilities. Thus, technological change is both creative and destructive—both an opportunity and a threat.

One of the most important impacts of technological change is that it can affect the height of barriers to entry and therefore radically reshape industry structure. The Internet, because it is so pervasive, has the potential for changing the competitive structure of many industries. It often lowers barriers to entry and reduces customer switching costs, changes that tend to increase the intensity of rivalry in an industry and lower both prices and profits.[31] For example, the Internet has lowered barriers to entry into the news industry. Providers of financial news now have to compete for advertising dollars and customer attention with new Internet-based media organizations that sprang up during the 1990s, such as TheStreet.com, the Motley Fool, and Yahoo!'s financial section. The resulting increase in rivalry has given advertisers more choices, enabling them to bargain down the prices that they must pay to media companies. Similarly, in the automobile industry, the ability of customers to comparison-shop for cars online and purchase cars online from a number of distributors such as Auto Nation has increased the ability of customers to find the best value for their money. Customers' increased bargaining power enables them to put downward pressure on car prices and squeeze profits out of the automobile industry.

Demographic Forces

Demographic forces are outcomes of changes in the characteristics of a population, such as age, gender, ethnic origin, race, sexual orientation, and social class. Like the other forces in the general environment, demographic forces present managers with opportunities and threats and can have major implications for organizations. Over the past thirty years, for example, women have entered the work force in increasing numbers. Between 1973 and 2006, the percentage of women in the work force increased from 44 to 60% in the United States (with similar increases in many other developed nations).[32] This dramatic increase has brought issues such as equal pay for equal work and sexual harassment at work to the forefront of issues that managers must address if they are to attract and make full use of the talents of female workers.

Changes in the age distribution of a population are another example of a demographic force that affects managers and organizations. Currently, most industrialized nations are experiencing the aging of their populations as a consequence of falling birth- and deathrates and the aging of the babyboom generation. In Germany, for example, the percentage of the population over age 65 is expected to rise from 15.4% in 1990 to 20.7% in 2010. Comparable figures for Canada are 11.4 and 14.4%; for Japan, 11.7 and 19.5%; and for the United States, 12.6 and 13.5%.[33]

The aging of the population is increasing opportunities for organizations that cater to older people; the home health care and recreation industries, for example, are seeing an upswing in demand for their services. As the babyboom generation from the late 1950s to the early 1960s has aged, it has created a host of opportunities and threats. During the 1980s, many baby boomers were getting married and creating an upsurge in demand for the customer appliances normally bought by couples marrying for the first time. Companies such as Whirlpool Corporation and General Electric capitalized on the resulting upsurge in demand for washing machines, dishwashers, dryers, and the like. In the 1990s, many of these same baby boomers were starting to save for retirement, creating an inflow of money into mutual funds and creating a boom in the mutual fund industry. In the next twenty years, many of these same baby boomers will retire, creating a boom in retirement communities.

● Social Forces

Social forces refer to the way in which changing social mores and values affect an industry. Like the other macroenvironmental forces discussed here, social change creates opportunities and threats. One of the major social movements of recent decades has been the trend toward greater health consciousness. Its impact has been immense, and companies that recognized the opportunities early have often reaped significant gains. Philip Morris, for example, capitalized on the growing health consciousness trend when it acquired Miller Brewing Company and then redefined competition in the beer industry with its introduction of low-calorie beer (Miller Lite). Similarly, PepsiCo was able to gain market share from its rival, Coca-Cola, by being the first to introduce diet colas and fruit-based soft drinks. At the same time, the health trend has created a threat for many industries. The tobacco industry, for example, is in decline as a direct result of greater customer awareness of the health implications of smoking.

● Political and Legal Forces

Political and legal forces are outcomes of changes in laws and regulations. They result from political and legal developments within society and significantly affect managers and companies.

Political processes shape a society's laws, which constrain the operations of organizations and managers and thus create both opportunities and threats.[34] For example, throughout much of the industrialized world, there has been a strong trend toward deregulation of industries previously controlled by the state and privatization of organizations once owned by the state. In the United States, deregulation of the airline industry in 1979 allowed twenty-nine new airlines to enter the industry between 1979 and 1993. The increase in passenger-carrying capacity after deregulation led to excess capacity on many routes, intense competition, and fare wars. To respond to this more competitive task environment, airlines have had to look for ways to reduce operating costs. The development of hub-and-spoke systems, the rise of nonunion airlines, and the introduction of no-frills discount service are all responses to increased competition in the airlines' task environment. Despite these innovations, the airline industry still experiences intense fare wars, which have lowered profits and caused numerous airline company bankruptcies. The global telecommunications service industry is now experiencing the same kind of turmoil following the deregulation of that industry in the United States and elsewhere.

In most countries, the interplay between political and legal forces, on the one hand, and industry competitive structure, on the other, is a two-way process in which the government sets regulations that influence competitive structure, and firms in an industry often seek to influence the regulations that governments enact by a number of means. First, when permitted, they may provide financial support to politicians or political parties that espouse views favorable to the industry and lobby government legislators directly to shape government regulations. For example, during the 1990s and early 2000s, the now-bankrupt energy trading company Enron lobbied government legislators to persuade them to deregulate energy markets in the United States, an action that Enron would benefit from. Second, companies and industries may lobby the government through industry associations. In 2002, the United States Steel Industry Association was a prime mover in persuading President Bush to enact a 30% tariff on imports of foreign steel into the United States. The purpose of the tariff was to protect American steel makers from foreign competitors, thereby reducing the intensity of rivalry in the United States steel markets.

Summary of Chapter

1. An industry can be defined as a group of companies offering products or services that are close substitutes for each other. Close substitutes are products or services that satisfy the same basic customer needs.

2. The main technique used to analyze competition in the industry environment is the five forces model. The five forces are (1) the risk of new entry by potential competitors, (2) the extent of rivalry among established firms, (3) the bargaining power of buyers, (4) the bargaining power of suppliers, and (5) the threat of substitute products. The stronger each force is, the more competitive the industry and the lower the rate of return that can be earned.

3. The risk of entry by potential competitors is a function of the height of barriers to entry. The higher the barriers to entry are, the lower is the risk of entry and the greater are the profits that can be earned in the industry.

4. The extent of rivalry among established companies is a function of an industry's competitive structure, demand conditions, cost conditions, and barriers to exit. Strong demand conditions moderate the competition among established companies and create opportunities for expansion. When demand is weak, intensive competition can develop, particularly in consolidated industries with high exit barriers.

5. Buyers are most powerful when a company depends on them for business but they themselves are not dependent on the company. In such circumstances, buyers are a threat.

6. Suppliers are most powerful when a company depends on them for business but they themselves are not dependent on the company. In such circumstances, suppliers are a threat.

7. Substitute products are the products of companies serving customer needs similar to the needs served by the industry being analyzed. The more similar the substitute products are to each other, the lower is the price that companies can charge without losing customers to the substitutes.

8. Some argue for a sixth competitive force of some significance: the power, vigor, and competence of complementors. Powerful and vigorous complementors may have a strong positive impact on demand in an industry.

9. Most industries are composed of strategic groups: groups of companies pursuing the same or a similar strategy. Companies in different strategic groups pursue different strategies.

10. The members of a company's strategic group constitute its immediate competitors. Because different strategic groups are characterized by different opportunities and threats, it may pay for a company to switch strategic groups. The feasibility of doing so is a function of the height of mobility barriers.

11. Industries go through a well-defined life cycle: from an embryonic stage, through growth, shakeout, and maturity, and eventually decline. Each stage has different implications for the competitive structure of the industry, and each gives rise to its own set of opportunities and threats.

12. The five forces, strategic group, and industry life cycles models all have limitations. The five forces and strategic group models present a static picture of competition that de-emphasizes the role of innovation. Yet innovation can revolutionize industry structure and completely change the strength of different competitive forces. The five forces and strategic group models have been criticized for de-emphasizing the importance of individual company differences. A company will not be profitable just because it is based in an attractive industry or strategic group; much more is required. The industry life cycle model is a generalization that is not always followed, particularly when innovations revolutionize an industry.

13. The macroenvironment affects the intensity of rivalry within an industry. Included in the macroenvironment are the global environment, the technological environment, the demographic and social environment, and the political and legal environment.

Discussion Questions

1. Under what environmental conditions are price wars most likely to occur in an industry? What are the implications of price wars for a company? How should a company try to deal with the threat of a price war?

2. Discuss Porter's five forces model with reference to what you know about the U.S. beer industry (see the Opening Case). What does the model tell you about the level of competition in this industry?

3. Identify a growth industry, a mature industry, and a declining industry. For each industry, identify the following: (a) the number and size distribution of companies, (b) the nature of barriers to entry, (c) the height of

barriers to entry, and (d) the extent of product differentiation. What do these factors tell you about the nature of competition in each industry? What are the implications for the company in terms of opportunities and threats?

4. Assess the impact of macroenvironmental factors on the likely level of enrollment at your university over the next decade. What are the implications of these factors for the job security and salary level of your professors?

Practicing Strategic Management

SMALL-GROUP EXERCISE
Competing with Microsoft

Break up into groups of three to five and discuss the following scenario. Appoint one group member as a spokesperson who will communicate the groups findings to the class.

You are a group of managers and software engineers at a small start-up. You have developed a revolutionary new operating system for personal computers that offers distinct advantages over Microsoft's Windows operating system: it takes up less memory space on the hard drive of a personal computer; it takes full advantage of the power of the personal computer's microprocessor, and in theory it can run software applications much faster than Windows; it is much easier to install and use than Windows; and it responds to voice instructions with an accuracy of 99.9%, in addition to input from a keyboard or mouse. The operating system is the only product offering that your company has produced.

Complete the following exercises:

1. Analyze the competitive structure of the market for personal computer operating systems. On the basis of this analysis, identify what factors might inhibit adoption of your operating system by customers.
2. Can you think of a strategy that your company might pursue, either alone or in conjunction with other enterprises, in order to beat Microsoft? What will it take to execute that strategy successfully?

ARTICLE FILE 2

Find an example of an industry that has become more competitive in recent years. Identify the reasons for the increase in competitive pressure.

STRATEGIC MANAGEMENT PROJECT
Module 2

This module requires you to analyze the industry environment in which your company is based using the information you have already gathered:

1. Apply the five forces model to the industry in which your company is based. What does this model tell you about the nature of competition in the industry?
2. Are any changes taking place in the macroenvironment that might have an impact, positive or negative, on the industry in which your company is based? If so, what are these changes, and how might they affect the industry?
3. Identify any strategic groups that might exist in the industry. How does the intensity of competition differ across these strategic groups?
4. How dynamic is the industry in which your company is based? Is there any evidence that innovation is reshaping competition or has done so in the recent past?
5. In what stage of its life cycle is the industry in which your company is based? What are the implications of this for the intensity of competition both now and in the future?
6. Is your company based in an industry that is becoming more global? If so, what are the implications of this change for competitive intensity?
7. Analyze the impact of national context as it pertains to the industry in which your company is based. Does national context help or hinder your company in achieving a competitive advantage in the global marketplace?

ETHICS EXERCISE

In the summer of 2006, word began to spread about a new type of beer soon to hit the market—a beer that answered the low-carb, aftertaste, and calorie concerns of today's beer drinkers all at once. Although a number of beers focusing on one issue, such as low-carb concerns, had recently been released, a beer addressing all three concerns at once could blow the market wide open. Chris, a long-time employee of the company behind the new beer, began to formulate a plan.

Over the next week, Chris spent much of his time chatting with a mid-level secretary named Clare. "Listen, Clare, we've both worked here a long time, and what have they shown us in the way of appreciation? Have you been promoted at all? I haven't had a raise since 2001! This is our chance, Clare! Our chance to really make some money and stick it to the higher-ups at the same time!" By Friday afternoon, Chris could see that Clare was on board. She agreed to come in over the weekend and, using an executive assistant's set of keys, find and copy the new beer formula.

Chris and Clare's plan seemed perfect. Clare had copied the necessary documents, and Chris, through a friend working at a rival brewery, had set up a meeting with one of the company's many executives. At the meeting a few days later, the executive expressed great interest in buying the formula at significant profit to its sellers, and Chris and Clare began to get excited. Much to their surprise, on Thursday morning, security met Chris and Clare as they entered the building in which they worked. The executive at the rival brewery had notified their superiors and the game was up!

1. Discuss the ethical dilemma presented in this case.
2. Why do you think the rival brewery notified the brewery at which Chris and Clare worked rather than taking the formula and using it to its own advantage?
3. What do you think the brewery at which Chris and Clare worked might do to ensure that it is protected against actions such as that taken by Chris and Clare?

CLOSING CASE

The Pharmaceutical Industry

Historically, the pharmaceutical industry has been a profitable one. Between 2002 and 2006, the average rate of return on invested capital (ROIC) for firms in the industry was 16.45%. Put differently, for every dollar of capital invested in the industry, the average pharmaceutical firm generated 16.45 cents of profit. This compares with an average return on invested capital of 12.76% for firms in the computer hardware industry, 8.54% for grocers, and 3.88% for firms in the electronics industry. However, the average level of profitability in the pharmaceutical industry has been declining of late. In 2002, the average ROIC in the industry was 21.6%; by 2006, it had fallen to 14.5%.

The profitability of the pharmaceutical industry can be best understood by looking at several aspects of its underlying economic structure. First, demand for pharmaceuticals has been strong and has grown for decades. Between 1990 and 2003, there was a 12.5% annual increase in spending on prescription drugs in the United States. This growth was driven by favorable demographics. As people grow older, they tend to need and consume more prescription medicines, and the population in most advanced nations has been growing older as the post–World War II baby-boom generation ages. Looking forward, projections suggest that spending on prescription drugs will increase between 10 and 11% annually through 2013.

Second, successful new prescription drugs can be extraordinarily profitable. Lipitor, the cholesterol-lowering drug sold by Pfizer, was introduced in 1997, and by 2005, this drug had generated a staggering $12.2 billion in annual sales for Pfizer. The costs of manufacturing, packing, and distributing Lipitor amounted to only about 10% of revenues. Pfizer spent close to $500 million on promoting Lipitor and perhaps as much again on maintaining a sales force to sell the product. That still left Pfizer with a gross profit of perhaps $10 billion. Since the drug is protected from direct competition by a twenty-year patent, Pfizer has a temporary monopoly and can charge a high price. Once the patent expires, which is scheduled to occur in 2010, other firms will be able to produce generic versions of Lipitor and the price will fall—typically by 80% within a year.

Competing firms can produce drugs that are similar (but not identical) to a patent-protected drug. Drug firms patent a specific molecule, and competing firms can patent similar, but not identical, molecules that have a similar pharmacological effect. Thus, Lipitor does have competitors in the market for cholesterol-lowering drugs, such as Zocor sold by Merck and Crestor sold by AstraZeneca. But these competing drugs are also patent-protected. Moreover, the high costs and risks associated with developing a new drug and bringing it to market limit new competition. Out of every five thousand compounds tested in the laboratory by a drug company, only five enter clinical trials, and only one of these will ultimately make it to the market. On average, estimates suggest that it costs some $800 million and takes anywhere from ten to fifteen years to bring a new drug to market. Once on the market, only three out of ten drugs ever recoup their R&D and marketing costs and turn a profit. Thus, the high profitability of the pharmaceutical industry rests on a handful of blockbuster drugs. At Pfizer, the world's largest pharmaceutical company, 55% of revenues were generated from just eight drugs.

To produce a blockbuster, a drug company must spend large amounts of money on research, most of which fails to produce a product. Only very large companies can shoulder the costs and risks of doing so, making it difficult for new companies to enter the industry. Pfizer, for example, spent some $7.44 billion on R&D in 2005 alone, equivalent to 14.5% of its total revenues. In a testament to just how difficult it is to get into the industry, although a large number of companies have been started in the last twenty years in the hope that they might develop new pharmaceuticals, only two of these companies, Amgen and Genentech, were ranked among the top twenty in the industry in terms of sales in 2005. Most have failed to bring a product to market.

In addition to R&D spending, the incumbent firms in the pharmaceutical industry spend large amounts of money on advertising and sales promotion. While the $500 million a year that Pfizer spends promoting Lipitor is small relative to the drug's revenues, it is a large amount for a new competitor to match, making market entry difficult unless the competitor has a significantly better product.

There are also some big opportunities on the horizon for firms in the industry. New scientific breakthroughs in genomics are holding out the promise that within the next decade, pharmaceutical firms might be able to bring new drugs to market that treat some of the most intractable medical conditions, including Alzheimer's, Parkinson's disease, cancer, heart disease, stroke, and AIDS.

However, there are some threats to the long-term dominance and profitability of industry giants like Pfizer. First, as spending on health care rises, politicians are looking for ways to limit health care costs, and one possibility is some form of price control on prescription drugs. Price controls are already in effect in most developed nations, and although they have not yet been introduced in the United States, they could be.

Second, between 2006 and 2009, twelve of the top thirty-five selling drugs in the industry will loose their patent protection. By one estimate, some 28% of the global drug industry's sales of $307 billion will be exposed to generic challenge in America alone, due to drugs going off patent between 2006 and 2012. It is not clear to many industry observers whether the established drug companies have enough new drug prospects in their pipelines to replace revenues from drugs going off patent. Moreover, generic drug companies have been aggressive in challenging the patents of proprietary drug companies and in pricing their generic offerings. As a result, their share of industry sales has been growing. In 2005, they accounted for more than half of all drugs prescribed by volume in the United States, up from one-third in 1990.

Third, the industry has come under renewed scrutiny following studies showing that some FDA-approved prescription drugs, known as COX-2 inhibitors, were associated with a greater risk of heart attacks. Two of these drugs, Vioxx and Bextra, were pulled from the market in 2004.[35]

Case Discussion Questions

1. Drawing on the five forces model, explain why the pharmaceutical industry has historically been a very profitable industry.

2. After 2002, the profitability of the industry, measured by ROIC, started to decline. Why do you think this occurred?

3. What are the prospects for the industry in the future? What are the opportunities? What are the threats? What must pharmaceutical firms do to exploit the opportunities and counter the threats?

Internal Analysis: Distinctive Competencies, Competitive Advantage, and Profitability

Southwest Airlines

Southwest Airlines has long been one of the standout performers in the U.S. airline industry. It is famous for its low fares, which are often about 30% beneath those of its major rivals. These are balanced by an even lower cost structure, which has enabled it to record superior profitability even in bad years such as 2002, when the industry faced slumping demand in the wake of the September 11 terrorist attacks. Indeed, during 2001 to 2005, quite possibly the worst four years in the history of the airline industry, when every other major airline lost money, Southwest made money every year and earned a return on invested capital of 5.8%.

What is the source of Southwest's competitive advantage? Many people immediately point to the company's business model and low cost structure. With regard to their business model, while operators like American Airlines and United route passengers through congested hubs, Southwest Airlines flies point-to-point, often through smaller airports. By competing in a way that other airlines do not, Southwest has found that it can capture enough demand to keep its planes full. Moreover, because it avoids many hubs, Southwest has experienced fewer delays. In the first eight months of 2006, Southwest planes arrived on schedule 80% of the time, compared to 76% at United and 74% at Continental.

As for Southwest's low cost structure, this has a number of sources. Unlike most airlines, Southwest flies only one type of plane, the Boeing 737. This reduces training costs, maintenance costs, and inventory costs while increasing efficiency in crew and flight scheduling. The operation is nearly ticketless and there is no seat assignment, which reduces cost and back-office accounting functions. There are no meals or movies in flight, and the airline will not transfer baggage to other airlines, reducing the need for baggage handlers.

The most important source of the company's low cost structure, however, seems to be very high employee productivity. One way airlines measure employee productivity is by the ratio of employees to passengers carried. According to figures from company 10-K statements, in 2005, Southwest had an employee-to-passenger ratio of 1 to 2,400, the best in the industry. By comparison, the ratio at United Airlines during 2005 was 1 to 1,175 and at Continental, it was 1 to

1,125. These figures suggest that holding size constant, Southwest runs its operation with far fewer people than competitors. How does it do this?

First, Southwest devotes enormous attention to the people it hires. On average, the company hires only 3% of those interviewed in a year. When hiring, it emphasizes teamwork and a positive attitude. Southwest rationalizes that skills can be taught but a positive attitude and a willingness to pitch in cannot. Southwest also creates incentives for its employees to work hard. All employees are covered by a profit-sharing plan, and at least 25% of an employee's share of the profit-sharing plan has to be invested in Southwest Airlines stock. This gives rise to a simple formula: the harder employees work, the more profitable Southwest becomes, and the richer the employees get. The results are clear. At other airlines, one would never see a pilot helping to check passengers onto the plane. At Southwest, pilots and flight attendants have been known to help clean the aircraft and check in passengers at the gate. They do this to turn around an aircraft as quickly as possible and get it into the air again because an aircraft doesn't make money when it is sitting on the ground. This flexible and motivated work force leads to higher productivity and reduces the company's need for more employees.

Second, because Southwest because flies point-to-point rather than through congested airport hubs, there is no need for dozens of gates and thousands of employees to handle banks of flights that come in and then disperse within a two-hour window, leaving the hub empty until the next flights a few hours later. The result: Southwest can operate with far fewer employees than airlines that fly through hubs.[1]

OVERVIEW

Why, within a particular industry or market, do some companies outperform others? What is the basis of their (sustained) competitive advantage? The Opening Case provides some clues. The competitive advantage of Southwest Airlines comes from efficiency, customer responsiveness, and reliability. Southwest's efficiency is primarily due to high labor productivity, which translates into lower operating costs. Southwest is responsive to customers because it flies point-to-point, and does not force passengers to fly through congested hubs that might lengthen their journey. Southwest is more reliable because a greater proportion of its flights arrive on time, in part because the company tries to avoid congested hubs, and partly because the company's flexible work force can turn around a plane at the gate in fifteen minutes, making sure that planes that arrive late leave closer to their scheduled departure time. As you will see in this chapter, efficiency, customer responsiveness, and reliability, which is an aspect of product quality, are three of the four main building blocks of competitive advantage. The other building block is innovation.

This chapter focuses on internal analysis, which is concerned with identifying the strengths and weaknesses of the company. Together with an analysis of the company's external environment, internal analysis gives managers the information they need to choose the business model and strategies that will enable their company to attain a sustained competitive advantage. Internal analysis is a three-step process. First, managers must understand the process by which companies create value for customers and profit for themselves, and they need to understand the role of resources, capabilities, and distinctive competencies in this process. Second, they need to understand how important superior efficiency, innovation, quality, and customer responsiveness are in creating value and generating high profitability. Third, they must be able to analyze the sources of their company's competitive advantage to identify what is driving the profitability of their enterprise and where opportunities for improvement might lie. In other words, they must be able to identify how the strengths of the enterprise boost its profitability and how any weaknesses lead to lower profitability.

Three more critical issues in internal analysis are addressed in this chapter. First, what factors influence the durability of competitive advantage? Second, why do successful companies often lose their competitive advantage? Third, how can companies avoid competitive failure and sustain their competitive advantage over time?

After reading this chapter, you will understand the nature of competitive advantage and why managers need to perform internal analysis, just as they must conduct industry analysis, to achieve superior performance and profitability.

The Roots of Competitive Advantage

A company has a *competitive advantage* over its rivals when its profitability is greater than the average profitability of all companies in its industry. It has a *sustained competitive advantage* when it is able to maintain above-average profitability over a number of years, as Dell has done in the personal computer industry and Southwest Airlines has done in the airline industry. The primary objective of strategy is to achieve a sustained competitive advantage, which in turn will result in superior profitability and profit growth. What are the sources of competitive advantage, and what is the link among strategy, competitive advantage, and profitability?

● **Distinctive Competencies**

Competitive advantage is based on distinctive competencies. **Distinctive competencies are firm-specific strengths that allow a company to differentiate its products from those offered by rivals, and/or achieve substantially lower costs than its rivals.** Southwest Airlines, for example, has a distinctive competence in managing its work force, which leads to higher employee productivity and lower costs (see the Opening Case). Similarly, it can be argued that Toyota, which is the standard outperformer in the automobile industry, has distinctive competencies in the development and operation of manufacturing processes. Toyota pioneered a whole range of manufacturing techniques, such as just-in-time inventory systems, self-managing teams, and reduced setup times for complex equipment. These competencies, collectively known as the Toyota lean production system, helped it attain superior efficiency and product quality, which are the basis of its competitive advantage in the global automobile industry.[2] Distinctive competencies arise from two complementary sources: resources and capabilities.[3]

RESOURCES   **Resources** refer to the assets of a company. A company's resources can be divided into two types: tangible and intangible. **Tangible resources** are physical entities, such as land, buildings, plant, equipment, inventory, and money. **Intangible resources** are nonphysical entities that are created by managers and other employees, such as brand names; the reputation of the company; the knowledge that employees have gained through experience; and the intellectual property of the company, including intellectual property protected through patents, copyrights, and trademarks.

Resources are particularly valuable when they enable a company to create strong demand for its products and/or to lower its costs. Toyota's valuable tangible resources include the equipment associated with its lean production system, much of which has been engineered specifically by Toyota for exclusive use in its factories. These valuable tangible resources allow Toyota to lower its costs relative to competitors. Similarly, Microsoft has a number of valuable intangible resources, including its brand name and the software code that underlies its Windows operating system. These valuable resources allow Microsoft to sell more of its products, relative to competitors.

Valuable resources are more likely to lead to a sustainable competitive advantage if they are rare, in the sense that competitors do not possess them, and difficult for rivals to imitate; that is, if there are *barriers to imitation* (we will discuss the source of barriers to imitation in more detail later in this chapter). For example, the software code underlying Windows is rare because only Microsoft has full access to it. The code is also difficult to imitate. A rival cannot simply copy the software code underlying Windows and sell its own version of Windows because the code is protected by copyright law, and copying it is illegal. Similarly, Toyota's specialized production equipment is rare (only Toyota has it), and it is difficult for competitors to imitate because Toyota does not allow competitors to examine the details of that equipment.

CAPABILITIES   **Capabilities** refer to a company's skills at coordinating its resources and putting them to productive use. These skills reside in an organization's rules, routines, and procedures, that is, the style or manner through which it makes decisions and manages its internal processes to achieve organizational objectives.[4] More generally, a company's capabilities are the product of its organizational structure, processes, control systems and hiring systems. They specify how and where decisions are made within a company, the kind of behaviors the company rewards, and the company's cultural norms and values. (We discuss how organizational structure and control systems help a company obtain capabilities in Chapters 12 and 13.) Capabilities are intangible. They reside not so much in individuals as in the way individuals interact, cooperate, and make decisions within the context of an organization.[5]

Like resources, capabilities are particularly valuable if they enable a company to create strong demand for its products and/or to lower its costs. The competitive advantage of Southwest Airlines is based in large part on its capability to select, motivate, and manage its work force in such a way that leads to high employee productivity and lower costs (see the Opening Case). As with resources, valuable capabilities are also more likely to lead to a sustainable competitive advantage if they are both rare and protected from copying by barriers to imitation.

RESOURCES, CAPABILITIES, AND COMPETENCIES   The distinction between resources and capabilities is critical to understanding what generates a distinctive competency. A company may have firm-specific and valuable resources, but unless it has the capability to use those resources effectively, it may not be able to create a distinctive competency. It is also important to recognize that a company may not need firm-specific and valuable resources to establish a distinctive competency so long as it does have capabilities that no competitor possesses. For example, the steel mini-mill operator Nucor is widely acknowledged to be the most cost-efficient steel maker in the United States. Its distinctive competency in low-cost steel making does not come from any firm-specific and valuable resources. Nucor has the same resources (plant, equipment, skilled employees, know-how) as many other mini-mill operators. What distinguishes Nucor is its unique capability to manage its resources in a highly productive way. Specifically, Nucor's structure, control systems, and culture promote efficiency at all levels within the company.

In sum, for a company to have a distinctive competency, it must, at a minimum, have either (1) a firm-specific and valuable resource and the capabilities (skills) necessary to take advantage of that resource or (2) a firm-specific capability to manage resources (as exemplified by Nucor). A company's distinctive competency is strongest

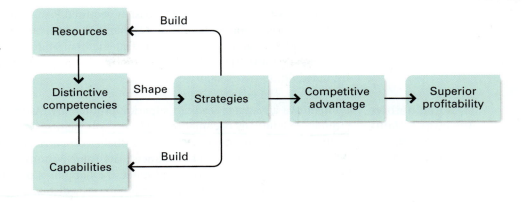

when it possesses both firm-specific and valuable resources and firm-specific capabilities to manage those resources.

THE ROLE OF STRATEGY Figure 3.1 illustrates the relationship of a company's strategies, distinctive competencies, and competitive advantage. Distinctive competencies shape the strategies that the company pursues, which lead to competitive advantage and superior profitability. However, it is also very important to realize that the strategies a company adopts can build new resources and capabilities or strengthen the existing resources and capabilities of the company, thereby enhancing the distinctive competencies of the enterprise. Thus, the relationship between distinctive competencies and strategies is not a linear one; rather, it is a reciprocal one in which distinctive competencies shape strategies, and strategies help to build and create distinctive competencies.[6]

The history of The Walt Disney Company since the 1980s illustrates the way this process works. In the early 1980s, Disney suffered a string of poor financial years that culminated in a 1984 management shakeup when Michael Eisner was appointed CEO. Four years later, Disney's sales had increased from $1.66 billion to $3.75 billion, its net profits had increased from $98 million to $570 million, and its stock market valuation had increased from $1.8 billion to $10.3 billion. What brought about this transformation was the company's deliberate attempt to use its resources and capabilities more aggressively: Disney's enormous film library, its brand name, and its filmmaking skills, particularly in animation. Under Eisner, many old Disney classics were re-released, first in movie theaters and then on video, earning the company millions in the process. Then Eisner reintroduced the product that had originally made Disney famous: the full-length animated feature. Putting together its brand name and in-house animation capabilities, Disney produced a stream of major box office hits, including *The Little Mermaid, Beauty and the Beast, Aladdin, Pocahontas,* and *The Lion King.* Disney also started a cable television channel, the Disney Channel, to use this library and capitalize on the company's brand name. In other words, Disney's existing resources and capabilities shaped its strategies.

Through his choice of strategies, Eisner also developed new competencies in different parts of the business. In the filmmaking arm of Disney, for example, Eisner created a new low-cost film division under the Touchstone label, and the company had a string of low-budget box office hits. It entered into a long-term agreement with the computer animation company Pixar to develop a competency in computer-generated animated films. This strategic collaboration produced several hits, including *Toy Story* and *Monsters Incorporated* (in 2004, Disney acquired Pixar). In sum, Disney's transformation was based not only on strategies that took advantage of the company's existing resources and capabilities but also on strategies that built new resources and capabilities, such as those that underlie the company's competency in computer-generated animated films.

● **Competitive Advantage, Value Creation, and Profitability**

Competitive advantage leads to superior profitability. At the most basic level, how profitable a company becomes depends on three factors: (1) the value customers place on the company's products, (2) the price that a company charges for its products, and (3) the costs of creating those products. The value customers place on a product reflects the utility they get from a product, the happiness or satisfaction gained from consuming or owning the product. Utility must be distinguished from price. Utility is something that customers get from a product. It is a function of the attributes of the product, such as its performance, design, quality, and point-of-sale and after-sale service. For example, most customers would place a much higher utility value on a top-end Lexus car from Toyota than on a low-end basic economy car from General Motors (they would value it more) precisely because they perceive the Lexus to have better performance and superior design, quality, and service. A company that strengthens the utility (or value) of its products in the eyes of customers has more pricing options: it can raise prices to reflect that utility (value) or hold prices lower to induce more customers to purchase its products, thereby expanding unit sales volume.

Whatever pricing option a company chooses, however, the price a company charges for a good or service is typically less than the utility value placed on that good or service by the customer because the customer captures some of that utility in the form of what economists call a consumer surplus.[7] The customer is able to do this because the company is competing with other companies for the customer's business, so the company must charge a lower price than it could were it a monopoly supplier. Moreover, it is normally impossible to segment the market to such a degree that the company can charge each customer a price that reflects that individual's unique assessment of the utility of a product—what economists refer to as a customer's reservation price. For these reasons, the price that gets charged tends to be less than the utility value placed on the product by many customers. Nevertheless, remember the basic principle here: the more utility that consumers get from a company's products or services, the more pricing options the company has.

These concepts are illustrated in Figure 3.2: U is the average utility value per unit of a product to a customer, P is the average price per unit that the company decides

FIGURE 3.2

Value Creation per Unit

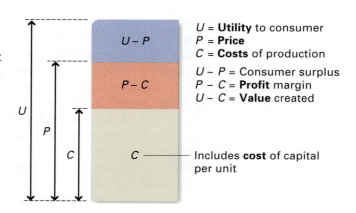

U = **Utility** to consumer
P = **Price**
C = **Costs** of production

$U - P$ = Consumer surplus
$P - C$ = **Profit** margin
$U - C$ = **Value** created

Includes **cost** of capital per unit

to charge for that product, and C is the average unit cost of producing that product (including actual production costs and the cost of capital investments in production systems). The company's average profit per unit is equal to $P - C$, and the consumer surplus is equal to $U - P$. In other words, $U - P$ is a measure of the value the consumer captures, and $P - C$ is a measure of the value the company captures. The company makes a profit so long as P is more than C, and its profitability will be greater the lower C is relative to P. Bear in mind that the difference between U and P is in part determined by the intensity of competitive pressure in the marketplace; the lower the intensity of competitive pressure, the higher the price that can be charged relative to U, but the difference between U and P is also determined by the company's pricing choice.[8] As we shall see, a company may choose to keep prices low relative to volume because lower prices enable the company to sell more products, attain scale economies, and boost its profit margin by lowering C relative to P.

Note also that the value created by a company is measured by the difference between the utility a consumer gets from the product (U) and the costs of production (C), that is, $U - C$. A company creates value by converting factors of production that cost C into a product from which customers get a utility of U. A company can create more value for its customers by lowering C or making the product more attractive through superior design, performance, quality, service, and the like. When customers assign a greater utility to the product (U increases), they are willing to pay a higher price (P increases). This discussion suggests that a company has a competitive advantage and high profitability when it creates more value for its customers than its rivals do.[9]

The company's pricing options are captured in Figure 3.3. Suppose a company's current pricing option is the one pictured in the middle column of Figure 3.3. Imagine that the company decides to pursue strategies to increase the utility of its product offering from U to U^* in order to boost its profitability. Increasing utility initially raises production costs because the company has to spend money to increase product performance, quality, service, and other factors. Now there are two different pricing options that the company can pursue. Option 1 is to raise prices to reflect the higher utility: the company raises prices more than its costs increase, and profit per unit ($P - C$) increases. Option 2 involves a very different set of choices: the company lowers

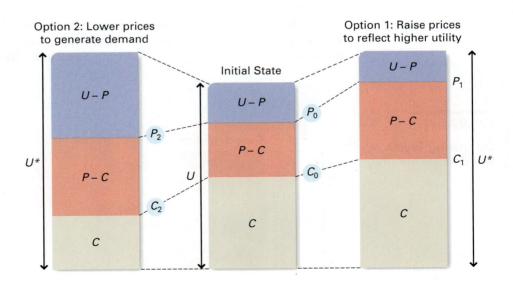

FIGURE 3.3

Value Creation and Pricing Options

prices in order to expand unit volume. Basically, what is happening is that customers recognize that they are getting a great bargain because price is now much lower than utility (the consumer surplus has increased), so they rush out to buy more (demand has increased). As unit volume expands due to increased demand, the company is able to realize scale economies and reduce its average unit costs. Although creating the extra utility initially costs more and prices are now lowered, profit margins widen because the average unit costs of production fall as volume increases and scale economies are attained.

Managers need to understand the dynamic relationships among utility, pricing, demand, and costs and make decisions on the basis of that understanding to maximize competitive advantage and profitability. Option 2 in Figure 3.3, for example, might not be a viable strategy if demand did not increase rapidly with lower prices or if there are few economies of scale to be had by increasing volume. Managers must understand how value creation and pricing decisions affect demand and also how unit costs change with increases in volume. In other words, they must have a good grasp of the demand for the company's product and its cost structure at different levels of output if they are to make decisions that maximize profitability.

Consider the automobile industry. According to a 2006 study by Harbour & Associates, in 2005, Toyota made $1,200 in profit on every vehicle it manufactured in North America. General Motors, in contrast, lost $2,496 on every vehicle it made.[10] What accounts for the difference? First, Toyota has the best reputation for quality in the industry. According to annual surveys issued by J. D. Power and Associates, Toyota consistently tops the list in terms of quality, while GM cars are at best in the middle of the pack. The higher quality translates into a higher utility and allows Toyota to charge 5 to 10% higher prices than General Motors for equivalent cars. Second, Toyota has a lower cost per vehicle than General Motors in part because of its superior labor productivity. For example, in Toyota's North American plants, it took an average of 29.40 employee hours to build a car, compared to 33.19 at GM plants in North America. That 3.49 hour productivity advantage translates into much lower labor costs for Toyota and, hence, a lower overall cost structure. Therefore, as summarized in Figure 3.4, Toyota's advantage over GM derives from greater utility (U), which has allowed the company to charge a higher price (P) for its cars, and from a lower cost structure (C), which taken together implies significantly greater profitability per vehicle ($P - C$).

Toyota's decisions with regard to pricing are guided by its managers' understanding of the relationship of utility, prices, demand, and costs. Given its ability to build more utility into its products, Toyota could have charged even higher prices

FIGURE 3.4

Comparing Toyota
and General Motors

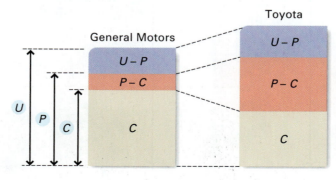

than illustrated in Figure 3.4, but that might have led to lower sales volume, fewer scale economies, higher unit costs, and lower profit margins. Toyota's managers have sought to find the pricing option that enables the company to maximize its profits given their assessment of demand for its products and its cost function. Thus, to create superior value, a company does not have to have the lowest cost structure in an industry or create the product with the highest utility in the eyes of customers. All that is necessary is that the gap between perceived utility (U) and costs of production (C) is greater than the gap attained by competitors.

Note that Toyota has differentiated itself from General Motors by its superior quality, which allows it to charge higher prices, and its superior productivity translates into a lower cost structure. Thus, its competitive advantage over General Motors is the result of strategies that have led to distinctive competencies, resulting in greater differentiation and a lower cost structure.

Indeed, at the heart of any company's business model is the combination of congruent strategies aimed at creating distinctive competencies that (1) differentiate its products in some way so that its consumers derive more utility from them, which gives the company more pricing options, and (2) result in a lower cost structure, which also gives it a broader range of pricing choices.[11] Achieving a sustained competitive advantage and superior profitability requires the right choices with regard to utility through differentiation and pricing given the demand conditions in the company's market and the company's cost structure at different levels of output. This issue is addressed in detail in the following chapters.

The Value Chain

All of the functions of a company—such as production, marketing, product development, service, information systems, materials management, and human resources-have a role in lowering the cost structure and increasing the perceived utility (value) of the products through differentiation. As the first step in examining this concept, consider the value chain, which is illustrated in Figure 3.5.[12] The term **value chain** refers to the idea that a company is a chain of activities for transforming inputs into outputs that customers value. The transformation process involves a number of primary activities and support activities that add value to the product.

● **Primary Activities**   **Primary activities** have to do with the design, creation, and delivery of the product; its marketing; and its support and after-sales service. In the value chain illustrated in

FIGURE 3.5

The Value Chain

Figure 3.5, the primary activities are broken down into four functions: research and development (R&D), production, marketing and sales, and customer service.

RESEARCH AND DEVELOPMENT **Research and development** is concerned with the design of products and production processes. Although we think of R&D as being associated with the design of physical products and production processes in manufacturing enterprises, many service companies also undertake R&D. For example, banks compete with each other by developing new financial products and new ways of delivering those products to customers. Online banking and smart debit cards are two recent examples of the fruits of new-product development in the banking industry. Earlier examples of innovation in the banking industry were ATM machines, credit cards, and debit cards.

By creating superior product design, R&D can increase the functionality of products, which makes them more attractive to customers, thereby adding value. Alternatively, the work of R&D may result in more efficient production processes, thereby lowering production costs. Either way, the R&D function can help to lower costs or raise the utility of a product and permit a company to charge higher prices. At Intel, for example, R&D creates value by developing ever more powerful microprocessors and helping to pioneer ever more efficient manufacturing processes (in conjunction with equipment suppliers).

It is important to emphasize that R&D is not just about enhancing the features and functions of a product; it is also about the elegance of a product's design, which can create an impression of superior value in the minds of consumers. For example, part of the success of Apple Computer's iPod player has been based on the elegance and appeal of the iPod design, which has turned this piece of electronic equipment into a fashion accessory. For another example of how design elegance can create value, see Strategy in Action 3.1, which discusses value creation at the fashion house, Burberry.

PRODUCTION **Production** is concerned with the creation of a good or service. For physical products, when we talk about production, we generally mean manufacturing. For services such as banking or retail operations, production typically takes place when the service is delivered to the customer, as when a bank makes a loan to a customer. By performing its activities efficiently, the production function of a company helps to lower its cost structure. For example, the efficient production operations of Honda and Toyota help those automobile companies achieve higher profitability relative to competitors such as General Motors. The production function can also perform its activities in a way that is consistent with high product quality, which leads to differentiation (and higher value) and lower costs.

MARKETING AND SALES There are several ways in which the marketing and sales functions of a company can help to create value. Through brand positioning and advertising, the marketing function can increase the value that customers perceive to be contained in a company's product (and thus the utility they attribute to the product). Insofar as these help to create a favorable impression of the company's product in the minds of customers, they increase utility. For example, in the 1980s, the French company Perrier persuaded U.S. customers that slightly carbonated bottled water was worth $1.50 per bottle rather than a price closer to the $0.50 that it cost to collect, bottle, and distribute the water. Perrier's marketing function essentially increased the perception of utility that customers ascribed to the product. Similarly, by helping to rebrand the company and its product offering, the marketing department at Burberry

Strategy in Action

3.1

Value Creation at Burberry

When Rose Marie Bravo, the highly regarded president of Saks Fifth Avenue, announced in 1997 that she was leaving to become CEO of ailing British fashion house Burberry, people thought she was crazy. Burberry, best known as a designer of raincoats with their trademark tartan linings, had been described as an outdated, stuffy business with a fashion cachet of almost zero. When she stepped down in 2006, Bravo was heralded in Britain and the United States as one of the world's best managers. In her tenure at Burberry, she had engineered a remarkable turnaround, leading a transformation of Burberry into what one commentator called an "achingly hip" high-end fashion brand whose famous tartan bedecks everything from raincoats to bikinis, and handbags to luggage in a riot of color from pink to blue to purple. In less than a decade, Burberry had become one of the most valuable luxury fashion brands in the world.

When asked how she achieved the transformation, Bravo explains that there was hidden value in the brand that was unleashed by constant creativity and innovation. Bravo hired world-class designers to redesign Burberry's tired fashion line and bought in Christopher Bailey, one of the very best, to lead the design team. The marketing department worked closely with advertisers to develop hip ads that would appeal to a younger well-heeled audience. The ads featured supermodel Kate Moss promoting the line, and Burberry hired a top fashion photographer to shoot Moss in Burberry. Burberry exercised tight control over distribution, pulling its products from stores whose image was not consistent with the Burberry brand, and expanding its own chain of Burberry stores.

Bravo also noted that "creativity doesn't just come from designers . . . ideas can come from the sales floor, the marketing department, even from accountants, believe it or not. People at whatever level they are working have a point of view and have something to say that is worth listening to." Bravo emphasized the importance of teamwork. "One of the things I think people overlook is the quality of the team. It isn't one person, and it isn't two people. It is a whole group of people—a team that works cohesively towards a goal—that makes something happen or not." She notes that her job is to build the team and then motivate them, "keeping them on track, making sure that they are following the vision."[a]

helped to create value (see Strategy in Action 3.1). Marketing and sales can also create value by discovering customer needs and communicating them back to the R&D function of the company, which can then design products that better match those needs.

CUSTOMER SERVICE. The role of the service function of an enterprise is to provide after-sales service and support. This function can create superior utility by solving customer problems and supporting customers after they have purchased the product. For example, Caterpillar, the U.S.-based manufacturer of heavy earthmoving equipment, can get spare parts to any point in the world within twenty-four hours, thereby minimizing the amount of downtime its customers have to face if their Caterpillar equipment malfunctions. This is an extremely valuable support capability in an industry where downtime is very expensive. It has helped to increase the utility that customers associate with Caterpillar products, and thus the price that Caterpillar can charge for its products.

● **Support Activities**   The **support activities** of the value chain provide inputs that allow the primary activities to take place. These activities are broken down into four functions: materials management (or logistics), human resources, information systems, and company infrastructure (see Figure 3.5).

MATERIALS MANAGEMENT (LOGISTICS) The materials-management (or logistics) function controls the transmission of physical materials through the value chain, from procurement through production and into distribution. The efficiency with which this is carried out can significantly lower cost, thereby creating more value. Dell Computer has a very efficient materials-management process. By tightly controlling the flow of component parts from its suppliers to its assembly plants, and into the hands of consumers, Dell has dramatically reduced its inventory holding costs. Lower inventories mean lower costs, and hence greater value creation. Another company that has benefited from very efficient materials management, the Spanish fashion company Zara, is discussed in Strategy in Action 3.2.

HUMAN RESOURCES The human resources function can help an enterprise to create more value in several ways. This function ensures that the company has the right mix of skilled people to perform its value creation activities effectively. It is also the job of the human resources function to ensure that people are adequately trained, motivated, and compensated to perform their value creation tasks. If the human resources

Strategy in Action

3.2

Competitive Advantage at Zara

The fashion retailer Zara is one of Spain's fastest growing and most successful companies, with sales of about $8.5 billion and a network of 2,800 stores in sixty-four countries. Zara's competitive advantage centers around one thing—speed. While it takes most fashion houses six to nine months to go from design to having merchandise delivered to a store, Zara can pull off the entire process in just five weeks. This rapid response time enables Zara to quickly respond to changing fashions.

Zara achieves this by breaking many of the rules of operation in the fashion business. While most fashion houses outsource production, Zara has its own factories and keeps about half of its production in-house. Zara also has its own designers and stores. Its designers are in constant contact with the stores, not only tracking what is selling on a real-time basis through information systems but also talking to store managers once a week to get their subjective impressions of what is hot. This information supplements data gathered from other sources, such as fashion shows.

Drawing on this information, Zara's designers create approximately 40,000 new designs a year, from which 10,000 are selected for production. Zara then purchases basic textiles from global suppliers but performs capital-intensive production activities in its own factories. These factories use computer-controlled machinery to cut pieces for garments. Zara does not produce in large volumes to attain economies of scale; instead it produces in small lots. Labor-intensive activities, such as sewing, are performed by subcontractors located close to Zara's factories. Zara makes a practice of having more production capacity than necessary so that if it spots an emerging fashion trend, it can quickly respond by designing garments and ramping up production.

Once a garment has been made, it is delivered to one of Zara's own warehouses and then shipped to its own stores once a week. Zara deliberately underproduces products, supplying small batches of products in hot demand before quickly shifting to the next fashion trend. Often its merchandise sells out quickly. The empty shelves in Zara stores create a scarcity value, which helps to generate demand. Customers quickly snap up products they like because they known they may soon be out of stock and not produced again.

As a result of this strategy, which is supported by competencies in design, information systems, and logistics management, Zara carries fewer inventories than competitors (Zara's inventory amounts to about 10% of sales, compared to 15% at rival stores like The Gap and Benetton). This means fewer price reductions to move products that haven't sold and higher profit margins.[b]

function operates well, employee productivity rises (which lowers costs) and customer service improves (which raises utility), thereby enabling the company to create more value. As we saw in the Opening Case, much of the competitive advantage of Southwest Airlines lies in its human resources practices, which have created a highly productive work force.

INFORMATION SYSTEMS Information systems are the largely electronic systems for managing inventory, tracking sales, pricing products, selling products, dealing with customer service inquiries, and so on. Information systems, when coupled with the communications features of the Internet, are holding out the promise of being able to improve the efficiency and effectiveness with which a company manages its other value creation activities. Again, Dell uses Web-based information systems to efficiently manage its global logistics network and increase inventory turnover. World-class information systems are also an aspect of Zara's competitive advantage (see Strategy in Action 3.2).

COMPANY INFRASTRUCTURE Company infrastructure is the companywide context within which all the other value creation activities take place: the organizational structure, control systems, and company culture. Because top management can exert considerable influence in shaping these aspects of a company, top management should also be viewed as part of the infrastructure of a company. Indeed, through strong leadership, top management can shape the infrastructure of a company and, through that, the performance of all other value creation activities that take place within it. A good example of this process is given in Strategy in Action 3.1, which looks at how Rose Marie Bravo helped to engineer a turnaround at Burberry.

The Building Blocks of Competitive Advantage

Four factors help a company to build and sustain competitive advantage—superior efficiency, quality, innovation, and customer responsiveness. Each of these factors is the product of a company's distinctive competencies. Indeed, in a very real sense, they are "generic" distinctive competencies. These generic competencies allow a company to (1) differentiate its product offering, and hence offer more utility to its customers, and (2) lower its cost structure (see Figure 3.6). These factors can be considered generic distinctive competencies because any company, regardless of its industry or the products or services it produces, can pursue them. Although they are discussed sequentially below, they are highly interrelated, and the important ways they affect each other should be noted. For example, superior quality can lead to superior efficiency, and innovation can enhance efficiency, quality, and responsiveness to customers.

● **Efficiency**   In one sense, a business is simply a device for transforming inputs into outputs. Inputs are basic factors of production such as labor, land, capital, management, and technological know-how. Outputs are the goods and services that the business produces. The simplest measure of efficiency is the quantity of inputs that it takes to produce a given output, that is, Efficiency = outputs/inputs. The more efficient a company is, the fewer the inputs required to produce a given output.

The two most important components of efficiency for many companies are employee productivity and capital productivity. **Employee productivity** refers to the

FIGURE 3.6

Building Blocks of
Competitive
Advantage

output produced per employee. For example, if it takes General Motors thirty hours of employee time to assemble a car and it takes Ford twenty-five hours, we can say that Ford has higher employee productivity than GM and is thus more efficient. As long as other things are equal, such as wage rates, we can assume from this information that Ford will have a lower cost structure than GM. Thus, employee productivity helps a company attain a competitive advantage through a lower cost structure. You will recall from the Opening Case that Southwest Airline's low cost structure was due in large part to higher labor productivity.

Capital productivity refers to the sales produced per dollar of capital invested in a business. An analysis of financial statements suggests that in 2005, Dell Computer generated $12.07 of sales for every dollar of capital it invested in its business, whereas its competitor Hewlett-Packard generated $2.14 of sales for every dollar of capital it invested in its business. Dell was far more efficient than Hewlett-Packard in the way it used its capital to generates sales revenues. Other things being equal, this will lead to lower costs and higher profitability (for a full comparison of Dell and Hewlett-Packard, see the Running Case in this chapter).

The concept of productivity is not limited to employee and capital productivity. Pharmaceutical companies, for example, often talk about the productivity of their R&D spending, by which they mean how many new drugs they develop from their investment in R&D. Other companies talk about their sales force productivity, which means how many sales they generate from every sales call, and so on. The important point to remember is that high productivity leads to greater efficiency and lower costs.

● **Quality as Excellence and Reliability**

A product can be thought of as a bundle of attributes.[13] The attributes of many physical products include their form, features, performance, durability, reliability, style, and design.[14] A product is said to have *superior quality* when customers perceive that its attributes provide them with higher utility than the attributes of products sold by rivals. For example, a Rolex watch has attributes-such as design, styling, performance, and reliability—that customers perceive as being superior to the same attributes in many other watches. Thus, we can refer to a Rolex as a high-quality product: Rolex has differentiated its watches by these attributes.

When customers evaluate the quality of a product, they commonly measure it against two kinds of attributes: those related to *quality as excellence* and those related to *quality as reliability*. From a quality-as-excellence perspective, the important attributes are things such as a product's design and styling, its aesthetic appeal, its features and functions, the level of service associated with the delivery of the product, and so on. For example, customers can purchase a pair of imitation leather boots for $20 from Wal-Mart, or they can buy a handmade pair of butter-soft leather boots from Nordstrom for $500. The boots from Nordstrom will have far superior styling, feel more comfortable, and look much better than those from Wal-Mart. The utility consumers will get from the Nordstrom boots will in all probability be much greater than the utility derived from the Wal-Mart boots but, of course, they will have to pay far more for them. That is the point: when excellence is built into a product offering, consumers have to pay more to own or consume it.

With regard to quality as reliability, a product can be said to be reliable when it consistently does the job it was designed for; does it well; and rarely, if ever, breaks down. As with excellence, reliability increases the utility a consumer gets from a product and thus the price the company can charge for that product. Toyota's cars, for example, have the highest reliability ratings in the automobile industry, and therefore consumers are prepared to pay more for them than for cars that are very similar in other attributes. As we shall see, increasing product reliability has been the central goal of an influential management philosophy that came out of Japan in the 1980s and is commonly referred to as **total quality management**.

The position of a product against two dimensions, reliability and other attributes, can be plotted on a figure similar to Figure 3.7. For example, a Lexus has attributes—such as design, styling, performance, and safety features—that customers perceive as demonstrating excellence in quality and that are viewed as being superior to those of most other cars. Lexus is also a very reliable car. Thus, the overall level of quality of the Lexus is very high, which means that the car offers consumers significant utility, and that gives Toyota the option of charging a premium price for the Lexus. Toyota also produces another very reliable vehicle, the Toyota Corolla, but this is aimed at less wealthy customers and it lacks many of the superior attributes of the Lexus.

FIGURE 3.7

A Quality Map for Automobiles

Thus, although the Corolla is also a high-quality car in the sense of being reliable, it is not as high quality as a Lexus in the sense of being an excellent product. At the other end of the spectrum, we can find poor-quality products that have both low reliability and inferior attributes, such as poor design, performance, and styling. An example is the Proton, which is built by the Malaysian car firm of the same name. The design of the car is over a decade old and has a dismal reputation for styling and safety. Moreover, Proton's reliability record is one of the worst of any car, according to J. D. Power.[15]

The concept of quality applies whether we are talking about Toyota automobiles, clothes designed and sold by The Gap, the customer service department of Citibank, or the ability of airlines to arrive on time. Quality is just as relevant to services as it is to goods.[16] The impact of high product quality on competitive advantage is twofold.[17] First, providing high-quality products increases the utility those products provide to customers, which gives the company the option of charging a higher price for them. In the automobile industry, for example, Toyota can charge a higher price for its cars because of the higher quality of its products.

The second impact of high quality on competitive advantage comes from the greater efficiency and the lower unit costs associated with reliable products. When products are reliable, less employee time is wasted making defective products or providing substandard services and less time has to be spent fixing mistakes, which translates into higher employee productivity and lower unit costs. Thus, high product quality not only enables a company to differentiate its product from that of rivals, but if the product is reliable, it also lowers costs.

The importance of reliability in building competitive advantage has increased dramatically over the past decade. Indeed, so crucial is the emphasis placed on reliability by many companies that achieving high product reliability can no longer be viewed as just one way of gaining a competitive advantage. In many industries, it has become an absolute imperative for survival.

● **Innovation**   Innovation refers to the act of creating new products or processes. There are two main types of innovation: product innovation and process innovation. **Product innovation** is the development of products that are new to the world or have superior attributes to existing products. Examples are Intel's invention of the microprocessor in the early 1970s; Cisco's development of the router for routing data over the Internet in the mid 1980s; Palm's development of the PalmPilot, the first commercially successful hand-held computer, in the mid 1990s; and Apple's development of the iPod in the early 2000s. **Process innovation** is the development of a new process for producing products and delivering them to customers. Examples include Toyota, which developed a range of new techniques collectively known as the Toyota lean production system for making automobiles: just-in-time inventory systems, self-managing teams, and reduced setup times for complex equipment.

Product innovation creates value by creating new products or enhanced versions of existing products that customers perceive as having more utility, thus increasing the company's pricing options. Process innovation often allows a company to create more value by lowering production costs. Toyota's lean production system, for example, helped to boost employee productivity, thus giving Toyota a cost-based competitive advantage.[18] Similarly, Staples's application of the supermarket business model to retail office supplies dramatically lowered the cost of selling office supplies. Staples passed on some of this cost saving to customers in the form of lower prices, which enabled the company to increase its market share rapidly.

In the long run, innovation of products and processes is perhaps the most important building block of competitive advantage.[19] Competition can be viewed as a process driven by innovations. Although not all innovations succeed, those that do can be a major source of competitive advantage because, by definition, they give a company something unique—something its competitors lack (at least until they imitate the innovation). Uniqueness can allow a company to differentiate itself from its rivals and charge a premium price for its product or, in the case of many process innovations, reduce its unit costs far below those of competitors.

● **Customer Responsiveness**

To achieve superior responsiveness to customers, a company must be able to do a better job than competitors of identifying and satisfying its customers' needs. Customers will then attribute more utility to its products, creating a differentiation based on competitive advantage. Improving the quality of a company's product offering is consistent with achieving responsiveness, as is developing new products with features that existing products lack. In other words, achieving superior quality and innovation is integral to achieving superior responsiveness to customers.

Another factor that stands out in any discussion of responsiveness to customers is the need to customize goods and services to the unique demands of individual customers or customer groups. For example, the proliferation of soft drinks and beers can be viewed partly as a response to this trend. Automobile companies have become more adept at customizing cars to the demands of individual customers. For instance, following the lead of Toyota, the Saturn division of General Motors builds cars to order for individual customers, letting them choose from a wide range of colors and options.

An aspect of responsiveness to customers that has drawn increasing attention is **customer response time**: the time that it takes for a good to be delivered or a service to be performed.[20] For a manufacturer of machinery, response time is the time it takes to fill customer orders. For a bank, it is the time it takes to process a loan or that a customer must stand in line to wait for a free teller. For a supermarket, it is the time that customers must stand in checkout lines. For a fashion retailer, it is the time required to take a new product through from design to a retail store (see Strategy in Action 3.2 for a discussion of how the Spanish fashion retailer Zara minimizes response time). Customer survey after customer survey has shown slow response time to be a major source of customer dissatisfaction.[21]

Other sources of enhanced responsiveness to customers are superior design, superior service, and superior after-sales service and support. All of these factors enhance responsiveness to customers and allow a company to differentiate itself from its less responsive competitors. In turn, differentiation enables a company to build brand loyalty and charge a premium price for its products. Consider how much more people are prepared to pay for next-day delivery of Express Mail as opposed to delivery in three to four days. In 2006, a two-page letter sent by overnight Express Mail within the United States cost about $12, compared with 39 cents for regular mail. Thus, the price premium for express delivery (reduced response time) was $11.61, or a premium of 3,079% over the regular price.

● **Business Models, the Value Chain, and Generic Distinctive Competencies**

As noted in Chapter 1, a business model is managers' conception, or gestalt, of how the various strategies that a firm pursues fit together into a congruent whole, thus enabling the firm to achieve a competitive advantage. More precisely, a business model represents the way in which managers configure the value chain of the firm through strategy, as well as the investments they make to support that configuration,

FIGURE 3.8

Competitive Advantage and the Value Creation Cycle

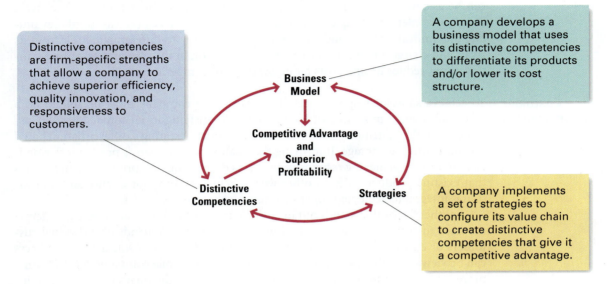

Distinctive competencies are firm-specific strengths that allow a company to achieve superior efficiency, quality innovation, and responsiveness to customers.

A company develops a business model that uses its distinctive competencies to differentiate its products and/or lower its cost structure.

A company implements a set of strategies to configure its value chain to create distinctive competencies that give it a competitive advantage.

so that they can build the distinctive competencies necessary to attain the efficiency, quality, innovation, and customer responsiveness required to support the firm's low-cost or differentiated position, thereby achieving a competitive advantage and generating superior profitability (see Figure 3.8).

For example, the main strategic goal of Wal-Mart is to be the lowest-cost operator offering a wide display of general merchandise in the retail industry. Wal-Mart's business model involves offering general merchandise in a self-service supermarket type of setting. Wal-Mart's strategies flesh out this business model and help the company to attain its strategic goal. For example, to reduce costs, Wal-Mart limits investments in the fittings and fixtures of its stores. One of the keys to generating sales and lowering costs in this setting is rapid inventory turnover, which is achieved through strategic investments in logistics and information systems. Wal-Mart in fact makes major investments in process innovation to improve the effectiveness of its information and logistics systems, which enables the company to respond to customer demands for low-priced goods when they walk in the door and to do so in a very efficient manner.

Wal-Mart's business model is very different from that found at a retailer such as Nordstrom. Nordstrom's business model is to offer high quality, and high-priced apparel, in a full-service and sophisticated setting. This implies differences in the way the value chain is configured. Nordstrom devotes far more attention to in-store customer service than Wal-Mart does, which implies significant investments in its salespeople. Moreover, Nordstrom invests far more in the furnishings and fittings for its stores, as opposed to Wal-Mart, whose stores have a basic warehouse feel to them. Nordstrom recaptures the costs of this investment by charging higher prices for higher-quality merchandise. Thus, even though Wal-Mart and Nordstrom both sell apparel (Wal-Mart is in fact the biggest seller of apparel in the United States), their business models imply a very different positioning in the marketplace and a very different configuration of value chain activities and investments.

Analyzing Competitive Advantage and Profitability

If a company's managers are to perform a good internal analysis, they need to be able to analyze the financial performance of their company, identifying how its strategies contribute (or not) to profitability. To identify strengths and weaknesses effectively, they need to be able to compare, or benchmark, the performance of their company against that of competitors and the historic performance of the company itself. This will help them determine whether they are more or less profitable than competitors and whether the performance of the company has been improving or deteriorating through time, whether their company strategies are maximizing the value being created, whether their cost structure is out of line with those of competitors, and whether they are using the resources of the company to the greatest effect.

As we noted in Chapter 1, the key measure of a company's financial performance is its profitability, which captures the return that a company is generating on its investments. Although several different measures of profitability exist, such as return on assets and return on equity, many authorities on the measurement of profitability argue that return on invested capital (ROIC) is the best measure because "it focuses on the true operating performance of the company."[22] (However, return on assets is very similar in formulation to return on invested capital.)

ROIC is defined as net profit over invested capital, or ROIC = net profit/invested capital. Net profit is calculated by subtracting the total costs of operating the company away from its total revenues (total revenues − total costs). *Net profit* is what is left over after the government takes its share in taxes. *Invested capital* is the amount that is invested in the operations of a company: property, plant, equipment, inventories, and other assets. Invested capital comes from two main sources: interest-bearing debt and shareholders' equity. Interest-bearing debt is money the company borrows from banks and those who purchase its bonds. Shareholders' equity is the money raised from selling shares to the public, plus earnings that the company has retained in prior years and can use to fund current investments. ROIC measures the effectiveness with which a company is using the capital funds that it has available for investment. As such, it is recognized to be an excellent measure of the value a company is creating.[23]

A company's ROIC can be algebraically decomposed into two major components: return on sales and capital turnover.[24] Specifically:

$$\text{ROIC} = \text{net profits/invested capital}$$

$$= \text{net profits/revenues} \times \text{revenues/invested capital}$$

where net profits/revenues is the return on sales, and revenues/invested capital is capital turnover. Return on sales measures how effectively the company converts revenues into profits. Capital turnover measures how effectively the company employs its invested capital to generate revenues. These two ratios can be further decomposed into some basic accounting ratios, as shown in Figure 3.9 (the terms in these ratios are defined in Table 3.1).[25]

The decomposition of ROIC shown in Figure 3.9 was first developed by managers at the DuPont Company in the early 1900s as a methodology for identifying the drivers of profitability, and the decomposition formula is sometimes referred to as "the DuPont Formula." Figure 3.9 says that a company's managers can increase ROIC by pursuing strategies that increase the company's return on sales. To increase the

FIGURE 3.9

Drivers of Profitability
(ROIC)

company's return on sales, they can pursue strategies that reduce the cost of goods sold (COGS) for a given level of sales revenues (COGS/sales); reduce the level of spending on sales force, marketing, general, and administrative expenses (SG&A) for a given level of sales revenues (SG&A/sales); and reduce R&D spending for a given level of sales revenues (R&D/sales). Alternatively, they can increase return on sales by pursuing strategies that increase sales revenues more than they increase the costs of the business, as measured by COGS, SG&A, and R&D expenses. That is, they

TABLE 3.1

Definitions of Basic Accounting Terms

Term	Definition	Source
Cost of goods sold (COGS)	Total costs of producing products.	Income statement
Sales, general, and administrative expenses (SG&A)	Costs associated with selling products and administering the company.	Income statement
R&D expenses (R&D)	Research and development expenditure.	Income statement
Working capital	The amount of money the company has to work with in the short term: Current assets — current liabilities.	Balance sheet
Property, plant, and equipment (PPE)	The value of investments in the property, plant, and equipment that the company uses to manufacture and sell its products. Also know as *fixed capital*.	Balance sheet
Return on sales (ROS)	Net profit expressed as a percentage of sales. Measures how effectively the company converts revenues into profits.	Ratio
Capital turnover	Revenues divided by invested capital. Measures how effectively the company uses its capital to generate revenues.	Ratio
Return on invested capital (ROIC)	Net profit divided by invested capital.	Ratio
Net profit	Total revenues minus total costs before tax.	Income statement
Invested capital	Interest-bearing debt plus shareholders equity.	Balance sheet

can increase the return on sales by pursuing strategies that lower costs or increase value through differentiation, and thus allow the company to increase its prices more than its costs.

Figure 3.9 also tells us that a company's managers can boost the profitability of their company by getting greater sales revenues from their invested capital, thereby increasing capital turnover. They do this by pursuing strategies that reduce the amount of working capital, such as the amount of capital invested in inventories, needed to generate a given level of sales (working capital/sales) and then pursuing strategies that reduce the amount of fixed capital that they have to invest in plant, property, and equipment (PPE) to generate a given level of sales (PPE/sales). That is, they pursue strategies that reduce the amount of capital that they need to generate every dollar of sales, and thus their cost of capital. Now recall that cost of capital is part of the cost structure of a company (see Figure 3.2), so strategies designed to increase capital turnover also lower the cost structure.

To see how these basic drivers of profitability help us to understand what is going on in a company and to identify its strengths and weaknesses, read the Running Case, which compares the financial performance of Dell Computer against its major rival, Hewlett-Packard.

RUNNING CASE

Comparing Dell to Hewlett-Packard

Figure 3.10 compares the financial performance of Dell Computer to that of its rival, Hewlett-Packard, for 2005. Note first that Dell was much more profitable than HP, measured by ROIC. Indeed, Dell's ROIC of 77.1% was astoundingly high. HP earned a mediocre ROIC of 5.91%, which may have been less than its cost of capital.

To explain this performance difference, first look at the difference in return on sales. Dell's ROS, at 6.39%, was more than double that of HP's at 2.77%. Why? It certainly is not because Dell is charging customers a high markup over its cost of goods sold. Indeed, Dell's COGS/sales ratio is higher than HP's, suggesting that Dell is pricing its products aggressively. However, Dell spends far less on SG&A expenses and on R&D than its rival. This lower level of spending reflects important strategic choices. Because Dell sells direct, it does not have a big sales forces; hence its SG&A expenses are much lower than HP's. In addition, Dell has decided not to spend heavily on R&D primarily because it sees itself as being in a commodity business. In Dell's view, R&D is something that its suppliers, such as Intel and Microsoft, undertake. HP is moving toward this view, but its higher level of R&D reflects the company's traditional strategic posture that it tries to compete in part through product innovation. Dell does not.

Now look at the difference in capital turnover. Here, the difference is striking. Dell generates $12.07 of sales for every dollar of capital invested in the business, HP just $2.14 of sales for every dollar. This difference drives most of the difference in ROIC. Why is Dell so much more efficient that HP in its use of capital? There are two reasons. First, Dell undertakes only final assembly, with everything else being outsourced to suppliers. Consequently, it has to invest less in property, plant, and equipment (PPE) than does HP.

Second, Dell is very efficient at managing its inventory, which is why its working capital to sales ratio is so much lower than HP's. Because Dell sells direct, it can build to order—it does not have to fill a retail channel with inventory. Moreover, it takes order information received over its website, and through telephone sales, and transmits

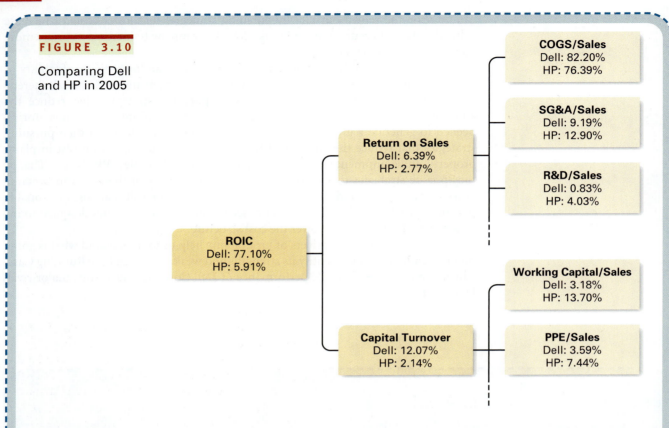

FIGURE 3.10

Comparing Dell and HP in 2005

that instantaneously to suppliers located throughout the world, who then adjust their own production schedules accordingly. Dell coordinates the entire process so that parts arrive at Dell's factories just when they are required and not before. There they are quickly assembled into machines and then shipped out the door in a few days. As a result, Dell turns over its inventory much more rapidly than HP does—88.81 times a year in 2005, compared to just 9.5 times a year at HP. Put another way, HP has a large amount of capital tied up in parts inventory that is waiting to be assembled into computers, or in finished inventory that is in distribution, or sitting in retail channels. Dell does not.

Dell's working capital requirements are reduced even further because many of its customers pay by credit card, and those cards are charged when a machine leaves Dell's factory, which is long before Dell has to pay its suppliers, enabling Dell to use this money to finance its day-to-day operations. In contrast, due to its lower inventory turnover,

HP probably has to pay its suppliers before it receives money from the sale of machines, which raises the company's need for working capital.

Despite Dell's superior profitability, in 2005 and 2006, HP's stock price outperformed that of Dell. The reason: Dell's profit growth stalled in 2005 and 2006, whereas HP's was accelerating, suggesting that down the road, Dell's ROIC will contract while HP's will expand. HP was gaining ground on Dell because it could offer businesses integrated services, which went beyond supplying computer hardware, to embrace designing and installing entire corporate information systems, including software. HP did this through its consulting operations. This was a resource that Dell, with its direct sales model, lacked. Dell did not need this resource to serve consumers and small businesses—long its core customer base—but this market was now maturing, and Dell needed to expand its presence in large businesses to keep growing, where it was at a disadvantage versus HP.[c]

The Durability of Competitive Advantage

The next question we must address is: How long will a competitive advantage last once it has been created? In other words, what is the durability of competitive advantage given that other companies are also seeking to develop distinctive competencies that will give them a competitive advantage? The answer depends on three factors: barriers to imitation, the capability of competitors, and the general dynamism of the industry environment.

● **Barriers to Imitation**

A company with a competitive advantage will earn higher-than-average profits. These profits send a signal to rivals that the company has some valuable distinctive competency that allows it to create superior value. Naturally, its competitors will try to identify and imitate that competency and, insofar as they are successful, ultimately their increased success may whittle away the company's superior profits.[26]

How quickly rivals will imitate a company's distinctive competencies is an important issue because the speed of imitation has a bearing on the durability of a company's competitive advantage. Other things being equal, the more rapidly competitors imitate a company's distinctive competencies, the less durable its competitive advantage will be, and the more important it is that the company endeavor to improve its competencies to stay one step ahead of the imitators. It is important to stress at the outset that ultimately almost any distinctive competency can be imitated by a competitor. The critical issue is time: the longer it takes competitors to imitate a distinctive competency, the greater the opportunity the company has to build a strong market position and reputation with customers, which are then more difficult for competitors to attack. Moreover, the longer it takes to achieve an imitation, the greater is the opportunity for the imitated company to improve on its competency or build other competencies, thereby staying one step ahead of the competition.

Barriers to imitation are a primary determinant of the speed of imitation. Barriers to imitation are factors that make it difficult for a competitor to copy a company's distinctive competencies; the greater the barriers to imitation, the more sustainable is a company's competitive advantage.[27] Barriers to imitation differ depending on whether a competitor is trying to imitate resources or capabilities.

IMITATING RESOURCES In general, the easiest distinctive competencies for prospective rivals to imitate tend to be those based on possession of firm-specific and valuable tangible resources, such as buildings, plant, and equipment. Such resources are visible to competitors and can often be purchased on the open market. For example, if a company's competitive advantage is based on sole possession of efficient-scale manufacturing facilities, competitors may move fairly quickly to establish similar facilities. Although Ford gained a competitive advantage over General Motors in the 1920s by being the first to adopt an assembly line manufacturing technology to produce automobiles, General Motors quickly imitated that innovation, competing away Ford's distinctive competency in the process. A similar process is occurring in the auto industry now as companies try to imitate Toyota's famous production system. However, Toyota has slowed down the rate of imitation by not allowing competitors access to its latest equipment.

Intangible resources can be more difficult to imitate. This is particularly true of brand names, which are important because they symbolize a company's reputation. In the heavy earthmoving equipment industry, for example, the Caterpillar brand name is synonymous with high quality and superior after-sales service and support. Similarly, the St. Michael's brand name used by Marks & Spencer, Britain's largest clothing retailer, symbolizes high-quality but reasonably priced clothing. Customers often display a preference for the products of such companies because the brand name is an important guarantee of high quality. Although competitors might like to imitate well-established brand names, the law prohibits them from doing so.

Marketing and technological know-how are also important intangible resources and can be relatively easy to imitate. The movement of skilled marketing personnel between companies may facilitate the general dissemination of marketing know-how. For example, in the 1970s, Ford was acknowledged as the best marketer among the big three U.S. auto companies. In 1979, it lost a lot of its marketing know-how to Chrysler when its most successful marketer, Lee Iacocca, joined Chrysler and subsequently hired many of Ford's top marketing people to work with him at Chrysler. More generally, successful marketing strategies are relatively easy to imitate because they are so visible to competitors. Thus, Coca-Cola quickly imitated PepsiCo's Diet Pepsi brand with the introduction of its own brand, Diet Coke.

With regard to technological know-how, the patent system in theory should make technological know-how relatively immune to imitation. Patents give the inventor of a new product a twenty-year exclusive production agreement. For example, the biotechnology company Immunex discovered and patented Enbrel, which is capable of halting the disease-causing mechanism that leads to rheumatoid arthritis. All prior treatments simply provided patients with some relief from the symptoms of rheumatoid arthritis. Approved by the Food and Drug Administration in 1998, Enbrel racked up sales of over $400 million in its first year on the market and may ultimately generate annual revenues of $4 billion. (In 2002, Immunex was acquired by Amgen.) Despite the large market, Immunex's patent stops potential competitors from introducing their own version of Enbrel. Whereas it is relatively easy to use the patent system to protect a biological product from imitation, this is not true of many other inventions. In electrical and computer engineering, for example, it is often possible to invent around patents: that is, produce a product that is functionally equivalent but does not rely on the patented technology. One study found that 60% of patented innovations were successfully invented around in four years.[28] This suggests that, in general, distinctive competencies based on technological know-how can be relatively short-lived.

IMITATING CAPABILITIES   Imitating a company's capabilities tends to be more difficult than imitating its tangible and intangible resources chiefly because capabilities are based on the way in which decisions are made and processes managed deep within a company. It is hard for outsiders to discern them.

On its own, the invisible nature of capabilities would not be enough to halt imitation; competitors could still gain insights into how a company operates by hiring people away from that company. However, a company's capabilities rarely reside in a single individual. Rather, they are the product of how numerous individuals interact within a unique organizational setting.[29] It is possible that no one individual within a company may be familiar with the totality of a company's internal operating routines and procedures. In such cases, hiring people away from a successful company in order to imitate its key capabilities may not be helpful.

• Capability of Competitors

According to work by Pankaj Ghemawat, a major determinant of the capability of competitors to imitate a company's competitive advantage rapidly is the nature of the competitors' prior strategic commitments.[30] By strategic commitment, Ghemawat means a company's commitment to a particular way of doing business—that is, to developing a particular set of resources and capabilities. Ghemawat's point is that once a company has made a strategic commitment, it will have difficulty responding to new competition if doing so requires a break with this commitment. Therefore, when competitors have long-established commitments to a particular way of doing business, they may be slow to imitate an innovating company's competitive advantage. Its competitive advantage will thus be relatively durable.

The U.S. automobile industry again offers an example. From 1945 to 1975, the industry was dominated by the stable oligopoly of General Motors, Ford, and Chrysler, all of which geared their operations to the production of the large cars that American customers demanded at the time. When the market shifted from large cars to small, fuel-efficient ones during the late 1970s, U.S. companies lacked the resources and capabilities required to produce these cars. Their prior commitments had built the wrong kind of skills for this new environment. As a result, foreign producers, and particularly the Japanese, stepped into the market breach by providing compact, fuel-efficient, high-quality, and low-cost cars. The failure of U.S. auto manufacturers to react quickly to the distinctive competency of Japanese auto companies gave the latter time to build a strong market position and brand loyalty, which subsequently have proved difficult to attack.

Another determinant of the ability of competitors to respond to a company's competitive advantage is the absorptive capacity of competitors.[31] **Absorptive capacity** refers to the ability of an enterprise to identify, value, assimilate, and use new knowledge. For example, in the 1960s and 1970s, Toyota developed a competitive advantage based on its innovation of lean production systems. Competitors such as General Motors were slow to imitate this innovation primarily because they lacked the necessary absorptive capacity. General Motors was such a bureaucratic and inward-looking organization that it was very difficult for the company to identify, value, assimilate, and use the knowledge that underlay lean production systems. Indeed, long after General Motors had identified and understood the importance of lean production systems, it was still struggling to assimilate and use that new knowledge. Put differently, internal inertial forces can make it difficult for established competitors to respond to a rival whose competitive advantage is based on new products or internal processes—that is, on innovation.

Taken together, factors such as existing strategic commitments and low absorptive capacity limit the ability of established competitors to imitate the competitive advantage of a rival, particularly when that competitive advantage is based on innovative products or processes. This is why when innovations reshape the rules of competition in an industry, value often migrates away from established competitors and toward new enterprises that are operating with new business models.

• Industry Dynamism

A dynamic industry environment is one that is changing rapidly. We examined the factors that determine the dynamism and intensity of competition in an industry in Chapter 2 when we discussed the external environment. The most dynamic industries tend to be those with a very high rate of product innovation—for instance, the customer electronics industry and the personal computer industry. In dynamic industries, the rapid rate of innovation means that product life cycles are shortening and that competitive advantage can be fleeting. A company that has a competitive advantage today may find its market position outflanked tomorrow by a rival's innovation.

In the personal computer industry, the rapid increase in computing power during the past two decades has contributed to a high degree of innovation and a turbulent environment. Reflecting the persistence of innovation, Apple Computer in the late 1970s and early 1980s had an industrywide competitive advantage due to its innovation. In 1981, IBM seized the advantage by introducing its first personal computer. By the mid 1980s, IBM had lost its competitive advantage to high-power clone manufacturers such as Compaq that had beaten IBM in the race to introduce a computer based on Intel's 386 chip. In turn, in the 1990s, Compaq subsequently lost its competitive advantage to Dell, which pioneered new low-cost ways of delivering computers to customers using the Internet as a direct-selling device.

● **Summarizing Durability of Competitive Advantage**

The durability of a company's competitive advantage depends on the height of barriers to imitation, the capability of competitors to imitate its innovation, and the general level of dynamism in the industry environment. When barriers to imitation are low, capable competitors abound, and the environment is dynamic, with innovations being developed all the time, then competitive advantage is likely to be transitory. But even within such industries, companies can build a more enduring competitive advantage if they are able to make investments that build barriers to imitation.

During the 1980s, Apple Computer built a competitive advantage based on the combination of a proprietary disk operating system and an intangible product image. The resulting brand loyalty enabled Apple to carve out a fairly secure niche in an industry where competitive advantage has otherwise proven to be very fleeting. However, by the mid-1990s, its strategy had been imitated primarily because of the introduction of Microsoft's Windows operating system, which imitated most of the features that had enabled Apple to build brand loyalty. By 1996, Apple was in financial trouble, providing yet another example that no competitive advantage lasts forever. Ultimately, anything can be imitated. However, Apple has shown remarkable resilience; in the late 1990s, it clawed its way back from the brink of bankruptcy to establish a viable position within its niche once again, a position it still held on to by the mid 2000s.

Avoiding Failure and Sustaining Competitive Advantage

How can a company avoid failure and escape the traps that have snared so many once successful companies? How can managers build a sustainable competitive advantage? Much of the remainder of this book deals with these issues. Here, we make a number of key points that set the scene for the coming discussion.

● **Why Companies Fail**

When a company loses its competitive advantage, its profitability falls. The company does not necessarily fail; it may just have average or below-average profitability and can remain in this mode for a considerable time, although its resource and capital base is shrinking. Failure implies something more drastic. A failing company is one whose profitability is now substantially lower than the average profitability of its competitors; it has lost the ability to attract and generate resources so that its profit margins and invested capital are shrinking rapidly.

Why does a company lose its competitive advantage and fail? The question is particularly pertinent because some of the most successful companies of the last half-century have seen their competitive position deteriorate at one time or another. IBM, General Motors, American Express, Digital Equipment, and Sears, among many others, at one time were held up as examples of managerial excellence but then have gone through periods where their financial performance was poor and they clearly lacked any competitive advantage. We explore three related reasons for failure: inertia, prior strategic commitments, and the Icarus paradox.

INERTIA The inertia argument says that companies find it difficult to change their strategies and structures in order to adapt to changing competitive conditions.[32] IBM is a classic example of this problem. For thirty years, it was viewed as the world's most successful computer company. Then in the space of a few years, its success turned into a disaster: it lost $5 billion in 1992, leading to layoffs of more than 100,000 employees. IBM's troubles were caused by a dramatic decline in the cost of computing power as a result of innovations in microprocessors. With the advent of powerful low-cost microprocessors, the locus of the computer market shifted from mainframes to small, low-priced personal computers, leaving IBM's huge mainframe operations with a diminished market. Although IBM had, and still has, a significant presence in the personal computer market, it had failed to shift the focus of its efforts away from mainframes and toward personal computers. This failure meant deep trouble for one of the most successful companies of the twentieth century (IBM has now executed a successful turnaround with a repositioning as a provider of e-commerce infrastructure and solutions).

One reason that companies find it so difficult to adapt to new environmental conditions seems to be the role of capabilities in causing inertia. Organizational capabilities—the way a company makes decisions and manages its processes—can be a source of competitive advantage, but they are difficult to change. IBM always emphasized close coordination among operating units and favored decision processes that stressed consensus among interdependent operating units as a prerequisite for a decision to go forward.[33] This capability was a source of advantage for IBM during the 1970s, when coordination among its worldwide operating units was necessary to develop, manufacture, and sell complex mainframes. But the slow-moving bureaucracy that it had spawned was a source of failure in the 1990s, when organizations had to adapt readily to rapid environmental change.

Capabilities are difficult to change because a certain distribution of power and influence is embedded within the established decision-making and management processes of an organization. Those who play key roles in a decision-making process clearly have more power. It follows that changing the established capabilities of an organization means changing its existing distribution of power and influence, and those whose power and influence would diminish resist such change. Proposals for change trigger turf battles. This power struggle and the political resistance associated with trying to alter the way in which an organization makes decisions and manages its process—that is, trying to change its capabilities—bring on inertia. This is not to say that companies cannot change. However, because change is so often resisted by those who feel threatened by it, change in most cases has to be induced by a crisis. By then, the company may already be failing, as happened at IBM.

Prior Strategic Commitments A company's prior strategic commitments not only limit its ability to imitate rivals but may also cause competitive disadvantage.[34] IBM, for instance, had major investments in the mainframe computer business, so when the market shifted, it was stuck with significant resources specialized for that particular business: its manufacturing facilities were geared to the production of mainframes, its research organization was similarly specialized, and so was its sales force. Because these resources were not well suited to the newly emerging personal computer business, IBM's difficulties in the early 1990s were in a sense inevitable. Its prior strategic commitments locked it into a business that was shrinking. Shedding these resources was bound to cause hardship for all organization stakeholders.

The Icarus Paradox Danny Miller has postulated that the roots of competitive failure can be found in what he termed the Icarus paradox.[35] Icarus is a figure in Greek mythology who used a pair of wings, made for him by his father, to escape from an island where he was being held prisoner. He flew so well that he went higher and higher, ever closer to the sun, until the heat of the sun melted the wax that held his wings together and he plunged to his death in the Aegean Sea. The paradox is that his greatest asset, his ability to fly, caused his demise. Miller argues that the same paradox applies to many once successful companies. According to Miller, many companies become so dazzled by their early success that they believe more of the same type of effort is the way to future success. As a result, they can become so specialized and inner-directed that they lose sight of market realities and the fundamental requirements for achieving a competitive advantage. Sooner or later, this leads to failure.

Miller identifies four major categories among the rising and falling companies, which he labels craftsmen, builders, pioneers, and salesmen. The craftsmen, such as Texas Instruments and Digital Equipment Corporation (DEC), achieved early success through engineering excellence. But then they became so obsessed with engineering details that they lost sight of market realities. (The story of DEC's demise is summarized in Strategy in Action 3.3.) Among the builders are Gulf & Western and ITT. Having built successful, moderately diversified companies, they then became so enchanted with diversification for its own sake that they continued to diversify far beyond the point at which it was profitable to do so. Miller's third group are the pioneers like Wang Labs. Enamored of their own originally brilliant innovations, managers here continued to search for additional brilliant innovations and ended up producing novel but completely useless products. The final category comprises the salesmen, exemplified by Procter & Gamble and Chrysler. They became so convinced of their ability to sell anything that they paid scant attention to product development and manufacturing excellence and, as a result, spawned a proliferation of bland, inferior products.

● **Steps to Avoid Failure**

Given that so many traps wait for companies, an important question arises: How can strategic managers use internal analysis to find them and escape them? We now look at several tactics that managers can use.

Focus on the Building Blocks of Competitive Advantage Maintaining a competitive advantage requires a company to continue focusing on all four generic building blocks of competitive advantage—efficiency, quality, innovation, and responsiveness to customers—and to develop distinctive competencies that contribute to superior performance

Strategy in Action

3.3

The Road to Ruin at DEC

Digital Equipment Corporation (DEC) was one of the premier computer companies of the 1970s and 1980s. DEC's original success was founded on the minicomputer, a cheaper, more flexible version of its mainframe cousins that Ken Olson and his brilliant team of engineers invented in the 1960s. They then improved on their original minicomputers until they could not be beat for quality and reliability. In the 1970s, their VAX series of minicomputers was widely regarded as the most reliable series of computers ever produced, and DEC was rewarded by high profit rates and rapid growth. By 1990, it was number 27 on the *Fortune 500* list of the largest corporations in America.

Buoyed by its success, DEC turned into an engineering monoculture: its engineers became idols; its marketing and accounting staff, however, were barely tolerated. Component specs and design standards were all that senior managers understood. Technological fine-tuning became such an obsession that the needs of customers for smaller, more economical, user-friendly computers were ignored. DEC's personal computers, for example, bombed because they were out of touch with the needs of customers, and the company failed to respond to the threat to its core market presented by the rise of computer workstations and client-server architecture. Indeed, Ken Olson was known for dismissing such new products. He once said, "We always say that customers are right, but they are not always right." Perhaps. But DEC, blinded by its early success, failed to remain responsive to its customers and changing market conditions. In another famous statement, when asked about personal computers in the early 1980s, Olson said, "I can see of no reason why anybody would ever want a computer on their desk."

By the early 1990s, DEC was in deep trouble. Olson was forced out in July 1992, and the company lost billions of dollars between 1992 and 1995. It returned to profitability in 1996 primarily because of the success of a turnaround strategy aimed at reorienting the company to serve precisely those areas that Olson had dismissed. In 1998, the company was acquired by Compaq Computer Corporation (which was subsequently purchased by Hewlett-Packard) and disappeared from the business landscape as an independent entity.[d]

in these areas. One of the messages of Miller's Icarus paradox is that many successful companies become unbalanced in their pursuit of distinctive competencies. DEC, for example, focused on engineering quality at the expense of almost everything else, including, most important, responsiveness to customers. Other companies forget to focus on any distinctive competency at all.

INSTITUTE CONTINUOUS IMPROVEMENT AND LEARNING The only constant in the world is change. Today's source of competitive advantage may soon be rapidly imitated by capable competitors or made obsolete by the innovations of a rival. In such a dynamic and fast-paced environment, the only way that a company can maintain a competitive advantage over time is to continually improve its efficiency, quality, innovation, and responsiveness to customers. The way to do this is to recognize the importance of learning within the organization.[36] The most successful companies do not stand still, resting on their laurels; they are always seeking out ways of improving their operations and in the process are constantly upgrading the value of their distinctive competencies or creating new competencies. Companies such as General Electric and Toyota have a reputation for being learning organizations. This means that they are continually analyzing the processes that underlie their efficiency, quality, innovation, and responsiveness to customers. Their objective is to learn from prior mistakes and to seek out ways to improve their processes over time. This has enabled Toyota, for example, to continually upgrade its employee productivity and product quality, and thus stay ahead of imitators.

TRACK BEST INDUSTRIAL PRACTICE AND USE BENCHMARKING   One of the best ways to develop distinctive competencies that contribute to superior efficiency, quality, innovation, and responsiveness to customers is to identify and adopt best industrial practice. Only in this way will a company be able to build and maintain the resources and capabilities that underpin excellence in efficiency, quality, innovation, and responsiveness to customers. (We discuss what constitutes best industrial practice in some depth in Chapter 4.) It requires tracking the practice of other companies, and perhaps the best way to do so is through benchmarking: measuring the company against the products, practices, and services of some of its most efficient global competitors. For example, when Xerox was in trouble in the early 1980s, it decided to institute a policy of benchmarking to identify ways to improve the efficiency of its operations. Xerox benchmarked L. L. Bean for distribution procedures, Deere & Company for central computer operations, Procter & Gamble for marketing, and Florida Power & Light for total quality management processes. By the early 1990s, Xerox was benchmarking 240 functions against comparable areas in other companies. This process has been credited with helping it dramatically improve the efficiency of its operations.[37]

OVERCOME INERTIA   Overcoming the internal forces that are a barrier to change within an organization is one of the key requirements for maintaining a competitive advantage. Suffice it to say here that identifying barriers to change is an important first step. Once this step has been taken, implementing change requires good leadership, the judicious use of power, and appropriate changes in organizational structure and control systems.

The Role of Luck

A number of scholars have argued that luck plays a critical role in determining competitive success and failure.[38] In its most extreme version, the luck argument devalues the importance of strategy altogether. Instead, it states that, in the face of uncertainty, some companies just happen to pick the correct strategy.

Although luck may be the reason for a company's success in particular cases, it is an unconvincing explanation for the persistent success of a company. Recall our argument that the generic building blocks of competitive advantage are superior efficiency, quality, innovation, and responsiveness to customers. Keep in mind also that competition is a process in which companies are continually trying to outdo each other in their ability to achieve high efficiency, superior quality, outstanding innovation, and quick responsiveness to customers. It is possible to imagine a company getting lucky and coming into possession of resources that allow it to achieve excellence on one or more of these dimensions. However, it is difficult to imagine how sustained excellence on any of these four dimensions could be produced by anything other than conscious effort, that is, by strategy. Luck may indeed play a role in success, and managers must always exploit a lucky break. (Strategy in Action 3.4 discusses the role of luck in the early history of Microsoft and how Bill Gates exploited that luck.) However, to argue that success is entirely a matter of luck is to strain credibility. As the golfing great Gary Player once said, "The harder I work, the luckier I seem to get." Managers who strive to formulate and implement strategies that lead to a competitive advantage are more likely to be lucky.

Strategy in Action   3.4

Bill Gates's Lucky Break

The product that launched Microsoft into its leadership position in the software industry was MS-DOS, the operating system for IBM and IBM-compatible PCs. The original DOS program, however, was developed not by Microsoft but by Seattle Computer, where it was known as Q-DOS (which stood for "quick and dirty operating system"). When IBM was looking for an operating system to run its original PC, it talked to a number of software companies, including Microsoft, about developing such a system. Seattle Computer was not one of those companies. Bill Gates knew that Seattle Computer had developed a disk operating system and took action: he borrowed $50,000 from his father, a senior partner in a prominent Seattle law firm, and then went to see the CEO of Seattle Computer and offered to purchase the rights to the company's Q-DOS system. He did not, of course, reveal that IBM was looking for a disk operating system. Seattle Computer, short of cash, quickly agreed. Gates then renamed the system MS-DOS, upgraded it, and licensed it to IBM. The rest, as they say, is history.

So was Gates lucky? Of course he was. It was lucky that Seattle Computer had not heard about IBM's request. It was lucky that IBM approached Microsoft. It was lucky that Gates knew about Seattle Computer's operating system. And it was lucky that Gates had a father wealthy enough to lend him $50,000 on short notice. On the other hand, Gates's luck was hardly random. Microsoft was already a player in the embryonic personal computer software industry, and its first software program, Microsoft Basic, had been a bestseller. IBM came to Microsoft because the company had already earned respect in the industry. Moreover, to attribute all of Microsoft's subsequent success to luck would be wrong. Although MS-DOS gave Microsoft a tremendous head start in the industry, it did not guarantee that Microsoft would continue to enjoy the kind of worldwide success that it has. To do that, Microsoft had to build the appropriate set of resources and capabilities required to produce a continual stream of innovative software, which is precisely what the company did with the cash generated from MS-DOS.[e]

Summary of Chapter

1. Distinctive competencies are the firm-specific strengths of a company. Valuable distinctive competencies enable a company to earn a profit rate that is above the industry average.

2. The distinctive competencies of an organization arise from its resources (its financial, physical, human, technological, and organizational assets) and capabilities (its skills at coordinating resources and putting them to productive use).

3. In order to achieve a competitive advantage, a company needs to pursue strategies that build on its existing resources and capabilities and formulate strategies that build additional resources and capabilities (develop new competencies).

4. The source of a competitive advantage is superior value creation.

5. To create superior value, a company must lower its costs or differentiate its product so that it creates more value and can charge a higher price, or do both simultaneously.

6. Managers must understand how value creation and pricing decisions affect demand and how costs change with increases in volume. They must have a good grasp of the demand conditions in the company's market and the cost structure of the company at different levels of output if they are to make decisions that maximize the profitability of their enterprise.

7. The four building blocks of competitive advantage are efficiency, quality, innovation, and responsiveness to customers. These are generic distinctive competencies. Superior efficiency enables a company to lower its costs, superior quality allows it to charge a higher price and lower its costs, and superior customer

service lets it charge a higher price. Superior innovation can lead to higher prices, particularly in the case of product innovations, or lower unit costs, particularly in the case of process innovations.

8. If a company's managers are to perform a good internal analysis, they need to be able to analyze the financial performance of their company, identifying how the strategies of the company relate to its profitability as measured by the return on invested capital.

9. The durability of a company's competitive advantage depends on the height of barriers to imitation,

the capability of competitors, and environmental dynamism.

10. Failing companies typically earn low or negative profits. Three factors seem to contribute to failure: organizational inertia in the face of environmental change, the nature of a company's prior strategic commitments, and the Icarus paradox.

11. Avoiding failure requires a constant focus on the basic building blocks of competitive advantage, continuous improvement, identification and adoption of best industrial practice, and victory over inertia.

Discussion Questions

1. What are the main implications of the material discussed in this chapter for strategy formulation?
2. When is a company's competitive advantage most likely to endure over time?
3. It is possible for a company to be the lowest-cost producer in its industry and simultaneously have an output

that is the most valued by customers. Discuss this statement.

4. Why is it important to understand the drivers of profitability as measured by the return on invested capital?
5. Which is more important in explaining the success and failure of companies: strategizing or luck?

Practicing Strategic Management

SMALL-GROUP EXERCISE
Analyzing Competitive Advantage

Break up into groups of three to five. Drawing on the concepts introduced in this chapter, analyze the competitive position of your business school in the market for business education. Then answer the following questions:

1. Does your business school have a competitive advantage?
2. If so, on what is this advantage based, and is this advantage sustainable?
3. If your school does not have a competitive advantage in the market for business education, identify the inhibiting factors that are holding it back.
4. How might the Internet change the way in which business education is delivered?
5. Does the Internet pose a threat to the competitive position of your school in the market for business education, or is it an opportunity for your school to enhance its competitive position? (Note that it can be both.)

ARTICLE FILE 3

Find a company that has sustained its competitive advantage for more than ten years. Identify the source of the competitive advantage, and explain why it has lasted so long.

STRATEGIC MANAGEMENT PROJECT
Module 3

This module deals with the competitive position of your company. With the information you have at your disposal, perform the tasks and answer the following questions:

1. Identify whether your company has a competitive advantage or disadvantage in its primary industry. Its primary industry is the one in which it has the most sales.
2. Evaluate your company against the four generic building blocks of competitive advantage: efficiency, quality, innovation, and responsiveness to customers. How

does this exercise help you understand the performance of your company relative to its competitors?

3. What are the distinctive competencies of your company?

4. What role have prior strategies played in shaping the distinctive competencies of your company? What has been the role of luck?

5. Do the strategies your company is pursuing now build on its distinctive competencies? Are they an attempt to build new competencies?

6. What are the barriers to imitating the distinctive competencies of your company?

7. Is there any evidence that your company finds it difficult to adapt to changing industry conditions? If so, why do you think this is the case?

ETHICS EXERCISE

John, an official at a national beverage chain, had been working to convince a national sandwich restaurant chain to carry his company's newest beverage, Slushy Soda. Originally, John hoped that the sandwich chain would simply agree to carry the frozen soda drink, but the sandwich chain was hesitant. Together, John and the sandwich chain agreed to do a test run on the new beverage in Atlanta, where the hot weather might assist in the soda's promotion. With each purchase, the sandwich chain would offer a coupon for a free Slushy Soda. If enough coupons were redeemed, the company would consider adding the beverage to its lineup.

John and his company had a lot of money invested in this new beverage; in fact, John's job was on the line. If he could not convince the sandwich chain to pick up the beverage, he could lose his job. After a week of the test run, the numbers were less than promising. In a moment of desperation, John sent several of his employees to Atlanta, ordering them to redeem as many of the beverage coupons as possible. They were also instructed to pass out coupons and cash to customers outside the sandwich shops in the hope that they would then redeem the coupons.

It didn't take long for the sandwich chain to figure out what was going on. John's employees were called home. John became responsible not only for his own termination but for those of his employees as well. And Slushy Soda never made it out of the starting gate.

1. Define the ethical dilemma presented in this case

2. Should John and his employees have been fired for attempting to manipulate the test run?

3. What does it say about John's company that he felt he needed to behave unethically to retain his job?

CLOSING CASE

Starbucks

In 2006, Starbucks, the ubiquitous coffee retailer, closed a decade of astounding financial performance. Sales had increased from $697 million to $7.8 billion, and net profits, from $36 million to $540 million. In 2006, Starbucks was earning a return on invested capital of 25.5%, which was impressive by any measure, and the company was forecasted to continue growing earnings and maintain high profits through the end of the decade. How did this come about?

Thirty years ago, Starbucks was a single store in Seattle's Pike Place Market selling premium roasted coffee. Today, it is a global roaster and retailer of coffee with more than 12,000 retail stores, some 3,000 of which are to be found in forty countries outside the United States. Starbucks Corporation set out on its current course in the 1980s when the company's director of marketing, Howard Schultz, came back from a trip to Italy enchanted with the Italian coffeehouse experience. Schultz, who later became CEO, persuaded the company's owners to experiment with the coffeehouse format—and the Starbucks experience was born.

Schultz's basic insight was that people lacked a "third place" between home and work where they could have their own personal time-out, meet with friends, relax, and have a sense of gathering. The business model that evolved out of this was to sell the company's own premium roasted coffee, along with freshly brewed espresso-style coffee beverages, a variety of pastries, coffee accessories, teas, and other products, in a coffeehouse setting. The company devoted, and continues to devote, considerable attention to the design of its stores to create a relaxed, informal, and comfortable atmosphere. Underlying this approach was a belief that Starbucks was selling far more than coffee—it was selling an experience. The premium price that Starbucks charged for its coffee reflected this fact.

From the outset, Schultz also focused on providing superior customer service in stores. Reasoning that motivated employees provide the best customer service, Starbucks executives developed employee hiring and training programs that were the best in the restaurant industry. Today, all Starbucks employees are required to attend training classes that teach them not only how to make a good cup of coffee but also the service-oriented values of the company. Beyond this, Starbucks provides progressive compensation policies that gave even part-time employees stock option grants and medical benefits—a very innovative approach in an industry where most employees are part-time, earn minimum wage, and have no benefits.

Unlike many restaurant chains, which expanded very rapidly through franchising arrangements once they established a basic formula that appears to work, Schultz believed that Starbucks needed to own its stores. Although it has experimented with franchising arrangements in some countries and in some situations in the United States such as at airports, the company still prefers to own its own stores whenever possible.

This formula met with spectacular success in the United States, where Starbucks went from obscurity to one of the best-known brands in the country in a decade. As it grew, Starbucks found that it was generating an enormous volume of repeat business. Today, the average customer comes into a Starbucks store around twenty times a month. The customers themselves are a fairly well-heeled group—their average income is about $80,000.

As the company grew, it started to develop a very sophisticated location strategy. Detailed demographic analysis was used to identify the best locations for Starbucks stores. The company expanded rapidly to capture as many premium locations as possible before its imitators could. Astounding many observers, Starbucks would even sometimes locate stores on opposite corners of the same busy street—so that it could capture traffic going in different directions down the street.

By 1995, with almost 700 stores across the United States, Starbucks began exploring foreign opportunities. The first stop was Japan, where Starbucks proved that the basic value proposition could be applied to a different cultural setting (there are now 600 stores in Japan). Next, Starbucks embarked on a rapid development strategy in Asia and Europe. By 2001, the magazine *Brandchannel* named Starbucks one of the ten most influential global brands, a position it has held ever since. But this is only the beginning. In October 2006, with 12,000 stores in operation, the company announced that its long term goal was to have 40,000 stores worldwide. Looking forward, it expects 50% of all new store openings to be outside the United States.[39]

Case Discussion Questions

1. Identify the resources, capabilities, and distinctive competencies of Starbucks.
2. How do Starbucks's resources, capabilities, and distinctive competencies translate into superior financial performance?
3. How secure is Starbucks's competitive advantage? What are the barriers to imitation?

Building Competitive Advantage Through Functional-Level Strategy

OPENING CASE

Boosting Efficiency at Matsushita

When Kunio Nakamura became CEO at the venerable Japanese electronics giant, Matsushita, in 2000, it was a company in deep trouble. Earnings had been going south for years and the company's market capitalization had shrunk to less than half of that of long-time rival Sony. Employees were frustrated and morale was poor. By the time he retired in June 2006, Matsushita was delivering its best financial performance in more than a decade. After losing $3.7 billion in 2002, in the year ending March 2006 the company registered profits of $1.37 billion. Moreover, earnings were projected to grow 20%, to $1.7 billion, in the year ending March 2007.

Nakamura achieved this transformation by relentlessly focusing on efficiency improvements. Early in his tenure, he put an end to the internal rivalries that had led different divisions to develop identical products. The resulting duplication wasted precious research and development (R&D) money and limited the ability of the company to realize economies of scale. He reduced the number of layers in the management hierarchy and slashed the domestic workforce by 19%—a tough thing to do at Matsushita, where life time employment had been the norm—and closed thirty factories. Then he pushed factory managers to do everything possible to raise productivity.

Matsushita's factory in Saga, Japan, exemplifies the obsession with productivity improvements. By 2004, employees at the factory, which makes cordless phones, faxes, and security cameras, had already doubled productivity since 2000 by introducing robots into the assembly line, but factory managers were not happy. An analysis of flow in the production system showed that bottlenecks on the assembly line meant that robots sat idle for longer than they were working. So the plant's managers ripped out the assembly line conveyer belts and replaced them with clusters of robots grouped into cells. The cells allowed them to double up on slower robots to make the entire manufacturing process run more smoothly. Then they developed software to synchronize production so that each robot jumped into action as soon as the previous step was completed. If one robot broke down, the work flow could be shifted to another to do the same job.

The results were impressive. The time that it took to build products was drastically reduced. It used to take two and a half days in a production run before the first finished products came off the assembly line; now it takes as little as forty minutes. Phones, for example, can now be assembled in one-third of the time, doubling weekly output from the same plant with the same number of employees. Shorter cycle times enabled the factory to slash inventories. Work-in-progress, such as partly finished products, along with components such as chipsets, keypads, and circuit boards, now spent far less time in the factory.

The Saga factory is known as a mother plant within Matsushita. Once process improvements have been refined at a mother plant, they have to be transferred to other plants within the group as quickly as possible. There are six other plants in the Saga group: in China, Malaysia, Mexico, and Britain. Most were able to quickly copy what was done at Saga and saw similar cuts in inventory and boosts in productivity.

Despite the faster pace of work, the factory employees paid close attention to product quality. The short cycle times helped employees to identify the source of defective products and quickly fix any errors that led to quality problems. Consequently, at less than 1% of output, by 2006, defect rates were at an all-time low in every factory. The reduction in waste further boosted productivity and helped the company to strengthen its reputation for producing high-quality merchandise.[1]

OVERVIEW

In this chapter, we take a close look at **functional-level strategies**: those aimed at improving the effectiveness of a company's operations and thus its ability to attain superior efficiency, quality, innovation, and customer responsiveness.

It is important to keep in mind the relationships among functional strategies, distinctive competencies, differentiation, low cost, value creation, and profitability (see Figure 4.1). Note that distinctive competencies shape the functional-level strategies

FIGURE 4.1

The Roots of Competitive Advantage

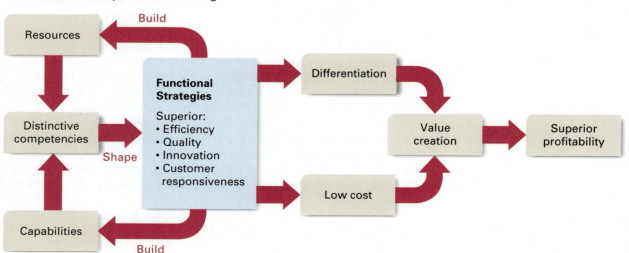

that a company can pursue and that managers, through their choices with regard to functional-level strategies, can build resources and capabilities that enhance a company's distinctive competencies. Note also that the ability of a company to attain superior efficiency, quality, innovation, and customer responsiveness will determine if its product offering is differentiated from that of rivals and if it has a low-cost structure. Recall that companies that increase the utility consumers get from their products through differentiation, while simultaneously lowering their cost structure, create more value than their rivals, and this leads to a competitive advantage and superior profitability and profit growth.

The Opening Case illustrates some of these relationships. Managers at Matsushita's Saga factory in Japan pursued functional-level strategies that raised productivity, thus increasing the efficiency of their production process while also reducing defect rates and boosting the reliability of their final product offering. The superior efficiency enabled the factory (and others like it around the world) to lower costs, while superior reliability enhanced product quality, helped to differentiate the product offering, and boosted sales volume. The result: Matsushita created more value, and its profitability increased.

Consistent with the Matsushita example, much of this chapter is devoted to looking at the basic strategies that can be adopted at the operating level to improve competitive position. By the end of this chapter, you will understand how functional-level strategies can be used to build a sustainable competitive advantage.

Achieving Superior Efficiency

A company is a device for transforming inputs (labor, land, capital, management, and technological know-how) into outputs (the goods and services produced). The simplest measure of efficiency is the quantity of inputs that it takes to produce a given output; that is, Efficiency = outputs/inputs. The more efficient a company is, the fewer the inputs required to produce a given output and therefore the lower its cost structure will be. Put another way, an efficient company has higher productivity, and therefore lower costs, than its rivals. Here we review the steps that companies can take at the functional level to increase their efficiency and thereby lower their cost structure.

● **Efficiency and Economies of Scale**

Economies of scale are unit cost reductions associated with a large scale of output. Recall from the last chapter that it is very important for managers to understand how the cost structure of their enterprise varies with output because this understanding should help to drive strategy. For example, if unit costs fall significantly as output is expanded—that is, if there are significant economies of scale—a company may benefit by keeping prices down and increasing volume.

One source of economies of scale is the ability to spread fixed costs over a large production volume. **Fixed costs** are costs that must be incurred to produce a product whatever the level of output; examples are the costs of purchasing machinery, setting up machinery for individual production runs, building facilities, advertising, and R&D. For example, Microsoft spent approximately $5 billion to develop the latest version of its Windows operating system, Windows Vista. It can realize substantial scale economies by spreading the fixed costs associated with developing the new operating system over the enormous unit sales volume it expects for this system

(95% of the world's 250 million personal computers use a Microsoft operating system). These scale economies are significant because of the trivial incremental (or marginal) cost of producing additional copies of Windows Vista: once the master copy has been produced, additional CDs containing the operating system can be produced for a few cents. The key to Microsoft's efficiency and profitability (and that of other companies with high fixed costs and trivial incremental or marginal costs) is to increase sales rapidly enough that fixed costs can be spread out over a large unit volume and substantial scale economies can be realized.

Another source of scale economies is the ability of companies producing in large volumes to achieve a greater division of labor and specialization. Specialization is said to have a favorable impact on productivity mainly because it enables employees to become very skilled at performing a particular task. The classic example of such economies is Ford's Model T car. The world's first mass-produced car, the Model T Ford was introduced in 1923. Until then, Ford had made cars using an expensive hand-built craft production method. By introducing mass-production techniques, the company achieved greater division of labor (it split assembly into small, repeatable tasks) and specialization, which boosted employee productivity. Ford was also able to spread the fixed costs of developing a car and setting up production machinery over a large volume of output. As a result of these economies, the cost of manufacturing a car at Ford fell from $3,000 to less than $900 (in 1958 dollars).

These examples illustrate that economies of scale can boost profitability, as measured by return on invested capital (ROIC), in a number of ways. Economies of scale exist in production, sales and marketing, and R&D, and the overall effect of realizing scale economies is to reduce spending as a percentage of revenues on cost of goods sold (COGS), sales, general, and administrative expenses (SG&A), and R&D expenses, thereby boosting return on sales and, by extension, ROIC (see Figure 3.9). Moreover, by making more intensive use of existing capacity, a company can increase the amount of sales generated from its property, plant, and equipment (PPE), thereby reducing the amount of capital it needs to generate a dollar of sales, and thus increasing its capital turnover and its ROIC.

The concept of scale economies is illustrated in Figure 4.2, which shows that as a company increases its output, unit costs fall. This process comes to an end at an output of Q1, where all scale economies are exhausted. Indeed, at outputs of greater

FIGURE 4.2

Economies and Diseconomies of Scale

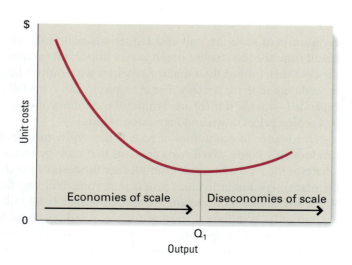

than Q1, the company may encounter **diseconomies of scale,** which are the unit cost increases associated with a large scale of output. Diseconomies of scale occur primarily because of the increasing bureaucracy associated with large-scale enterprises and the managerial inefficiencies that can result.[2] Larger enterprises have a tendency to develop extensive managerial hierarchies in which dysfunctional political behavior is commonplace, information about operating matters is accidentally and deliberately distorted by the number of managerial layers through which it has to travel to reach top decisionmakers, and poor decisions are the result. Past some point (such as Q1 in Figure 4.2), the inefficiencies that result from such developments outweigh any additional gains from economies of scale, and unit costs start to rise as output expands. This was what had occurred at Matsushita. When Kunio Nakamura became CEO in 2000, he reduced the number of layers in the management hierarchy in an attempt to eliminate diseconomies of scale (see the Opening Case).

Managers must know not only the extent of economies of scale but also where diseconomies of scale begin to occur. At Nucor Steel, for example, the realization that diseconomies of scale exist has led to a decision not to build plants that employ more than 300 individuals. The belief is that it is more efficient to build two plants, each employing 300 people, than one plant employing 600 people. Although the larger plant might theoretically be able to reap greater scale economies, Nucor's management believes that these would be swamped by the diseconomies of scale that come with larger organizational units.

● Efficiency and Learning Effects

Learning effects are cost savings that come from learning by doing. Labor, for example, learns by repetition how best to carry out a task. Therefore, labor productivity increases over time, and unit costs fall as individuals learn the most efficient way to perform a particular task. Equally important, management in new manufacturing facilities typically learns over time how best to run the new operation. Hence, production costs decline because of increasing labor productivity and management efficiency. Japanese companies like Toyota are noted for making learning a central part of their operating philosophy.

Learning effects tend to be more significant when a technologically complex task is repeated because there is more to learn. Thus, learning effects will be more significant in an assembly process that has 1,000 complex steps than in one with 100 simple steps. Although learning effects are normally associated with the manufacturing process, there is every reason to believe that they are just as important in service industries. For example, one famous study of learning in the context of the health care industry found that more experienced medical providers posted significantly lower mortality rates for a number of common surgical procedures, suggesting that learning effects are at work in surgery.[3] The authors of this study used the evidence to argue for establishing regional referral centers for the provision of highly specialized medical care. These centers would perform many specific surgical procedures (such as heart surgery), replacing local facilities with lower volumes and presumably higher mortality rates. Another recent study found strong evidence of learning effects in a financial institution. The study looked at a newly established document-processing unit with 100 staff members and found that, over time, documents were processed much more rapidly as the staff learned the process. Overall, the study concluded that unit costs fell every time the cumulative number of documents processed doubled.[4] Strategy in Action 4.1 looks at the determinants of differences in learning effects across a sample of hospitals performing cardiac surgery.

Strategy in Action

Learning Effects in Cardiac Surgery

A study carried out by researchers at the Harvard Business School tried to estimate the importance of learning effects in the case of a specific new technology for minimally invasive heart surgery that was approved by federal regulators in 1996. The researchers looked at sixteen hospitals and obtained data on the operations for 660 patients. They examined how the time required to undertake the procedure varied with cumulative experience. Across the sixteen hospitals, they found that average time fell from 280 minutes for the first procedure with the new technology to 220 minutes by the time a hospital had performed fifty procedures (note that not all of the hospitals performed fifty procedures, and the estimates represent an extrapolation based on the data).

Next they looked at differences across hospitals. Here they found evidence of very large differences in learning effects. One hospital, in particular, stood out. This hospital, which they called Hospital M, reduced its net procedure time from 500 minutes on case 1 to 132 minutes by case 50. Hospital M's eighty-eight-minute procedure time advantage over the average hospital at case 50 translated into a cost saving of approximately $2,250 per case, and allowed surgeons at the hospital to do one more revenue-generating procedure per day.

The researchers tried to find out why Hospital M was so superior. They noted that all hospitals had similar state-of-the-art operating rooms and used the same set of FDA-approved devices, that all adopting surgeons went through the same training courses, and that all surgeons came from highly respected training hospitals. Follow-up interviews suggested, however, that Hospital M differed in how it implemented the new procedure. The team was handpicked by the adopting surgeon to perform the surgery. It had significant prior experience working together (indeed, that was apparently a key criterion for team members). The team trained together to perform the new surgery. Before undertaking a single procedure, they met with the operating room nurses and anesthesiologists to discuss the procedure. Moreover, the adopting surgeon mandated that the surgical team and surgical procedure were stable in the early cases. The initial team went through fifteen procedures before new members were added or substituted and twenty cases before the procedures were modified. The adopting surgeon also insisted that the team meet prior to each of the first ten cases, and they also meet after the first twenty cases to debrief.

The picture that emerges is one of a core team that was selected and managed to maximize the gains from learning. Unlike other hospitals where there was less stability of team members and procedures, and where there was not the same attention to briefing, debriefing, and learning, surgeons at Hospital M both learned much faster and ultimately achieved higher productivity than their peers in other institutions. Clearly, differences in the implementation of the new procedure were very important.[a]

In terms of the unit cost curve of a company, although economies of scale imply a movement along the curve (say, from A to B in Figure 4.3), the realization of learning effects implies a downward shift of the entire curve (B to C in Figure 4.3) as both labor and management become more efficient over time at performing their tasks at every level of output. In accounting terms, learning effects in a production setting will reduce the cost of goods sold as a percentage of revenues, enabling the company to earn a higher return on sales and return on invested capital.

No matter how complex the task is, however, learning effects typically die out after a limited period of time. Indeed, it has been suggested that they are really important only during the start-up period of a new process and then cease after two or three years.[5] When changes occur to a company's production system—as a result of merger or the use of new information technology, for example—the learning process has to begin again.

FIGURE 4.3

FIGURE 4.3

The Impact of
Learning and Scale
Economies on
Unit Costs

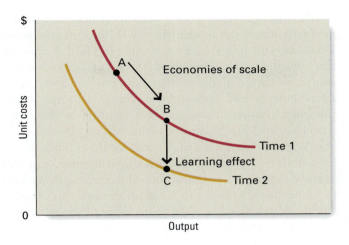

● **Efficiency and the Experience Curve**

The **experience curve** refers to the systematic lowering of the cost structure, and consequent unit cost reductions, that have been observed to occur over the life of a product.[6] According to the experience-curve concept, unit manufacturing costs for a product typically decline by some characteristic amount each time accumulated output of the product is doubled (accumulated output is the total output of a product since its introduction). This relationship was first observed in the aircraft industry, where it was found that each time accumulated output of airframes was doubled, unit costs declined to 80 percent of their previous level.[7] Thus, the fourth airframe typically cost only 80 percent of the second airframe to produce, the eighth airframe only 80 percent of the fourth, the sixteenth only 80 percent of the eighth, and so on. The outcome of this process is a relationship between unit manufacturing costs and accumulated output similar to that illustrated in Figure 4.4. Economies of scale and learning effects underlie the experience-curve phenomenon. Put simply, as a company increases the accumulated volume of its output over time, it is able to realize both economies of scale (as volume increases) and learning effects. Consequently, unit costs and cost structure fall with increases in accumulated output.

FIGURE 4.4

The Experience Curve

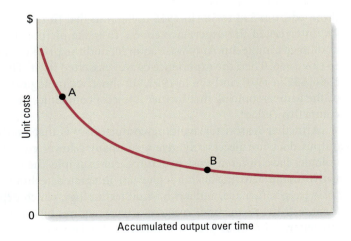

The strategic significance of the experience curve is clear: increasing a company's product volume and market share will lower its cost structure relative to its rivals. Thus, company B in Figure 4.4, because it is farther down the experience curve, has a cost advantage over company A because of its lower cost structure. The concept is very important in industries that mass-produce a standardized output (for example, the manufacture of semiconductor chips). A company that wishes to become more efficient and lower its cost structure must try to ride down the experience curve as quickly as possible. This means constructing efficient scale manufacturing facilities even before it has generated demand for the product and aggressively pursuing cost reductions from learning effects. It might also need to adopt an aggressive marketing strategy, cutting prices to the bone and stressing heavy sales promotions and extensive advertising in order to build up demand, and hence accumulated volume, as quickly as possible. The need to be aware of the relationship of demand, price options, and costs noted in Chapter 3 is clear.

Once down the experience curve because of its superior efficiency, the company is likely to have a significant cost advantage over its competitors. For example, it has been argued that Intel uses such tactics to ride down the experience curve and gain a competitive advantage over its rivals in the market for microprocessors. Similarly, one reason Matsushita came to dominate the global market for VHS videotape recorders is that it based its strategy on the experience curve.[8]

However, there are three reasons why managers should not become complacent about efficiency-based cost advantages derived from experience effects. First, since neither learning effects nor economies of scale go on forever, the experience curve is likely to bottom out at some point; indeed, it must do so by definition. When this occurs, further unit cost reductions from learning effects and economies of scale will be hard to come by. Thus, in time, other companies can lower their cost structures and match the cost leader. Once this happens, a number of low-cost companies can have cost parity with each other. In such circumstances, a sustainable competitive advantage must rely on strategic factors besides the minimization of production costs by using existing technologies—factors such as better responsiveness to customers, product quality, or innovation.

Second, as noted in Chapter 2, changes that are always taking place in the external environment disrupt a company's business model, so cost advantages gained from experience effects can be made obsolete by the development of new technologies. The price of television picture tubes followed the experience-curve pattern from the introduction of the television in the late 1940s until 1963. The average unit price dropped from $34 to $8 (in 1958 dollars) in that time. However, the advent of color TV interrupted the experience curve. To make picture tubes for color TVs, a new manufacturing technology was required, and the price of color TV tubes shot up to $51 by 1966. Then the experience curve reasserted itself. The price dropped to $48 in 1968, $37 in 1970, and $36 in 1972.[9] In short, technological change can alter the rules of the game, requiring that former low-cost companies take steps to reestablish their competitive edge.

A further reason for avoiding complacency is that producing a high volume of output does not necessarily give a company a lower cost structure. Different technologies have different cost structures. For example, the steel industry has two alternative manufacturing technologies: an integrated technology, which relies on the basic oxygen furnace, and a mini-mill technology, which depends on the electric arc furnace. Whereas the basic oxygen furnace requires high volumes to attain maximum efficiency, mini-mills are cost efficient at relatively low volumes. Moreover, even when both technologies are producing at their most efficient output levels, steel companies with basic oxygen furnaces do not have a cost advantage over mini-mills. Consequently, the pursuit of experience economies by an integrated company using basic oxygen technology may not bring the kind of cost advantages that a naive reading of the experience-curve phenomenon would lead the company to expect. Indeed, there have been significant periods of time when integrated companies have not been able to get enough orders to run at optimum capacity. Hence, their production costs have been considerably higher than those of mini-mills.[10] As we discuss next, in many industries new flexible manufacturing technologies hold out the promise of allowing small manufacturers to produce at unit costs comparable to those of large assembly line operations.

● **Efficiency, Flexible Production Systems, and Mass Customization**

Central to the concept of economies of scale is the idea that the best way to achieve high efficiency and a lower cost structure is through the mass production of a standardized output. The tradeoff implicit in this idea is between unit costs and product variety. Producing greater product variety from a factory implies shorter production runs, which implies an inability to realize economies of scale and higher costs. That is, a wide product variety makes it difficult for a company to increase its production efficiency and thus reduce its unit costs. According to this logic, the way to increase efficiency and achieve a lower cost structure is to limit product variety and produce a standardized product in large volumes (see Figure 4.5a).

This view of production efficiency has been challenged by the rise of flexible production technologies. The term **flexible production technology**—or lean production, as it is sometimes called—covers a range of technologies designed to reduce setup times for complex equipment, increase the use of individual machines through better scheduling, and improve quality control at all stages of the manufacturing

FIGURE 4.5

Tradeoff Between Costs and Product Variety

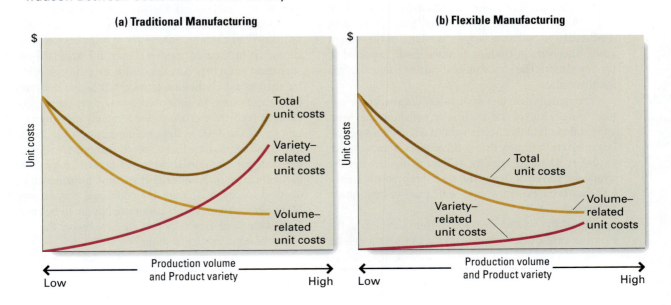

process.[11] Flexible production technologies allow the company to produce a wider variety of end-products at a unit cost that at one time could be achieved only through the mass production of a standardized output (see Figure 4.5b). Indeed, research suggests that the adoption of flexible production technologies may increase efficiency and lower unit costs relative to what can be achieved by the mass production of a standardized output, while at the same time enabling the company to customize its product offering to a much greater extent than was once thought possible. The term **mass customization** has been coined to describe the ability of companies to use flexible manufacturing technology to reconcile two goals that were once thought to be incompatible: low cost and differentiation through product customization.[12] For an extended example of the benefits of mass customization, see Strategy in Action 4.2, which looks at mass customization at Lands' End.

Strategy in Action   4.2

Mass Customization at Lands' End

Years ago, almost all clothing was made to individual order by a tailor (a job shop production method). Then along came the twentieth century and techniques for mass production, mass marketing, and mass selling. Production in the industry shifted toward larger volume and less variety based on standardized sizes. The benefits in terms of production cost reductions were enormous, but the customer did not always win. Offset against lower prices was the difficulty of finding clothes that fit as well as tailored clothes once did. Look around you and you will see that people come in a bewildering variety of shapes and sizes; then go into a store to purchase a shirt, and you get to choose between just four sizes: small, medium, large, and extra large! It is estimated the current sizing categories in clothing fit only about one-third of the population. The rest of us wear clothes where the fit is less than ideal.

The mass-production system has drawbacks for apparel manufacturers and retailers as well. Year after year, apparel firms find themselves saddled with billions of dollars in excess inventory that is either thrown away, or put on fire sale, because retailers had too many items of the wrong size and color. To try and solve this problem, Lands' End has been experimenting with mass-customization techniques.

To purchase customized clothes from Lands' End, the customer provides information on the Lands' End website by answering a series of fifteen questions (for pants) or twenty-five questions (for shirts), covering about everything from waist to inseam. The process takes about twenty minutes the first time through, but once the information is saved by Lands' End, it can be quickly accessed for repeat purchases. The customer information is then analyzed by an algorithm that pinpoints a person's body dimensions by taking these data points and running them against a huge database of typical sizes to create a unique, customized pattern. The analysis is done automatically by a computer, which then transmits the order to one of five contract manufacturer plants in the United States and elsewhere, which cut and sew the finished garment, and ship the finished product directly to the customer.

Today, customization is available for most categories of Lands' End clothing. Some 40% of its online shoppers choose a customized garment over the standard-size equivalent when they have the choice. Even though prices for customized clothes are at least $20 higher and they take about three to four weeks to arrive, customized clothing reportedly accounts for a rapidly growing percentage of the $500 million online business for Lands' End. Land's End states that its profit margins are roughly the same for customized clothes as regular clothes, but the reductions in inventories that come from matching demand to supply account for additional cost savings. Moreover, customers who customize appear to be more loyal, with reordering rates that are 34% higher than for buyers of standard-size clothing.[b]

Flexible machine cells are a common flexible production technology. Flexible machine cell is a grouping of various types of machinery, a common materials handler, and a centralized cell controller (a computer). Each cell normally contains four to six machines capable of performing a variety of operations but dedicated to producing a family of parts or products. The settings on the machines are computer-controlled, which allows each cell to switch quickly between the production of different parts or products.

Improved capacity utilization and reductions in work-in-progress (that is, stockpiles of partly finished products) and waste are major efficiency benefits of flexible machine cells. Improved capacity utilization arises from the reduction in setup times and from the computer-controlled coordination of production flow between machines, which eliminates bottlenecks. The tight coordination between machines also reduces work-in-progress. Reductions in waste are due to the ability of computer-controlled machinery to identify ways to transform inputs into outputs while producing a minimum of unusable waste material. Freestanding machines might be in use 50% of the time; the same machines, when grouped into a cell, can be used more than 80% of the time and produce the same end-product with half the waste, thereby increasing efficiency and resulting in lower costs.

The effects of installing flexible production technology on a company's cost structure can be dramatic. The Opening Case tells how Matsushita doubled its productivity by putting flexible machine cells in its factories. Ford Motor Company is currently introducing flexible production technologies into its automotive plants around the world. These new technologies should allow Ford to produce multiple models from the same line and to switch production from one model to another much more quickly than in the past. In total, Ford hopes to take $2 billion out of its cost structure by 2010.[13]

More generally, in terms of the profitability framework developed in Chapter 3, flexible production technology should boost profitability (measured by ROIC) by reducing the cost of goods sold as a percentage of revenues, reducing the working capital needed to finance work-in-progress (because there is less of it), and reducing the amount of capital that needs to be invested in property, plant, and equipment to generate a dollar of sales (because less space is needed to store inventory).

● **Marketing and Efficiency**   The marketing strategy that a company adopts can have a major impact on efficiency and cost structure. **Marketing strategy** refers to the position that a company takes with regard to pricing, promotion, advertising, product design, and distribution. Some of the steps leading to greater efficiency are fairly obvious. For example, riding down the experience curve to achieve a lower cost structure can be facilitated by aggressive pricing, promotions, and advertising, all of which are the task of the marketing function. Other aspects of marketing strategy have a less obvious but no less important impact on efficiency. One important aspect is the relationship of customer defection rates, cost structure and unit costs.[14]

Customer defection rates (or churn rates) are the percentage of a company's customers who defect every year to competitors. Defection rates are determined by customer loyalty, which in turn is a function of the ability of a company to satisfy its customers. Because acquiring a new customer entails certain one-time fixed costs for advertising, promotions, and the like, there is a direct relationship between defection rates and costs. The longer a company holds on to a customer, the greater is the volume of customer-generated unit sales that can be set against these fixed costs, and the lower the average unit cost of each sale. Thus, lowering customer defection rates allows a company to achieve a lower cost structure.

One consequence of the defection-cost relationship depicted is illustrated in Figure 4.6. Because of the relatively high fixed costs of acquiring new customers, serving customers who stay with the company only for a short time before switching to competitors often leads to a loss on the investment made to acquire those customers. The longer a customer stays with the company, the more the fixed costs of acquiring that customer can be spread out over repeat purchases, boosting the profit per customer. Thus, there is a positive relationship between the length of time that a customer stays with a company and profit per customer. If a company can reduce customer defection rates, it can make a much better return on its investment in acquiring customers and thereby boost its profitability. In terms of the profitability framework developed in Chapter 3, reduced customer defection rates mean that the company needs to spend less on sales, general, and administrative expenses to generate a dollar of sales revenue, which increases both return on sales and return on invested capital.

For an example, consider the credit card business.[15] Most credit card companies spend an average of $50 to recruit a customer and set up a new account. These costs come from the advertising required to attract new customers, the credit checks required for each customer, and the mechanics of setting up an account and issuing a card. These one-time fixed costs can be recouped only if a customer stays with the company for at least two years. Moreover, when customers stay a second year, they tend to increase their use of the credit card, which raises the volume of revenues generated by each customer over time. As a result, although the credit card business loses $50 per customer in year 1, it makes a profit of $44 in year 3 and $55 in year 6.

Another economic benefit of long-time customer loyalty is the free advertising that customers provide for a company. Loyal customers can dramatically increase the volume of business through referrals. A striking example is Britain's largest retailer, the clothing and food company Marks & Spencer, whose success is built on a well-earned reputation for providing its customers with high-quality goods at reasonable prices. The company has generated such customer loyalty that it does not need to advertise in Britain, a major source of cost saving.

The key message, then, is that reducing customer defection rates and building customer loyalty can be major sources of a lower cost structure. One study has estimated that a 5% reduction in customer defection rates leads to the following increases in profits per customer over average customer life: 75% in the credit card business, 50% in the insurance brokerage industry, 45% in the industrial laundry business, and 35% in the computer software industry.[16]

A central component of developing a strategy to reduce defection rates is to identify customers who have defected, find out why they defected, and act on that information so that other customers do not defect for similar reasons in the future. To take these measures, the marketing function must have information systems capable of tracking customer defections.

● **Materials Management, Just-in-Time, and Efficiency**

The contribution of materials management (logistics) to boosting the efficiency of a company can be just as dramatic as the contribution of production and marketing. Materials management encompasses the activities necessary to get inputs and components to a production facility (including the costs of purchasing inputs), through the production process, and out through a distribution system to the end-user.[17] Because there are so many sources of cost in this process, the potential for reducing costs through more efficient materials-management strategies is enormous. For a typical manufacturing company, materials and transportation costs account for 50 to 70% of its revenues, so even a small reduction in these costs can have a substantial impact on profitability. According to one estimate, for a company with revenues of $1 million, a return on invested capital of 5%, and materials-management costs that amount to 50% of sales revenues (including purchasing costs), increasing total profits by $15,000 would require either a 30% increase in sales revenues or a 3% reduction in materials costs.[18] In a typical competitive market, reducing materials costs by 3% is usually much easier than increasing sales revenues by 30%.

Improving the efficiency of the materials-management function typically requires the adoption of a **just-in-time** (**JIT**) inventory system, which is designed to economize on inventory holding costs by having components arrive at a manufacturing plant just in time to enter the production process or to have goods arrive at a retail store only when stock is almost depleted. The major cost saving comes from increasing inventory turnover, which reduces inventory holding costs, such as warehousing and storage costs, and the company's need for working capital. For example, through efficient logistics, Wal-Mart can replenish the stock in its stores at least twice a week; many stores receive daily deliveries if they are needed. The typical competitor replenishes its stock every two weeks, so it has to carry a much higher inventory and needs more working capital per dollar of sales. Compared to its competitors, Wal-Mart can maintain the same service levels with a lower investment in inventory, a major source of its lower cost structure. Thus, faster inventory turnover has helped Wal-Mart achieve an efficiency-based competitive advantage in the retailing industry.[19]

More generally, in terms of the profitability model developed in Chapter 3, JIT inventory systems reduce the need for working capital (since there is less inventory to finance) and the need for fixed capital to finance storage space (since there is less to store), which reduces capital needs; increases capital turnover; and, by extension, boosts the return on invested capital.

The drawback of JIT systems is that they leave a company without a buffer stock of inventory. Although buffer stocks are expensive to store, they can help tide a company over shortages on inputs brought about by disruption among suppliers (for instance, a labor dispute at a key supplier) and can help a company respond quickly to increases in demand. However, there are ways around these limitations. For example, to reduce the risks linked to dependence on just one supplier for an important input, a company might decide to source inputs from multiple suppliers.

Recently, the efficient management of materials and inventory has been recast in terms of **supply-chain management**: the task of managing the flow of inputs and components from suppliers into the company's production processes to minimize inventory holding and maximize inventory turnover. One of the exemplary companies in terms of supply-chain management is Dell, whose goal is to streamline its supply chain to such an extent that it *replaces inventory with information.*

R&D Strategy and Efficiency

The role of superior research and development (R&D) in helping a company achieve a greater efficiency and a lower cost structure is twofold. First, the R&D function can boost efficiency by designing products that are easy to manufacture. By cutting down on the number of parts that make up a product, R&D can dramatically decrease the required assembly time, which translates into higher employee productivity, lower costs, and higher profitability. For example, after Texas Instruments redesigned an infrared sighting mechanism that it supplies to the Pentagon, it found that it had reduced the number of parts from forty-seven to twelve, the number of assembly steps from fifty-six to thirteen, the time spent fabricating metal from 757 minutes per unit to 219 minutes per unit, and unit assembly time from 129 minutes to twenty minutes. The result was a substantial decline in production costs. Design for manufacturing requires close coordination between the production and R&D functions of the company, of course. Cross-functional teams with production and R&D personnel who work jointly on the problem best achieve this objective.

The second way in which the R&D function can help a company achieve a lower cost structure is by pioneering process innovations. A process innovation is an innovation in the way production processes operate that improves their efficiency. Process innovations have often been a major source of competitive advantage. Toyota's competitive advantage is based partly on the company's invention of new flexible manufacturing processes that dramatically reduced setup times. This process innovation enabled it to obtain efficiency gains associated with flexible manufacturing systems years ahead of its competitors.

Human Resources Strategy and Efficiency

Employee productivity is one of the key determinants of an enterprise's efficiency, cost structure, and profitability.[20] Productive manufacturing employees can lower the cost of goods sold as a percentage of revenues, a productive sales force can increase sales revenues for a given level of expenses, and productive employees in the company's R&D function can boost the percentage of revenues generated from new products for a given level of R&D expenses. Thus, productive employees lower the costs of generating revenues; increase the return on sales; and, by extension, boost the company's return on invested capital. The challenge for a company's human resources function is to devise ways to increase employee productivity. Among the choices it has are using certain hiring strategies, training employees, organizing the work force into self-managing teams, and linking pay to performance.

HIRING STRATEGY Many companies that are well-known for their productive employees devote considerable attention to hiring. Southwest Airlines hires people who have a positive attitude and work well in teams because it believes that people who have a positive attitude will work hard and interact well with customers, therefore helping to create customer loyalty. Nucor hires people who are self-reliant and goal-oriented because its employees work in self-managing teams where they have to be self-reliant and goal-oriented to perform well. As these examples suggest, it is important to make sure that the hiring strategy of the company is consistent with its own internal organization, culture, and strategic priorities. The people a company hires should have attributes that match the strategic objectives of the company.

EMPLOYEE TRAINING Employees are a major input into the production process. Those who are highly skilled can perform tasks faster and more accurately and are more likely to learn the complex tasks associated with many modern production methods than individuals with lesser skills. Training upgrades employee skill levels, bringing the company productivity-related efficiency gains from learning and experimentation.[21]

SELF-MANAGING TEAMS The use of **self-managing teams,** whose members coordinate their own activities and make their own hiring, training, work, and reward decisions, has been spreading rapidly. The typical team comprises five to fifteen employees who produce an entire product or undertake an entire task. Team members learn all team tasks and rotate from job to job. Because a more flexible work force is one result, team members can fill in for absent coworkers and take over managerial duties such as scheduling work and vacation, ordering materials, and hiring new members. The greater responsibility thrust on team members and the empowerment it implies are seen as motivators. (Empowerment is the process of giving lower-level employees decision-making power.) People often respond well to being given greater autonomy and responsibility. Performance bonuses linked to team production and quality targets work as an additional motivator.

The effect of introducing self-managing teams is reportedly an increase in productivity of 30% or more and a substantial increase in product quality. Further cost savings arise from eliminating supervisors and creating a flatter organizational hierarchy, which also lowers the cost structure of the company. In manufacturing companies, perhaps the most potent way to lower the cost structure is to combine self-managing teams with flexible manufacturing cells. For example, after the introduction of flexible manufacturing technology and work practices based on self-managing teams, a General Electric plant in Salisbury, North Carolina, increased productivity by 250% compared with GE plants that produced the same products four years earlier.[22]

Still, teams are no panacea; in manufacturing companies, self-managing teams may fail to live up to their potential unless they are integrated with flexible manufacturing technology. Also, teams put a lot of management responsibilities on team members, and helping team members to cope with these responsibilities often requires substantial training—a fact that many companies often forget in their rush to drive down costs, with the result that the teams don't work out as well as planned.[23]

PAY FOR PERFORMANCE It is hardly surprising that linking pay to performance can help increase employee productivity, but the issue is not quite so simple as just introducing incentive pay systems. It is also important to define what kind of job performance is to be rewarded and how. Some of the most efficient companies in the world, mindful that cooperation among employees is necessary to realize productivity gains, link pay to group or team (rather than individual) performance. Nucor divides its work force into teams of thirty or so, with bonus pay, which can amount to 30 percent of base pay, linked to the ability of the team to meet productivity and quality goals. This link creates a strong incentive for individuals to cooperate with each other in pursuit of team goals; that is, it facilitates teamwork.

● **Information Systems and Efficiency**

With the rapid spread of computers, the explosive growth of the Internet and corporate intranets (internal corporate computer networks based on Internet standards), and the spread of high-bandwidth fiber optics and digital wireless technology, the information systems function is moving to center stage in the quest for operating efficiencies and a lower cost structure.[24] The impact of information systems on productivity is wide-ranging and potentially affects all other activities of a company. For example, Cisco Systems has been able to realize significant cost savings by moving its ordering and customer service functions online. The company has just 300 service agents handling all of its customer accounts, compared to the 900 it would need if sales were not handled online. The difference represents an annual saving of $20 million a year. Moreover, without automated customer service functions, Cisco calculates that it would need at least 1,000 additional service engineers, which would cost around $75 million.[25] Dell Computer also makes extensive use of the Internet both to lower its cost structure and to differentiate itself from rivals (see the Running Case in this chapter).

Like Cisco and Dell, many companies are using web-based information systems to reduce the costs of coordination between the company and its customers and the company and its suppliers. By using web-based programs to automate customer and supplier interactions, they can substantially reduce the number of people required to manage these interfaces, thereby reducing costs. This trend extends beyond high-tech companies. Banks and financial service companies are finding that they can substantially reduce costs by moving customer accounts and support functions online. Such a move reduces the need for customer service representatives, bank tellers, stockbrokers, insurance agents, and others. For example, it costs an average of about $1.07 to execute a transaction at a bank, such as shifting money from one account to another; executing the same transaction over the Internet costs $0.01.[26]

Similarly, the theory behind Internet-based retailers such as Amazon.com is that by replacing physical stores and their supporting personnel with an online virtual store and automated ordering and checkout processes, a company can take significant costs out of the retailing system. Cost savings can also be realized by using web-based information systems to automate many internal company activities, from managing expense reimbursements to benefits planning and hiring processes, thereby reducing the need for internal support personnel.

● **Infrastructure and Efficiency**

A company's infrastructure—that is, its structure, culture, style of strategic leadership, and control system—determines the context within which all other value creation activities take place. It follows that improving infrastructure can help a company increase efficiency and lower its cost structure. Above all, an appropriate infrastructure can help foster a companywide commitment to efficiency and promote cooperation among different functions in pursuit of efficiency goals. These issues are addressed at length in later chapters.

For now, it is important to note that strategic leadership is especially important in building a companywide commitment to efficiency. The leadership task is to articulate a vision that recognizes the need for all functions of a company to focus on improving efficiency (this is what happen at Matsushita when Kunio Nakamura became CEO in 2000—see the Opening Case). It is not enough to improve the efficiency of production or of marketing or of R&D in a piecemeal fashion. Achieving superior efficiency requires a companywide commitment to this goal that must be articulated by general and functional managers. A further leadership task is to facilitate the cross-functional cooperation needed to achieve superior efficiency. For example, designing products that are easy to manufacture requires that production and R&D

RUNNING CASE

Dell's Utilization of the Internet

Dell Computer is famous for being the first company to implement online selling in the PC industry. Launched in June 1994, today more than 85% of Dell's computers are sold online. According to Michael Dell, "As I saw it, the Internet offered a logical extension of the direct [selling] model, creating even stronger relationships with our customers. The Internet would augment conventional telephone, fax, and face-to-face encounters, and give our customers the information they wanted faster, cheaper, and more efficiently." Dell's website allows customers to customize their orders to a degree that would have been unthinkable before the Web. Customers can mix and match product features such as microprocessors, memory, monitors, internal hard drives, CD and DVD drives, keyboard and mouse format, and so on, in order to get the system that best suits their particular requirements. By allowing customers to configure their order, Dell increases its customer responsiveness, thereby differentiating itself from rivals. Dell has also put much of its customer service functions online, reducing the need for telephone calls to customer service representatives and saving costs in the process. Each week some 200,000 people access Dell's troubleshooting tips online. Each of these visits to Dell's website saves the company a potential $15, which is the average cost of a technical support call. If just 10% of these online visitors were to call Dell by telephone instead, it would cost the company $15.6 million per year.

Dell also uses the Internet to manage its supply chain, feeding real-time information about order flow to its suppliers. Dell's suppliers use this information to better schedule their own production on a real-time basis, providing components to Dell on a just-in-time basis, thereby taking inventory out of the system and reducing Dell's need for working capital and space to store the inventory. Dell's ultimate goal is to drive all inventories out of the supply chain, apart from that in transit between suppliers and Dell, effectively replacing inventory with information. By doing so, Dell can drive significant costs out of its system.

Internet-based customer ordering and procurement systems have also allowed the company to synchronize demand and supply to an extent that few other companies can. For example, if Dell sees that it is running out of a particular component, say, seventeen-inch monitors from Sony, it can manipulate demand by offering a nineteen-inch model at a lower price until Sony delivers more seventeen-inch monitors. By taking such steps to fine-tune the balance between demand and supply, Dell can meet customers' expectations and maintain its differential advantage. Moreover, balancing supply and demand allows the company to minimize excess and obsolete inventory. Dell writes off between 0.05% and 0.1% of total materials costs in excess or obsolete inventory. Its competitors write off between 2 and 3%, which again gives Dell a significant cost advantage.[c]

personnel communicate, integrating JIT systems with production scheduling requires close communication between materials management and production, designing self-managing teams to perform production tasks requires close cooperation between human resources and production, and so on.

● **Summary: Achieving Efficiency**   Table 4.1 summarizes the primary roles that various functions must take to achieve superior efficiency. Bear in mind that achieving superior efficiency is not something that can be tackled on a function-by-function basis. It requires an organizationwide commitment and an ability to ensure close cooperation among functions. Top management, by exercising leadership and influencing the infrastructure, plays a major role in this process.

TABLE 4.1

Primary Roles of Value Creation Functions in Achieving Superior Efficiency

Value Creation Function	Primary Roles
Infrastructure (leadership)	1. Provide companywide commitment to efficiency 2. Facilitate cooperation among functions
Production	1. Where appropriate, pursue economies of scale and learning economics 2. Implement flexible manufacturing systems
Marketing	1. Where appropriate, adopt aggressive marketing to ride down the experience curve 2. Limit customer defection rates by building brand loyalty
Materials management	1. Implement JIT systems 2. Implement supply-chain coordination
R&D	1. Design products for ease of manufacture 2. Seek process innovations
Information systems	1. Use information systems to automate processes 2. Use information systems to reduce costs of coordination
Human resources	1. Institute training programs to build skills 2. Implement self-managing teams 3. Implement pay for performance

Achieving Superior Quality

In Chapter 3, we noted that quality can be thought of in terms of two dimensions: *quality as reliability* and *quality as excellence.* High-quality products are reliable in the sense that they do the job they were designed for and do it well, and are also perceived by consumers to have superior attributes. We also noted that superior quality gives a company two advantages. First, a strong reputation for quality allows a company to differentiate its products from those offered by rivals, thereby creating more utility in the eyes of customers, which gives the company the option of charging a premium price for its products. Second, eliminating defects or errors from the production process reduces waste, increases efficiency, and lowers the cost structure of the company and increases its profitability. For example, reducing the number of defects in a company's manufacturing process lowers the cost of goods sold as a percentage of revenues, thereby raising the company's return on sales and return on invested capital. In this section, we look in more depth at what managers can do to enhance the reliability and other attributes of the company's product offering.

● **Attaining Superior Reliability**

The principal tool that most managers now use to increase the reliability of their product offering is the Six Sigma quality improvement methodology. The Six Sigma methodology is a direct descendant of the total quality management (TQM) philosophy that was widely adopted, first by Japanese companies and then by American companies, during the 1980s and early 1990s.[27] The TQM concept was developed by a number of American management consultants, including W. Edwards Deming, Joseph Juran, and A. V. Feigenbaum.[28]

Originally, these consultants won few converts in the United States. However, managers in Japan embraced their ideas enthusiastically and even named their premier annual prize for manufacturing excellence after Deming. The philosophy underlying TQM, as articulated by Deming, is based on the following five-step chain reaction:

1. Improved quality means that costs decrease because of less rework, fewer mistakes, fewer delays, and better use of time and materials.

2. As a result, productivity improves.

3. Better quality leads to higher market share and allows the company to raise prices.

4. This increases the company's profitability and allows it to stay in business.

5. Thus the company creates more jobs.[29]

Deming identified a number of steps that should be part of any quality improvement program:

- A company should have a clear business model to specify where it is going and how it is going to get there.

- Management should embrace the philosophy that mistakes, defects, and poor-quality materials are not acceptable and should be eliminated.

- Quality of supervision should be improved by allowing more time for supervisors to work with employees and giving them appropriate skills for the job.

- Management should create an environment in which employees will not fear reporting problems or recommending improvements.

- Work standards should not only be defined as numbers or quotas but should also include some notion of quality to promote the production of defect-free output.

- Management is responsible for training employees in new skills to keep pace with changes in the workplace.

- Achieving better quality requires the commitment of everyone in the company.

It took the rise of Japan to the top rank of economic powers in the 1980s to alert western business to the importance of the TQM concept. Since then, quality improvement programs have spread rapidly throughout western industry. Strategy in Action 4.3 describes one of the most successful implementations of a quality improvement process, General Electric's Six Sigma program.

Despite such instances of spectacular success, quality improvement practices are not universally accepted. A study by the American Quality Foundation found that only 20% of U.S. companies regularly review the consequences of quality performance, compared with 70% of Japanese companies.[30] Another study, this one by Arthur D. Little, of 500 American companies using TQM found that only 36% believed that TQM was increasing their competitiveness.[31] A prime reason for this, according to the study, was that many companies had not fully understood or embraced the TQM concept. They were looking for a quick fix, whereas implementing a quality improvement program is a long-term commitment.

Strategy in Action

4.3

General Electric's Six Sigma Quality Improvement Process

Six Sigma, a quality and efficiency program adopted by several major corporations, including Motorola, General Electric, and Allied Signal, aims to reduce defects, boost productivity, eliminate waste, and cut costs throughout a company. "Sigma" comes from the Greek letter that statisticians use to represent a standard deviation from a mean: the higher the number of sigmas, the smaller the number of errors. At 6 sigma, a production process would be 99.99966 percent accurate, creating just 3.4 defects per million units. Although it is almost impossible for a company to achieve such perfection, several companies strive toward that goal.

General Electric is perhaps the most fervent adopter of Six Sigma programs. Under the direction of long-serving CEO Jack Welch, GE spent nearly $1 billion between 1994 and 1998 to convert all of its divisions to the Six Sigma faith. Welch credits the program with raising GE's operating profit margins to 16.6% in 1998, up from 14.4% three years earlier.

One of the first products designed from start to finish using Six Sigma processes was a $1.25 million diagnostic computer tomography (CT) scanner, the Lightspeed, which produces rapid three-dimensional images of the human body. The new scanner captures multiple images simultaneously, requiring only twenty seconds to do full-body scans that once took three minutes—an important time reduction because patients must remain perfectly still during the scan. GE spent $50 million to run 250 separate Six Sigma analyses designed to improve the reliability and lower the manufacturing cost of the new scanner. Its efforts were rewarded when the Lightspeed's first customers soon noticed that it ran without

downtime from the start, a testament to the reliability of the product.

Achieving that reliability took a lot of work. GE's engineers deconstructed the scanner into its basic components and tried to improve the reliability of each component through a detailed step-by-step analysis. For example, the most important parts of CT scanners are vacuum tubes that focus x-ray waves. The tubes that GE used in previous scanners, which cost $60,000 each, suffered from low reliability. Hospitals and clinics wanted the tubes to operate for twelve hours a day for at least six months, but typically they lasted only half that long. Moreover, GE was scrapping some $20 million in tubes each year because they failed preshipping performance tests, and a disturbing number of faulty tubes were slipping past inspection, only to be pronounced unusable on arrival.

To try to solve the reliability problem, the Six Sigma team took the tubes apart. They knew that one problem was a petroleum-based oil used in the tube to prevent short circuits by isolating the anode, which has a positive charge, from the negatively charged cathode. The oil often deteriorated after a few months, leading to short circuits, but the team did not know why. By using statistical what-if scenarios on all parts of the tube, the researchers learned that the lead-based paint on the inside of the tube was adulterating the oil. Acting on this information, the team developed a paint that would preserve the tube and protect the oil.

By pursuing this and other improvements, the Six Sigma team was able to extend the average life of a vacuum tube in the CT scanner from three months to over a year. Although the improvements increased the cost of the tube from $60,000 to $85,000, the increased cost was outweighed by the reduction in replacement costs, making it an attractive proposition for customers.[d]

● **Implementing Reliability Improvement Methodologies**
Among companies that have successfully adopted quality improvement methodologies, certain imperatives stand out. These are discussed below in the order in which they are usually tackled in companies implementing quality improvement programs. What needs to be stressed first, however, is that improvement in product reliability is a cross-functional process. Its implementation requires close cooperation among all functions in the pursuit of the common goal of improving quality; it is a process that cuts across functions. The roles played by the different functions in implementing reliability improvement methodologies is summarized in Table 4.2.

TABLE 4.2

Roles Played by Different Functions in Implementing Reliability Improvement Methodologies

Infrastructure (leadership)	1. Provide leadership and commitment to quality
	2. Find ways to measure quality
	3. Set goals and create incentives
	4. Solicit input from employees
	5. Encourage cooperation among functions
Production	1. Shorten production runs
	2. Trace defects back to source
Marketing	1. Focus on the customer
	2. Provide customers' feedback on quality
Materials management	1. Rationalize suppliers
	2. Help suppliers implement quality improvement methodologies
	3. Trace defects back to suppliers
R&D	1. Design products that are easy to manufacture
Information systems	1. Use information systems to monitor defect rates
Human resources	1. Institute quality improvement training programs
	2. Identify and train "black belts"
	3. Organize employees into quality teams

BUILD ORGANIZATIONAL COMMITMENT TO QUALITY There is evidence that quality improvement programs will do little to improve the performance of a company unless everyone in the organization embraces it.[32] When Xerox launched its quality program, its first step was to educate the entire work force, from top management down, in the importance and operation of the program. It did so by forming groups, beginning with a group at the top of the organization that included the CEO. The top group was the first to receive basic TQM training. Each member of this group was then given the task of training a group at the next level in the hierarchy, and so on down throughout the organization, until all 100,000 employees had received basic TQM training. Both top management and the human resources function of the company can play a major role in this process. Top management has the responsibility of exercising the leadership required to make a commitment to quality an organizationwide goal. The human resources function must take on responsibility for companywide training in TQM techniques.

CREATE QUALITY LEADERS If a quality improvement program is to be successful, individuals must be identified to lead the program. Under the Six Sigma methodology, exceptional employees are identified and put through a "black belt" training course on the Six Sigma methodology. The black belts are taken out of their normal job roles and assigned to work solely on Six Sigma projects for the next two years. In effect, they become internal consultants and project leaders. Because they are dedicated to Six Sigma programs, they are not distracted from the task at hand by day-to-day operating responsibilities. To make a black belt assignment attractive, many companies now use it as a step in a career path. Successful black belts do not return to their prior job after two years but instead are promoted and given more responsibility.

FOCUS ON THE CUSTOMER Quality improvement practitioners see a focus on the customer as the starting point, and indeed, the raison d'être, of the whole quality philosophy.[33] The marketing function, because it provides the primary point of contact with the customer, should play a major role here. It needs to identify what customers want from the good or service that the company provides, what the company actually provides to customers, and the gap between what customers want and what they get, which could be called the quality gap. Then, together with the other functions of the company, it needs to formulate a plan for closing the quality gap.

IDENTIFY PROCESSES AND THE SOURCE OF DEFECTS One of the hallmarks of the Six Sigma quality improvement methodology is identifying discrete repetitive processes that can be improved. This is normally done by using flowchart methodology to break an operation into its constituent parts. Thus, as noted in Strategy in Action 4.3, to improve its Lightspeed CT scanner, GE's engineers deconstructed the scanner into its basic components and tried to improve the reliability of each component through a detailed step-by-step analysis.

Quality improvement methodologies preach the need to identify defects that arise from processes, trace them to their source, find out what caused them, and make corrections so that they do not recur. Production and materials management typically have primary responsibility for this task.

To uncover defects, Deming advocated the use of statistical procedures to pinpoint variations in the quality of goods or services. Deming viewed variation as the enemy of quality.[34] The Six Sigma methodology also relies heavily on statistical analysis of variation. Once variations have been identified, they must be traced to their source and eliminated. One technique that helps greatly in tracing defects to their source is reducing lot sizes for manufactured products. With short production runs, defects show up immediately. Consequently, they can be quickly traced to the source, and the problem can be addressed. Reducing lot sizes also means that, when defective products are produced, their number will not be large, thus decreasing waste. Flexible manufacturing techniques, discussed earlier, can be used to reduce lot sizes without raising costs. Consequently, adopting flexible manufacturing techniques is an important aspect of a TQM program.

JIT inventory systems also play a part. Under a JIT system, defective parts enter the manufacturing process immediately; they are not warehoused for several months before use. Hence, defective inputs can be quickly spotted. The problem can then be traced to the supply source and corrected before more defective parts are produced. Under a more traditional system, the practice of warehousing parts for months before they are used may mean that many defects are produced by a supplier before they enter the production process.

FIND WAYS TO MEASURE QUALITY Another imperative of any quality improvement program is to create a metric that can be used to measure quality. This is relatively easy in manufacturing companies, where quality can be measured by criteria such as defects per million parts. It tends to be more difficult in service companies, but with a little creativity, suitable metrics can be devised. For example, one of the metrics Florida Power & Light uses to measure quality is meter-reading errors per month. Another is the frequency and duration of power outages. L. L. Bean, the Freeport, Maine, mail-order retailer of outdoor gear, uses the percentage of orders that are correctly filled as one of its quality measures. For some banks, the key measures are the number of customer defections per year and the number of statement errors per thousand customers. The common theme that runs through all these examples is identifying what quality means from a customer's perspective and devising a method to gauge this.

SET GOALS AND CREATE INCENTIVES Once a metric has been devised, the next step is to set a challenging quality goal and create incentives for reaching it. Xerox again provides an example. When it introduced its TQM program, its initial goal was to reduce defective parts from 25,000 per million to 1,000 per million. Under Six Sigma programs, the goal is 3.4 defects per million units. One way of creating incentives to attain such a goal is to link rewards, like bonus pay and promotional opportunities, to the goal. Thus, within many companies that have adopted self-managing teams, the bonus pay of team members is determined in part by their ability to attain quality goals. Setting goals and creating incentives are key tasks of top management.

SOLICIT INPUT FROM EMPLOYEES Employees can be a vital source of information regarding the sources of poor quality. Therefore, a framework must be established for soliciting employee suggestions for improvements. Quality circles, which are meetings of groups of employees, have often been used to achieve this goal. Other companies have used self-managing teams as forums for discussing quality improvement ideas. Whatever forum is used, soliciting input from employees requires that management be open to receiving, and acting on, bad news and criticism from employees. According to Deming, one problem with U.S. management is that it has grown used to "killing the bearer of bad tidings." But, he argues, managers who are committed to the quality concept must recognize that bad news is a gold mine of information.[35]

BUILD LONG-TERM RELATIONSHIPS WITH SUPPLIERS A major source of poor-quality finished goods is poor-quality component parts. To decrease product defects, a company has to work with its suppliers to improve the quality of the parts they supply. The primary responsibility in this area falls on the materials-management function, which interacts with suppliers.

To implement JIT systems with suppliers and to get suppliers to adopt their own quality improvement programs, two steps are necessary. First, the number of suppliers has to be reduced to manageable proportions. Second, the company must commit to building a cooperative long-term relationship with the suppliers that remain. Asking suppliers to invest in JIT and quality improvement programs is asking them to make major investments that tie them to the company. For example, in order to implement a JIT system fully, the company may ask a supplier to relocate its manufacturing plant so that it is next-door to the company's assembly plant. Suppliers are likely to be hesitant about making such investments unless they feel that the company is committed to an enduring, long-term relationship with them.

DESIGN FOR EASE OF MANUFACTURE The more assembly steps a product requires, the more opportunities there are for making mistakes. Designing products with fewer parts should make assembly easier and result in fewer defects. Both R&D and manufacturing need to be involved in designing products that are easy to manufacture.

BREAK DOWN BARRIERS AMONG FUNCTIONS Implementing quality improvement methodologies requires organizationwide commitment and substantial cooperation among functions. R&D has to cooperate with production to design products that are easy to manufacture, marketing has to cooperate with production and R&D so that customer problems identified by marketing can be acted on, human resources management has to cooperate with all the other functions of the company in order to devise suitable quality-training programs, and so on. The issue of achieving cooperation among subunits within a company is explored in Chapter 12. What needs stressing at this point is that ultimately it is the responsibility of top management to ensure that such cooperation occurs. Strategy in Action 4.4 describes the efforts of a service company to put quality improvement programs into practice and the benefits it has gained as a result.

● **Improving Quality as Excellence**

As we stated in Chapter 3, a product is a bundle of different attributes, and reliability is just one of them, albeit an important one. Products can also be *differentiated* by attributes that collectively define product excellence. These attributes include the form, features, performance, durability, and styling of a product. In addition, a company can create quality as excellence by emphasizing attributes of the service associated with the product, such as ordering ease, prompt delivery, easy installation, the availability of customer training and consulting, and maintenance services. Dell Computer, for example, differentiates itself on ease of ordering (via the Web), prompt delivery, easy installation, and the ready availability of customer support and maintenance services. Differentiation can also be based on the attributes of the people in the company

Strategy in Action   4.4

Six Sigma at Mount Carmel Health

Following the lead of General Electric, a number of health care organizations have adopted the Six Sigma approach or similar quality improvement tools as a way of trying to improve the quality of their service offerings. One of the first was Mount Carmel Health, a three hospital 9,000 employee health care provider in Ohio. Mount Carmel Health implemented a Six Sigma program after suffering from poor financial performance in 2000. It was initiated in late 2000, and by early 2001, forty-four employees had been trained in Six Sigma principles. These "black belts" were pulled out of their original positions and were not replaced. By the second half of 2001, they were leading some sixty projects in different phases of implementation.

One of the first projects focused on a simple and common problem among health care providers: timely and accurate reimbursement of costs. Mount Carmel discovered that it was writing off large amounts of potential revenues from the government-run Medicare programs as uncollectible because the charges were denied by Medicare administrators. Mount Carmel had low expectations for this business anyway, so it had never analyzed why the write-offs were so high. After conducting a careful analysis as part of a Six Sigma project, it discovered that a significant portion of the denials were due to the incorrect coding of reports submitted to Medicare. If the reports were coded correctly—that is, if fewer errors were made in the production of forms—the Six Sigma team estimated that annual income would be some $300,000 higher, so they devised improved processes for coding the forms to reduce the error rate. The result was that net income rose by over $800,000. It appeared that improving the coding process for this one parameter improved the reporting of many other parameters and led to a reimbursement rate much higher than anticipated.

In another example, by examining a process flowchart, employees at Mount Carmel were able to improve patient throughput through CT scanners from 1.8 to 2.7 patients per hour, which resulted in an annual net revenue improvement of $2.4 million per scanner. A three-week patient wait-time for CT scanners was also reduced to one or two days, greatly increasing customer responsiveness.

By 2005, Mount Carmel had over 550 Six Sigma quality improvement projects either completed or ongoing. The organization estimates that since it launched the process in July 2000, it has reduced costs by some $63 million.[e]

TABLE 4.3

Attributes Associated with a Product Offering

Product Attributes	Service Attributes	Associated Personnel Attributes
Form	Ordering ease	Competence
Features	Delivery	Courtesy
Performance	Installation	Credibility
Durability	Customer training	Reliability
Reliability	Customer consulting	Responsiveness
Style	Maintenance and repair	Communication

whom customers interact with when making a product purchase, such as their competence, courtesy, credibility, responsiveness, and communication. Singapore Airlines, for example, enjoys an excellent reputation for quality service largely because passengers perceive their flight attendants as competent, courteous, and responsive to their needs. Thus, we can talk about the product attributes, service attributes, and personnel attributes associated with a company's product offering (see Table 4.3).

For a product to be regarded as high in the excellence dimension, a company's product offering must be seen as superior to that of rivals. Achieving a perception of high quality on any of these attributes requires specific actions by managers. First, it is important for managers to collect marketing intelligence indicating which of these attributes are most important to customers. For example, consumers of personal computers may place a low weight on durability because they expect their PC to be made obsolete by technological advances within three years, but they may place a high weight on features and performance. Similarly, ease of ordering and timely delivery may be very important attributes for customers of online booksellers (as they are indeed for customers of Amazon.com), whereas customer training and consulting may be very important attributes for customers who purchase complex business-to-business software to manage their relationships with suppliers.

Second, once the company has identified the attributes that are important to customers, it needs to design its products, and the associated services, so that those attributes are embodied in the product, and it needs to make sure that personnel in the company are appropriately trained so that the correct attributes are emphasized. This requires close coordination between marketing and product development (the topic of the next section) and the involvement of the human resources management function in employee selection and training.

Third, the company must decide which of the significant attributes to promote and how best to position them in the minds of consumers, that is, how to tailor the marketing message so that it creates a consistent image in the minds of customers.[36] At this point, it is important to recognize that although a product might be differentiated on the basis of six attributes, covering all of those attributes in the company's communication messages may lead to an unfocused message. Many marketing experts advocate promoting only one or two central attributes to customers. For example, Volvo consistently emphasizes the safety and durability of its vehicles in all marketing messages, creating the perception in the minds of consumers (backed by product design) that Volvo cars are safe and durable. Volvo cars are also very reliable and have high performance, but the company does not emphasize these attributes in its marketing messages. In contrast, Porsche emphasizes performance and styling in all of its marketing messages; thus, a Porsche is positioned differently in the minds of consumers than a Volvo is. Both are regarded as high-quality products because both have superior attributes, but the attributes that the two companies have chosen to emphasize are very different. They are differentiated from the average car in different ways.

Finally, it must be recognized that competition does not stand still but instead produces continual improvement in product attributes and often the development of new-product attributes. This is obvious in fast-moving high-tech industries where product features that were considered leading edge just a few years ago are now obsolete, but the same process is also at work in more stable industries. For example, the rapid diffusion of microwave ovens during the 1980s required food companies to build new attributes into their frozen food products: They had to maintain their texture and consistency while being microwaved. A product could not be considered high quality unless it could do that. This speaks to the importance of having a strong R&D function in the company that can work with marketing and manufacturing to continually upgrade the quality of the attributes that are designed into the company's product offerings. Exactly how to achieve this goal is covered in the next section.

Achieving Superior Innovation

In many ways, building distinctive competencies that result in innovation is the most important source of competitive advantage because innovation can result in new products that better satisfy customer needs, can improve the quality (attributes) of existing products, or can reduce the costs of making products that customers want. Thus, the ability to develop innovative new products or processes gives a company a major competitive advantage that allows it to (1) differentiate its products and charge a premium price and/or (2) lower its cost structure below that of its rivals. Competitors, however, attempt to imitate successful innovations and often succeed. Therefore, maintaining a competitive advantage requires a continuing commitment to innovation.

Robert Cooper found that successful new-product launches are major drivers of superior profitability. Cooper looked at more than 200 new-product introductions and found that of those classified as successes, some 50% achieve a return on investment in excess of 33%, half have a payback period of two years or less, and half achieve a market share in excess of 35%.[37] Many companies have established a track record for successful innovation. Among them are DuPont, which has produced a steady stream of successful innovations, such as cellophane, Nylon, Freon, and Teflon; Sony, whose successes include the Walkman, the compact disc, and the PlayStation; Nokia, which has been a leader in the development of wireless phones; Pfizer, a drug company that produced eight blockbuster new drugs during the 1990s and early 2000s; 3M, which has applied its core competency in tapes and adhesives to developing a wide range of new products; Intel, which has consistently managed to lead in the development of innovative new microprocessors to run personal computers; and Cisco Systems, whose innovations helped to pave the way for the rapid growth of the Internet.

● **The High Failure Rate of Innovation**   Although promoting innovation can be a source of competitive advantage, the failure rate of innovative new products is high. One study of product development in the chemical, drug, petroleum, and electronics industries suggested that only about 20% of major R&D projects ultimately result in a commercially successful product or process.[38] An in-depth case study of product development in three companies (one in chemicals and two in drugs) reported that about 60% of R&D projects reached technical completion, 30% were commercialized, and only 12% earned a profit that exceeded the company's cost of capital.[39] Another study concluded that one in nine major R&D projects, or about 11%, produced commercially successful products.[40] In sum, the evidence suggests that only 10 to 20% of major R&D projects give rise to a commercially successful product. Well-publicized product failures include Apple Computer's Newton, a personal digital assistant; Sony's Betamax format in the video player and recorder market; and Sega's Dreamcast videogame console. While many reasons have been advanced to explain why so many new products fail to generate an economic return, five explanations for failure appear on most lists: uncertainty, poor commercialization, poor positioning strategy, technological myopia, and being slow to market.[41]

UNCERTAINTY   New-product development is an inherently risky process. It requires testing a hypothesis whose answer is impossible to know prior to market introduction: Have we tapped an unmet customer need? Is there sufficient market demand for this new technology? Although good market research can reduce the uncertainty about likely future demand for a new technology, uncertainty cannot be eradicated, so a certain failure rate is to be expected.

The failure rate is higher for quantum product innovations than for incremental innovations. A **quantum innovation** represents a radical departure from existing technology—the introduction of something that is new to the world. The development of the World Wide Web can be considered a quantum innovation in communications technology. Other quantum innovations include the development of the first photocopier by Xerox, the first contact lenses by Bausch and Lomb, and the first microprocessor by Intel in 1971. **Incremental innovation** refers to an extension of existing technology. For example, Intel's Pentium Pro microprocessor is an incremental product innovation because it builds on the existing microprocessor architecture of Intel's X86 series. The uncertainty of future demand for a new product is much greater if that product represents a quantum innovation that is new to the world than if it is an incremental innovation designed to replace an established product whose demand profile is already well known. Consequently, the failure rate tends to be higher for quantum innovations.

POOR COMMERCIALIZATION   A second reason frequently cited to explain the high failure rate of new-product introductions is **poor commercialization**—something that occurs when there is definite customer demand for a new product, but the product is not well adapted to customer needs because of factors such as poor design and poor quality. For instance, many of the early personal computers failed to sell because customers needed to understand computer programming to use them. Steve Jobs at Apple Computer understood that if the technology could be made user friendly (if it could be commercialized), there would be an enormous market for it. Hence, the original personal computers that Apple marketed incorporated little in the way of radically new technology, but they made existing technology accessible to the average person. Paradoxically, the failure of Apple Computer to establish a market for the Newton, the hand-held personal digital system that Apple introduced in the summer of 1993, can be traced to poor commercialization of a potentially attractive technology. Apple predicted a $1 billion market for the Newton, but sales failed to materialize when it became clear that the Newton's handwriting software, an attribute that Apple chose to emphasize in its marketing promotions, could not adequately recognize messages written on the Newton's message pad.

POOR POSITIONING STRATEGY   Poor positioning strategy arises when a company introduces a potentially attractive new product, but sales fail to materialize because it is poorly positioned in the marketplace. **Positioning strategy** is the specific set of options a company adopts for a product on four main dimensions of marketing: price, distribution, promotion and advertising, and product features. Apart from poor product quality, another reason for the failure of the Apple Newton was poor positioning strategy. The Newton was introduced at such a high initial price (close to $1,000) that there would probably have been few buyers even if the technology had been adequately commercialized.

TECHNOLOGICAL MYOPIA   Another reason that many new-product introductions fail is that companies often make the mistake of marketing a technology for which there is not enough customer demand. **Technological myopia** occurs when a company gets blinded by the wizardry of a new technology and fails to examine whether there is customer demand for the product. This problem may have been a factor in the failure of the desktop computer introduced by NeXT in the late 1980s (NeXT was founded by Steve Jobs, the founder of Apple Computer). Technologically, the NeXT machines were clearly ahead of their time, with advanced software and hardware features that would not be incorporated into most PCs for another decade. However, customer acceptance was very slow primarily because of the complete lack of applications software such as spreadsheet and word-processing programs to run on the machines. Management at NeXT was so enthused by the technology incorporated in their new computer that they ignored this basic market reality. After several years of slow sales, NeXT eventually withdrew the machines from the marketplace. Ironically, the company itself was ultimately acquired by Apple Computer, and in 2001 a new version of the NeXT operating system, known as OS X, became the operating system for Apple's computers.

BEING SLOW TO MARKET   Finally, companies fail when they are slow to get their products to market. The more time that elapses between initial development and final marketing—that is, the slower the cycle time—the more likely it is that someone else will beat the company to market and gain a first-mover advantage.[42] By and large, slow innovators update their products less frequently than fast innovators do. Consequently, they can be perceived as technical laggards relative to the fast innovators. In the car industry, General Motors has suffered from being a slow innovator. Its product development cycle has been about five years, compared with two to three years at Honda, Toyota, and Mazda and three to four years at Ford. Because they are based on five-year-old technology and design concepts, GM cars are already out of date when they reach the market.

● **Building Competencies in Innovation**   Companies can take a number of steps to build a competency in innovation and avoid failure. Six of the most important steps are (1) building skills in basic and applied scientific research, (2) developing a good process for project selection and project management, (3) achieving cross-functional integration, (4) using product development teams, (5) using partly parallel development processes, and (6) learning from experience.[43]

SKILLS IN BASIC AND APPLIED RESEARCH Building skills in basic and applied research requires the employment of research scientists and engineers and the establishment of a work environment that fosters creativity. To the extent that firms can do this, it increases their *absorptive capacity*, which we noted in Chapter 3 is the ability of an enterprise to identify, value, assimilate, and use new knowledge. A number of top companies try to achieve this by setting up university-style research facilities, where scientists and engineers are given time to work on their own research projects, in addition to projects that are linked directly to ongoing company research. At Hewlett-Packard, for example, company labs are open to engineers around the clock. Hewlett-Packard even encourages its corporate researchers to devote 10% of company time to exploring their own ideas and does not penalize them if they fail. 3M allows researchers to spend 15% of the workweek researching any topic that intrigues them, as long as there is the potential of a payoff for the company. The most famous outcome of this policy is the ubiquitous Post-it Notes. The idea for them evolved from a researcher's desire to find a way to keep the bookmark from falling out of his hymnal. Post-it Notes are now a major 3M business, with annual revenues of around $300 million. Google has copied this philosophy, and allows its engineers to spend 20% of their time working on projects of their own choosing that are not part of their core task. Among the products that have come out of this process are Google News and Google Earth.

PROJECT SELECTION AND MANAGEMENT Project management is the overall management of the innovation process, from generation of the original concept through development, and into final production and shipping. Project management requires three important skills: the ability to generate as many good ideas as possible, the ability to select among competing projects at an early stage of development so that the most promising receive funding and potential costly failures are killed off, and the ability to minimize time to market. The concept of the development funnel, divided into three phases, summarizes what is required to build these skills (see Figure 4.7).[44]

The objective in phase I is to widen the mouth of the funnel to encourage as much idea generation as possible. To this end, a company should solicit input from all its functions, as well as from customers, competitors, and suppliers. At gate 1, the funnel narrows. Here ideas are reviewed by a cross-functional team of managers who did not participate in the original concept development. Concepts that are ready to

FIGURE 4.7

The Development
Funnel

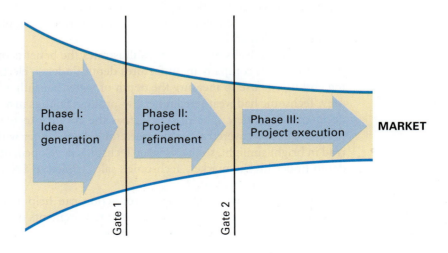

proceed then move to phase II, where the details of the project proposal are worked out. Note that gate 1 is not a go/no-go evaluation point. At this screen, ideas may be sent back for further concept development and then resubmitted for evaluation.

During phase II, which typically lasts only one or two months, the data and information from phase I are put into a form that will enable senior management to evaluate proposed projects against competing projects. Normally, this requires the development of a careful project plan, complete with details of the proposed target market, attainable market share, likely revenues, development costs, production costs, key milestones, and the like. The next big selection point, gate 2, is a go/no-go evaluation point. Senior managers review the projects under consideration and select those that seem likely winners and make the most sense from a strategic perspective, given the long-term goals of the company. The overriding objective is to select projects whose successful completion will help to maintain or build a competitive advantage for the company. A related objective is to ensure that the company does not spread its scarce capital and human resources too thinly over too many projects and instead concentrates resources on projects where the probability of success and potential returns is most attractive. Any project selected to go forward at this stage will be funded and staffed, the expectation being that it will be carried through to market introduction. In phase III, the project development proposal is executed by a cross-functional product development team.

Cross-Functional Integration Tight cross-functional integration among R&D, production, and marketing can help a company to ensure that:

1. Product development projects are driven by customer needs.

2. New products are designed for ease of manufacture.

3. Development costs are kept in check.

4. Time to market is minimized.

5. Close integration between R&D and marketing is achieved to ensure that product development projects are driven by the needs of customers.

A company's customers can be one of its primary sources of new-product ideas. The identification of customer needs, and particularly unmet needs, can set the context within which successful product innovation takes place. As the point of contact with customers, the marketing function can provide valuable information. Moreover, integrating R&D and marketing is crucial if a new product is to be properly commercialized. Otherwise, a company runs the risk of developing products for which there is little or no demand.

The case of Techsonic Industries illustrates the benefits of integrating R&D and marketing. This company manufactures depth finders—electronic devices that fishing enthusiasts use to measure the depth of water beneath a boat and to track their prey. Techsonic had weathered nine new-product failures in a row when the company decided to interview sportspeople across the country to identify what it was they needed. They discovered an unmet need for a depth finder with a gauge that could be read in bright sunlight, so that is what Techsonic developed. In the year after the $250 depth finder hit the market, Techsonic's sales tripled to $80 million, and its market share surged to 40 percent.[45]

Integration between R&D and production can help a company to ensure that products are designed with manufacturing requirements in mind. Design for manufacturing lowers manufacturing costs and leaves less room for mistakes and thus can lower costs and increase product quality. Integrating R&D and production can help lower development costs and speed products to market. If a new product is not designed with manufacturing capabilities in mind, it may prove too difficult to build, given existing manufacturing technology. In that case, the product will have to be redesigned, and both overall development costs and time to market may increase significantly. For example, making design changes during product planning could increase overall development costs by 50% and add 25% to the time it takes to bring the product to market.[46] Moreover, many quantum product innovations require new processes to manufacture them, which makes it all the more important to achieve close integration between R&D and production because minimizing time to market and development costs may require the simultaneous development of new products and new processes.[47]

PRODUCT DEVELOPMENT TEAMS One of the best ways to achieve cross-functional integration is to establish cross-functional product development teams composed of representatives from R&D, marketing, and production. The objective of a team should be to take a product development project from the initial concept development to market introduction. A number of attributes seem to be important in order for a product development team to function effectively and meet all its development milestones.[48]

First, a **heavyweight project manager**—one who has high status within the organization and the power and authority required to get the financial and human resources that the team needs to succeed—should lead the team and be dedicated primarily, if not entirely, to the project. The leader should believe in the project (a champion) and be skilled at integrating the perspectives of different functions and helping personnel from different functions work together for a common goal. The leader should also be able to act as an advocate of the team in dealings with senior management.

Second, the team should be composed of at least one member from each key function. The team members should have a number of attributes, including an ability to contribute functional expertise, high standing within their function, a willingness to share responsibility for team results, and an ability to put functional advocacy aside. It is generally preferable if core team members are 100% dedicated to the project for its duration. Such dedication ensures that their focus is on the project, not on the ongoing work of their function.

Third, the team members should be located in the same physical area to create a sense of camaraderie and facilitate communication. Fourth, the team should have a clear plan and clear goals, particularly with regard to critical development milestones and development budgets. The team should have incentives to attain those goals, such as pay bonuses when major development milestones are hit. Fifth, each team needs to develop its own processes for communication and conflict resolution. For example, one product development team at Quantum Corporation, a California-based manufacturer of disk drives for personal computers, instituted a rule that all major decisions would be made and conflicts resolved at meetings that were held every Monday afternoon. This simple rule helped the team to meet its development goals.[49]

Finally, there is always a danger that a new product development team can develop shared cognitive biases that leads to a lack of objectivity and emotional commitment to a project (see Chapter 1 for a discussion of cognitive biases).[50] To guard against this possibility, it is a good idea to have well-regarded outsiders periodically evaluate the product and decide whether to proceed or not.

FIGURE 4.8

Sequential and Partly
Parallel Development
Processes

(a) A Sequential Process

Opportunity identification → Concept development → Product design → Process design → Commercial production

(b) A Partly Parallel Process

Opportunity identification
Concept development
Product design
Process design
Commercial production

PARTLY PARALLEL DEVELOPMENT PROCESSES One way in which a product development team can compress the time it takes to develop a product and bring it to market is to use a partly parallel development process. Traditionally, product development processes have been organized on a sequential basis, as illustrated in Figure 4.8a. A problem with this kind of process is that product development proceeds without manufacturing issues in mind. Most significantly, because the basic design of a product is completed prior to the design of a manufacturing process and full-scale commercial production, there is no early warning system to indicate manufacturability. As a consequence, the company may find that it cannot manufacture the product cost-efficiently and may have to send it back to the design stage for redesign. The cycle time lengthens as the product bounces back and forth between stages.

To solve this problem, companies typically use a process similar to that illustrated in Figure 4.8b. In the partly parallel development process, development stages overlap so that, for example, work starts on the development of the production process before the product design is finalized. By reducing the need for expensive and time-consuming product redesigns, such a process can significantly reduce the time it takes to develop a new product and bring it to market.

For an example, consider what occurred after Intel Corporation introduced its 386 microprocessor in 1986. A number of companies, including IBM and Compaq, were racing to be the first to introduce a 386-based personal computer. Compaq beat IBM by six months and gained a major share of the high-power market mainly because it used a cross-functional team and a partly parallel process to develop the product. The team included engineers (R&D) and marketing, production, and finance people. Each function worked in parallel rather than sequentially. While engineers were designing the product, production people were setting up the manufacturing facilities, marketing people were working on distribution and planning marketing campaigns, and finance people were working on project funding.

LEARNING FROM EXPERIENCE Evidence strongly suggests that developing competencies in innovation requires managers to take proactive steps to learn from their experience with product development, and to incorporate the lessons from past successes and failures in future new product development processes.[51] This is easier said than done. To learn, managers need to undertake an objective postmortem of a product development project, identify key success factors and the root causes of failures, and allocate resources toward fixing failures. Leaders also need to admit their own failures if they are to encourage others to step up to the plate and identify what they did wrong. Strategy in Action 4.5 looks at how Corning learned from a prior mistake to develop a potentially promising new product.

The primary role that the various functions play in achieving superior innovation is summarized in Table 4.4. The table makes two matters clear. First, top management must bear primary responsibility for overseeing the whole development process. This entails both managing the development funnel and facilitating cooperation among the functions. Second, the effectiveness of R&D in developing new products and processes depends on its ability to cooperate with marketing and production.

Strategy in Action   4.5

Corning: Learning from Innovation Failures

In 1998, Corning, then the world's largest supplier of fiber-optic cable, decided to diversify into the development and manufacture of DNA microarrays (DNA chips). DNA chips are used to analyze the function of genes and are an important research tool in the drug development process. Corning tried to develop a DNA chip that could print all 28,000 human genes onto a set of slides. By 2000, Corning had invested over $100 million in the project and its first chips were on the market, but the project was a failure and in 2001 it was pulled.

What went wrong? Corning was late to market—a critical mistake. The market was dominated by Affymetrix, which had been in the businesses since the early 1990s. By 2000, Affymetrix's DNA chips were the dominant design—researchers were familiar with them, they performed well, and few people were willing to switch to chips from unproven competitors. Corning was late because it adhered to its long-established innovation processes, which were not entirely appropriate in the biological sciences. In particular, Corning's own in-house experts in the physical sciences insisted on sticking to rigorous quality standards that customers and life scientists felt were higher than necessary. These quality standards proved to be very difficult to achieve and, as a result, the product launch was delayed, giving Affymetrix time to consolidate its hold on the market. Moreover, Corning failed to give prototypes of its chips to potential customers, and consequently it missed incorporating some crucial features that customers wanted.

After reviewing this failure, Corning decided that it needed to bring customers into the development process earlier. And it needed to hire more outside experts if it was diversifying into an area where it lacked competencies, and to give those experts a larger say in the development process.

The project was not a total failure, however, for through it Corning discovered a vibrant and growing market—the market for drug discovery. By combining what it had learned about drug discovery with another failed businesses, photonics, which manipulates data using light waves, Corning created a new product called Epic. Epic is a revolutionary technology for drug testing that uses light waves instead of fluorescent dyes (the standard industry practice). Epic promises to accelerate the process of testing potential drugs and saving pharmaceutical companies valuable R&D money. Unlike its DNA microarray project, Corning had eighteen pharmaceutical companies test Epic before development was finalized. Corning used this feedback to refine Epic. The company believes that ultimately Epic could generate $500 million annually.[f]

Functional Roles for Achieving Superior Innovation

Value Creation Function	Primary Roles
Infrastructure (leadership)	1. Manage overall project (i.e., manage the development function)
	2. Facilitate cross-functional cooperation
Production	1. Cooperate with R&D on designing products that are easy to manufacture
	2. Work with R&D to develop process innovations
Marketing	1. Provide market information to R&D
	2. Work with R&D to develop new products
Materials management	No primary responsibility
R&D	1. Develop new products and processes
	2. Cooperate with other functions, particularly marketing and manufacturing, in the development process
Information systems	1. Use information systems to coordinate cross-functional and cross-company product development work
Human resources	1. Hire talented scientists and engineers

Achieving Superior Responsiveness to Customers

To achieve superior responsiveness to customers, a company must give customers what they want, when they want it, and at a price they are willing to pay—so long as the company's long-term profitability is not compromised in the process. Customer responsiveness is an important differentiating attribute that can help to build brand loyalty. Strong product differentiation and brand loyalty give a company more pricing options; it can charge a premium price for its products or keep prices low to sell more goods and services to customers. Either way, the company that is more responsive to its customers' needs than are rivals will have a competitive advantage, all else being equal.

Achieving superior responsiveness to customers means giving customers value for money, and steps taken to improve the efficiency of a company's production process and the quality of its products should be consistent with this aim. In addition, giving customers what they want may require the development of new products with new features. In other words, achieving superior efficiency, quality, and innovation are all part of achieving superior responsiveness to customers. There are two other prerequisites for attaining this goal. First, a company has to develop a competency in listening to and focusing on its customers and in investigating and identifying their needs. Second, it constantly needs to seek better ways to satisfy those needs.

● **Focusing on the Customer** A company cannot be responsive to its customers' needs unless it knows what those needs are. Thus, the first step to building superior responsiveness to customers is to motivate the whole company to focus on the customer. The means to this end are demonstrating leadership, shaping employee attitudes, and using mechanisms for bringing customers into the company.

DEMONSTRATING LEADERSHIP Customer focus must start at the top of the organization. A commitment to superior responsiveness to customers brings attitudinal changes throughout a company that ultimately can be built only through strong leadership. A mission statement that puts customers first is one way to send a clear message to employees about the desired focus. Another avenue is top management's own actions. For example, Tom Monaghan, the founder of Domino's Pizza, stayed close to the customer by visiting as many stores as possible every week, running some deliveries himself, insisting that other top managers do the same, and eating Domino's pizza regularly.[52]

SHAPING EMPLOYEE ATTITUDES   Leadership alone is not enough to attain a superior customer focus. All employees must see the customer as the focus of their activity and be trained to focus on the customer, whether their function is marketing, manufacturing, R&D, or accounting. The objective should be to make employees think of themselves as customers—to put themselves in customers' shoes. At that point, employees will be better able to identify ways to improve the quality of a customer's experience with the company.

To reinforce this mindset, incentive systems within the company should reward employees for satisfying customers. For example, senior managers at the Four Seasons hotel chain, who pride themselves on their customer focus, like to tell the story of Roy Dyment, a door attendant in Toronto who neglected to load a departing guest's briefcase into his taxi. The door attendant called the guest, a lawyer, in Washington, D.C., and found that he desperately needed the briefcase for a morning meeting. Dyment hopped on a plane to Washington and returned it—without first securing approval from his boss. Far from punishing Dyment for making a mistake and for not checking with management before going to Washington, the Four Seasons responded by naming Dyment Employee of the Year.[53] This action sent a powerful message to Four Seasons employees about the importance of satisfying customer needs.

BRINGING CUSTOMERS INTO THE COMPANY   "Know thy customer" is one of the keys to achieving superior responsiveness to customers. Knowing the customer not only requires that employees think like customers themselves; it also demands that they listen to what their customers have to say and, as much as possible, bring them into the company. Although this may not involve physically bringing customers into the company, it does mean bringing in customers' opinions by soliciting feedback from customers on the company's goods and services and by building information systems that communicate the feedback to the relevant people.

For an example, consider direct-selling clothing retailer Lands' End. Through its catalog, the Internet, and customer service telephone operators, Lands' End actively solicits comments from its customers about the quality of its clothing and the kind of merchandise they want it to supply. Indeed, it was customers' insistence that initially prompted the company to move into the clothing segment. Lands' End used to supply equipment for sailboats through mail-order catalogs. However, it received so many requests from customers to include outdoor clothing in its offering that it responded by expanding the catalog to fill this need. Soon clothing became the main business, and Lands' End dropped the sailboat equipment. Today, the company still pays close attention to customer requests. Every month, a computer printout of customer requests and comments is given to managers. This feedback helps the company to fine-tune the merchandise it sells. Indeed, new lines of merchandise are frequently introduced in response to customer requests.[54]

● **Satisfying Customer Needs**   Once a focus on the customer is an integral part of the company, the next requirement is to satisfy the customer needs that have been identified. As already noted, efficiency, quality, and innovation are crucial competencies that help a company satisfy customer needs. Beyond that, companies can provide a higher level of satisfaction if they differentiate their products by (1) customizing them, where possible, to the requirements of individual customers and (2) reducing the time it takes to respond to or satisfy customer needs.

CUSTOMIZATION Customization is varying the features of a good or service to tailor it to the unique needs or tastes of groups of customers or, in the extreme case, individual customers. Although extensive customization can raise costs, the development of flexible manufacturing technologies has made it possible to customize products to a much greater extent than was feasible ten to fifteen years ago without experiencing a prohibitive rise in cost structure (particularly when flexible manufacturing technologies are linked with web-based information systems). For example, online retailers such as Amazon.com have used web-based technologies to develop a homepage customized for each user. When a customer accesses amazon.com, he or she is offered a list of recommendations for books or music to purchase based on an analysis of prior buying history, a powerful competency that gives Amazon.com a competitive advantage.

The trend toward customization has fragmented many markets, particularly customer markets, into ever smaller niches. An example of this fragmentation occurred in Japan in the early 1980s when Honda dominated the motorcycle market there. Second-place Yamaha decided to go after Honda's lead. It announced the opening of a new factory that, when operating at full capacity, would make Yamaha the world's largest manufacturer of motorcycles. Honda responded by proliferating its product line and stepping up its rate of new-product introduction. At the start of what became known as the motorcycle wars, Honda had sixty motorcycles in its product line. Over the next eighteen months, it rapidly increased its range to 113 models, customizing them to ever smaller niches. Honda was able to accomplish this without bearing a prohibitive cost penalty because it has a competency in flexible manufacturing. The flood of Honda's customized models pushed Yamaha out of much of the market, effectively stalling its bid to overtake Honda.[55]

RESPONSE TIME Giving customers what they want, when they want it, requires speed of response to customer demands. To gain a competitive advantage, a company must often respond to customer demands very quickly, whether the transaction is a furniture manufacturer's delivery of a product once it has been ordered, a bank's processing of a loan application, an automobile manufacturer's delivery of a spare part for a car that broke down, or the wait in a supermarket checkout line. We live in a fast-paced society, where time is a valuable commodity. Companies that can satisfy customer demands for rapid response build brand loyalty, differentiate their products, and can charge higher prices for them.

Increased speed often lets a company choose a premium pricing option, as the mail delivery industry illustrates. The air express niche of the mail delivery industry is based on the notion that customers are often willing to pay considerably more for overnight Express Mail as opposed to regular mail. Another example of the value of rapid response is Caterpillar, the manufacturer of heavy earthmoving equipment, which can get a spare part to any point in the world within twenty-four hours. Downtime for heavy construction equipment is very costly, so Caterpillar's ability to respond quickly in the event of equipment malfunction is of prime importance to its customers. As a result, many of them have remained loyal to Caterpillar despite the aggressive low-price competition from Komatsu of Japan.

TABLE 4.5

Primary Roles of Different Functions in Achieving Superior Responsiveness to Customers

Value Creation Function	Primary Roles
Infrastructure (leadership)	1. Through leadership by example, build a companywide commitment to responsiveness to customers
Production	1. Achieve customization through implementation of flexible manufacturing 2. Achieve rapid response through flexible manufacturing
Marketing	1. Know the customer 2. Communicate customer feedback to appropriate functions
Materials management	1. Develop logistics systems capable of responding quickly to unanticipated customer demands (JIT)
R&D	1. Bring customers into the product development process
Information systems	1. Use web-based information systems to increase responsiveness to customers
Human resources	1. Develop training programs that get employees to think like customers themselves

In general, reducing response time requires (1) a marketing function that can quickly communicate customer requests to production, (2) production and materials-management functions that can quickly adjust production schedules in response to unanticipated customer demands, and (3) information systems that can help production and marketing in this process.

Table 4.5 summarizes the steps different functions must take if a company is to achieve superior responsiveness to customers. Although marketing plays the critical role in helping a company attain this goal, primarily because it represents the point of contact with the customer, Table 4.5 shows that the other functions also have major roles. Moreover, like achieving superior efficiency, quality, and innovation, achieving superior responsiveness to customers requires top management to lead in building a customer orientation within the company.

Summary of Chapter

1. A company can increase efficiency through a number of steps: exploiting economies of scale and learning effects, adopting flexible manufacturing technologies, reducing customer defection rates, implementing just-in-time systems, getting the R&D function to design products that are easy to manufacture, upgrading the skills of employees through training, introducing self-managing teams, linking pay to performance, building a companywide commitment to efficiency through strong leadership, and designing structures that facilitate cooperation among different functions in pursuit of efficiency goals.

2. Superior quality can help a company lower its costs, differentiate its product, and charge a premium price.

3. Achieving superior quality demands an organization-wide commitment to quality and a clear focus on the customer. It also requires metrics to measure quality goals and incentives that emphasize quality, input from employees regarding ways in which quality can be improved, a methodology for tracing defects to their source and correcting the problems that produce them, a rationalization of the company's supply base, cooperation with the suppliers that remain to implement total quality management programs, products

that are designed for ease of manufacturing, and substantial cooperation among functions.

4. The failure rate of new-product introductions is high because of factors such as uncertainty, poor commercialization, poor positioning strategy, slow cycle time, and technological myopia.

5. To achieve superior innovation, a company must build skills in basic and applied research, design good processes for managing development projects, and achieve close integration among the different functions of the company primarily through the adoption of cross-functional product development teams and partly parallel development processes.

6. To achieve superior responsiveness to customers often requires that the company achieve superior efficiency, quality, and innovation.

7. To achieve superior responsiveness to customers, a company needs to give customers what they want, when they want it. It must ensure a strong customer focus, which can be attained by emphasizing customer focus through leadership, training employees to think like customers, bringing customers into the company through superior market research, customizing products to the unique needs of individual customers or customer groups, and responding quickly to customer demands.

Discussion Questions

1. How are the four generic building blocks of competitive advantage related to each other?

2. What role can top management play in helping a company achieve superior efficiency, quality, innovation, and responsiveness to customers?

3. In the long run, will adoption of Six Sigma quality improvement processes give a company a competitive advantage, or will it be required just to achieve parity with competitors?

4. In what sense might innovation be called the single most important building block of competitive advantage?

Practicing Strategic Management

SMALL-GROUP EXERCISE
Identifying Excellence

Break up into groups of three to five. Appoint one group member as a spokesperson who will communicate your findings to the class.

You are the management team of a start-up company that will produce hard disk drives for the personal computer industry. You will sell your product to manufacturers of personal computers (original equipment manufacturers). The disk drive market is characterized by rapid technological change, product life cycles of only six to nine months, intense price competition, high fixed costs for manufacturing equipment, and substantial manufacturing economies of scale. Your customers, the original equipment manufacturers, issue very demanding technological specifications that your product has to comply with. They also pressure you to deliver your product on time so that it fits in with their own product introduction schedule.

1. In this industry, what functional competencies are the most important for you to build?

2. How will you design your internal processes to ensure that those competencies are built within the company?

ARTICLE FILE 4

Choose a company that is widely regarded as excellent. Identify the source of its excellence, and relate it to the material discussed in this chapter. Pay particular attention to the role played by the various functions in building excellence.

STRATEGIC MANAGEMENT PROJECT
Module 4

This module deals with the ability of your company to achieve superior efficiency, quality, innovation, and responsiveness to customers. With the information you have at your disposal, answer the questions and perform the tasks listed:

1. Is your company pursuing any of the efficiency-enhancing practices discussed in this chapter?
2. Is your company pursuing any of the quality-enhancing practices discussed in this chapter?
3. Is your company pursuing any of the practices designed to enhance innovation discussed in this chapter?
4. Is your company pursuing any of the practices designed to increase responsiveness to customers discussed in this chapter?
5. Evaluate the competitive position of your company in the light of your answers to questions 1–4. Explain what, if anything, the company needs to do to improve its competitive position.

ETHICS EXERCISE

A group of men and women from the beverage company ColaSmart were sitting around a large conference table suggesting marketing ideas for their new green-tea soft drink. The group was getting nowhere. Suddenly, Frank, the group's leader, called out, "Okay, what will get consumers fired up? What's one of the main concerns of adults in today's society? Fat loss, right? So what about referring to our drink as 'the fat burner?'"

A couple of people perked up. "Yeah, people will certainly buy it if they think it will help them burn fat and lose weight!"

One man, sitting at the end of the table, raised his hand. "What's up, Mike?" Frank called out.

"What if," Mike began, "people buy our drink, thinking it will burn fat, and it doesn't? If we're going to make a claim like that, shouldn't we do some tests first—make sure our claim will stand up under scrutiny?"

"Nah!" Frank scoffed. "We're selling to suckers, people who will want to believe it and who will blame themselves if it doesn't work. They'll keep trying it again and again because they'll want to believe that fat loss can be as easy as consuming a drink."

Most of the people in the room, eager for the profits the drink could provide, piped up in favor of the fat-burning claim. Only Mike and another woman from the group were against the idea.

1. Describe the ethical dilemmas presented in this case.
2. Should Mike voice his concerns to the company before the marketing campaign is solidified?
3. Do you think making an unsubstantiated claim is a breach of ethics?

CLOSING CASE

Verizon Wireless

In the wireless telecommunications industry, one metric above all others determines a company's profitability: customer churn, or the number of subscribers who leave a service within a given time period. Churn is important because it costs between $300 and $400 to acquire a customer. With monthly bills in the United States averaging $50, it can take six to eight months just to recoup the fixed costs of a customer acquisition. If churn rates are higher, profitability is eaten up by the costs of acquiring customers who do not stay long enough to provide a profit to the service provider.

The risk of churn increased significantly in the United States after November 2003, when the Federal Communications Commission allowed wireless subscribers to take their numbers with them when they switched to a new service provider. Over the next few years, a clear winner emerged in the battle to limit customer defections: Verizon Wireless. By mid-2006,

Verizon's churn rate was 0.87% a month, implying that 12% of the company's customers were leaving the service each year. While this might sound high, it was considerably lower than the churn rate at its competitors. The monthly churn rate at Cingular Wireless was 1.5%, at Sprint Nextel it was 2.1%, and at T-Mobile it was 2.2%.

Verizon's low churn rate has enabled the company to grow its subscriber base faster than rivals, which allows the company to better achieve economies of scale by spreading the fixed costs of building a wireless network over a larger customer base. In the quarter ending June 30, 2006, Verizon added 1.8 million customers, bringing its total up to 54 million. These customer additions easily outpaced those of its rivals Cingular, which added 1.5 million subscribers to bring its base up to 57 million, and Sprint, which added 0.7 million subscribers to bring its base up to 52 million.

There are several reasons for Verizon's success. First, in its early years, the company invested heavily in building a high-quality nationwide wireless network. It has the largest coverage area of any wireless provider and has successfully differentiated itself on the quality of its service. Customers report clearer connections and fewer dropped calls on the Verizon network than on any other network.

A technological choice has also played into this advantage. Verizon is one of two U.S. wireless companies that took a chance and bet on a new wireless technology know as CDMA (the other was Sprint). CDMA is less costly to install than a competing wireless technology, known as GSM, and is well suited to providing broadband services, such as wireless connections to the Internet. When Verizon chose to build a nationwide CDMA network, the technology was unproven and critics questioned its reliability and cost. But the critics were wrong, and Verizon now has an advantage over most of its competitors, who opted for the more established GSM technology. Utilizing the broadband capabilities of its CDMA network, in 2005, Verizon was the first wireless provider to offer a nationwide broadband service that allows subscribers to connect to the Internet in major metropolitan areas via a laptop or cell phone. This may well prove to be another source of differential advantage.

Verizon has communicated its coverage and quality advantage to customers with its "Test Man" advertisements. In these ads, a Verizon Test Man wearing horn-rimmed glasses and a Verizon uniform wanders around remote spots in the nation asking on his Verizon cell phone, "Can you hear me now?" Verizon says that the Test Man is actually the personification of a crew of fifty Verizon employees who each drive some 100,000 miles annually in specially outfitted vehicles to test the reliability of Verizon's network.

To further reduce customer churn, Verizon has invested heavily in its customer care function. Almost as soon as new customers receive their first monthly bill, Verizon Wireless representatives are on the phone, asking how they like the service. In that same call, a Verizon representative will ask what parts of the service a customer isn't using. If someone isn't yet using voice mail, for example, the representative will offer to set it up and get it working.

In addition, Verizon's automated software programs analyze the call habits of individual customers. Using that information, Verizon representatives will contact customers and suggest alternative calling plans that might better suit their needs. For example, Verizon might contact a customer and say, "We see that because of your heavy use on weekends, an alternative calling plan might make more sense for you and help reduce your monthly bills." The goal is to anticipate customer needs and proactively satisfy them, rather than have the customer take the initiative and possibly switch to another service provider.[56]

Case Discussion Questions

1. Do Verizon have a distinctive competency? If so, what is the source of that competency?

2. How do Verizon's customer service capabilities and coverage affect the quality of its service offering? How do you think they affect Verizon's cost structure? What are the implications for Verizon's long-run profitability and profit growth?

3. How would you characterize Verizon's business-level strategy (note, we discuss business-level strategy in detail in the next chapter)? How do the company's functional strategies enable it to implement its business-level strategy?

4. Do you think that Verizon has a sustainable competitive advantage in the wireless business?

Building Competitive Advantage Through Business-Level Strategy

Chapter 5: Building Competitive Advantage ... In December 2006, it had invested ...

OPENING CASE

E*Trade's Changing Business Strategies

In many industries, new entrants have taken advantage of the opportunities opened up by the Internet to overcome barriers to entry and compete successfully against market leaders. Consider the situation of E*Trade, the online brokerage company. For many years, large, established bricks-and-mortar brokerages like Merrill Lynch and Shearson Lehman had dominated the industry and used their protected positions to charge high brokerage fees, often over $100 per stock trade. Then in the 1990s, online entrepreneurs began to develop software that would allow them to offer online brokerage service, and one of the first online brokers was E*Trade, whose Internet software trading platform allowed customers to make their own trades online and to do so at a price that originally was set at $19.95—many times lower than before.

The low-cost competition story in the online brokerage industry did not stop there. In the last decade, E*Trade has repeatedly come under pressure from a succession of new online brokerage houses such as Schwab, TD Ameritrade, and Scottrade, which offered stock trades for fees that range from $9.95 to $4.95, undercutting E*Trade's prices by 100% or more. How could E*Trade, which had made its reputation by being the low-cost leader in the industry, compete against companies that now boasted that they were the new cost leaders?

E*Trade was forced to reduce its fee to $9.95 per trade, but to avoid further decreases, it decided to pursue a business model based on enhancing its differentiated appeal to customers by offering them a higher quality of service and a broader product line. E*Trade introduced new improved software that made it even easier for customers to use the Internet to research and trade shares, and it began offering them personalized financial advice. In addition, E*Trade's new package offered customers more financial research tools, such as streaming stock quotes that provide information on changes in stock prices in real time so that customers could take advantage of second-to-second changes in stock prices. It also provided them with investment reports that gave them access to more information about specific companies to improve their investment decisions. Finally, E*Trade decided to merge with an online bank, TeleBank, so that it could offer its customers a broad range of online banking services, such as online bill paying, CDs, and check-writing services, and thus become a one-stop online shopping site for all of a customer's financial needs. It also took over a variety of other financial service companies to offer its customers a broad financial service product line, such as auto and mortgage loans.

The realization that it could not just be a low-cost company but also had to create a differentiation advantage in the quickly evolving online financial services industry paid off for E*Trade. All these strategies helped to increase its customers' switching costs and keep them loyal; they did not move to the lowest-cost online broker because they perceived that they were receiving extra value in terms of service and reliability for the $9.95 price, and E*Trade's customer accounts increased steadily over time—as did its stock price.

In December 2006, it faced a new challenge, however, when Bank of America moved aggressively into the online brokerage business by offering customers *free* online brokerage service, with up to 30 free trades per month, provided they agreed to open an account with the bank and keep at least $25,000 in the account. This was a major challenge to E*Trade, (and all the other discount brokers) from a well-known brand name, and its stock price fell sharply as investors questioned if its competitive advantage is sustainable. In January 2007, the jury was still out, E*Trade announced it would not match Bank of America's offer of free online brokerage service, and the latter was beginning to aggressively roll out its free service nationally.[1]

OVERVIEW

As the Opening Case suggests, this chapter examines how a company selects and pursues a business model that will allow it to compete effectively in an industry and grow its profits and profitability. A successful business model results from business-level strategies that create a competitive advantage over rivals and achieve superior performance in an industry.

In Chapter 2, we examined how the competitive forces at work inside an industry affect its profitability. As industry forces change, so they change the profitability of an industry, and thus the profitability of any particular business model. Industry analysis is vital in formulating a successful business model because it determines (1) how existing companies will decide to change their business-level strategies to improve the performance of their business model over time, (2) whether or not established companies outside an industry may decide to create a business model to enter it, and (3) whether entrepreneurs can devise a business model that will allow them to compete successfully against existing companies in an industry.

In Chapter 3, we examined how competitive advantage depends on a company developing a business model that allows it to achieve superior efficiency, quality, innovation, and customer responsiveness, the building blocks of competitive advantage. And in Chapter 4, we discussed how every function must develop the distinctive competencies that allow a company to implement a business model that will lead to superior performance and competitive advantage in an industry.

In this chapter, we examine the competitive decisions involved in creating a business model that will attract and retain customers, and continue to do so over time, so that a company enjoys growing profits and profitability. To create a successful business model, strategic managers must (1) formulate business-level strategies that will allow a company to attract customers away from other companies in the industry (its competitors), and (2) implement those business-level strategies, which also involves the use of functional-level strategies to increase responsiveness to customers, efficiency, innovation, and quality.

By the end of this chapter, you will be able to distinguish between the principal generic business models and business-level strategies that a company uses to obtain a competitive advantage over its rivals. You will also understand why, and under what circumstances, strategic leaders of companies like E*Trade and Bank of America change their companies' strategies over time to pursue different kinds of business models to try to increase their competitive advantage over industry rivals.

Competitive Positioning and the Business Model

To create a successful business model, managers must choose a set of business-level strategies that work together to give a company a competitive advantage over its rivals; that is, they must optimize **competitive positioning**. As we noted in Chapter 1, to craft a successful business model, a company must first define its business, which entails decisions about (1) customers' needs, or what is to be satisfied; (2) customer groups, or who is to be satisfied; and (3) distinctive competencies, or how customer needs are to be satisfied.[2] The decisions managers make about these three issues determine which set of strategies they formulate and implement to put a company's business model into action and create value for customers. Consequently, we need to examine the principal choices facing managers as they make these three decisions.

● **Formulating the Business Model: Customer Needs and Product Differentiation**

Customer needs are desires, wants, or cravings that can be satisfied by means of the attributes or characteristics of a product—a good or service. For example, a person's craving for something sweet can be satisfied by a box of Godiva chocolates, a carton of Ben & Jerry's ice cream, a Snickers bar, or a spoonful of sugar. Two factors determine which product a customer chooses to satisfy these needs: (1) the way a product is differentiated from other products of its type so that it appeals to customers, and (2) the price of the product. All companies must differentiate their products to a certain degree to attract customers. Some companies, however, decide to offer customers a low-priced product and do not engage in much product differentiation. Companies that seek to create something unique about their product differentiate their products to a much greater degree than others so that they satisfy customers' needs in ways other products cannot.

Product differentiation is the process of designing products to satisfy customers' needs. A company obtains a competitive advantage when it creates, makes, and sells a product in a way that better satisfies customer needs than its rivals do. Here, the four building blocks of competitive advantage come into play because a company's decision to pursue one or more of these building blocks determines its approach to product differentiation. If managers devise strategies to differentiate a product by innovation, excellent quality, or responsiveness to customers, they are choosing a business model based on offering customers *differentiated products*. On the other hand, if managers base their business model on finding ways to increase efficiency and reliability to reduce costs, they are choosing a business model based on offering customers *low-priced products*.

Creating unique or distinctive products can be achieved in countless different ways, which explains why there are usually many different companies competing in an industry. Distinctiveness obtained from the physical characteristics of a product commonly results from pursuing innovation or quality, such as when a company focuses on developing state-of-the-art car safety systems or on engineering an SUV to give it sports-car-like handling, something Porsche and BMW strive to achieve.

Similarly, companies might try to design their cars with features such as butter-soft, hand-sewn leather interiors; fine wood fittings; and sleek, exciting body styling to appeal to customers' psychological needs, such as a personal need for prestige, status, or to declare a particular lifestyle, something Mercedes-Benz and Lexus strive for.[3]

Differentiation has another important aspect. Companies that invest their resources to create something distinct or different about their products can often charge a *higher,* or *premium, price* for their product. For example, superb design or technical sophistication allows companies to charge more for their products because customers are willing to pay these higher prices. Porsche and Mercedes-Benz buyers pay a high premium price to enjoy their sophisticated vehicles, as do customers of Godiva chocolates, which retail for about $26 a pound—much more than, say, a box of Whitman's candies or Hershey chocolates.

Consider the high-price segment of the car market, where customers are willing to pay more than $35,000 to satisfy their needs for a personal luxury vehicle. In this segment, Cadillac, Mercedes-Benz, Infiniti, BMW, Jaguar, Lexus, Lincoln, Audi, Volvo, Acura, and others are engaged in a continuing battle to design the perfect luxury vehicle—the one that best meets the needs of those who want such a vehicle. Over time, the companies that attract the most luxury car buyers—because they have designed the cars that possess the innovative features or excellent quality and reliability these customers desire the most—are the ones that achieve a sustained competitive advantage over rivals. For example, some customers value a sporty ride and performance handling; Mercedes-Benz and BMW, because of their cutting-edge technical design, can offer this driving experience better than any other automaker. Toyota's Lexus division is well known for the smoothness and quietness of its cars and their exceptional reliability. Lexus cars consistently outrank all other cars in published reliability rankings, and this excellence appeals to a large group of customers who appreciate these qualities. Volvo has a reputation for producing safe cars, and Rolls-Royce has a reputation for prestige cars. Other luxury carmakers have not fared so well. Cadillac, Lincoln, Audi, Acura, and Infiniti have found it more difficult to differentiate their cars, which sometimes compare unfavorably to their rivals in terms of ride, comfort, safety, or reliability. Although these less successful companies still sell many cars, customers often find their needs better satisfied by the attributes and qualities of their rivals' cars, and it is the latter that make above-average industry profits.

Even in the luxury car segment, however, carmakers must be concerned with efficiency because price affects a buying decision, even for highly differentiated products. Luxury carmakers compete to offer customers the car with the ride, performance, and features that provide them with the most value (satisfies their needs best) given the price of the car. Thus, Lexus cars are always several thousand dollars less than comparable cars, and Toyota can price these cars lower because of its low cost structure. For example, the Lexus LS430, introduced in 2006 at around $56,000, is about $20,000 less than the BMW 7 Series and Mercedes S Class, its nearest rivals. Most customers are discriminating and match price to differentiation even in the luxury car segment of the market, so BMW and Mercedes have to offer customers something that justifies their vehicles' higher prices.

At every price range in the car market—under $15,000, from $15,000 to $25,000, $25,000 to $35,000, and the luxury segment above $35,000—many models of cars compete to attract customers. For each price range, a carmaker has to decide how best to differentiate a particular car model to suit the needs of customers in that price range. Typically, the more differentiated a product is, the more it will cost to design and produce, and so differentiation leads to a higher cost structure. Thus, if a carmaker is to stay within the $15,000 to $25,000 price range and yet design and produce a differentiated car that will give it a competitive advantage and allow it to outperform its rivals in the same price range, its strategic managers have to make crucial and difficult decisions. They have to forecast what features customers will most value; for example, they may decide to trade off styling, safety, and performance so that the car will not cost too much to produce, enabling them to make a profit and to still sell the car for less than $25,000.

In sum, in devising a business model, strategic managers are always constrained by the need to differentiate their products against the need to keep their cost structure under control so that they can offer the product at a competitive price—a price that offers customers as much or more value than the products of its rivals. Companies that have built a competitive advantage through innovation, quality, and reliability can differentiate their products more successfully than their rivals can. In turn, because customers perceive there is more value in their products, these companies can charge a premium price.

● **Formulating the Business Model: Customer Groups and Market Segmentation**

The second main choice involved in formulating a successful business model is to decide which kind of product(s) to offer to which customer group(s). Customer groups are the sets of people who share a similar need for a particular product. Because a particular product usually satisfies several different kinds of desires and needs, many different customer groups normally exist in a market. In the car market, for example, some customers want basic transportation, some want top-of-the-line luxury, and others want the thrill of driving a sports car: these are three of the customer groups in the car market.

In the athletic shoe market, the two main customer groups are those people who use them for sporting purposes and those who like to wear them because they are casual and comfortable. Each customer group often includes subgroups composed of people who have an even more specific need for a product. Inside the group of people who buy athletic shoes for sporting purposes, for example, are subgroups of people who buy shoes suited to a specific kind of activity, such as running, aerobics, walking, and soccer (see Figure 5.1).

A company searching for a successful business model has to group customers according to the similarities or differences in their needs to discover what kinds of

FIGURE 5.1

Identifying Customer Groups and Market Segments

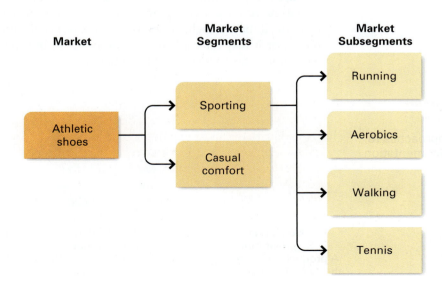

products to develop for different kinds of customers. The marketing function performs research to discover a group of customers' primary needs for a product, how they will use it, and their income or buying power (to determine the balance between differentiation and price). Other important attributes of a customer group are then identified that more narrowly target their specific needs. Once a group of customers who share a similar or specific need for a product has been identified, this group is treated as a market segment. Companies then decide whether to make and sell a product designed to satisfy the specific needs of this customer segment.

THREE APPROACHES TO MARKET SEGMENTATION Market segmentation is the way a company decides to group customers, based on important differences in their needs or preferences, in order to gain a competitive advantage.[4] First, the company must segment the market according to how much customers are able and willing to pay for a particular product—such as the different price ranges for cars mentioned above. Once price has been taken into consideration, customers can be segmented according to the specific needs that are being satisfied by a particular product, such as the economy, luxury, or speed of the cars mentioned above.

In crafting a business model, managers have to think strategically about which segments they are going to compete in and how they will differentiate their products for each segment. In other words, once market segments have been identified, a company has to decide how *responsive it should be to the needs of customers in the different segments.* This decision determines a particular company's product range. There are three main approaches toward market segmentation in devising a business model (see Figure 5.2):

- First, a company might choose not to recognize that different market segments exist and make a product targeted at the average or typical customer. In this case, customer responsiveness is at a *minimum*, and the focus is on price, not differentiation.

- Second, a company can choose to recognize the differences between customer groups and make a product targeted toward most or all of the different market segments. In this case, customer responsiveness is *high* and products are being *customized* to meet the specific needs of customers in each group, so the emphasis is on differentiation, not price.

- Third, a company might choose to target just *one or two market segments* and devote its resources to developing products for customers in just these segments. In this case, it may be highly responsive to the needs of customers in only these segments, or it may offer a bare-bones product to undercut the prices charged by companies who do focus on differentiation.

FIGURE 5.2

Three Approaches to
Market Segmentation

**No Market
Segmentation**
A product is targeted at
the "average customer."

**High Market
Segmentation**
A different product is offered
to each market segment.

**Focused Market
Segmentation**
A product is offered to one
or a few market segments.

Since a company's cost structure and operating costs increase when it makes a different product for each market segment rather than just one product for the whole market, why would a company devise a business model based on serving customers in multiple market segments? The answer is that, although operating costs increase, the decision to produce a range of products that are closely aligned with the needs of customers in different market segments attracts many more customers (because responsiveness to customers increases), and therefore sales revenues and profits increase. A car company that offers a wide range of cars customized to the needs of customers in different market segments increases the number of cars it can sell. As long as a company's revenues increase faster than its operating costs as its product range expands, profitability increases.

This does *not* mean that all companies should decide to produce a wide range of products aimed at each market segment to increase their profitability. It depends on how much customer needs for a product differ in a particular market or industry. In some industries, like cars, customer needs differ widely. There are considerable differences in buyers' primary needs for a car: income levels, lifestyles, ages, and so on. For this reason, major global carmakers broaden their product range and make vehicles to serve most market segments. A company that produces just one car model, compared to a company that produces twenty-five models, may find itself at a serious competitive disadvantage.

On the other hand, in some markets, customers have similar needs for a product and so the relative price of competing products drives their buying choices. In this situation, a company that chooses to use its resources to make and sell a single product as inexpensively as possible might gain a major competitive advantage. The average customer buys the product because it's a good value for the money. This is the business model followed by companies that specialize in making a low-cost product, such as BIC, which makes low-cost razors and ballpoint pens, and Arm & Hammer, which makes baking soda. These are products that most people use in the same way. This is also the business model followed by companies like Wal-Mart, with its mission to buy products from suppliers as cheaply as possible and then sell them to customers at the lowest possible prices. BIC and Wal-Mart do not segment the market; they decide to serve the needs of customers who want to buy products as inexpensively as possible. Wal-Mart promises everyday low prices and price rollbacks; BIC promises the lowest-priced razor blades that work acceptably.

The third approach to market segmentation is to target a product just at one or two market segments. To pursue this approach, a company must develop something very special or distinctive about its product to attract a large share of customers in those particular market segments. In the car market, for example, Rolls-Royce and Porsche target their products at specific market segments. Porsche, for example, targets its well-known sports cars at buyers in the high-priced sports car segment. In a similar way, specialty retailers compete for customers in a particular market segment, such as the segment composed of affluent people who can afford to buy expensive handmade clothing, or people who enjoy wearing trendy shoes such as Nike's Converse brand. A retailer might also specialize in a particular style of clothing, such as western wear, beachwear, or accessories. In many markets, these are enormous opportunities for small companies to specialize in satisfying the needs of a specific market segment. Often, these companies can better satisfy their customers' needs because they are so close to them and understand how their needs are changing over time.

Market segmentation is an evolving, ongoing process that presents considerable opportunities for strategic managers to improve their company's business model. For example, in the car industry, savvy strategists often identify a new customer group whose specific needs have not been met and who have had to "satisfice" and buy a model that does not meet their needs exactly but is a reasonable compromise. Now a car company can decide to treat this group as a market segment and create a product designed to meet group members' specific needs; if it makes the right choice, it has a blockbuster product. This was the origin of the minivan, sports utility vehicle, and all the recently introduced hybrid vehicles like the Honda Pilot, Toyota Prius, or Dodge Magnum. In the case of SUVs, many car buyers wanted a more rugged and powerful vehicle capable of holding many people or towing heavy loads. They liked the comfort of a car but also the qualities of a pickup; by combining the characteristics of both, carmakers created the SUV market segment. If managers make mistakes, however, and design a product for a market segment that is much smaller than they expected, the opposite can occur. In 2005, for example, Ford announced that it was ending production of its expensive luxury Lincoln truck and Excursion SUV because sales had been only in the hundreds a year, not the thousands a year it had projected.

● Implementing the Business Model: Building Distinctive Competencies

To develop a successful business model, strategic managers have to devise a set of strategies that determine (1) how to differentiate and price their product and (2) how much to segment a market and how wide a range of products to develop. Whether these strategies will result in a profitable business model now depends on strategic managers' ability to implement their business model, that is, to choose strategies that will create products that provide customers with the most value, while keeping their cost structure viable (because of the need to be price competitive).

In practice, this involves deciding how to invest a company's capital to build and shape distinctive competencies that result in a competitive advantage based on superior efficiency, quality, innovation, and/or responsiveness to customers. Hence, implementing a company's business model sets in motion *the specific set of functional-level strategies needed to create a successful differentiation and low-cost business strategy.* We discussed how functional strategies can build competitive advantage in Chapter 4. The better the fit between a company's business strategy and its functional-level strategies, the more value and profit a company creates.

Figure 5.3 illustrates Wal-Mart's business model. Sam Walton, the company's founder, devised a business model based on the strategy of keeping operating costs to a minimum so that he could offer customers everyday low prices and continuous price rollbacks. To this end, Walton chose business-level strategies to increase efficiency, such as having low product differentiation (Wal-Mart chooses minimal advertising and low responsiveness to customers) and targeting the mass market. His discount retail business model was based on the idea that lower costs mean lower prices.

Having devised a way to compete for customers, Walton's task was now to implement the business model in ways that would create a low-cost structure to allow him to charge lower prices. One business-level strategy he implemented was to locate his stores outside large cities, in small towns where there were no low-cost competitors; a second was to find ways to manage the value chain to reduce the costs of getting products from manufacturers to customers; and a third was to design and staff store operations to increase efficiency. The task of all functional managers in logistics, materials management, sales and customer service, store management, and so on, was to implement specific functional-level strategies that supported the low-cost/low-price business model. Figure 5.3 illustrates some of the thousands of specific choices that Wal-Mart has made to allow it to implement its business model successfully.

FIGURE 5.3

Wal-Mart's Business Model

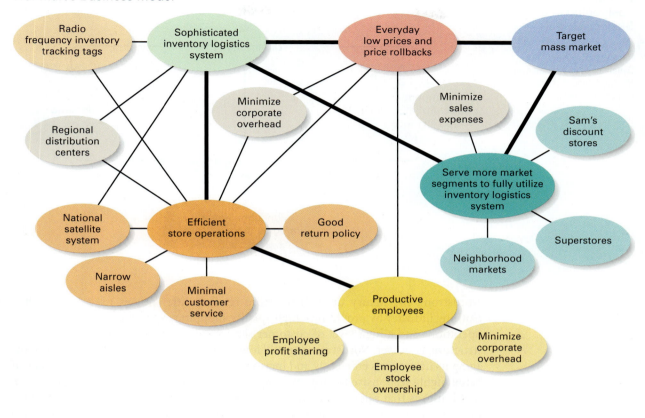

Competitive Positioning and Business-Level Strategy

Figure 5.4 presents a way of thinking about the competitive positioning decisions that strategic managers make to create a successful business model.[5] The decision to differentiate a product increases its perceived value to the customer so that market demand for the product increases. Differentiation is expensive, however; for example, additional expenditures on resources are needed to improve product quality or support a higher level of service. Therefore, the decision to increase product differentiation also raises a company's cost structure and results in a higher unit cost. In some cases, however, if increased demand for the product allows a company to make large volumes of the product and achieve economies of scale, these economies can offset some of these extra costs; this effect is showed by the dotted line in Figure 5.4.[6]

To maximize profitability, managers must choose a premium pricing option that compensates for the extra costs of product differentiation but is not so high that it chokes off the increase in expected demand (to prevent customers from deciding that the extra differentiation is not worth the higher price). Once again, to increase profitability, managers must also search for other ways to reduce the cost structure, but not in ways that will harm the differentiated appeal of their products. There are many specific functional strategies a company can adopt to achieve this. For example,

FIGURE 5.4

Competitive
Positioning at the
Business Level

Source: Copyright © C. W. L.
Hill and G. R. Jones, "The
Dynamics of Business-Level
Strategy" (unpublished
manuscript, 2005).

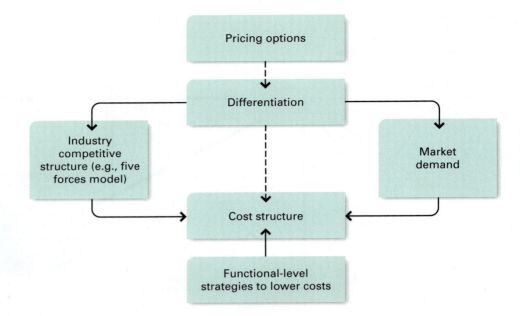

Nordstrom, the luxury department store retailer, differentiates itself in the retail clothing industry by providing a high-quality shopping experience with elegant store operations and a high level of customer service, all of which raise Nordstrom's cost structure. However, Nordstrom can still lower its cost structure by, for example, managing its inventories efficiently and increasing inventory turnover. Also, its strategy of being highly responsive to customers results in more customers and higher demand, which means that sales per square foot increase, and this revenue enables it to make more intensive use of its facilities and salespeople, which in turn leads to scale economies and lower costs. Thus, no matter what level of differentiation a company chooses to pursue in its business model, it always has to recognize the way its cost structure will vary as a result of its choice of differentiation and the other specific strategies it adopts to lower its cost structure; in other words, *differentiation and cost structure decisions affect one another.*

The last main dynamic shown in Figure 5.4 concerns the impact of the industry's competitive structure on a company's differentiation, cost structure, and pricing choices. Recall that strategic decision making takes place in an environment where watchful and agile competitors exist; therefore, one company's choice of competitive positioning is always made *with reference to those of its competitors.* If, for example, competitors start to offer products with new or improved features, a company may be forced to increase its level of differentiation to remain competitive, even if this reduces its profitability. Similarly, if competitors decide to develop products for new market segments, the company will have to follow suit or lose its competitive edge. Thus, because differentiation increases costs, increasing industry competition can drive up a company's cost structure. When that happens, a company's ability to charge a premium price to cover these high costs depends on whether its profitability increases or decreases.

In sum, maximizing the profitability of a company's business model is about making the right choices with regard to value creation through differentiation, costs, and pricing given both the demand conditions in the company's market and the competitive conditions in the company's industry. Because *all the different variables in Figure 5.4 change as the others change,* managers can never accurately predict the outcome of their decisions. This is why devising and managing a successful business model is such a difficult thing to do—and why effective strategic leadership is vital.

Competitive Positioning: Generic Business-Level Strategies

As we discussed above, a successful business model is the result of the way a company formulates and implements a set of business-level strategies to achieve a fit among its differentiation, cost, and pricing options. While no diagram can ever model all the complexities involved in business-level strategy decisions, Figure 5.5 represents a way to bring together the three issues involved in developing a successful business model. In the figure, the vertical and horizontal axes represent, respectively, the decisions of strategic managers to position a company's products in relation to the tradeoff between differentiating products (higher costs/higher prices) and achieving the lowest cost structure or cost leadership (lower costs/lower prices). In Figure 5.5, the curve connecting the axes represents the value creation frontier: the maximum amount of value that the products of different companies in an industry can provide at any one time with different business models. In other words, companies on the value frontier are those that have the most successful and profitable business models in a particular industry.

As Figure 5.5 illustrates, the value creation frontier is reached by pursuing one or more of the four building blocks of competitive advantage (quality has been split

FIGURE 5.5

Competitive Positioning and the Value Creation Frontier

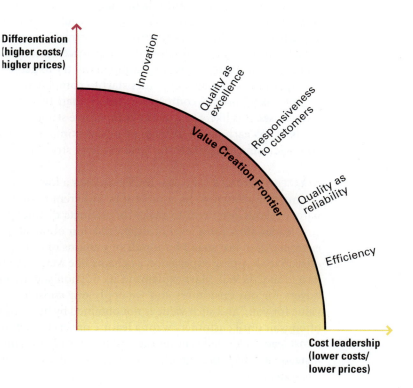

into two), which have been listed from top to bottom according to how much they can contribute to the creation of a differentiation or cost-leadership advantage. Thus innovation, a costly process that results in unique products, is closest to the differentiation axis, followed by quality as excellence, customer responsiveness, and quality as reliability; efficiency is closest to the cost-leadership axis.

To reach the value creation frontier and thus achieve above-average profitability, a company must formulate and implement a business model using one or a combination of three generic business-level strategies: cost leadership, differentiation, and focused differentiation. A **generic business-level strategy** gives a company a specific form of competitive position and advantage vis-à-vis its rivals that results in above-average profitability.[7] *Generic* means that all companies can potentially pursue these strategies regardless of whether they are manufacturing, service, or nonprofit enterprises; they are also generic because they can be pursued across different kinds of industries.

● **Cost Leadership**

A company pursuing a cost-leadership business model chooses strategies that do everything possible to lower its cost structure so it can make and sell goods or services at a lower cost than its competitors. These strategies include both functional strategies designed to improve its operating performance and competitive strategies intended to influence industry competition in its favor. In essence, a company seeks to achieve a competitive advantage and above-average profitability by developing a cost-leadership business model that positions it on the value creation frontier as close as possible to the lower costs/lower prices axis.

Two advantages accrue from pursuing cost leadership. First, if a company's closest rivals, such as those that compete in the same price range or for the same customer group, charge similar prices for their products, the cost leader will be more profitable than its competitors because of its lower costs. Second, the cost leader gains a competitive advantage by being able to charge a lower price than its competitors because of its lower cost structure. As discussed earlier, offering customers the same kind of value from a product but at a lower price attracts many more customers, so that even though the company has chosen a lower price option, the increased volume of sales will cause profits to surge. If its competitors try to get lost customers back by reducing their prices and all companies start to compete on price, the cost leader will still be able to withstand competition better than the other companies because of its lower costs. It is likely to win any competitive struggle. For these reasons, cost leaders are likely to earn above-average profits. A company becomes a cost leader when its strategic managers pursue the business-level strategic choices discussed below.

STRATEGIC CHOICES The cost leader chooses a low to moderate level of product differentiation relative to its competitors. Differentiation is expensive; the more a company expends resources to make its products distinct, the more its costs rise.[8] The cost leader aims for a level of differentiation obtainable at low cost.[9] Wal-Mart, for example, does not spend hundreds of millions of dollars on store design to create an attractive shopping experience, as chains like Macy's, Dillard's, or Saks Fifth Avenue have done. As Wal-Mart explains in its mission statement, "We think of ourselves as buyers for our customers and we apply our considerable strengths to get the best value for you," and such value is not obtained by building lavish stores.[10] Cost leaders often wait until customers want a feature or service before providing it. For example, a cost leader like Dell is never the first to offer high-quality graphics or video in a PC; instead, it adds such graphic or video capabilities only when it is obvious that customers demand it.

The cost leader also ignores the many different market segments in an industry. It positions its products to appeal to the average customer to reduce the costs of developing and selling many different products tailored to the needs of different market segments. In targeting the average customer, strategic managers try to produce or provide the least or smallest number of products that will be desired by the highest number of customers—which is at the heart of Dell's approach to building its computers or Wal-Mart's approach to stocking its stores. Thus, although customers may not get exactly the products they want, they are attracted by the lower prices.

To implement cost leadership, the overriding goal of the cost leader must be to choose strategies to increase its efficiency and lower its cost structure compared with its rivals. The development of distinctive competencies in manufacturing, materials management, and information technology is central to achieving this goal. For example, manufacturing companies pursuing a cost-leadership strategy concentrate on doing all they can to continually ride down the experience curve so that their cost structure keeps getting lower and lower. Achieving a cost-leadership position requires that a company develop skills in flexible manufacturing, adopt efficient materials-management techniques, and do all it can to increase inventory turnover and reduce the cost of goods sold. (Table 4.1 outlined the ways in which a company's functions can be used to increase efficiency.)

Consequently, for companies that make products, the manufacturing and materials-management functions are the center of attention, and the other functions shape their distinctive competencies to meet the needs of manufacturing and materials management.[11] The sales function, for example, may develop the competency of capturing large, stable sets of customers' orders. In turn, this allows manufacturing to make longer production runs and so achieve economies of scale and reduce costs. At Dell, for example, online customers are provided with a limited set of choices so that Dell can customize PCs to a customer's needs at low cost. Finding ways to customize products at low cost is an important task for managers pursuing a cost-leadership strategy. The human resources function may focus on instituting training programs and compensation systems that lower costs by improving employees' productivity, and the research and development function may specialize in process improvements to lower the manufacturing costs.

By contrast, companies supplying services, such as retail stores like Wal-Mart, must develop distinctive competencies in whatever functions contribute most to their cost structure. For Wal-Mart, this is the cost of purchasing products, so the logistics or materials-management function becomes of central importance. Wal-Mart has taken advantage of advances in information technology to lower the costs associated with getting goods from manufacturers to customers, just as Dell, the cost leader in the PC industry, uses the Internet to lower the cost of selling its computers. Another major source of cost savings in pursuing cost leadership is to choose an organizational structure and culture to implement this strategy in the most cost-efficient way. Thus, a low-cost strategy implies minimizing the number of managers in the hierarchy and the rigorous use of budgets to control production and selling costs. An interesting example of the way a company can craft a business model to become the cost leader in an industry is Ryanair, discussed in Strategy in Action 5.1.

COMPETITIVE ADVANTAGES AND DISADVANTAGES Porter's five forces model, introduced in Chapter 2, explains why each of the business models allows a company to pursue competitive strategies that help it reach the value creation frontier shown in Figure 5.5.[12] The five forces are threats from competitors, powerful suppliers, powerful

Strategy in Action

5.1

Ryanair Takes Control over the Sky in Europe

Ryanair, based in Dublin, Ireland, imitated and improved on the cost-leadership business model pioneered by Southwest Airlines in the United States and used it to become a leading player in the European air travel market. Ryanair's CEO, the flamboyant Michael O'Leary, saw the specific strategies Southwest had developed to cut costs and used the same strategies to position Ryanair as the lowest-cost, lowest-priced European airline. Today, the average cost of a Ryanair ticket within Europe is $48, compared to $330 on British Airways and $277 on Lufthansa, which have long dominated the European air travel market. The result is that Ryanair now flies more passengers inside Britain than British Airways, and its share of the European market is growing as fast as it can gain access to new landing spots and buy the new planes needed to service its expanding route structure.

O'Leary has managed to improve on Southwest's low-cost business model. Ryanair imitated the main elements of Southwest's model, such as using only one plane, the 737, to reduce maintenance costs, selling tickets directly to customers, and eliminating seat assignments and free in-flight meals. It also avoids high-cost airports like Heathrow and chooses smaller ones outside big cities, such as Luton, its London hub, just as Wal-Mart chose to move into smaller towns. However, to reduce cleanup costs, O'Leary also eliminated the seat-back pockets that often contain trash left by previous passengers, as well as blankets, pillows, free sodas and snacks, and even sick bags—anything at all a passenger might expect to receive on a more differentiated airline. "You get what you pay for" is Ryanair's philosophy. To implement his cost-leadership strategy, O'Leary and all employees are expected to find ways to wipe out or reduce the small, incremental expenses that arise in performing the tens of thousands of specific operations needed to run an airline. His goal is to eliminate all the differentiated qualities of an airline that can raise costs. Through all these tactics, Ryanair has lowered its cost structure so far that no other European airline can come close to offering its low-cost fares and break even, let alone make a profit.

The other side of Ryanair's business model is to add to its revenues by getting its customers to spend as much as possible while they are on its flights. To this end, Ryanair offers snacks, meals, and a variety of drinks to encourage customers to open their wallets. In addition, to cut costs his planes have no seatback LCD screens for viewing movies and playing games; passengers can rent a digital hand-held device for $6 a flight to watch movies and sitcoms or play games or music. Fourteen percent of its revenues come from these sources; they are so important that the airline gives away millions of its unsold seats free to customers so that it can at least get some revenue from passengers sitting in what would otherwise be empty seats.

How have competitors reacted to Ryanair's cost-leadership strategy? Some airlines have started a low-price subsidiary, just as United's TED division was created to compete with Southwest in the United States. However, this often results in cannibalization as their passengers move from the high-price to the low-price service. Some airlines that pursue the differentiation strategy, like British Airways, are not suffering because they are solidly profitable in the business segment of the market. However, other airlines, such as Air France and Alitalia, Italy's flagship airline, are close to bankruptcy, and Irish carrier Aer Lingus had to cut costs by 50% just to survive. The power of Ryanair was evident in 2006 when O'Leary announced he wanted to buy Aer Lingus, something the Irish government prevented. But it has become clear throughout the world that the cost-leadership business model is the only one that will fare well in the future, and all large national and U.S. airlines are rushing to adopt strategies that will allow them to pursue it.[a]

buyers, substitute products, and new entrants. The cost leader is protected from industry competitors by its cost advantage. Its lower costs also mean that it will be less affected than its competitors by increases in the price of inputs if there are powerful suppliers, and less affected by a fall in the prices it can charge if there are powerful buyers. Moreover, since cost leadership usually requires a large market share, the cost leader purchases in relatively large quantities, increasing its bargaining power over suppliers. If substitute products begin to come onto the market, the cost leader can reduce its price to compete with them and retain its market share. Finally, the leader's cost advantage constitutes a barrier to entry because other companies are unable to enter the industry and match the leader's costs or prices. The cost leader is therefore relatively safe as long as it can maintain its low-cost advantage.

The principal dangers of the cost-leadership approach lurk in competitors' ability to pursue new strategies that lower their cost structures and beat the cost leader at its own game—which is what happened to E*Trade in the Opening Case. For instance, if technological change makes experience-curve economies obsolete, new companies may apply lower-cost technologies that give them a cost advantage. The steel mini-mills discussed in Chapter 4 pursued this strategy to obtain a competitive advantage. Competitors may also draw a cost advantage from labor-cost savings. Global competitors located in countries overseas often have very low labor costs; wage costs in the United States are roughly 600% more than they are in Malaysia, China, or Mexico. Most U.S. companies now assemble their products abroad as part of their low-cost strategy; many are forced to do so simply to compete and stay in business.

Competitors' ability to imitate the cost leader's methods easily is another threat to the cost-leadership strategy. For example, companies in China routinely take apart the electronic products of Japanese companies like Sony and Panasonic to see how they are designed and assembled. Then, using Chinese-made components and a huge pool of inexpensive domestic labor, they manufacture clones of these products and flood the U.S. market with inexpensive tape players, radios, phones, and DVD players.

Finally, the pursuit of cost leadership carries a risk that strategic managers, in their single-minded desire to reduce costs, might make decisions that decrease costs but then drastically reduce demand for the product. This happened to Gateway in the early 2000s when, to reduce the costs of customer service, customer support people were instructed not to help customers who were experiencing problems with their new Gateway computers if they had installed their own new software on the machines. New buyers, most of whom install their own software, began to complain vociferously, and Gateway's sales began to fall as word spread. Within six months, managers had reversed their decision, and once again Gateway began offering full customer support.

● **Focused Cost Leadership**

A cost leader is not always a large, national company that targets the average customer. Sometimes a company can pursue a **focused cost leadership** business model based on combining the cost leadership and focused business-level strategies to compete for customers in just one or a few market segments. Focused cost leaders concentrate on a narrow market segment, which can be defined geographically, by type of customer, or by segment of the product line.[13] In Figure 5.6, focused cost leaders are represented by the smaller circles next to the cost leader's circle. For example, since a geographic niche can be defined by region or even by locality, a cement-making company, a carpet-cleaning business, or a pizza chain can pursue a cost-leadership strategy in one or more cities in a region. Figure 5.7 compares a focused cost-leadership business model with a pure cost-leadership model.

If a company uses a focused cost-leadership approach, it competes against the cost leader in the market segments where it can operate at no cost disadvantage. For example, in local lumber, cement, bookkeeping, or pizza delivery markets, the focuser may have lower materials or transportation costs than the national cost leader. The focuser may also have a cost advantage because it is producing complex or custom-built products that do not lend themselves easily to economies of scale in production and

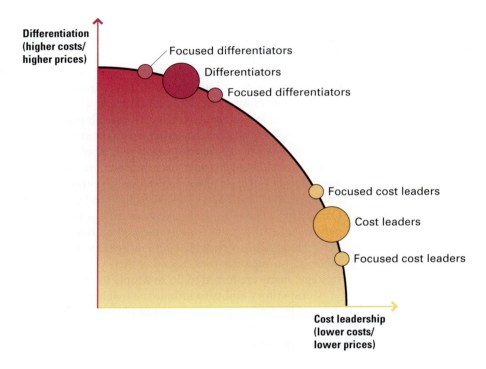

FIGURE 5.6

Generic Business Models and the Value Creation Frontier

therefore offer few cost-saving possibilities. The focused cost leader concentrates on small-volume custom products, for which it has a cost advantage, and leaves the large-volume standardized market to the national cost leader—for example, low-priced Mexican food specials versus Big Macs.

Because it has no cost disadvantage in its market segments, a focused cost leader also operates on the value creation frontier and so earns above-average profits. Such a company has a great opportunity to develop its own niche and compete against companies pursuing cost-leadership or differentiated strategies. Ryanair, for example, began as a focus company because at first it operated flights only between Dublin and London. Since there was no cost leader in the European market, it was able to quickly expand its operations; today, it is the European cost leader and its future goal seems to be to become the global cost leader! Similarly, Southwest began as a focused cost leader within the Texas market, but now it is a national air carrier and competes against new companies that pursue focused cost leadership, such as JetBlue and Song.[14]

FIGURE 5.7

Why Focus Strategies Are Different

Because a focused company makes and sells only a relatively small quantity of a product, its cost structure will often be higher than that of the cost leader. In some industries, like cars, this can make it very difficult or impossible to compete with the cost leader. Sometimes, however, by targeting some new market segment or by implementing a business model in a superior way—such as by adopting a more advanced technology—focused companies can be a threat to large cost leaders. For example, flexible manufacturing systems have opened up many new opportunities for focused companies because small production runs become possible at a lower cost. The steel mini-mills discussed in Chapter 4 provide another good example of how a focused company, in this case Nucor, can grow so efficient by specializing in one market that it becomes *the* cost leader. Similarly, the growth of the Internet has opened up many new opportunities for focused companies to develop business models based on being the cost leader compared to bricks-and-mortar companies. Amazon.com shows how effectively a company can craft a business model to become the cost leader.

IMPLICATIONS AND CONCLUSIONS To pursue cost leadership, strategic managers need to devote enormous efforts to incorporate all the latest information, materials management, and manufacturing technology into their operations to find new ways to reduce costs. Often, as we saw in Chapter 4, using new technology will also raise quality and increase responsiveness to customers. A low-cost approach requires ongoing strategic thinking to make sure the business model is aligned with changing environmental opportunities and threats.

Strategic managers in companies throughout the industry are watching the cost leader and will move quickly to imitate its innovations because they also want to reduce their costs. Today, a differentiator cannot let a cost leader obtain too great a cost advantage because the leader might then be able to use its high profits to invest more in product differentiation and beat the differentiator at its own competitive game. For example, Toyota and Honda began as cost leaders by manufacturing simple low-priced cars. Their cars sold well, and they then invested their profits to design and make new models of cars that became increasingly differentiated based on features and quality. Today, Toyota and Honda, with cars in every market segment, pursue a differentiation strategy, although Toyota also has the lowest cost structure of any global car company.

A cost leader must also respond to the strategic moves of its differentiated competitors and increase the quality and features of its products if it is to prosper in the long run. Even low-priced products, such as Timex watches and BIC razors, cannot be too inferior to the more expensive Seiko watches or Gillette razors if the lower-costs/lower-prices policy is to succeed. Companies in an industry watch the strategies their rivals are pursuing and the changes they make to those strategies. If Seiko or Swatch introduces a novel kind of LCD watch dial or Gillette introduces a three- or four-blade razor, managers at Timex and BIC will respond within months by incorporating these innovations into their low-priced products if required. This situation is also very common in the high-priced women's fashion industry. As soon as the famous designers like Gucci and Dior have shown their spring and fall collections, their designs are copied and the plans transmitted to factories in Malaysia, where workers are ready to manufacture low-priced imitations that, within months, will reach low-price clothing retail stores around the world.

A business model like cost leadership should be thought of as a specific set of strategic choices that helps a company stay focused on how to compete most effectively over time. It is all too easy for strategic managers, flush with the success of pursuing cost leadership, to become less vigilant and lose sight of changes in the five forces of competition and in the macroenvironment that change the rules of the competitive game. McDonald's, long the cost leader in the fast-food industry, was surprised when rivals like Taco Bell began to offer 99-cent daily specials. McDonald's had to learn how to make fast food more cheaply to compete, and its managers have adopted new cooking techniques and food management practices that have ratcheted it down the experience curve, so that today 99-cent meals are a permanent fixture on the McDonald's menu.

● **Differentiation**

A **differentiation** business model is based on pursuing a business-level strategy that allows a company to achieve a competitive advantage by creating a product that customers perceive as different or distinct in some important way. A differentiator (that is, a differentiated company) has the ability to satisfy customers' needs in a way that its competitors cannot. This means that it can charge a premium price (one higher than that charged by its closest rivals). The ability to increase revenues by charging premium prices (rather than by reducing costs, as the cost leader does) allows the differentiator to reach the value frontier, outperform its competitors, and achieve superior profitability, as shown in Figure 5.6. As noted earlier, customers pay a premium price when they believe the product's differentiated qualities are worth the extra money. Consequently, differentiated products are often priced on the basis of what the market will bear.[15]

Mercedes-Benz cars are more expensive than the cars of its closest rivals because customers believe they offer more features and confer more status on their owners. Similarly, a BMW is not much more expensive to produce than a Honda, but its high price determined by customers who want its distinctive sporty ride and the prestige of owning a BMW. (In fact, in Japan, BMW prices its entry cars quite modestly to attract young, well-heeled Japanese customers away from Honda.) Similarly, Rolex watches do not cost much to produce, their design has not changed very much for years, and their gold content represents only a small fraction of the price. Customers buy a Rolex, however, because of the distinct qualities they perceive in it: its beautiful design, and its ability to hold its value as well as to confer status on its wearer.

STRATEGIC CHOICES A differentiator invests its resources to gain a competitive advantage from superior innovation, excellent quality, and responsiveness to customer needs—the three principal routes to high product differentiation. For example, Procter & Gamble claims that its product quality is high and that its Ivory soap is 99.44% pure. Maytag stresses reliability and the best repair record of any other washer on the market. IBM promotes the quality service provided by its well-trained sales force. Innovation is commonly the source of differentiation for technologically complex products, and many people pay a premium price for new and innovative products, such as a state-of-the-art gaming PC, HD-DVD player, or car.

When differentiation is based on responsiveness to customers, a company offers comprehensive after-sales service and product repair. This is an especially important consideration for complex products such as cars and domestic appliances, which are likely to break down periodically. Maytag, Dell, and BMW all excel in responsiveness to customers. In service organizations, quality-of-service attributes are also very important. Neiman Marcus, Nordstrom, and FedEx can charge premium prices because they offer an exceptionally high level of service. Firms of lawyers, accountants, and consultants stress the service aspects—their knowledge, professionalism, and reputation— of their operations to clients.

Finally, a product's appeal to customers' psychological desires is a source of differentiation. The appeal can be prestige or status, as it is with BMWs and Rolex watches; safety of home and family, as with Aetna or Prudential Insurance; or simply providing a superior shopping experience, as with Target and Macy's. Differentiation can also be tailored to age groups and socioeconomic groups. Indeed, the bases of differentiation are endless.

A company pursuing a business model based on differentiation frequently strives to differentiate itself along as many dimensions as possible. The less it resembles its rivals, the more it is protected from competition and the wider is its market appeal. Thus, BMWs offer more than prestige; they also offer technological sophistication, luxury, reliability, and good (albeit very expensive) repair service. All these bases of differentiation help increase sales.

Generally, a differentiator chooses to divide its market into many segments and niches and to offer different products in each segment, just as Toyota and Dell do. Strategic managers recognize how much revenue can be increased when each of a company's products, targeted at different market segments, can attract more customers. A differentiator only targets the market segments in which customers are willing to pay a premium price, however. For example, Sony produces many TV models, but it targets only the niches from mid-priced to high-priced sets, and its lowest-priced model is always a few hundred dollars above that of its competitors, thus bringing into play the premium-price factor. Customers have to pay extra for a Sony.

Finally, in choosing how to implement its business model, a differentiated company concentrates on developing distinctive competencies in the functions that provide the source of its competitive advantage. Differentiation on the basis of innovation and technological competency depends on the R&D function, as discussed in Chapter 4. Efforts to improve service to customers depend on the quality of the sales and customer service function.

Pursuing a business model based on differentiation is expensive, so a differentiator has a cost structure that is higher than that of a cost leader. Building new competencies in the functions necessary to sustain a company's differentiated appeal does not mean neglecting the cost structure, however. Even differentiators benchmark how cost leaders operate to find ways to imitate their cost-saving innovations while preserving the source of their competitive advantage. A differentiator must control its cost structure to ensure that the price of its products does not exceed the price that customers are willing to pay for them, as noted in Nordstrom's case. Also, superior profitability is a function of a company's cost structure, so it is important to keep costs under control but not to reduce them so far that a company loses the source of its differentiated appeal.[16] The owners of the famous Savoy Hotel in London, England, face just this problem. The Savoy's reputation has always been based on the incredibly high level of service it offers its customers. Three hotel employees serve the needs of each guest, and in every room, a guest can summon a waiter, maid, or valet by pressing a button at bedside. The cost of offering this level of service has been so high that the hotel used to make less than 1% net profit every year; to increase profit, a room today costs at least $500 a night![17] Its owners try to find ways to reduce costs to increase profits, but if they reduce the number of hotel staff (the main source of the Savoy's high costs), they may destroy the main source of its differentiated appeal.

COMPETITIVE ADVANTAGES AND DISADVANTAGES The advantages of the differentiation strategy can also be discussed in the context of the five forces model. Differentiation safeguards a company against competitors to the degree that customers develop brand loyalty for its products, a valuable asset that protects the company on all fronts. Powerful suppliers are less of a problem because the differentiated company's strategy is geared more toward the price it can charge than toward costs. Also, differentiators can often pass on price increases to customers because they are willing to pay the premium price. Thus, a differentiator can tolerate moderate increases in input prices better than the cost leader can. Differentiators are unlikely to experience problems with powerful buyers because they offer a distinct product; only they can supply the product and it commands brand loyalty. Differentiation and brand loyalty also create a barrier for other companies seeking to enter the industry. A new company has to find a way to make its own product distinctive to be able to compete, which involves an expensive investment in building some kind of distinctive competence.

Finally, substitute products are a threat only if a competitor can develop a product that satisfies a customer need like the differentiator's product does and so customers switch to the lower-priced product. Wired phone companies have suffered as lower-cost alternative ways of making phone calls, through digital fiber-optic cable, satellite, and the Internet, are becoming increasingly available. The issue is how much of a premium price a company can charge for distinctness before customers switch products. In the phone industry, the answer is: Not much. The large carriers have reduced prices drastically; 2.5 cents a minute is a common rate, down from 37 cents just a decade ago.

The main problems with a differentiation strategy center on how well strategic managers can maintain a product's perceived difference or distinctness in the eyes of customers. In the 2000s, it has become clear that it is easier than ever for agile competitors to imitate and copy successful differentiators. This has happened across many industries, such as retailing, computers, cars, home electronics, telecommunications, and pharmaceuticals. Patents and first-mover advantages (the advantages of being the first to market a product or service) last only so long, and as the overall quality of competing products increases, brand loyalty declines. The problems L. L. Bean has had in maintaining its competitive advantage, described in Strategy in Action 5.2, highlight many of the threats that face a differentiator.

IMPLICATIONS AND CONCLUSIONS   A business model based on differentiation requires a company to make strategic choices that reinforce each other and together increase the value of a good or service in the eyes of customers. When a product is distinctive in customers' eyes, differentiators can charge a premium price. The disadvantages of pursuing differentiation are the ease with which competitors can imitate a differentiator's product and the difficulty of maintaining a premium price. When differentiation stems from the design or physical features of the product, differentiators are at great risk because imitation is easy. An increasing risk is that over time products such as HD-DVD players or LCD televisions become commodity-like products, for which the importance of differentiation diminishes as customers become more price sensitive. However, when differentiation stems from functional-level strategies that lead to superior service or reliability, or from any intangible source, such as FedEx's guarantee or the prestige of a Rolex, a company is much more secure. It is difficult to imitate intangible products, and a differentiator can often reap the benefits of this for a long time. Nevertheless, all differentiators must watch for imitators and be careful that they do not charge a price higher than the market will bear.

● **Focused Differentiation**   As in the case of the focused cost leader, a company that pursues a business model based on **focused differentiation** chooses to combine the differentiation and focused generic business-level strategies and specializes in making distinctive products for one or two market segments. All the means of differentiation that are open to the differentiator are available to the focused differentiator. The point is that the focused company develops a business model that allows it to successfully position itself to

Strategy in Action   5.2

L. L. Bean's New Business Model

In 1911, Leon Leonwood Bean, a hunter who grew weary of walking miles to hunt game as his feet became wetter and wetter, decided he would create a waterproof boot. The one he invented had leather uppers attached to a large, rounded rubber base and sole. Soon he began selling his shoes through mail order. Word spread about their reliability. Backed by his policy of being responsive to customers who complained (often replacing their boots years after a sale), his company's reputation spread even faster. As the years went by, L. L. Bean expanded its now well-known product line to include products such as its canvas tote bags and, of course, its flannel dog bed. By 2000, the company's mail-order revenues exceeded $1 billion a year, and L. L. Bean became known for offering one of the broadest and highest-quality product lines of sporting clothes and accessories.

To display its product line, the company built a 160,000-square-foot signature store in Freeport, Maine, that stocks hundreds of versions of its backpacks, fleece vests, shirts, moccasins, tents, and other items, and over 3 million visitors a year shop its store. L. L. Bean established this store partly to give customers hands-on access to its products so that they would have a better understanding of the high quality they were being offered. Of course, L. L. Bean expects to command a premium price for offering such a wide variety of high-quality products, and historically it has enjoyed high profit margins. Customers buy its products for their personal use but also as gifts for friends and relatives.

Bean's business model began to suffer in the mid-1990s, however, when there was an explosion in the number of companies touting high-quality, high-priced products to customers, and Bean's catalog lost its unique appeal. Furthermore, the growth of the Internet through the 1990s gave customers access to many more companies that offered quality products, often at much lower prices, such as Lands' End, which also began to feature fleece vests, dog beds, and so on in its product lineup. The problem facing any differentiator is how to protect the distinctiveness of its products from imitators who are always searching for ways to steal away its customers by offering them similar kinds of products at reduced prices.

Finding ways to protect Bean's business model proved to be a major challenge. Its catalog sales were stagnant for several years as customers switched loyalty to low-priced companies. Bean's current CEO, Chris McCormick, has crafted new strategies to help the company rebuild its competitive advantage. One is to build a chain of L. L. Bean stores in major urban locations to allow more potential customers to examine the quality of its products and so attract them—either to buy them in the stores or to use its website.

So far, this approach has not proved to be easy because physical retail stores have a high cost structure, and Bean has had to search for the right way to implement its strategy. It has also had to lower the price of its sporting clothes and accessories in these stores; the days of premium prices are gone. Another strategy has been to launch an aggressive advertising campaign aimed at younger customers who may not know the Bean story. With physical stores, the Internet, and its catalog, it may have a better chance of getting their business.

The jury is still out, however. Not only are other differentiated sporting goods chains expanding, such as Dick's Sporting Goods and Gander Mountain, but sites like Amazon.com and Landsend.com, now owned by Sears, are offering lower-priced products. Whether McCormick will be able to successfully change L. L. Bean's business model to allow it to reach the value creation frontier remains to be seen.[b]

---

compete with the differentiator in just one or a few segments. For example, Porsche, a focused differentiator, competes against Toyota and GM in the sports car and luxury SUV segments of the car market.

For the focused differentiator, selecting a niche often means focusing on one type of customer, such as serving only the very rich, the very young, or the very adventurous, or focusing on only a segment of the product line, such as only on organic or vegetarian foods or very fast cars, designer clothes, or designer sunglasses. Focused differentiators are able to reach the value frontier when they are able to develop a distinctive product that better meets the needs of customers in a particular segment than the differentiator can (Figure 5.6). This may happen, for example, when a focused differentiator gains better knowledge of the needs of a small customer set (such as sports car buyers), knowledge of a region, or expertise in a particular field (such as corporate law, management consulting, or website management for retail customers or restaurants). Alternatively, it might develop superior skills in responsiveness to customers based on its ability to serve the particular needs of regional or industry customers in ways that a national differentiator would find very expensive. Similarly, concentration on a narrow range of products sometimes allows a focuser to develop innovations more quickly than a large differentiator can.

The focuser does not attempt to serve all market segments because that would bring it into direct competition with the differentiator. Instead, it concentrates on building market share in one market segment; if it is successful, it may begin to serve more and more market segments and chip away at the differentiator's competitive advantage. However, if it is too successful at what it does, or if it does try to compete with the differentiator, it may run into trouble because the differentiator has the resources to imitate the focused company's business model. For example, when Ben & Jerry's created a luxury ice cream, their huge success led other companies like Häagen-Dazs and Godiva to produce their own competing products. A good example of the way competition is changing even between focused differentiators that make a similar luxury product, in this case, designer clothing, is profiled in Strategy in Action 5.3.

In summary, a focused differentiator can protect its competitive advantage and niche to the extent that it can provide a product or service that its rivals cannot, for example, by being close to its customers and responding to their changing needs. However, if the focuser's niche disappears over time because of technological change or changes in customers' tastes, it cannot move easily to new niches, and this can be a major challenge. For example, clothing store chain Brooks Brothers, whose focus was on providing formal business attire, ran into great difficulty in the 1990s when business casual became the clothing norm at most companies. It found it hard to adapt to the changing market and was bought out in 2001. Similarly, corner diners have become almost a thing of the past because they are unable to compete with the low prices and speed of fast-food chains like McDonald's and the upscale atmosphere of Starbucks. The disappearance of niches is one reason that so many small companies fail.

The Dynamics of Competitive Positioning

Companies that successfully pursue one of the business models just discussed are able to outperform their rivals and reach the value creation frontier. They have developed business-level strategies that result in competitive advantage and above-average profitability; they are usually the most successful and well-known companies in their industry. While some companies are able to develop the business model and strategies that allow them to reach the value creation frontier, many others cannot and so only achieve average or below-average profitability. As Figure 5.8 illustrates, the most successful companies in the retail industry, such as Neiman Marcus, Macy's, Target, Wal-Mart, and Costco, have reached the value frontier, but their competitors, such as Nordstrom, Sack's, Dillard's, JCPenney's, and Sears/Kmart, have not.

Why are some companies in an industry able to reach this frontier while others fail, even *when they appear to be using the same business model, for example, differentiation or focus differentiation*? Moreover, few companies are able to continually outperform

Strategy in Action

Zara Uses IT to Change the World of Fashion

Well-known fashion houses like Chanel, Dior, Gucci, and Armani charge thousands of dollars for the fashionable suits and dresses that they introduce twice yearly in the fall and spring. Since only the very rich can afford such differentiated and expensive clothing, most luxury designers produce less expensive lines of clothing and accessories that are sold in upscale fashion retailers such as Neiman Marcus, Nordstrom, and Saks Fifth Avenue. In the 2000s, however, these luxury designers, which all pursue focus differentiation, have come under increasing pressure from small, agile fashion designers, such as England's Jaeger and Laura Ashley and Spain's Zara, which have developed capabilities in using IT (information technology) that allow them to pursue a focused differentiation strategy but at a much lower cost than the luxury fashion houses. This has allowed them to circumvent barriers to entry into the high-fashion segment and develop well-received brand names that still command a premium price.

Zara, in particular, has achieved significant success. Its sales have soared because it has created innovative information systems that lower costs and speed time to market so that it can produce fashionable clothes at lower prices and sell them in its own chain of clothing stores. Zara uses IT to manage the interface between its design and manufacturing operations efficiently. Major fashion houses like Dior and Gucci can take six or more months to design their collections and then three to six months more before their moderately-priced lines become available in upscale retailers. Zara's designers closely watch the trends in the high-fashion industry and the kinds of innovations that the major houses are introducing. Then, using its IT that is linked to its suppliers and the low-cost manufacturers abroad that make its clothing, Zara's designers can create a new collection in only five weeks. These clothes can then be made in a week and delivered to stores soon after. This short time to market gives Zara great flexibility and has allowed it to compete effectively in the rapidly changing fashion market, where customer tastes evolve quickly.

IT also gives Zara instant feedback on which of its clothes are selling well and in which countries. This information enables Zara to engage in continual product development and remain at the cutting edge of fashion, a major source of differentiation advantage. For example, Zara can manufacture more of a particular kind of dress or suit to meet high customer demand, and it can keep up with fashion by constantly changing its mix of clothes in its rapidly expanding global network of stores. Moreover, since it is following a focused strategy, it can do this at relatively small output levels. Its IT has allowed Zara to minimize the inventory it has to carry, which is the major cost of goods sold for a clothing maker/retailer. Because of the quick manufacturing-to-sales cycle and just-in-time fashion, Zara has been able to offer its collections at comparatively low prices and still make profits that are the envy of the fashion clothing industry. When Zara went public in 2001, its stock price soared because of its high ROIC, and investors believe this will continue as Zara continues to open its stores in most major cities around the world.[c]

their rivals and remain on the value creation frontier; companies such as Toyota, Dell, and Wal-Mart are rare. Why is it so hard for companies to sustain their competitive advantage over time and remain on the frontier? To understand why some companies perform better than others and why the performance of one company can change over time, it is necessary to understand the dynamics involved in positioning a company's business model so that it can compete successfully over time. In this section, we first explore another business model that helps explain why some companies are able to sustain and increase their competitive advantage over time. Second, we examine how the business model a company pursues puts it into a strategic group of competitors that affect its performance. Finally, we examine why differences in performance among companies in an industry are to be expected and why some companies run into major competitive problems that affect their very survival.

FIGURE 5.8

The Dynamics of
Competitive
Positioning

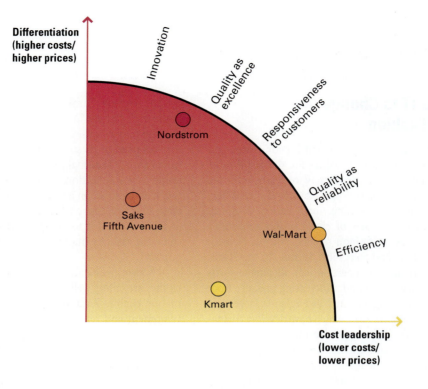

Differentiation
(higher costs/
higher prices)

Innovation

Quality as excellence

Responsiveness to customers

Quality as reliability

Nordstrom

Saks
Fifth Avenue

Wal-Mart

Efficiency

Kmart

Cost leadership
(lower costs/
lower prices)

● **Competitive
Positioning for
Superior
Performance:
Broad Differentiation**

Companies that pursue cost leadership pursue a different business model and strategies than companies that choose differentiation, yet each business model is a path to superior performance and profitability. As we have emphasized throughout this chapter, however, no matter what business model a company pursues, it cannot afford to ignore its cost structure. Managers must always try to find ways to reduce costs in this era of intense global competition in which new (focused) companies might appear with some kind of differentiation or cost advantage and use it to become a dominant competitor, as Toyota and Wal-Mart did. At the same time, all companies need to differentiate their products to some degree to attract customers, increase their market share, and grow their profits over time. Thus, a company that can combine the strategies necessary to pursue both cost leadership and differentiation successfully will develop the most profitable business model in its industry.

Today, many of the most successful companies in an industry have found ways to achieve this. These companies are well known because they can offer customers excellent-quality products at very reasonable prices; that is, they can offer customers a superior "value proposition" compared to all their rivals. The middle of the value creation frontier is occupied by **broad differentiators,** the companies that have developed business-level strategies to improve their differentiation and cost structure simultaneously. Broad differentiators operate on the value creation frontier because they have chosen a level of differentiation that gives them a competitive advantage in the market segments they have targeted, but they have achieved this *in a way that has allowed them to lower their cost structure over time* (see Figure 5.9). Thus, although they may have higher costs than cost leaders, and although they may offer a less-differentiated product than differentiators do, they have found a competitive position that offers their customers as much and normally more value than industry rivals. Broad differentiators continually use their distinctive competencies to increase the range of their products, and they are constantly seeking to enter new market segments

FIGURE 5.9

The Broad
Differentiation
Business Model

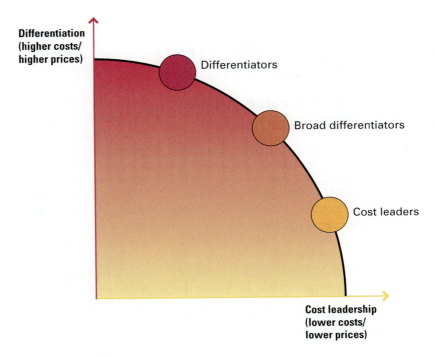

FIGURE 5.9

The Broad
Differentiation
Business Model

to increase their market share to grow their profits. At the same time, they also work continuously to find ways to lower their cost structure and increase their ROIC.

The companies that have formulated and implemented the business-level strategies that enable them to get to this middle, or broadly differentiated, position become an increasing threat to both differentiators and cost leaders over time. These companies make a differentiated product that allows them to charge a premium price for their product compared to a cost leader. However, because of their low cost structure, they can choose to price their product with just *some "small" premium* over the price charged by cost leaders—and, of course, a much lower price than a differentiator has to charge to cover its higher cost structure. As a result, customers often perceive the value offered by the broad differentiator's products to be well worth the premium price (superior value proposition) and so are attracted away from the cost leader's product. At the same time, those customers who are reluctant to pay the high premium price that differentiators command may decide that the qualities of the broad differentiator's product (and its price) more than make up for the loss of the extra differentiated features of the luxury premium-priced products—and choose a Mazda MX5 over a Porsche Boxter, or a box of See's chocolates over Godiva chocolates, and halve the cost of their purchase in the process.

As a result, if strategic managers have the skills to pursue this business model successfully, their companies, as broad differentiators, can steadily increase their market share and profitability over time. This provides them with more capital to reinvest in their business, and so they can continually improve their business model. For example, over time their growing profits allow broad differentiators to invest in new technology that both increases their differentiation advantage and lowers their cost structure; this weakens the competitive position of their rivals. As they build their competitive advantage and become able to offer customers a better value proposition, they push the value creation frontier to the right and knock their competitors off the frontier so they become less profitable. Toyota, profiled in Strategy in Action 5.4, is a good example of a company that used a broad differentiation business model that has increasingly put its rivals at a competitive disadvantage. The result today is that it has replaced Ford as

Strategy in Action

Toyota's Goal? A High-Value Vehicle to Match Every Customer Need

The car industry has always been one of the most competitive in the world because of the huge revenues and profits that are at stake: in 2005, annual global car sales were over $350 billion. It is small wonder, then, that industry rivalry has been increasing as carmakers have been fighting to develop new car models that better satisfy the needs of particular groups of buyers. One company at the forefront of these endeavors is Toyota.

Toyota, which pioneered lean production, produced its first car over thirty years ago: an ugly, boxy affair that was, however, inexpensive. As the quality of its car became apparent, sales increased, and Toyota, which was then a focused cost leader, plowed its profits back into improving the styling of its vehicles and into efforts to continually reduce production costs. Over time, it used its low cost structure, including its efficient design processes, to produce an ever increasing range of reasonably priced vehicles tailored to different segments of the car market. By the 1980s, its ability to go from the initial design stage to the production stage in two to three years allowed it to bring out new models faster than its competitors and to capitalize on the development of new market segments. Low costs and fast time to market have also allowed it to correct mistakes quickly if it designs a car that proves to have little market appeal—and Toyota has made mistakes.

In 1999, for example, Toyota brought out the Echo, a subcompact car that featured state-of-the-art engineering to deliver exceptional fuel economy: around fifty to sixty miles per gallon. The Echo was designed to be inexpensive to run and buy, and Toyota targeted this vehicle at buyers in their twenties, expecting them to appreciate these qualities. Its designers were disappointed when this age group displayed little enthusiasm for the car; its styling did not appeal to them even if its performance did fit their budget. The Echo's buyers turned out to be individuals in their forties who appreciated its economy and found it a useful second car to get around in.

Recognizing that they failed to position their product to hit the important market segment of young adults, the main car buyers of the future, Toyota's designers went back to the drawing board. Analyzing changing market trends and demographics, they sought to find the styling and features for a car that was good-looking and fun to drive for this market segment and that could be sold for $16,000 to $18,000. Toyota (and several other carmakers) realized that perhaps the time was ripe for the return to the hatchback, but an updated version of it. Hatchbacks had been very popular in the early 1980s; however, the cars then were small and often had an ungainly appearance. Sales of hatchbacks had dropped off quickly when carmakers began to offer new sports utility vehicles and updated small sedans. By 1995, relatively few hatchbacks were available.

Drawing on its design and manufacturing competencies, Toyota's engineers updated and shaped the hatchback to suit the needs of young adults in their twenties: the result was the Toyota Matrix, introduced in 2002 at a price starting at $17,000. The Matrix features revolutionary body styling reflective of much more expensive, sporty cars. It is spacious inside and geared to the needs of its intended young buyers; for example, seats fold back to allow for carrying a large cargo volume, and many storage bins and two-prong plugs for power outlets allow for the use of VCRs, MP3 players, and other devices. The message is that the Matrix is designed to be functional, fun, and a sporty ride. Then, in 2003, Toyota introduced a new car, the Scion, once again a car designed to appeal to young people.

Toyota has also been a leader in positioning its whole range of vehicles to take advantage of emerging market segments. In the sports utility segment, its first offering was the expensive Toyota Land Cruiser, priced at over $35,000. Realizing the need for sports utility vehicles in other price ranges, it next introduced the 4Runner, priced at $20,000 and designed for the average sports utility customer; the RAV4, a small sports utility vehicle in the low $20,000 range, followed; then came the Sequoia, a bigger, more powerful version of the 4Runner in the upper $20,000 range. Finally, taking the technology from its Lexus R3000 vehicle, it introduced the luxury Highlander sports utility vehicle in the low $30,000 range. It now offers six models of sports utility vehicles, each offering a particular combination of price, size, performance, styling, and luxury to appeal to a particular customer group within the sports utility segment of the car market. Toyota also positions its sedans to appeal to different sets of buyers. For example, the Camry, one of the best-selling cars in the United States, is targeted toward the middle of the market, to customers who can afford to pay about $25,000 and want a balance of luxury, performance, safety, and reliability. The Camry also has a small premium price relative to similar cars of its U.S. competitors, such as the Ford 500 and the GM Impala.

Toyota's broad differentiation business model is based, on the demand side, on making a range of vehicles that optimizes the amount of value it can create for different groups of customers. On the supply side, the number of models it makes is constrained by the need to maintain a low cost structure and to choose the car-pricing options that will generate maximum sales revenues and profits. The decision about how many kinds of vehicles to produce is also affected by the strategies of its rivals because they are also trying to determine the optimum range of cars to produce. Toyota was not alone in its decision to produce a hatchback in 2002: other noticeable competitors included BMW, which introduced the redesigned Mini Cooper; Honda's new Civic hatchbacks; the already well-received PT Cruiser from Daimler-Chrysler; and Ford's Fusion. In fact, the number of hatchback models doubled in the 2000s, as did the expected number of sales (up to 750,000 vehicles). Competition in this market segment is now intense. Each car company needs to anticipate the actions of its rivals, and each hopes, like Toyota, that it has made the right choices to obtain a large share of customers in this important market segment.[d]

the second largest global carmaker by sales after GM, but it is many times as profitable as GM, Ford, and most other carmakers.

Why has Toyota been so successful in pursuing a business model based on broad differentiation? Toyota is a leader in continuously improving manufacturing techniques to lower its cost structure. Recall that changes in technology, such as the constantly improving flexible manufacturing technologies we discussed in Chapter 4, as well as new digital, electronic, and information technologies (which we examine in detail in Chapter 7), have made it possible for all companies to reduce their cost structure if they can implement it in the right way. New technologies also provide many opportunities to increase product differentiation while maintaining a low cost structure. Technological developments often provide many ways for a company that has traditionally pursued a pure differentiation strategy to do so at a significantly lower cost so that it can choose a lower pricing option and build demand.

Companies like Toyota are continuously experimenting with new ways to reduce costs and segment their markets. The use of robots and flexible manufacturing cells reduces the costs of retooling the production line, and the costs associated with small production runs make it much easier to produce a wide variety of vehicle models and maintain an efficient cost structure. Today, flexible manufacturing enables a company pursuing differentiation to manufacture a range of products at a cost comparable to that of the cost leader. BMW, for example, has taken advantage of flexible manufacturing technologies to reduce its costs, and it has also chosen to charge only a modest premium price to boost its sales revenues. This new strategy has worked: its market share and profitability have increased in recent years.

Indeed, the ability of flexible manufacturing to substantially reduce the costs of differentiating products has promoted the trend toward market fragmentation and niche marketing in many consumer goods industries, such as mobile phones, computers, and appliances. Another way that a differentiated producer may be able to realize significant economies of scale is by standardizing many of the component parts used in its end products. Toyota's various models of sports utility vehicles are built on only three different car platforms. As a result, Toyota is able to realize significant economies of scale in the manufacture and bulk purchase of standardized component parts, despite its high level of market segmentation.

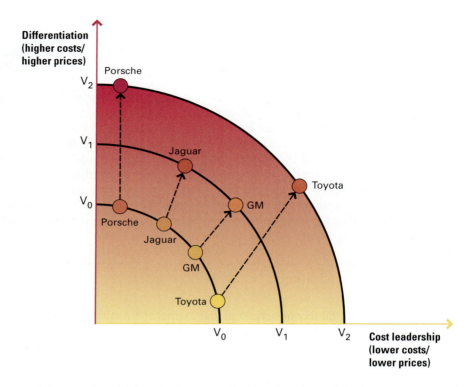

The way in which a business model based on broad differentiation can disrupt industry competition and change the rules of the competitive game is illustrated in Figure 5.10, which contrasts the car industry as it was in the days of mass production with the industry in the days of lean production. The value frontier (V_0) represents the most value that could be produced using mass-production technology, and at that time, GM was the broad differentiator, with its five divisions producing cars that gave it an 80% share of the U.S. car market. Toyota is shown as the focused cost leader on the value creation frontier because it was learning the skills involved in lean production. On the other hand, Porsche and Jaguar are shown as the differentiators on the value creation frontier: their pricey cars sold because of their innovative features, exceptional styling, and European origin.

On the V_0 frontier, GM was the dominant company, but as Toyota grew, its continuous ability to make high-quality cars efficiently and then to expand into more and more market segments changed the rules of the competitive game. Today, in an era of lean production, Toyota is the successful broad differentiator and has pushed out the value frontier to V_2, meaning that customers now receive substantially more performance, safety, and luxury from their cars than they did ten or twenty years ago; in essence, they get more value for their money. Where is GM today? To survive, GM has had to develop skills in lean manufacturing, and this has allowed it to move up to the V_1 frontier. However, GM cannot match Toyota's low cost structure, and it has also had to dramatically cut the number of models it offers to customers because it cannot sell its cars at profitable prices. By 2004, its market share had fallen to 26%, and today it is creating far less value than Toyota, something reflected in its ROIC and stock price.

Jaguar, now owned by Ford, is also in a desperate position. Ford has tried to reduce Jaguar's cost structure and strengthen its styling and image, which has always been the key to its cars' differentiated appeal. By 2004, it was clear its strategies had not worked: demand for Jaguars had been falling, while demand for BMWs, Mercedes, and Lexus cars had been soaring. As for Porsche, it also had to learn lean production skills; however, its task is a little easier because it only produces a few sports car models. In addition, its engineers have kept their performance and handling at the leading edge of technological developments, so that today Porsche enjoys record sales and profits. Toyota and Porsche are on the value frontier at V_2; although GM and Jaguar have moved forward to V_1, their enormous losses in the last twenty years because of their failure to reach the value creation frontier have led to major falls in their market share and profits. Intense competition from ever advancing technology and from countries like China that have low-cost labor has been transforming competition in many industries, including the car industry. Carmakers have been trying to find ways to compete with Toyota and reach the new value frontier—however, Toyota is continually pushing the frontier out to the right.

One set of business-level strategies that a broad differentiator commonly uses to maintain a low cost structure is to make a vehicle targeted at one segment of the global market and then allow only limited customization of that vehicle. For example, carmakers throughout the world are offering customers a mid-priced sedan with an economy, luxury, or sports package to appeal to this principal market segment. Package offerings substantially lower manufacturing costs because long production runs of the various packages are possible. Once again, the company sees gains from both differentiation and low cost. Just-in-time inventory systems can also help reduce costs and improve the quality and reliability of a company's products. Toyota's cost of goods sold is the lowest of any carmaker, and although Ford and Chrysler have spent billions to lower their costs, Toyota continues to push the value frontier out to the right, as already mentioned. In 2004, for example, its hybrid car, the Prius, which is powered by both a gasoline engine and a battery, became popular because of rising gas prices. Toyota has licensed the rights to use its hybrid technology to Ford and GM, and more and more companies are planning to bring out a range of hybrid vehicles.

Finally, many companies, such as Dell and Amazon.com, have been using the Internet and e-commerce as a way of becoming a broad differentiator. Both companies have been rapidly expanding the range of products they offer to customers and taking advantage of their highly efficient materials-management systems to drive down costs compared to bricks-and-mortar retailers. The Internet is a highly cost-effective way to inform millions of potential customers about the nature and quality of a company's products. Also, when customers do their own work on the Internet, such as by managing their own finances, stock trades, bill paying, travel booking, and purchasing, a company has shifted these costs to the customer and is no longer bearing them. Direct selling to the customer also avoids the need to use wholesalers and other intermediaries, which results in great cost savings. It has been estimated that 40% of the profit in a new car goes to the dealership that sells the car and covers costs such as those associated with marketing the car.

● Competitive Positioning and Strategic Groups

As this whole discussion suggests, competition in an industry is dynamic. New developments such as (1) technological innovations that permit increased product differentiation, (2) the identification of new customer groups and market segments, and (3) the continual discovery of better ways to implement a business model to lower the cost structure continually change the competitive forces at work in an industry. In such a dynamic situation, the competitive position of companies can change rapidly. Higher-performing companies are able to gain from positioning themselves competitively to pursue broad differentiation. On the other hand, poorer-performing companies are often slow to recognize how their competitive position is changing because of the actions of their rivals, so they often find their competitive advantage disappearing. Strategic group analysis, which we discussed in Chapter 2, is a useful tool to help companies in an industry better understand the dynamics of competitive positioning so they can change their business models to position themselves to achieve superior performance.

A company's business model determines how it will compete for customers in a particular market segment, market, or industry, and typically several companies are competing for the same set of customers. This means that the business-level strategies pursued by one company affect the strategies pursued by the others, and over time companies competing for the same customers become rivals locked in a competitive struggle. The goal is to be the company that reaches or pushes out the value creation frontier to obtain a competitive advantage and achieve above-average profitability.

Within most industries, strategic groups emerge, with all companies within each group pursuing a similar business model.[18] All companies in an industry competing to be the cost leader form one strategic group, all those seeking some form of differentiation advantage form another, and companies that have developed a broad differentiation strategy constitute another strategic group. Companies pursuing focused differentiation or focused cost leadership form yet other strategic groups.

The concept of strategic groups has a number of implications for competitive positioning. First, strategic managers must map their competitors according to their choice of business model. They can then identify the sets of strategies their rivals have decided to pursue, such as what customer needs to satisfy, which customer groups to serve, and which distinctive competencies to develop. They can then use this knowledge to position themselves closer to customer and differentiate themselves from their competitors. In other words, careful strategic-group analysis allows managers to uncover the most important bases of competition in an industry and to identify products and market segments where they can compete most successfully for customers. Such analysis also helps to reveal what competencies are likely to be most valuable in the future so that companies can make the right investment decision. For example, the need to develop new models of cars that can be sold across the world and can be assembled reliably by low-cost labor has dominated competitive positioning in the global car industry. U.S. car companies have bought or formed alliances with almost every foreign car manufacturer to obtain marketing, design, or manufacturing knowledge.

Second, once a company has mapped its competitors, it can better understand how changes taking place in the industry are affecting its relative standing vis-à-vis differentiation and cost structure, as well as identify opportunities and threats. Often a company's nearest competitors are those companies in its strategic group that are pursuing a similar business model. Customers tend to view the products of such companies as direct substitutes for each other. Thus, a major threat to a company's profitability can arise from within its own strategic group when one or more companies find ways to either improve product differentiation and get closer to customers or lower their cost structure. This is why companies today benchmark their closest competitors on major performance dimensions to determine if they are falling behind in some important respect. For example, UPS and FedEx are constantly examining each other's performance.

Because strategic-group analysis also forces managers to focus on the activities of companies in other strategic groups, it helps them to identify emerging threats from companies outside their strategic group, such as when a focused company has devised a business model that will bring sweeping changes to the industry. It also helps them understand opportunities that might be arising because of changes in the environment; in response to these changes, they might purchase a focused company and implement its business model across the entire company to absorb the threat.

Recall from Chapter 2 that different strategic groups can have a different standing with respect to each of Porter's five competitive forces because these forces affect companies in different ways. In other words, the risk of new entry by potential competitors, the degree of rivalry among companies within a group, the bargaining power of buyers, the bargaining power of suppliers, and the competitive force of substitute products can all vary in intensity among different strategic groups within the same industry. In the global car industry, for example, the smaller focused differentiators and cost leaders ran into trouble in the 1990s. Their input costs were rising, and they could not afford billions of dollars to design new models and build the new flexible manufacturing plants needed to produce them. Indeed, some European, Korean, and even Japanese companies started to lose billions of dollars. Large U.S. and European carmakers, which were also suffering from the emergence of Toyota and Honda as broad differentiators, realized that they had to reduce their cost structure to survive. The need to compete with Toyota and Honda led to a huge wave of global merger activity that has left just a handful of global giants to compete in the 2000s. For example, Daimler Benz took over Chrysler Suzuki, GM took control of Isuzu and Saab, Ford merged with Mazda and took over Jaguar and Volvo, and Renault took a controlling stake in Nissan to learn lean production techniques. Thus, the strategic-group map in the global car industry changed dramatically. Today, only a handful of focused companies like BMW and Porsche remain, and even they have forged alliances with other carmakers. If they make a mistake in managing their business models, they will also become a target for one of the large global companies seeking to increase product differentiation.

In sum, strategic-group analysis involves identifying and charting the business models and business-level strategies that industry rivals are pursuing. Managers can then determine which strategies are successful and unsuccessful and why a certain business model is working or not. They can also analyze how the relative competitive position of industry rivals, both those pursuing the same business model and those pursuing different business models, is changing over time. This knowledge allows them to either fine-tune or radically alter their business models and strategies to improve their own competitive position.

● Failures in Competitive Positioning

Successful competitive positioning requires that a company achieve a fit between its strategies and its business model. Thus, a cost leader cannot strive for a high level of market segmentation, as a differentiator does, and provide a wide range of products because those choices would raise its cost structure too much and the company would lose its low-cost advantage. Similarly, a differentiator with a competency in innovation that tries to reduce its expenditures on research and development, or one with a competency in after-sales service that seeks to economize on its sales force to decrease costs, is asking for trouble because it has implemented its business model in the wrong way.

To pursue a successful business model, managers must be careful to ensure that the set of business-level strategies they have formulated and implemented are working in harmony to support each other and do not result in conflicts that ruin the competitive position the company is aiming for through its choice of business model. Many companies, through neglect, ignorance, or error—or perhaps because of the Icarus paradox discussed in Chapter 1—do not work to continually improve their business model, do not perform strategic-group analysis, and often fail to identify and respond to changing opportunities and threats in the industry environment. As a result, the company's business model starts to fail because its business-level strategies do not work together and its profitability starts to decline. Sometimes its performance can decline so quickly that the company is taken over by other companies or goes bankrupt.

These companies have lost their position on the value creation frontier either because they have lost the source of their competitive advantage or because their rivals have found ways to push out the value creation frontier and leave them behind. Sometimes these companies initially pursued a successful cost-leadership or differentiation business model but then gradually began to pursue business-level strategies that worked against them. Unfortunately, it seems that most companies lose control of their business models over time, often because they become large, complex companies that are difficult to manage or because the environment is changing faster than they can change their business model—such as by adjusting product and market choices to suit changing industry conditions. This is why it is so important that managers *think strategically*.

In Chapter 1, we defined *strategic intent* as the way managers think about where they want their organization to be in the future and what kinds of resources and capabilities they will need to achieve this vision. Strategic intent provides a company with a sense of direction and stretches managers at all levels to be more inventive or innovative and to make better use of resources. Moreover, it "implies a competitive distinct point of view about the future; it holds out to employees the promise of exploring new competitive territory."[19] The experience of Holiday Inns, described in Strategy in Action 5.5, shows how a company can lose control of its business model but also how managers can change it to suit the changing competitive landscape.

There are many factors that can cause a company to make competitive positioning errors. While some focused companies may succeed spectacularly for a time, a focuser can also make a major error when, in its rush to implement its business model, it over-expands and so loses control of its business model. Take People Express, a U.S. airline that was the first cost leader to emerge after deregulation of the U.S. airline industry. It started out as a specialized air carrier serving a narrow market niche: low-priced travel on the eastern seaboard. In pursuing focused cost leadership, it was very successful, but in its rush to expand to other geographic regions, it decided to take over other airlines. These airlines were differentiators that had never pursued cost leadership; the purchases raised the company's cost structure and it lost its competitive advantage against the other national carriers. In the end, People Express was swallowed up by Texas Air and incorporated into Continental Airlines. Herb Kelleher, the founder of Southwest Airlines, watched how People Express had failed, and he stuck to the cost-leadership business model. He took *twenty* years to build his national airline, but he never deviated from the strategies necessary to pursue cost leadership.

In 2004, Southwest announced it might do away with its strategy of no seat reservations and might make other changes to deal with its expanding route structure. This means that its top managers need to be vigilant in managing its cost structure. Another focus differentiator that ran into problems was Krispy Kreme Doughnuts, which began to expand the number of its stores rapidly in the 2000s as demand for its tasty product soared. By 2004, its cost structure was out of control. Its failure to implement its business model, combined with the fall in the demand for doughnuts because of the popularity of the Atkins diet, resulted in its first loss and its stock price has plummeted.

Differentiators can also fail in the market and end up stuck in the middle if focused competitors attack their markets with more specialized or low-cost products that blunt their competitive edge. This happened to IBM in the large-frame computer market when PCs became more powerful and able to do the job of the much more expensive mainframes. Of course, the increasing movement toward flexible manufacturing has aggravated the problems facing both cost leaders and differentiators.

Strategy in Action

5.5

Holiday Inns on Six Continents

The history of the Holiday Inns motel chain is one of the great success stories in U.S. business. Its founder, Kemmons Wilson, found motels to be small, expensive, and of unpredictable quality when he vacationed in the early 1950s. This discovery, along with the prospect of unprecedented highway travel that would come with the new interstate highway program, triggered a realization: there was an unmet customer need—a gap in the market for quality accommodations. Holiday Inns was founded to meet that need. From the beginning, Holiday Inns set the standard for offering motel features such as air conditioning and icemakers while keeping room rates reasonable. These amenities enhanced the motels' popularity, and motel franchising, Wilson's invention, made rapid expansion possible. By 1960, Holiday Inns could be found in almost every city and on every major highway. Before the 1960s ended, more than one thousand of them were in full operation, and occupancy rates averaged 80%. The concept of mass accommodation had arrived.

The service that Holiday Inns offered appealed to the average traveler, who wanted a standardized product (a room) at an average price—the middle of the hotel room market. But by the 1970s, travelers were beginning to make different demands on hotels and motels. Some wanted luxury and were willing to pay higher prices for better accommodations and service. Others sought low prices and accepted rock-bottom quality and service in exchange. As the market fragmented into different groups of customers with different needs, Holiday Inns was still offering an undifferentiated, average-cost, average-quality product.

Although Holiday Inns missed the change in the market and thus failed to respond appropriately to it, the competition did not. Companies such as Hyatt siphoned off the top end of the market, where quality and service sold rooms. Chains such as Motel 6 and Days Inns captured the basic-quality, low-price end of the market. In between were many specialty chains that appealed to business travelers, families, or self-caterers (people who want to be able to cook in their hotel rooms). Holiday Inns' position was attacked from all sides. As occupancy rates dropped drastically with increasing competition, profitability declined.

Wounded but not dead, Holiday Inns began a counterattack. The original chain was upgraded to suit quality-oriented travelers. Then, to meet the needs of different kinds of travelers, Holiday Inns created new hotel and motel chains: the luxury Crowne Plazas, the Hampton Inns serving the low-priced end of the market, and the all-suite Embassy Suites. Thus, Holiday Inns attempted to meet the demands of the many niches, or segments, of the hotel market that have emerged as customers' needs have changed over time. These moves were successful in the early 1990s, and Holiday Inns grew to become one of the largest suppliers of hotel rooms in the industry. However, by the late 1990s, falling revenues made it clear that with intense competition in the industry from other chains such as Marriott, Holiday Inns was once again losing its differentiated appeal.

In the fast-changing hotel and lodging market, positioning each hotel brand or chain to maximize customer demand is a continuing endeavor. In 2000, the pressure on all hotel chains to adapt to the challenges of global competition and become globally differentiated brands led to the takeover of Holiday Inns and its incorporation into the international Six Continents Hotels chain. Today, around the globe, more than 3,200 hotels flying the flags of Holiday Inns, Holiday Inns Express, Crowne Plaza, Staybridge Suites by Holiday Inns, and luxury Inter-Continental Hotels and Resorts are positioning themselves to offer the services, amenities, and lodging experiences that will cater to almost every travel occasion and guest need. In the 2000s, the company has undertaken a massive modernization campaign in the United States to take existing full-service Holiday Inns to their next evolution. Holiday Inns plans to have a room to meet the need of every segment of the lodging market anywhere in the world.[e]

No company is safe in the jungle of competition, and each must be constantly on the lookout to take advantage of competitive advantages as they arise.

In sum, strategic managers must employ the tools discussed in this book to continually monitor how well the business-level strategies that formulate and implement their company's business model are working. No task is more important than ensuring that their company is optimally positioned against its rivals to compete for customers. And, as we have discussed, the constant changes occurring in the external environment, as well as through the actions of competitors who work to push out the value creation frontier, make competitive positioning a complex, demanding task that requires the highest degree of strategic thinking. This is why companies pay tens of millions of dollars a year to CEOs and other top managers who have demonstrated their ability to create and sustain successful business models.

Summary of Chapter

1. To create a successful business model, managers must choose business-level strategies that give a company a competitive advantage over its rivals; that is, they must optimize competitive positioning. They must first decide on (1) customer needs, or what is to be satisfied; (2) customer groups, or who is to be satisfied; and (3) distinctive competencies, or how customer needs are to be satisfied. These decisions determine which strategies they formulate and implement to put a company's business model into action.

2. Customer needs are desires, wants, or cravings that can be satisfied through the attributes or characteristics of a product. Customers choose a product based on (1) the way a product is differentiated from other products of its type and (2) the price of the product. Product differentiation is the process of designing products to satisfy customers' needs in ways that competing products cannot. Companies that create something distinct or different can often charge a higher, or premium, price for their product.

3. If managers devise strategies to differentiate a product by innovation, excellent quality, or responsiveness to customers, they are choosing a business model based on offering customers differentiated products. If managers base their business model on finding ways to reduce costs, they are choosing a business model based on offering customers low-priced products.

4. The second main choice in formulating a successful business model is to decide which kind of product(s) to offer to which customer group(s). Market segmentation is the way a company decides to group customers, based on important differences in their needs or preferences, in order to gain a competitive advantage.

5. There are three main approaches toward market segmentation. First, a company might choose to ignore differences and make a product targeted at the average or typical customer. Second, a company can choose to recognize the differences between customer groups and make a product targeted toward most or all of the different market segments. Third, a company might choose to target just one or two market segments.

6. To develop a successful business model, strategic managers have to devise a set of strategies that determine (1) how to differentiate and price their product, and (2) how much to segment a market and how wide a range of products to develop. Whether these strategies will result in a profitable business model now depends on strategic managers' ability to provide customers with the most value while keeping their cost structure viable.

7. The value creation frontier represents the maximum amount of value that the products of different companies inside an industry can give customers at any one time by using different business models. Companies on the value creation frontier are those that have the most successful business models in a particular industry.

8. The value creation frontier can be reached by choosing among four *generic competitive strategies:* cost leadership, focused cost leadership, differentiation, and focused differentiation.

9. A cost-leadership business model is based on lowering the company's cost structure so it can make and sell goods or services at a lower cost than its rivals. A cost leader is often a large, national company that targets the average customer. Focused cost leadership is developing the right strategies to serve just one or two market segments.

10. A differentiation business model is based on creating a product that customers perceive as different or distinct in some important way. Focused differentiation is providing a differentiated product for just one or two market segments.

11. The middle of the value creation frontier is occupied by broad differentiators; they have pursued their differentiation strategy in a way that has also allowed them to lower their cost structure over time.

12. Strategic-group analysis helps companies in an industry better understand the dynamics of competitive positioning. In strategic-group analysis, managers identify and chart the business models and business-level strategies their industry rivals are pursuing. Then they can determine which strategies are successful and

unsuccessful and why a certain business model is working or not. In turn, this allows them to either fine-tune or radically alter their business models and strategies to improve their competitive position.

13. Many companies, through neglect, ignorance, or error, do not work to continually improve their business model, do not perform strategic-group analysis, and often fail to identify and respond to changing opportunities and threats. As a result, their business-level strategies do not work together, their business model starts to fail, and their profitability starts to decline. There is no more important task than ensuring that one's company is optimally positioned against its rivals to compete for customers.

Discussion Questions

1. Why does each generic business model require a different set of business-level strategies? Give examples of pairs of companies in (a) the computer industry, (b) the electronics industry, and (c) the fast-food industry that pursue different types of business models.

2. How do changes in the environment affect the success of a company's business model?

3. What is the value creation frontier? How does each of the four generic business models allow a company to reach this frontier?

4. How can companies pursuing cost leadership and differentiation lose their place on the value frontier? In what ways can they regain their competitive advantage?

5. How can a focused company push the value creation frontier to the right? How does this affect other industry competitors? On the other hand, how can changes in the value creation frontier threaten focused companies?

6. Why is strategic-group analysis important for superior competitive positioning?

7. What are some of the reasons companies lose control over their business models, and thus their competitive advantage, over time?

Practicing Strategic Management

SMALL-GROUP EXERCISE
Finding a Strategy for a Restaurant

Break up into groups of three to five and discuss the following scenario. You are a group of partners contemplating opening a new restaurant in your city. You are trying to decide how to position your restaurant to give it the best competitive advantage.

1. Create a strategic-group map of the restaurants in your city by analyzing their generic business models and strategies. What are the similarities or differences between these groups?

2. Identify which restaurants you think are the most profitable and why.

3. On the basis of this analysis, decide what kind of restaurant you want to open and why.

ARTICLE FILE 5

Find an example (or several examples) of a company pursuing one of the generic business models. What set of business-level strategies does the company use to formulate and implement its business model? How successful has the company been?

STRATEGIC MANAGEMENT PROJECT
Module 5

This part of the project focuses on the nature of your company's business model and business-level strategies. If your company operates in more than one business, concentrate on either its core, or most central, business or on its most important businesses. Using all the information you have collected on your company so far, answer the following questions:

1. How differentiated are the products or services of your company? What is the basis of its differentiated appeal?

2. What is your company's strategy toward market segmentation? If it segments its market, on what basis does it do so?

3. What distinctive competencies does your company have? (Use the information on functional-level strategy in the last chapter to answer this question.) Is efficiency, quality, innovation, responsiveness to customers, or a combination of these factors the main driving force in your company?

4. What generic business model is your company pursuing? How has it formulated and implemented a set of business-level strategies to pursue this business model?

5. What are the advantages and disadvantages associated with your company's choice of business model and strategies?

6. Is your company a member of a strategic group in an industry? If so, which one?

7. How could you improve your company's business model and strategies to strengthen its competitive advantage?

ETHICS EXERCISE

George Vargus had just been hired as a salesperson for a large construction company in town. His assignment was to go out and land large contracts for the company. For the first few months, George would be shadowing the company's other salesperson, Bill Carle. During George's first week, Bill, with George in tow, attended at least one meeting per day. Most of these meetings occurred during lunch or dinner and lasted for hours. George enjoyed the easy pace of the job, along with the good food and abundant drink that seemed to be an integral part of the process. Compared to his last job working as a salesperson for a home renovation store, this job was heaven.

During his second week on the job, George began to have second thoughts. He and Bill continued to attend long, enjoyable lunches and dinners, but George was beginning to wonder if this was the way that he wanted to conduct business. Extraordinary amounts of money were being spent wining and dining potential clients and it almost felt like bribery. He asked Bill about it, wondering if they should be taking clients down to sites currently under construction and showing them recent buildings, among other things, but Bill simply said, "Hey, this is sanctioned by the higher ups—I'm certainly not going to turn down the chance to do business like a king."

Finally it was George's last week shadowing Bill. As usual, they took a group of people looking to build a high-end condominium complex downtown to a five-star restaurant. As the evening began to wind down, one of the group members asked Bill, "Can you hook us up with the nightlife, if you know what I mean?" When Bill agreed, George knew that this just wasn't the job for him. The next day, he resigned.

1. Define the ethical issue presented in this case.
2. Do you think George should have quit his job?
3. What would you have done in George's position?
4. Do you think Bill's method of conducting business was ethically inappropriate? Why or why not.

CLOSING CASE

Samsung Changes Its Business Model Again and Again

In the 2000s, Samsung, based in Seoul, Korea, has risen to become the most profitable consumer electronics company in the world. Since 1999, its revenues have doubled, and it has become the second most profitable global technology company after Microsoft.[20] The story of how Samsung's business model has changed over time explains how the company has reached its enviable position.

In the 1980s, Samsung watched as Japanese companies like Sony and Matsushita (the maker of Panasonic and JVC products) turned out thousands of innovative new consumer electronics such as the Walkman, home video recorders, high-quality televisions, and compact disk players. Samsung's strategy was to see which of these products and which of their specific features, such

as a TV with a hard disk that can store movies, customers liked the best. Then Samsung's engineers would find ways to imitate this technology, just as Japanese companies had imitated U.S. electronics companies in the 1950s when they were the world's leading electronics makers. Samsung would make a low-cost copy of these products and sell them at lower prices than Japanese companies. While this strategy was profitable, however, Samsung was not in the league of Japanese companies like Sony, which could charge premium prices for their electronics and then continually plow their enormous profits back into research to make ever more advanced state-of-the-art electronics—and thus increase their profitability.

Samsung continued to pursue its low-cost strategy until the mid-1990s, when its chair, Lee Kun Hee, made a major decision. Sensing the emerging threat posed by China and other Asian countries whose cheap labor would rob Samsung of its low-cost advantage, Lee realized that Samsung needed to find a way to enter the big leagues and compete directly against the Japanese giants. The question was: How could Samsung do this, given that companies like Sony, Panasonic, and Hitachi were leaders in electronics research and development?

Lee began his new strategy by closing down thirty-two unprofitable product divisions and laying off 40% of Samsung's work force. Having lowered its cost structure, Samsung could now invest much more of its capital in product research. Lee decided to concentrate Samsung's research budget on new-product opportunities in areas like microprocessors, LCD screens, and other new kinds of digital components that he sensed would be in demand in the coming digital revolution. Today, Samsung is a major supplier of chips and LCD screens to all global electronics makers, and it can produce these components at a much lower cost than electronics makers can because it is farther down the experience curve.

The focus of Lee's new strategy, however, was on developing research and engineering skills that would allow the company to quickly capitalize on the technology being innovated by Sony, Matsushita, Phillips, and Nokia. His engineers would take this technology and rapidly develop and improve it to create new and improved products that were more advanced than those offered by Japanese competitors. Samsung would produce a wider variety of products than competitors but only in relatively small quantities. Then, as its new products were sold in stores, newer electronic models that were still more advanced would replace them. One advantage of speeding products to market is that inventory does not sit in Samsung's warehouses or stores, nor does Samsung need to stock large quantities of components because it needs only enough to make its budgeted output of a particular product. So by making speed the center of its differentiation strategy, Samsung was able to make more efficient use of its capital even as it introduced large numbers of new products to the market.

At the same time, Samsung's ability to innovate a large number of advanced products attracts customers and has allowed it to build its market share. Today, for example, while Nokia can claim to be a leading cell phone innovator, Samsung was the first to realize that customers wanted a color screen for their phone to allow them to play games and a built-in camera that would allow them to send photographs to their friends. Both these incremental advances have allowed Samsung to dramatically increase its share of the cell phone market. To compete with Samsung, Nokia has had to learn how to innovate new models of cell phones rapidly. Although in the 2000s Nokia has introduced new phones more quickly, Samsung has been able to do so even faster.[21]

By making speed of new-product development the center of its business model, Samsung also was able to move ahead of its other major competitors like Sony. Because of its focus on developing new technology and because of the slow speed of decision making typical in Japanese companies, Sony was hard hit by Samsung's success, and its profitability and stock price declined sharply in the 2000s. Today, Samsung is not just imitating Sony's leading-edge technology but is also developing its own, as shown by the fact that in 2004, Sony and Samsung announced a major agreement to share the costs of basic research into improving LCDs, which run into billions of dollars.

Today, Samsung is in the first tier of electronics makers and is regarded by many as one of the most innovative companies in the world. Almost a quarter of Samsung's 80,000 employees work in one of its four research divisions—semiconductors, telecommunications, digital media, and flat-screen panels. Because many of its products require components developed by all four divisions, it brings researchers, designers, engineers, and marketers from all its divisions together in teams at its research facility outside Seoul to spur the innovation that is the major source of its success. At the same time, it can still make many electronic components at a lower cost than its competitors, which has further contributed to its high profitability. Given the rapid technological advances in China, however, it appears that Chinese companies may soon be able to make some of their components at a lower cost than Samsung, thus doing to Samsung what Samsung did to companies like Sony. Samsung is relying on the speed of its research and engineering to fight off their challenge, but all global electronics makers are now in a race to speed their products to market.

Case Discussion Questions

1. How has Samsung's business model and strategies changed over time?

2. What is the basis of Samsung's current business model? In what ways is it trying to improve its competitive advantage? (Go to the Internet and update the case.)

Business-Level Strategy and the Industry Environment

OPENING CASE

Competition Gets Ugly in the Toy Business

The rapid pace at which the world is changing is forcing strategic managers at all kinds of companies to speed up their decision making, otherwise they get left behind by agile competitors who do respond faster to changing customer fads and fashions. Nowhere is this truer than in the global toy industry, where in the doll business, worth over $10 billion a year in sales, vicious combat is raging. The largest global toy company, Mattel, has earned tens of billions of dollars from the world's best-selling doll, Barbie, since it introduced her almost fifty years ago.[1] Mothers who played with the original dolls bought them for their daughters, and then granddaughters, and Barbie became an American icon. However, Barbie's advantage as best-selling global doll led Mattel's managers to make major strategic errors in the 2000s.

Barbie and all Barbie accessories accounted for almost 50% of Mattel's toy sales in the 1990s, so protecting its star product was crucial. The Barbie doll was created in the 1960s when most women were homemakers, and her voluptuous shape was a response to a dated view of what the "ideal" woman should look like. Barbie's continuing success, however, led Bob Eckert, Mattel's CEO, and his top managers to underestimate how much the world had altered. Changing cultural views about the role of girls, women, sex, marriage, and working women in the last decades shifted the tastes of doll buyers. But Mattel's managers continued to bet on Barbie's eternal appeal and collectively bought into an "If it's not broken, don't fix it" approach. In fact, given that Barbie was the best-selling doll, they thought it might be dangerous to make major changes to her appearance; customers might not like these product development changes and might stop buying her. Mattel's top managers decided not to rock the boat, they left the brand and business model unchanged and focused their efforts on developing new digital kinds of toys.

So Mattel was unprepared when a challenge came along in the form of a new kind of doll, the Bratz doll, introduced by MGA Entertainment. Many competitors of Barbie had emerged over the years—the doll business is highly profitable—but no other doll had matched Barbie's appeal to young girls (or their mothers). The marketers and designers behind the Bratz line of dolls had spent a lot of time discovering what the new generation of girls, especially those aged seven to eleven, wanted from a doll, however. And it turned out that the Bratz dolls they designed met the desires of these girls. Bratz dolls have larger heads and oversized eyes, wear lots of makeup and short dresses, and are multicultural to give each doll "personality and attitude."[2] The dolls were designed to appeal to a new generation of girls brought up in a fast-changing fashion, music, and television market/age. The Bratz dolls met the untapped needs of "tween" girls and the new line took off. MGA quickly licensed the rights to make and sell the doll to toy companies overseas, and Bratz quickly became a serious competitor of Barbie.

Now Mattel was in trouble. Its strategic managers had to change its business model and strategies and bring Barbie up to date. Mattel's designers must have been wishing they had been adventurous and made more radical changes earlier when they did not need to change. However, they decided to change Barbie's "extreme" vital statistics; they killed off her old-time boyfriend Ken and replaced him with Blaine, an Aussie surfer, and so on.[3] They also recognized they had waited much too long to introduce their own new lines of dolls to meet the changing needs of tween and other girls in the 2000s. So in 2002, they rushed out the My Scene line of dolls, which were obvious imitations of Bratz dolls. This new line has

not matched the popularity of Bratz dolls. Mattel also introduced a new line called Flava in 2003 to appeal to even younger girls, but this line flopped completely. At the same time, the decisions that they made to change Barbie and her figure, looks, clothing, and boyfriends came too late, and sales of Barbie dolls continued to fall.

By 2006, sales of the Barbie collection had dropped 30%, a serious matter because Mattel's profits and stock price hinge on Barbie's success, and so they both plunged. Analysts argue that Mattel had not paid enough attention to its customers' changing needs and to introducing the new and improved products necessary to keep a company on top of its market. Mattel brought back Ken in 2006. Then, in a sign of its mounting problems, in November 2006 Mattel's lawyers filed suit against MGA Entertainment arguing that the Bratz dolls' copyright rightfully belonged to them. Mattel complained that the head designer of Bratz was a Mattel employee when he made the initial drawings for the dolls and that they had applied for copyright protection on a number of early Bratz drawings. In addition, they claimed that MGA hired key Mattel employees away from the firm and that these employees stole sensitive sales information and transferred it to MGA. Clearly, competition in the doll business is getting ugly.

OVERVIEW

As Mattel's problems with its Barbie doll suggests, a company's business model cannot just be created and left to take care of itself. If strategic managers do create a successful business model, they still face another challenge: the need to continually formulate and implement business-level strategies to sustain their competitive advantage over time in different kinds of industry environments. Different industry environments present particular kinds of opportunities and threats for companies, and a company's business model and strategies have to adapt and change to meet the changing environment.

This chapter first examines how companies in fragmented industries can develop new kinds of business-level strategies to strengthen their business models. It then considers the challenges of developing and sustaining a competitive advantage in embryonic, growth, mature, and declining industries. By the end of this chapter, you will understand how forces in the changing industry environment require managers to pursue new kinds of business-level strategies to strengthen their company's business model and keep it at the value creation frontier.

Strategies in Fragmented Industries

A *fragmented industry* is one composed of a large number of small and medium-sized companies—for example, the dry cleaning, restaurant, health club, and legal services industries. There are several reasons that an industry may consist of many small companies rather than a few large ones.[4]

First, fragmented industries are characterized by low barriers to entry because of the lack of economies of scale. Many homebuyers, for example, prefer dealing with local real estate agents, whom they perceive as having better local knowledge than national chains. Second, in some industries, there may even be diseconomies of scale. In the restaurant business, for example, customers often prefer the unique food and style of a popular local restaurant rather than the standardized offerings of some national chain. Third, low entry barriers that permit constant entry by new companies also serve to keep an industry fragmented. The restaurant industry exemplifies this situation. The costs of opening a restaurant are moderate and can be borne by a single entrepreneur. High transportation costs, too, can keep an industry fragmented, and local or regional production may be the only efficient way to satisfy customers' needs, as in the cement business. Finally, an industry may be fragmented because customers' needs are so specialized that only small job lots of products are required, and thus there is no room for a large mass-production operation to satisfy the market.

For some fragmented industries, these factors dictate that the focus business model will be the most profitable to pursue. Companies may specialize by customer group, customer need, or geographic region, so that many small specialty companies operate in local or regional markets. All kinds of custom-made products—furniture, clothing, hats, boots, and so on—fall into this category, as do all small service operations that cater to particular customers' needs, such as laundries, restaurants, health clubs, and furniture rental stores. Indeed, service companies make up a large proportion of the enterprises in fragmented industries because they provide personalized service to clients and therefore need to be responsive to customers' needs.

However, strategic managers are eager to gain the cost advantages of pursuing cost leadership or the sales/revenue-enhancing advantages of differentiation by circumventing the competitive conditions that have allowed focus companies to dominate an industry. Essentially, companies have searched for new business-level strategies that will allow them to consolidate a fragmented industry in order to enjoy the much higher potential returns possible in a consolidated industry. These companies include large retailers such as Wal-Mart and Target; fast-food chains such as McDonald's and Burger King; movie rental chains such as Blockbuster and Hollywood Video; chains of health clubs such as Bally's, and President and First Lady; repair shops like Midas Muffler; and even lawyers, consultants, and tax preparers.

To grow, consolidate their industries, and become the industry leaders, these companies have developed strategies such as chaining, franchising, creating horizontal mergers, and also using the Internet and information technology (IT) in order to realize the advantages of a cost-leadership or differentiation business model. In doing so, these companies have pushed out the value creation frontier to the right, with the result that many focus companies have lost their competitive advantage and have disappeared.

Many of the new leaders pioneered a new business model in an industry that lowers costs or confers a differentiation advantage (or both). They do this by competing in a very different way from established rivals. Managers in a fragmented industry must seek out cost or differentiation advantages that others have not recognized.

● **Chaining**   Companies such as Wal-Mart and Midas International pursue a **chaining** strategy to obtain the advantages of cost leadership. They establish networks of linked merchandising outlets that are so interconnected by advanced IT that they function as one large business entity. The consolidated buying power that these companies possess through their nationwide store chains allows them to negotiate large price reductions with their suppliers, which promotes their competitive advantage. They overcome the barrier of high transportation costs by establishing sophisticated regional distribution centers, which can economize on inventory costs and maximize responsiveness to the needs of stores and customers. They also realize economies of scale from sharing managerial skills across the chain and from using nationwide, rather than local, advertising.

The U.S. food retail business during the 1950s, when supermarkets revolutionized the business model behind the selling of food products, is a good example of the advantages of chaining. Prior to the development of supermarkets, the food retail industry was fragmented, with many small mom-and-pop retailers selling a limited range of products and providing full service to customers, including home delivery. The first supermarkets were usually regionally based, with fewer than 100 stores, and they differentiated themselves by offering a much larger selection of items in a big store layout. At the same time, they lowered their costs by moving from a full-service to a self-service strategy (they needed far fewer employees to run a store), and they passed on those cost savings to customers in the form of lower prices. In other words, the supermarkets competed in a very different way from established food retailers: they adopted a new business model.

As the supermarkets started to grow, opening hundreds of more stores, they were able to capture scale economies that were not available to smaller retailers. For example, by clustering their stores around central distribution warehouses in different cities and eventually regions, they were able to gain distribution efficiencies and reduce the amount of inventory they had to hold in a store. Also, by buying from vendors in large quantities, they were able to demand deep price discounts that they passed on to customers in the form of lower prices, enabling the supermarkets to gain even more market share from smaller retailers. In the 1970s and 1980s, the supermarkets were also the first to introduce information systems based on point-of-sale terminals that tracked the sale of individual items. The information provided by the point-of-sale terminals enabled the supermarkets to optimize their stocking of items, quickly cutting back on items that were not selling and devoting more shelf space to items that were selling faster. Reducing the need to hold inventory took even more costs out of the systems and ensured a good match between customer demands and items in the supermarket, which further differentiated the supermarkets from smaller retailers. Although these information systems were expensive to implement, the supermarkets could spread the costs over a large volume of sales. The small mom-and-pop retailers could not afford such systems because their sales base was too small. As a consequence of these developments, the food retail industry was becoming consolidated by the 1980s, a trend that is accelerating today. The small mom-and-pop food retailer is now almost extinct.

The new supermarket business model that provided cost and differentiation advantages over the old established mom-and-pop model has been applied to a wide range of retail industries, consolidating one after the other. Barnes & Noble and Borders applied the supermarket business model to book retailing; Staples applied it to office supplies; Best Buy, to electronics retailing; Home Depot, to building supplies; and so on. In each case, the companies that pursued a business model based on cost leadership or differentiation changed the competitive structure of the industry to its advantage, consolidating the industry and weakening the five forces of competition in the process.

● **Franchising**

Like chaining, franchising is a business-level strategy that allows companies, particularly service companies such as McDonald's or Century 21 Real Estate, to enjoy the competitive advantages that result from cost leadership or differentiation. In franchising, the franchiser (parent) grants to its franchisees the right to use the parent's name, reputation, and business model in a particular location or area in return for a sizable franchise fee and often a percentage of the profits.[5]

One particular advantage of this strategy is that, because franchisees essentially own their businesses, they are strongly motivated to make the companywide business model work effectively and make sure that quality and standards are consistently high so that customers' needs are always satisfied. Such motivation is particularly critical for a differentiator that must continually work to maintain its unique or distinctive appeal. In addition, franchising lessens the financial burden of swift expansion and so permits rapid growth of the company. Finally, a nationwide franchised company can reap the advantages of large-scale advertising, as well as economies in purchasing, management, and distribution, as McDonald's does very efficiently in pursuing its cost-leadership model.

● **Horizontal Merger**

Companies such as Anheuser-Busch, Dillard's, and Blockbuster chose a strategy of *horizontal merger* to consolidate their respective industries. For example, Dillard's arranged the merger of regional store chains in order to form a national company. By pursuing horizontal merger, companies are able to obtain economies of scale or secure a national market for their product. As a result, they are able to pursue a cost-leadership or a differentiation business model (although Dillard's has been struggling to pursue its differentiation model effectively). The many important strategic implications of horizontal mergers are discussed in detail in Chapter 9.

● **Using Information Technology and the Internet**

The arrival of new technology often gives a company the opportunity to develop new business strategies to consolidate a fragmented industry. Amazon.com and eBay, for example, used the Internet, and the associated strategies e-commerce makes possible, to pursue a cost-leadership model and consolidate the fragmented auction and bookselling industries. Before eBay, the auction business was extremely fragmented, with local auctions in cities being the principal way in which people could dispose of their antiques and collectibles. By harnessing the Internet, eBay can now assure sellers that they are getting wide visibility for their collectibles and are likely to receive a higher price for their product. Similarly, Amazon.com's success in the book market has accelerated the consolidation of the book retail industry, and many small bookstores have closed because they cannot compete by price or selection. Clear Channel Communications, profiled in Strategy in Action 6.1, used many of the strategies discussed above to become the biggest radio broadcaster in the United States.

The challenge in a fragmented industry is to figure out the best set of strategies to overcome a fragmented market so that the competitive advantages associated with pursuing one of the different business models can be realized. It is difficult to think of any major service activities—from consulting and accounting firms to businesses satisfying the smallest customer need, such as beauty parlors and car repair shops—that have not been consolidated by companies seeking to pursue a more profitable business model.

Strategy in Action

6.1

Clear Channel Creates a National Chain of Local Radio Stations

Clear Channel Communications started out with only one radio station in San Antonio in 1995, following a pattern that was then typical of the radio broadcasting industry. Historically, the industry was fragmented because a federal law prevented any company from owning more than forty stations nationwide; as a result, a large proportion of the local radio stations were independently owned and operated. Clear Channel took advantage of the repeal of this law in 1996 to start buying radio stations and, most importantly, to develop a business model (which today is one of *broad differentiation*) that would allow it to obtain the gains from consolidating this fragmented industry. By 2005, it operated over 1,200 U.S. radio stations.

Clear Channel's strategic managers recognized from the beginning that the major way to increase the profitability of city and small town radio stations was to obtain economies of scale from operating and marketing on a national level. The issue was to find ways to raise the quality of its programming to increase its value to listeners, increase the number of listeners, and thus increase advertising revenues (because advertising rates are based on the number of listeners). At the same time, it needed to find ways to reduce each station's high operating costs, that is, lower its cost structure. How to do both simultaneously was the challenge.

On the value side of the equation, an important issue was how to achieve economies of scale from having a national reach while maintaining local ties to the community. Many listeners like to feel they are listening to a local station that understands who they are and what their needs are. Yet if all programming and service are handled on a local level, how can economies of scale from a national base be achieved? Most cost savings come from standardizing service across stations, from broadcasting uniform content. In addition, local listeners often become used to the glitzy, slick productions put on by national cable television broadcasting companies such as MTV and the main television networks. Because they are national, these companies can afford to pay large sums to stars and celebrities and invest heavily in developing quality products. Such large expenditures are beyond most radio stations' budgets and simply increase the cost of goods sold too much. Moreover, advertising rates had to be kept at a level that both large national companies and small local ones would find acceptable; they could not simply be raised to cover higher costs.

Clear Channel's managers began to experiment with information technology and the Internet and took advantage of emerging digital technology that allowed for the easy and rapid manipulation and transfer of large volumes of data. By the late 1990s, music and programming could easily be recorded, stored in digital format, and edited. Its managers hit on a strategy called voice tracking. To obtain economies of scale, Clear Channel employed popular regional or national DJs to record its daily programs, and these same DJs customized their productions to suit the needs of local markets. For example, one technology allows DJs to isolate and listen to the end of one track and the beginning of the next; then they can insert whatever talk, news, or information is appropriate between tracks as and when they like. The local stations supply this local information; after they have customized their program, the DJs send it over the Internet, where the local operators handle it. This practice has enormous advantages. On the cost side, the programming costs of a limited number of popular DJs are much lower than the cost of employing an army of local DJs. On the differentiation side, the quality of programming is much higher because Clear Channel can invest more in its programming and because the appeal of some DJs is much higher than others. Over time, higher-quality programming increases the number of listeners, and this attracts more national advertisers, whose digital advertisements can be easily inserted in the programming by local operators.

In addition, Clear Channel developed its own proprietary brand name, KISS, across its radio stations so that when people travel, they will be attracted to its local stations wherever they are. It hoped that the resulting increased customer demand would drive up advertising revenues, thereby lowering its cost structure and increasing its future profitability. Clear Channel received a major shock in the 2000s when the growing popularity of MP3 players like the iPod, web surfing, and online videos began to sharply reduce the size of its listening audience, hurting its advertising revenues. It has been forced to experiment with new ways of tailoring radio advertising to listeners, experimenting with short sound bites, and is also allying with Google to find ways to better tailor advertising to the particular needs of the local market. Once again, nothing stays the same for long in any competitive industry environment. [a]

Strategies in Embryonic and Growth Industries

As we discussed in Chapter 2, an embryonic industry is one that is just beginning to develop, and a growth industry is one in which first-time demand is expanding rapidly as many new customers enter the market. In choosing the strategies needed to pursue a business model, embryonic and growth industries pose special challenges because the *attributes of customers change* as market demand expands and *new groups of customers* who have different and evolving needs emerge. Also, other factors affect the rate at which a market grows and expands. Strategic managers have to be aware of the way competitive forces in embryonic and growth industries change over time because they commonly have to build and develop new kinds of competencies and refine their business models to compete effectively in the long term.

Most embryonic industries emerge when a technological innovation creates new product or market opportunities. For example, a century ago, the car industry was born following the development of a new technology, the internal combustion engine, which gave rise to many new products, including the motorcar and motorbus. In 1975, the PC industry was born after new microprocessor technology was developed to build the world's first commercially available PC, the Altair 8800, sold by MITS. Shortly afterward, the PC software industry was born when a Harvard dropout, Bill Gates, and his old school friend, Paul Allen, wrote a version of a popular computer language, BASIC, that would run on the Altair 8800.[6] In 1986, the Internet protocol (IP) network equipment industry was born following the development of the router, an IP switch, by an obscure California start-up, Cisco Systems.

Customer demand for the products of an embryonic industry is frequently limited at first, for a variety of reasons. Moreover, strategic managers who understand how markets develop are in a much better position to pursue a business model and strategies that will lead to a sustained competitive advantage. Reasons for slow growth in market demand include (1) the limited performance and poor quality of the first products, (2) customer unfamiliarity with what the new product can do for them, (3) poorly developed distribution channels to get the product to customers, (4) a lack of complementary products to increase the value of the product for customers, and (5) high production costs because of small volumes of production.

Customer demand for the first cars, for example, was limited by their poor performance (they were no faster than a horse, far noisier, and frequently broke down); a lack of important complementary products, such as a network of paved roads and gas stations; and high production costs, which made them a luxury item. Similarly, demand for the first PCs was limited because buyers had to be able to program a computer to use it, and there were no software application programs that could be purchased to run on the PCs. Because of such problems, early demand for the products of embryonic industries comes from a small set of technologically sophisticated customers who are willing to put up with, and may even enjoy, imperfections in the product. Computer hobbyists, who got great joy out of tinkering with their imperfect machines and finding ways to make them work, bought the first PCs.

An industry moves from an embryonic to a growth stage when a *mass market* starts to develop for the industry's product (a mass market is one in which large numbers of customers enter the market). Mass markets typically start to develop when three things occur: (1) ongoing technological progress makes a product easier to use and increases the value of the product to the average customer; (2) key complementary products are developed that do the same; and (3) companies in the industry strive to find ways to reduce production costs so they can lower their cost structure and choose a low price option, and this stimulates high demand.[7] For example, a mass market for cars emerged when (1) technological progress increased the performance of cars; (2) a network of paved roads and gas stations was established, which meant a car could go more places and thus had more value; and (3) Henry Ford began to mass-produce cars, which dramatically lowered production costs and allowed him to reduce prices, causing the demand for cars to surge. Similarly, the mass market for PCs started to emerge when technological advances made them easier to use, a supply of complementary software such as spreadsheets and word processing programs was developed that increased the value of owning a PC, and companies in the industry started to use mass production to build PCs at low cost.

Strategic managers who understand how the demand for a product is affected by changing customer needs and groups can focus their energies on developing new strategies to protect and strengthen their business models, such as building competencies in low-cost manufacturing or speedy product development. One strategy, for example, would be to share information about new products under development with the companies that supply complementary products so that customers will be convinced the new product is worth buying. Another strategy would be to involve customers in the product development process to gain their input and their acceptance of a new product.

● The Changing Nature of Market Demand

The development of most markets follows an S-shaped growth curve similar to that illustrated in Figure 6.1. As the stage of market development moves from embryonic to mature, customer demand first accelerates and then decelerates as a market approaches saturation. As we noted in Chapter 2, in a saturated market, most customers have already bought the product, and demand is limited to replacement demand; the market is mature. Figure 6.1 shows that different groups of customers who have different needs enter the market over time—and this has major implications for a company's product differentiation and market segmentation decisions.

The first group of customers to enter the market are referred to as the *innovators*. Innovators are technocrats who get great delight from being the first to purchase and experiment with products based on a new technology, even though that technology

FIGURE 6.1

Market Development and Customer Groups

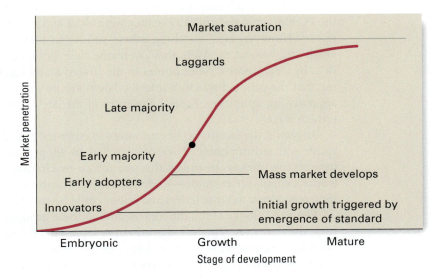

is imperfect and expensive. They often have an engineering mindset and want to own the technology for its own sake. In the PC industry, the first customers were software engineers and computer hobbyists who wanted to write computer code at home.[8]

The *early adopters* are the second group of customers to enter the market. Early adopters understand that the technology might have important future applications and are willing to experiment with it to see if they can pioneer uses for it, often by finding new ways to satisfy customer needs. Early adopters are often visionaries who appreciate how the technology may be used in the future and try to be the first to profit from its use. Jeff Bezos, the founder of Amazon.com, was an early adopter of the Internet and web-based technology, who saw in 1994 that the Internet could be used in innovative ways to sell books. He saw this possibility before anyone else and was one of the first dot-com pioneers to purchase web servers and related software and use them to sell products over the Internet. Amazon.com was thus an early adopter.

Both innovators and early adopters enter the market while the industry is in its embryonic stage. The next group of customers, the *early majority*, represents the leading wave or edge of the mass market; their entry signifies the beginning of the growth stage. Customers in the early majority are comfortable with the new technology and products. However, they are pragmatists: they weigh the benefits of adopting new products against their costs and wait to enter the market until they are confident that products will offer them tangible benefits. Once they start to enter the market, however, they do so in large numbers. This is what happened in the PC market after IBM's introduction of the PC in 1981. For the early majority, IBM's entry into the market legitimized the technology and signaled that the benefits of adoption would be worth the costs of purchasing and learning to use the product. The growth of the PC market was then given further impetus by the development of important applications that added value to it, such as new spreadsheet and word processing programs. These applications transformed the PC from a hobbyist's toy into a business productivity tool.

Once the mass market attains a critical mass, with something like 30% of the potential market penetrated, the next wave of customers enters the market. This wave is characterized as the *late majority*: the customers who purchase a new technology or product only when it is clear it will be around for a long time. Examples of the members of a typical late majority customer group are the customers who started to enter the PC market in the mid-1990s; they were older and somewhat intimidated by computers. However, after watching others similar to themselves buying PCs to send email and browse the Web, they overcame their hesitancy and started to purchase PCs. By 2002, some 65% of homes in the United States had at least one PC, suggesting that the product was well into the late majority group and that the market was approaching saturation. Indeed, the entry of the late majority signals the end of the growth stage.

Laggards, the last group of customers to enter the market, are inherently conservative and technophobic. They often refuse to adopt a new technology even if its benefits are obvious or unless they are forced by circumstances—to reply to a colleague's email, for example—to do so. People who stick to using typewriters rather than computers to write letters and books could be considered laggards today.

Figure 6.2 looks at the differences among these groups of consumers in a somewhat different way. The bell-shaped curve represents the total market, and the divisions in the curve show the percentage of customers who, on average, fall into each customer group. The early adopters are a very small percentage of the total customers

FIGURE 6.2

Market Share of
Different Customer
Segments

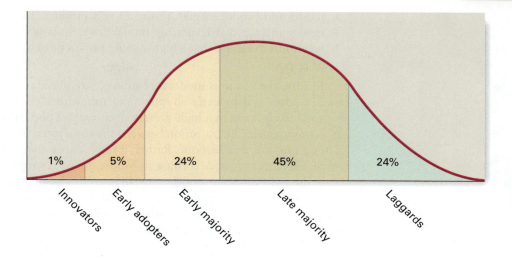

| 1% | 5% | 24% | 45% | 24% |

Innovators   Early adopters   Early majority   Late majority   Laggards

who will ultimately buy the product. Thus, the figure illustrates a vital competitive fact: *Most market demand and industry profits arise when members of the early and late majority enter the market.* And research has found that, although many of the early pioneering companies do well in attracting innovators and early adopters, many of these companies often *fail* to attract a significant share of early and late majority customers and ultimately go out of business.

● **Strategic Implications: Crossing the Chasm**

Why are pioneering companies often unable to create a business model that allows them to be successful over time and remain the market leaders? *Innovators and early adopters have very different customer needs from the early majority.* In an influential book, Geoffrey Moore argues that because of the differences in customer needs between these groups, the business-level strategies required for companies to succeed in the emerging mass market are quite different from those required to succeed in the embryonic market.[9] Pioneering companies that do not change the strategies they use to pursue their business model will therefore lose their competitive advantage to those companies that implement new strategies that push the value creation frontier out to the right. Different strategies are often required to support and strengthen a company's business model as a market develops over time, for the following reasons:

● Innovators and early adopters are technologically sophisticated individuals who are willing to tolerate engineering imperfections in the product. The early majority, however, values ease of use and reliability. Companies competing in an embryonic market typically pay more attention to increasing the performance of a product than to its ease of use and reliability. Those competing in a mass market need to make sure that the product is reliable and easy to use. Thus, the product development strategies required for success are different as a market develops over time.

● Innovators and early adopters are typically reached through specialized distribution channels, and products are often sold by word of mouth. Reaching the early majority requires mass-market distribution channels and mass-media advertising campaigns that require a different set of marketing and sales strategies.

● Because innovators and the early majority are relatively few in number and are not particularly price sensitive, companies serving them typically pursue a focus model and produce small quantities of a product. To serve the rapidly growing mass market, a cost-leadership model based on large-scale mass production may be critical to ensure that a high-quality product can be produced reliably at a low price point.

In sum, the business model and strategies required to compete in an embryonic market populated by early adopters and innovators are very different from those required to compete in a high-growth mass market populated by the early majority. As a consequence, the transition between the embryonic market and the mass market is not a smooth, seamless one. Rather, it represents a *competitive chasm*, or gulf, that companies must cross. According to Moore, many companies do not or cannot develop the right business model; they fall into the chasm and go out of business. This insight is consistent with the observation that, although embryonic markets are frequently populated by large numbers of small companies, once the mass market begins to develop, the number of companies in the marketplace drops off sharply.[10]

Figure 6.3, which compares the strategies of AOL Time Warner and Prodigy, illustrates Moore's thesis by showing that a wide chasm exists between innovators and the early majority, that is, between the embryonic market and the rapidly growing mass market. Note also that other smaller chasms exist between other sets of customers, and that these too represent important, although less dramatic, breaks in the nature of the market that require changes in business-level strategy (for example, a different approach to market segmentation). The implication of Moore's thesis is that a company must often formulate and implement new strategies, and build new competencies, if it is to create a business model that can successfully cross the chasm. Strategy in Action 6.2 describes how the early leader in online services, Prodigy, fell into the chasm, while AOL successfully built a business model to cross it.

To cross this chasm successfully, managers must correctly identify the customer needs of the first wave of early majority users—the leading edge of the mass market. Once companies have identified these customers' needs, they must alter their business model by developing new strategies to redesign products and create distribution channels and marketing campaigns to reach the early majority. In this way, they will have ready a suitable product, at a reasonable price, that they can sell to the members of the early majority as they start to enter the market in large numbers. In sum, industry pioneers must abandon their old focused business model that was directed solely toward the needs of their early or initial customers because this focus may lead

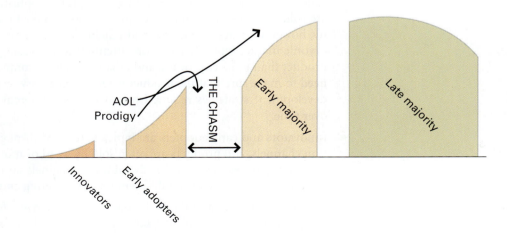

FIGURE 6.3

The Chasm Between Innovators and the Early Majority: AOL and Prodigy

Strategy in Action

6.2

How Prodigy Fell into the Chasm Between Innovators and the Early Majority

Before America Online (AOL) became a household name, Prodigy Communications was a market leader. Founded in 1984, Prodigy was a joint venture among Sears, IBM, and CBS. CBS soon dropped out, but IBM and Sears stuck with it, investing $500 million in developing the network and finally launching it in 1990. Prodigy's business model was differentiation, and the goal was to build the largest proprietary online shopping network: the system would give its customers the ability to buy anything, even plane tickets, online. IBM knew about computers, and Sears knew about retail. It seemed like the perfect marriage.

Launched in the fall of 1990, the service quickly accumulated half a million users. There was little sense of competition at the time. The largest competitor, CompuServe, was conservatively managed, and it pursued a focused business model based on servicing the needs of technical users and financial services (CompuServe was owned by H&R Block, America's largest tax return service). There was another small competitor, AOL, but in the words of one Prodigy executive, "It was just a little thing off to the side." Ten years later, the little thing had become the largest online service in the world, with 33 million members, and Prodigy had exited the online business altogether after IBM and Sears had invested, and lost, some $1.2 billion on the venture.

Why did Prodigy fail? The company appeared to be focusing on the mass market. Its target customers were not computer-oriented early adopters but typical middle-class Americans. And its business model to sell products online seemed correct; surely this ultimately had to become a major application of the Internet. The problem was that Prodigy's managers did not choose the right set of strategies to formulate the business model; in particular, they did not understand the full range of needs customers were trying to satisfy by using the Internet.

One of the surprise early drivers of customer demand for online services, and a major factor in creating the mass market, was email. AOL's strategy was to offer its members unlimited email, but Prodigy charged members a fee for sending more than thirty emails per month—a big difference in business models. Another important application of online service was chatrooms, a service that customers were increasingly embracing. AOL saw chatrooms as one of the unique possibilities of online service for satisfying customer needs, and its strategy was to quickly implement the software that would soon make chatrooms one of its most popular features.

The lawyers at Prodigy's corporate headquarters, however, feared that Prodigy might be held legally liable for comments made in chatrooms or events that arose from them, and they discouraged Prodigy from offering this service. This censorship, lack of chatrooms, and charges for email rankled Prodigy subscribers, who soon started to switch in droves to AOL.

The nature of the software interface used to allow customers to connect to an online service also became a critical competitive issue as the market developed. When it was introduced, Prodigy's primitive graphical user interface was acceptable by the PC standards of the time, which were based on Microsoft's MS-DOS operating system. When Microsoft introduced its much more user-friendly Windows 3.0 systems in 1990, AOL moved quickly to redesign its software interface to be compatible with Windows, and this made AOL much easier to use. Prodigy was part owned by IBM, however, which at that time was trying to promote its own new PC operating system, the ill-fated OS/2. So Prodigy dragged its feet. It waited to implement a Windows version of its own interface until December 1993, by which time it had lost the majority of Windows users to AOL.

By 1996, the battle was effectively over: AOL was growing by leaps and bounds, and Prodigy was losing customers at a rapid pace because its strategies had pushed out the value creation frontier. AOL, by correctly sensing the way customer needs were changing and then providing a differentiated product that met those needs, crossed the chasm with ease.[b]

FIGURE 6.4

Differences in Diffusion Rates for Different Products

Automobile (1886)
Cell phone (1983)
Electricity (1873)
Microwave (1953)
PC (1975)
Radio (1905)
Telephone (1876)
Television (1926)
VCR (1952)

Source: Peter Brimelow, "The Silent Boom," *Forbes,* July 7, 1997, pp. 170–171. Reprinted by permission of *Forbes Magazine* © 2002 Forbes, Inc.

them to ignore the needs of the early majority users and the need to pursue a differentiation or cost-leadership model to become the dominant competitor in the future.

● **Strategic Implications of Market Growth Rates**

A final important issue that strategic managers must understand in embryonic and growth industries is that different markets develop at different rates. The speed at which a market develops can be measured by its growth rate, that is, the rate at which the industry's product is bought by customers in that market. Figure 6.4 charts the growth rates of several important products in the United States from their initial introduction to the present time. Although many of these products display the classic S-shaped growth curve, their markets have grown at different rates. For example, demand for TVs has grown more rapidly than demand for cars. The market growth rates for new kinds of products seem to have accelerated over time, probably because the increasing use of the mass media and low-cost mass production help to accelerate the demand for new products. However, there are also differences in the growth rate for new products introduced at around the same time. For example, the cell phone was introduced somewhat later than the PC, and yet market demand has grown more rapidly.

● **Factors Affecting Market Growth Rates**

A number of factors explain the variation in market growth rates for different products and thus the speed with which a particular industry develops. It is important for strategic managers to understand the source of these differences because, by their choice of business model and strategies, they can accelerate or retard the rate at which a particular market grows.[11] *In other words, business-level strategy is a major determinant of industry profitability.*

The first factor that accelerates customer demand is a new product's *relative advantage,* that is, the degree to which a new product is perceived as better at satisfying customer needs than the product it supersedes. For example, the early growth in demand for cell phones was partly driven by their economic benefits. Studies showed that because business customers could always be reached by cell phone, they made better use of their time—for instance, by not showing up at a meeting that had been cancelled at the last minute—and saved two hours per week that would otherwise have been wasted. For busy executives, the early adopters, the productivity benefits of owning a cell phone outweighed the costs. Cell phones also diffused rapidly for social reasons, in particular, because they conferred glamour or prestige on their users (something that also drives demand for advanced kinds of hand-held computers and smart phones).

Another factor driving growth in demand is *compatibility*, the degree to which a new product is perceived as being consistent with the current needs or existing values of potential adopters. Demand for cell phones grew rapidly because their operation was compatible with the prior experience of potential adopters who used traditional wire-line phones.

Complexity is a third factor. Complexity is the degree to which a new product is perceived as difficult to understand and use. Early PCs, with their clunky operating system interfaces, were complex to use and so were slow to be adopted. The first cell phones were simple to use and were adopted quickly.

A fourth factor is *trialability*, which is the degree to which a new product can be experimented with on a hands-on trial basis. Many people first used cell phones by borrowing one from a colleague to make a call, and this positive experience helped accelerate growth rates. In contrast, early PCs were more difficult to experiment with because they were rare and expensive and because some training was needed to use them. These complications led to slower growth rates.

The last factor is *observability*, the degree to which the results of using and enjoying a new product can be seen and appreciated by other people. The Palm Pilot, and later the BlackBerry, diffused rapidly because it was easy to observe how quickly its users could schedule meetings, enter addresses, record expenses, and so on. The convenience of the device was clear, and the same was true of the cell phone, so they were rapidly adopted.

Young companies must be sure to devise strategies that address these issues if they are to grow their market share. At the beginning, Nike's founders, for example, worked hard to show customers how its new sneakers offered major advantages in sports performance and were compatible with the sporting lifestyle that was sweeping the United States. Obviously, trialability was easy and complexity was low because Nike's shoes were conveniently displayed and could be tried on in stores. Nike also used dramatic guerrilla-style marketing campaigns to increase the observability of its products, and as people watched others wearing Nike shoes, a kind of contagion effect spread as people had to have a pair of Nike shoes. Thus, Nike was highly successful in using these strategies to pursue its differentiation business model.

● **Strategic Implications of Differences in Growth Rates**

From a strategic perspective, companies can increase the demand for a new product if they develop business-level strategies to clearly show its relative advantage, make it as compatible as possible with customers' prior needs and experiences, reduce its complexity, and make it possible for customers to try or observe others using the product. These considerations must drive the product development process that takes a product from the design stage and puts it into customers' hands. Companies that develop the distinctive competencies needed to do this gain a competitive advantage and thus increased market share.

Apple Computer succeeded at first because the less complex design of its Apple II PC made it easier to use than competing designs, and also because some key complements (particularly VisiCalc, the first business spreadsheet) soon became available for the machine. Similarly, the growing popularity of Sony's first PlayStation was due in part to the fact that Sony pioneered the marketing strategy of setting up displays in retail stores where potential customers could try a PlayStation and others could observe them enjoying it.

Another important strategic issue at the growth stage is that the popularity of a new product often increases or spreads in a way that is analogous to a *viral model of infection.* Lead adopters (the first customers who buy a product) in a market become "infected" or enthused with the product. Subsequently, they infect other people by telling them about its advantages, and after having observed the benefits of the product, these people also adopt it. A good example of this model of diffusion occurred with Hotmail, when its developers decided to add a tag line on the bottom of an email that read, "get your free email at Hotmail.com." This tag line proved to be remarkably effective in recruiting new members. Someone would sign up at one institution, say, the University of Washington, and send email via Hotmail to friends. Some of the recipients would also sign up. Within a few days, there would be ten members at the University of Washington, then one hundred, and within a month a thousand—all "infected" from the original user.

Companies promoting new products can take advantage of this viral diffusion phenomenon by identifying and aggressively courting potential opinion leaders in a community—customers whose views command respect. For example, when the manufacturers of new high-tech medical equipment, such as an MRI scanner, start to sell a new product, they first try to get well-known doctors at major research and teaching hospitals to use the product. They may give these opinion leaders free machines for their research purposes and work closely with them in developing the technology. Once these opinion leaders commit to the product and give it their stamp of approval, doctors at many other hospitals often follow.

In sum, understanding competitive dynamics in embryonic and growth industries is an important strategic issue. The ways in which different kinds of customer groups emerge and customer needs change are important determinants of the strategies that need to be pursued to make a business model successful over time. Similarly, understanding the factors that affect a market's growth rate allows managers to tailor their business model to a changing industry environment. (Much more is said about competition in dynamic, changing, high-tech industries in the next chapter.)

Navigating Through the Life Cycle to Maturity

Another crucial decision that faces strategic managers at each stage of the industry life cycle is which investment strategy to pursue. An investment strategy determines the amount and type of resources and capital—human, functional, and financial—that must be spent to configure a company's value chain so that it can pursue a business model successfully over time.[12] In deciding on an investment strategy, managers must evaluate the potential return (on invested capital) from investing in a generic business model against the cost. In this way, they can determine whether pursuing a certain business model strategy is likely to be profitable and how the profitability of a particular business model will change as competition within the industry changes.

Two factors are crucial in choosing an investment strategy: the competitive advantage a company's business model gives it in an industry relative to its competitors, and the stage of the industry's life cycle in which the company is competing.[13] In determining the strength of a company's relative competitive position, market share and distinctive competencies become important. A large market share signals greater potential returns from future investment because it suggests a company has brand loyalty and is in a strong position to grow its profits in the future. Similarly, the more difficult it is to imitate a company's distinctive competencies, such as those in research and development (R&D) or manufacturing and marketing, the more sustainable is the competitive advantage supplied by its business model and the greater the likelihood that investment in it will lead to a higher ROIC. These two attributes also reinforce one another; for example, a large market share may help a company to create and develop distinctive competencies that strengthen its business model over time because high demand allows it to ride down the experience curve and lower its cost structure. Also, a large market share can create a large cash flow, which may allow for more investment to develop competencies in R&D or elsewhere. In general, companies with the largest market share and the strongest distinctive competencies are in the best position to build and sustain their competitive advantage. Companies with a small market share and little potential for developing a distinctive competency are in a much weaker competitive position.[14]

Because different kinds of opportunities and threats are found in each life cycle stage, the stage of the industry life cycle also influences a company's choice of how much to invest in its business model. Therefore, each stage has different implications for the investment of resources needed to obtain a competitive advantage. Competition is strongest in the shakeout stage of the life cycle and least important in the embryonic stage, for example. The *risks* associated with pursuing a certain business model therefore change over time. The difference in risk explains why the potential returns from investing in a particular business model depend on the life cycle stage.

● **Embryonic Strategies**

In the embryonic stage, all companies, weak and strong, emphasize the development of a distinctive competency and an associated business model. During this stage, investment needs are great because a company has to establish a competitive advantage. Many fledgling companies in the industry are seeking resources to develop a distinctive competency. Thus, the appropriate business-level investment strategy is a **share-building strategy**. The aim is to build market share by developing a stable and distinctive competitive advantage to attract customers who have no knowledge of the company's products.

Companies require large amounts of capital to develop R&D or sales and service competencies. They cannot generate much of this capital internally. Thus, a company's success depends on its ability to demonstrate a distinctive competency to attract outside investors or venture capitalists. If a company gains the resources to develop a distinctive competency, it will be in a relatively stronger competitive position. If it fails, its only option may be to exit the industry. In fact, companies in weak competitive positions at all stages in the life cycle may choose to exit the industry to cut their losses.

● **Growth Strategies**

At the growth stage, the task facing a company is to strengthen its business model to provide the base it needs to survive the coming shakeout. Thus, the appropriate investment strategy is the **growth strategy**. The goal is to maintain its relative competitive position in a rapidly expanding market and, if possible, to increase it—in other words, to grow with the expanding market. However, other companies are entering the market and catching up with the industry's innovators. As a result, the companies first into the market with a particular kind of product often require successive waves of capital infusion to maintain the momentum generated by their success in the embryonic stage. For example, differentiators need to engage in extensive research and development to maintain their technological lead, and cost leaders need to invest in state-of-the-art machinery and computers to obtain new experience-curve economies. All this investment to strengthen their business model is very expensive. And, as we discuss above, many companies fail to recognize the changing needs of customers in the market and invest their capital in ways that do not lead to the distinctive competencies required for long-term success.

The growth stage is also the time when companies attempt to secure their grip over customers in existing market segments and enter new segments so that they can increase their market share. Increasing the level of market segmentation to become a broad differentiator is expensive as well. A company has to invest resources to develop a new sales and marketing competency, for example. Consequently, at the growth stage, companies must make investment decisions about the relative advantages of differentiation, cost-leadership, or focus business models given their financial needs and relative competitive position. If one or a few companies have emerged as the clear cost leaders, for example, other companies might realize that it is futile to compete head-to-head with these companies and instead decide to pursue a growth strategy using a differentiation or focus approach and invest resources in developing other competencies. As a result, strategic groups start to develop in an industry as each company seeks the best way to invest its scarce resources to maximize its competitive advantage.

Companies must spend a lot of money just to keep up with growth in the market, and finding additional resources to develop new skills and competencies is a difficult task for strategic managers. Consequently, companies in a weak competitive position at this stage engage in a **market concentration** strategy to find a viable competitive position. They seek to specialize in some way and adopt a focus business model to reduce their investment needs. If they are very weak, they may also choose to exit the industry and sell out to a stronger competitor.

● **Shakeout Strategies**   By the shakeout stage, demand is increasing slowly, and competition by price or product characteristics becomes intense. Companies in strong competitive positions need resources to invest in a **share-increasing strategy** to attract customers from weak companies exiting the market. In other words, companies attempt to maintain and increase market share despite fierce competition. The way companies invest their resources depends on their business model.

For cost leaders, investment in cost control is crucial if they are to survive the shakeout stage because of the price wars that can occur; they must do all they can to reduce costs. Differentiators in a strong competitive position choose to forge ahead and increase their market share by investing in marketing, and they are likely to develop a sophisticated after-sales service network. Differentiators in a weak position reduce their investment burden by withdrawing to a focused model, the market concentration strategy, to specialize in a particular market segment. A market concentration strategy generally indicates that a company is trying to turn its business around so that it can survive in the long run.

Weak companies exiting the industry engage in a harvest strategy. A company using a **harvest strategy** must limit or decrease its investment in a business and extract, or milk, the investment as much as it can. For example, a company reduces to a minimum the assets it employs in the business and forgoes investment to reduce its cost structure.[15] Then the company harvests all the sales revenues it can profitably obtain before it liquidates all its assets and exits the industry. Companies that have lost their cost-leadership position to more efficient companies are more likely to pursue a harvest strategy because a smaller market share means higher costs and they are unable to move to a focus strategy. Differentiators, in contrast, have a competitive advantage in this stage if they can move to a focus model.

● **Maturity Strategies**   By the maturity stage, companies want to reap the rewards of their previous investments in developing the business models that have made them dominant industry competitors. Until now, profits have been reinvested in the business, and dividends have been small. Investors in leading companies have obtained their rewards through the appreciation of the value of their stock because the company has reinvested most of its capital to maintain and increase market share. As market growth slows in the maturity stage, a company's investment strategy depends on the level of competition in the industry and the source of the company's competitive advantage.

In environments in which competition is high because of technological change or low barriers to entry, companies need to defend their competitive position. Strategic managers need to continue to invest heavily in maintaining the company's competitive advantage. Both cost leaders and differentiators adopt a **hold-and-maintain strategy** to defend their business models and to ward off threats from focused companies who might be appearing. They expend resources to develop their distinctive competency and thus remain the market leaders. For example, differentiated companies may invest in improved after-sales service, and low-cost companies may invest in the latest production technologies.

At this point, too many companies realize the benefits that can be obtained by investing resources to become broad differentiators to protect themselves from aggressive competitors (both at home and abroad) that are watching for any opportunity or perceived weakness to take the lead in the industry. Differentiators enter new market segments to increase their market share; they also take advantage of their growing profits to develop flexible manufacturing systems to reduce their production costs. Cost leaders also begin to enter more market segments and increase product differentiation to expand their market share. For example, Gallo moved from the bulk wine segment and began marketing premium wines and wine coolers to take advantage of its low production costs. Soon Gallo's new premium brands, like Falling Leaf chardonnay, became the best-selling wines in the United States. As time goes on, the competitive positions of the leading differentiators and cost leaders become closer, and the pattern of industry competition changes yet again, as we discuss in the next section.

Strategy in Mature Industries

As a result of fierce competition in the shakeout stage, an industry becomes consolidated, and so a mature industry is commonly dominated by a small number of large companies. Although it may also contain many medium-sized companies and a host of small, specialized ones, the large companies determine the nature of competition in the industry because they can influence the five competitive forces. Indeed, these large companies owe their leading positions to the fact that they have developed the most successful business models and strategies in the industry.

By the end of the shakeout stage, companies have learned how important it is to analyze each other's business model and strategies. They also know that if they change their strategies, their actions are likely to stimulate a competitive response from industry rivals. For example, a differentiator that starts to lower its prices because it has adopted a more cost-efficient technology not only threatens other differentiators but may also threaten cost leaders that see their competitive advantage being eroded. Hence, by the mature stage of the life cycle, companies have learned the meaning of competitive independence.

As a result, in mature industries, business-level strategy revolves around understanding how established companies *collectively* try to reduce the strength of industry competition to preserve both company and industry profitability. Interdependent companies can help protect their competitive advantage and profitability by adopting strategies and tactics, first, to deter entry into an industry and, second, to reduce the level of rivalry within an industry.

● **Strategies to Deter Entry: Product Proliferation, Price Cutting, and Maintaining Excess Capacity**

Companies can use three main methods to deter entry by potential rivals and hence maintain and increase industry profitability: product proliferation, price cutting, and maintaining excess capacity (see Figure 6.5). Of course, *potential entrants* will try to circumvent such entry-deterring strategies by incumbent companies. Competition is rarely a one-way street.

PRODUCT PROLIFERATION   As we noted above, in the maturity stage, most companies move to increase their market share by producing a wide range of products targeted at different market segments. Sometimes, however, to reduce the threat of entry, existing companies ensure that they are offering a product targeted at every segment in the market. This creates a barrier to entry because potential competitors find it hard to break into an industry and establish themselves when there is no obvious group of customers whose needs are not being met by existing companies.[16] This strategy of "filling the niches," or catering to the needs of customers in all market segments to deter entry, is known as **product proliferation**.

Because the large U.S. carmakers were so slow to fill the small-car niches (they did *not* pursue a product proliferation strategy), they were vulnerable to the entry of the Japanese into these market segments in the United States in the 1980s. Ford and GM really had no excuse for this situation because, in their European operations, they had a long history of small-car manufacturing. Managers should have seen the opening and filled it ten years earlier, but the (mistaken) view was that "small cars mean small profits." Better small profits than no profits! In the soap and detergent industry,

FIGURE 6.5

Strategies for Deterring
Entry of Rivals

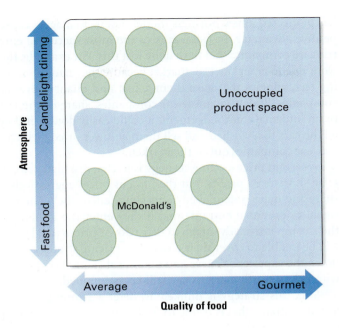

FIGURE 6.6

Product Proliferation
in the Restaurant
Industry

on the other hand, competition is based on the production of new kinds of soaps and
detergents to satisfy or create new desires by customers. Thus, the number of soaps
and detergents, and especially the way they are packaged (powder, liquid, or tablets),
proliferates, making it very difficult for prospective entrants to attack a new market
segment.

Figure 6.6 indicates how product proliferation can deter entry. It depicts product
space in the restaurant industry along two dimensions: atmosphere, which ranges
from fast food to candlelight dining, and quality of food, which ranges from average
to gourmet. The circles represent product spaces filled by restaurants located along
the two dimensions. Thus, McDonald's is situated in the average-quality/fast-food
area. A gap in the product space gives a potential entrant or an existing rival an opportunity to enter the market and make inroads. The shaded, unoccupied product
space represents areas where new restaurants can enter the market. When all the
product spaces are filled, this barrier to entry makes it much more difficult for a new
company to gain a foothold in the market and differentiate itself.

PRICE CUTTING In some situations, pricing strategies can be used to deter entry by
other companies, thus protecting the profit margins of companies already in an industry. One entry-deterring strategy is to cut prices every time a new company enters
the industry or, even better, every time a potential entrant is *contemplating* entry, and
then raise prices once the new or potential entrant has withdrawn. The goal here is to
send a signal to potential entrants that new entry will be met with price cuts. If incumbent companies in an industry consistently pursue such a strategy, potential entrants will come to understand that their entry will spark off a price war, the threat of
new entry will be reduced, average prices will be higher, and industry profitability
will increase.

However, a price-cutting strategy will not keep out an entrant that plans to adopt
a new technology that will give it a cost advantage over established companies or that

has pioneered a new business model that its managers expect will also give it a competitive advantage. In fact, many of the most successful entrants into mature industries are companies that have done just this. For example, the Japanese car companies were able to enter the U.S. market because they had pioneered new lean manufacturing technologies that gave them a cost and quality advantage over established U.S. companies. Today, Japanese car companies' share of the U.S. market is limited only by an informal trade agreement; it could easily double if they were allowed to import all the cars they wished and sell them at lower prices, which might drive one or more U.S. car companies out of the market.

A second price-cutting strategy is to charge a high price initially for a product and seize short-term profits, but then to cut prices aggressively in order to build market share and deter potential entrants simultaneously.[17] The incumbent companies thus signal to potential entrants that if they enter the industry, the incumbents will use their competitive advantage to drive down prices to a level at which new companies will be unable to cover their costs. This pricing strategy also allows a company to ride down the experience curve and obtain substantial economies of scale. Since costs fall with prices, profit margins can still be maintained.

Still, this strategy is unlikely to deter a strong potential competitor—an established company that is trying to find profitable investment opportunities in other industries. It is difficult, for example, to imagine 3M's being afraid to enter an industry because companies there threaten to drive down prices. A company such as 3M has the resources to withstand any short-term losses. Dell also had few worries about entering the highly competitive electronics industry and starting to sell televisions, digital cameras, and so on, because of its powerful set of distinctive competencies. Hence, when faced with such a scenario, it may be in the interests of incumbent companies to accept new entry gracefully, giving up market share gradually to the new entrants to prevent price wars from developing and thus saving their profits, if this is feasible. As Strategy in Action 6.3 details, Toys "R" Us has been forced to give up market share in the toy market, and it has lost much of its prominence as a result.

MAINTAINING EXCESS CAPACITY A third competitive technique that allows companies to deter entry involves maintaining excess capacity, that is, maintaining the physical capability to produce more of a product than customers currently demand. Existing industry companies may deliberately develop some limited amount of excess capacity to warn potential entrants that if they enter the industry, existing firms can retaliate by increasing output and forcing down prices until entry would become unprofitable. However, the threat to increase output has to be *credible*; that is, companies in an industry must collectively be able to raise the level of production quickly if entry appears likely.

● **Strategies to Manage Rivalry**

Beyond seeking to deter entry, companies also wish to develop strategies to manage their competitive interdependence and decrease price rivalry. Unrestricted competition over prices reduces both company and industry profitability. Several strategies are available to companies to manage industry rivalry. The most important are price signaling, price leadership, nonprice competition, and capacity control (Figure 6.7).

PRICE SIGNALING A company's ability to choose the price option that leads to superior performance is a function of several factors, including the strength of demand for a product and the intensity of competition among rivals. Price signaling is the first means by which companies attempt to control rivalry among competitors to allow the *industry* to choose the most favorable pricing option.[18] **Price signaling** is

Strategy in Action

New Competitors for Toys "R" Us

Toys "R" Us, based in Paramus, New Jersey, grew at an astonishing 25% annual rate to become the market leader in the retail toy market in 1990, with a 20% share. To reach its dominant position, the company consolidated the fragmented toy market by developing a nationwide chain of retail outlets so that it could pursue a cost-leadership strategy. To lower its cost structure, Toys "R" Us developed efficient materials-management techniques for ordering and distributing toys to its stores, and it provided a low level of customer service compared to traditional small toy shops. This business model allowed it to achieve a low expense-to-sales ratio of 17%, and it then used this favorable cost structure to promote a philosophy of everyday low pricing. The company deliberately set out to undercut the prices of its rivals, and it succeeded: two of its largest competitors, Child World and Lionel, went bankrupt.

With its dominant position in the industry established, Toys "R" Us continued to build its chain of toy stores, and it began stocking an ever larger and more complex array of products. This would raise its costs; nevertheless, its managers reasoned that they could afford to do so because they were in the driver's seat, and customers would find more value in a wider toy selection. Moreover, raising prices of the toys could offset any cost increases, or perhaps the company could negotiate higher price discounts from toymakers like Mattel or Parker Bros.

The company received a shock in 1995 when its commanding position was threatened by the entry of a new set of rivals. Recognizing the high profits that Toys "R" Us was earning, rapidly expanding companies such as Wal-Mart, Kmart, and Target began to make toy selling a major part of their business model. What could Toys "R" Us do to stop them? Not much. Because of its failure to control costs, Toys "R" Us could not stop their entry into its business by reducing its prices; in other words, by failing to pursue its cost-leadership strategy faithfully, it had lost its ability to play pricing games as it had done with its earlier rivals. The entry of these other companies also reduced its power over its suppliers, the toymakers, because they now had important new customers. Finally, some of the new entrants, Wal-Mart in particular, were now the cost leaders in the retail industry, and their size gave them the resources to withstand any problems if Toys "R" Us attempted to start a price war. In fact, Wal-Mart simply imitated the earlier approach of Toys "R" Us and began selling toys at prices that were below those of Toys "R" Us! By 2000, Wal-Mart became the leading price-setter in the toy market.

To survive, Toys "R" Us has tried to lower its cost structure in its core toy business. It installed new IT to increase the efficiency of its purchasing and distribution operations. It reduced the number of items its stores carry by over 30% to slash its cost structure. At the same time, recognizing that it will never be able to match Wal-Mart's low costs, it changed its business model to try to create customer value by developing other kinds of stores for related market segments, such as Kids "R" Us and Babies "R" Us. It also went online and attempted to develop a major Web presence. However, faced with the high costs of online selling today, it partnered with Amazon.com; toys bought in its shop on Amazon's website can be picked up at any Toys "R" Us store.

By 2004, it was clear that these moves had not halted the decline in the company's market share and profitability. In fact, in 2004, it made the surprise announcement that it was thinking of getting out of the toy business and would henceforth focus on its specialty Kids "R" Us and Babies "R" Us stores, which were making money. However, in November 2004, it still had not found a buyer for its toy stores, and in 2005, it finally announced that it was selling the entire company to a group of investors led by the KKR venture capitalist group; their goal is to reorganize the now private company to rebuild the profitability of its business model.[c]

the process by which companies increase or decrease product prices to convey their intentions to other companies and so influence the way they price their products.[19] Companies use price signaling to improve industry profitability.

Companies may use price signaling to announce that they will respond vigorously to hostile competitive moves that threaten them. For example, they may signal that if one company starts to cut prices aggressively, they will respond in kind. A

FIGURE 6.7

Strategies for
Managing Industry
Rivalry

tit-for-tat strategy is a well-known price signaling strategy in which a company does exactly what its rivals do: if its rivals cut prices, the company follows; if its rivals raise prices, the company follows. By pursuing this strategy consistently over time, a company sends a clear signal to its rivals that it will match any pricing moves they make, the idea being that, sooner or later, rivals will learn that the company will always pursue a tit-for-tat strategy. Because rivals now know that the company will match any price reductions and that cutting prices will only reduce profits, price cutting becomes less common in the industry. A tit-for-tat strategy also signals to rivals that price increases will be imitated, increasing the probability that rivals will initiate price increases to raise profits. Thus, a tit-for-tat strategy can be a useful way of shaping pricing behavior in an industry.[20]

The airline industry is a good example of the power of price signaling, when prices typically rise and fall depending on the current state of customer demand. If one carrier signals the intention to lower prices, a price war frequently ensues as other carriers copy each other's signals. If one carrier feels demand is strong, it tests the waters by signaling an intention to increase prices, and price signaling becomes a strategy to obtain uniform price increases. Nonrefundable tickets, another strategy adopted to obtain a more favorable pricing option, originated as a market signal by one company that was quickly copied by all other companies in the industry. Carriers recognized that they could stabilize their revenues and earn interest on customers' money if they collectively acted to force customers to assume the risk of buying airline tickets in advance. In essence, price signaling allows companies to give one another information that enables them to understand each other's competitive product or market strategy and make coordinated, price-competitive moves.

PRICE LEADERSHIP **Price leadership**—in which one company assumes the responsibility for choosing the most favorable industry pricing option—is a second tactic used to reduce price rivalry and thus enhance the profitability of companies in a mature industry.[21] Formal price leadership, or price setting by companies jointly, is illegal under antitrust laws, so the process of price leadership is often very subtle. In the car industry, for example, prices are set by imitation. The price set by the weakest company—that is, the one with the highest cost structure—is often used as the basis for competitors' pricing. Thus, U.S. carmakers set their prices, and Japanese carmakers then set theirs with reference to the U.S. prices. The Japanese are happy to do this because they have lower costs than U.S. companies, so they make higher profits than U.S. carmakers without competing with them on price. Pricing is done by market segment. The prices of different auto models in the model range indicate the customer segments that the companies are aiming for and the price range they believe the market segment can tolerate. Each manufacturer prices a model in the segment with reference to the prices charged by its competitors, not by reference to competitors' costs. Price leadership also allows differentiators to charge a premium price.

Although price leadership can stabilize industry relationships by preventing head-to-head competition and thus raise the level of profitability within an industry, it has its dangers. It helps companies with high cost structures, allowing them to survive without having to implement strategies to become more productive and efficient. In the long term, such behavior makes them vulnerable to new entrants that have lower costs because they have developed new low-cost production techniques. That is what happened in the U.S. car industry after the Japanese entered the market. After years of tacit price fixing, with GM as the price leader, the carmakers were subjected to growing low-cost Japanese competition, to which they were unable to respond. Indeed, most U.S. carmakers survived only because the Japanese carmakers were foreign firms. Had the foreign firms been new U.S. entrants, the government would probably not have taken steps to protect Chrysler, Ford, or GM.

NONPRICE COMPETITION A third very important aspect of product and market strategy in mature industries is the use of **nonprice competition** to manage rivalry within an industry. The use of strategies to try to prevent costly price cutting and price wars does not preclude competition by product differentiation. Indeed, in many industries, product differentiation strategies are the principal tool companies use to deter potential entrants and manage rivalry within their industry.

Product differentiation allows industry rivals to compete for market share by offering products with different or superior features, such as the features of the Bratz dolls, or by applying different marketing techniques. In Figure 6.8, product and market segment dimensions are used to identify four nonprice competitive strategies based on product differentiation: market penetration, product development, market development, and product proliferation. (Notice that this model applies to new market segments, not new markets.)[22]

Market penetration. When a company concentrates on expanding market share in its existing product markets, it is engaging in a strategy of market penetration.[23] **Market penetration** involves heavy advertising to promote and build product differentiation, which Mattel has actively pursued through its aggressive marketing campaign for Barbie, for example. In a mature industry, advertising aims to influence customers' brand choice and create a brand-name reputation for the company and its products. In this way, a company can increase its market share by attracting the

FIGURE 6.8

Four Nonprice Competitive Strategies

customers of its rivals. Because brand-name products often command premium prices, building market share in this situation is very profitable, which is why Mattel is trying to meet the challenge from MG Entertainment's Bratz doll.

In some mature industries—for example, soap and detergent, disposable diapers, and beer brewing—a market-penetration strategy becomes a way of life.[24] In these industries, all companies engage in intensive advertising and battle for market share. Each company fears that if it does not advertise, it will lose market share to rivals who do. Consequently, in the soap and detergent industry, Procter & Gamble spends more than 20% of sales revenues on advertising, with the aim of maintaining and perhaps building market share. These huge advertising outlays constitute a barrier to entry for prospective entrants.

Product development. **Product development** is the creation of new or improved products to replace existing ones.[25] The wet-shaving industry depends on product replacement to create successive waves of customer demand, which then create new sources of revenue for companies in the industry. Gillette, for example, periodically comes out with a new and improved razor, such as its new vibrating razor that competes with Schick's four-bladed razor, to try to boost its market share. In the car industry, each major car company replaces its models every three to five years to encourage customers to trade in their old models and buy the new one.

Product development is crucial for maintaining product differentiation and building market share. For instance, the laundry detergent Tide has gone through more than fifty changes in formulation during the past forty years to improve its performance. The product is always advertised as Tide, but it is a different product each year. Refining and improving products is a crucial strategy that companies use to fine-tune and improve their business models in a mature industry, but this kind of competition can be as vicious as a price war because it is very expensive and can dramatically increase a company's cost structure. One of Mattel's central strategies is product development, and in the 2000s, its cost structure soared as it spent tens of millions of dollars to develop successful new kinds of dolls and toys to compete in a changing environment.

Market development. **Market development** finds new market segments for a company's products. A company pursuing this strategy wants to capitalize on the brand name it has developed in one market segment by locating new market segments in which to compete—just as Mattel and Nike do by entering many different segments of the toy and shoe markets, respectively. In this way, companies can leverage the product differentiation advantages of their brand name. The Japanese auto manufacturers provide an interesting example of the use of market development. When they entered the market, each Japanese manufacturer offered a car model aimed at the economy segment of the auto market, such as the Toyota Corolla and the Honda Accord. Then they upgraded each model over time, and now each is directed at a more expensive market segment. The Accord is a leading contender in the midsize car segment, and the Corolla fills the small-car segment that used to be occupied by the Celica, which is now aimed at a sportier market segment. By redefining their product offerings, Japanese manufacturers have profitably developed their market segments and successfully attacked their industry rivals, wresting market share from these companies. Although the Japanese used to compete primarily as cost leaders, market development has allowed them to become differentiators as well. In fact, as we noted in

FIGURE 6.9

Toyota's Product Lineup

Price	Sports Utility Vehicles	Passenger/ Sports Sedans	Passenger Vans	Personal Luxury Vehicles	Sporty Cars	Pickup Trucks
$11–20K	RAV4, Scion xB	Echo, Matrix, Corolla, Prism, Scion xA			Celica GT	Tacoma
$21–30K	4-Runner, Highlander	Camry, Avalon	Sienna	Avalon	MR2, Spyder	Tundra
$31–45K	Sequoia, RX330	GS 300, IS 300		ES 330	Camry, Solara	Tundra Double Cab
$46–75K	Land Cruiser, GX, LX	GS 430		LS 430	SC 430	

the last chapter, Toyota has used market development to become a broad differentiator. Figure 6.9 illustrates how, over time, Toyota has used market development to develop a vehicle for almost every main segment of the car market.

Product proliferation. **Product proliferation** can be used to manage rivalry within an industry and to deter entry. The strategy of product proliferation generally means that large companies in an industry all have a product in each market segment or niche and compete head-to-head for customers. If a new niche develops, such as sports utility vehicles, designer sunglasses, or Internet websites, then the leader gets a first-mover advantage, but soon all the other companies catch up. Once again, competition is stabilized, and rivalry within the industry is reduced. Product proliferation thus allows the development of stable industry competition based on product differentiation, not price—that is, nonprice competition based on the development of new products. The competitive battle is over a product's perceived uniqueness, quality, features, and performance and not over its price, something that is becoming increasingly important in the PC business, as the Running Case discusses.

CAPACITY CONTROL Although nonprice competition helps mature industries avoid the cutthroat price cutting that reduces company and industry levels of profitability, price competition does periodically break out when excess capacity exists in an industry. Excess capacity arises when companies collectively produce too much output and, to dispose of it, they cut prices. When one company cuts prices, the others quickly follow (a game theory prediction: see the discussion in a later section of this chapter) because they fear that the price cutter will be able to sell its entire inventory while they will be left with unwanted goods. The result is that a price war develops.

Excess capacity may be caused by a shortfall in demand, as when a recession lowers the demand for cars and causes car companies to give customers price incentives to purchase a new car. In this situation, companies can do nothing except wait for better times. By and large, however, excess capacity results from companies within an industry simultaneously responding to favorable conditions: they all invest in new plants to be able to take advantage of the predicted upsurge in demand. Paradoxically, each individual company's effort to outperform the others means that, collectively, the companies create industry overcapacity, which hurts them all.

RUNNING CASE

Dell Has to Rethink Its Business-Level Strategies

As we have discussed in our story of Dell so far, the company achieved its position as the cost leader on the value creation frontier because of its ability to manage its supply chain and thus make and sell a PC at a lower price than its competitors. In the 1990s, its low-cost advantage resulted in many of its competitors, such as IBM, being driven from the market, and others, like HP and Gateway, struggled to reduce their cost structures to remain profitable. By the early 2000s, however, things had changed. Dell found that its main rival HP had learned how to manage its supply chain and could now build a PC at a price competitive with Dell's, one important reason being that it used powerful low-cost chips made by AMD. Dell also found that Apple computer's new sleek designs were attracting more and more customers, especially because in 2006, Apple began to use Intel's chips, which made its machines Windows-compatible. Dell was now feeling the heat on all sides. Analysts started to criticize the pedestrian look of its computers, which were almost always plain black boxes, and make unfavorable comparisons with HP's and Apple's redesigned computers.

So, starting in 2006, Dell decided to improve the look and design of its PCs and invest resources to make them more differentiated—even though this would increase costs. It hired 500 new design engineers to beef up its internal team of industrial designers, recruiting specialists from carmakers and consumer products companies to make them more attractive and functional. And it also bought the PC focus differentiator Alienware Corp., which made high-powered/high-priced gaming PCs whose sleek futuristic machines, modeled after the beast from the movie Alien, were regarded by many as the best looking PCs on the market. One result was that in 2006, Dell introduced the $3,500 XPS M2010, a cross between a desktop and laptop targeted at entertainment enthusiasts, which features a detachable wireless keyboard and a monitor with adjustable height. And with its black, leatherlike exterior, it resembles a luxury briefcase when closed. Dell then began to introduce innovative lower-priced models such as the new $1,990 XPS 700 desktop,

also aimed at hard-core video gamers. Its new designs allowed Dell to charge a premium price for its top-of-the-line machines, which represent only about 1% of Dell's total 2005 sales of $55.9 billion.

Dell's eventual goal, however, is for all these design innovations to trickle down into its principle lines of PCs so that it can charge higher prices for them and so increase its overall profit margins. By focusing more on product development and differentiation, Dell hopes not only to increase its profits, but also to fight back the challenge from HP and Apple so that it will occupy the middle of the value creation frontier and thus strengthen its competitive advantage. With its mass-market PCs, Dell's goal is also to make them easier and more comfortable to use; for example, Dell set out to make the controls for laptop touchpads, PC keyboards, and LCD monitors more functional and easier to use. Another battle Dell has had to fight to stay on the value creation frontier is to increase the level of its customer service after it outsourced most of this function to companies in India. Long the leader in customer service, Dell lost its lead to HP and Gateway in 2005 as customer complaints about poor quality service increased. Even though its goal is to squeeze out every cent of costs, in 2006, Dell pumped back over $250 million into improved customer service and brought the corporate customer service department back to the United States to protect its dominating position in the important business server and PC market segment.

Only time will tell if Dell's new business-level strategies will work. Its stock price plummeted in 2006 as its profit margins shrank and those of HP and Apple increased. But by the fall, there were increasing signs that its new lines of PCs were attracting customers back. It also began to use AMD's chips, breaking its long alliance with Intel, to keep the cost of its new machines low and competitive. Product and market development, as well as product proliferation, is a never-ending process, especially when technology changes quickly, as it does in the computer industry.

Although demand is rising, the consequence of each company's decision to increase capacity is a surge in industry capacity, which drives down prices. To prevent the accumulation of costly excess capacity, companies must devise strategies that let them control—or at least benefit from—capacity expansion programs. Before we examine these strategies, however, we need to consider in greater detail the factors that cause excess capacity.[26]

Factors causing excess capacity. The problem of excess capacity often derives from technological developments. Sometimes new low-cost technology is the culprit because all companies invest in it simultaneously to prevent being left behind. Excess capacity occurs because the new technology can produce more than the old. In addition, new technology is often introduced in large increments, which generates overcapacity. For instance, an airline that needs more seats on a route must add another plane, thereby adding hundreds of seats even if only fifty are needed. To take another example, a new chemical process may operate efficiently only at the rate of 1,000 gallons a day, whereas the previous process was efficient at 500 gallons a day. If all companies within an industry change technologies, industry capacity may double, and enormous problems can result.

Overcapacity may also be caused by competitive factors within an industry. Entry into an industry is one such factor. The entry of South Korean companies into the global semiconductor industry in the 1990s caused massive overcapacity and price declines. Similarly, the entry of steel producers from the former Soviet Union countries into the global steel market produced excess capacity and plunging prices in the world steel market in the late 1990s and early 2000s. Sometimes the age of a company's plant is the source of the problem. For example, in the hotel industry, given the rapidity with which the quality of hotel furnishings declines, customers are always attracted to new hotels. When new hotel chains are built alongside the old chains, excess capacity can result. Often companies are simply making simultaneous competitive moves based on industry trends, but those moves eventually lead to head-to-head competition. Most fast-food chains, for instance, establish new outlets whenever demographic data show population increases. However, the companies seem to forget that all other chains use the same data (they are not fully anticipating their rivals' actions). Thus, a locality that has no fast-food outlets may suddenly see several being built at the same time. Whether they can all survive depends on the growth rate of demand relative to the growth rate of the chains.

Choosing a capacity-control strategy. Given the various ways in which capacity can expand, companies clearly need to find some means of controlling it. If they are always plagued by price cutting and price wars, they will be unable to recoup the investments in their generic strategies. Low profitability within an industry caused by overcapacity forces not just the weakest companies but also sometimes the major players to exit the industry. In general, companies have two strategic choices: (1) each company individually must try to preempt its rivals and seize the initiative, or (2) the companies collectively must find indirect means of coordinating with each other so that they are all aware of the mutual effects of their actions.

To *preempt* rivals, a company must forecast a large increase in demand in the product market and then move rapidly to establish large-scale operations that will be able to satisfy the predicted demand. By achieving a first-mover advantage, the company may deter other firms from entering the market because the preemptor will usually be able to move down the experience curve, reduce its costs (and thus its prices, too), and threaten a price war if necessary.

This strategy, however, is extremely risky because it involves investing resources before the extent and profitability of the future market are clear. Wal-Mart preempted Sears and Kmart, with its strategy of locating in small rural towns to tap an underexploited market for discount goods. Wal-Mart has been able to engage in market penetration and market expansion because of the secure base it established in its rural strongholds.

A preemptive strategy is also risky if it does not deter competitors and they decide to enter the market. If the competitors have a stronger generic strategy or more resources, such as Microsoft or Intel, they can make the preemptor suffer. Thus, for the strategy to succeed, the preemptor must generally be a credible company with enough resources to withstand a possible price war.

To *coordinate* with rivals as a capacity-control strategy, caution must be exercised because collusion on the timing of new investments is illegal under antitrust law. However, tacit coordination is practiced in many industries as companies attempt to understand and forecast one another's competitive moves. Generally, companies use market signaling to secure coordination. They make announcements about their future investment decisions in trade journals and newspapers. In addition, they share information about their production levels and their forecasts of demand within an industry to bring supply and demand into equilibrium. Thus, a coordination strategy reduces the risks associated with investment in the industry. This is very common in the chemical refining and oil business, where new capacity investments frequently cost hundreds of millions of dollars.

Game Theory

As we have discussed, companies are in a constant competitive struggle with rivals in their industry to gain more business from customers. A useful way of viewing this struggle is as a competitive game between companies, in which companies are continually using competitive moves and tactics to compete effectively in an industry. Companies that understand the competitive nature of the game they are playing can often improve their competitive positioning and increase the profitability of their business models. For example, managers can implement better strategies to pursue cost leadership or differentiation.

A branch of work in the social sciences known as *game theory* can be used to model competition between a company and its rivals and help managers improve their business models and strategies.[27] From a game theory perspective, companies in an industry can be viewed as players that are all simultaneously making choices about which business models and strategies to pursue to maximize their profitability. The problem strategic managers face is that the potential profitability of each business model is not some fixed amount; it varies depending on the strategies one company selects and also the strategies that its rivals select. There are two basic types of game: sequential move games and simultaneous move games. In a *sequential move game*, such as chess, players move in turn, and one player can select a strategy to pursue after considering its rival's choice of strategies. In a *simultaneous move game*, the players act at the same time, in ignorance of their rival's current actions. The classic game of rock-paper-scissors is a simultaneous move game.

In the business world, both sequential and simultaneous move games are commonplace as strategic managers jockey for competitive position in the industry. Indeed, game theory is particularly useful in analyzing situations in which a company is competing against a limited number of rivals and a considerable level of interdependence exists in the industry, as occurs in a mature industry. Several of the basic principles that underlie game theory are examined below; these principles can be useful in determining which business model and strategies managers should pursue.

LOOK FORWARD AND REASON BACK   One of the most basic messages of game theory is that managers need to think strategically in two related ways: (1) look forward, think ahead, and anticipate how rivals will respond to whatever strategic moves they make; and (2) reason backward to determine which strategic moves to pursue today given their assessment of how the company's rivals will respond to various future strategic moves. Managers who take both of these approaches should be able to discover the specific competitive strategy that will lead to the greatest potential returns. This cardinal principle of game theory is known as *look forward and reason back*. To understand its importance, consider the following scenario.

Two large companies, UPS and FedEx, which specialize in next-day delivery of packages, dominate the U.S. air express industry. They have a very high fixed cost structure because they need to invest in a capital-intensive nationwide network of aircraft, trucks, and package-sorting facilities. The key to their profitability is to increase volume sufficiently so that these fixed costs can be spread out over a large number of packages, reducing the unit cost of transporting each package.

Imagine that a bright young manager at UPS calculates that if UPS cuts prices for next-day delivery service by 15%, the volume of packages the company ships will grow by over 30%, and so will UPS's total revenues and profitability. Is this a smart move? The answer depends on whether the bright young manager has remembered to look forward and reason back, and think through how FedEx would respond to UPS's price cuts.

Because UPS and FedEx are competing directly against each other, their strategies are interdependent. If UPS cuts prices, FedEx will lose market share, its volume of shipments will decline, and its profitability will suffer. FedEx is unlikely to accept this result: if UPS cuts prices by 15%, FedEx is likely to follow and cut its prices by 15% to hold on to market share. The net result is that the average level of prices in the industry will fall by 15%, as will revenues, and both players will see their profitability decline—a lose-lose situation. By looking forward and reasoning back, the new manager discovers that the strategy of cutting prices is not a good one.

Decision trees can be used to help in the process of looking forward and reasoning back. Figure 6.10 maps out the decision tree for the simple game analyzed above from the perspective of UPS. (Note that this is a sequential move game.) UPS moves first, and then FedEx must decide how to respond. Here, you see that UPS has to choose between two strategies: cutting prices by 15% or leaving them unchanged. If it leaves prices unchanged, it will continue to earn its current level of profitability, which is $100 million. If it cuts prices by 15%, one of two things can happen: FedEx matches the price cut, or FedEx leaves its prices unchanged. If FedEx matches UPS's price cut (FedEx decides to fight a price war), profits are lost in the price competition, and UPS's profit will be $0. If FedEx does not respond and leaves its prices unaltered, UPS will gain market share and its profits will rise to $180 million. So the best pricing strategy for UPS to pursue depends on its assessment of FedEx's likely response.

Figure 6.10 assigns probabilities to the different responses from FedEx: specifically, there is a 70% chance that FedEx will match UPS's price cut and a 30% chance that it will do nothing. These probabilities come from an assessment of how UPS's price cut will affect FedEx's sales volume and profitability. The bigger the negative impact of UPS's price cut is on FedEx's sales volume and profitability, the more likely it is that FedEx will match UPS's price cuts. This is another example of the principle

FIGURE 6.10

A Decision Tree for
UPS's Pricing Strategy

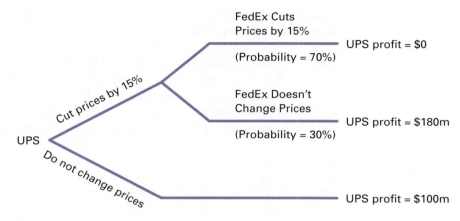

of looking forward and reasoning back. Assigning a 70% probability to the top branch in Figure 6.10 assumes that the price cut from UPS will have a significant negative impact on FedEx's business and will force the company to respond with a price cut of its own. The probabilities can also come from looking at the history of FedEx's responses to UPS's price moves. If FedEx has a long history of matching UPS's price cuts, the probability that it will do so this time is high. If FedEx does not have a history of matching UPS's price cuts, the probability will be lower.

Now let us revisit the question of what strategy UPS should pursue. If UPS does not cut prices, its profits are $100 million. If it cuts prices, its expected profits are $(.70) \times \$0 + (.30) \times \$180 = \$60$ million. Since $60 million is less than $100 million, UPS should not pursue the price-cutting strategy. If it did, FedEx would probably respond, and the net effect would be to depress UPS's profitability. Another way of looking at this scenario is to ask: Under what assumptions about the probability of FedEx's responding would it be worthwhile for UPS to cut prices by 15%? For UPS to move forward with its price cuts, the expected profits from doing so must be greater than $100 million, which is the profit from doing nothing. The way to work this out is to find the probability for which UPS is indifferent between leaving prices unaltered or changing them. We use p to signify probability: $\$100m = p \times \$180m$. Solving for p, we get $p = \$100m/\$180m = 0.556$. In other words, for UPS to go ahead with the proposed price cut, the probability that FedEx will do nothing must be greater than 55.6%.

KNOW THY RIVAL At this juncture, the question of whether this example is rather contrived might arise. After all, could UPS managers *really* anticipate how FedEx's profits could be affected if UPS cut its prices by 15%? And could UPS really assign a probability to FedEx's likely response? The answer is that, although UPS's managers cannot calculate exactly what the profit impact and probabilities would be, they can make an informed decision by collecting competitive information and thinking strategically. For example, they could estimate FedEx's cost structure by looking at FedEx's published financial accounts. And because they are in the same business as FedEx, they can assess the effect of falling demand on FedEx's cost structure and bottom line. Moreover, by looking at the history of FedEx's competitive behavior, they can assess how FedEx will respond to a price cut.

This illustrates a second basic principle of game theory: know thy rivals. In other words, in thinking strategically, managers must put themselves in the position of a rival to answer the question of how that rival is likely to act in a particular situation. If a company's managers are to be effective at looking forward and reasoning back, they must have a good understanding of what their rival is likely to do under different scenarios, and they need to be able to extrapolate their rival's future behavior based on this understanding.

FIND THE DOMINANT STRATEGY   A **dominant strategy** is one that makes you better off than you would be if you played any other strategy, *no matter what strategy your opponent uses.* To grasp this concept, consider a simultaneous move game based on a situation that developed in the U.S. car industry in the early 1990s and has been going on ever since (so far we have been considering a sequential move game). Two car companies, Ford and GM (both differentiators), have to decide whether to introduce cash-back rebate programs in November to move unsold inventory that is building up on the lots of car dealers nationwide. Each company can make one of two moves: offer cash rebates or do not offer cash rebates. Because the advanced planning associated with launching such a strategy is fairly extensive, both companies must make a decision about what to do by mid-October, which is before each has had a chance to see what its rival is doing.

In each of the previous four years, both companies have introduced just such programs on November 1 and kept them in place until December 31. Customers have become conditioned to expect these programs and increasingly have held back their new car purchases in anticipation of the cash-rebate programs beginning in November. This learned behavior by customers has increased the strategic importance of the rebate programs and made such programs increasingly expensive for the automobile companies—hence the billions of dollars GM and Ford have lost in the 2000s. Figure 6.11 lays out a payoff matrix associated with each strategy.

The four cells in this matrix represent the four possible outcomes of pursuing or not pursuing a cash-rebate strategy. The numbers in parentheses in the center of each cell represent the profit that General Motors and Ford, respectively, will get in each case (in millions of dollars). If both General Motors and Ford decide not to introduce cash rebates (cell 1), each will get $800 million in profit for the November 1–December 31 period. If GM introduces a cash-rebate program but Ford doesn't, GM will gain market share at Ford's expense, and GM will get $1,000 million in profit, while Ford gets just $200 million (cell 2). The converse holds if Ford introduces a rebate program but GM doesn't (cell 3). If both companies introduce rebate programs, both get $400 million (see cell 4; remember, the rebates are expensive and essentially represent deep price discounting to move unsold inventory). Finally, the

FIGURE 6.11

A Payoff Matrix for a Cash-Rebate Program for GM and Ford

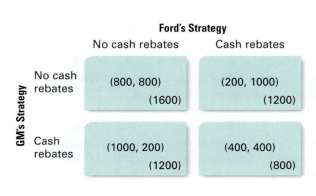

	Ford's Strategy	
GM's Strategy	No cash rebates	Cash rebates
No cash rebates	(800, 800) (1600)	(200, 1000) (1200)
Cash rebates	(1000, 200) (1200)	(400, 400) (800)

figures in parentheses in the lower right-hand corner of each cell represent the joint profit associated with each outcome.

You can see in this payoff matrix that GM's dominant strategy is to offer cash rebates because whatever strategy Ford pursues, GM does better if it offers cash rebates than if it doesn't. If Ford's strategy is to offer no cash rebates, GM's best strategy is to offer rebates and capture a profit of $1,000 million. If Ford's strategy is to offer cash rebates, GM's best strategy is again to offer cash rebates and get a profit of $400 million. So whatever Ford does, GM's best strategy is to offer cash rebates.

An interesting aspect of this game is that Ford also goes through the same reasoning process. Indeed, the payoff matrix shows that Ford's dominant strategy is also to offer cash rebates. The net result is that while both players get $400 million profit, the combined payoff of $800 million is the lowest of any combination! Clearly, both automakers could have done better if they had cooperated and jointly decided not to offer cash rebates. Why didn't they cooperate about this decision? There are two reasons. First, cooperation to set prices is illegal under U.S. antitrust law. Second, even though neither party will gain from offering rebates, *it cannot trust the other party not to offer a cash rebate because then it would be even worse off*. As the payoff matrix shows, if Ford does not offer cash rebates, GM has a very big incentive to do so, and vice versa. So both companies assume that the other will offer rebates, both end up doing so, and customers receive the value and are the winners!

The payoff structure in this game is famous. It is known as the *prisoner's dilemma game* because it was first explained using an example of two suspects, or prisoners, who are being interrogated for possible involvement in a crime. In the original exposition, the prisoners can confess to the crime and also implicate their partner in the crime to get a reduced sentence, or not confess or implicate the other. If the other prisoner also doesn't either confess or implicate the other, they both go free. The problem is that neither prisoner can trust the other not to implicate the partner to get a reduced sentence. So to reduce their losses (length of jail time), both end up confessing and implicating the other, and both go to jail.

The prisoner's dilemma is thought to capture the essence of many situations where two or more companies are competing against each other and their dominant strategy is to fight a price war, even if they would collectively be better off by *not* doing so. In other words, the prisoner's dilemma can be used to explain the mutually destructive price competition that breaks out in many industries from time to time. It also raises the question of whether companies can do anything to extricate themselves from such a situation. This brings us to the final principle of game theory, which is explored in the following section.

STRATEGY SHAPES THE PAYOFF STRUCTURE OF THE GAME An important lesson of game theory is that, through its choice of strategy, a company can alter the payoff structure of the competitive game being played in the industry. To understand this concept, consider once more the cash-rebate game played by Ford and GM, in which both companies are compelled to choose a dominant strategy that depresses total payoffs. How can they extricate themselves from this predicament? They can do it by changing the behavior of customers.

Recall that rebates were necessary only because customers had come to expect them and held off purchasing a car until the rebates were introduced. In a self-fulfilling prophecy, this depresses demand and forces the companies to introduce rebates to move unsold inventory on the lots of car dealers. If these expectations could be changed, customers would not hold off their purchases in anticipation of the rebates being introduced in November of each year, and companies would no longer have to introduce rebates to move unsold inventory on the lots of car dealers. A company can change customer behavior through its choice of strategy.

This is what GM actually did. After several years of rebate wars, GM decided to issue a new credit card that allowed cardholders to apply 5% of their charges toward buying or leasing a new GM car, up to $500 a year with a maximum of $3,500. The credit card launch was one of the most successful in history: within two years, there were 9 million GM credit card holders, and the card had replaced the other incentives that GM offered, principally the end-of-year cash rebates. Because of the card, price-sensitive customers who typically waited for the rebates could purchase a reduced-price car any time of the year. Moreover, once they had the card, they were much more likely to buy from GM than Ford. This strategy changed customer behavior. Customers no longer waited for rebates at the end of the year before buying, an inventory of unsold cars did not build up on the lots of dealers, and GM was not forced into fighting a rebate war to clear inventory.

If this strategy was so successful, what was to stop Ford from imitating it? Nothing! Ford began to offer its own credit card soon after GM did. In this case, however, imitation of the strategy led to increased profitability because both GM and Ford had found a clever way to differentiate themselves from each other: by issuing credit cards that created stronger brand loyalty. With the new cards, a GM cardholder was more likely to buy a GM car and a Ford cardholder was more likely to buy a Ford car. By reducing the tendency of customers to play GM and Ford dealers against each other, the card also had the effect of enabling both GM and Ford to raise their prices. Figure 6.12 illustrates how strategy can change the payoff matrix.

By issuing credit cards and strengthening the differentiation component of their strategy, both Ford and GM reduced the value of cash rebates and made it less likely that customers would switch to the company that offers rebates. The payoff structure of the game changed, and so did the dominant strategy. Now that GM's dominant strategy is not to offer cash rebates, whatever Ford does, GM is better off not offering rebates. The same is true for Ford. In other words, by their choice of strategy, General Motors and Ford have changed their dominant strategy in a way that boosts their profitability.

More generally, this example suggests that the way out of mutually destructive price competition associated with a prisoner's dilemma type of game is for the players to change their business models and differentiate their product offerings in the minds of customers, thereby reducing their sensitivity to price competition. In other words, by their choice of strategy and business model (one principally based on differentiation),

FIGURE 6.12

Altered Payoff Matrix for GM and Ford

Ford's Strategy

		No cash rebates	Cash rebates
GM's Strategy	No cash rebates	(1200, 1200) (2400)	(800, 1000) (1800)
	Cash rebates	(1000, 800) (1800)	(400, 400) (800)

companies can alter the payoff structure associated with the game, alter their dominant strategy, and move away from a prisoner's dilemma type of game structure.

This insight also points to the need for companies to think through how their choice of business strategy might change the structure of the competitive game they are playing. Although we have looked at how strategy can transform the payoff structure of the game in a way that is more favorable, the opposite can and does occur. Companies often unintentionally change their business models and pursue strategies that change the payoff structure of the game in a way that is much less favorable to them and comes to resemble a prisoner's dilemma, as the competitive dynamics between Coca-Cola and PepsiCo in the soft drink industry did; see Strategy in Action 6.4.

The Pepsi challenge changed the long-established competitive rules in the industry. As the basis of competition shifted from differentiation by abstract lifestyle advertising to direct product comparisons, then to price competition, the payoff structure associated with their game changed and became more of a prisoner's dilemma type of structure. Had Pepsi's managers looked ahead and reasoned back, they might have realized that price competition would be the outcome of its new aggressive strategy and they might not have launched the Pepsi challenge, especially because the company was gaining market share from Coke, albeit slowly. However, because Pepsi's strategy changed the nature of differentiation in the industry, it led to a lose-lose situation.

Strategy in Action   6.4

Coca-Cola and PepsiCo Go Head-to-Head

For thirty years, until the late 1970s, the cola segment of the soft drink industry went through a golden age in which the main players, Coca-Cola and PepsiCo, were very profitable. These two companies competed against each other by advertising their respective products, Coke and Pepsi, based on abstract lifestyle product attributes. PepsiCo would introduce advertisements showing that it was cool to drink Pepsi, and Coca-Cola would produce advertisements with catchy jingles such as "things go better with Coke." Neither company competed on price. Coke led the market throughout the period, although by the mid-1970s, Pepsi was closing in.

At this point, Pepsi launched a new and innovative strategy: the Pepsi challenge. The Pepsi challenge was a taste test in which customers were blindfolded and asked which drink they preferred, Pepsi or Coke. In the test, about 55% of customers consistently said they preferred Pepsi, a significant result given that Pepsi trailed Coke in market share. Pepsi test-marketed the Pepsi challenge in Dallas, and it was so successful that in the late 1970s, Pepsi rolled out the challenge nationally, a situation that presented a real dilemma for Coke. It could not respond with its own blind taste test because in the tests, the majority of people preferred Pepsi. Moreover, the Pepsi challenge had changed the nature of competition in the industry. After thirty years of competition through product differentiation based on lifestyle product attributes with no direct (and aggressive) product comparisons, Pepsi had shifted to a direct product comparison based on a real attribute of the product: taste.

PepsiCo had altered its business model and changed how it chose to differentiate its product from Coke. As Pepsi was now gaining market share, Coca-Cola's managers decided to make an aggressive response: deep price discounts for Coke in local markets where they controlled the Coke bottler and the local Pepsi bottler was weak. This was a successful move; in markets where price discounting was used, Coke started to gain its share back. PepsiCo then decided to respond in kind and cut prices too. Before long, price discounting was widespread in the industry. Customers were coming to expect price discounting, brand loyalty had been eroded, and the value associated with differentiation had been reduced. Both Coke and Pepsi experienced declining profitability.[d]

So how did the soft drink manufacturers try to extricate themselves from this situation? Over the course of a few years, they once more shifted the way in which they differentiated their products. They introduced new products, such as Diet Coke and Cherry Coke, to rebuild brand loyalty, and they reemphasized abstract advertising by using celebrities to help create a brand image for their soda, thus differentiating it from their competitors' offerings and reducing customer price sensitivity. They are still doing this today—Pepsi, for example, uses the dancing and music of Britney Spears as a device for building a brand image that differentiates its offering from Coke. However, it took several years for Pepsi and Coke to do this, and in the interim they had to grapple with a payoff structure that reduced profitability in the industry. Moreover, price discounting is still common today.

Strategies in Declining Industries

Sooner or later, many industries enter into a decline stage, in which the size of the total market starts to shrink. Examples are the railroad industry, the tobacco industry, and the steel industry. Industries start declining for a number of reasons, including technological change, social trends, and demographic shifts. The railroad and steel industries began to decline when technological changes brought viable substitutes for their products. The advent of the internal combustion engine drove the railroad industry into decline, and the steel industry fell into decline with the rise of plastics and composite materials. As for the tobacco industry, changing social attitudes toward smoking, which are themselves a product of growing concerns about the health effects of smoking, have caused a decline in tobacco usage.

● **The Severity of Decline**   When the size of the total market is shrinking, competition tends to intensify in a declining industry and profit rates tend to fall. The intensity of competition in a declining industry depends on four critical factors, which are indicated in Figure 6.13. First, the intensity of competition is greater in industries in which decline is rapid as opposed to industries, such as tobacco, in which decline is slow and gradual.

Second, the intensity of competition is greater in declining industries in which exit barriers are high. As we noted in Chapter 2, high exit barriers keep companies locked into an industry even when demand is falling. The result is the emergence of excess productive capacity and, hence, an increased probability of fierce price competition.

Third, and related to the previous point, the intensity of competition is greater in declining industries in which fixed costs are high (as in the steel industry). The reason

FIGURE 6.13

Factors That Determine the Intensity of Competition in Declining Industries is that the need to cover fixed costs, such as the costs of maintaining productive capacity, can make companies try to use any excess capacity they have by slashing prices, which can trigger a price war.

Finally, the intensity of competition is greater in declining industries in which the product is perceived as a commodity (as it is in the steel industry) in contrast to industries in which differentiation gives rise to significant brand loyalty, as was true until very recently of the declining tobacco industry.

Not all segments of an industry typically decline at the same rate. In some segments, demand may remain reasonably strong despite decline elsewhere. The steel industry illustrates this situation. Although bulk steel products, such as sheet steel, have suffered a general decline, demand has actually risen for specialty steels, such as those used in high-speed machine tools. Vacuum tubes provide another example. Although demand for them collapsed when transistors replaced them as a key component in many electronics products, vacuum tubes still had some limited applications in radar equipment for years afterward. Consequently, demand in this vacuum tube segment remained strong despite the general decline in the demand for vacuum tubes. The point, then, is that there may be pockets of demand in an industry in which demand is declining more slowly than in the industry as a whole or is not declining at all. Price competition thus may be far less intense among the companies serving such pockets of demand than within the industry as a whole.

● Choosing a Strategy

There are four main strategies that companies can adopt to deal with decline: (1) a **leadership strategy**, by which a company seeks to become the dominant player in a declining industry; (2) a **niche strategy**, which focuses on pockets of demand that are declining more slowly than the industry as a whole; (3) a **harvest strategy**, which optimizes cash flow; and (4) a **divestment strategy**, by which a company sells off the business to others. Figure 6.14 provides a simple framework for guiding strategic choice. Note that the intensity of competition in the declining industry is measured

FIGURE 6.14

Strategy Selection in a Declining Industry

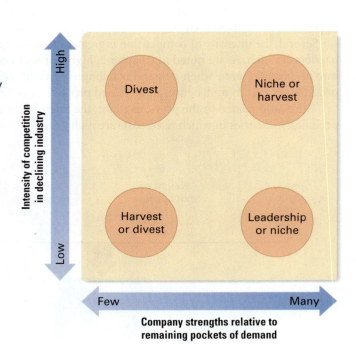

on the vertical axis and that a company's strengths relative to remaining pockets of demand are measured on the horizontal axis.

LEADERSHIP STRATEGY A leadership strategy aims at growing in a declining industry by picking up the market share of companies that are leaving the industry. A leadership strategy makes most sense (1) when the company has distinctive strengths that allow it to capture market share in a declining industry and (2) the speed of decline and the intensity of competition in the declining industry are moderate. Philip Morris has pursued such a strategy in the tobacco industry. Through aggressive marketing, Philip Morris has increased its market share in a declining industry and earned enormous profits in the process.

The tactical steps companies might use to achieve a leadership position include using aggressive pricing and marketing to build market share, acquiring established competitors to consolidate the industry, and raising the stakes for other competitors—for example, by making new investments in productive capacity. Such competitive tactics signal to other competitors that the company is willing and able to stay and compete in the declining industry. These signals may persuade other companies to exit the industry, which would further enhance the competitive position of the industry leader. Strategy in Action 6.5 offers an example of a company, Richardson Electronics, that has prospered by taking a leadership position in a declining industry. It is one of the last companies in the vacuum tube business.

Strategy in Action | 6.5

How to Make Money in the Vacuum Tube Business

At its peak in the early 1950s, the vacuum tube business was a major industry in which companies such as Westinghouse, General Electric, RCA, and Western Electric had a large stake. Then along came the transistor, making most vacuum tubes obsolete, and one by one all the big companies exited the industry. One company, however, Richardson Electronics, not only stayed in the business but also demonstrated that high returns are possible in a declining industry. Primarily a distributor (although it does have some manufacturing capabilities), Richardson bought the remains of a dozen companies in the United States and Europe as they exited the vacuum tube industry, and it now has a warehouse that stocks more than 10,000 different types of vacuum tubes. The company is the world's only supplier of many of them, which helps explain why its gross margin is in the 35 to 40% range.

Richardson survives and prospers because vacuum tubes are vital parts of some older electronics equipment that would be costly to replace with solid-state equipment. In addition, vacuum tubes still outperform semiconductors in some limited applications, including radar and welding machines. The U.S. government and GM are big customers of Richardson.

Speed is the essence of Richardson's business. The company's Illinois warehouse offers overnight delivery to some 40,000 customers, and it processes 650 orders a day at an average price of $550. Customers such as GM do not really care whether a vacuum tube costs $250 or $350; what they care about is the $40,000 to $50,000 downtime loss that they face when a key piece of welding equipment isn't working. By responding quickly to the demands of such customers and being the only major supplier of many types of vacuum tubes, Richardson has placed itself in a monopoly position that many companies in growing industries would envy. However, a new company, Westrex Corp., was formed to take advantage of the growing popularity of vacuum tubes in high-end stereo systems, and today it is competing head-to-head with Richardson in some market segments. Clearly, good profits can be made even in a declining industry.[e]

NICHE STRATEGY A niche strategy focuses on pockets of demand in the industry in which demand is stable or declining less rapidly than in the industry as a whole. The strategy makes sense when the company has some unique strengths relative to those niches where demand remains relatively strong. As an example, consider Naval, a company that manufactures whaling harpoons and small guns to fire them and makes money doing so. This might be considered rather odd because the world community has outlawed whaling. However, Naval survived the terminal decline of the harpoon industry by focusing on the one group of people who are still allowed to hunt whales, although only in very limited numbers: North American Eskimos. Eskimos are permitted to hunt bowhead whales, provided that they do so only for food and not for commercial purposes. Naval is the sole supplier of small harpoon whaling guns to Eskimo communities, and its monopoly position allows it to earn a healthy return in this small market.

HARVEST STRATEGY As we noted earlier, a harvest strategy is the best choice when a company wishes to get out of a declining industry and optimize cash flow in the process. This strategy makes the most sense when the company foresees a steep decline and intense future competition or lacks strengths relative to remaining pockets of demand in the industry. A harvest strategy requires the company to cut all new investments in capital equipment, advertising, R&D, and the like. The inevitable result is that it will lose market share, but because it is no longer investing in this business, initially its positive cash flow will increase. Essentially, the company is taking cash flow in exchange for market share. Ultimately, cash flows will start to decline, and at this stage it makes sense for the company to liquidate the business. Although this strategy is very appealing in theory, it can be somewhat difficult to put into practice. Employee morale in a business that is being run down may suffer. Furthermore, if customers catch on to what the company is doing, they may defect rapidly. Then market share may decline much faster than the company expected.

DIVESTMENT STRATEGY A divestment strategy rests on the idea that a company can recover most of its investment in an underperforming business by selling it early, before the industry has entered into a steep decline. This strategy is appropriate when the company has few strengths relative to whatever pockets of demand are likely to remain in the industry and when the competition in the declining industry is likely to be intense. The best option may be to sell out to a company that is pursuing a leadership strategy in the industry. The drawback of the divestment strategy is that it depends for its success on the ability of the company to spot its industry's decline before it becomes serious and to sell out while the company's assets are still valued by others.

Summary of Chapter

1. In fragmented industries composed of a large number of small and medium-sized companies, the principal forms of competitive strategy are chaining, franchising, and horizontal merger, as well as using the Internet.

2. In embryonic and growth industries, strategy is determined partly by market demand. The innovators and early adopters have different needs from those in the early and the late majority, and a company must be prepared to cross the chasm between the two. Similarly, managers must understand the factors that affect a market's growth rate so they can tailor their business model to a changing industry environment.

3. Companies need to navigate the difficult road from growth to maturity by choosing an investment strategy that supports their business model. In choosing this strategy, managers must consider the company's competitive position in the industry and the stage of the industry's life cycle. Some main types of investment strategy are share building, growth, market concentration, share increasing, harvest, and hold-and-maintain.

4. Mature industries are composed of a few large companies whose actions are so highly interdependent that the success of one company's strategy depends on the responses of its rivals.

5. The principal strategies used by companies in mature industries to deter entry are product proliferation, price cutting, and maintaining excess capacity.

6. The principal strategies used by companies in mature industries to manage rivalry are price signaling, price leadership, nonprice competition, and capacity control.

7. Game theory suggests several management principles: look forward and reason back, know thy rival, pursue your dominant strategy, remember that strategy can alter the payoff structure of the game, and use strategy to change the payoff structure in a way that increases the profitability of your dominant strategy.

8. In declining industries, in which market demand has leveled off or is falling, companies must tailor their price and nonprice strategies to the new competitive environment. They also need to manage industry capacity to prevent the emergence of capacity expansion problems.

9. There are four main strategies a company can pursue when demand is falling: leadership, niche, harvest, and divestment. The choice is determined by the severity of industry decline and the company's strengths relative to the remaining pockets of demand.

Discussion Questions

1. Why are industries fragmented? What are the main ways in which companies can turn a fragmented industry into a consolidated one?

2. What are the key problems in maintaining a competitive advantage in embryonic and growth industry environments? What are the dangers associated with being the leader?

3. In managing their growth through the life cycle, what investment strategies should be made by (a) differentiators in a strong competitive position and (b) differentiators in a weak competitive position?

4. Discuss how companies can use (a) product differentiation and (b) capacity control to manage rivalry and increase an industry's profitability.

5. What insights would game theory offer (a) a small pizza restaurant operating in a crowded college market and (b) a detergent manufacturer seeking to bring out new products in established markets?

Practicing Strategic Management

SMALL-GROUP EXERCISE
How to Keep the Salsa Hot

Break up into groups of three to five, appoint one group member to be the spokesperson who will communicate your findings to the class, and discuss the following scenario. You are the managers of a company that has pioneered a new kind of salsa for chicken that has taken the market by storm. The salsa's differentiated appeal has been based on a unique combination of spices and packaging that has allowed you to charge a premium price. Over the past three years, your salsa has achieved a national reputation, and now major food companies such as Kraft and Nabisco, seeing the potential of this market segment, are beginning to introduce new salsas of their own, imitating your product.

1. Describe your business model and the strategies you are pursuing.

2. Describe the industry environment in which you are competing.

3. What kinds of competitive strategies can you adopt to strengthen your business model in this kind of environment?

ARTICLE FILE 6

Choose a company or group of companies in a particular industry environment, and explain how it has adopted a competitive strategy to protect or enhance its business-level strategy.

STRATEGIC MANAGEMENT PROJECT
Module 6

This part of the project considers how conditions in the industry environment affect the success of your company's business model and strategies. With the information you have at your disposal, perform the tasks and answer the questions listed:

1. In what kind of industry environment (for example, embryonic, mature) does your company operate? Use the information from Strategic Management Project: Module 2 to answer this question.

2. Discuss how your company has attempted to develop strategies to protect and strengthen its business model. For example, if your company is operating in an embryonic industry, how has it attempted to increase its competitive advantage over time? If it operates in a mature industry, discuss how it has tried to manage industry competition.

3. What new strategies would you advise your company to pursue and thus increase its competitive advantage? For example, how should it attempt to differentiate its products in the future or lower its cost structure?

4. On the basis of this analysis, do you think your company will be able to maintain its competitive advantage in the future? Why or why not?

ETHICS EXERCISE

Beverly answered her office phone to find an executive from Grey Industries on the line. "Ms. Jones," he began after pleasantries has been exchanged, "we would be honored if you would consider joining our corporate board." After gathering information, Beverly agreed. As the president of the Natural History Museum, a nonprofit organization in Denver, Colorado, she was used to receiving these requests. In fact, she currently served on two other boards.

A month later, Grey Industries donated half a million dollars to the museum. Beverly, on behalf of the museum, had received large donations from the other companies on whose boards she served. Although she knew it was good for the museum, she wondered if the companies were simply being generous or had ulterior motives. Beverly had managed to remain impartial and serve objectively despite such donations, but she knew other presidents and directors of nonprofit organizations had not and had made decisions based on donation promises. Beverly knew that the Nasdaq Stock Market was encouraging companies to put limits on their donations to nonprofit organizations if presidents and directors of those organizations served on their boards, but firm rules had yet to be put into place. Beverly thought this move would be a smart one on the part of corporations and helpful to board members.

To further complicate matters, Beverly had some serious reservations about the ways in which Grey Industries conducted business. The company's business model hadn't been updated in years, and the competition was beginning to take over. Despite obvious issues, Grey Industries was holding on to its top-level managers—individuals who had been with the company since the beginning. These very same managers seemed incapable of implementing the changes necessary to keep Grey Industries in the running. Having accepted the company's donation, Beverly had to make a difficult decision. Should she resign from the board? Or should she follow her gut instinct and insist that Grey Industries replace these managers immediately or lose to the competition?

1. Define the ethical dilemmas presented in this case.

2. Do you think presidents and directors of nonprofit organizations can remain objective despite promises of large donations?

3. What are the pros and cons of corporations offering donations to nonprofit organizations?

4. How do you think Beverly should approach the situation? Why?

CLOSING CASE

Nike's Winning Ways

Nike, headquartered in Beaverton, Oregon, was founded over thirty years ago by Bill Bowerman, a former University of Oregon track coach, and Phil Knight, an entrepreneur in search of a profitable business opportunity. Bowerman's goal was to dream up a new kind of sneaker tread that would enhance a runner's traction and speed, and he came up with the idea for Nike's waffle tread after studying the waffle iron in his home. Bowerman and Knight made their shoe and began selling it out of the trunks of their car at track meets. From this small beginning, Nike has grown into a company that sold over $12 billion worth of shoes in the $35 billion athletic footwear and apparel industries in 2004.[28]

Nike's amazing growth came from its business model, which has always been based on two original functional strategies: to create state-of-the-art athletic shoes and then to publicize the qualities of its shoes through dramatic guerrilla-style marketing. Nike's marketing is designed to persuade customers that its shoes are not only superior but also a high fashion statement and a necessary part of a lifestyle based on sporting or athletic interests. A turning point came in 1987 when Nike increased its marketing budget from $8 million to $48 million to persuade customers its shoes were the best. A large part of this advertising budget soon went to pay celebrities like Michael Jordan millions of dollars to wear and champion its products. The company has consistently pursued this strategy: in 2003 it signed basketball star LeBron James to a $90 million endorsement contract, and many other sports stars, such as Tiger Woods and Serena Williams, are already part of its charmed circle.

Nike's strategy to emphasize the uniqueness of its product has obviously paid off; its market share soared and its revenues hit $9.6 billion in 1998. However, 1998 was also a turning point because in that year, sales began to fall. Nike's $200 Air Jordans no longer sold like they used to, and inventory built up in stores and warehouses. Suddenly it seemed much harder to design new shoes that customers perceived to be significantly better. Nike's stunning growth in sales was actually reducing its profitability; somehow it had lost control of its business model. Phil Knight, who had resigned his management position, was forced to resume the helm and lead the company out of its troubles. He recruited a team of talented top managers from leading consumer products companies to help him improve Nike's business model. As a result, Nike has changed its business model in some fundamental ways.

In the past, Nike shunned sports like golf, soccer, rollerblading, and so on, and it focused most of its efforts on making shoes for the track and basketball markets to build its market share in these areas. However, when its sales started to fall, it realized that using marketing to increase sales in a particular market segment can grow sales and profits only so far; it needed to start selling more types of shoes to more segments of the athletic shoe market. So Nike took its design and marketing competencies and began to craft new lines of shoes for new market segments. For example, it launched a line of soccer shoes and perfected their design over time, and by 2004, it had won the biggest share of the soccer market from its arch-rival Adidas.[29] Also in 2004, it launched its Total 90 III shoes, which are aimed at the millions of casual soccer players throughout the world who want a shoe they can just "play" in. Once more, Nike's dramatic marketing campaigns aim to make their shoes part of the soccer lifestyle, to persuade customers that traditional sneakers do not work because soccer shoes are sleeker and fit the foot more snugly.[30]

To take advantage of its competencies in design and marketing, Nike then decided to enter new market segments by purchasing other footwear companies offering shoes that extended or complemented its product lines. For example, it bought Converse, the maker of retro-style sneakers; Hurley International, which makes skateboards and Bauer in-line and hockey skates; and Official Starter, a licensor of athletic shoes and apparel whose brands include the low-priced Shaq brand. Allowing Converse to take advantage of Nike's in-house competencies has resulted in dramatic increases in the sales of its sneakers, and Converse has made an important contribution to Nike's profitability.[31]

Nike had also entered another market segment when it bought Cole Haan, the dress shoemaker, in the 1980s. Now it is searching for other possible acquisitions. It decided to enter the athletic apparel market to use its skills there, and by 2004, sales were over $1 billion. In making all these changes to its business model, Nike was finding ways to invest its capital in new products where it could increase its market share and profitability. Its new focus on developing new and improved products for new market segments is working. Nike's ROIC has soared from 14% in 2000 to 24% in 2006, and it makes over $1 billion profit.

Case Discussion Questions

1. What business model and strategies is Nike pursuing?

2. How has Nike's business model changed the nature of industry competition?

3. What new strategies have emerged in the shoe industry as a result?

Strategy and Technology

Format War—Blu-Ray Versus HD-DVD

A format war is developing in the consumer electronics industry between two different versions of next-generation high-definition DVD players and discs. In one camp is Sony with its Blu-ray format; in the other is Toshiba, which is championing the rival HD-DVD format. Both high-definition formats offer a dramatic improvement in picture and sound quality over established DVD technology and are designed to work with high-definition televisions. Although each new format will play old DVDs, the two standards are incompatible with each other. Blu-ray players will not accept DVDs formatted for HD-DVD, and vice versa.

Format wars like this have occurred many times in the past. VHS versus Betamax in the videocassette market and Windows versus Macintosh in personal computer operating systems are classic examples. If history is any guide, format wars tend to be "winner-takes-all" contests, with the loser being vanquished to a niche (as in the case of Apple's Macintosh operating system), or exiting the market altogether (as in the case of Sony's Betamax format). Format wars are a high-stakes game.

Both Sony and Toshiba have been working hard to ensure that their format gains an early lead in sales. In turn, so the thinking goes, this will increase the supply of preformatted discs designed to play on one format or the other, which should lead to a further increase in sales of the format that has the largest share of the market, and thus to its eventual dominance. A key strategy of both companies has been to line up film studios and get them to commit to issuing discs based on their format.

Initially it looked as if Sony had the early advantage. Prior to the technology being launched in the market, Columbia Pictures and MGM (both owned by Sony), along with Disney and Fox Studios, all committed exclusively to Blu-ray. By late 2005, several other studios that had initially committed exclusively to HD-DVD, including Warner Brothers and Paramount, also indicated that they would support Blu-ray as well. Warner and Paramount cited Blu-ray's momentum among other studios and its strong copyright protection mechanisms. This left just Universal Studios committed exclusively to HD-DVD.

To further strengthen its hand, Sony announced that it would incorporate Blu-ray technology in its next-generation P3 videogame console and its Vaio line of personal computers. Hewlett-Packard and Dell Computer also indicated that they would support the Blu-ray format. Sony even licensed the Blu-ray format to several other consumer electronics firms, including Samsung, in a bid to increase the supply of Blu-ray players in stores.

Then things began to go wrong for Sony. The company had to delay delivery of its P3 videogame console by a year due to engineering problems, which sapped some of the momentum from Blu-ray. Microsoft took advantage of this misstep, announcing that it would market an HD-DVD player that would work with its own videogame console, Xbox 360. In mid-2006, the first Blu-ray and HD-DVD players hit the market—the Blu-ray

players were more expensive, as much as twice the price of entry-level HD-DVD players. According to Toshiba, HD-DVD players and discs are cheaper to manufacture, although Sony disputes this. To complicate matters, one of the first Blu-ray players, made by Sony licensee Samsung, was shipped with a bad chip that marred its image quality.

By late 2006, some firms were beginning to hedge their bets. Hewlett-Packard reversed its earlier position and said that it would support both standards. So who will win this war? At this stage, it is too early to say. One possibility, however, is that neither format will win. Faced with two incompatible formats, consumers may do what they have in the past: wait. And without consumer dollars to drive adoption of one format over the other, the market may fail to gain traction.[1]

The format war now unfolding in the consumer electronics industry between two competing and incompatible versions of next-generation high-definition DVDs is typical of the nature of competition in high-technology industries (see the Opening Case). In this chapter, we will take a close look at the nature of competition and strategy in high-technology industries. **Technology** refers to the body of scientific knowledge used in the production of goods or services. **High-technology (high-tech) industries** are those in which the underlying scientific knowledge that companies in the industry use is advancing rapidly, and by implication, so are the attributes of the products and services that result from its application. The computer industry is often thought of as the quintessential example of a high-technology industry. Other industries often considered high-tech are telecommunications, where new technologies based on wireless and the Internet have proliferated in recent years; consumer electronics, where the digital technology underlying products from high-definition DVD players to videogame terminals and digital cameras is advancing rapidly; pharmaceuticals, where new technologies based on cell biology, recombinant DNA, and genomics are revolutionizing the process of drug discovery; power generation, where new technologies based on fuel cells and cogeneration may change the economics of the industry; and aerospace, where the combination of new composite materials, electronics, and more efficient jet engines are giving birth to a new era of superefficient commercial jet aircraft such as Boeing's 787.

This chapter focuses on high-technology industries for a number of reasons. First, technology is accounting for an ever larger share of economic activity. Estimates suggest that 12 to 15% of total economic activity in the United States is accounted for by information technology industries.[2] This figure actually underestimates the true impact of technology on the economy because it ignores the other high-technology areas we just mentioned. Moreover, as technology advances, many low-technology industries are becoming more high-tech. For example, the development of biotechnology and genetic engineering transformed the production of seed corn, long considered a low-technology business, into a high-technology business. Retailing used to be considered a low-technology business, but the shift to online retailing, led by companies like Amazon, has changed this. Moreover, high-technology products are making their way into a wide range of businesses; today a Ford Explorer contains more computing power than the multimillion-dollar mainframe computers used in the Apollo space program, and the competitive advantage of physical stores, such as Wal-Mart, is based on their use of information technology. The circle of high-technology industries is both large and expanding, and even in industries not thought of as high-tech, technology is revolutionizing aspects of the product or production system.

Although high-tech industries may produce very different products, when it comes to developing a business model and strategies that will lead to a competitive advantage and superior profitability and profit growth, they often face a similar situation. For example, winner-take-all format wars are common in many high-technology industries, such as the consumer electronics and computer industries (see the Opening Case for an example of an ongoing format war). This chapter examines the competitive features found in many high-tech industries and the kinds of strategies that companies must adopt to build business models that will allow them to achieve superior profitability and profit growth.

When you have completed this chapter, you will have an understanding of the nature of competition in high-tech industries and the strategies that companies can pursue to succeed in those industries.

Technical Standards and Format Wars

Especially in high-tech industries, ownership of **technical standards**—a set of technical specifications that producers adhere to when making the product or a component of it—can be an important source of competitive advantage.[3] Indeed, in many cases, the source of product differentiation is based on the technical standard. As in the high-definition DVD market, often only one standard will come to dominate a market, so many battles in high-tech industries revolve around companies competing to be the one that sets the standard.

Battles to set and control technical standards in a market are referred to as **format wars**; they are essentially battles to control the source of differentiation and thus the value that such differentiation can create for the customer. Because differentiated products often command premium prices and are often expensive to develop, the competitive stakes are enormous. The profitability and very survival of a company may depend on the outcome of the battle. For example, the outcome of the battle now being waged over the establishment and ownership of the standard for high-definition DVDs will help determine which companies will be leaders for the next decade in that marketplace (see the Opening Case).

● **Examples of Standards** A familiar example of a standard is the layout of a computer keyboard. No matter what keyboard you buy, the letters are all in the same pattern.[4] The reason is quite obvious. Imagine if each computer maker changed the ways the keys were laid out—if some started with QWERTY on the top row of letters (which is indeed the format used and is known as the QWERTY format), some with YUHGFD, and some with ACFRDS. If you learned to type on one layout, it would be irritating and time-consuming to have to relearn on a YUHGFD layout. The standard format (QWERTY) makes it easy for people to move from computer to computer because the input medium, the keyboard, is set out in a standard way.

Another example of a technical standard concerns the dimensions of containers used to ship goods on trucks, railcars, and ships: all have the same basic dimensions—the same height, length, and width—and all make use of the same locking mechanisms to hold them onto a surface or to bolt against each other. Having a standard ensures that containers can be moved easily from one mode of transportation to another—from trucks to railcars, to ships, and back to railcars. If containers lacked standard dimensions and locking mechanisms, it would suddenly become much more difficult to ship containers around the world. Shippers would have to make sure that they had the right kind of container to go on the ships, trucks, and railcars scheduled to carry a particular container around the world—very complicated indeed.

Consider, finally, the personal computer. Most share a common set of features: an Intel or Intel-compatible microprocessor, random access memory (RAM), a Microsoft operating system, an internal hard drive, a floppy disk drive, a CD drive, a keyboard, a monitor, a mouse, a modem, and so on. We call this set of features the dominant design for personal computers (a **dominant design** refers to a common set of features or design characteristics). Embedded in this design are several technical standards (see Figure 7.1). For example, the Wintel technical standard is based on an Intel microprocessor and a Microsoft operating system. Microsoft and Intel "own" that standard, which is central to the personal computer. Developers of software applications, component parts, and peripherals such as printers adhere to this standard when developing their own products because this guarantees that their products will work well with a personal computer based on the Wintel standard. Another technical standard for connecting peripherals to the PC is the Universal Serial Bus (USB), established by an industry standards-setting board. No one owns it; the standard is in the public domain. A third technical standard is for communication between a PC and the Internet via a modem. Known as TCP/IP, this standard was also set by an industry association and is in the public domain. Thus, as with many other products, the PC is actually based on several technical standards. It is also important to note that when a company owns a standard, as Microsoft and Intel do with the Wintel standard, it may be a source of competitive advantage and high profitability.

FIGURE 7.1

Technical Standards for Personal Computers

Dominant Design

Microsoft operating system
Intel microprocessor
Internal hard drive
Monitor
QWERTY keyboard
Wintel Standard
USB
TCP/IP
Slots for connecting peripherals
Ram
Mouse
CD drive
Floppy disk drive
Modem

● **Benefits of Standards**

Standards emerge because there are economic benefits associated with them. First, having a technical standard helps to guarantee compatibility between products and their complements—other products used with them. For example, containers are used with railcars, trucks, and ships, and PCs are used with software applications. Compatibility has the tangible economic benefit of reducing the costs associated with making sure that products work well with each other.

Second, having a standard can help to reduce confusion in the minds of consumers. A few years ago, several consumer electronics companies were vying with each other to produce and market the first generation of DVD players, and they were championing different variants of the basic DVD technology—different standards—that were incompatible with each other; a DVD disk designed to run on a DVD player made by Toshiba would not run on a player made by Sony, and vice versa. The companies feared that selling these incompatible versions of the same technology would produce confusion in the minds of consumers, who would not know which version to purchase and might decide to wait and see which technology ultimately dominated the marketplace. With lack of demand, the technology might fail to gain traction in the marketplace and would not be successful. To avoid this possibility, the developers of DVD equipment established a standard-setting body for the industry, the DVD Forum, which established a common technical standard for DVD players and disks that all companies adhered to. The result was that when DVDs were introduced, they adhered to a common standard, which avoided confusion in consumers' minds. This helped to boost demand for DVD players, making them one of the fastest-selling technologies of the late 1990s and early 2000s. However, the DVD Forum has not been able to agree on a common standard for high-definition DVDs (see the Opening Case).

Third, the emergence of a standard can help to reduce production costs. Once a standard emerges, products based on that standard design can be mass-produced, enabling the manufacturers to realize substantial economies of scale and lower their cost structures. The fact that there is a central standard for PCs (the Wintel standard) means that the component parts for a PC can be mass-produced. A manufacturer of internal hard drives, for example, can mass-produce drives for Wintel PCs and thus can realize substantial scale economies. If there were several competing and incompatible standards, each of which required a unique type of hard drive, production runs for hard drives would be shorter, unit costs would be higher, and the cost of PCs would go up.

Fourth, the emergence of standards can help to reduce the risks associated with supplying complementary products and thus increase the supply for those products. Consider the risks associated with writing software applications to run on personal computers. This is a risky proposition, requiring the investment of considerable sums of money for developing the software before a single unit is sold. Imagine what would occur if there were ten different operating systems in use for PCs, each with only 10% of the market, rather than the current situation, where 95% of the world's PCs adhere to the Wintel standard. Software developers would be faced with the need to write ten different versions of the same software application, each for a much smaller market segment. This would change the economics of software development, increase its risks, and reduce potential profitability. Moreover, because of their higher cost structure and fewer economies of scale, the price of software programs would increase.

Thus, although many people complain about the consequences of Microsoft's near monopoly of PC operating systems, that monopoly does have at least one good effect: it substantially reduces the risks facing the makers of complementary products and the costs of those products. In fact, standards lead to both low-cost and differentiation advantages for individual companies and can help raise the level of industry profitability.

● **Establishment of Standards**

Standards emerge in an industry in three main ways. First, recognizing the benefits of establishing a standard, companies in an industry might lobby the government to mandate an industry standard. In the United States, for example, the Federal Communications Commission (FCC), after detailed discussions with broadcasters and consumer electronics companies, has mandated a single technical standard for digital television broadcasts (DTV) and required broadcasters to have capabilities in place for broadcasting digital signals based on this standard by 2006. The FCC took this step because it believed that without government action to set the standard, the roll-out of DTV would be very slow. With a standard set by the government, consumer electronics companies can have greater confidence that a market will emerge, and this should encourage them to develop DTV products.

Second, technical standards are often set by cooperation among businesses, without government help, often through the medium of an industry forum, such as the DVD Forum. Companies cooperate in this way when they decide that competition among them to create a standard might be harmful because of the uncertainty that it would create in the minds of consumers.

When standards are set by the government or an industry association, they fall into the **public domain**, meaning that any company can freely incorporate into its products the knowledge and technology on which the standard is based. For example, no one owns the QWERTY format, and therefore no one company can profit from it directly. Similarly, the language that underlies the presentation of text and graphics on the Web, hypertext markup language (HTML), is in the public domain; it is free for all to use. The same is true for TCP/IP, the communications standard used for transmitting data on the Internet.

Often, however, the industry standard is selected competitively by the purchasing patterns of customers in the marketplace—that is, by market demand. In this case, the strategy and business model a company has developed for promoting its technological standard are of critical importance because ownership of an industry standard that is protected from imitation by patents and copyrights is a valuable asset—a source of sustained competitive advantage and superior profitability. Microsoft and Intel, for example, both owe their competitive advantage to format wars, which exist between two or more companies competing against each other to get their designs adopted as the industry standard. Format wars are common in high-tech industries because of the high stakes. The Wintel standard became the dominant standard for PCs only after Microsoft and Intel won format wars against Apple Computer's proprietary system and later against IBM's OS/2 operating system. Microsoft and Real Networks are currently competing head-to-head in a format war to establish rival technologies—Windows Media Player and RealPlayer—as the standard for streaming video and audio technology on the Web. The Opening Case tells how Sony and Toshiba are currently engaged in a format war as they try to get their respective technologies established as the standard for high-definition DVDs.

● **Network Effects, Positive Feedback, and Lockout**

It is increasingly apparent that when standards are set by competition between companies promoting different formats, network effects are a primary determinant of how standards are established.[5] **Network effects** arise in industries where the size of the network of complementary products is a primary determinant of demand for an industry's product. For example, the demand for automobiles early in the twentieth century was an increasing function of the network of paved roads and gas stations. Similarly, the demand for telephones is an increasing function of the number of other numbers that can be called with that phone, that is, of the size of the telephone network (the telephone network is the complementary product). When the first telephone service was introduced in New York City, only a hundred numbers could be called. The network was very small because of the limited number of wires and telephone switches, which made the telephone a relatively useless piece of equipment. As more and more people got telephones and as the network of wires and switches expanded, the value of a telephone connection increased. This led to an increase in demand for telephone lines, which further increased the value of owning a telephone, setting up a positive feedback loop.

To understand why network effects are important in the establishment of standards, consider the classic example of a format war: the battle between Sony and Matsushita to establish their respective technology for videocassette recorders (VCRs) as the standard in the marketplace. Sony was first to market with its Betamax technology, followed by Matsushita with its VHS technology. Both companies sold VCR recorder-players, and movie studios issued films prerecorded on VCR tapes for rental to consumers. Initially, all tapes were issued in Betamax format to play on Sony's machine. Sony did not license its Betamax technology, preferring to make all of the player-recorders itself. When Matsushita entered the market, it realized that it would have to encourage movie studios to issue movies for rental on VHS tapes to make its VHS format players valuable to consumers. The only way to do that, Matsushita's managers reasoned, was to increase the installed base of VHS players as rapidly as possible. They believed that the greater the installed base of VHS players, the greater the incentive would be for movie studios to issue movies for rental on VHS format tapes. The more prerecorded VHS tapes available for rental, the greater the value of a VHS player to consumers, and therefore, the greater the demand would be for VHS players (see Figure 7.2). Matsushita wanted to exploit a positive feedback loop.

To do this, Matsushita chose a licensing strategy under which any consumer electronics company was allowed to manufacture VHS format players under license. The strategy worked. A large number of companies agreed to manufacture VHS players,

FIGURE 7.2

Positive Feedback in the Market for VCRs

and soon far more VHS players were available for purchase in stores than Betamax players. As sales of VHS players started to grow, movie studios issued more films for rental in VHS format, and this stoked demand. Before long, it was clear to anyone who walked into a video rental store that there were more and more VHS tapes available for rent and fewer and fewer Betamax tapes. This served to reinforce the positive feedback loop, and ultimately Sony's Betamax technology was shut out of the market. The pivotal difference between the two companies was strategy: Matsushita chose a licensing strategy, and Sony did not. As a result, Matsushita's VHS technology became the de facto standard for VCRs, while Sony's Betamax technology was locked out.

The general principle that emerges from this example is that when two or more companies are competing with each other to get their technology adopted as a standard in an industry, and when network effects and positive feedback loops are important, the company that wins the format war will be the one whose strategy best exploits positive feedback loops. It turns out that this is a very important strategic principle in many high-technology industries, particularly computer hardware, software, telecommunications, and consumer electronics. Microsoft is where it is today because it exploited a positive feedback loop. So did Dolby (see Strategy in Action 7.1).

An important implication of the positive feedback process is that as the market settles on a standard, companies promoting alternative standards can become locked out of the market when consumers are unwilling to bear the switching costs required for them to abandon the established standard and adopt the new standard. In this context, switching costs are the costs that consumers must bear to switch from a product based on one technological standard to a product based on another.

To illustrate, imagine that a company developed an operating system for personal computers that was both faster and more stable (crashed less) than the current standard in the marketplace, Microsoft Windows. Would this company be able to gain significant market share from Microsoft? Only with great difficulty. Consumers buy personal computers not for their operating system but for the applications that run on that system. A new operating system would initially have a very small installed base, so few developers would be willing to take the risks in writing word-processing programs, spreadsheets, games, and other applications for that operating system. Because there would be very few applications available, consumers who did make the switch would have to bear the switching costs associated with giving up some of their applications—something that they might not be willing to do. Moreover, even if applications were available for the new operating system, consumers would have to bear the costs of purchasing those applications, another source of switching costs. In addition, they would have to bear the costs associated with learning to use the new operating system, yet another source of switching costs. Thus, many consumers would be unwilling to switch even if the new operating system performed better than Windows, and the company promoting the new operating system would thus be locked out of the market.

Consumers will bear switching costs if the benefits of adopting the new technology outweigh the costs of switching. For example, in the late 1980s and early 1990s, millions of people switched from analog record players to digital CD players even though the switching costs were significant: they had to purchase the new player technology, and many people purchased duplicate copies of their favorite music recordings. They nevertheless made the switch because for many people, the perceived benefit—the incredibly better sound quality associated with CDs—outweighed the costs of switching.

Strategy in Action

7.1

How Dolby Became the Standard in Sound Technology

Inventor Ray Dolby's name has become synonymous with superior sound in homes, movie theaters, and recording studios. The technology produced by his company, Dolby Laboratories, is part of nearly every music cassette and cassette recorder; prerecorded videotape; and, most recently, DVD movie disk and player. Since 1976, close to 1.5 billion audio products that use Dolby's technology have been sold worldwide. More than 44,000 movie theaters now show films in Dolby Digital Surround Sound, and some 50 million Dolby Digital home theater receivers have been sold since 1999. Dolby technology has become the de facto industry standard for high-quality sound in the music and film industry. How did Dolby build this technology franchise?

The story goes back to 1965, when Dolby Laboratories was founded in London by Ray Dolby (the company's headquarters moved to San Francisco in 1976). Dolby, who had a Ph.D. in physics from Cambridge University in England, had invented a technology for reducing the background hiss in professional tape recording without compromising the quality of the material being recorded. In 1968, Dolby reached an agreement to license his noise-reduction technology to KLH, a highly regarded American producer of audio equipment (record players and tape decks) for the consumer market. Soon other manufacturers of consumer equipment started to approach Dolby to license the technology. Dolby briefly considered manufacturing record players and tape decks for the consumer market, but as he later commented, "I knew that if we entered that market and tried to make something like a cassette deck, we would be in competition with any licensee that we took on. . . . So we had to stay out of manufacturing in that area in order to license in that area."

Dolby adopted a licensing business model and then had to determine what licensing fee to charge. He decided to charge a modest fee to reduce the incentive that manufacturers would have to develop their own technology. Then there was the question of which companies to license to. Dolby wanted the Dolby name associated with superior sound, so he needed to make sure that licensees adhered to quality standards. Therefore, the company set up a formal quality control program for its licensees' products. Licensees have to agree to have their products tested by Dolby, and the licensing agreement states that they cannot sell products that do not pass Dolby's quality tests. By preventing products with substandard performance from reaching the market, Dolby has maintained the quality image of products featuring Dolby technology and trademarks. Today, Dolby Laboratories tests samples of hundreds of licensed products every year under this program. By making sure that the Dolby name is associated with superior sound quality, Dolby's quality assurance strategy has increased the power of the Dolby brand, making it very valuable to license.

Another key aspect of Dolby's strategy was born in 1970 when Dolby began to promote the idea of releasing prerecorded cassettes encoded with Dolby noise-reduction technology so that they would have low noise when played on players equipped with Dolby noise-reduction technology. Dolby decided to license the technology on prerecorded tapes for free, instead collecting licensing fees just from the sales of tape players that used Dolby technology. This strategy was hugely successful and set up a positive feedback loop that helped to make Dolby technology ubiquitous. Growing sales of prerecorded tapes encoded with Dolby technology created a demand for players that contained Dolby technology, and as the installed base of players with Dolby technology grew, the proportion of prerecorded tapes that were encoded with Dolby technology surged, further boosting demand for players incorporating Dolby technology. By the mid-1970s, almost all prerecorded tapes were encoded with Dolby noise-reduction technology. This strategy remains in effect today for all media recorded with Dolby technology and encompasses not only videocassettes but also videogames and DVD releases encoded with Dolby Surround or Dolby Digital.

As a result of its licensing and quality assurance strategies, Dolby has become the standard for high-quality sound in the music and film industries. Although the company is small—its revenues were $327 million in 2005—its influence is large. It continues to push the boundaries of sound-reduction technology (it has been a leader in digital sound since the mid-1980s) and has successfully extended its noise-reduction franchise, first into films, then into DVD and videogame technology, and finally onto the Web, where it has licensed its digital technology to a wide range of media companies for digital music delivery and digital audio players, such as those built into personal computers and hand-held music players. Dolby has also licensed its technology for use in next-generation DVD players—high-definition DVDs.[a]

As this process started to get under way, a positive feedback loop started to develop, with the growing installed base of CD players leading to an increase in the number of music recordings issued on CDs, as opposed to or in addition to vinyl records. Past some point, the installed base of CD players got so big that music companies started to issue recordings only on CDs. Once this happened, even those who did not want to switch to the new technology were required to if they wished to purchase new music recordings. The industry standard had shifted: the new technology had locked in as the standard, and the old technology was locked out. It follows that despite its dominance, the Wintel standard for personal computers could one day be superseded if a competitor finds a way of providing sufficient benefits that enough consumers are willing to bear the switching costs associated with moving to a new operating system.

Strategies for Winning a Format War

From the perspective of a company pioneering a new technological standard in a marketplace where network effects and positive feedback loops operate, the key question becomes, "What strategy should we pursue to establish our format as the dominant one?" The various strategies that companies should adopt to win format wars revolve around *finding ways to make network effects work in their favor and against their competitors*. Winning a format war requires a company to build the installed base for its standard as rapidly as possible, thereby leveraging the positive feedback loop, inducing consumers to bear switching costs, and ultimately locking the market into its technology. It requires the company to jump-start and then accelerate demand for its technological standard or format so that it becomes established as quickly as possible as the industry standard, thereby locking out competing formats. Several key strategies and tactics can be adopted to try to achieve this.[6]

Ensure a Supply of Complements

It is important for the company to make sure that, in addition to the product itself, there is an adequate supply of complements. For example, no one will buy the Sony PlayStation 3 unless there is an adequate supply of games to run on that machine. And no one will purchase a Palm hand-held computer unless there are enough software applications to run on it. Companies normally take two steps to ensure an adequate supply of complements.

First, they may diversify into the production of complements and seed the market with sufficient supply to help jump-start demand for their format. Before Sony produced the original PlayStation in the early 1990s, it established its own in-house unit to produce videogames for the PlayStation. When it launched the PlayStation, Sony also simultaneously issued sixteen games to run on the machine, giving consumers a reason to purchase the format. Second, companies may create incentives or make it easy for independent companies to produce complements. Sony also licensed the right to produce games to a number of independent game developers, charged the developers a lower royalty rate than they had to pay to competitors such as Nintendo and Sega, and provided them with software tools that made it easier for them to develop the games. Thus, the launch of the Sony PlayStation was accompanied by the simultaneous launch of thirty or so games, which quickly helped to stimulate demand for the machine.

Leverage Killer Applications

Killer applications are applications or uses of a new technology or product that are so compelling that they persuade customers to adopt the new format or technology in droves, thereby "killing" demand for competing formats. Killer applications often help to jump-start demand for the new standard. For example, in the late 1990s, hand-held computers based on the Palm operating system became the dominant format in the market for personal digital assistants (PDAs). The killer applications that drove adoption of the Palm format were the personal information management functions and a pen-based input medium (based on Graffiti) that Palm bundled with its original PalmPilot, which it introduced in 1996. There had been PDAs before the PalmPilot, including Apple Computer's ill-fated Newton, but the applications and ease of use of the PalmPilot persuaded many consumers to enter this market. Within eighteen months of its initial launch, more than 1 million PalmPilots had been sold, making for a faster demand ramp-up than occurred for the first cell phones and pagers. Similarly, the killer applications that induced consumers to sign up for online services such as AOL were email, chatrooms, and the ability to browse the Web.

Ideally, the company promoting a technological standard will want to develop the killer applications itself—that is, develop the appropriate complementary products, as Palm did with the PalmPilot. However, it may also be able to leverage the applications that others develop. For example, the early sales of the IBM PC following its 1981 introduction were driven primarily by IBM's decision to license two important software programs for the PC, VisiCalc (a spreadsheet program) and Easy Writer (a word-processing program), both developed by independent companies. IBM saw that they were driving rapid adoption of rival personal computers, such as the Apple II, so it quickly licensed them, produced versions that would run on the IBM PC, and sold them as complements to the IBM PC, a strategy that was to prove very successful.

● Aggressively Price and Market

A common tactic to jump-start demand is to adopt a **razor and blade strategy**: pricing the product (razor) low in order to stimulate demand and increase the installed base, and then trying to make high profits on the sale of complements (razor blades), which are priced relatively high. This strategy owes its name to the fact that it was pioneered by Gillette to sell its razors and razor blades. Many other companies have followed this strategy—for example, Hewlett-Packard typically sells its printers at cost but makes significant profits on the subsequent sale of its replacement cartridges. In this case, the printer is the "razor," and it is priced low to stimulate demand and induce consumers to switch from their existing printer; the cartridges are the "blades," which are priced high to make profits. The inkjet printer represents a proprietary technological format because only Hewlett-Packard cartridges can be used with the printers, and not cartridges designed for competing inkjet printers, such as those sold by Canon. A similar strategy is used in the videogame industry: manufacturers price videogame consoles at cost to induce consumers to adopt their technology, while making profits on the royalties they receive from the sales of games that run on their system.

Aggressive marketing is also a key factor in jump-starting demand to get an early lead in an installed base. Substantial upfront marketing and point-of-sales promotion techniques are often used to try to get potential early adopters to bear the switching costs associated with adopting the format. If these efforts are successful, they can be the start of a positive feedback loop. Again, the Sony PlayStation provides a good example. Sony linked the introduction of the PlayStation with nationwide television advertising aimed at its primary demographic (eighteen- to thirty-four-year-olds) and in-store displays that allowed potential buyers to play games on the machine before making a purchase.

● Cooperate with Competitors

Companies have been close to simultaneously introducing competing and incompatible technological standards a number of times. A good example is the compact disk. Initially four companies—Sony, Philips, JVC, and Telefunken—were developing CD players using different variations of the underlying laser technology. If this situation had persisted, they might have ultimately introduced incompatible technologies into the marketplace, so a CD made for a Philips CD player would not play on a Sony CD player. Understanding that the nearly simultaneous introduction of such incompatible technologies can create significant confusion among consumers and often leads them to delay their purchases, Sony and Philips decided to join forces with each other and cooperate on developing the technology. Sony contributed its error-correction technology, and Philips contributed its laser technology. The result of this cooperation was that momentum among other players in the industry shifted toward the Sony-Philips alliances; JVC and Telefunken were left with little support. Most importantly, recording labels announced that they would support the Sony-Philips format but not the Telefunken or JVC format. Telefunken and JVC subsequently decided to abandon their efforts to develop CD technology. The cooperation between Sony and Philips was important because it reduced confusion in the industry and allowed a single format to come to the fore, which speeded up adoption of the technology. The cooperation was a win-win situation for both Philips and Sony, which eliminated the competitors and allowed them to share in the success of the format.

License the Format

Another strategy often adopted is to license the format to other enterprises so that they can produce products based on it. The company that pioneered the format gains from the licensing fees and from the enlarged supply of the product, which can stimulate demand and help accelerate market adoption. This was the strategy that Matsushita adopted with its VHS format for the videocassette recorder. In addition to producing VCRs at its own factory in Osaka, Matsushita let a number of other companies produce VHS format players under license (Sony decided not to license its competing Betamax format and produced all Betamax format players itself), and so VHS players were more widely available. More people purchased VHS players, which created an incentive for film companies to issue more films on VHS tapes (as opposed to Betamax tapes), which further increased demand for VHS players, and hence helped Matsushita to lock in VHS as the dominant format in the marketplace. Sony, ironically the first to market, saw its position marginalized by the reduced supply of the critical complement, prerecorded films, and ultimately withdrew Betamax players from the consumer marketplace.

As we saw in Strategy in Action 7.1, Dolby adopted a similar licensing strategy to get its noise-reduction technology adopted as the technological standard in the music and film industries. By charging a modest licensing fee for use of the technology in recording equipment and forgoing licensing fees on media recorded using Dolby technology, Dolby deliberately sought to reduce the financial incentive that potential competitors might have to develop their own, possibly superior, technology. Dolby calculated that its long-run profitability would be maximized by adopting a licensing strategy that limited the incentive of competitors to enter the market.

The correct strategy to pursue in a particular scenario requires that the company consider all of these different strategies and tactics and pursue those that seem most appropriate given the competitive circumstances prevailing in the industry and the likely strategy of rivals. Although no mix of strategies and tactics can be called the best, the company must keep the goal of rapidly increasing the installed base of products based on its standard as the primary goal. By helping to jump-start demand for its format, a company can induce consumers to bear the switching costs associated with adopting its technology and leverage any positive feedback process that might exist. Also important is not pursuing strategies that have the opposite effect. For example, pricing high to capture profits from early adopters, who tend not to be as price sensitive as later adopters, can have the unfortunate effect of slowing demand growth and letting a more aggressive competitor pick up market share and establish its format as the industry standard.

Costs in High-Technology Industries

In many high-tech industries, the fixed costs of developing the product are very high, but the costs of producing one extra unit of the product are very low. This is most obvious in the case of software. For example, it reportedly cost Microsoft $5 billion to develop Windows Vista, the latest version of its Windows operating system, but the cost of producing one more copy of Windows Vista is virtually zero. Once Windows Vista was completed, Microsoft produced master disks that it sent out to PC manufacturers, such as Dell Computer, which then loaded a copy of Windows Vista onto every PC it sold. The cost to Microsoft was effectively zero, and yet it receives a significant licensing fee for each copy of Windows Vista installed on a PC.[7] For Microsoft, the marginal cost of making one more copy of Windows Vista is close to zero, although the fixed costs of developing the product are $5 billion.

Many other high-technology products have similar cost economics: very high fixed costs and very low marginal costs. Most software products share these features, although if the software is sold through stores, the costs of packaging and distribution will raise the marginal costs, and if it is sold by a sales force direct to end-users, this too will raise the marginal costs. Many consumer electronics products have the same basic economics. The fixed costs of developing a DVD player or a videogame console can be very expensive, but the costs of producing an incremental unit are very low. The costs of developing a new drug, such as Viagra, can run to over $800 million, but the marginal cost of producing each additional pill is at most a few cents.

● **Comparative Cost Economics**

To grasp why this cost structure is strategically important, a company must understand that, in many industries, marginal costs rise as a company tries to expand output (economists call this the law of diminishing returns). To produce more of a good, a company has to hire more labor and invest in more plant and machinery. At the margin, the additional resources used are not as productive, so this leads to increasing marginal costs. However, the law of diminishing returns often does not apply in many high-tech settings, such as the production of software or sending one more bit of data down a digital telecommunications network.

Consider two companies, α and β (see Figure 7.3). Company α is a conventional producer and faces diminishing returns, so as it tries to expand output, its marginal costs rise. Company β is a high-tech producer, and its marginal costs do not rise at all as output is increased. Note that in Figure 7.3, company β's marginal cost curve is drawn as a straight line near the horizontal axis, implying that marginal costs are close to zero and do not vary with output, whereas company α's marginal costs rise as output is expanded, illustrating diminishing returns. Company β's flat and low marginal cost curve means that its average cost curve will fall continuously over all ranges of output as it spreads its fixed costs out over greater volume. In contrast, the rising marginal costs encountered by company α mean that its average cost curve is the U-shaped curve familiar from basic economics texts. For simplicity, assume that both companies sell their product at the same price, Pm, and both sell exactly the same quantity of output, 0 (Q1). You can see from Figure 7.3 that at an output of Q1, company β has much lower average costs than company α and as a consequence is making far more profit (profit is the shaded area in Figure 7.3).

FIGURE 7.3

Cost Structures in High-Technology Industries

● **Strategic Significance** If a company can shift from a cost structure where it encounters increasing marginal costs to one where fixed costs may be high but marginal costs are much lower, its profitability may increase. In the consumer electronics industry, such a shift has been playing out for two decades. Music recordings used to be based on analog technology, where marginal costs rose as output expanded due to diminishing returns (as in the case of company α in Figure 7.3). Since the 1980s, digital systems such as CD players have replaced analog systems. Digital systems are software based, and this implies much lower marginal costs of producing one more copy of a recording. As a result, the music labels have been able to lower prices, expand demand, and see their profitability increase (their production system has more in common with company β in Figure 7.3).

This process is still unfolding. The latest technology for making copies of music recordings is based on distribution over the Internet (for example, by downloading onto an iPod). Here, the marginal costs of making one more copy of a recording are lower still. In fact, they are close to zero and do not increase with output. The only problem is that the low costs of copying and distributing music recordings have created a copyright problem that the major music labels have yet to solve (we discuss this in more detail shortly when we consider intellectual property rights). The same shift is now beginning to affect other industries. Some companies are building their strategies around trying to exploit and profit from this shift. For an example, see Strategy in Action 7.2, which looks at SonoSite.

When a high-tech company faces high fixed costs and low marginal costs, its strategy should emphasize the low-cost option: deliberately drive prices down to drive volume up. Look again at Figure 7.3 and you will see that the high-tech company's average costs fall rapidly as output expands. This implies that prices can be reduced to stimulate demand, and as long as prices fall less rapidly than average costs, per-unit profit margins will expand as prices fall. This is a consequence of the fact

Strategy in Action

7.2

Lowering the Cost of Ultrasound Equipment Through Digitalization

The ultrasound unit has been an important piece of diagnostic equipment in hospitals for some time. Ultrasound units use the physics of sound to produce images of soft tissues in the human body. They can produce detailed three-dimensional color images of organs and, by using contrast agents, track the flow of fluids through an organ. A cardiologist, for example, can use an ultrasound in combination with contrast agents injected into the bloodstream to track the flow of blood through a beating heart. In additional to the visual diagnosis, ultrasound also produces an array of quantitative diagnostic information of great value to physicians.

Modern ultrasound units are sophisticated instruments that cost around $250,000 to $300,000 each for a top-line model. They are fairly bulky instruments, weighing some 300 pounds, and are wheeled around hospitals on carts.

A few years back, a group of researchers at ATL, one of the leading ultrasound companies, came up with an idea for reducing the size and cost of a basic unit. They theorized that it might be possible to replace up to 80% of the solid circuits in an ultrasound unit with software, in the process significantly shrinking the size and reducing the weight of machines and thereby producing portable ultrasound units. Moreover, by digitalizing much of the ultrasound (replacing hardware with software), they could considerably drive down the marginal costs of

making additional units and would thus be able to make a good profit at much lower price points.

The researchers reasoned that a portable and inexpensive ultrasound unit would find market opportunities in totally new niches. For example, a small, inexpensive ultrasound unit could be placed in an ambulance or carried into battle by an army medic, or purchased by family physicians for use in their offices. Although they realized that it would be some time, perhaps decades, before such small, inexpensive machines could attain the image quality and diagnostic sophistication of top-of-the-line machines, they saw the opportunity in terms of creating market niches that previously could not be served by ultrasound companies because of the high costs and bulk of the product.

The researchers ultimately became a project team within ATL and were then spun out of ATL as an entirely new company, SonoSite. In late 1999, they introduced their first portable product, weighing just six pounds and costing around $25,000. SonoSite targeted niches that full-sized ultrasound products could not reach: ambulatory care and foreign markets that could not afford the more expensive equipment. In 2005, the company sold $150 million worth of its product.

In the long run, SonoSite plans to build more features and greater image quality into the small hand-held machines, primarily by improving the software. This could allow the units to penetrate U.S. hospital markets that currently purchase the established technology, much as client-server systems based on PC technology came to replace mainframes for some functions in business corporations.[b]

that the firm's marginal costs are low and do not rise with output. This strategy of pricing low to drive volume up and reap wider profit margins is central to the business model of some very successful high-technology companies, including Microsoft.

Managing Intellectual Property Rights

Ownership of a technology can be a source of sustained competitive advantage and superior profitability, particularly when the company owns a technology that is the standard in an industry, such as Microsoft and Intel's Wintel standard for personal computers and Dolby's ownership of the standard for noise-reduction technology in the music and film recording industries. Even if a technology is not standard but is valued by a sufficient number of consumers, ownership of that technology can still be very profitable. Apple's current personal computer technology is by no means the standard in the marketplace, much as Apple would like it to be. In fact, the company's iMac technology accounted for only about 5% of the personal computers sold in 2006. But that small slice of a very large market is still a valuable niche for Apple.

● Intellectual Property Rights

Because new technology is the product of intellectual and creative effort, we call it intellectual property. The term **intellectual property** refers to the product of any intellectual and creative effort and includes not only new technology but also a wide range of intellectual creations, including music, films, books, and graphic art. As a society, we value the products of intellectual and creative activity. Intellectual property is seen as a very important driver of economic progress and social wealth.[8] But it is also often expensive, risky, and time-consuming to create intellectual property.

For example, a new drug to treat a dangerous medical condition such as cancer can take twelve to sixteen years to develop and cost as much as $800 million. Moreover, only 20% of new drugs that are tested in humans actually make it to the market.[9] The remainder of these drugs fail because they are found to be unsafe or ineffective. Given the costs, risks, and time involved in this activity, few companies would be willing to develop a new drug and bring it to market unless they could be reasonably sure that if they were successful in developing the drug, their investment would be profitable. If the minute they introduced a successful cancer drug, their competitors produced imitations of that drug, no company would even consider making the initial investment.

To make sure that this does not happen, we grant the creators of intellectual property certain rights over their creation. These rights, which stop competitors from copying or imitating the creation for a number of years, take the legal forms of patents, copyrights, and trademarks, which all serve the same basic objective: to give individuals and companies an incentive to engage in the expensive and risky business of creating new intellectual property.

The creation of intellectual property is a central endeavor in high-technology industries, and the management of intellectual property rights has moved to center stage in many of these companies. Developing strategies to protect and enforce intellectual property rights can be an important aspect of competitive advantage. For many companies, this amounts to making sure that their patents and copyrights are respected. It is not uncommon, therefore, to see high-technology companies bringing lawsuits against their competitors for patent infringement. In general, companies often use such lawsuits not only to sanction those they suspect of violating the company's intellectual property rights, but also to signal to potential violators that the company will aggressively defend its property. Legal action alone suffices to protect intellectual property in many industries, but in others, such as software, the low costs of illegally copying and distributing intellectual property call for more creative strategies to manage intellectual property rights.

● Digitalization and Piracy Rates

Protecting intellectual property has become more complicated in the past few decades because of **digitalization**, that is, the rendering of creative output in digital form. This can be done for music recordings, films, books, newspapers, magazines, and computer software. Digitalization has dramatically lowered the cost of copying and distributing digitalized intellectual property or digital media. As we have seen, the marginal cost of making one more copy of a software program is very low, and the same is true for any other intellectual property rendered in digital form. Moreover, digital media can be distributed at a very low cost (again, almost zero), for example, by distributing over the Internet. Reflecting on this, one commentator has described the

Internet as a "giant out-of-control copying machine."[10] The low marginal costs of copying and distributing digital media have made it very easy to sell illegal copies of such property. In turn, this has helped to produce a high level of piracy (in this context, piracy refers to the theft of intellectual property).

The International Federation of the Phonographic Industry claims that about one-third of all recorded music products sold worldwide in 2005 were pirated (illegal) copies, suggesting that piracy costs the industry over $4.5 billion annually.[11] The computer software industry also suffers from lax enforcement of intellectual property rights. Estimates suggest that violations of intellectual property rights cost personal computer software firms revenues equal to $35 billion in 2005.[12] According to the Business Software Alliance, a software industry association, in 2005, some 35% of all software applications used in the world were pirated. The worst region was Latin America, where the piracy rate was 68% (see Figure 2.2). One of the worst countries was China, where the piracy rate in 2005 ran at 86% and cost the industry more than $3.9 billion in lost sales, up from $444 million in 1995. Although at 21% the piracy rate was much lower in the United States, the value of sales lost was more significant because of the size of the market, reaching an estimated $6.9 billion in 2005.[13]

The scale of this problem is so large that simply resorting to legal tactics to enforce intellectual property rights has amounted to nothing more than a partial solution to the piracy problem. Many companies now build sophisticated encryption software into their digital products, which can make it more difficult for pirates to copy digital media and thereby can raise the costs of stealing. But the pirates too are sophisticated and often seem to be able to find their way around encryption software. This raises the question of whether there are additional strategies that can be adopted to manage digital rights and thereby limit piracy.

Strategies for Managing Digital Rights

One strategy is simply to recognize that while the low costs of copying and distributing digital media make some piracy inevitable, the same attributes can be used to the company's advantage.[14] The basic strategy here represents yet another variation of the basic razor and blades principle: give something away for free to boost the sales of a complementary product. A familiar example concerns Adobe Acrobat Reader, the software program for reading documents formatted by Adobe Acrobat (that is, PDF-formatted documents). Adobe developed Adobe Acrobat to allow people to format documents in a manner that resembled a high-quality printed page and to display and distribute these documents over the Web. Moreover, Adobe documents are formatted in a read-only format, meaning that they cannot be altered by individuals, nor can parts of those documents be copied and pasted to other documents. Its strategy has been to give away Adobe Acrobat Reader for free and then make money by selling its Acrobat software for formatting documents. The strategy has worked extremely well. Anyone can download a copy of Acrobat Reader from Adobe's website. Because the marginal costs of copying and distributing this software over the Web are extremely low, the process is almost free for both Adobe and its customers. The result is that the Acrobat Reader has diffused very rapidly and is now the dominant format for viewing high-quality documents distributed and downloaded over the Web. As the installed base of Acrobat Readers has grown, sales of Adobe Acrobat software have soared as more and more organizations and individuals realize that formatting their digital documents in Acrobat makes sense.

Another strategy is to take advantage of the low costs of copying and distributing digital media to drive down the costs of purchasing those media, thereby reducing the incentive that consumers have to steal. When coupled with encryption software that makes piracy more difficult and vigorous legal actions to enforce intellectual property regulations, this can slow the piracy rate and generate incremental revenues that cost little to produce. A third strategy might be to alter the firm's business model in a way that makes piracy more difficult. As discussed in Strategy in Action 7.3, the videogame industry has seen a shift from selling games outright, to renting them online.

Strategy in Action   7.3

Battling Piracy in the Videogame Industry

Over the past decade, the videogame industry has grown into a global colossus worth more than $25 billion a year in revenues. For the three biggest players in the industry, Sony with its PlayStation, Microsoft with Xbox, and Nintendo, this potentially represents a huge growth engine, but the engine is threatened by a rise in piracy, which cost the videogame industry an estimated $4 billion in 2005.

The piracy problem is particularly serious in East Asia (except for Japan), where videogame consoles are routinely "chipped"—sold with modified chips, called mod chips, that override the console's security system, allowing it to play illegally copied games and CDs. Importers or resellers, who charge a small markup for making the modification, illegally install the mod chips. In some areas, such as Hong Kong, it is almost impossible to find a console that hasn't been modified.

Because they allow users to play illegally copied games, consoles with mod chips offer a gaping gateway for software pirates, and they directly threaten the profitability of console and game makers. The big three in the industry all follow a razor and blades business model, where the console (razor) is sold at a loss, and profit is made on the sale of the game (razor blades). In the case of Microsoft's Xbox, estimates suggest the company loses as much as $200 on each Xbox it sells. To make profits, Microsoft collects royalties on the sale of games developed under license, in addition to producing and selling some games itself. Games typically retail for about $50, and Microsoft must sell six to twelve games to each Xbox user to recoup the $200 loss on the initial sale and start making a profit. If those users are purchasing pirated games and playing them on "chipped" Xbox consoles, Microsoft collects nothing in royalties and may never reach the breakeven point. Sony and Nintendo face similar problems. In East Asia, some 70% of game software sold in the region may be pirated thanks to the popularity of "chipped" consoles and the low price of pirated games, which may sell for one-third the price of the legal game.

Historically, all the big videogame companies tried to deal with the piracy problem in East Asia by ignoring the market. Sony launched its PlayStation II in East Asia two years after its Japanese launch, and Microsoft delayed its East Asian launch for a year after it launched elsewhere in the world. But this tactic is increasingly questionable in a region where there may soon be more gamers than in the United States. Industry estimates suggest that Asian gamers spent more on videogame software in 2005 than U.S. gamers did, much of it on low-priced pirated games.

Another tactic that both Sony and Microsoft are now using is to regularly alter the hardware specifications of its consoles, rendering the existing mod chips useless. But the companies have found this is just a temporary solution: within a few weeks, mod chips made to override the new specifications are available on the market.

A third tactic is to push local authorities to legally enforce existing intellectual property rights law that in theory outlaws the mod chip practice. For example, Microsoft, Sony, and Nintendo joined forces to sue the Hong Kong company, Lik Sang, which sells mod chips through its website and is one of the world's largest distributors of the chips. Some observers question the value of this tactic, however; they argue that if Lik Sang is shut down, many others in Hong Kong may be willing to take its place. What is needed, they argue, is concerted government action to stop the pirates, and so far East Asian governments have not been quick to act.

A final way of dealing with piracy is to change the business model. All three main players in the industry are now starting to push online games, where customers pay a subscription fee to play online, as opposed to a one-time fee to purchase a game. This business model makes piracy much less of an issue and it may drive growth forward in places like China, where piracy is endemic. Indeed, current estimates suggest that there are already 29 million gamers in China, most of whom play pirated games, and that this figure will increase to 55 million by 2009. If a good percentage switch to online gaming, the revenues could be significant.[c]

Capturing First-Mover Advantages

In high-technology industries, companies often compete by striving to be the first to develop revolutionary new products, that is, to be a **first mover**. By definition, the first mover, with regard to a revolutionary product, is in a monopoly position. If the new product satisfies unmet consumer needs and demand is high, the first mover can capture significant revenues and profits. Such revenues and profits signal to potential rivals that there is money to be made by imitating the first mover. As illustrated in Figure 7.4, in the absence of strong barriers to imitation, this implies that imitators will rush into the market created by the first mover, competing for the first mover's monopoly profits and leaving all participants in the market with a much lower level of returns.

Despite imitation, some first movers have the ability to capitalize on and reap substantial first-mover advantages—the advantages of pioneering new technologies and products that lead to an enduring competitive advantage. Intel introduced the world's first microprocessor in 1971 and today still dominates the microprocessor segment of the semiconductor industry. Xerox introduced the world's first photocopier and for a long time enjoyed a leading position in the industry. Cisco introduced the first Internet protocol network router in 1986 and still dominates the market for that equipment today. Some first movers can reap substantial advantages from their pioneering activities that lead to an enduring competitive advantage. They can, in other words, limit or slow the rate of imitation.

But there are plenty of counterexamples suggesting that first-mover advantages might not be easy to capture and, in fact, that there might be **first-mover disadvantages**—the competitive disadvantages associated with being first. For example, Apple Computer was the first company to introduce a hand-held computer, the Apple Newton, but the product failed; a second mover, Palm, succeeded where Apple had failed. In the market for commercial jet aircraft, DeHavilland was first to market with the Comet, but the second mover, Boeing, with its 707 jetliner, went on to dominate the market.

Clearly, being a first mover does not by itself guarantee success. As we shall see, the difference between innovating companies that capture first-mover advantages and those that fall victim to first-mover disadvantages in part turns on the strategy that the first mover pursues. Before considering the strategy issue, however, we need to take a closer look at the nature of first-mover advantages and disadvantages.[15]

FIGURE 7.4

The Impact of Imitation on the Profits of a First Mover

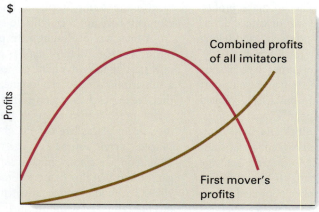

● **First-Mover Advantages**

There are five main sources of first-mover advantages.[16] First, the first mover has an opportunity to exploit network effects and positive feedback loops, locking consumers into its technology. In the VCR industry, Sony could have exploited network effects by licensing its technology, but instead the company ceded its first-mover advantage to the second mover, Matsushita.

Second, the first mover may be able to establish significant brand loyalty, which is expensive for later entrants to break down. Indeed, if the company is successful in this endeavor, its name may become closely associated with the entire class of products, including those produced by rivals. People still talk of "Xeroxing" when they are going to make a photocopy or "FedExing" when they are going to send a package by overnight delivery.

Third, the first mover may be able to ramp up sales volume ahead of rivals and thus reap cost advantages associated with the realization of scale economies and learning effects (see Chapter 4). Once the first mover has these cost advantages, it can respond to new entrants by cutting prices to hold on to its market share and still earn significant profits.

Fourth, the first mover may be able to create switching costs for its customers that subsequently make it difficult for rivals to enter the market and take customers away from the first mover. Wireless service providers, for example, will give new customers a "free" wireless phone, but customers must sign a contract agreeing to pay for the phone if they terminate the service contract within a specified time period, such as a year. Because the real cost of a wireless phone may run from $100 to $200, this represents a significant switching cost that later entrants have to overcome.

Finally, the first mover may be able to accumulate valuable knowledge related to customer needs, distribution channels, product technology, process technology, and so on. This accumulated knowledge gives it a knowledge advantage that later entrants might find difficult or expensive to match. Sharp, for example, was the first mover in the commercial manufacture of active matrix liquid crystal displays used in laptop computers. The process for manufacturing these displays is very difficult, with a high reject rate for flawed displays. Sharp has accumulated such an advantage with regard to production processes that it has been very difficult for later entrants to match it on product quality, and thus costs.

● **First-Mover Disadvantages**

Balanced against these first-mover advantages are a number of disadvantages.[17] First, the first mover has to bear significant pioneering costs that later entrants do not. The first mover has to pioneer the technology, develop distribution channels, and educate customers about the nature of the product. All of this can be expensive and time-consuming. Later entrants, by way of contrast, might be able to free-ride on the first mover's investments in pioneering the market and customer education.

Related to this, first movers are more prone to make mistakes because there are so many uncertainties in a new market. Later entrants may be able to learn from the mistakes made by first movers, improve on the product or the way in which it is sold, and come to market with a superior offering that captures significant market share from the first mover. For example, one of the reasons that the Apple Newton failed was that the handwriting software in the hand-held computer failed to recognize human handwriting. The second mover in this market, Palm, learned from Apple's error. When it introduced the PalmPilot, it used software that recognized letters written in a particular way, Graffiti, and then persuaded customers to learn this method of inputting data into the hand-held computer.

Third, first movers run the risk of building the wrong resources and capabilities because they are focusing on a customer set that is not going to be characteristic of the mass market. This is the crossing-the-chasm problem that we discussed in the previous chapter. Recall that the customers in the early market—those we categorized as innovators and early adopters—have different characteristics from the first wave of the mass market, the early majority. The first mover runs the risk of gearing its resources and capabilities to the needs of innovators and early adopters and not being able to switch when members of the early majority enter the market. As a result, first movers run a greater risk of plunging into the chasm that separates the early market from the mass market.

Finally, the first mover may invest in inferior or obsolete technology. This can happen when its product innovation is based on underlying technology that is advancing rapidly. By basing its product on an early version of the technology, it may lock itself into something that rapidly becomes obsolete. In contrast, later entrants may be able to leapfrog the first mover and introduce products that are based on later versions of the underlying technology. This happened in France during the 1980s when, at the urging of the government, France Telecom introduced the world's first consumer online service, Minitel. France Telecom distributed crude terminals to consumers for free, which they could hook up to their phone line and use to browse phone directories. Other simple services were soon added, and before long the French could conduct online shopping, banking, travel, weather, and news—all years before the Web was invented. The problem was that by the standards of the Web, Minitel was very crude and inflexible, and France Telecom, as the first mover, suffered. The French were very slow to adopt personal computers and then the Internet primarily because Minitel had such a presence. As late as 1998, only one-fifth of French households had a computer, compared with two-fifths in the United States, and only 2% of households were connected to the Internet, compared to over 30% in the United States. As the result of a government decision, France Telecom, and indeed an entire nation, was slow to adopt a revolutionary new online medium, the Web, because they were the first to invest in a more primitive version of the technology.[18]

Strategies for Exploiting First-Mover Advantages

The task facing a first mover is how to exploit its lead to capitalize on first-mover advantages and build a sustainable long-term competitive advantage while simultaneously reducing the risks associated with first-mover disadvantages. There are three basic strategies available: (1) develop and market the innovation itself, (2) develop and market the innovation jointly with other companies through a strategic alliance or joint venture, and (3) license the innovation to others and let them develop the market.

The optimal choice of strategy depends on the answers to three questions:

1. Does the innovating company have the complementary assets to exploit its innovation and capture first-mover advantages?

2. How difficult is it for imitators to copy the company's innovation? In other words, what is the height of the barriers to imitation?

3. Are there capable competitors that could rapidly imitate the innovation?

 COMPLEMENTARY ASSETS Complementary assets are the assets required to exploit a new innovation and gain a competitive advantage.[19] Among the most important complementary assets are competitive manufacturing facilities capable of handling rapid growth in customer demand while maintaining high product quality. State-of-the-art manufacturing facilities enable the first mover to move quickly down the experience curve without encountering production bottlenecks or problems with the quality of the product. The inability to satisfy demand because of these problems, however, creates the opportunity for imitators to enter the marketplace. For example, in 1998, Immunex was the first company to introduce a revolutionary new biological treatment for rheumatoid arthritis. Sales for this product, Enbrel, ramped up very rapidly, hitting $750 million in 2001. However, Immunex had not invested in sufficient manufacturing capacity. In mid-2000, it announced that it lacked the capacity to satisfy demand and that creating additional capacity would take at least two years. This manufacturing bottleneck gave the second mover in the market, Johnson & Johnson, the opportunity to expand demand for its product rapidly, which was outselling Enbrel by early 2002. Immunex's first-mover advantage had been partly eroded because it lacked an important complementary asset, the manufacturing capability required to satisfy demand.

Complementary assets also include marketing know-how, an adequate sales force, access to distribution systems, and an after-sales service and support network. All of these assets can help an innovator build brand loyalty and achieve market penetration more rapidly.[20] In turn, the resulting increases in volume facilitate more rapid movement down the experience curve and the attainment of a sustainable cost-based advantage due to scale economies and learning effects. One of the reasons that EMI, the first mover in the market for CT scanners, ultimately lost out to established medical equipment companies, such as GE Medical Systems, was that it lacked the marketing know-how, sales force, and distribution systems required to compete effectively in the world's largest market for medical equipment, the United States.

Developing complementary assets can be very expensive, and companies often need large infusions of capital for this purpose. That is why first movers often lose out to late movers that are large, successful companies in other industries with the resources to develop a presence in the new industry quickly. Microsoft and 3M exemplify companies that can move quickly to capitalize on the opportunities when other companies open up new product markets, such as compact disks or floppy disks. For example, although Netscape pioneered the market for Internet browsers with the Netscape Navigator, Microsoft's Internet Explorer ultimately dominated the market for Internet browsers.

HEIGHT OF BARRIERS TO IMITATION Recall from Chapter 3 that barriers to imitation are factors that prevent rivals from imitating a company's distinctive competencies and innovations. Although ultimately any innovation can be copied, the higher the barriers are, the longer it takes for rivals to imitate, and the more time the first mover has to build an enduring competitive advantage.

Barriers to imitation give an innovator time to establish a competitive advantage and build more enduring barriers to entry in the newly created market. Patents, for example, are among the most widely used barriers to imitation. By protecting its photocopier technology with a thicket of patents, Xerox was able to delay any significant imitation of its product for seventeen years. However, patents are often easy to "invent around." For example, one study found that this happened to 60% of patented innovations within four years.[21] If patent protection is weak, a company might try to slow imitation by developing new products and processes in secret. The most famous example of this approach is Coca-Cola, which has kept the formula for Coke a secret for generations. But Coca-Cola's success in this regard is an exception. A study of 100 companies has estimated that proprietary information about a company's decision to develop a major new product or process is known to its rivals within about twelve to eighteen months of the original development decision.[22]

CAPABLE COMPETITORS **Capable competitors** are companies that can move quickly to imitate the pioneering company. Competitors' capability to imitate a pioneer's innovation depends primarily on two factors: (1) research and development (R&D) skills and (2) access to complementary assets. In general, the greater the number of capable competitors with access to the R&D skills and complementary assets needed to imitate an innovation, the more rapid imitation is likely to be.

In this context, R&D skills refer to the ability of rivals to reverse-engineer an innovation to find out how it works and quickly develop a comparable product. As an example, consider the CT scanner. GE bought one of the first CT scanners produced by EMI, and its technical experts reverse-engineered it. Despite the product's technological complexity, GE developed its own version, which allowed it to imitate EMI quickly and ultimately to replace EMI as the major supplier of CT scanners.

With regard to complementary assets, the access that rivals have to marketing, sales know-how, or manufacturing capabilities is one of the key determinants of the rate of imitation. If would-be imitators lack critical complementary assets, not only do they have to imitate the innovation, but they may also have to imitate the innovator's complementary assets. This is expensive, as AT&T discovered when it tried to enter the personal computer business in 1984. AT&T lacked the marketing assets (sales force and distribution systems) necessary to support personal computer products. The lack of these assets and the time it takes to build them partly explain why, four years after it entered the market, AT&T had lost $2.5 billion and still had not emerged as a viable contender. It subsequently pulled out of this business.

THREE INNOVATION STRATEGIES The way in which these three factors—complementary assets, height of barriers to imitation, and the capability of competitors—influence the choice of innovation strategy is summarized in Table 7.1. The competitive strategy of developing and marketing the innovation alone makes most sense when (1) the innovator has the complementary assets necessary to develop the innovation, (2) the barriers to imitating a new innovation are high, and (3) the number of capable competitors is limited. Complementary assets allow rapid development and promotion of the innovation. High barriers to imitation buy the innovator time to establish a competitive advantage and build enduring barriers to entry through brand loyalty or experience-based cost advantages. The fewer the capable competitors, the less likely it is that any one of them will succeed in circumventing barriers to imitation and quickly imitating the innovation.

TABLE 7.1

Strategies for Profiting from Innovation

Strategy	Does the Innovator Have the Required Complementary Assets?	What Is the Likely Height of Barriers to Imitation?	How Many Capable Competitors Exist in the Industry?
Going it alone	Yes	High	Very few
Entering into an alliance	No	High	Moderate number
Licensing the innovation	No	Low	Many

The competitive strategy of developing and marketing the innovation jointly with other companies through a strategic alliance or joint venture makes most sense when (1) the innovator lacks complementary assets, (2) barriers to imitation are high, and (3) there are several capable competitors. In such circumstances, it makes sense to enter into an alliance with a company that already has the complementary assets—in other words, with a capable competitor. Theoretically, such an alliance should prove to be mutually beneficial, and each partner can share in high profits that neither could earn on its own. Moreover, such a strategy has the benefit of co-opting a potential rival. For example, had EMI teamed up with a capable competitor to develop the market for CT scanners, such as GE Medical Systems, instead of going it alone, the company might not only have been able to build a more enduring competitive advantage, but it would also have co-opted a potentially powerful rival into its camp.

The third strategy, licensing, makes most sense when (1) the innovating company lacks the complementary assets, (2) barriers to imitation are low, and (3) there are many capable competitors. The combination of low barriers to imitation and many capable competitors makes rapid imitation almost certain. The innovator's lack of complementary assets further suggests that an imitator will soon capture the innovator's competitive advantage. Given these factors, and because rapid diffusion of the innovator's technology through imitation is inevitable, the innovator can at least share in some of the benefits of this diffusion by licensing its technology.[23] Moreover, by setting a relatively modest licensing fee, the innovator may be able to reduce the incentive that potential rivals have to develop their own competing, and possibly superior, technology. This seems to have been the strategy Dolby adopted to get its technology established as the standard for noise reduction in the music and film businesses (see Strategy in Action 7.1).

Technological Paradigm Shifts

Technological paradigm shifts occur when new technologies come along that revolutionize the structure of the industry, dramatically alter the nature of competition, and require companies to adopt new strategies to survive. A good example of a paradigm shift that is currently unfolding is the shift from chemical to digital photography (another example of digitalization). For over half a century, the large incumbent enterprises in the photographic industry such as Kodak and Fuji film have generated most of their revenues from selling and processing film using traditional silver halide technology. The rise of digital photography is a huge threat to their business models. Digital cameras do not use film, the mainstay of Kodak's and Fuji's business. Moreover, these cameras are more like specialized computers than conventional cameras and are thus based on scientific knowledge that Kodak and Fuji have little knowledge of. Although both Kodak and Fuji are investing heavily in the development of digital cameras, they are facing intense competition from companies such as Sony, Canon, and Hewlett-Packard, which have developed their own digital cameras; from software developers such as Adobe and Microsoft, which make the software for manipulating digital images; and from printer companies such as Hewlett-Packard and Canon, which are making the printers that consumers can use to print out their own high-quality pictures at home. As digital substitution gathers speed in the photography industry, it is not clear that the traditional incumbents will be able to survive this shift; the new competitors might well rise to dominance in the new market.

If Kodak and Fuji do decline, they will not be the first large incumbents to be felled by a technological paradigm shift in their industry. In the early 1980s, the computer industry was revolutionized by the arrival of personal computer technology, which gave rise to client-server networks that replaced traditional mainframe and minicomputers for many business uses. Many incumbent companies in the mainframe era, such as Wang, Control Data, and DEC, ultimately did not survive, and even IBM went through a decade of wrenching changes and large losses before it reinvented itself as a provider of ebusiness solutions. In their place, new entrants such as Microsoft, Intel, Dell, and Compaq rose to dominance in this new computer industry.

Examples such as these raise four questions:

1. When do paradigm shifts occur, and how do they unfold?

2. Why do so many incumbents go into decline following a paradigm shift?

3. What strategies can incumbents adopt to increase the probability that they will survive a paradigm shift as profitable enterprises and emerge on the other side of the market abyss created by the arrival of new technology?

4. What strategies can new entrants into a market adopt to profit from a paradigm shift?

We shall answer each of these questions in the remainder of this chapter.

● Paradigm Shifts and the Decline of Established Companies

Paradigm shifts appear to be more likely to occur in an industry when one or both of the following conditions are in place: First, the established technology in the industry is mature and approaching or at its "natural limit," and second, a new "disruptive technology" has entered the marketplace and is taking root in niches that are poorly served by incumbent companies using the established technology.[24]

THE NATURAL LIMITS TO TECHNOLOGY Richard Foster has formalized the relationship between the performance of a technology and time in terms of what he calls the technology S-curve (see Figure 7.5).[25] This curve shows the relationship over time of cumulative investments in R&D and the performance (or functionality) of a given technology. Early in the evolution of a new technology, R&D investments in a new technology tend to yield rapid improvements in performance as basic engineering problems are solved. After a time, diminishing returns to cumulative R&D begin to set in, the rate of improvement in performance slows, and the technology starts to approach its natural limit, where further advances are not possible. For example, one can argue that there was more improvement in the first fifty years of the commercial

FIGURE 7.5

The Technology S-Curve

aerospace business following the pioneering flight by the Wright Brothers than there has been in the second fifty years. Indeed, the world's largest commercial jet aircraft, the Boeing 747, is based on a 1960s design, as is the world's fastest commercial jet aircraft, the Concorde. In commercial aerospace, therefore, we are now in the region of diminishing returns and may be approaching the natural limit to improvements in the technology of commercial aerospace.

Similarly, it can be argued that we are approaching the natural limit to technology in the performance of silicon-based semiconductor chips. Over the past two decades, the performance of semiconductor chips has been increased dramatically by packing ever more transistors onto a single small silicon chip. This process has helped to increase the power of computers, lower their cost, and shrink their size. But we are starting to approach limits to the ability to shrink the width of lines on a chip and therefore pack ever more transistors onto a single chip. The limit is imposed by the natural laws of physics. Light waves are used to help etch lines onto a chip, and one cannot etch a line that is smaller than the wavelength of light being used. Semiconductor companies are already using light with very small wavelengths, such as extreme ultraviolet, to etch lines onto a chip, but there are limits to how far this technology can be pushed, and many believe that we will reach those limits within the decade. Does this mean that our ability to make smaller, faster, cheaper computers is coming to an end? Probably not. It is more likely that we will find another technology to replace silicon-based computing and enable us to continue building smaller, faster, cheaper computers. In fact, several exotic competing technologies are already being developed that may replace silicon-based computing. These include self-organizing molecular computers, three-dimensional microprocessor technology, quantum computing technology, and the use of DNA to perform computations.[26]

What does all of this have to do with paradigm shifts? According to Foster, when a technology approaches its natural limit, research attention turns to possible alternative technologies, and sooner or later one of those alternatives might be commercialized and replace the established technology. That is, the probability that a paradigm shift will occur increases. Thus, sometime in the next decade or two, another paradigm shift might shake the very foundations of the computer industry as exotic computing technology replaces silicon-based computing. If and when this happens, and if history is any guide, many of the incumbents in today's computer industry will go into decline, and new enterprises will rise to dominance.

Foster pushes this point a little further, noting that, initially, the contenders for the replacement technology are not as effective as the established technology in producing the attributes and features that consumers demand in a product. For example, in the early years of the twentieth century, automobiles were just starting to be produced. They were valued for their ability to move people from place to place, but so were the horse and cart (the established technology). When automobiles originally appeared, the horse and cart were still quite a bit better than the automobile at moving people from place to place (see Figure 7.6). After all, the first cars were slow, noisy, and likely to break down. Moreover, they needed a network of paved roads and gas stations to be really useful, and that network didn't exist, so for most applications, the horse and cart were still the preferred mode of transportation—to say nothing of the fact that they were cheaper.

However, this comparison ignored the fact that in the early twentieth century, automobile technology was at the very start of its S-curve and was about to experience dramatic improvements in performance as major engineering problems were solved (and those paved roads and gas stations were built). In contrast, after 3,000 years of

FIGURE 7.6

Established and
Successor
Technologies

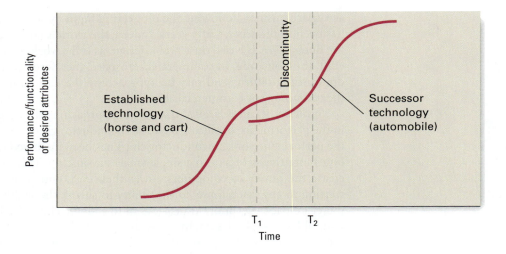

continuous improvement and refinement, the horse and cart were almost definitely
at the end of their technological S-curve. The result was that the rapidly improving
automobile soon replaced the horse and cart as the preferred mode of transportation. At time T1 in Figure 7.6, the horse and cart were still superior to the automobile. By time T2, the automobile had surpassed the horse and cart.

Foster notes that because the successor technology is initially less efficient than the
established technology, established companies and their customers often make the
mistake of dismissing it, only to be taken off-guard by its rapid performance improvement. A final point is that more than one potential successor technology appears, usually a swarm of potential successor technologies, only one of which might ultimately
come to the fore (see Figure 7.7). When this is the case, established companies are put
at a disadvantage. Even if they recognize that a paradigm shift is imminent, they may
not have the resources to invest in all the potential replacement technologies. If they
invest in the wrong one (something that is easy to do given the uncertainty that sur-
rounds the entire process), they may be locked out of subsequent development.

 DISRUPTIVE TECHNOLOGY Clayton Christensen has built on Foster's insights and his
own research to develop a theory of disruptive technology that has become very

FIGURE 7.7

Swarm of Successor
Technologies

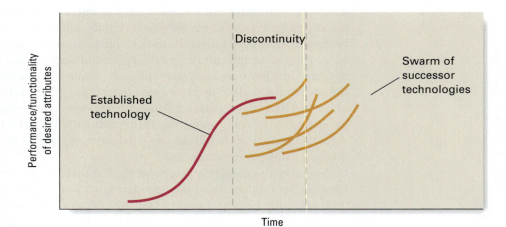

influential in high-technology circles.[27] Christensen uses the term *disruptive technology* to refer to a new technology that gets its start away from the mainstream of a market and then, as its functionality improves over time, invades the main market. Such technologies are disruptive because they revolutionize industry structure and competition, often causing the decline of established companies. They cause a technological paradigm shift.

Christensen's greatest insight is that established companies are often aware of the new technology but do not invest in it because they listen to their customers, and their customers do not want it. Of course, this arises because the new technology is early in its development, and thus only at the beginning of the S-curve for that technology. Once the performance of the new technology improves, customers do want it, but by this time, new entrants, as opposed to established companies, have accumulated the knowledge required to bring the new technology into the mass market. Christensen supports his view with several detailed historical case studies, one of which is summarized in Strategy in Action 7.4.

Strategy in Action   7.4

Disruptive Technology in Mechanical Excavators

Excavators are used to dig foundations for large buildings, trenches to lay large pipes for sewers and the like, and foundations and trenches for residential construction and farm work. Prior to the 1940s, the dominant technology used to manipulate the bucket on a mechanical excavator was based on a system of cables and pulleys. Although these mechanical systems could lift large buckets of earth, the excavators themselves were quite large, cumbersome, and expensive. Thus, they were rarely used to dig small trenches for house foundations, irrigation ditches for farmers, and the like. In most cases, these small trenches were dug by hand.

In the 1940s, a new technology made its appearance: hydraulics. In theory, hydraulic systems had certain advantages over the established cable and pulley systems. Most important, their energy efficiency was higher: for a given bucket size, a smaller engine would be required for a hydraulic system. However, the initial hydraulic systems also had drawbacks. The seals on hydraulic cylinders were prone to leaking under high pressure, effectively limiting the size of the bucket that could be lifted using hydraulics. Notwithstanding this drawback, when hydraulics first appeared, many of the incumbent firms in the mechanical excavation industry took the technology seriously enough to ask their primary customers whether they would be interested in

products based on hydraulics. Because the primary customers of incumbents needed excavators with large buckets to dig out the foundations for buildings and large trenches, their reply was no. For this customer set, the hydraulic systems of the 1940s were not reliable or powerful enough. Consequently, after consulting with their customers, the established companies in the industry made the strategic decision not to invest in hydraulics. Instead, they continued to produce excavation equipment based on the dominant cable and pulley technology.

It was left to a number of new entrants, which included J. I. Case, John Deere, J. C. Bamford, and Caterpillar, to pioneer hydraulic excavation equipment. Because of the limits on bucket size imposed by the seal problem, these companies initially focused on a poorly served niche in the market that could make use of small buckets: residential contractors and farmers. Over time, these new entrants were able to solve the engineering problems associated with weak hydraulic seals, and as they did so, they manufactured excavators with larger buckets. Ultimately, they invaded the market niches served by the old-line companies: general contractors that dug the foundations for large buildings, sewers, and so on. At this point, Case, Deere, Caterpillar, and their kin rose to dominance in the industry, while the majority of established companies from the prior era lost share. Of the thirty or so manufacturers of cable-actuated equipment in the United States in the late 1930s, only four survived to the 1950s.[d]

In addition to listening too closely to their customers, Christensen also identifies a number of other factors that make it very difficult for established companies to adopt a new disruptive technology. He notes that many established companies declined to invest in new disruptive technologies because initially they served such small market niches that it seemed unlikely that they would have an impact on the company's revenues and profits. As the new technology started to improve in functionality and invade the main market, their investment was often hindered by the fact that exploiting the new technology required a new business model totally different from the company's established model, and thus was very difficult to implement.

Both of these points can be illustrated by referring to one more example: the rise of online discount stockbrokers, such as Ameritrade and E*Trade, which made use of a new technology, the Internet, during the 1990s to allow individual investors to trade stocks for a very low commission fee. In contrast, full-service stockbrokers, such as Merrill Lynch, where orders had to be placed through a stockbroker who earned a commission for performing the transaction, did not.

Christensen also notes that a new network of suppliers and distributors typically grows up around the new entrants. Not only do established companies initially ignore disruptive technology, but so do their suppliers and distributors. This creates an opportunity for new suppliers and distributors to enter the market to serve the new entrants. As the new entrants grow, so does the associated network. Ultimately, Christensen suggests, the new entrants and their network may replace not only established enterprises, but also the entire network of suppliers and distributors associated with established companies. Taken to its logical extreme, this view suggests that disruptive technologies may result in the demise of the entire network of enterprises associated with established companies in an industry.

The established companies in an industry that is being rocked by a technological paradigm shift often have to cope with internal inertia forces that limit their ability to adapt, but the new entrants do not and thereby have an advantage. They do not have to deal with an established and conservative customer set and an obsolete business model. Instead, they can focus on optimizing the new technology, improving its performance, and riding the wave of disruptive technology into new market segments until they invade the main market and challenge the established companies, by which time they may be well equipped to beat them.

● **Strategic Implications for Established Companies**

Although Christensen has uncovered an important tendency, it is by no means written in stone that all established companies are doomed to fail when faced with disruptive technologies, as we have seen with IBM and Merrill Lynch. Established companies must meet the challenges created by the emergence of disruptive technologies.[28]

First, having access to the knowledge about how disruptive technologies can revolutionize markets is itself a valuable strategic asset. Many of the established companies that Christensen examined failed because they took a myopic view of the new technology and asked their customers the wrong question. Instead of asking, "Are you interested in this new technology?" they should have recognized that the new technology was likely to improve rapidly over time and instead asked, "Would you be interested in this new technology if it improves its functionality over time?" If they had done so, they may have made very different strategic decisions.

Second, it is clearly important for established enterprises to invest in newly emerging technologies that may ultimately become disruptive technologies. Companies have to hedge their bets about new technology. As we have noted, at any time, there may be a swarm of emerging technologies, any one of which might ultimately become a disruptive technology. Large, established companies that are generating significant cash flows can and often should establish and fund central R&D operations to invest in and develop such technologies. In addition, they may wish to acquire newly emerging companies that are pioneering potentially disruptive technologies or enter into alliances with them to develop the technology jointly. The strategy of acquiring companies that are developing potentially disruptive technology is one that Cisco Systems, a dominant provider of Internet network equipment, is famous for pursuing. At the heart of this strategy must be recognition on the part of the incumbent enterprise that it is better for the company to develop disruptive technology and then cannibalize its established sales base than to have that sales base taken away by new entrants.

However, Christensen makes the very important point that even when established companies do undertake R&D investments in potentially disruptive technologies, they often fail to commercialize those technologies because of internal forces that suppress change. For example, managers in the parts of the business that are currently generating the most cash may claim that they need the greatest R&D investment to maintain their market position and may lobby top management to delay investment in a new technology. Early in the S-curve, when it is very unclear what the long-term prospects of a new technology may be, this can be a powerful argument. The consequence, however, may be that the company fails to build a competence in the new technology and will suffer accordingly.

In addition, Christensen argues that the commercialization of new disruptive technology often requires a radically different value chain with a completely different cost structure—a new business model. For example, it may require a different manufacturing system, a different distribution system, and different pricing options and involve very different gross margins and operating margins. Christensen argues that it is almost impossible for two distinct business models to coexist within the same organization. When they try to do that, almost inevitably the established business model will suffocate the business model associated with the disruptive technology.

The solution to this problem is to separate the disruptive technology and place it in its own autonomous operating division. For example, during the early 1980s, Hewlett-Packard (HP) built a very successful laser printer business. Then along came inkjet technology. Some in the company believed that inkjet printers would cannibalize sales of laser printers and consequently argued that HP should not produce inkjet printers. Fortunately for HP, senior management at the time saw inkjet technology for what it was: a potential disruptive technology. Instead, they allocated significant R&D funds toward its commercialization. Furthermore, when the technology was ready for market introduction, they established an autonomous inkjet division at a different geographic location with its own manufacturing, marketing, and distribution activities. They accepted that the inkjet division might take sales away from the laser printer division and decided that it was better to have an HP division cannibalize the sales of another HP division than have those sales cannibalized by another company. Luckily for HP, it turns out that inkjet printers cannibalize sales of laser printers only on the margin and that both have profitable market niches. This outcome, however, does not detract from the message of the story: if your company is developing a potentially disruptive technology, the chances of success will be enhanced if it is placed in a stand-alone product division and given its own mandate.

● **Strategic
Implications for
New Entrants**

This work just discussed also holds implications for new entrants. The new entrants, or attackers, have several advantages over established enterprises. Pressures to continue the existing out-of-date business model do not hamstring new entrants, which do not have to worry about product cannibalization issues. They do not have to worry about their established customer base or relationships with established suppliers and distributors. Instead, they can focus all their energies on the opportunities offered by the new disruptive technology, ride the S-curve of technology improvement, and grow rapidly with the market for that technology. This does not mean that the new entrants have no problems to solve. They may be constrained by a lack of capital or have to manage the organizational problems associated with rapid growth; most importantly, they may need to find a way to take their technology from a small out-of-the-way niche into the mass market.

Perhaps one of the most important issues facing new entrants is the choice of whether to partner with an established company or go it alone in their attempt to develop and profit from a new disruptive technology. Although a new entrant may enjoy all of the advantages of the attacker, it may lack the resources required to exploit them fully. In such a case, it might want to consider forming a strategic alliance with a larger, established company to gain access to those resources. The main issues here are the same as those that we discussed earlier when examining the three strategies that companies can pursue to capture first-mover advantages: go it alone, enter into a strategic alliance, or license the technology.

Summary of Chapter

1. Technical standards are important in many high-tech industries: they guarantee compatibility, reduce confusion in the minds of customers, allow for mass production and lower costs, and reduce the risks associated with supplying complementary products.

2. Network effects and positive feedback loops often determine which standard comes to dominate a market.

3. Owning a standard can be a source of sustained competitive advantage.

4. Establishing a proprietary standard as the industry standard may require the company to win a format war against a competing and incompatible standard. Strategies for doing this include producing complementary products, leveraging killer applications, using aggressive pricing and marketing, licensing the technology, and cooperating with competitors.

5. Many high-tech products are characterized by high fixed costs of development but very low or zero marginal costs of producing one extra unit of output. These cost economics create a presumption in favor of strategies that emphasize aggressive pricing to increase volume and drive down average total costs.

6. Many digital products suffer from very high piracy rates because of the low marginal costs of copying and distributing such products. Piracy can be reduced by

the appropriate combination of strategy, encryption software, and vigorous defense of intellectual property rights.

7. It is very important for a first mover to develop a strategy to capitalize on first-mover advantages. A company can choose from three strategies: develop and market the technology itself, do so jointly with another company, or license the technology to existing companies. The choice depends on the complementary assets required to capture a first-mover advantage, the height of barriers to imitation, and the capability of competitors.

8. Technological paradigm shifts occur when new technologies come along that revolutionize the structure of the industry, dramatically alter the nature of competition, and require companies to adopt new strategies to survive.

9. Technological paradigm shifts are more likely to occur when progress in improving the established technology is slowing because it is giving diminishing returns and a new disruptive technology is taking root in a market niche.

10. Established companies can deal with paradigm shifts by hedging their bets with regard to technology or setting up a stand-alone division to exploit the technology.

Discussion Questions

1. What is different about high-tech industries? Were all industries once high tech?
2. Why are standards so important in many high-tech industries? What are the competitive implications of this?
3. You work for a small company that has the leading position in an embryonic market. Your boss believes that the company's future is ensured because it has a 60% share of the market, the lowest cost structure in the industry, and the most reliable and highest-valued product. Write a memo to him outlining why his assumptions might be incorrect.
4. You are working for a small company that has developed an operating system for PCs that is faster and more stable than Microsoft's Windows operating system. What strategies might the company pursue to unseat Windows and establish its new operating system as the dominant technical standard in the industry?
5. You are a manager for a major music record label. Last year, music sales declined by 10%, primarily because of very high piracy rates for CDs. Your boss has asked you to develop a strategy for reducing piracy rates. What would you suggest that the company do?
6. Reread the Opening Case on the emerging format war for high-definition DVD players. On the basis of the information contained in this case, who do you think is most likely to win this format war, Sony or Toshiba? Why?

Practicing Strategic Management

SMALL-GROUP EXERCISE
Digital Books

Break up into groups of three to five, appoint one group member to be the spokesperson who will communicate your findings to the class, and discuss the following scenario. You are a group of managers and software engineers at a small start-up that has developed software that enables customers to easily download and view digital books on a variety of digital devices, from PCs to iPods and e-book readers. The same software also allows customers to share digital books using peer-to-peer technology (the same technology that allows people to share music files on the Web), and to burn digital books onto DVDs.

1. How do you think the market for this software is likely to develop? What factors might inhibit adoption of this software?
2. Can you think of a strategy that your company might pursue in combination with book publishers that will enable your company to increase revenues and with film companies to reduce piracy rates?

ARTICLE FILE 7

Find an example of an industry that has undergone a technological paradigm shift in recent years. What happened to the established companies as that paradigm shift unfolded?

STRATEGIC MANAGEMENT PROJECT
Module 7

This module requires you to analyze the industry environment in which your company is based and determine if it is vulnerable to a technological paradigm shift. With the information you have at your disposal, answer the following questions:

1. What is the dominant product technology used in the industry in which your company is based?
2. Are technical standards important in your industry? If so, what are they?
3. What are the attributes of the majority of customers purchasing the product of your company (for example, are they early adopters, early majority members, late majority members)? What does this tell you about the strategic issues that the company is likely to face in the future?
4. Did the dominant technology in your industry diffuse rapidly or slowly? What drove the speed of diffusion?
5. Where is the dominant technology in your industry on its S-curve? Are alternative competing technologies being developed that might give rise to a paradigm shift in your industry?
6. Are intellectual property rights important for your company? If so, what strategies is it adopting to protect those rights? Is it doing enough?

ETHICS EXERCISE

Sue had been hoping to get into investing for some time, but she simply didn't know how to get started. Her nephew had recommended that she visit his financial planner, and today she had her first appointment. She arrived fifteen minutes early and was shown into a spacious and classy waiting area. The receptionist offered her a choice of beverages and soon returned with a steaming cup of tea. Although initially nervous about turning over her investment decisions to a stranger, Sue was feeling more confident by the minute.

After a short wait, a tailored, middle-aged woman arrived to show Sue into an office bright with sunshine. Coming from behind the desk was a young man who promptly introduced himself as Dave. Sue was taken aback by his youth and casual attitude, but she had heard great things about this man from her nephew. As they settled themselves, Dave asked Sue about her investment wishes. He listened intently and immediately began to recommend a number of mutual funds and other investment opportunities. He also suggested that she conduct the majority of her investment activity online at his

direction. Dave was friendly and attentive, and Sue found herself being swept up by his presentation. He seemed so confident about the earning potential of these investments that Sue agreed readily to his suggestions.

Some weeks later, after seeing some initial returns on her investments, Sue began to lose money. Not knowing what to think, she called her nephew to get his opinion. He was experiencing the same run of bad luck. After digging for information from his friends in the financial industry, Sue's nephew discovered that Dave was known for recommending mutual funds for which he received extra payments from the fund firms themselves, regardless of the viability of the funds. Fortunately, Sue and her nephew were able to retrieve some of their money, and both considered that they had learned a valuable lesson.

1. Define the ethical issue presented in this case.
2. Should promoting funds to receive extra payments be legal?
3. How might an investor protect him- or herself from what happened to Sue and her nephew?

CLOSING CASE

The Failure of Friendster

In 2002, Jonathan Abrams thought that he was in the right place at the right time. With seed money raised from a wealthy Silicon Valley investor, the thirty-something engineer was developing a social networking site. The site, which debuted in March 2003, was called Friendster. It enabled people to post their profiles online, to link up with friends online, and introduce their friends to each other. Abrams's motivation for starting Friendster was that he wanted to meet girls, and he thought that a social networking site would be a pretty cool way to do it.

The site soon became one of the hot Internet properties of 2003. By the fall of 2003, Friendster had signed up over 3 million users. Publications including *Time, Esquire, Vanity Fair*, and *U.S. Weekly* were writing about Friendster before anybody had ever heard of MySpace. By November 2003, Friendster had attracted significant

investment from a clutch of high-profile venture capitalists (VCs), including the legendary John Dorr, perhaps the most successful venture capitalist in the history of Silicon Valley, who took a seat on Friendster's board. Dorr was joined by several other high-profile board members.

The buzz around Friendster led to a bid from another fast-growing VC-funded Silicon Valley start-up, Google, which wanted to buy the company for $30 million. The board, populated by venture capitalists like Dorr who were all looking for the next big thing, urged Abrams not to sell. It wasn't hard; Abrams thought Friendster would be worth much more in a short time, and he said no to Google. Three short years later, Abrams probably regrets that decision. Had he taken the Google offer, which was in stock, he would be worth about $1.5 billion today. Instead,

Abrams is no longer at Friendster, and the pioneering social networking site has been totally eclipsed by rivals like MySpace, Facebook, and Flickr. In September 2006, Friendster had just 1 million registered users; MySpace, which went live a year after Friendster, had 55.9 million!

One of Friendster's problems was that the site was soon overwhelmed by rapid growth. With 3 million users, it could take as long as forty seconds for pages to download. Another was the lack of new features on Friendster: while MySpace was rapidly introducing new features like blogs and tools that people could use to jazz up their profiles, Friendster stood still. Part of the problem was that new tools and features would only slow down Friendster even more. As for why Friendster was so slow, in part that was due to Friendster's closed system. Users at Friendster could only view the profiles of those on a relatively short chain of acquaintances. In contrast, MySpace uses an open system where anybody can look at anybody else's profile—which is much simpler to execute.

In addition, MySpace, which organized users around favorite bands, tapped into a much more energetic demographic: those in their teens and early twenties. Friendster's users, meanwhile, were somewhat older.

Other observers wonder about management problems at Friendster. The high-powered board was apparently preoccupied with big strategic issues and spent little time talking about the mundane technological problems that stymied the company's growth. There was also a revolving door for CEOs. The board felt Abrams was out of his depth, and quickly replaced him in March 2004 with one of their own, Tim Koogle, the former CEO of Yahoo. Koogle, always a caretaker CEO, stepped down after three months to be replaced by Scott Sassa, a former TV executive, who lasted just a year before being replaced by Taek Kwan, who lasted all of six months. By 2006, Friendster was on its fifth CEO, Kent Lindstrom.

The board considered shutting Friendster down, but in early 2006, they decided to keep the company afloat and injected $3.1 million into the enterprise. This was followed by an additional $10 million of venture capital funding in August 2006. Partly fueling this new investment is a feeling that while Friendster may be down, it is not yet out. Early on, Friendster filed about a dozen patent applications covering various aspects of social networking. By mid-2006, the U.S. Patent Office was starting to grant some of these patents, and Lindstrom was clearly wondering whether they could be used to extract royalties from rivals. The first patent to be granted covers "a method and apparatus for calculating and displaying and acting upon relationships in a social network." As for Friendster's service, it has been repositioned as a service for twenty-five to forty–year-olds who cannot spend hours every day online.[29]

Case Discussion Questions

1. Friendster was the first mover in the social networking space. Could it have become the dominant enterprise? In retrospect, what might the company have done differently?

2. What first-mover disadvantages did Friendster fall victim to?

3. Why did second-mover MySpace grow so much more rapidly than Friendster?

4. How might the revolving door of CEOs have hurt the young company?

5. What is the outlook for Friendster now? Do you think it is possible for the company to regain momentum? How?

Strategy in the Global Environment

MTV—A Global Brand Goes Local

MTV Networks has become a symbol of globalization. Established in 1981, the U.S.-based music TV network has been expanding outside its North American base since 1987, when it opened MTV Europe. Now owned by media conglomerate Viacom, MTV Networks, which includes siblings Nickelodeon and VH1, the music station for the aging baby boomers, generates more than $2 billion in revenues outside the United States. Since 1987, MTV has become the most ubiquitous cable programmer in the world. By 2006, the network reached a combined total of 443 million households, some 289 million of which were in 140 other countries.

While the United States still leads in number of households, the most rapid growth is elsewhere, particularly in Asia, where nearly two-thirds of the region's 3 billion people are under age thirty-five, the middle class is expanding quickly, and TV ownership is spreading rapidly. MTV Networks figures that every second of every day, over 2 million people are watching MTV around the world, the majority outside the United States.

Despite its international success, MTV's global expansion got off to a weak start. In 1987, it piped a single feed across Europe composed almost entirely of American programming with English-speaking veejays. Naïvely, the network's U.S. managers thought Europeans would flock to the American programming. But while viewers in Europe shared a common interest in a handful of global superstars, who at the time included Madonna and Michael Jackson, their tastes turned out to be surprisingly local. What was popular in Germany might not be popular in Great Britain. Many staples of the American music scene left Europeans cold. MTV suffered as a result. Soon local copycat stations were springing up in Europe that focused on the music scene in individual countries. They took viewers and advertisers away from MTV. As explained by Tom Freston, the former chair of MTV Networks, "We were going for the most shallow layer of what united viewers and brought them together. It didn't go over too well."

In 1995, MTV changed its strategy and broke Europe into regional feeds, of which there are around twenty-five, including feeds for the United Kingdom and Ireland; another for Germany, Austria, and Switzerland; one for Italy; one for France; one for Spain; one for Holland; and one for Russia. The network adopted the same localization strategy elsewhere in the world. For example, in Asia, it has ten feeds—an English-Hindi channel for India, separate Mandarin feeds for China and Taiwan, a Korean feed for South Korea, a Bahasa-language feed for Indonesia, a Japanese feed for Japan, and so on. Digital and satellite technology have made the localization of programming cheaper and easier. MTV Networks can now beam half a dozen feeds off one satellite transponder.

While MTV Networks exercises creative control over these different feeds, and while all the channels have the same familiar frenetic look and feel of MTV in the United States, a significant share of the programming and content is now local. When MTV opens a local station now, it begins with expatriates from elsewhere in the world to do a "gene transfer" of company culture and operating principles. Once these are established, however, the network switches to local employees and the expatriates move on. The idea is to discover the tastes of the local population and produce programming that matches those tastes.

Although many of the programming ideas still originate in the United States, with staples such as *The Real*

World having equivalents in different countries, an increasing share of programming is local in conception. In Italy, *MTV Kitchen* combines cooking with a music countdown. *Erotica* airs in Brazil and features a panel of youngsters discussing sex. The Indian channel produces twenty-one homegrown shows hosted by local veejays who speak Hinglish, a city-bred breed of Hindi and English. Hit shows include *MTV Cricket in Control*, appropriate for a land where cricket is a national obsession; *MTV Housefull*, which hones in on Hindi film stars (India has the biggest film industry outside Hollywood), and *MTV Bakra*, which is modeled after *Candid Camera*.

This localization push reaped big benefits for MTV, allowing the network to capture viewers back from local imitators. In India, for example, ratings increased by more than 700% between 1996, when the localization push began, and 2000. In turn, localization helps MTV to capture more of those all-important advertising revenues, even from other multinationals such as Coca-Cola, whose own advertising budgets are often locally determined.[1]

OVERVIEW

This chapter begins with a discussion of ongoing changes in the global competitive environment and discusses models that managers can use for analyzing competition in different national markets. Next, the chapter discusses the various ways in which international expansion can increase a company's profitability and profit growth. It also looks at the advantages and disadvantages of different strategies that companies can pursue to gain a competitive advantage in the global marketplace. This is followed by a discussion of two related strategic issues: (1) how managers decide which foreign markets to enter, when to enter them, and on what scale, and (2) what kind of vehicle or means a company should use to expand globally and enter a foreign country. Once a company has entered a foreign market, it becomes a **multinational company**, that is, a company that does business in two or more national markets. The vehicles that companies can employ to enter foreign markets and become multinationals include exporting, licensing, setting up a joint venture with a foreign company, and setting up a wholly owned subsidiary. The chapter closes with a discussion of the benefits and costs of entering into strategic alliances with other global companies. By the time you have completed this chapter, you will have a good understanding of the various strategic issues that companies face when they decide to expand their operations abroad to achieve competitive advantage and superior profitability.

MTV Networks, profiled in the Opening Case, previews many of the issues that we will explore in this chapter. Like many other companies, MTV moved into other countries because it saw huge growth opportunities there, and it thought it could create value by transferring its business model and American style of music programming to foreign markets. MTV initially treated foreign markets much like the United States, right down to airing the same music videos worldwide, but it soon found that this was not the correct approach. Many American music stars drew big yawns in Europe and Asia, where most of the stars were local. These national differences in customer tastes and preferences required MTV to change its approach to programming. It moved away from its one-size-fits-all strategy of global standardization and became more local in its orientation, adapting its programming to different markets, with different music videos and programs being aired in different markets. As one MTV manager has stated, "[D]espite being a global brand, we are local in our approach. We reflect the tastes and demands of our viewers and this differs in each market. Thus the need to create specific channels [in each country] that meet the need of our target audience."[2] At the same time, MTV's foreign affiliates still have the same look, feel, and overall programming philosophy of the U.S. parent. Striking the right balance between global standardization and local responsiveness let MTV reap big dividends, enabling the network to gain viewers and advertisers at the expense of competitors. As we shall see, many other enterprises have sought to do the same.

The Global and National Environments

Fifty years ago, most national markets were isolated from each other by significant barriers to international trade and investment. In those days, managers could focus on analyzing just those national markets in which their company competed. They did not need to pay much attention to entry by global competitors because there were few and entry was difficult. Nor did they need to pay much attention to entering foreign markets because that was often prohibitively expensive. All of this has now changed. Barriers to international trade and investment have tumbled, huge global markets for goods and services have been created, and companies from different nations are entering each other's home markets on a hitherto unprecedented scale, increasing the intensity of competition. Rivalry can no longer be understood merely in terms of what happens within the boundaries of a nation; managers now need to consider how globalization is affecting the environment in which their company competes and what strategies their company should adopt to exploit the unfolding opportunities and counter competitive threats. In this section, we look at the changes ushered in by falling barriers to international trade and investment, and we discuss a model for analyzing the competitive situation in different nations.

● **The Globalization of Production and Markets**

The past half-century has seen a dramatic lowering of barriers to international trade and investment. For example, the average tariff rate on manufactured goods traded between advanced nations has fallen from around 40% to under 4%. Similarly, in nation after nation, regulations prohibiting foreign companies from entering domestic markets and establishing production facilities, or acquiring domestic companies, have been removed. As a result of these two developments, there has been a surge in both the volume of international trade and the value of foreign direct investment. The volume of world merchandise trade has grown faster than the world economy since 1950.[3] From 1970 to 2005, the volume of world merchandise trade expanded twenty-sevenfold, outstripping the expansion of world production, which grew about 7.5 times in real terms. Moreover, between 1992 and 2005, the total flow of foreign direct investment from all countries increased over 500%, while world trade by value grew by some 140% and world output by around 40%.[4] These two trends have led to the globalization of production and the globalization of markets.[5]

The globalization of production has been increasing as companies take advantage of lower barriers to international trade and investment to disperse important parts of their production processes around the globe. Doing so enables them to take advantage of national differences in the cost and quality of factors of production such as labor, energy, land, and capital, which allows them to lower their cost structures and boost profits. For example, some 30% of the Boeing Company's commercial jet aircraft, the 777, is built by foreign companies. For its next jet airliner, the 787, Boeing is pushing this trend even further, with some 65% of the total value of the aircraft scheduled to be outsourced to foreign companies, 35% of which will go to three major Japanese companies, and another 20% going to companies located in Italy, Singapore, and the United Kingdom.[6] Part of Boeing's rationale for outsourcing so much production to foreign suppliers is that these suppliers are the best in the world at performing their particular activity. Therefore, the result of having foreign suppliers build specific parts is a better final product and higher profitability for Boeing.

As for the globalization of markets, it has been argued that the world's economic system is moving from one in which national markets are distinct entities, isolated from each other by trade barriers and barriers of distance, time, and culture, toward a system in which national markets are merging into one huge global marketplace. Increasingly, customers around the world demand and use the same basic product offerings. Consequently, in many industries, it is no longer meaningful to talk about the German market, the U.S. market, or the Japanese market; there is only the global market. The global acceptance of Coca-Cola, Citigroup credit cards, blue jeans, Starbucks, McDonald's hamburgers, the Nokia wireless phone, and Microsoft's Windows operating system are examples of this trend.[7]

The trend toward the globalization of production and markets has several important implications for competition within an industry. First, industry boundaries do not stop at national borders. Because many industries are becoming global in scope, actual and potential competitors exist not only in a company's home market but also in other national markets. Managers who analyze only their home market can be caught unprepared by the entry of efficient foreign competitors. The globalization of markets and production implies that companies around the globe are finding their home markets under attack from foreign competitors. For example, in Japan, Merrill Lynch and Citicorp are making inroads against Japanese financial service institutions. In the United States, Finland's Nokia has taken market share from Motorola in the market for wireless phone handsets (see Strategy in Action 8.1). In the European Union, the once-dominant Dutch company Philips has seen its market share in the customer electronics industry taken by Japan's JVC, Matsushita, and Sony.

Second, the shift from national to global markets has intensified competitive rivalry in industry after industry. National markets that once were consolidated oligopolies, dominated by three or four companies and subjected to relatively little foreign competition, have been transformed into segments of fragmented global industries in which a large number of companies battle each other for market share in country after country. This rivalry has threatened to drive down profitability and made it all the more critical for companies to maximize their efficiency, quality, customer responsiveness, and innovative ability. The painful restructuring and downsizing that has been going on at companies such as Kodak and Xerox is as much a response to the increased intensity of global competition as it is to anything else. However, not all global industries are fragmented. Many remain consolidated oligopolies, except that now they are consolidated global, rather than national, oligopolies. In the videogame industry,

Strategy in Action

Finland's Nokia

The wireless phone market is one of the great growth stories of the last decade. Starting from a very low base in 1990, annual global sales of wireless phones surged to reach 825 million units in 2005. By the end of 2005, there were over 1.7 billion wireless subscribers worldwide, up from less than 10 million in 1990. Nokia is one of the dominant players in the world market for mobile phones. Nokia's roots are in Finland, not normally a country that comes to mind when one talks about leading-edge technology companies. In the 1980s, Nokia was a rambling Finnish conglomerate with activities that embraced tire manufacturing, paper production, consumer electronics, and telecommunications equipment. By 2006, it had transformed itself into a focused telecommunications equipment manufacturer with a global reach, sales of over $40 billion, earnings of more than $5 billion, and a 34% share of the global market for wireless phones. How has this former conglomerate emerged to take a global leadership position in wireless telecommunications equipment? Much of the answer lies in the history, geography, and political economy of Finland and its Nordic neighbors.

In 1981, the Nordic nations cooperated to create the world's first international wireless telephone network. They had good reason to become pioneers: it cost far too much to lay down a traditional wire line telephone service in those sparsely populated and inhospitably cold countries. The same features made telecommunications all the more valuable: people driving through the Arctic winter and owners of remote northern houses needed a telephone to summon help if something went wrong. As a result, Sweden, Norway, and Finland became the first nations in the world to take wireless telecommunications seriously. They found, for example, that although it cost up to $800 per subscriber to bring a traditional wire line service to remote locations, the same locations could be linked by wireless cellular for only $500 per person. As a consequence, 12% of the people in Scandinavia owned

cellular phones by 1994, compared with less than 6% in the United States, the world's second most developed market. This lead continued over the next decade. By the end of 2005, 90% of the population in Finland owned a wireless phone, compared with 70% in the United States.

Nokia, a long-time telecommunications equipment supplier, was well positioned to take advantage of this development from the start, but there were other forces at work that helped Nokia develop its competitive edge. Unlike almost every other developed nation, Finland has never had a national telephone monopoly. Instead, the country's telephone services have long been provided by about fifty or so autonomous local telephone companies whose elected boards set prices by referendum (which naturally means low prices). This army of independent and cost-conscious telephone service providers prevented Nokia from taking anything for granted in its home country. With typical Finnish pragmatism, its customers were willing to buy from the lowest-cost supplier, whether that was Nokia, Ericsson, Motorola, or some other company. This situation contrasted sharply with that prevailing in most developed nations until the late 1980s and early 1990s, where domestic telephone monopolies typically purchased equipment from a dominant local supplier or made it themselves. Nokia responded to this competitive pressure by doing everything possible to drive down its manufacturing costs while staying at the leading edge of wireless technology.

The consequences of these forces are clear. Nokia is now a leader in digital wireless technology. Many now regard Finland as the lead market for wireless telephone services. If you want to see the future of wireless, you don't go to New York or San Francisco; you go to Helsinki, where Finns use their wireless handsets not just to talk to each other but also to browse the Web, execute e-commerce transactions, control household heating and lighting systems, or purchase Coke from a wireless-enabled vending machine. Nokia has gained this lead because Scandinavia started switching to digital technology five years before the rest of the world.[a]

for example, three companies are battling for global dominance: Microsoft from the United States and Nintendo and Sony from Japan. In the market for wireless handsets, Nokia of Finland does global battle against Motorola of the United States, Samsung and LG from South Korea, and Sony-Ericsson, a joint venture between Sony of Japan and Ericsson of Sweden.

Finally, although globalization has increased both the threat of entry and the intensity of rivalry within many formerly protected national markets, it has also created enormous opportunities for companies based in those markets. The steady decline in barriers to cross-border trade and investment has opened up many once-protected markets to companies based outside them. Thus, for example, in recent years, western European, Japanese, and U.S. companies have accelerated their investments in the nations of Eastern Europe, Latin America, and Southeast Asia as they try to take advantage of growth opportunities in those areas.

● National Competitive Advantage

Despite the globalization of production and markets, many of the most successful companies in certain industries are still clustered in a small number of countries. For example, many of the world's most successful biotechnology and computer companies are based in the United States, and many of the most successful customer electronics companies are based in Japan and South Korea. Germany is the base for many successful chemical and engineering companies. These facts suggest that the nation-state within which a company is based may have an important bearing on the competitive position of that company in the global marketplace.

In a study of national competitive advantage, Michael Porter identified four attributes of a national or country-specific environment that have an important impact on the global competitiveness of companies located within that nation:[8]

- *Factor endowments*: A nation's position in factors of production such as skilled labor or the infrastructure necessary to compete in a given industry
- *Local demand conditions*: The nature of home demand for the industry's product or service
- *Related and supporting industries*: The presence or absence in a nation of supplier industries and related industries that are internationally competitive
- *Firm strategy, structure, and rivalry*: The conditions in the nation that govern how companies are created, organized, and managed and the nature of domestic rivalry

Porter speaks of these four attributes as constituting the diamond, arguing that companies from a given nation are most likely to succeed in industries or strategic groups in which the four attributes are favorable (see Figure 8.1). He also argues that the diamond's attributes form a mutually reinforcing system in which the effect of one attribute is dependent on the state of the others.

FACTOR ENDOWMENTS Factor endowments—the cost and quality of factors of production—are prime determinants of the competitive advantage that certain countries might have in certain industries. Factors of production include basic factors, such as land, labor, capital, and raw materials, and advanced factors, such as technological know-how, managerial sophistication, and physical infrastructure (roads, railways, and ports). The competitive advantage that the United States enjoys in biotechnology might be explained by the presence of certain advanced factors of production—for example, technological know-how—in combination with some basic factors, which might be a pool of relatively low-cost venture capital that can be used to fund risky start-ups in industries such as biotechnology.

LOCAL DEMAND CONDITIONS Home demand plays an important role in providing the impetus for upgrading competitive advantage. Companies are typically most sensitive to the needs of their closest customers. Thus, the characteristics of home demand are particularly important in shaping the attributes of domestically made products

FIGURE 8.1

National Competitive
Advantage

Source: Adapted from
M. E. Porter, "The Competitive
Advantage of Nations,"
Harvard Business Review
(March–April 1990): 77.

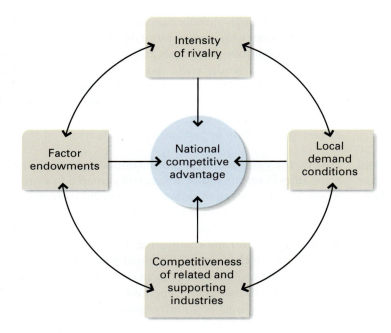

and creating pressures for innovation and quality. A nation's companies gain competitive advantage if their domestic customers are sophisticated and demanding and pressure local companies to meet high standards of product quality and produce innovative products. Japan's sophisticated and knowledgeable buyers of cameras helped stimulate the Japanese camera industry to improve product quality and introduce innovative models. A similar example can be found in the cellular phone equipment industry, where sophisticated and demanding local customers in Scandinavia helped push Nokia of Finland and Ericsson of Sweden to invest in cellular phone technology long before demand for cellular phones took off in other developed nations. As a result, Nokia and Ericsson, together with Motorola, are significant players in the global cellular telephone equipment industry. (The case of Nokia was reviewed in more depth in Strategy in Action 8.1.)

COMPETITIVENESS OF RELATED AND SUPPORTING INDUSTRIES The third broad attribute of national advantage in an industry is the presence of internationally competitive suppliers or related industries. The benefits of investments in advanced factors of production by related and supporting industries can spill over into an industry, thereby helping it achieve a strong competitive position internationally. Swedish strength in fabricated steel products (such as ball bearings and cutting tools) has drawn on strengths in Sweden's specialty steel industry. Switzerland's success in pharmaceuticals is closely related to its previous international success in the technologically related dye industry. One consequence of this process is that successful industries within a country tend to be grouped into clusters of related industries. Indeed, this was one of the most pervasive findings of Porter's study. One such cluster is the German textile and apparel sector, which includes high-quality cotton, wool, synthetic fibers, sewing machine needles, and a wide range of textile machinery.

INTENSITY OF RIVALRY The fourth broad attribute of national competitive advantage in Porter's model is the intensity of rivalry of firms within a nation. Porter makes two important points here. First, different nations are characterized by different management ideologies, which either help them or do not help them to build national competitive advantage. For example, Porter noted the predominance of engineers in top management at German and Japanese firms. He attributed this to these firms' emphasis on improving manufacturing processes and product design. In contrast, Porter noted a predominance of people with finance backgrounds leading many U.S. firms. He linked this to U.S. firms' lack of attention to improving manufacturing processes and product design. He argued that the dominance of finance led to an overemphasis on maximizing short-term financial returns. According to Porter, one consequence of these different management ideologies was a relative loss of U.S. competitiveness in those engineering-based industries where manufacturing processes and product design issues are all-important (such as the automobile industry).

Porter's second point is that there is a strong association between vigorous domestic rivalry and the creation and persistence of competitive advantage in an industry. Rivalry induces companies to look for ways to improve efficiency, which makes them better international competitors. Domestic rivalry creates pressures to innovate, improve quality, reduce costs, and invest in upgrading advanced factors. All this helps to create world-class competitors. The stimulating effects of strong domestic competition are clear in the story of the rise of Nokia of Finland in the market for wireless handsets and telephone equipment (see Strategy in Action 8.1).

● **Using the Framework**

The framework just described can help managers to identify where their most significant global competitors are likely to come from. For example, there is an emerging cluster of computer service and software companies in Bangalore, India, that includes two of the fastest-growing information technology companies in the world, Infosys and Wipro. These companies are emerging as aggressive competitors on the global stage. Indeed, there are signs that this is already happening, because both companies have recently opened offices in the European Union and United States so they can better compete against the likes of IBM and EDS.

The framework can also be used to help managers decide where they might want to locate certain productive activities. Seeking to take advantage of U.S. expertise in biotechnology, many foreign companies have set up research facilities in San Diego, Boston, and Seattle, where U.S. biotechnology companies tend to be clustered. Similarly, in an attempt to take advantage of Japanese success in customer electronics, many U.S. electronics companies have set up research and production facilities in Japan, often in conjunction with Japanese partners.

Finally, the framework can help a company assess how tough it might be to enter certain national markets. If a nation has a competitive advantage in certain industries, it might be challenging for foreigners to enter those industries. For example, the highly competitive retailing industry in the United States has proved to be a very difficult one for foreign companies to enter. Successful foreign retailers such as Britain's Marks & Spencer and IKEA from Sweden have found it tough going in the United States, precisely because the U.S. retailing industry is the most competitive in the world.

Increasing Profitability and Profit Growth Through Global Expansion

Here we look at a number of ways in which expanding globally can enable companies to increase their profitability and grow their profits more rapidly. At the most basic level, global expansion increases the size of the market that a company is addressing, thereby boosting profit growth. As we shall see, global expansion also offers opportunities for reducing the cost structure of the enterprise or adding value through differentiation, thereby potentially boosting profitability.

● Expanding the Market: Leveraging Products

A company can increase its growth rate by taking goods or services developed at home and selling them internationally. Indeed, almost all multinationals started out doing just this. Procter & Gamble, for example, developed most of its best-selling products at home and then sold them around the world (Pampers and Ivory Soap being cases in point; see Strategy in Action 8.2). Similarly, from its earliest days, Microsoft has always focused on selling its software around the world. Automobile companies like Ford, Volkswagen, and Toyota also grew by developing products at home and then selling them in international markets. The returns from such a strategy are likely to be greater if indigenous competitors in the nations a company enters lack comparable products. Thus, Toyota has grown its profits by entering the large automobile markets of North America and Europe and by offering products that are differentiated from those offered by local rivals (Ford and GM) by their superior quality and reliability.

It is important to note that the success of many multinational companies is based not just on the goods or services that they sell in foreign nations, but also on the distinctive competencies (unique skills) that underlie the production and marketing of those goods or services. Thus, Toyota's success is based on its distinctive competency in manufacturing automobiles, and expanding internationally can be seen as a way of generating greater returns from this competency. Similarly, Procter & Gamble's global success was based on more than its portfolio of consumer products; it was also based on the company's skills in mass-marketing consumer goods. P&G grew rapidly in international markets between 1950 and 1990 because it was one of the most skilled mass-marketing enterprises in the world and could "outmarket" indigenous competitors in the nations it entered. Global expansion was thus a way of generating higher returns from its competency in marketing.

Pushing this further, one could say that because distinctive competencies are in essence the most valuable aspects of a company's business model, the successful global expansion by manufacturing companies like Toyota and P&G was based on their ability to transfer aspects of their business model and apply it to foreign markets. The same can be said of companies engaged in the service sectors of an economy, such as financial institutions, retailers, restaurant chains, and hotels. Expanding the market for their services often means replicating their business model in foreign nations (albeit with some changes to account for local differences, which we will discuss in more detail shortly). Starbucks, for example, is expanding rapidly outside the United States by taking the basic business model it developed at home and using it as a blueprint for establishing international operations. Similarly, McDonald's is famous for its international expansion strategy, which has taken the company into more than 120 nations that collectively generate over half of the company's revenues.

● Realizing Cost Economies from Global Volume

In addition to growing profits more rapidly, expanding its sales volume through international expansion can help a company realize cost savings from economies of scale, thereby boosting profitability. Such scale economies come from several sources. First, by spreading the fixed costs associated with developing a product and setting up production facilities over its global sales volume, a company can lower its average unit cost. Thus, Microsoft can garner significant scale economies by spreading the $5 billion it cost to develop Windows Vista over global demand.

Second, by serving a global market, a company can potentially utilize its production facilities more intensively, which leads to higher productivity, lower costs, and greater profitability. For example, if Intel sold microprocessors only in the United States, it might be able to keep its factories open for only one shift, five days a week. But by serving a global market from the same factories, it might be able to utilize those assets for two shifts, seven days a week. In other words, the capital invested in those factories is used more intensively if Intel sells to a global as opposed to a national market, which translates into higher capital productivity and a higher return on invested capital.

Third, as global sales increase the size of the enterprise, so its bargaining power with suppliers increases, which may allow it to bargain down the cost of key inputs and boost profitability. Wal-Mart has been able to use its enormous sales volume as a lever to bargain down the price it pays suppliers for merchandise sold through its stores.

In addition to the cost savings that come from economies of scale, companies that sell to a global as opposed to a local marketplace may be able to realize further cost savings from learning effects. We first discussed learning effects in Chapter 4, where we noted that employee productivity increases with cumulative increases in output over time (for example, it costs considerably less to build the one-hundredth aircraft on a Boeing assembly line than the tenth because employees learn how to perform their tasks more efficiently over time). By selling to a global market, a company may be able to increase its sales volume more rapidly, and thus the cumulative output from its plants, which in turn should result in quicker learning, higher employee productivity, and a cost advantage over competitors that are growing more slowly because they lack international markets.

● Realizing Location Economies

Earlier in this chapter, we discussed how countries differ from each other along a number of dimensions, including differences in the cost and quality of factors of production. These differences imply that some locations are more suited than others to producing certain goods and services.[9] **Location economies** are the economic benefits that arise from performing a value creation activity in the optimal location for that activity, wherever in the world that might be (transportation costs and trade barriers permitting). Locating a value creation activity in the optimal location for that activity can have one of two effects: (1) it can lower the costs of value creation, thus helping the company to achieve a low-cost position, or (2) it can enable a company to differentiate its product offering, which gives it the option of charging a premium price or keeping the price low and using differentiation as a means of increasing sales volume. Thus, efforts to realize location economies are consistent with the business-level strategies of low cost and differentiation. In theory, a company that realizes location economies by dispersing each of its value creation activities to the optimal location for that activity should have a competitive advantage over a company that bases all of its value creation activities at a single location. It should be able to differentiate its product offering better and lower its cost structure more than its single-location competitor. In a world where competitive pressures are increasing, such a strategy may well become an imperative for survival.

For an example of how this works in an international business, consider Clear Vision, a manufacturer and distributor of eyewear. Started in the 1970s by David Glassman, the firm now generates annual gross revenues of more than $100 million. Not exactly small, but no corporate giant either, Clear Vision is a multinational firm with production facilities on three continents and customers around the world. Clear Vision began its move toward becoming a multinational in the early 1980s. The strong dollar at that time made U.S.-based manufacturing very expensive. Low-priced imports were taking an ever larger share of the U.S. eyewear market, and Clear Vision realized it could not survive unless it also began to import. Initially the firm bought from independent overseas manufacturers, primarily in Hong Kong. However, it became dissatisfied with these suppliers' product quality and delivery. As Clear Vision's volume of imports increased, Glassman decided that the best way to guarantee quality and delivery was to set up Clear Vision's own manufacturing operation overseas. Accordingly, Clear Vision found a Chinese partner, and together they opened a manufacturing facility in Hong Kong, with Clear Vision being the majority shareholder.

The choice of the Hong Kong location was influenced by its combination of low labor costs, a skilled work force, and tax breaks given by the Hong Kong government. The firm's objective at this point was to lower production costs by locating value creation activities at an appropriate location. After a few years, however, the increasing industrialization of Hong Kong and a growing labor shortage had pushed up wage rates to the extent that it was no longer a low-cost location. In response, Glassman and his Chinese partner moved part of their manufacturing to a plant in mainland China to take advantage of the lower wage rates there. Again, the goal was to lower production costs. The parts for eyewear frames manufactured at this plant are shipped to the Hong Kong factory for final assembly and then distributed to markets in North and South America. The Hong Kong factory now employs eighty people, and the China plant, between 300 and 400.

At the same time, Clear Vision was looking for opportunities to invest in foreign eyewear firms with reputations for fashionable design and high quality. Its objective was not to reduce production costs but to launch a line of high-quality, differentiated, designer eyewear. Clear Vision did not have the design capability in-house to support such a line, but Glassman knew that certain foreign manufacturers did. As a result, Clear Vision invested in factories in Japan, France, and Italy, holding a minority shareholding in each case. These factories now supply eyewear for Clear Vision's Status Eye division, which markets high-priced designer eyewear.[10]

SOME CAVEATS Introducing transportation costs and trade barriers complicates this picture somewhat. New Zealand might have a comparative advantage for low-cost car assembly operations, but high transportation costs make it an uneconomical location from which to serve global markets. Factoring transportation costs and trade barriers into the cost equation helps explain why many U.S. companies have been shifting their production from Asia to Mexico. Mexico has three distinct advantages over many Asian countries as a location for value creation activities: low labor costs; Mexico's proximity to the large U.S. market, which reduces transportation costs; and the North American Free Trade Agreement (NAFTA), which has removed many trade barriers among Mexico, the United States, and Canada, increasing Mexico's attractiveness as a production site for the North American market. Thus, although the relative costs of value creation are important, transportation costs and trade barriers also must be considered in location decisions.

Another caveat concerns the importance of assessing political and economic risks when making location decisions. Even if a country looks very attractive as a production location when measured against cost or differentiation criteria, if its government is unstable or totalitarian, companies are usually well advised not to base production there. Similarly, if a particular national government appears to be pursuing inappropriate social or economic policies, this might be another reason for not basing production in that location, even if other factors look favorable.

● **Leveraging the Skills of Global Subsidiaries**

Initially, many multinational companies develop the valuable competencies and skills that underpin their business model in their home nation and then expand internationally, primarily by selling products and services based on those competencies.

However, for more mature multinational enterprises that have already established a network of subsidiary operations in foreign markets, the development of valuable skills can just as well occur in foreign subsidiaries.[11] Skills can be created anywhere within a multinational's global network of operations, wherever people have the opportunity and incentive to try new ways of doing things. The creation of skills that help to lower the costs of production, or to enhance perceived value and support higher product pricing, is not the monopoly of the corporate center.

Leveraging the skills created within subsidiaries and applying them to other operations within the firm's global network may create value. For example, McDonald's is finding more and more often that its foreign franchisees are a source of valuable new ideas. Faced with slow growth in France, its local franchisees have begun to experiment not only with the menu but also with the layout and theme of restaurants. Gone are the ubiquitous Golden Arches; gone too are many of the utilitarian chairs and tables and other plastic features of the fast-food giant. Many McDonald's restaurants in France now have hardwood floors, exposed brick walls, and even armchairs. Half of the 930 or so outlets in France have been upgraded to a level that would make them unrecognizable to an American. The menu, too, has been changed to include premier sandwiches, such as chicken on focaccia bread, priced some 30% higher than the average hamburger. In France at least, the strategy seems to be working. Following the changes, increases in same-store sales rose from 1% annually to 3.4%. Impressed with the impact, McDonald's executives are now considering adopting similar changes at other McDonald's restaurants in markets where same-store sales growth is sluggish, including the United States.[12]

For the managers of a multinational enterprise, this phenomenon creates important new challenges. First, they must have the humility to recognize that valuable skills can arise anywhere within the firm's global network, not just at the corporate center. Second, they must establish an incentive system that encourages local employees to acquire new competencies. This is not as easy as it sounds. Creating new competencies involves a degree of risk. Not all new skills add value. For every valuable idea created by a McDonald's subsidiary in a foreign country, there may be several failures. The management of the multinational must install incentives that encourage employees to take the necessary risks, and the company must reward people for successes and not sanction them unnecessarily for taking risks that did not pan out. Third, managers must have a process for identifying when valuable new skills have been created in a subsidiary, and finally, they need to act as facilitators, helping to transfer valuable skills within the firm.

Cost Pressures and Pressures for Local Responsiveness

Companies that compete in the global marketplace typically face two types of competitive pressures: *pressures for cost reductions* and *pressures to be locally responsive* (see Figure 8.2).[13] These competitive pressures place conflicting demands on a company. Responding to pressures for cost reductions requires that a company try to minimize its unit costs. To attain this goal, it may have to base its productive activities at the most favorable low-cost location, wherever in the world that might be. It may also have to offer a standardized product to the global marketplace in order to realize the cost savings that come from economies of scale and learning effects. On the other hand, responding to pressures to be locally responsive requires that a company differentiate its product offering and marketing strategy from country to country in an effort to accommodate the diverse demands arising from national differences in consumer

FIGURE 8.2

Pressures for Cost
Reductions and Local
Responsiveness

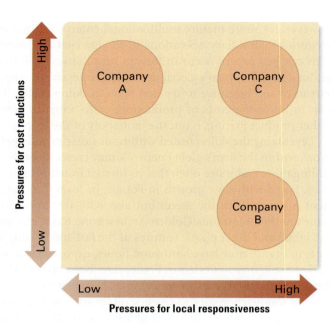

tastes and preferences, business practices, distribution channels, competitive conditions, and government policies. Because differentiation across countries can involve
significant duplication and a lack of product standardization, it may raise costs.

Some companies, such as Company A in Figure 8.2, face high pressures for cost
reductions and low pressures for local responsiveness, and others, such as Company
B, face low pressures for cost reductions and high pressures for local responsiveness.
But many companies are in the position of Company C: they face high pressures for
both cost reductions and local responsiveness. Dealing with these conflicting and
contradictory pressures is a difficult strategic challenge, primarily because being locally responsive tends to raise costs.

● Pressures for Cost
        Reductions

In competitive global markets, international businesses often face pressures for cost
reductions. To respond to these pressures, a firm must try to lower the costs of value
creation. A manufacturer, for example, might mass-produce a standardized product
at the optimal location in the world, wherever that might be, to realize economies of
scale and location economies. Alternatively, it might outsource certain functions to
low-cost foreign suppliers in an attempt to reduce costs. Thus, many computer companies have outsourced their telephone-based customer service functions to India,
where qualified technicians who speak English can be hired at a lower wage rate
than in the United States. In the same vein, a retailer like Wal-Mart might push its
suppliers (who are manufacturers) to also lower their prices. (In fact, the pressure
that Wal-Mart has placed on its suppliers to reduce prices has been cited as a major
cause of the trend among North American manufacturers to shift production to
China.)[14] A service business, such as a bank, might move some back-office functions,
like information processing, to developing nations where wage rates are lower.

Cost reduction pressures can be particularly intense in industries producing
commodity-type products where meaningful differentiation on nonprice factors is
difficult and price is the main competitive weapon. This tends to be the case for
products that serve universal needs. Universal needs exist when the tastes and preferences of consumers in different nations are similar if not identical, such as for bulk

chemicals, petroleum, steel, sugar, and the like. They also exist for many industrial and consumer products: for example, hand-held calculators, semiconductor chips, personal computers, and liquid crystal display screens. Pressures for cost reductions are also intense in industries where major competitors are based in low-cost locations, where there is persistent excess capacity, and where consumers are powerful and face low switching costs. Many commentators have argued that the liberalization of the world trade and investment environment in recent decades, by facilitating greater international competition, has generally increased cost pressures.[15]

● **Pressures for Local Responsiveness**

Pressures for local responsiveness arise from differences in consumer tastes and preferences, infrastructure and traditional practices, distribution channels, and host government demands. Responding to pressures to be locally responsive requires that a company differentiate its products and marketing strategy from country to country to accommodate these factors, all of which tends to raise a company's cost structure.

DIFFERENCES IN CUSTOMER TASTES AND PREFERENCES Strong pressures for local responsiveness emerge when customer tastes and preferences differ significantly between countries, as they may for historic or cultural reasons. In such cases, a multinational company's products and marketing message have to be customized to appeal to the tastes and preferences of local customers. The company is then typically pressured to delegate production and marketing responsibilities and functions to a company's overseas subsidiaries.

For example, the automobile industry in the 1980s and early 1990s moved toward the creation of so-called world cars. The idea was that global companies such as General Motors, Ford, and Toyota would be able to sell the same basic vehicle the world over, sourcing it from centralized production locations. If successful, the strategy would have enabled automobile companies to reap significant gains from global scale economies. However, this strategy frequently ran aground upon the hard rocks of consumer reality. Consumers in different automobile markets seem to have different tastes and preferences, and these require different types of vehicles. North American consumers show a strong demand for pickup trucks. This is particularly true in the South and West, where many families have a pickup truck as a second or third car. But in European countries, pickup trucks are seen purely as utility vehicles and are purchased primarily by firms rather than individuals. As a consequence, the product mix and marketing message need to be tailored to account for the different nature of demand in North America and Europe. Another example of the need to respond to national differences in tastes and preferences is given in Strategy in Action 8.2, which looks at the experience of Swedish retailer IKEA in foreign markets.

Notwithstanding the experiences of companies such as MTV and IKEA, some commentators have argued that customer demands for local customization are on the decline worldwide.[16] According to this argument, modern communications and transport technologies have created the conditions for a convergence of the tastes and preferences of customers from different nations. The result is the emergence of enormous global markets for standardized consumer products. The worldwide acceptance of McDonald's hamburgers, Coca-Cola, Gap clothes, Nokia cell phones, and Sony televisions, all of which are sold globally as standardized products, are often cited as evidence of the increasing homogeneity of the global marketplace. Others, however, consider this argument to be extreme. For example, Christopher Bartlett and Sumantra Ghoshal have observed that in the consumer electronics industry, buyers reacted to an overdose of standardized global products by showing a renewed preference for products that are differentiated according to local conditions.[17]

Strategy in Action

Localization at IKEA

IKEA may be the world's most successful global retailer. Established by Ingvar Kamprad in Sweden in 1943 when he was just seventeen years old, the home-furnishing superstore has grown into a global cult brand, with 230 stores in thirty-three countries that host 410 million shoppers a year and generated sales of €14.8 billion ($17.7 billion) in 2005. Kamprad himself, who still owns the private company, is rumored to be the world's richest man.

IKEA's target market is the global middle class who are looking for low-priced but attractively designed furniture and household items. The company applies the same basic formula worldwide: open, large warehouse stores, festooned in the blue and yellow colors of the Swedish flag, that offer 8,000 to 10,000 items, from kitchen cabinets to candlesticks. Use wacky promotions to drive traffic into the stores. Configure the interior of the stores so that customers have to pass through each department to get to the checkout. Add restaurants and child-care facilities so that shoppers stay as long as possible. Price the items as low as possible. Make sure that product design reflects the simple clean Swedish lines that have become IKEA's trademark. And then watch the results: customers who enter the store planning to buy a $40 coffee table and end up spending $500 on everything from storage units to kitchen ware.

IKEA aims to reduce the price of its offerings by 2 to 3% per year, which requires relentless attention to cost cutting. With a network of 1,300 suppliers in fifty-three countries, IKEA devotes considerable attention to finding the right manufacturer for each item. Consider the company's best-selling Klippan love seat. Designed in 1980, the Klippan, with its clean lines, bright colors, simple legs, and compact size, has sold some 1.5 million units since its introduction. Originally manufactured in Sweden, IKEA soon transferred production to lower-cost suppliers in Poland. As demand for the Klippan grew, IKEA then decided that it made more sense to work with suppliers in each of the company's big markets to avoid the costs associated with shipping the product all over the world. Today, there are five suppliers of the frames in Europe, plus three in the United States and two in China. To reduce the cost of the cotton slipcovers, production has been concentrated in four core suppliers in China and Europe. The resulting efficiencies from these global sourcing decisions enabled IKEA to reduce the price of the Klippan by some 40% between 1999 and 2005.

Despite its standard formula, however, IKEA has found that global success requires that it adapt its offerings to the tastes and preferences of consumers in different nations. IKEA first discovered this in the early 1990s, when it entered the United States. The company soon found that its European style offerings didn't always resonate with American consumers. Beds were measured in centimeters, not the king, queen, and twin sizes that Americans are familiar with. Sofas weren't big enough, wardrobe drawers were not deep enough, glasses were too small, curtains were too short, and kitchens didn't fit U.S. size appliances. Since then, IKEA has redesigned its offerings in the United States to appeal to American consumers, and it has been rewarded with stronger store sales. The same process is now unfolding in China, where the company plans to have ten stores by 2010. The store layout in China reflects the layout of many Chinese apartments, and since many Chinese apartments have balconies, IKEA's Chinese stores include a balcony section. IKEA has had to adapt its locations to China, where car ownership is still not widespread. In the West, IKEA stores are generally located in suburban areas and have lots of parking space, but in China they are located near public transportation, and IKEA offers delivery services so that Chinese customers can get their purchases home.[b]

DIFFERENCES IN INFRASTRUCTURE AND TRADITIONAL PRACTICES Pressures for local responsiveness also arise from differences in infrastructure or traditional practices among countries, creating a need to customize products accordingly. To meet this need, companies may have to delegate manufacturing and production functions to foreign subsidiaries. For example, in North America, consumer electrical systems are based on 110 volts, whereas in some European countries, 240-volt systems are standard. Thus, domestic electrical appliances have to be customized to take this difference in infrastructure into account. Traditional practices also often vary across nations. For example, in Britain, people drive on the left-hand side of the road, creating a demand for right-hand-drive cars, whereas in France (and the rest of Europe), people drive on the right-hand side of the road and therefore want left-hand-drive cars. Obviously, automobiles have to be customized to take this difference in traditional practices into account.

Although many of the country differences in infrastructure are rooted in history, some are quite recent. For example, in the wireless telecommunications industry, different technical standards are found in different parts of the world. A technical standard known as GSM is common in Europe, and an alternative standard, CDMA, is more common in the United States and parts of Asia. The significance of these different standards is that equipment designed for GSM will not work on a CDMA network, and vice versa. Thus, companies such as Nokia, Motorola, and Ericsson, which manufacture wireless handsets and infrastructure such as switches, need to customize their product offerings according to the technical standard prevailing in a given country.

DIFFERENCES IN DISTRIBUTION CHANNELS A company's marketing strategies may have to be responsive to differences in distribution channels among countries, which may necessitate delegating marketing functions to national subsidiaries. In the pharmaceutical industry, for example, the British and Japanese distribution system is radically different from the U.S. system. British and Japanese doctors will not accept or respond favorably to a U.S.-style high-pressure sales force. Thus, pharmaceutical companies have to adopt different marketing practices in Britain and Japan compared with the United States—soft sell versus hard sell.

Similarly, Poland, Brazil, and Russia all have similar per-capita income on a purchasing power parity basis, but there are big differences in distribution systems across the three countries. In Brazil, supermarkets account for 36% of food retailing; in Poland, for 18%; and in Russia, for less than 1%.[18] These differences in channels require that companies adapt their own distribution and sales strategy.

HOST GOVERNMENT DEMANDS Finally, economic and political demands imposed by host country governments may require local responsiveness. For example, pharmaceutical companies are subject to local clinical testing, registration procedures, and pricing restrictions, all of which make it necessary that the manufacturing and marketing of a drug meet local requirements. Moreover, because governments and government agencies control a significant proportion of the health care budget in most countries, they are in a powerful position to demand a high level of local responsiveness.

More generally, threats of protectionism, economic nationalism, and local content rules (which require that a certain percentage of a product be manufactured locally) dictate that international businesses manufacture locally. As an example, consider Bombardier, the Canadian-based manufacturer of railcars, aircraft, jet boats, and snowmobiles. Bombardier has twelve railcar factories across Europe. Critics of the company argue that the resulting duplication of manufacturing facilities leads to high costs and helps explain why Bombardier makes lower profit margins on its railcar operations than on its other business lines. In reply, managers at Bombardier argue that in Europe, informal rules with regard to local content favor employers who hire local workers. To sell railcars in Germany, they claim, you must manufacture in Germany. The same goes for Belgium, Austria, and France. To try to address its cost structure in Europe, Bombardier has centralized its engineering and purchasing functions, but it has no plans to centralize manufacturing.[19]

Choosing a Global Strategy

Pressures for local responsiveness imply that it may not be possible for a firm to realize the full benefits from economies of scale and location economies. It may not be possible to serve the global marketplace from a single low-cost location, producing a globally standardized product, and marketing it worldwide to achieve economies of scale. In practice, the need to customize the product offering to local conditions may work against the implementation of such a strategy. For example, automobile firms have found that Japanese, American, and European consumers demand different kinds of cars, and this necessitates producing products that are customized for local markets. In response, firms like Honda, Ford, and Toyota are pursuing a strategy of establishing top-to-bottom design and production facilities in each of these regions so that they can better serve local demands. Although such customization brings benefits, it also limits the ability of a firm to realize significant scale economies and location economies.

In addition, pressures for local responsiveness imply that it may not be possible to leverage skills and products associated with a firm's distinctive competencies wholesale from one nation to another. Concessions often have to be made to local conditions. Even McDonald's, despite being depicted as a leader for the proliferation of standardized global products, has found that it has to customize its product offerings (its menu) in order to account for national differences in tastes and preferences.

Given the need to balance the cost and differentiation (value) sides of a company's business model, how do differences in the strength of pressures for cost reductions versus those for local responsiveness affect the choice of a company's strategy? Companies typically choose among four main strategic postures when competing internationally: a global standardization strategy, a localization strategy, a transnational strategy, and an international strategy.[20] The appropriateness of each strategy varies with the extent of pressures for cost reductions and local responsiveness. Figure 8.3 illustrates the conditions under which each of these strategies is most appropriate.

FIGURE 8.3

Four Basic Strategies

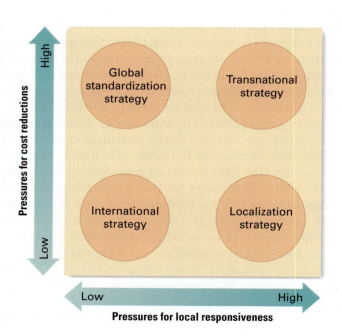

● **Global Standardization Strategy**

Companies that pursue a **global standardization strategy** focus on increasing profitability by reaping the cost reductions that come from economies of scale and location economies; that is, their business model is based on pursuing a low-cost strategy on a global scale. The production, marketing, and research and development (R&D) activities of companies pursuing a global strategy are concentrated in a few favorable locations. These companies try not to customize their product offering and marketing strategy to local conditions because customization, which involves shorter production runs and the duplication of functions, can raise costs. Instead, they prefer to market a standardized product worldwide so that they can reap the maximum benefits from economies of scale. They also tend to use their cost advantage to support aggressive pricing in world markets. Dell Computer is a good example of a company that pursues such a strategy (see the Running Case).

RUNNING CASE

Dell's Global Business Strategy

Dell has been expanding its presence outside the United States since the early 1990s. In fiscal 2006, 41% of Dell's $56 billion in revenue was generated outside the United States. Dell's strategic goal is to be the low-cost player in the global industry. It does not alter its business model from country to country; instead, it uses the same direct-selling and supply chain model that worked so well in the United States. Dell is thus pursuing a global standardization strategy.

Dell's basic approach to overseas expansion has been to serve foreign markets from a handful of regional manufacturing facilities, each established as a wholly owned subsidiary. To support its global business, it operates three final assembly facilities in the United States, one in Brazil (serving South America), two in Ireland (serving Europe), one in Malaysia (serving Southeast Asia), and two in China (serving China). Each of these plants is large enough to attain significant economies of scale. When demand in a region gets large enough, Dell considers opening a second plant; thus, it has three plants in the United States to serve North America, and two in Ireland to serve Europe. With sales growing rapidly in India, the company will bring an Indian plant online in 2007.

Each plant uses exactly the same supply chain management processes that have made Dell famous. Taking advantage of its supply chain management software, Dell schedules production of every line in every factory around the world every two hours. Every factory is run with no more than a few hours of inventory on hand, including work in progress. To serve Dell's global factories, many of Dell's largest suppliers have also located their facilities close to Dell's manufacturing plants so that they can better meet the company's demands for just-in-time inventory.

Dell has set up customer service centers in each region to handle phone and online orders and to provide technical assistance. In general, each center serves an entire region, which Dell has found to be more efficient than locating a customer service center in each country where the company does business. Beginning in 2001, Dell started to experiment with outsourcing some of its customer service functions for English-language customers to call centers in India. Although the move helped the company to lower costs, it also led to dissatisfaction from customers, particularly in the United States, who could not always follow the directions given over the phone from someone with an Indian accent. Subsequently, Dell moved its call centers for English-language businesses back to the United States and the United Kingdom. Dell continues to invest in Indian call centers for its retail customers, however, and in 2006, it announced that it was opening a fourth Indian call center.[c]

This strategy makes the most sense when there are strong pressures for cost reductions and demand for local responsiveness is minimal. Increasingly, these conditions prevail in many industrial goods industries, whose products often serve universal needs. In the semiconductor industry, for example, global standards have emerged, creating enormous demands for standardized global products. Accordingly, companies such as Intel, Texas Instruments, and Motorola all pursue a global strategy.

As both MTV and IKEA have discovered, however, in many consumer goods markets, demand for local responsiveness remains high. In these markets, the global standardization strategy is inappropriate.

Localization Strategy

A **localization strategy** focuses on increasing profitability by customizing the company's goods or services so that they provide a good match to the tastes and preferences in different national markets. Localization is most appropriate when there are substantial differences across nations with regard to consumer tastes and preferences and where cost pressures are not too intense. By customizing the product offering to local demands, the company increases the value of that product in the local market. On the downside, because it involves some duplication of functions and smaller production runs, customization limits the ability of the company to capture the cost reductions associated with mass-producing a standardized product for global consumption. The strategy may make sense, however, if the added value associated with local customization supports higher pricing, which would enable the company to recoup its higher costs, or if it leads to substantially greater local demand, enabling the company to reduce costs through the attainment of some scale economies in the local market.

MTV is a good example of a company that has had to pursue a localization strategy (see the Opening Case). If MTV had not localized its programming to match the demands of viewers in different nations, it would have lost market share to local competitors, its advertising revenues would have fallen, and its profitability would have declined. Thus, even though it raised costs, localization became a strategic imperative at MTV.

At the same time, it is important to realize that companies like MTV still have to keep a close eye on costs. Companies pursuing a localization strategy still need to be efficient and, whenever possible, capture some scale economies from their global reach. As noted earlier, many automobile companies have found that they have to customize some of their product offerings to local market demands—for example, by producing large pickup trucks for U.S. consumers and small, fuel-efficient cars for Europeans and the Japanese. At the same time, these companies try to get some scale economies from their global volume by using common vehicle platforms and components across many different models and by manufacturing those platforms and components at efficiently scaled factories that are optimally located. By designing their products in this way, these companies have been able to localize their product offering, yet simultaneously capture some scale economies.

Transnational Strategy

We have argued that a global standardization strategy makes the most sense when cost pressures are intense and demands for local responsiveness are limited. Conversely, a localization strategy makes the most sense when demands for local responsiveness are high but cost pressures are moderate or low. What happens, however, when the company simultaneously faces both strong cost pressures and strong pressures for local responsiveness? How can managers balance such competing and inconsistent demands? According to some researchers, the answer is by pursuing what has been called a transnational strategy.

Two of these researchers, Christopher Bartlett and Sumantra Ghoshal, argue that in today's global environment, competitive conditions are so intense that, to survive, companies must do all they can to respond to pressures for both cost reductions and local responsiveness. They must try to realize location economies and economies of scale from global volume, transfer distinctive competencies and skills within the company, and simultaneously pay attention to pressures for local responsiveness.[21]

Bartlett and Ghoshal also note that, in the modern multinational enterprise, distinctive competencies and skills do not reside just in the home country but can develop in any of the company's worldwide operations. Thus, they maintain that the flow of skills and product offerings should not be all one way, from home company to foreign subsidiary. Rather, the flow should also be from foreign subsidiary to home country, and from foreign subsidiary to foreign subsidiary. Transnational companies, in other words, must also focus on leveraging subsidiary skills.

In essence, companies that pursue a **transnational strategy** are trying to develop a business model that simultaneously achieves low costs, differentiates the product offering across geographic markets, and fosters a flow of skills between different subsidiaries in the company's global network of operations. As attractive as this may sound, the strategy is not an easy one to pursue because it places conflicting demands on the company. Differentiating the product to respond to local demands in different geographic markets raises costs, which runs counter to the goal of reducing costs. Companies like Ford and ABB (one of the world's largest engineering conglomerates) have tried to embrace a transnational strategy and have found it difficult to implement in practice.

Indeed, how best to implement a transnational strategy is one of the most complex questions that large global companies are grappling with today. It may be that few if any companies have perfected this strategic posture. But some clues to the right approach can be gleaned from a number of companies. Consider, for example, the case of Caterpillar. The need to compete with low-cost competitors such as Komatsu of Japan forced Caterpillar to look for greater cost economies. However, variations in construction practices and government regulations across countries meant that Caterpillar also had to be responsive to local demands. Therefore, Caterpillar confronted significant pressures for cost reductions and for local responsiveness. To deal with cost pressures, Caterpillar redesigned its products to use many identical components and invested in a few large-scale component-manufacturing facilities, sited at favorable locations, to fill global demand and realize scale economies. At the same time, the company augments the centralized manufacturing of components with assembly plants in each of its major global markets. At these plants, Caterpillar adds local product features, tailoring the finished product to local needs. Thus, Caterpillar is able to realize many of the benefits of global manufacturing while reacting to pressures for local responsiveness by differentiating its product among national markets.[22] Caterpillar started to pursue this strategy in 1979, and over the next twenty years, it succeeded in doubling output per employee, significantly reducing its overall cost structure in the process. Meanwhile, Komatsu and Hitachi, which are still wedded to a Japan-centric global strategy, have seen their cost advantages evaporate and have been steadily losing market share to Caterpillar.

However, building an organization capable of supporting a transnational strategy is a complex and challenging task. Indeed, some would say it is too complex because the strategy implementation problems of creating a viable organizational structure and the control systems to manage this strategy are immense. We shall return to this issue in Chapter 13.

● International Strategy

Sometimes it is possible to identify multinational companies that find themselves in the fortunate position of being confronted with low-cost pressures and low pressures for local responsiveness. Typically these enterprises are selling a product that serves universal needs, but because they do not face significant competitors, they are not confronted with pressures to reduce their cost structure. Xerox found itself in this position in the 1960s after its invention and commercialization of the photocopier. The technology underlying the photocopier was protected by strong patents, so for several years, Xerox did not face competitors—it had a monopoly. Because the product was highly valued in most developed nations, Xerox was able to sell the same basic product the world over and charge a relatively high price for it. At the same time, because it did not face direct competitors, the company did not have to deal with strong pressures to minimize its costs.

Historically, companies like Xerox have followed a similar developmental pattern as they build their international operations. They tend to centralize product development functions such as R&D at home. However, they also tend to establish manufacturing and marketing functions in each major country or geographic region in which they do business. Although they may undertake some local customization of product offering and marketing strategy, this tends to be rather limited in scope. Ultimately, in most international companies, the head office retains tight control over marketing and product strategy.

Other companies that have pursued this strategy include Procter & Gamble, which historically always developed innovative new products in Cincinnati and then transferred them wholesale to local markets. Another company that has followed a similar strategy is Microsoft. The bulk of Microsoft's product development work takes place in Redmond, Washington, where the company is headquartered. Although some localization work is undertaken elsewhere, this is limited to producing foreign-language versions of popular Microsoft programs such as Office.

● Changes in Strategy over Time

The Achilles heel of the international strategy is that, over time, competitors inevitably emerge, and if managers do not take proactive steps to reduce their cost structure, their company may be rapidly outflanked by efficient global competitors. This is exactly what happened to Xerox. Japanese companies such as Canon ultimately invented their way around Xerox's patents, produced their own photocopiers in very efficient manufacturing plants, priced them below Xerox's products, and rapidly took global market share from Xerox. Xerox's demise was not due to the emergence of competitors, because ultimately that was bound to occur, but rather to its failure to proactively reduce its cost structure in advance of the emergence of efficient global competitors. The message in this story is that an international strategy may not be viable in the long term, and to survive, companies that are able to pursue it need to shift toward a global standardization strategy, or perhaps a transnational strategy, in advance of competitors (see Figure 8.4).

The same can be said about a localization strategy. Localization may give a company a competitive edge, but if it is simultaneously facing aggressive competitors, the company will also have to reduce its cost structure, and the only way to do that may be to adopt more of a transnational strategy. Thus, as competition intensifies, international and localization strategies tend to become less viable, and managers need to orientate their companies toward either a global standardization strategy or a transnational strategy.

FIGURE 8.4

Changes over Time

FIGURE 8.4

Changes over Time

Basic Entry Decisions

A company contemplating foreign expansion must make three basic decisions: which overseas markets to enter, when to enter those markets, and on what scale.

● **Which Overseas Markets to Enter**

There are over 200 nation-states in the world, and they do not all hold out the same profit potential for a company contemplating foreign expansion. The choice of foreign markets must be based on an assessment of their long-run profit potential. The attractiveness of a country as a potential market for international business depends on balancing the benefits, costs, and risks associated with doing business in that country. The long-run economic benefits of doing business in a country are a function of factors such as the size of a market (in terms of demographics), the existing wealth (purchasing power) of consumers in that market, and the likely future wealth of consumers. Some markets are very large when measured by numbers of consumers (such as China and India), but low living standards may imply limited purchasing power and therefore a relatively small market when measured in economic terms. The costs and risks associated with doing business in a foreign country are typically lower in economically advanced and politically stable democratic nations and greater in less developed and politically unstable nations.

By performing benefit-cost-risk calculations, a company can come up with a ranking of countries in terms of their attractiveness and long-run profit potential.[23] Obviously, preference is given to entering markets that rank highly. For an example, consider the case of the American financial services company Merrill Lynch. Although Merrill Lynch has long had international operations, these were in its investment banking business and not its private client business (which deals with the investment needs of individuals). During the late 1990s, Merrill Lynch entered the private-client business in the United Kingdom, Canada, and Japan. All three of these countries have a large pool of private savings and exhibit relatively low political and economic risks, so it makes sense that they would be attractive to Merrill Lynch. By offering financial service products, such as mutual funds and investment advice, to individuals, Merrill Lynch has been able to capture a large enough proportion of the private savings pool in each country to justify its investment in setting up business there.

One other factor of importance is the value that a company's business model can create in a foreign market. This depends on the suitability of its business model to that market and the nature of indigenous competition.[24] Most importantly, if the company can offer a product that has not been widely available in that market and satisfies an unmet need, the value of that product to consumers is likely to be much greater than if the company simply offers the same type of product that indigenous competitors and other foreign entrants are already offering. Greater value translates into an ability to charge higher prices or build up unit sales volume more rapidly (or both).

● Timing of Entry

Once a set of attractive national markets has been identified, it is important to consider the timing of entry: early (before other overseas companies) or late (after other international businesses have already established themselves in the market). Several first-mover advantages are frequently associated with entering a market early.[25] One advantage is the ability to preempt rivals and capture demand by establishing a strong brand name. A second is the ability to build up demand, sales revenue, and market share in that country and ride down the experience curve ahead of future rivals. Both factors give the early entrant a cost advantage over later entrants, which may enable it to respond to later entry by cutting prices below those of later entrants and drive them out of the market. A third advantage is the ability of early entrants to create switching costs that tie customers into their products or services. Such switching costs make it difficult for later entrants to win business.

The case of Merrill Lynch illustrates these ideas. Merrill Lynch was one of the first western firms to set up a private-client business in Japan. Merrill entered by acquiring fifty branch offices and 2,000 employees from the bankrupt Japanese investment firm, Yamaichi Securities. By entering the private-client market in Japan before competitors, Merrill hoped to establish a brand name that later entrants would find difficult to match. Moreover, by entering early with a valuable product offering, Merrill hoped to build up its sales volume rapidly, which would enable it to realize scale economies from establishing a network of Japanese branches. Finally, Merrill's business model is based on establishing close relationships between its financial advisers (that is, stockbrokers) and private clients. Merrill's financial advisers are taught to get to know the needs of their clients and help manage their finances more effectively. Once these relationships are established, people rarely change. In other words, because of *switching costs*, they are unlikely to shift their business to later entrants. This effect is likely to be particularly strong in a country like Japan, where long-term relationships have traditionally been very important in business and social settings. For all of these reasons, Merrill Lynch hoped to capture first-mover advantages relative to its western competitors that would enable it to enjoy a strong competitive position in Japan for years to come.

There can also be first-mover disadvantages associated with entering a foreign market before other global companies.[26] These disadvantages are associated with pioneering costs, which an early entrant has to bear and which a later entrant can avoid. **Pioneering costs** arise when the business system in a foreign country is so different from that in a company's home market that a company has to devote considerable effort, time, and expense to learning the rules of the game. Pioneering costs also include the costs of business failure if the company, because of its ignorance of the overseas environment, makes major strategic mistakes. Thus, a global company that is one of the first to enter a national market has a certain liability.[27] Research evidence suggests that the probability of survival increases if an international business enters a national market after several other overseas companies have already done so.[28] The late entrant, it would appear, benefits by observing and learning from the mistakes made by early entrants.

Pioneering costs also include the costs of promoting and establishing a product offering, including the costs of educating customers. These can be significant when the product being promoted is unfamiliar to local consumers. In contrast, later entrants may be able to ride on an early entrant's investments in learning and customer education by watching how the early entrant proceeded in the market, by avoiding costly mistakes made by the early entrant, and by exploiting the market potential created by the early entrant's investments in customer education. For example, KFC introduced the Chinese to American-style fast food, but a later entrant, McDonald's, has capitalized on the market in China.

● **Scale of Entry and Strategic Commitments**

The final issue that a company needs to consider when contemplating market entry is the scale of entry. Entering a market on a large scale involves the commitment of significant resources to that venture. Not all companies have the resources necessary to enter on a large scale, and even some large companies prefer to enter overseas markets on a small scale and then build their presence slowly over time as they become more familiar with the market.

The consequences of entering on a significant scale are associated with the value of the resulting strategic commitments.[29] A strategic commitment is a decision that has a long-term impact and is difficult to reverse. Deciding to enter a foreign market on a significant scale is a major strategic commitment. Strategic commitments, such as large-scale market entry, can have an important influence on the nature of competition in a market. For example, by entering Japan's private client business on a significant scale with fifty offices and 2,000 employees, Merrill signaled its commitment to the market. Merrill hoped this would have several effects. On the positive side, it would make it easier for Merrill to attract clients. The scale of entry gives potential clients reason for believing that Merrill will remain in the market for the long run. It may also give other overseas institutions considering entry into Japan's market pause for thought because now they will have to compete not only against Japan's indigenous institutions but also against an aggressive and successful U.S. institution. On the negative side, the move may wake up Japan's financial institutions and elicit a vigorous competitive response from them (which has occurred). Moreover, by committing itself heavily to Japan, Merrill may have fewer resources available to support expansion in other desirable markets. In other words, Merrill's commitment to Japan limits its strategic flexibility.

As this example suggests, significant strategic commitments are neither unambiguously good nor bad. Rather, they tend to change the competitive playing field and unleash a number of changes, some of which may be desirable and some of which may not. Therefore, it is important for a company to think through the implications of large-scale entry into a market and act accordingly. Of particular relevance is trying to identify how actual and potential competitors might react to large-scale entry into a market. It is also important to bear in mind a connection between large-scale entry and first-mover advantages. Specifically, the large-scale entrant is more likely than the small-scale entrant to be able to capture first-mover advantages associated with demand preemption, scale economies, and switching costs.

Balanced against the value and risks of the commitments associated with large-scale entry are the benefits of entering on a small scale. Small-scale entry has the advantage of allowing a company to learn about a foreign market while simultaneously limiting the company's exposure to that market. In this sense, small-scale entry can be seen as a way of gathering more information about a foreign market before deciding whether to enter on a significant scale and how best to enter that market. In other words, by giving the company time to collect information, small-scale entry reduces the risks associated with a subsequent large-scale entry. On the other hand, the lack of commitment associated with small-scale entry may make it more difficult for the small-scale entrant to build market share and capture first-mover or early-mover advantages. The risk-averse company that enters a foreign market on a small scale may limit its potential losses, but it may also lose the chance to capture first-mover advantages.

The Choice of Entry Mode

The issue of when and how to enter a new national market raises the question of how to determine the best mode or vehicle for such entry. There are five main choices of entry mode: exporting, licensing, franchising, entering into a joint venture with a host country company, and setting up a wholly owned subsidiary in the host country. Each mode has its advantages and disadvantages, and managers must weigh these carefully when deciding which mode to use.[30]

● **Exporting**   Most manufacturing companies begin their global expansion as exporters and only later switch to one of the other modes for serving a foreign market. Exporting has two distinct advantages: it avoids the costs of establishing manufacturing operations in the host country, which are often substantial, and it may be consistent with scale economies and location economies. By manufacturing the product in a centralized location and then exporting it to other national markets, the company may be able to realize substantial scale economies from its global sales volume. That is how Sony came to dominate the global television market, how many Japanese auto companies originally made inroads into the U.S. auto market, and how Samsung gained share in the market for computer memory chips.

There are also a number of drawbacks to exporting. First, exporting from the company's home base may not be appropriate if there are lower-cost locations for manufacturing the product abroad (that is, if the company can realize location economies by moving production elsewhere). Thus, particularly in the case of a company pursuing a global standardization or transnational strategy, it may pay to manufacture in a location where conditions are most favorable from a value creation perspective and then export from that location to the rest of the globe. This is not so much an argument against exporting as an argument against exporting from the company's home country. For example, many U.S. electronics companies have moved some of their manufacturing to Asia because low-cost but highly skilled labor is available there. They export from that location to the rest of the globe, including the United States.

Another drawback is that high transport costs can make exporting uneconomical, particularly in the case of bulk products. One way of getting around this problem is to manufacture bulk products on a regional basis, thereby realizing some economies from large-scale production while limiting transport costs. Many multinational chemical companies manufacture their products on a regional basis, serving several countries in a region from one facility.

Tariff barriers, too, can make exporting uneconomical, and a government's threat to impose tariff barriers can make the strategy very risky. Indeed, the implicit threat from the U.S. Congress to impose tariffs on Japanese cars imported into the United States led directly to the decision by many Japanese auto companies to set up manufacturing plants in the United States.

Finally, a common practice among companies that are just beginning to export also poses risks. A company may delegate marketing activities in each country in which it does business to a local agent, but there is no guarantee that the agent will act in the company's best interest. Often foreign agents also carry the products of competing companies and thus have divided loyalties. Consequently, they may not do as good a job as the company would if it managed marketing itself. One way to solve this problem is to set up a wholly owned subsidiary in the host country to handle local marketing. In this way, the company can reap the cost advantages that arise from manufacturing the product in a single location and exercise tight control over marketing strategy in the host country.

● Licensing

International licensing is an arrangement whereby a foreign licensee buys the rights to produce a company's product in the licensee's country for a negotiated fee (normally, royalty payments on the number of units sold). The licensee then puts up most of the capital necessary to get the overseas operation going.[31] The advantage of licensing is that the company does not have to bear the development costs and risks associated with opening up a foreign market. Licensing therefore can be a very attractive option for companies that lack the capital to develop operations overseas. It can also be an attractive option for companies that are unwilling to commit substantial financial resources to an unfamiliar or politically volatile foreign market where political risks are particularly high.

Licensing has three serious drawbacks, however. First, it does not give a company the tight control over manufacturing, marketing, and strategic functions in foreign countries that it needs to have in order to realize scale economies and location economies—as companies pursuing both global standardization and transnational strategies try to do. Typically, each licensee sets up its own manufacturing operations. Hence, the company stands little chance of realizing scale economies and location economies by manufacturing its product in a centralized location. When these economies are likely to be important, licensing may not be the best way of expanding overseas.

Second, competing in a global marketplace may make it necessary for a company to coordinate strategic moves across countries so that the profits earned in one country can be used to support competitive attacks in another. Licensing, by its very nature, severely limits a company's ability to coordinate strategy in this way. A licensee is unlikely to let a multinational company take its profits (beyond those due in the form of royalty payments) and use them to support an entirely different licensee operating in another country.

A third problem with licensing is the risk associated with licensing technological know-how to foreign companies. For many multinational companies, technological know-how forms the basis of their competitive advantage, and they would want to maintain control over the use to which it is put. By licensing its technology, a company can quickly lose control over it. RCA, for instance, once licensed its color television technology to a number of Japanese companies. The Japanese companies quickly assimilated RCA's technology and then used it to enter the U.S. market. Now the Japanese have a bigger share of the U.S. market than the RCA brand does.

There are ways of reducing this risk. One way is by entering into a cross-licensing agreement with a foreign firm. Under a cross-licensing agreement, a firm might license some valuable intangible property to a foreign partner and, in addition to a royalty payment, also request that the foreign partner license some of its valuable know-how to the firm. Such agreements are believed to reduce the risks associated with licensing technological know-how because the licensee realizes that if it violates the spirit of a licensing contract (by using the knowledge obtained to compete directly with the licensor), the licensor can do the same to it. Put differently, cross-licensing agreements enable firms to hold each other hostage, thereby reducing the probability that they will behave opportunistically toward each other.[32] Such cross-licensing agreements are increasingly common in high-technology industries. For example, the U.S. biotechnology firm Amgen has licensed one of its key drugs, Nuprogene, to Kirin, the Japanese pharmaceutical company. The license gives Kirin the right to sell Nuprogene in Japan. In return, Amgen receives a royalty payment and, through a licensing agreement, it gains the right to sell certain of Kirin's products in the United States.

● Franchising

In many respects, franchising is similar to licensing, although franchising tends to involve longer-term commitments than licensing does. Franchising is basically a specialized form of licensing in which the franchiser not only sells intangible property to the franchisee (normally a trademark), but also insists that the franchisee agree to abide by strict rules about how it does business. The franchiser will also often assist the franchisee to run the business on an ongoing basis. As with licensing, the franchiser typically receives a royalty payment, which amounts to some percentage of the franchisee's revenues.

Whereas licensing is a strategy pursued primarily by manufacturing companies, franchising, which resembles it in some respects, is a strategy employed chiefly by service companies. McDonald's provides a good example of a firm that has grown by using a franchising strategy. McDonald's has set down strict rules about how franchisees should operate a restaurant. These rules extend to control over the menu, cooking methods, staffing policies, and restaurant design and location. McDonald's also organizes the supply chain for its franchisees and provides management training and financial assistance.[33]

The advantages of franchising are similar to those of licensing. Specifically, the franchiser does not have to bear the development costs and risks of opening up a foreign market on its own because the franchisee typically assumes those costs and risks. Thus, using a franchising strategy, a service company can build up a global presence quickly and at a low cost.

The disadvantages are less pronounced than in the case of licensing. Since franchising is often used by service companies, there is no reason to consider the need for coordination of manufacturing to achieve experience curve and location economies. But franchising may inhibit the firm's ability to take profits out of one country to support competitive attacks in another. A more significant disadvantage of franchising is quality control. The foundation of franchising arrangements is that the firm's brand name conveys a message to consumers about the quality of the firm's product. Thus, a business traveler checking in at a Four Seasons hotel in Hong Kong can reasonably expect the same quality of room, food, and service that she would receive in New York. The Four Seasons name is supposed to guarantee consistent product quality. This presents a problem because foreign franchisees may not be as concerned about quality as they are supposed to be, and the result of poor quality can extend beyond lost sales in a particular foreign market to a decline in the firm's worldwide reputation. For example, if the business traveler has a bad experience at the Four Seasons in Hong Kong, she may never go to another Four Seasons hotel and may urge her colleagues to do likewise. The geographical distance of the firm from its foreign franchisees can make poor quality difficult to detect. In addition, the sheer numbers of franchisees—in the case of McDonald's, tens of thousands—can make quality control difficult. Due to these factors, quality problems may persist.

To reduce the extent of quality problems, a company can set up a subsidiary in each country or region in which it is expanding. The subsidiary, which might be wholly owned by the company or a joint venture with a foreign company, then assumes the rights and obligations to establish franchisees throughout that particular country or region. The combination of proximity and the limited number of independent franchisees that have to be monitored reduces the quality control problem. Besides, because the subsidiary is at least partly owned by the company, the company can place its own managers in the subsidiary to ensure the kind of quality monitoring it wants. This organizational arrangement has proved very popular in practice. It has been used by McDonald's, KFC, and Hilton Hotels Corp. to expand their international operations, to name just three examples.

● **Joint Ventures**   Establishing a joint venture with a foreign company has long been a favored mode for entering a new market. One of the most famous long-term joint ventures is the Fuji-Xerox joint venture to produce photocopiers for the Japanese market. The most typical form of joint venture is a 50/50 joint venture, in which each party takes a 50% ownership stake and operating control is shared by a team of managers from both parent companies. Some companies have sought joint ventures in which they have a majority shareholding (for example, a 51% to 49% ownership split), which permits tighter control by the dominant partner.[34]

Joint ventures have a number of advantages. First, a company may feel that it can benefit from a local partner's knowledge of a host country's competitive conditions, culture, language, political systems, and business systems. Second, when the development costs and risks of opening a foreign market are high, a company might gain by sharing these costs and risks with a local partner. Third, in some countries, political considerations make joint ventures the only feasible entry mode. For example, historically many U.S. companies found it much easier to get permission to set up operations in Japan if they went in with a Japanese partner than if they tried to enter on their own. This is why Xerox originally teamed up with Fuji to sell photocopiers in Japan.

Despite these advantages, there are major disadvantages with joint ventures. First, as with licensing, a firm that enters into a joint venture risks giving control of its technology to its partner. Thus, a proposed joint venture in 2002 between Boeing and Mitsubishi Heavy Industries to build a new wide-body jet raised fears that Boeing might unwittingly give away its commercial airline technology to the Japanese. However, joint-venture agreements can be constructed to minimize this risk. One option is to hold majority ownership in the venture. This allows the dominant partner to exercise greater control over its technology. But it can be difficult to find a foreign partner who is willing to settle for minority ownership. Another option is to keep secret from a partner the technology that is central to the core competence of the firm while sharing other technology.

A second disadvantage is that a joint venture does not give a firm the tight control over subsidiaries that it might need to realize experience-curve or location economies. Nor does it give a firm the tight control over a foreign subsidiary that it might need for engaging in coordinated global attacks against its rivals. Consider the entry of Texas Instruments (TI) into the Japanese semiconductor market. When TI established semiconductor facilities in Japan, it did so for the dual purpose of checking Japanese manufacturers' market share and limiting their cash available for invading TI's global market. In other words, TI was engaging in global strategic coordination. To implement this strategy, TI's subsidiary in Japan had to be prepared to take instructions from corporate headquarters regarding competitive strategy. The strategy also required the Japanese subsidiary to run at a loss if necessary. Few if any potential joint-venture partners would have been willing to accept such conditions because it would have necessitated a willingness to accept a negative return on investment. Indeed, many joint ventures establish a degree of autonomy that would make such direct control over strategic decisions all but impossible to establish.[35] Thus, to implement this strategy, TI set up a wholly owned subsidiary in Japan.

• Wholly Owned Subsidiaries

A wholly owned subsidiary is one in which the parent company owns 100% of the subsidiary's stock. To establish a wholly owned subsidiary in a foreign market, a company can either set up a completely new operation in that country or acquire an established host country company and use it to promote its products in the host market.

Setting up a wholly owned subsidiary offers three advantages. First, when a company's competitive advantage is based on its control of a technological competency, a wholly owned subsidiary will normally be the preferred entry mode because it reduces the company's risk of losing this control. Consequently, many high-tech companies prefer wholly owned subsidiaries to joint ventures or licensing arrangements. Wholly owned subsidiaries tend to be the favored entry mode in the semiconductor, computer, electronics, and pharmaceutical industries.

Second, a wholly owned subsidiary gives a company the kind of tight control over operations in different countries that it needs if it is going to engage in global strategic coordination—taking profits from one country to support competitive attacks in another.

Third, a wholly owned subsidiary may be the best choice if a company wants to realize location economies and the scale economies that flow from producing a standardized output from a single or limited number of manufacturing plants. When pressures on costs are intense, it may be more beneficial for a company to configure its value chain so that value added at each stage is maximized. Thus, a national subsidiary may specialize in manufacturing only part of the product line or certain components of the end product, and then exchanging parts and products with other subsidiaries in the company's global system. Establishing such a global production system requires a high degree of control over the operations of national affiliates. Different national operations have to be prepared to accept centrally determined decisions about how they should produce, how much they should produce, and how their output should be priced for transfer between operations. A wholly owned subsidiary would have to comply with these mandates, whereas licensees or joint-venture partners would most likely shun such a subservient role.

On the other hand, establishing a wholly owned subsidiary is generally the most costly method of serving a foreign market. The parent company must bear all the costs and risks of setting up overseas operations—in contrast to joint ventures, where the costs and risks are shared, or licensing, where the licensee bears most of the costs and risks. But the risks of learning to do business in a new culture diminish if the company acquires an established host country enterprise. Acquisitions, though, raise a whole set of additional problems, such as trying to marry divergent corporate cultures, and these problems may more than offset the benefits. (The problems associated with acquisitions are discussed in Chapter 10.)

● **Choosing an Entry Strategy**
The advantages and disadvantages of the various entry modes are summarized in Table 8.1. Tradeoffs are inevitable in choosing one entry mode over another. For example, when considering entry into an unfamiliar country with a track record of nationalizing foreign-owned enterprises, a company might favor a joint venture with a local enterprise. Its rationale might be that the local partner will help it establish operations in an unfamiliar environment and speak out against nationalization should the possibility arise. But if the company's distinctive competency is based on proprietary technology, entering into a joint venture might mean risking loss of control over that technology to the joint-venture partner, which would make this strategy

TABLE 8.1

The Advantages and Disadvantages of Different Entry Modes

Entry Mode	Advantages	Disadvantages
Exporting	● Ability to realize location- and scale-based economies	● High transport costs ● Trade barriers ● Problems with local marketing agents
Licensing	● Low development costs and risks	● Inability to realize location-and scale-based economies ● Inability to engage in global strategic coordination ● Lack of control over technology
Franchising	● Low development costs and risks	● Inability to engage in global strategic coordination ● Lack of control over quality
Joint ventures	● Access to local partner's knowledge ● Shared development costs and risks ● Political dependency	● Inability to engage in global strategic coordination ● Inability to realize location- and scale-based economies ● Lack of control over technology
Wholly owned subsidiaries	● Protection of technology ● Ability to engage in global strategic coordination ● Ability to realize location- and scale-based economies	● High costs and risks

unattractive. Despite such hazards, some generalizations can be offered about the optimal choice of entry mode.

DISTINCTIVE COMPETENCIES AND ENTRY MODE   When companies expand internationally to earn greater returns from their differentiated product offerings, entering markets where indigenous competitors lack comparable products, the companies are pursuing an international strategy. The optimal entry mode for such companies depends to some degree on the nature of their distinctive competency. In particular, we need to distinguish between companies with a distinctive competency in technological know-how and those with a distinctive competency in management know-how.

If a company's competitive advantage—its distinctive competency—derives from its control of proprietary technological know-how, licensing and joint-venture arrangements should be avoided if possible to minimize the risk of losing control of that technology. Thus, if a high-tech company is considering setting up operations in a foreign country to profit from a distinctive competency in technological know-how, it should probably do so through a wholly owned subsidiary.

However, this rule should not be viewed as a hard and fast one. For instance, a licensing or joint-venture arrangement might be structured so that it reduces the risks that a company's technological know-how will be expropriated by licensees or joint-venture partners. We consider this kind of arrangement in more detail later in the chapter when we discuss the issue of structuring strategic alliances. To take another exception to the rule, a company may perceive its technological advantage as being only transitory and expect rapid imitation of its core technology by competitors. In this situation, the company might want to license its technology as quickly as possible to foreign companies to gain global acceptance of its technology before imitation occurs.[36] Such a strategy has some advantages. By licensing its technology to competitors, the company may deter them from developing their own, possibly superior, technology. It also may be able to establish its technology as the dominant design in the industry (as Matsushita did with its VHS format for VCRs), thus ensuring a steady stream of royalty payments. Except for these situations, however, the attractions of licensing are probably outweighed by the risks of losing control of technology, and therefore licensing should be avoided.

The competitive advantage of many service companies, such as McDonald's or Hilton Hotels, is based on management know-how. For such companies, the risk of losing control of their management skills to franchisees or joint-venture partners is not that great. The reason is that the valuable asset of such companies is their brand name, and brand names are generally well protected by international laws pertaining to trademarks. Given this fact, many of the issues that arise in the case of technological know-how do not arise in the case of management know-how. As a result, many service companies favor a combination of franchising and subsidiaries to control franchisees within a particular country or region. The subsidiary may be wholly owned or a joint venture. In most cases, however, service companies have found that entering into a joint venture with a local partner to set up a controlling subsidiary in a country or region works best because a joint venture is often politically more acceptable and brings a degree of local knowledge to the subsidiary.

PRESSURES FOR COST REDUCTION AND ENTRY MODE   The greater the pressures for cost reductions, the more likely it is that a company will want to pursue some combination of exporting and wholly owned subsidiaries. By manufacturing in the locations where factor conditions are optimal and then exporting to the rest of the world, a company may be able to realize substantial location economies and substantial scale economies. The company might then want to export the finished product to marketing subsidiaries based in various countries. Typically, these subsidiaries would be wholly owned and have the responsibility for overseeing distribution in a particular country. Setting up wholly owned marketing subsidiaries is preferable to a joint-venture arrangement or using a foreign marketing agent because it gives the company the tight control over marketing that might be required to coordinate a globally dispersed value chain. In addition, tight control over a local operation enables the company to use the profits generated in one market to improve its competitive position in another market. Hence, companies pursuing global or transnational strategies prefer to establish wholly owned subsidiaries.

Global Strategic Alliances

Global strategic alliances are cooperative agreements between companies from different countries that are actual or potential competitors. Strategic alliances run the gamut from formal joint ventures, in which two or more companies have an equity stake, to short-term contractual agreements, in which two companies may agree to cooperate on a particular problem (such as developing a new product).

● **Advantages of Strategic Alliances**

Companies enter into strategic alliances with competitors to achieve a number of strategic objectives.[37] First, strategic alliances may facilitate entry into a foreign market. For example, many firms feel that if they are to successfully enter the Chinese market, they need a local partner who understands business conditions and who has good connections (or *guanxi*—see Chapter 3). Thus, in 2004, Warner Brothers entered into a joint venture with two Chinese partners to produce and distribute films in China. As a foreign film company, Warner found that if it wanted to produce films on its own for the Chinese market, it had to go through a complex approval process for every film, and it had to farm out distribution to a local company, both of which made doing business in China very difficult. Due to the participation of Chinese firms, however, the joint-venture films will go through a streamlined approval process, and the venture will be able to distribute any films it produces. Moreover, the joint venture will be able to produce films for Chinese television, something that foreign firms are not allowed to do.[38]

Second, strategic alliances allow firms to share the fixed costs (and associated risks) of developing new products or processes. An alliance between Boeing and a number of Japanese companies to build Boeing's latest commercial jetliner, the 787, was motivated by Boeing's desire to share the estimated $8 billion investment required to develop the aircraft. For another example of cost sharing, see Strategy in Action 8.3, which discusses the strategic alliances between Cisco and Fujitsu.

Third, an alliance is a way to bring together complementary skills and assets that neither company could easily develop on its own.[39] In 2003, for example, Microsoft and Toshiba established an alliance aimed at developing embedded microprocessors (essentially tiny computers) that can perform a variety of entertainment functions in an automobile (e.g., run a back-seat DVD player or a wireless Internet connection). The processors will run a version of Microsoft's Windows CE operating system. Microsoft brings its software engineering skills to the alliance and Toshiba brings its skills in developing microprocessors.[40] The alliance between Cisco and Fujitsu was also formed to share know-how (see Strategy in Action 8.3).

Strategy in Action   8.3

Cisco and Fujitsu

In late 2004, Cisco Systems, the world's largest manufacturer of Internet routers, entered into an alliance with the Japanese computer, electronics, and telecommunications equipment firm, Fujitsu. The stated purpose of the alliance was to jointly develop next-generation high-end routers for sale in Japan. Routers are the digital switches that sit at the heart of the Internet and direct traffic—they are, in effect, the traffic cops of the Internet. Although Cisco has long held the leading share in the market for routers (indeed, it pioneered the original router technology), it faces increasing competition from other firms such as Juniper Technologies and China's fast growing Huawei Technologies. At the same time, demand in the market is shifting as more and more telecommunications companies adopt Internet-based telecommunications services. While Cisco has long had a strong global presence, management also felt that the company needed to have a better presence in Japan, which is shifting rapidly to second-generation high-speed Internet-based telecommunications networks.

By entering into an alliance with Fujitsu, Cisco feels it can achieve a number of goals. First, both firms can pool their R&D efforts, which will enable them to share complementary technology and develop products quicker, thereby gaining an advantage over competitors. Second,

by combining Cisco's proprietary leading-edge router technology with Fujitsu's production expertise, the companies believe that they can produce products that are more reliable than those currently offered. Third, Fujitsu will give Cisco a stronger sales presence in Japan. Fujitsu has good links with Japan's telecommunications companies and a well-earned reputation for reliability. It will leverage these assets to sell the routers produced by the alliance, which will be co-branded as Fujitsu-Cisco products. Fourth, sales may be further enhanced by bundling the co-branded routers together with other telecommunications equipment that Fujitsu sells and marketing an entire solution to customers. Fujitsu sells many telecommunications products, but it lacks a strong presence in routers. Cisco is strong in routers but lacks strong offerings elsewhere. The combination of the two company's products will enable Fujitsu to offer Japan's telecommunications companies end-to-end communications solutions. Since many companies prefer to purchase their equipment from a single provider, this should drive sales.

The alliance introduced its first products in May 2006. If it is successful, both firms should benefit. Development costs will be lower than if they did not cooperate. Cisco will grow its sales in Japan, and Fujitsu can use the co-branded routers to fill out its product line and sell more bundles of products to Japan's telecommunications companies.[d]

Fourth, it can make sense to form an alliance that will help the firm establish technological standards for the industry that will benefit the firm. For example, in 1999, Palm Computer, the leading maker of personal digital assistants (PDAs), entered into an alliance with Sony under which Sony agreed to license and use Palm's operating system in Sony PDAs. The motivation for the alliance was in part to help establish Palm's operating system as the industry standard for PDAs, as opposed to a rival Windows-based operating system from Microsoft.[41]

● **Disadvantages of Strategic Alliances**   The advantages we have discussed can be very significant. Despite this, some commentators have criticized strategic alliances on the grounds that they give competitors a low-cost route to new technology and markets.[42] For example, a few years ago, some commentators argued that many strategic alliances between U.S. and Japanese firms were part of an implicit Japanese strategy to keep high-paying, high-value-added jobs in Japan while gaining the project engineering and production process skills that underlie the competitive success of many U.S. companies.[43] They argued that Japanese success in the machine tool and semiconductor industries was built on U.S. technology acquired through strategic alliances. And they argued that U.S. managers were aiding the Japanese by entering alliances that channel new inventions to Japan and provide a U.S. sales and distribution network for the resulting products. Although such deals may generate short-term profits, so the argument goes, in the long run, the result is to "hollow out" U.S. firms, leaving them with no competitive advantage in the global marketplace.

These critics have a point; alliances have risks. Unless a firm is careful, it can give away more than it receives. But there are so many examples of apparently successful alliances between firms—including alliances between U.S. and Japanese firms—that their position seems extreme. It is difficult to see how the Microsoft–Toshiba alliance, the Boeing–Mitsubishi alliance for the 787, or the Fuji–Xerox alliance fit the critics' thesis. In these cases, both partners seem to have gained from the alliance. Why do some alliances benefit both firms while others benefit one firm and hurt the other? The next section provides an answer to this question.

● Making Strategic Alliances Work

The failure rate for international strategic alliances is quite high. For example, one study of forty-nine international strategic alliances found that two-thirds run into serious managerial and financial troubles within two years of their formation, and although many of these problems are ultimately solved, 33% are ultimately rated as failures by the parties involved.[44] The success of an alliance seems to be a function of three main factors: partner selection, alliance structure, and the manner in which the alliance is managed.

PARTNER SELECTION One of the keys to making a strategic alliance work is to select the right kind of partner. A good partner has three principal characteristics. First, a good partner helps the company achieve strategic goals such as gaining market access, sharing the costs and risks of new-product development, or gaining access to critical core competencies. In other words, the partner must have capabilities that the company lacks and that it values.

Second, a good partner shares the firm's vision for the purpose of the alliance. If two companies approach an alliance with radically different agendas, the chances are great that the relationship will not be harmonious and will end.

Third, a good partner is unlikely to try to exploit the alliance opportunistically for its own ends—that is, to expropriate the company's technological know-how while giving away little in return. In this respect, firms who have reputations for fair play—and want to maintain them—probably make the best partners. For example, IBM is involved in so many strategic alliances that it would not pay for the company to trample over individual alliance partners (in 2003, IBM reportedly had more than 150 major strategic alliances).[45] This would tarnish IBM's reputation of being a good ally and would make it more difficult for IBM to attract alliance partners. Because IBM attaches great importance to its alliances, it is unlikely to engage in the kind of opportunistic behavior that critics highlight. Similarly, their reputations make it less likely (but by no means impossible) that Japanese firms such as Sony, Toshiba, and Fuji, which have histories of alliances with non-Japanese firms, would opportunistically exploit an alliance partner.

To select a partner with these three characteristics, a company needs to conduct some comprehensive research on potential alliance candidates. To increase the probability of selecting a good partner, the company should collect as much pertinent, publicly available information about potential allies as possible; collect data from informed third parties, including companies that have had alliances with the potential

FIGURE 8.5

Structuring Alliances to Reduce Opportunism

partners, investment bankers who have had dealings with them, and some of their former employees; and get to know potential partners as well as possible before committing to an alliance. This last step should include face-to-face meetings between senior managers (and perhaps middle-level managers) to ensure that the chemistry is right.

ALLIANCE STRUCTURE   Having selected a partner, the alliance should be structured so that the company's risk of giving too much away to the partner is reduced to an acceptable level. Figure 8.5 depicts the four safeguards against opportunism by alliance partners that we discuss here. (**Opportunism**, which is often defined as self-interest seeking with guile, includes the expropriation of technology or markets.) First, alliances can be designed to make it difficult (if not impossible) to transfer technology not meant to be transferred. Specifically, the design, development, manufacture, and service of a product manufactured by an alliance can be structured to protect sensitive technologies to prevent their leakage to the other participant. In the alliance between General Electric and Snecma to build commercial aircraft engines, for example, GE reduced the risk of excess transfer by walling off certain sections of the production process. The modularization effectively cut off the transfer of what GE regarded as key competitive technology while permitting Snecma access to final assembly. Similarly, in the alliance between Boeing and the Japanese to build the 767, Boeing walled off research, design, and marketing functions considered central to its competitive position, while allowing the Japanese to share in production technology. Boeing also walled off new technologies not required for 767 production.[46]

Second, contractual safeguards can be written into an alliance agreement to guard against the risk of opportunism by a partner. For example, TRW has three strategic alliances with large Japanese auto component suppliers to produce seat belts, engine valves, and steering gears for sale to Japanese-owned auto assembly plants in the United States. TRW has clauses in each of its alliance contracts that bar the Japanese firms from competing with TRW to supply U.S.-owned auto companies with component parts. By doing this, TRW protects itself against the possibility that the Japanese companies are entering into the alliances merely as a way to gain access to the North American market to compete with TRW in its home market.

Third, both parties to an alliance can agree in advance to swap skills and technologies that the other covets, thereby ensuring a chance for equitable gain. Cross-licensing agreements are one way to achieve this goal.

Fourth, the risk of opportunism by an alliance partner can be reduced if the firm extracts a significant credible commitment from its partner in advance. The long-term alliance between Xerox and Fuji to build photocopiers for the Asian market perhaps best illustrates this. Rather than enter into an informal agreement or a licensing arrangement (which Fuji Photo initially wanted), Xerox insisted that Fuji invest in a 50/50 joint venture to serve Japan and East Asia. This venture constituted such a significant investment in people, equipment, and facilities that Fuji Photo was committed from the outset to making the alliance work in order to earn a return on its investment. By agreeing to the joint venture, Fuji essentially made a credible commitment to the alliance. Given this commitment, Xerox felt secure in transferring its photocopier technology to Fuji.

MANAGING THE ALLIANCE Once a partner has been selected and an appropriate alliance structure agreed on, the task facing the company is to maximize the benefits from the alliance. One important ingredient of success appears to be sensitivity to cultural differences. Many differences in management style are attributable to cultural differences, and managers need to make allowances for these differences in dealing with their partner. Beyond this, maximizing the benefits from an alliance seems to involve building trust between partners and learning from partners.[47]

Managing an alliance successfully requires building interpersonal relationships between the firms' managers, or what is sometimes referred to as relational capital.[48] This is one lesson that can be drawn from a successful strategic alliance between Ford and Mazda. Ford and Mazda set up a framework of meetings within which their managers not only discuss matters pertaining to the alliance but also have time to get to know each other better. The belief is that the resulting friendships help build trust and facilitate harmonious relations between the two firms. Personal relationships also foster an informal management network between the firms. This network can then be used to help solve problems arising in more formal contexts (such as in joint committee meetings between personnel from the two firms).

Academics have argued that a major determinant of how much knowledge a company gains from an alliance is based on its ability to learn from its alliance partner.[49] For example, in a five-year study of fifteen strategic alliances between major multinationals, Gary Hamel, Yves Doz, and C. K. Prahalad focused on a number of alliances between Japanese companies and western (European or American) partners.[50] In every case in which a Japanese company emerged from an alliance stronger than its western partner, the Japanese company had made a greater effort to learn. Few western companies in the study seemed to want to learn from their Japanese partners. They tended to regard the alliance purely as a cost-sharing or risk-sharing device rather than as an opportunity to learn how a potential competitor does business.

For an example of an alliance in which there was a clear learning asymmetry, consider the agreement between General Motors and Toyota Motor Corp. to build the Chevrolet Nova. This alliance was structured as a formal joint venture, New United Motor Manufacturing, in which both parties had a 50% equity stake. The venture owned an auto plant in Fremont, California. According to one of the Japanese managers, Toyota achieved most of its objectives from the alliance: "We learned about U.S. supply and transportation. And we got the confidence to manage U.S. workers." All that knowledge was then quickly transferred to Georgetown, Kentucky, where Toyota opened a plant of its own in 1988. By contrast, although General Motors got a new product, the Chevrolet Nova, some GM managers complained that their new knowledge was never put to good use inside GM. They say that they should have been kept together as a team to educate GM's engineers and workers about the Japanese system. Instead, they were dispersed to different GM subsidiaries.[51]

When entering into an alliance, a company must take some measures to ensure that it learns from its alliance partner and then puts that knowledge to good use within its own organization. One suggested approach is to educate all operating employees about the partner's strengths and weaknesses and make clear to them how acquiring particular skills will bolster their company's competitive position. For such learning to be of value, the knowledge acquired from an alliance has to be diffused throughout the organization—which did not happen at GM. To spread this knowledge, the managers involved in an alliance should be used as a resource in familiarizing others within the company about the skills of an alliance partner.

Summary of Chapter

1. For some companies, international expansion represents a way of earning greater returns by transferring the skills and product offerings derived from their distinctive competencies to markets where indigenous competitors lack those skills. As barriers to international trade have fallen, industries have expanded beyond national boundaries, and industry competition and opportunities have increased.

2. Because of national differences, it pays a company to base each value creation activity it performs at the location where factor conditions are most conducive to the performance of that activity. This strategy is known as focusing on the attainment of location economies.

3. By building sales volume more rapidly, international expansion can help a company gain a cost advantage through the realization of scale economies and learning effects.

4. The best strategy for a company to pursue may depend on the kind of pressures it must cope with: pressures for cost reductions or for local responsiveness. Pressures for cost reductions are greatest in industries producing commodity-type products, where price is the main competitive weapon. Pressures for local responsiveness arise from differences in consumer tastes and preferences, as well as from national infrastructure and traditional practices, distribution channels, and host government demands.

5. Companies pursuing an international strategy transfer the skills and products derived from distinctive competencies to foreign markets while undertaking some limited local customization.

6. Companies pursuing a localization strategy customize their product offering, marketing strategy, and business strategy to national conditions.

7. Companies pursuing a global standardization strategy focus on reaping the cost reductions that come from scale economies and location economies.

8. Many industries are now so competitive that companies must adopt a transnational strategy. This involves a simultaneous focus on reducing costs, transferring skills and products, and being locally responsive. Implementing such a strategy may not be easy.

9. The most attractive foreign markets tend to be found in politically stable developed and developing nations that have free market systems.

10. Several advantages are associated with entering a national market early, before other international businesses have established themselves. These advantages must be balanced against the pioneering costs that early entrants often have to bear, including the greater risk of business failure.

11. Large-scale entry into a national market constitutes a major strategic commitment that is likely to change the nature of competition in that market and limit the entrant's future strategic flexibility. The firm needs to think through the implications of such commitments before embarking on a large-scale entry. Although making major strategic commitments can yield many benefits, there are also risks associated with such a strategy.

12. There are five different ways of entering a foreign market: exporting, licensing, franchising, entering into a joint venture, and setting up a wholly owned subsidiary. The optimal choice of entry mode depends on the company's strategy.

13. Strategic alliances are cooperative agreements between actual or potential competitors. The advantages of alliances are that they facilitate entry into foreign markets,

enable partners to share the fixed costs and risks associated with new products and processes, facilitate the transfer of complementary skills between companies, and help companies establish technical standards.

14. The drawbacks of a strategic alliance are that the company risks giving away technological know-how and market access to its alliance partner while getting very little in return.

15. The disadvantages associated with alliances can be reduced if the company selects partners carefully, paying close attention to reputation, and structures the alliance to avoid unintended transfers of know-how.

Discussion Questions

1. Plot the position of the following companies on Figure 8.3: Microsoft, Google, Coca-Cola, Dow Chemicals, Pfizer, and McDonald's. In each case, justify your answer.

2. Identify whether the following are global standardization industries, or industries where localization is more important: bulk chemicals, pharmaceuticals, branded food products, moviemaking, television manufacture, personal computers, airline travel, and fashion retailing.

3. Discuss how the need for control over foreign operations varies with the strategy and distinctive competencies of a company. What are the implications of this relationship for the choice of entry mode?

4. Licensing proprietary technology to foreign competitors is the best way to give up a company's competitive advantage. Discuss this statement.

5. What kind of companies stand to gain the most from entering into strategic alliances with potential competitors? Why?

Practicing Strategic Management

SMALL-GROUP EXERCISE
Developing a Global Strategy

Break into groups of three to five, appoint one group member to be the spokesperson who will communicate your findings to the class, and discuss the following scenario. You work for a company in the soft drink industry that has developed a line of carbonated, fruit-based drinks. You have already established a significant presence in your home market, and now you are planning the global strategy development of the company in the soft drink industry. You need to decide the following:

1. The overall strategy to pursue: a global standardization strategy, a localization strategy, an international strategy, or a transnational strategy.
2. Which markets to enter first.
3. The entry strategy to pursue, for example, franchising, joint venture, wholly owned subsidiary.
4. What information do you need to make these decisions? On the basis of what you do know, what strategy would you recommend?

ARTICLE FILE 8

Find an example of a multinational company that in recent years has switched from a localization, international, or global standardization strategy to a transnational strategy. Identify why the company made the switch and any problems that the company may be encountering while it tries to change its strategic orientation.

STRATEGIC MANAGEMENT PROJECT
Module 8

This module requires you to identify how your company might profit from global expansion, the global strategy that your company should pursue, and the entry mode that it might favor. With the information you have at your disposal, answer the questions regarding the following two situations:

Your company is already doing business in other countries.

1. Is your company creating value or lowering the costs of value creation by realizing location

economies, transferring distinctive competencies abroad, or realizing cost economies from the economies of scale? If it is not creating value or lowering the costs of value creation, does it have the potential to do so?

2. How responsive is your company to differences among nations? Does it vary its product and marketing message from country to country? Should it?

3. What are the cost pressures and pressures for local responsiveness in the industry in which your company is based?

4. What strategy is your company pursuing to compete globally? In your opinion, is this the correct strategy, given cost pressures and pressures for local responsiveness?

5. What major foreign market does your company serve, and what mode has it used to enter this market? Why is your company active in these markets and not others? What are the advantages and disadvantages of using this mode? Might another mode be preferable?

Your company is not yet doing business in other countries.

1. What potential does your company have to add value to its products or lower the costs of value creation by expanding internationally?

2. On the international level, what are the cost pressures and pressures for local responsiveness in the industry in which your company is based? What implications do these pressures have for the strategy that your company might pursue if it chose to expand globally?

3. What foreign market might your company enter, and what entry mode should it use to enter this market? Justify your answer.

ETHICS EXERCISE

Bob was nearing retirement. Although he had enjoyed his job, he was growing bored and restless. In charge of so many people and projects, he was beginning to care less and less each day, and he knew that it was time to get out. Just the other day, he had accidentally allowed one of his managers to fire one of the company's best workers for reasons more personal than professional. Once done, the action could not be reversed. Now Bob was afraid of making more mistakes.

For years now, Bob had been in charge of his company's China office. He liked living in China and working with the Chinese people. In fact, he was thinking of staying on after retirement, although he was looking forward to moving out of the hustle and bustle of Beijing. "Only one more month to go," he thought, "and I'll be free! Can I keep it together until then?"

Suddenly, a day later, Bob had a desperate phone call from company headquarters in the United States. It had just been discovered that one of Bob's managers had been embezzling funds from the company. Bob's superiors were asking him to put off his retirement and to stay for at least six extra months to help clean up the problem caused by this manager.

Bob felt conflicted. On the one hand, he felt that he could no longer perform his job well, nor did he want to anymore. On the other hand, he owed his company a great deal. Should he focus on himself and leave his company in the lurch? Or should he pull it together and help the company that had given him so much?

1. Identify the ethical dilemma at stake in this case.
2. What would you do if you were in Bob's position?
3. Do you think Bob should keep his position in his current state?

CLOSING CASE

The Evolution of Strategy at Procter & Gamble

Founded in 1837, Cincinnati-based Procter & Gamble has long been one of the world's most international companies. Today, P&G is a global colossus in the consumer products business, with annual sales in excess of $68 billion, some 56% of which are generated outside the United States. P&G sells more than 300 brands—including Ivory soap, Tide, Pampers, IAMS pet food, Crisco, Gillette, and Folgers—to consumers in 180 countries. It has production operations in eighty countries and employs close to 138,000 people globally.

P&G established its first foreign factory in 1915 when it opened a plant in Canada to produce Ivory soap and Crisco. This was followed in 1930 by the establishment of the company's first foreign subsidiary in Britain. The pace of international expansion quickened in the 1950s and 1960s as P&G expanded rapidly in western Europe, and then again in the 1970s when the company entered Japan and other Asian nations. Sometimes P&G entered a nation by acquiring an established competitor and its brands, as occurred in the case of Great Britain and Japan, but more typically the company set up operations from the ground floor.

By the late 1970s, the strategy at P&G was well established. The company developed new products in Cincinnati and then relied on semiautonomous foreign subsidiaries to manufacture, market, and distribute those products in different nations. In many cases, foreign subsidiaries had their own production facilities and tailored the packaging, brand name, and marketing message to local tastes and preferences. For years, this strategy delivered a steady stream of new products and reliable growth in sales and profits. By the 1990s, however, profit growth at P&G was slowing.

The essence of the problem was simple; P&G's costs were too high because of extensive duplication of manufacturing, marketing, and administrative facilities in different national subsidiaries. The duplication of assets made sense in the world of the 1960s, when national markets were segmented from each other by barriers to cross-border trade. Products produced in Great Britain, for example, could not be sold economically in Germany due to high tariff duties levied on imports into Germany. By the 1980s, however, barriers to cross-border trade were falling rapidly worldwide and fragmented national markets were merging into larger regional or global markets. Also, the retailers through which P&G distributed its products, such as Wal-Mart, Tesco in the United Kingdom, and Carrefour in France, were growing larger and more global. These emerging global retailers were demanding price discounts from P&G.

In 1993, P&G embarked on a major reorganization in an attempt to control its cost structure and recognize the new reality of emerging global markets. The company shut down some thirty manufacturing plants around the globe, laid off 13,000 employees, and concentrated production in fewer plants that could better realize economies of scale and serve regional markets. These actions cut some $600 million a year out of P&G's cost structure. It wasn't enough! Profit growth remained sluggish.

In 1998, P&G launched its second reorganization of the decade. Named Organization 2005, its goal was to transform P&G into a truly global company. The company tore up its old organization, which was based on countries and regions, and replaced it with one based on seven self-contained global business units, ranging from baby care to food products. Each business unit was given complete responsibility for generating profits from its products, and for manufacturing, marketing, and product development. Each business unit was told to rationalize production, concentrating it in fewer, larger facilities; to build global brands wherever possible, thereby eliminating marketing differences among countries; and to accelerate the development and launch of new products. In 1999, P&G announced that, as a result of this initiative, it would close another ten factories and lay off 15,000 employees, mostly in Europe where there was still extensive duplication of assets. The annual cost savings were estimated to be about $800 million. P&G planned to use the savings to cut prices and increase marketing spending in an effort to gain market share and thus further lower costs through the attainment of scale economies. This time, the strategy seemed to be working. Between 2003 and 2006, P&G reported strong growth in both sales and profits. Significantly, P&G's global competitors, such as Unilever, Kimberly-Clark, and Colgate-Palmolive, were struggling in 2003 to 2006.[52]

Case Discussion Questions

1. What strategy was Procter & Gamble pursuing until the late 1990s?

2. Why did this strategy succeed for so many years? Why was it no longer working by the 1990s?

3. What strategy did P&G adopt in the late 1990s and early 2000s? Does this strategy make more sense? Why?

Corporate-Level Strategy: Horizontal Integration, Vertical Integration, and Strategic Outsourcing

Oracle Strives to Become the Biggest and the Best

Oracle Corp., based in Redwood City, California, is the world's largest maker of database software and the third largest global software company in terms of sales after Microsoft and IBM. This commanding position is not enough for Oracle, however, which has set its sights on becoming the global leader in the corporate applications software market. Here, Germany's SAP, which has 45% of the market, is the acknowledged leader and Oracle, with only 19%, is a distant second.[1] Corporate applications is a fast growing and highly profitable market, however, and Oracle has been snapping up leading companies in this segment at a fast pace. Its goal is to quickly build the distinctive competencies it needs to expand the range of products that it can offer to its existing customers and to attract new customers to compete with SAP. Beginning in 2005, Oracle's CEO Larry Ellison spent $19 billion to acquire fourteen leading suppliers of corporate software, including two of the top five companies: PeopleSoft, a leading human resources management (HRM) software supplier it bought for $10 billion, and Siebel Systems, a leader in customer relationship management (CRM) software, which cost Oracle $5.8 billion.

Oracle expects several competitive advantages to result from its use of acquisitions to pursue the corporate strategy of horizontal integration. First, it is now able to meld or bundle the best software applications of these acquired companies—with Oracle's own first-class set of corporate and database software programs—to create a new integrated suite of software that will allow corporations to manage all their functional activities such as accounting, marketing, sales, HRM, CRM, and supply-chain management. Second, through these acquisitions, Oracle obtained access to thousands of new customers—all the companies that currently use the software of the companies it acquired. All these companies now become potential new customers for all of Oracle's other database and corporate software offerings. Third, beyond increasing the range of its products and the number of its customers, Oracle's acquisitions have consolidated the corporate software industry. By taking over some of its largest rivals, Oracle has become the second largest supplier of corporate software, and so it is better positioned to compete with the leader SAP.

Achieving the advantages of its new strategy may not be easy, however. The person in charge of assembling Oracle's new unified software package and selling it to customers is John

Wookey, Oracle's senior vice president in charge of applications, who jokingly says that his "head is the one on the chopping block if this doesn't work." CEO Ellison has been quick to fire executives who haven't performed well in the past, and he expects a lot from his top executives. To grow Oracle's market share and profits, Wookey must draw on the best of the technology Oracle obtained from each of the companies it acquired to build its new suite of state-of-the-art corporate software applications. He also has to persuade customers not to switch software vendors—for example, not to jump ship to SAP—while Oracle builds its package and then to gradually adopt more and more of Oracle's software offerings to run their functional activities.

Wookey is well placed to implement Oracle's new strategy, however: he is known as a consensus builder and product champion both inside and outside the company, and when interacting with Oracle's customers. He spends his working day sharing information with the top managers of Oracle's various businesses, and meeting with his team of fourteen senior staff members, to work out how the whole package should be put together and what it should include. He also regularly visits major customers, especially those that came with its acquisitions, to gain their input into how and what kind of software package Oracle should build. Wookey even formed an advisory council of leading customers to help make sure the final package meets their needs. One of Wookey's notable achievements was retaining the top-rate software engineers who Oracle obtained from its acquired rivals. These employees could have easily found high-paying

jobs elsewhere, but most of the top engineers Oracle wanted stayed to help it achieve its new goals.

Nevertheless, by the end of 2006, there were signs that all was not going well with Oracle's new strategy. SAP is a powerful competitor; its popular software is fast becoming the industry standard, so unseating SAP in the $23.4 billion corporate software market will not be easy. SAP is still the leader in more advanced functional applications incorporating the latest technologies, and its proprietary technology is all homegrown, so it doesn't face the huge implementation issue of bringing together the applications from many different acquisitions. Preventing customers from switching to SAP may not be easy now that their loyalty to their old software supplier has been broken if it was acquired by Oracle.

Analysts also say that Oracle runs the risk of stretching itself too thin if it continues to purchase too many companies too quickly, because high-tech acquisitions are the most difficult to pull off in terms of management and execution. So, in December 2006, while Oracle announced that its second-quarter profit rose 21%, and sales rose to $4.16 billion from $3.29 billion in the previous year, it also announced that sales of corporate applications software slowed to 28% from 80%.[2] Larry Ellison is still under pressure to accelerate sales growth and surpass investors' expectations, and only if Oracle can put out corporate application software sales numbers that beat expectations will analysts regard its strategy as a success. Still, Oracle's stock gained 47% in 2006 compared to SAP's 15%, so investors clearly believe he and Wookey have a sporting chance.

OVERVIEW

Over the last few years, Oracle has acquired many companies in order to create a software empire. The overriding goal of Larry Ellison and his top managers is to maximize the value of the company for its shareholders, and Ellison embarked on his quest because he believes that by combining all these different businesses into one entity, Oracle, he will be able to increase its profitability. Clearly, the scale of Ellison's mission and vision for Oracle takes the issue of strategy formulation to a new level of complexity.

The Oracle story illustrates the use of corporate-level strategy to identify (1) which businesses and industries a company should compete in, (2) which value creation activities it should perform in those businesses, and (3) how it should enter or leave businesses or industries to maximize its long-run profitability. In formulating corporate-level strategy, managers must adopt a long-term perspective and consider how changes taking place in an industry and in its products, technology, customers, and competitors will affect their company's current business model and its future strategies. They then decide how to implement specific corporate-level strategies to redefine their company's business model so that it can achieve a competitive position in the changing industry environment by taking advantage of the opportunities and countering the threats. Thus, the principal goal of corporate-level strategy is to enable a company to sustain or promote its competitive advantage and profitability in its present business and in any new businesses or industries that it enters.

This chapter is the first of two that deals with the role of corporate-level strategy in repositioning and redefining a company's business model. We discuss three corporate-level strategies—horizontal integration, vertical integration, and strategic outsourcing—that are primarily directed toward improving a company's competitive advantage and profitability in its present business or product market. Diversification, which entails entry into new kinds of markets or industries, is examined in the next chapter, along with guidelines for choosing the most profitable way to enter new markets or industries or to exit others. By the end of this and the next chapter, you will understand how the different levels of strategy contribute to the creation of a successful and profitable business or multibusiness model. You will also be able to differentiate among the types of corporate strategies managers use to maximize long-term company profitability.

Corporate-Level Strategy and the Multibusiness Model

The formulation of corporate-level strategies is the final part of the strategy formulation process. These strategies drive a company's business model over time and determine the kinds of business- and functional-level strategies that will maximize long-run profitability. The relationship between business-level strategy and functional-level strategy was discussed in Chapter 5. Strategic managers develop a business model and strategies that use their company's distinctive competencies to strive for a cost-leadership position and/or to differentiate its products. Chapter 8 described how global strategy is also an extension of these basic principles. Throughout this chapter and the next, we repeatedly stress that to increase profitability, a corporate-level strategy should enable a company or one or more of its business divisions or units to perform value-chain functional activities (1) at a lower cost and/or (2) in a way that allows for differentiation. A company can then choose the pricing option (lowest, average, or premium) that allows it to maximize revenues and profitability. In addition, corporate-level strategy will boost profitability if it helps a company reduce industry rivalry and lowers the threat of damaging price competition. Thus, a company's corporate-level strategies should be chosen to promote the success of a company's business model and to allow it to achieve a sustainable competitive advantage at the business level. Competitive advantage leads to higher profitability.

At the corporate level, some companies like Oracle choose to compete only in one industry (the software industry in Oracle's case), but then they develop strategies to increase the profitability of their business model by entering new market segments and providing a wider range of goods and services. Oracle, for example, expanded its activities into the corporate applications software market segment to better satisfy the needs of existing customers and attract new customers.

Other companies, however, often choose to expand their business activities beyond one market or industry and enter others. When a company decides to expand into new industries, it must construct its business model at two levels. First, it must develop a business model and strategies for each business unit or division in every industry in which it competes. Second, it must also develop a higher-level *multibusiness model* that justifies its entry into different businesses and industries. This model should explain how and why entering the new industry will allow the company to use its existing functional competencies and business strategies to increase its return on investment. A multibusiness model should also explain any other ways in which a company's involvement in more than one business or industry can increase its profitability. Dell, for example, might argue that its entry into computer consulting and into the computer printer market will enable it to offer its customers a complete line of computer products and services, which will allow it to better compete with HP or IBM. This chapter first focuses on the advantages of staying in one industry by pursuing horizontal integration. It then looks at why companies use vertical integration and expand into new industries. In the next chapter, we will examine another important corporate strategy that companies employ to enter new industries to increase their profitability: diversification.

Horizontal Integration: Single-Industry Strategy

Managers use corporate-level strategy to identify which industries their company should compete in to maximize its long-run profitability. For many companies, profitable growth and expansion often entail finding ways to compete successfully within a single market or industry over time. In other words, a company confines its value creation activities to just one business or industry. Examples of such single-business companies include McDonald's, with its focus on the global fast-food restaurant business, and Wal-Mart, with its focus on global discount retailing.

Staying in one industry allows a company to focus its total managerial, financial, technological, and functional resources and capabilities on competing successfully in one area. This is important in fast-growing and changing industries, where demands on a company's resources and capabilities are likely to be substantial, but where the long-term profits from establishing a competitive advantage are also likely to be significant.

A second advantage of staying in a single industry is that a company "sticks to the knitting," meaning that it stays focused on what it knows and does best. It does not make the mistake of entering new industries where its existing resources and capabilities create little value and/or where a whole new set of competitive industry forces—new competitors, suppliers, and customers—present unanticipated threats. Both Coca-Cola and Sears, like many other companies, have committed this strategic error. Coca-Cola once decided to expand into the movie business and acquired Columbia Pictures, and it also acquired a large wine-producing business. Sears, the clothing seller, once decided to become a one-stop shopping place and bought Allstate Insurance, Coldwell Banker (a real estate company), and Dean Witter (a financial services enterprise). Both companies found that they not only lacked the competencies to compete successfully in their new industries, but also that they had not foreseen the different kinds of competitive forces that existed in these industries. They concluded that entry into these new industries dissipated rather than created value and lowered their profitability, and they ultimately sold off their new businesses at a loss.

Even when a company stays in one industry, sustaining a successful business model and strategies over time can be difficult because of changing conditions in the environment, such as advances in technology that allow new competitors into the market and blur the boundaries between different products or markets. A decade ago, the strategic issue facing telecommunications companies was how to shape their line of wired phone service products to best meet customer needs in the local and long-distance phone service market. However, a new kind of product, wireless phone service, was emerging. At first, it was so expensive that only business customers who really needed it could afford it. Within five years, however, wireless phone companies had developed a business model to lower the cost and price of wireless phone service and many customers switched to the new product, a trend that has accelerated.

At the same time, more and more people began to surf the Internet. At first, the Internet was not regarded as a substitute for wired or wireless phone service, but today millions of people are using VOIP technology to make phone calls over the Internet. And companies that want to attract customers must now include services like digital messaging and wireless email in their product line. Many of the leading phone companies did not predict how these changes in technology would affect industry competition and were late in changing their business models to add these new products and services. As a result, many have been swallowed up and acquired by companies like AT&T, WorldCom, and Verizon, which did predict the emerging threats.

Thus, even in one industry, it is all too easy for strategic managers to fail to see the "forest" (changing nature of the industry that results in new product/market opportunities) for the "trees" (focus on positioning current products). A focus on corporate-level strategy can help managers forecast future trends and position their company so it can compete successfully in a changing environment. Strategic managers must avoid becoming so immersed in positioning their company's *existing* product lines that they fail to consider new opportunities and threats. The task for corporate-level managers is to analyze how new emerging technologies might affect their business models, how and why these might change customer needs and customer groups in the future, and what kinds of new distinctive competencies will be needed to respond to these changes.

One corporate-level strategy that has been widely used to help managers better position their companies is horizontal integration. **Horizontal integration** is the process of acquiring or merging with industry competitors in an effort to achieve the competitive advantages that come with large scale and scope. An **acquisition** occurs when one company uses its capital resources, such as stock, debt, or cash, to purchase another company, and a **merger** is an agreement between equals to pool their operations and create a new entity. The Opening Case discusses how Larry Ellison made a series of major corporate software acquisitions so that Oracle could build up its competencies in all segments of the software industry, attract thousands of new customers, and compete better against SAP.

Mergers and acquisitions have occurred in many industries. In the car industry, Chrysler merged with Daimler-Benz to create DaimlerChrysler; in the aerospace industry, Boeing merged with McDonnell Douglas to create the world's largest aerospace company; in the pharmaceutical industry, Pfizer acquired Warner-Lambert to become the largest pharmaceutical firm; and in the computer hardware industry, Compaq acquired Digital Equipment Corporation and then itself was acquired by HP. In the 2000s, the rate of mergers and acquisitions has been increasing as companies jockey for global competitive advantage. Many of the largest mergers and acquisitions have been cross-border affairs as companies race to acquire overseas companies in the same industry. In 2000, companies from all nations spent around $1.1 trillion on 7,900 cross-border mergers and acquisitions, over 70% of them horizontal mergers and acquisitions; the rate has been accelerating ever since.[3]

The net result of this wave of mergers and acquisitions has been to increase the level of concentration in a wide range of industries. Consolidated oligopolies have been replacing more fragmented industry structures.[4] For example, twenty years ago, cable television was dominated by a patchwork of thousands of small, family-owned businesses, but by 2005, three companies controlled over two-thirds of the market. In 1990, the three big publishers of college textbooks accounted for 35% of the market; by 2005, they accounted for over 65%. In the manufacture of basic DRAM semiconductor chips, the four largest firms accounted for 85% of the global market by 2005 because of mergers and acquisitions, up from 45% in 1995. Why is this happening? An answer can be found by looking at the way horizontal integration can improve the competitive advantage and profitability of companies who choose to stay in one industry.

● Benefits of Horizontal Integration

In pursuing horizontal integration, managers have decided to invest their company's capital to purchase the assets of industry competitors as a way to increase the profitability of its single-business model. Profits and profitability increase when horizontal integration (1) lowers the cost structure, (2) increases product differentiation, (3) replicates the business model, (4) reduces rivalry within the industry, and (5) increases bargaining power over suppliers and buyers.

LOWER COST STRUCTURE Horizontal integration can lower a company's cost structure because it creates increasing *economies of scale.* Suppose there are five major competitors, each operating a manufacturing plant in some region of the United States, and none of these plants is operating at full capacity. If one competitor buys up another and shuts down that plant, it can operate its own plant at full capacity and so reduce its manufacturing costs. Achieving economies of scale is very important in industries that have a high fixed-cost structure. In such industries, large-scale production allows companies to spread their fixed costs over a large volume and in this way drive down average unit costs. In the telecommunications industry, for example, the fixed costs of building a fiber-optic or wireless network are very high, and to make such an investment pay off, a company needs a large volume of customers. Thus, companies like AT&T and Verizon acquired other telecommunications companies to gain access to their customers. These new customers increased its utilization rate and thus reduced the costs of serving each customer. Similar considerations were involved in Oracle's acquisitions and in the pharmaceutical industry, where mergers have resulted from the need to realize scale economies in sales and marketing. The fixed costs of building a nationwide pharmaceutical sales force are very high, and pharmaceutical companies need a good portfolio of products to effectively use that sales force. Pfizer acquired Warner-Lambert because its salespeople would then have more products to sell when they visited physicians and their productivity would therefore increase.

A company can also lower its cost structure when horizontal integration allows it to *reduce the duplication of resources* between two companies, such as by eliminating the need for two sets of corporate head offices, two separate sales forces, and so on. Thus, one way HP justified its strategy to acquire rival computer maker Compaq was that the acquisition would save the combined company $2.5 billion in annual expenses by eliminating redundant functions, as discussed in the Running Case.

RUNNING CASE

Beating Dell: Why HP Acquired Compaq

In 2001, Hewlett-Packard (now HP) shocked the business world when its former CEO, Carly Fiorina, announced that rival computer maker Compaq had agreed to be acquired by HP. The announcement came at the end of a year in which slumping demand and strong competition from Dell had buffeted both companies. The merged company would have annual revenues of about $87.4 billion, putting it in the same league as IBM, and would be able to provide customers with a full range of computer products and services. With the exception of printers, where HP is the market leader, there was significant product overlap between HP and Compaq.

To justify the acquisition, Fiorina claimed that it would yield a number of benefits. First, there would be significant cost savings. Some $2.5 billion a year would be taken out of annual expenses by eliminating redundant administrative functions and cutting 15,000 employees. In addition, combining the PC businesses of HP and Compaq would enable HP to capture significant scale economies and compete more efficiently with Dell. The same would be true in the computer server and storage businesses, areas where Dell was gaining share. Critics, however, were quick to point out that Dell's competitive advantage was based on its cost-leadership business model, which was based on the efficient management of its supply chain—an area where both HP and Compaq lagged behind Dell. Although achieving economies of scale is desirable, would the merger allow the new HP to reduce its cost structure, such as by increasing its supply-chain efficiency? If the new HP could not change its PC business model to match Dell's low costs, then the merger would not provide any real benefit.

In addition to the cost advantages of the merger, Fiorina argued that the acquisition would give HP a critical mass in the computer service and consultancy business, where it lagged behind leader IBM significantly. By being able to offer customers a total solution to their information technology needs, both hardware *and* services, Fiorina argued that HP could gain new market share among corporate customers, who would now buy its PCs as part of the total "computer package"; moreover, HP would be entering the higher-margin service business. Here, too, however, critics were quick to perceive flaws. They argued

that HP would still be a minnow in the service and consultancy area, with under 3% of market share.

In 2004, HP announced that it had achieved its cost savings target and that it was continuing to find ways to reduce the duplication of resources in the merged company. However, it also announced that Dell's entry into the printer business had hurt its profit margins and that the profit margins on the sales of its PCs were still well below those obtained by Dell. HP's stock price plunged, and its board of directors reacted by firing Fiorina and bringing in a new CEO, Mark Hurd, a person with proven skills in managing a company's cost structure. Hurd initiated another round of cost reductions by pruning HP's product line and work force. In the spring of 2006, the company astounded analysts when it announced much higher profit margins on its sales of PCs and higher profits across the company. Many of Fiorina's strategies had begun to pay off. HP's PCs were much more attractive to customers, and Dell's foray into printers had not proved highly successful against market leader HP. Neither had Dell's entry into other electronics industries, such as MP3 players, televisions, and so on.

The result was that competitive advantage in the PC industry seemed to be moving away from Dell toward HP. As we discussed in the Running Case in the last chapter, in response, Dell has been forced to find ways to increase its level of differentiation to increase the attractiveness of its machines and so defend its position against HP and Apple. Dell engaged in horizontal differentiation when it bought the upscale PC maker Alienware in one move to increase product differentiation: it also entered into physical retailing when it began to open Dell PC stores in major shopping malls in 2006, imitating Apple's strategy. To find even more cost savings, Dell also began to use AMD's cheaper chips and broke its long-term exclusive tie to Intel. Analysts worry that its move to increase product differentiation may hurt Dell's cost leadership position; despite its attempt to lower costs, they worry Dell might become stuck in the middle. However, Dell is still a strong competitor, and only time will tell how the battle for market share in the PC industry will play out as Dell, HP, and Apple work to find new ways to lower costs and differentiate their products to grow their sales, profits, and ROIC.[a]

Another example of using horizontal integration to reduce operating costs occurred in 2004 when Kmart and Sears announced that they were merging their companies to better position themselves to compete against Wal-Mart. One goal was to share common purchasing and distribution facilities and combine their HRM functions to reduce costs. Another goal was to increase differentiation, and by 2006, some Kmart stores began to carry some of Sears's well-known product lines, such as its appliances and Craftsman tools, while Sears's stores may soon begin to stock some of Kmart's designer lines, such as Martha Stewart.

INCREASED PRODUCT DIFFERENTIATION As the Sears/Kmart merger suggests, horizontal integration may also increase profitability when it increases product differentiation, for example, by allowing a company to combine the product lines of merged companies so that it can offer customers a wider range of products that can be bundled together. **Product bundling** involves offering customers the opportunity to buy a complete range of products at a single combined price. This increases the value of a company's product line because customers often obtain a price discount from buying a set of products and also become used to dealing with just one company and its representatives. A company may obtain a competitive advantage from increased product differentiation. A famous example of the value of product bundling is Microsoft Office, which is a bundle of different software programs, including a word processor, spreadsheet, and presentation program. In the early 1990s, Microsoft was number 2 or 3 in each of these product categories, behind companies such as WordPerfect (which led in the word-processing category), Lotus (which had the best-selling spreadsheet), and Harvard Graphics (which had the best-selling presentation software). By offering all three programs in a single-price package, Microsoft presented consumers with a superior value proposition, and its product bundle quickly gained market share, ultimately accounting for more than 90% of all sales of word processors, spreadsheets, and presentation software.

Another way to increase product differentiation is through **cross-selling**, which involves a company taking advantage of, or leveraging, its established relationship with customers by acquiring additional product lines or categories that it can sell to them. In this way, a company increases differentiation because it can provide a total solution and satisfy all customers' specific needs. Cross-selling and becoming a total-solution provider is an important rationale for horizontal integration in the computer sector, where information technology (IT) companies have tried to increase the value of their offerings by providing all of the hardware and service needs of corporate customers. Providing a total solution saves customers time and money because they do not have to deal with several suppliers, and a single sales team can ensure that all the different components of a customer's IT work seamlessly together. When horizontal integration increases the differentiated appeal and value of the company's products, the total-solution provider gains market share. This was the business model IBM pursued when it acquired many IT companies and is one of the main reasons for its current success in the computer sector.

REPLICATING THE BUSINESS MODEL Given the many ways in which horizontal integration can lead to both product differentiation and low-cost advantages, it can be very profitable to use this strategy to replicate a company's successful business model in *new market segments* within its industry. In the retail industry, for example, Wal-Mart took its low-cost/low-price discount retail business model to enter into the even lower-priced warehouse segment. It has also expanded the range of products it offers customers by entering the supermarket business and establishing a nationwide chain of Wal-Mart superstores that sell groceries and produce. It has replicated this business model globally by acquiring supermarket chains in several countries, such as the United Kingdom, Mexico, and most recently Japan, where it can use its efficient global materials-management processes to pursue its cost-leadership strategy. In the United States, it is currently experimenting with new small-size supermarkets it calls neighborhood markets to expand its presence in the supermarket segment.

REDUCED INDUSTRY RIVALRY Horizontal integration can help to reduce industry rivalry in two ways. First, acquiring or merging with a competitor helps to *eliminate excess capacity* in an industry, which often triggers price wars, as we discussed in Chapter 6. By taking excess capacity out of an industry, horizontal integration creates a more benign environment in which prices might stabilize or even increase.

Second, by reducing the number of competitors in an industry, horizontal integration often makes it easier to implement *tacit price coordination* among rivals, that is, coordination reached without communication (explicit communication to fix prices is illegal). In general, the larger the number of competitors in an industry, the more difficult it is to establish informal pricing agreements, such as price leadership by the dominant company, which reduces the possibility that a price war will erupt. By increasing industry concentration and creating an oligopoly, horizontal integration can make it easier to establish tacit coordination among rivals.

Both of these motives also seem to have been behind HP's acquisition of Compaq. The PC industry was suffering from significant excess capacity and a serious price war, triggered by Dell's desire to gain market share. By acquiring Compaq, HP hoped to be able to remove excess capacity in the industry and eventually impose some pricing discipline that would lead to higher prices. In fact, by 2004, the average price of PCs started to increase, and the major competitors began to look for ways to differentiate their products to compete better and to avoid new price wars breaking out.

INCREASED BARGAINING POWER Finally, some companies use horizontal integration because it allows them to obtain bargaining power over suppliers or buyers and so increase their profitability at the expense of suppliers or buyers. By consolidating the industry through horizontal integration, a company becomes a much larger buyer of suppliers' products and uses this as leverage to bargain down the price it pays for its inputs, thereby lowering its cost structure. Similarly, by acquiring its competitors, a company gains control over a greater percentage of an industry's product or output. Other things being equal, it then has more power to raise prices and profits because customers have less choice of supplier and are more dependent on the company for their products.

When a company has greater ability to raise prices to buyers or bargain down the prices paid for inputs, it has increased market power. For an example of how the process of consolidation through horizontal integration can play out, see Strategy in Action 9.1, which looks at the way in which health care providers in eastern Massachusetts have pursued horizontal integration to gain bargaining power, and hence market power, over insurance providers.

• Problems with Horizontal Integration

Although horizontal integration can clearly strengthen a company's business model in several ways, problems, limitations, and dangers are associated with this strategy. We discuss many of these dangers in detail in Chapter 10, but the important point to note here is that a wealth of data suggests that the majority of mergers and acquisitions do *not* create value and many actually *reduce* value.[5] For example, a well-known study by KPMG, a large accounting and management consulting company, looked at 700 large

Strategy in Action

9.1

Horizontal Integration in Health Care

In the United States, health maintenance organizations (HMOs) have become a powerful force in the health care sector. HMOs are health insurance companies that provide people with health care coverage, and often companies contract with HMOs on behalf of their employees for health insurance coverage. The HMOs then "supply" patients to health care providers. Thus, HMOs can be viewed as the suppliers of the critical input—patients—to health care providers. In turn, the revenues of health care providers are dependent on the number of patients who pass through their system. Clearly, it is in the interests of HMOs to bargain down the price they must pay health care providers for coverage, and to gain bargaining power, HMOs have used horizontal integration to merge with each other until, today, they control a large volume of patients. To fight back, however, health care providers have also resorted to horizontal integration, and the battle is raging.

As an example of how this process plays out, consider how the relationship between HMOs and hospitals evolved in eastern Massachusetts. In the early 1990s, three big HMOs controlled 75% of the market for health insurance in eastern Massachusetts. In contrast, there were thirty-four separate hospital networks in the region. Thus, the insurance providers were consolidated, while the health care providers were fragmented, giving the insurance providers considerable bargaining power. The HMOs used their bargaining power to demand deep discounts from health care providers. If a hospital wouldn't offer discounts to an HMO, the HMO would threaten to remove it from its list of providers. Because losing all of those potential patients would severely damage the revenues that a hospital could earn, the hospitals had little choice but to comply with the request.

This situation changed when two of the most prestigious hospitals in the region, Massachusetts General and Brigham & Women's Hospital, merged with each other to form Partners HealthCare System. Since then, Partners has continued to pursue the strategy of acquiring other hospitals to gain power over HMOs. By 2002, it had seven hospitals and some 5,000 doctors in its system. Other regional hospitals pursued a similar strategy, and the number of independent hospital networks in the region fell from thirty-four in 1994 to twelve by 2002.

In the 2000s, Partners has increasingly exercised its strengthened bargaining power by demanding that HMOs accept a fee increase for services offered by Partners hospitals. One of the biggest HMOs, Tufts, refused to accept the increase and informed nearly 200,000 of its 900,000 subscribers that they would no longer be able to use Partners hospitals or physicians affiliated with Partners. There was an enormous uproar from subscribers. Many employers threatened to pull out of the HMO and switch to another if the policy was not changed. Tufts quickly realized it had little choice but to accept the fee increase. Tufts went back to Partners and agreed to a 30% fee increase over three years. Thus, bargaining power in the system had shifted from the HMOs toward the hospital networks. However, the Massachusetts attorney general received so many complaints from employers about rising health care premiums that an investigation into market power and anticompetitive behavior among health care providers in eastern Massachusetts was started. Clearly, the battle is not over yet.[b]

acquisitions and found that while 30% of these did increase the profitability of the acquiring company, 31% reduced profitability, and the remainder had little impact on it.[6] The implication is that implementing a horizontal integration strategy is not an easy task for managers.

As we discuss in Chapter 10, mergers and acquisitions often fail to produce the anticipated gains for a number of reasons: problems associated with merging very different company cultures, high management turnover in the acquired company when the acquisition was a hostile one, and a tendency of managers to overestimate the benefits to be gained from a merger or acquisition and to underestimate the problems involved in merging their operation.

Another problem with horizontal integration is that, when a company uses it to become a dominant industry competitor, an attempt to keep using the strategy to grow even larger brings a company into conflict with the Federal Trade Commission, the government agency responsible for enforcing antitrust law. Antitrust authorities are concerned about the potential for abuse of market power; they believe that more competition is generally better for consumers than is less competition. They worry that large companies that dominate their industry may be in a position to abuse their market power and raise prices to consumers above the level that would exist in more competitive situations. They also believe that dominant companies can use their market power to crush potential competitors by, for example, cutting prices whenever new competitors enter a market and so force them out of business, and then raising prices again once the threat has been eliminated. Because of these concerns, any merger or acquisition that is perceived by the antitrust authorities as creating too much consolidation and the *potential* for future abuse of market power may be blocked. The proposed merger between AT&T and Bell South was held up for one year, until December 2006, because of concerns this problem would arise.

Vertical Integration: Entering New Industries to Strengthen the Core Business Model

Many companies that use horizontal integration to strengthen their business model and improve their competitive position also use the corporate-level strategy of vertical integration for the same purpose. In pursuing vertical integration, however, a company is entering new industries to support the business model of its core industry, the one that is the primary source of its competitive advantage and profitability. At this point, therefore, a company has to formulate a multibusiness model that explains how entry into a new industry will enhance its long-term profitability. The multibusiness model justifying vertical integration is based on a company entering industries that *add value* to its core products because this increases product differentiation and/or lowers its cost structure.

A company pursuing a strategy of **vertical integration** expands its operations either backward into an industry that produces inputs for the company's products (*backward vertical integration*) or forward into an industry that uses, distributes, or sells the company's products (*forward vertical integration*). To enter an industry, it may establish its own operations and build the value chain needed to compete effectively in that industry, or it may acquire or merge with a company that is already in the industry. A steel company that supplies its iron ore needs from company-owned iron ore mines exemplifies backward integration. A PC maker that sells its PCs through company-owned retail outlets illustrates forward integration. For example, in 2001, Apple Computer entered the retail industry when it decided to set up a chain of Apple Stores to sell its computers and iPods, something Dell has now imitated. IBM is a highly vertically integrated company; for example, it integrated backward into the chip and disk drive industry to produce the chips and drives that go into its computers, and it integrated forward into the computer software and consulting services industries.

Figure 9.1 illustrates four main stages in a typical raw-materials-to-customer value-added chain. For a company based in the final assembly stage, backward integration means moving into component parts manufacturing and raw materials production. Forward integration means moving into distribution and sales (retail). At each stage in the chain, *value is added* to the product, meaning that a company at that stage

FIGURE 9.1

Stages in the Raw-Materials-to-Customer Value-Added Chain

takes the product produced in the previous stage and transforms it in some way so that it is worth more to a company at the next stage in the chain and, ultimately, to the customer. It is important to note that each stage of the value-added chain is a separate industry or industries in which many different companies may be competing. Moreover, within each industry, every company has a value chain composed of the value creation activities we discussed in Chapter 3: research and development (R&D), production, marketing, customer service, and so on. In other words, we can think of a value chain that runs *across* industries, and embedded within that are the value chains of companies *within* each industry.

As an example of the value-added concept, consider how companies in each industry involved in the production of a PC contribute to the final product (Figure 9.2). At the first stage in the chain are the raw materials companies that make specialty ceramics, chemicals, and metal, such as Kyocera of Japan, which manufactures the ceramic substrate for semiconductors. These companies sell their products to the makers of PC component products, such as Intel and Micron Technology, which transform the ceramics, chemicals, and metals they purchase into PC components such as microprocessors, disk drives, and memory chips. In the process, they *add value* to the raw materials they purchase. At the third stage, these components are then sold to companies that assemble PCs, such as Gateway, Apple, Dell, and HP, and that take these components and transform them into PCs—that is, *add value* to the components they purchase. At the fourth stage, the finished PCs are then either sold directly to the final customer over the Internet or sold to retailers such as Best Buy and OfficeMax, which distribute and sell them to the final customer. Companies that distribute and sell PCs also *add value* to the product because they make it accessible to customers and provide customer service and support.

FIGURE 9.2

The Raw-Materials-to-Customer Value-Added Chain in the Personal Computer Industry

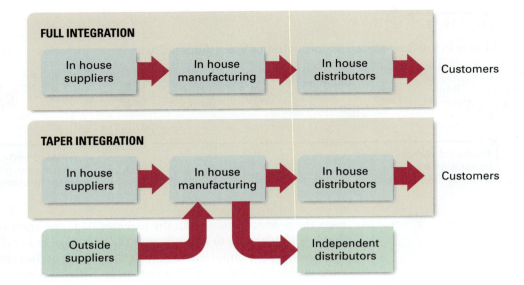

Thus, companies in different industries add value at each stage in the raw-materials-to-customer chain. Viewed in this way, vertical integration presents companies with a choice about which industries in the raw-materials-to-customer chain to operate and compete in. This choice is determined by how much establishing operations at a stage in the value chain will increase product differentiation or lower costs, as we discuss below.

Finally, it is also important to distinguish between full integration and taper integration (see Figure 9.3).[7] A company achieves **full integration** when it produces *all* of a particular input needed for its processes or disposes of *all* of its completed products through its own operations. In **taper integration**, a company buys from independent suppliers in addition to company-owned suppliers or disposes of its completed products through independent outlets in addition to company-owned outlets. The advantages of taper integration over full integration are discussed later in the chapter.

● **Increasing Profitability Through Vertical Integration**

As noted earlier, a company pursues vertical integration to strengthen the business model of its original or core business and to improve its competitive position.[8] Vertical integration increases product differentiation, lowers costs, or reduces industry competition when it (1) facilitates investments in efficiency-enhancing specialized assets, (2) protects product quality, and (3) results in improved scheduling.

FACILITATING INVESTMENTS IN SPECIALIZED ASSETS A specialized asset is one that is designed to perform a specific task and whose value is significantly reduced in its next-best use.[9] The asset may be a piece of equipment that has a firm-specific use or the know-how or skills that a company or employees have acquired through training and experience. Companies invest in specialized assets because these assets allow them to lower their cost structure or to better differentiate their products, which facilitates premium pricing. A company might invest in specialized equipment to lower its manufacturing costs, for example, or it might invest in a highly specialized technology that allows it to develop better-quality products than its rivals can. Thus, specialized assets can help a company achieve a competitive advantage at the business level.

Just as a company invests in specialized assets in its own industry to build competitive advantage, it is often necessary that suppliers invest in specialized assets to produce the inputs that a specific company needs. By investing in these assets, a supplier can make higher-quality inputs that give its customer a differentiation advantage, or it can now make inputs at a lower cost so it can charge its customer a lower price to keep its business. However, it is often difficult to persuade companies in adjacent stages of the raw-materials-to-customer value-added chain to undertake investments in specialized assets. Often, to realize the benefits associated with such investments, a company has to vertically integrate and enter into adjacent industries and make the investments itself. Why does this happen?

Imagine that Ford has developed a unique high-performance fuel-injection system that will dramatically increase fuel efficiency and differentiate Ford's cars from those of its rivals, giving it a major competitive advantage. Ford has to decide whether to make the system in-house (vertical integration) or contract with an independent supplier to make the system. Manufacturing these new systems requires a substantial investment in specialized equipment that can be used only for this purpose. In other words, because of its unique design, the equipment cannot be used to manufacture any other type of fuel-injection system for Ford or any other automaker. Thus, it is an investment in specialized assets.

Consider this situation from the perspective of an independent supplier deciding whether to make this investment. The supplier might reason that once it has made the investment, it will become dependent on Ford for business because *Ford is the only possible customer for the fuel-injection system made by this specialized equipment.* The supplier realizes that this puts Ford in a strong bargaining position and that Ford might use its power to demand lower prices for the fuel-injection systems. Given the risks involved, the supplier declines to make the investment in specialized equipment.

Now consider Ford's position. Ford might reason that if it contracts production of these systems to an independent supplier, it might become too dependent on that supplier for a vital input. Because specialized equipment is required to produce the fuel-injection systems, Ford cannot switch its order to other suppliers. Ford realizes that this increases the bargaining power of the independent supplier and that the supplier might use its power to demand higher prices.

The situation of *mutual dependence* that would be created by the investment in specialized assets makes Ford hesitant to allow efficient suppliers to make the product, and makes suppliers hesitant to undertake such a risky investment. The problem is a lack of trust—neither Ford nor the supplier can trust the other to play fair in this situation. The lack of trust arises from the risk of **holdup,** that is, being taken advantage of by a trading partner after the investment in specialized assets has been made.[10] Because of this risk, Ford reasons that the only safe way to get the new fuel-injection systems is to manufacture them itself.

To generalize from this example, if achieving a competitive advantage requires one company to make investments in specialized assets so it can trade with another, the risk of holdup may serve as a deterrent and the investment may not take place. Consequently, the potential for higher profitability from specialization will be lost. To prevent such loss, companies vertically integrate into adjacent stages in the value chain. Historically, the problems surrounding specific assets have driven automobile companies to vertically integrate backward into the production of component parts, steel companies to vertically integrate backward into the production of iron, computer companies to vertically integrate backward into chip production, and aluminum companies to vertically integrate backward into bauxite mining. The way specific asset issues have led to vertical integration in the aluminum industry is discussed in Strategy in Action 9.2.

Strategy in Action

9.2

Specialized Assets and Vertical Integration in the Aluminum Industry

The metal content and chemical composition of bauxite ore, used to produce aluminum, vary from deposit to deposit, so each type of ore requires a specialized refinery—that is, the refinery must be designed for a particular type of ore. Running one type of bauxite through a refinery designed for another type reportedly increases production costs by 20% to 100%. Thus, the value of an investment in a specialized aluminum refinery and the cost of the output produced by that refinery depend on receiving the right kind of bauxite ore.

Imagine that an aluminum company has to decide whether to invest in an aluminum refinery designed to refine a certain type of ore. Also assume that this ore is extracted by a company that owns a single bauxite mine. Using a different type of ore would raise production costs by 50%. Therefore, the value of the aluminum company's investment is dependent on the price it must pay the bauxite company for this bauxite. Recognizing this, once the aluminum company has made the investment in a new

refinery, what is to stop the bauxite company from raising bauxite prices? Nothing. Once it has made the investment, the aluminum company is locked into its relationship with its bauxite supplier. The bauxite supplier can increase prices because it knows that as long as the increase in the total production costs of the aluminum company is less than 50%, the aluminum company will continue to buy its ore. Thus, once the aluminum company has made the investment, the bauxite supplier can *hold up* the aluminum company.

How can the aluminum company reduce the risk of holdup? The answer is by purchasing the bauxite supplier. If the aluminum company can purchase the bauxite supplier's mine, it need no longer fear that bauxite prices will be increased after the investment in an aluminum refinery has been made. In other words, vertical integration, by eliminating the risk of holdup, makes the specialized investment worthwhile. In practice, it has been argued that these kinds of considerations have driven aluminum companies to pursue vertical integration to such a degree that, according to one study, 91% of the total volume of bauxite is transferred within vertically integrated aluminum companies.[c]

ENHANCING PRODUCT QUALITY By entering industries at other stages of the value-added chain, a company can often enhance the quality of the products in its core business and so strengthen its differentiation advantage. For example, the ability to control the reliability and performance of components such as fuel-injection systems may increase a company's competitive advantage in the luxury sedan market and enable it to charge a premium price. Conditions in the banana industry also illustrate the importance of vertical integration in maintaining product quality. Historically, a problem facing food companies that import bananas has been the variable quality of delivered bananas, which often arrive on the shelves of U.S. supermarkets too ripe or not ripe enough. To correct this problem, major U.S. food companies such as General Foods have integrated backward and now own banana plantations so they have control over the supply of bananas. As a result, they can now distribute and sell bananas of a standard quality at the optimal time to better satisfy customers. Knowing that they can rely on the quality of these brands, customers are willing to pay more for them. Thus, by vertically integrating backward into plantation ownership, banana companies have built customer confidence, which in turn has enabled them to charge a premium price for their product.

The same considerations can promote forward vertical integration. Ownership of retail outlets may be necessary if the required standards of after-sales service for complex products are to be maintained. For example, in the 1920s, Kodak owned retail outlets for distributing photographic equipment. The company felt that few established retail outlets had the skills necessary to sell and service its photographic equipment. By the 1930s, Kodak decided that it no longer needed to own its retail outlets because other retailers had begun to provide satisfactory distribution and service for Kodak products. It then withdrew from retailing.

IMPROVED SCHEDULING Sometimes important strategic advantages can be obtained when vertical integration makes it quicker, easier, and more cost effective to plan, coordinate, and schedule the transfer of a product, such as raw materials or component parts, between adjacent stages of the value-added chain.[11] Such advantages can be crucial when a company wants to realize the benefits of just-in-time inventory systems. For example, in the 1920s, Ford profited from the tight coordination and scheduling that are possible with backward vertical integration. Ford integrated backward into steel foundries, iron ore shipping, and iron ore mining. Deliveries at Ford were coordinated to such an extent that iron ore unloaded at Ford's steel foundries on the Great Lakes was turned into engine blocks within twenty-four hours, which helped to lower Ford's cost structure.

Very often, the improved scheduling that vertical integration makes possible also enables a company to respond better to sudden changes in demand. For example, if demand drops, a company can quickly cut production of components, or when demand increases, a company can quickly increase production capacity to get its products into the marketplace faster.[12]

● **Problems with Vertical Integration**

Vertical integration can often be used to strengthen a company's business model and increase profitability. However, the opposite can occur when vertical integration results in (1) an increasing cost structure, (2) disadvantages that arise when technology is changing fast, and (3) disadvantages that arise when demand is unpredictable. Sometimes these disadvantages are so great that vertical integration may reduce profitability rather than increase it—in which case, companies vertically disintegrate and exit industries adjacent to the industry value chain. For example, Ford, which was highly vertically integrated, sold all its companies involved in mining iron ore and making steel when more efficient and specialized steel producers emerged that were able to supply lower-priced steel.

INCREASING COST STRUCTURE Although vertical integration is often undertaken to lower a company's cost structure, it can raise costs if, over time, a company makes mistakes, such as continuing to purchase inputs from company-owned suppliers when low-cost independent suppliers can supply the same inputs. During the early 1990s, for example, General Motors's company-owned suppliers made 68% of the component parts for its vehicles; this figure was higher than for any other major carmaker and made General Motors (GM) the highest-cost global carmaker. In 1992, it was paying $34.60 an hour in United Auto Workers wages and benefits to its employees at company-owned suppliers for work that rivals could get from independent nonunionized suppliers at half that rate.[13] Thus, vertical integration can be a disadvantage when company-owned suppliers develop a higher cost structure than those of independent suppliers. Why would a company-owned supplier develop such a high cost structure?

One explanation is that company-owned or in-house suppliers know that they can always sell their components to the carmaking divisions of their company—they have a captive customer. When company-owned suppliers do not have to compete with independent suppliers for orders, they have much *less incentive* to look for new ways to reduce operating costs or increase quality. Indeed, in-house suppliers may simply pass on any cost increases to the carmaking divisions in the form of higher **transfer prices**, the prices one division of a company charges other divisions for its products. Unlike independent suppliers, which constantly have to increase their efficiency to protect their competitive advantage, in-house suppliers face no such competition, and the resulting rising cost structure reduces a company's profitability.

The term *bureaucratic costs* refers to the costs of solving the transaction difficulties that arise from managerial inefficiencies and the need to manage the handoffs or exchanges between business units to promote increased differentiation or to lower a company's cost structure. Bureaucratic costs become a significant component of a company's cost structure because considerable managerial time and effort must be spent to reduce or eliminate managerial inefficiencies—such as those that result when company-owned suppliers lose their incentive to increase efficiency or innovation.

This problem can be partially solved when a company pursues *taper*, rather than *full*, integration because now in-house suppliers do have to compete with independent suppliers. In essence, independent suppliers provide a benchmark against which a company can measure the relative efficiency of its in-house suppliers, providing an incentive for company-owned suppliers (or functions) to find ways to lower their cost structure.

TECHNOLOGICAL CHANGE When technology is changing fast, vertical integration may lock a company into an old, inefficient technology and prevent it from changing to a new one that would strengthen its business model.[14] Consider a radio manufacturer that, in the 1950s, integrated backward and acquired a manufacturer of vacuum tubes to reduce costs. When transistors replaced vacuum tubes as a major component in radios in the 1960s, this company found itself locked into a technologically outdated business. However, if it had switched to transistors, the company would have had to write off its investment in vacuum tubes, and so managers were reluctant to adopt the new technology. Instead, they continued to use vacuum tubes in their radios, while competitors that were not in the vacuum tube industry rapidly switched to the new technology. As a result, the company lost its competitive advantage, and its failing business model led to a rapid loss in market share. Thus, vertical integration can pose a serious disadvantage when it prevents a company from adopting new technology or changing its suppliers or distribution systems to match the requirements of changing technology.

DEMAND UNPREDICTABILITY Suppose the demand for a company's core product, such as cars or washing machines, is predictable and a company knows how many units it needs to make each month or year. Under these conditions, vertical integration, by allowing the company to schedule and coordinate the flow of products along the value-added chain, may result in major cost savings. However, suppose the demand for cars or washing machines fluctuates wildly and is unpredictable. Now, if demand for cars suddenly plummets, the carmaker may find itself burdened with warehouses full of component parts it no longer needs, and this is a major drain on profitability. Thus, vertical integration can be risky when demand is unpredictable because it is hard to manage the volume or flow of products along the value-added chain.

For example, an auto manufacturer might vertically integrate backward to acquire a supplier of fuel-injection systems that can make exactly the number of systems the carmaker needs each month. However, if demand for cars falls because gas prices soar, the carmaker finds itself locked into a business that is now inefficient because it is not producing at full capacity. Its cost structure then starts to rise. When demand is unpredictable, taper integration might be less risky than full integration because a company can keep its in-house suppliers running at full capacity and increase or reduce its orders from independent suppliers to match changing demand conditions.

● The Limits of Vertical Integration

Although vertical integration can strengthen a company's business model in many ways, it may weaken it when (1) bureaucratic costs increase because company-owned suppliers lack the incentive to reduce operating costs and (2) changing technology or uncertain demand reduces a company's ability to change its business model to protect its competitive advantage. It is clear that strategic managers have to carefully assess the advantages and disadvantages of expanding the boundaries of their company by entering adjacent industries, either backward (upstream) or forward (downstream), in the value-added chain. While the decision to enter a new industry to make crucial component parts might have been profitable in the past, it might make no economic sense today, when many low-cost global component parts suppliers can compete for a company's business. The risks and returns on investing in vertical integration have to be continually evaluated, and companies should be as willing to vertically disintegrate as vertically integrate to strengthen their core business model. Finally, it is worth noting that taper vertical integration rather than full vertical integration may decrease bureaucratic costs because it creates an incentive for in-house suppliers to reduce operating costs. There are other ways of achieving this, however, as we discuss next.

Alternatives to Vertical Integration: Cooperative Relationships

Is it possible to obtain the differentiation and cost-savings advantages associated with vertical integration without having to bear the problems and costs associated with this strategy? In other words, is there another corporate-level strategy that managers can use to obtain the advantages of vertical integration while allowing other companies to perform upstream and downstream activities? Today, many companies have found that they can realize many of the benefits associated with vertical integration by entering into long-term cooperative relationships with companies in industries along the value-added chain. **Strategic alliances**, discussed in Chapter 8, are long-term agreements between two or more companies to jointly develop new products that benefit all companies concerned. The advantages of strategic alliances can be clarified by contrasting them with the benefits obtained if a company decides to enter into short-term contracts with other companies.

• Short-Term Contracts and Competitive Bidding

Many companies use short-term contracts, which last for a year or less, to establish the prices and conditions under which they will purchase raw materials or components from suppliers or sell their final products to distributors. A classic example is the carmaker that uses a *competitive bidding strategy* in which independent component suppliers compete to be the company that will be chosen to supply a particular part, made to agreed-upon specifications, at the lowest price. For example, GM typically solicits bids from global suppliers to produce a particular component and awards a one-year contract to the supplier submitting the lowest bid. At the end of the year, the contract is put out for competitive bid again. There is no guarantee that the company that wins the contract one year will hold on to it the next.

The advantage of this strategy for GM is that it forces suppliers to compete over price, which drives the cost of its inputs down. However, GM has no long-term commitment to individual suppliers, and it drives a hard bargain. For this reason, prospective suppliers will likely be unwilling to make the expensive investment in specialized assets that are needed to produce higher-quality or better-designed component parts. In addition, they will be reluctant to agree to tight scheduling because that would allow GM to obtain the benefits from a just-in-time inventory system but would increase the suppliers' operating costs and so reduce their profitability. With no guarantee it will retain GM's business, the supplier may refuse to invest in specialized assets; thus, to realize differentiation and cost gains, GM will have to vertically integrate backward.

In other words, the strategy of short-term contracting and competitive bidding, *because it signals a company's lack of long-term commitment to its suppliers*, will make it difficult or impossible for that company to realize the gains associated with vertical integration. Of course, this is not a problem when there is minimal need for close co-operation and no need to invest in specialized assets to improve scheduling or product quality. In such cases, competitive bidding may be optimal. However, when this need is significant, a competitive bidding strategy can be a serious drawback.

In the past, GM did place itself at a competitive disadvantage when it used a competitive bidding approach to negotiate with its suppliers. In 1992, the company instructed its parts suppliers to cut their prices by 10%, regardless of prior pricing agreements. In effect, GM tore up existing contracts and threatened to stop doing business with suppliers that did not agree to the price reduction. Although its action gave it a short-term benefit from lower costs, in the longer term, the loss of trust and the hostility created between the company and its suppliers resulted in problems for GM. According to press reports, several suppliers claimed that they reduced the R&D spending necessary to design GM parts in the future, a form of specialized investment. They also indicated that they would first impart their new design knowledge to Chrysler (now DaimlerChrysler) and Ford, which both focused on forging cooperative long-term relationships with their suppliers.[15]

Strategic Alliances and Long-Term Contracting

As opposed to short-term contracts, strategic alliances are long-term cooperative relationships between two or more companies who agree to commit resources to develop new products. Typically, one company agrees to supply the other, and the other company agrees to continue purchasing from that supplier; both make a commitment to jointly seek ways to lower costs or increase input quality. A strategic alliance, by creating a stable long-term relationship, becomes a *substitute* for vertical integration; it allows both companies to share in the same kinds of benefits that result from vertical integration but avoids the problems linked with having to manage a company located in an adjacent industry in the value-added chain, such as lack of incentives or changing technology.

Consider the cooperative relationships, which often go back decades, that many Japanese carmakers have with their components suppliers (the *keiretsu* system), which exemplifies successful long-term contracting. Together, carmakers and suppliers work out ways to increase the value added—for example, by implementing just-in-time inventory systems or cooperating on component-parts designs to improve quality and lower assembly costs. As part of this process, the suppliers make substantial investments in specialized assets to better serve the needs of a particular carmaker. Any cost savings that result are shared by carmakers and suppliers. Thus, Japanese carmakers have been able to capture many of the benefits of vertical integration without having to enter and own companies in new industries. Similarly, the component suppliers also benefit because their business and profitability grow as the companies they supply grow.[16]

In contrast to their Japanese counterparts, U.S. carmakers have historically pursued vertical integration.[17] According to several studies, the result is that the ever increasing cost of managing scores or even hundreds of companies in different industries has put GM and Ford at a significant cost disadvantage relative to their Japanese competitors.[18] Moreover, even when U.S. auto companies decided not to integrate vertically, they tended to use their powerful position to pursue an aggressive competitive bidding strategy, playing off component suppliers against each other.[19] This mindset now seems to be changing. For details on how DaimlerChrysler has attempted to build long-term cooperative relationships with suppliers, see Strategy in Action 9.3.

Strategy in Action

9.3

DaimlerChrysler's U.S. *Keiretsu*

For most of its history, Chrysler (now DaimlerChrysler) managed suppliers through a competitive bidding process: suppliers were selected on the basis of their ability to supply components at the lowest possible cost to Chrysler. A supplier's track record on performance and quality was relatively unimportant in this process. Contracts were renegotiated every two years, with little or no commitment from Chrysler to continuing to do business with a particular supplier. As a result, the typical relationship between Chrysler and its suppliers was characterized by mutual distrust, suspicion, and reluctance on the part of suppliers to invest too much in their relationship with Chrysler.

Since the early 1990s, Chrysler has systematically reorganized its dealings with suppliers in an attempt to build stable long-term relationships. The aim of this new approach has been to try to get suppliers to help Chrysler develop new products and improve its production processes. To encourage suppliers to cooperate and make investments specific to Chrysler's needs, the company has moved away from its old adversarial approach. The average contract with suppliers has been lengthened from two years to over four and a half years. Furthermore, Chrysler has given 90% of its suppliers commitments that business will be extended for at least the life of a model, if not beyond. The company has also committed itself to sharing with suppliers the benefits of any process improvements they might suggest. The basic thinking behind offering suppliers such credible commitments is to align incentives between Chrysler and its suppliers to create a sense of shared destiny and to encourage mutual cooperation to increase the size of the financial pie that they will share in the future.

By 1996, the fruits of this new approach were beginning to appear. By involving suppliers early in product development and giving them greater responsibility for design and manufacturing, DaimlerChrysler was able to compress its product development cycle and substantially reduce the costs of the product development effort. DaimlerChrysler's U.S. division reduced the time it took to develop a new vehicle from 234 weeks during the mid-1980s to about 160 weeks by 1996. The total cost of developing a new vehicle also dropped by 20 to 40%, depending on the model. With development costs in the automobile industry running at between $1 and $2 billion, that translates into a huge financial savings. Many of these savings were the direct result of engineering improvements suggested by suppliers or improved coordination between the company and suppliers in the design process. To facilitate this process, the number of resident engineers from suppliers who work side by side with DaimlerChrysler engineers in cross-company design teams increased from thirty in 1989 to more than 300 by 1996.

In 1990, Chrysler began implementing a program known internally as the supplier cost reduction effort (SCORE), which focuses on cooperation between DaimlerChrysler and suppliers to identify opportunities for process improvements. In its first two years of operation, SCORE generated 875 ideas from suppliers that were worth $170.8 million in annual savings to suppliers. In 1994, suppliers submitted 3,786 ideas that produced $504 million in annual savings. By December 1995, Chrysler had implemented 5,300 ideas that have generated more than $1.7 billion in annual savings. One supplier alone, Magna International, submitted 214 proposals; Chrysler adopted 129 of them for a total cost savings of $75.5 million. Many of the ideas themselves have a relatively small financial impact; for example, a Magna suggestion to change the type of decorative wood grain used on minivans saved $0.5 million per year. But the cumulative impact of thousands of such ideas has had a significant impact on DaimlerChrysler's bottom line.

DaimlerChrysler has continued to pursue this approach aggressively, so much so that in 2004, it announced that its long-term goal was for its suppliers to take over a much higher percentage of actual car production—which includes making the car body and assembling most of its major components. Chrysler believes that this will give suppliers greater motivation than its own car divisions to control quality and reduce costs. Thus, it has a radical long-term business model: it wants to be a car designer and not a carmaker. The cars that come off the assembly line may have Chrysler's name on them, but it will have only designed them, not built them.[d]

The interesting question raised by the preceding discussion is: How does a company create a stable long-term strategic alliance with another company given the fear of holdup and the possibility of being cheated, which arise when one company makes an investment in specialized assets to trade with another? How have companies like Toyota managed to develop such enduring relationships with their suppliers?

Companies can take several steps to ensure the success of a long-term cooperative relationship and to lessen the chance that one company will renege on its agreement and try to cheat the other. One of those steps is for the company that makes the investment in specialized assets to demand a *hostage* from its partner. Another is to establish a *credible commitment* on both sides to build a trusting long-term relationship.[20]

HOSTAGE TAKING   Hostage taking is essentially a means of guaranteeing that a partner will keep its side of the bargain. The cooperative relationship between Boeing and Northrop illustrates this type of situation. Northrop is a major subcontractor for Boeing's commercial airline division, providing many components for the 747 and 767 aircraft. To serve Boeing's special needs, Northrop has had to make substantial investments in specialized assets. In theory, because of the sunk costs associated with such investments, Northrop is dependent on Boeing, and Boeing is in a position to renege on previous agreements and use the threat to switch orders to other suppliers as a way of driving down prices. In practice, however, Boeing is highly unlikely to do this because it is a major supplier to Northrop's defense division and provides many parts for the Stealth bomber. Boeing also has had to make substantial investments in specialized assets to serve Northrop's needs. Thus, the companies are *mutually dependent*. Boeing is unlikely to renege on any pricing agreements with Northrop because it knows that Northrop could respond in kind. Each company holds a hostage—the specialized investment the other has made—as insurance against any attempt by the other company to renege on its prior pricing agreements.

CREDIBLE COMMITMENTS   A credible commitment is a believable promise or pledge to support the development of a long-term relationship between companies. To understand the concept of credibility in this context, consider the following relationship between General Electric and IBM. GE is one of the major suppliers of advanced semiconductor chips to IBM, and many of the chips are customized to IBM's requirements. To meet IBM's specific needs, GE has had to make substantial investments in specialized assets that have little other value. As a consequence, GE is dependent on IBM and faces a risk that IBM will take advantage of this dependence to demand lower prices. In theory, IBM could back up its demand by threatening to switch its business to another supplier. However, GE reduced this risk by having IBM enter into a contractual agreement that committed IBM to purchase chips from GE for a ten-year period. In addition, IBM agreed to share the costs of the specialized assets needed to develop the customized chips, thereby reducing GE's investment. Thus, by publicly committing itself to a long-term contract and putting some money into the chip development process, IBM essentially made a *credible commitment* to continue purchasing those chips from GE.

MAINTAINING MARKET DISCIPLINE   Just as a company pursuing vertical integration faces the problem that its in-house suppliers might become lazy and inefficient, so a company that forms a strategic alliance with another to make its components runs the risk that the other company's costs will rise as it becomes progressively more lax or inefficient over time. This happens because the supplier knows it does not have to compete with other suppliers for the company's business. Consequently, a company seeking to form a long-term strategic alliance needs to possess some kind of power that it can use to discipline its partner should the need arise.

The company holds two strong cards over its supplier. First, even long-term contracts are periodically renegotiated, generally every four to five years, so the supplier knows that if it fails to live up to its commitments, the company may refuse to renew the contract. Second, some companies engaged in long-term relationships with suppliers use a **parallel sourcing policy**—that is, they enter into a long-term contract with *two* suppliers for the same part (as is the practice at Toyota, for example).[21] This arrangement gives the company a hedge against an uncooperative supplier because it knows that if it fails to comply with the agreement, the company can switch all its business to the other supplier. This threat rarely needs to be actualized because the mere fact that the company and its suppliers know that parallel sourcing is being used and that a supplier can be replaced at short notice injects an element of market discipline into their relationship.

The growing importance of just-in-time inventory systems as a way to reduce costs and enhance quality—and thus differentiation—is increasing the pressure on companies to form strategic alliances in a wide range of industries. The number of strategic alliances, especially global strategic alliances, formed each year is increasing, and the popularity of vertical integration may be falling because so many low-cost global suppliers now exist in countries like Malaysia, Korea, and China.

Strategic Outsourcing

Vertical integration and strategic alliances are alternative ways of managing the value chain *across industries* to strengthen a company's core business model. However, just as low-cost suppliers of component parts exist, so today many *specialized companies* exist that can perform one of a company's *own value-chain activities* in a way that contributes to a company's differentiation advantage or that lowers its cost structure.

Strategic outsourcing is the decision to allow one or more of a company's value-chain activities or functions to be performed by independent specialist companies that focus all their skills and knowledge on just one kind of activity. The activity to be outsourced may encompass an entire function, such as the manufacturing function, or it may be just one kind of activity that a function performs. For example, many companies outsource the management of their pension systems while keeping other HRM activities within the company. When a company chooses to outsource a value-chain activity, it is choosing to focus on *fewer* value creation activities to strengthen its business model.

Many companies have started to outsource activities that managers regard as noncore or nonstrategic, meaning they are not a source of a company's distinctive competencies and competitive advantage.[22] One survey found that some 54% of the companies polled had outsourced manufacturing processes or services in the past three years.[23] Another survey estimates that some 56% of all global product manufacturing is outsourced to manufacturing specialists.[24] Companies that outsource include Nike, which does not make its athletic shoes, and The Gap, which does not make its jeans and clothing; these products are made under contract at low-cost global locations. Similarly, many high-technology companies outsource much of their manufacturing activity to contract manufacturers that specialize in low-cost assembly. Cisco, the leader in the Internet router and switch business, does not actually manufacture routers and switches; rather, they are made by contract manufacturers such as Flextronics and Jabil Circuit.

While manufacturing is probably the most popular form of strategic outsourcing, as we noted earlier, many other kinds of noncore activities are also outsourced. Microsoft has long outsourced its entire customer technical support operation to an independent company, as does Dell. Both companies have extensive customer support operations in India that are staffed by skilled operatives who are paid a fraction of what their U.S. counterparts earn. BP Amoco outsourced almost all of its human resources function to Exult, a San Antonio company, in a five-year deal worth $600 million, and a few years later, Exult won a ten-year $1.1 billion contract to handle HRM activities for all Bank of America's 150,000 employees. Similarly, American Express outsourced its entire IT function to IBM in a seven-year deal worth $4 billion in 2002. The IT outsourcing market in North America was worth over $200 billion by 2006.[25] In 2006, IBM announced that it was outsourcing its purchasing function to an Indian company to save $2 billion a year.[26]

Companies engage in strategic outsourcing to strengthen their business models and increase their profitability. The process of strategic outsourcing typically begins with strategic managers identifying the value-chain activities that form the basis of a company's competitive advantage; these are obviously kept within the company to protect them from competitors. Managers then systematically review the noncore functions to assess whether they can be performed more effectively and efficiently by independent companies that specialize in those activities. Because these companies specialize in a particular activity, they can perform it in ways that lower costs or improve differentiation. If managers decide there are differentiation or cost advantages, these activities are outsourced to those specialists.

One possible outcome of this process is illustrated in Figure 9.4, which shows the primary value-chain activities and boundaries of a company before and after it has pursued strategic outsourcing. In this example, the company decided to outsource its production and customer service functions to specialist companies, leaving just R&D

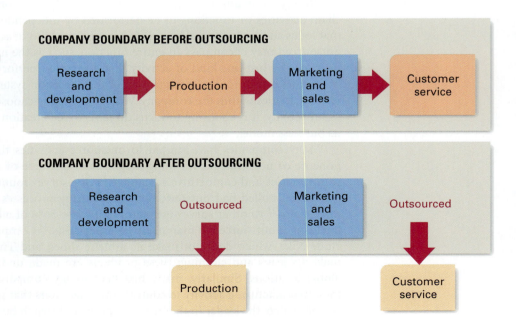

FIGURE 9.4

Strategic Outsourcing of Primary Value Creation Functions

and marketing and sales within the company. Once outsourcing has been executed, the relationships between the company and its specialists are then often structured as long-term contractual relationships, with rich information sharing between the company and the specialist organization to which it has contracted the activity. The term **virtual corporation** has been coined to describe companies that have pursued extensive strategic outsourcing.[27]

● **Benefits of Outsourcing**

Strategic outsourcing has several advantages. It can help a company to (1) lower its cost structure, (2) increase product differentiation,[28] and (3) focus on the distinctive competencies that are vital to its long-term competitive advantage and profitability.

LOWER COST STRUCTURE Outsourcing reduces costs when the price that must be paid to a specialist company to perform a particular value-chain activity is less than what it would cost the company to perform that activity itself, that is, internally. Specialists are often able to perform an activity at a lower cost than the company can because they are able to realize scale economies or other efficiencies not available to the company. For example, performing HRM activities, such as managing a pay and benefits system, requires a significant investment in sophisticated HRM IT, and purchasing this IT represents a considerable fixed cost for one company. But by aggregating the HRM IT needs of many individual companies, a company that specializes in HRM, such as Exult or Paycheck, can obtain huge economies of scale in IT that any single company could not hope to achieve. Some of these cost savings are then passed on to client companies in the form of lower prices, which reduces their cost structure. A similar dynamic is at work in the contract manufacturing business. Once again, manufacturing specialists like Solectron, Flextronics, and Jabil Circuit make large capital investments to build efficient-scale manufacturing facilities, but then they are able to spread those capital costs over a huge volume of output and drive down unit costs so that they can make a specific product—an Apple iPod or Motorola Krazr, for example, at a lower cost than the company can.

Specialists are also likely to obtain the cost savings associated with learning effects much more rapidly than a company that performs an activity just for itself (see Chapter 4 for a review of learning effects). For example, because a company like Flextronics is manufacturing similar products for several different companies, it is able to build up *cumulative* volume more rapidly, and it learns how to manage and operate the manufacturing process more efficiently than any of its clients could. This drives down the specialists' cost structure and also allows them to charge client companies a lower price for a product than if the client companies made it in-house.

Specialists are also often able to perform an activity at a lower cost than a specific company because they are based in low-cost global locations. Nike, for example, outsources the manufacture of its running shoes to companies based in China because of the much lower wage rates in China. The Chinese-based specialist can now assemble shoes, which is a very labor-intensive activity, at a much lower cost than if Nike assembled its shoes in the United States. Although Nike could establish its own operations in China to manufacture running shoes, this would require a major capital investment and limit its ability to switch production to an even lower-cost location later, say, Vietnam. So for Nike and most other consumer goods companies, outsourcing manufacturing activity to both lower costs and obtain the flexibility to switch to a more favorable location should labor costs change is the most efficient way to handle production.

ENHANCED DIFFERENTIATION A company may also be able to differentiate its final products better by outsourcing certain noncore activities to specialists. For this to occur, the *quality* of the activity performed by specialists must be greater than if that same activity were performed by the company. On the reliability dimension of quality, for example, a specialist may be able to achieve a lower error rate in performing an activity precisely because it focuses solely on that activity and has developed a strong distinctive competency in it. Again, this is one advantage claimed for contract manufacturers. Companies like Flextronics have adopted Six Sigma methodologies (see Chapter 4) and driven down the defect rate associated with manufacturing a product. Thus, they can provide more reliable products to their clients, which can now differentiate their products on the basis of their superior quality.

A company can also improve product differentiation by outsourcing to specialists when they stand out on the excellence dimension of quality. For example, the excellence of Dell's U.S. customer service is a differentiating factor, and Dell outsources its PC repair and maintenance function to specialist companies. A customer who has a problem with a product purchased from Dell can get excellent help over the phone, and if it turns out that there is a defective part in the computer, a maintenance person will be dispatched to replace the part within a few days. The excellence of this service differentiates Dell and helps to guarantee repeat purchases, which is why HP has worked hard to match Dell's level of service quality. In a similar way, carmakers often outsource specific kinds of vehicle component design activities, such as microchips or headlights, to specialists that have earned a reputation for design excellence in this particular activity.

FOCUS ON THE CORE BUSINESS A final advantage of strategic outsourcing is that it allows managers to focus their energies and their company's resources on performing those core activities that have the most potential to create value and competitive advantage. In other words, companies can enhance their core competencies and thus are able to push out the value creation frontier and create more value for their customers. For example, Cisco remains the dominant competitor in the Internet router industry because it has focused on building its competencies in product design, marketing and sales, and supply-chain management. Companies that focus on the core activities essential for competitive advantage in their industry are better able to drive down the costs of performing those activities and thus better differentiate their final products.

● Risks of Outsourcing

Although outsourcing noncore activities has many benefits, there are also risks associated with it, risks such as holdup and the possible loss of important information. Managers must assess these risks before they decide to outsource a particular activity. As we discuss below, however, these risks can be reduced when the appropriate steps are taken.

HOLDUP In the context of outsourcing, holdup refers to the risk that a company will become too dependent on the specialist provider of an outsourced activity and that the specialist will use this fact to raise prices beyond some previously agreed-on rate. As with strategic alliances, the risk of holdup can be reduced by outsourcing to several suppliers and pursuing a parallel sourcing policy, as DaimlerChrysler and Cisco do. Moreover, when an activity can be performed well by any one of several different providers, the threat that a contract will not be renewed in the future is normally sufficient to keep the chosen provider from exercising bargaining power over the company.

For example, although IBM enters into long-term contracts to provide IT services to a wide range of companies, it would be highly unlikely to try to raise prices after the contract has been signed because it knows full well that such an action would reduce its chance of getting the contract renewed in the future. Moreover, the fact that IBM has many strong competitors in the IT services business, such as EDS, Accenture, and HP, gives it a very strong incentive to deliver significant value to its client and not to practice holdup.

LOSS OF INFORMATION   A company that is not careful can lose important competitive information when it outsources an activity. For example, many computer hardware and software companies have outsourced their customer technical support function to specialists. Although this makes good sense from a cost and differentiation perspective, it may also mean that a critical point of contact with the customer, and a source of important feedback, is lost. Customer complaints can be useful pieces of information and valuable input into future product design, but if those complaints are not clearly communicated to the company by the specialists performing the technical support activity, the company can lose that information. Again, this is not an argument against outsourcing. Rather, it is an argument for making sure that there is good communication flow between the outsourcing specialist and the company. At Dell, for example, a great deal of attention is paid to making sure that the specialist responsible for providing technical support and onsite maintenance collects and communicates all relevant data regarding product failures and other problems to Dell, so that Dell can design better products.

Summary of Chapter

1. A corporate strategy should enable a company, or one or more of its business units, to perform one or more of the value creation functions at a lower cost or in a way that allows for differentiation and a premium price.
2. Horizontal integration can be understood as a way of trying to increase the profitability of a company by (a) reducing costs, (b) increasing the value of the company's products through differentiation, (c) replicating the business model, (d) managing rivalry within the industry to reduce the risk of price warfare, and (e) increasing bargaining power over suppliers and buyers.
3. There are two drawbacks associated with horizontal integration: the numerous pitfalls associated with mergers and acquisitions, and the fact that the strategy can bring a company into direct conflict with antitrust authorities.
4. Vertical integration can enable a company to achieve a competitive advantage by helping build barriers to entry, facilitating investments in specialized assets, protecting product quality, and helping to improve scheduling between adjacent stages in the value chain.

5. The disadvantages of vertical integration include increasing bureaucratic costs if a company's internal or in-house supplier becomes inefficient, and a lack of flexibility when technology is changing fast or demand is uncertain.
6. Entering into a long-term contract can enable a company to realize many of the benefits associated with vertical integration without having to bear the same level of bureaucratic costs. However, to avoid the risks associated with becoming too dependent on its partner, it needs to seek a credible commitment from its partner or establish a mutual hostage-taking situation.
7. The strategic outsourcing of noncore value creation activities may allow a company to lower its costs, better differentiate its products, and make better use of scarce resources, while also enabling it to respond rapidly to changing market conditions. However, strategic outsourcing may have a detrimental effect if the company outsources important value creation activities or becomes too dependent on the key suppliers of those activities.

Discussion Questions

1. Why was it profitable for GM and Ford to integrate backward into component-parts manufacturing in the past, and why are both companies now trying to buy more of their parts from outside suppliers?

2. Under what conditions might horizontal integration be inconsistent with the goal of maximizing profitability?

3. What value creation activities should a company outsource to independent suppliers? What are the risks involved in outsourcing these activities?

4. What steps would you recommend that a company take to build long-term cooperative relationships with its suppliers that are mutually beneficial?

Practicing Strategic Management

SMALL-GROUP EXERCISE
Comparing Vertical Integration Strategies

Break up into small groups of three to five people, appoint one group member as a spokesperson who will communicate your findings to the class, then read the following description of the activities of Seagate Technologies and Quantum Corporation, both of which manufacture computer disk drives. On the basis of this description, outline the pros and cons of a vertical integration strategy. Which strategy do you think makes most sense in the context of the computer disk drive industry?

Quantum Corporation and Seagate Technologies are major producers of disk drives for personal computers and workstations. The disk drive industry is characterized by sharp fluctuations in the level of demand, intense price competition, rapid technological change, and product life cycles of no more than twelve to eighteen months. In recent years, Quantum and Seagate have pursued very different vertical integration strategies.

Seagate is a vertically integrated manufacturer of disk drives, both designing and manufacturing the bulk of its own disk drives. Quantum specializes in design and outsources most of its manufacturing to a number of independent suppliers, including, most important, Matsushita Kotobuki Electronics (MKE) of Japan. Quantum makes only its newest and most expensive products in-house. Once a new drive is perfected and ready for large-scale manufacturing, Quantum turns over manufacturing to MKE. MKE and Quantum have cemented their partnership over eight years. At each stage in designing a new product, Quantum's engineers send the newest drawings to a production team at MKE. MKE examines the drawings and is constantly proposing changes that make new

disk drives easier to manufacture. When the product is ready for manufacture, eight to ten Quantum engineers travel to MKE's plant in Japan to spend at least a month to work on production ramp-up.

ARTICLE FILE 9

Find an example of a company whose horizontal or vertical integration strategy appears to have dissipated rather than created value. Identify why this has been the case and what the company should do to rectify the situation.

STRATEGIC MANAGEMENT PROJECT
Module 9

This module requires you to assess the horizontal and vertical integration strategies pursued by your company. With the information you have at your disposal, answer the questions and perform the tasks listed:

1. Has your company ever pursued a horizontal integration strategy? What was the strategic reason for pursuing this strategy?

2. How vertically integrated is your company? If your company does have vertically integrated operations, is it pursuing a strategy of taper or full vertical integration?

3. Assess the potential for your company to create value through vertical integration. In reaching your assessment, also consider the bureaucratic costs of managing vertical integration.

4. On the basis of your assessment in question 3, do you think your company should (a) outsource some operations that are currently performed in-house or (b) bring some operations in-house that are currently outsourced? Justify your recommendations.

5. Is your company involved in any long-term cooperative relationships with suppliers or buyers? If so, how are these relationships structured? Do you think that these relationships add value to the company? Why?

6. Is there any potential for your company to enter into (additional) long-term cooperative relationships with suppliers or buyers? If so, how might these relationships be structured?

ETHICS EXERCISE

Kelli had been out of college for five months and was desperately in need of a well paying job. She had always abhorred sales, but her mother's friend owned an insurance company and offered to train her as a medical insurance salesperson. Kelli knew the earning potential for a job like this one was good, and she needed the cash. After talking with friends and family, she decided to accept the job.

During her first week of training, Kelli began to see things that disturbed her. On Tuesday, she shadowed Bob, a salesperson with the company for ten years, as he reviewed and sold a policy to a young couple. During the discussion with the couple, Bob assured them that the policy covered severe injuries, various cancers, and other serious illnesses. Reading over the policy later, Kelli noticed that the policy did not cover many common illnesses—something Bob had neglected to mention to the couple. On Wednesday, Kelli shadowed another seasoned salesperson, Greta. In this case, Greta sold a policy to an elderly man without mentioning that it was not compatible with Medicare.

By Friday, Kelli was worried. She asked John, another salesperson almost as new as she was, about Bob and Greta's behavior and was told that this was simply how things were done. "You'll learn it soon enough, Kelli. The name of the game here is sell, sell, sell."

Kelli didn't know what to do. Was her mom's friend, who had been kind enough to give her a job despite inexperience, supportive of these business methods? If not, how could she tell her what was going on behind her back? If so, how could Kelli quit without making everyone angry?

1. Define the ethical issues presented in this case.
2. What do you think Kelli should do?
3. Do you think what Bob and Greta did was unethical? Why or why not?

CLOSING CASE

Read All About It News Corp.

Way before television and the Internet, "Read all about it" was the cry of street vendors eager to persuade news-hungry customers to buy the most recent version of their newspaper. Now, TV channels like CNN and Web portals like Yahoo! and Google provide almost instantaneous news from around the world. "Read the latest" might also describe the growth of News Corporation Limited, or News Corp., the company headed by controversial CEO Rupert Murdoch, who every year for the last several decades has engineered some kind of acquisition or divestiture that has created one of the four largest and most powerful entertainment media companies in the world. What is the news about News Corp.? What kinds of strategies did Murdoch use to create his media empire?

Rupert Murdoch was born into a newspaper family; his father owned and ran the *Adelaide News,* an Australian regional newspaper, and when his father died in 1952, Murdoch gained control of the paper. He quickly enlarged his customer base by acquiring more Australian newspapers. One of these had connections to a major British pulp newspaper, the *Mirror,* a paper similar to the *National Enquirer,* and Murdoch recognized that he had an opportunity to copy the *Mirror*'s business model but make his paper even more sensational. His business model worked, and Murdoch established the *Sun* as a leading British tabloid.

Murdoch's growing reputation as an entrepreneur showed that he could create a much higher return from the assets he controlled (ROIC) than his competitors and enabled him to borrow increasing amounts of money from investors. With this money, he bought well-known newspapers such as the *British Sunday Telegraph* and then his first U.S. newspaper, the *San Antonio Express*. Pursuing his sensational business model further, he launched the *National Star*. His growing profits and reputation allowed him to continue to borrow money, and in 1977, he bought the *New York Post*. Four years later, in 1981, he engineered a new coup when he bought the *Times* and *Sunday Times,* Britain's leading conservative publications—a far cry from the *Sun* tabloid.

Murdoch's strategy of horizontal integration through merger allowed him to create one of the world's biggest newspaper empires. However, he also realized that industries in the entertainment and media sector can be divided into those that provide media content, or "software" (books, movies, and television programs), and those that provide the media channels, or "hardware," necessary to bring software to customers (movie theaters, television channels, television cable, and satellite broadcasting). Murdoch decided that he could create the most profit by becoming involved in both the media software *and* hardware industries—that is, the entire value chain of the entertainment and media sector. This strategy of vertical integration gave him control over all the different industries, joined together like links in a chain that converted inputs such as stories into finished products like newspapers or books.

In the 1980s, Murdoch began purchasing global media companies in both the software and hardware stages of the entertainment sector. He also launched new ventures of his own. For example, sensing the potential of satellite broadcasting, he launched Sky in 1983, the first satellite television channel in the United Kingdom. He also began a new strategy of horizontal integration by purchasing companies that owned television stations. He paid $1.5 billion for Metromedia, which owned seven stations that reached over 20% of U.S. households. He scored another major coup in 1985 when he bought Twentieth Century Fox Movie Studios, a premium content provider. Now he had Fox's huge film library and its creative talents to make new films and television programming.

In 1986, Murdoch decided to create the FOX Broadcasting Company and buy or create his own U.S. network of FOX affiliates that would show programming developed by his own FOX movie studios. After a slow start, the FOX network gained popularity with sensational shows like *The Simpsons*, which became FOX's first blockbuster program. Then in 1994, FOX purchased the sole rights to broadcast all NFL games for over $1 billion, thereby shutting out NBC and becoming the fourth network. The FOX network has never looked back and, with Murdoch's sensational business model, was one of the first to create the reality programming that has proved so popular in the 2000s.

Realizing that he could create even more value by transmitting his growing media content over new channels, Murdoch also began to increase his company's presence in satellite broadcasting. In 1990, Murdoch merged his Sky satellite channel with British Satellite Broadcasting to form BSkyB, which has since become the leading satellite provider in the United Kingdom. Then, in 2003, News Corp. announced it would buy DIRECTV, one of the two largest satellite TV providers, for $6.6 billion. At the same time, News Corp. was also acquiring many other companies in both stages of the entertainment value chain to strengthen its competitive position in those industries.

By 2004, Murdoch's business model, based on strategies of horizontal and vertical integration, had created a global media empire. The company's profitability has ebbed and flowed because of the massive debt needed to fund Murdoch's acquisitions, debt that has frequently brought his company near financial ruin. However, banks that understand the value of his assets, such as Citibank, have provided the money needed to service those debts. Meanwhile, News Corp.'s ROIC has been steadily increasing through the 2000s and it has become the leading global media empire..

Case Discussion Questions

1. What kind of corporate-level strategies did News Corp. pursue to build its multibusiness model?

2. What are the advantages and disadvantages associated with these strategies?

Corporate-Level Strategy: Formulating and Implementing Related and Unrelated Diversification

Tyco's Rough Ride

Tyco International has experienced success and failure under different CEOs. Its multibusiness model was implemented differently by its former CEO Dennis Kozlowski, who took over in 1992. Tyco's sales expanded from $3.1 billion in 1992 to $38 billion in 2001, when it earned over $5 billion in profit. Much of this growth was driven by acquisitions that Kozlowski orchestrated to take Tyco into a diverse range of businesses, including medical supplies, security equipment, electronic components, plastics, financial services, and telecommunications.

Kozlowski's early success has been attributed to the way he applied a business model based on several consistent strategies. First, through its acquisitions, Tyco seeks to attain a critical mass in the industries in which it competes. Despite the fact that the company is diversified, Tyco became one of the largest providers of security systems, basic medical supplies, and electronic components in the United States. Indeed, Kozlowski used acquisitions to consolidate fragmented industries and attain economies of scale that give Tyco a cost-based advantage over smaller rivals.[1]

Second, Tyco sought out companies making basic products that have a strong market share, but the companies have been underperforming compared to their competitors—which indicates there is substantial room for improvement. Once Tyco identified a potential target, Kozlowski approached the company's managers to see if they supported the idea of being acquired. After its auditors had carefully examined the target's books and decided the company had potential, Tyco made a formal bid. When the acquisition had been completed, Tyco worked to find ways to improve the performance of the acquired unit. Corporate overhead and the company's work force were slashed, and the old top management team was removed. Unprofitable product lines were sold off or closed down, and factories and sales forces were merged with Tyco's existing operations to reduce costs and obtain scale economies. For example, within months of acquiring AMP (the world's largest manufacturer of electronic components) for $12 billion in 1999, Tyco had identified close to $1 billion in cost savings that could be implemented by closing unprofitable plants and reducing its work force by 8,000. Once costs were slashed, the new management team was then set tough goals and given strong incentives to boost profitability.

Throughout most of the 1990s, this business model worked well and Tyco's stock soared, but then in the late 1990s, things changed. Tyco's most recent acquisitions did not seem to be contributing much to profitability; the company was growing, but somehow its performance seemed to be flagging. Then, beginning in 1999, analysts began to criticize the company's top managers for using inappropriate accounting methods to disguise the fact that Tyco's business model was failing. Critics argued that Kozlowski and Tyco's chief financial officer Mark Swartz had started to systematically find ways to inflate the profitability of its operating units and new acquisitions to make Tyco's performance look better than it actually was. They were forced to resign in 2003, and in 2005, these accusations were borne out when both men were sentenced to prison for grand larceny, securities fraud, falsifying business records, and conspiring to defraud Tyco of hundreds of millions of dollars to fund lavish lifestyles.

Tyco was a ship adrift in the early 2000s; it seemed that there was no longer a rationale for keeping its empire together, its business model was a failure, and its stock price plummeted. The company's stock traded with a so-called diversification discount because investors found it impossible to evaluate the profitability of its individual business units. So, its new CEO, Edward Breen, decided that the best way to increase value to shareholders was to reverse the business model that been developed by Kozlowski.[2]

In 2006, Breen announced that he had decided to pursue a new, nondiversified business model. The company's four business units would be split into three separate companies, each of which would be headed by its own independent top management team. Tyco's electronics and health care units would be spun off in tax-free transactions, and Breen would continue to run its remaining operations, including its well-known ADT home alarm systems and security equipment, fire protection, and pump-and-valve businesses. Breen believes that the managers of each independent company will be better positioned to develop the most successful business model for their industry, and that the returns they will eventually generate will exceed those provided by Tyco's old multibusiness model, which by the end of Kozlowski's reign had simply resulted in growth without increased profitability. The spinoff is expected to take place in 2007.[3]

OVERVIEW

Tyco's current CEO Edward Breen has decided that the different businesses Tyco owns will be able to create more value if they are split into three separate companies, each of which will be managed by its own top management team. Breen believes that each of the new companies will then be better positioned in their respective industries to maintain and grow market share and improve their profit margins. Breen has developed a *multibusiness model* that will allow each company to pursue its own, industry-specific business model and thus allow it to gain a better position vis-à-vis industry competitors. As we discuss later, Breen has decided to abandon Tyco's corporate-level strategy of unrelated diversification and "de-diversify" to increase the profitability of each company and thus increase returns to shareholders.

In this chapter, we continue our discussion of how companies can utilize their distinctive competencies, and the business models that are based on them, by formulating and implementing new corporate-level strategies to grow their profits and free cash flow. Companies cannot stand still; they must continually search for ways to use their capital more efficiently and effectively. In a competitive environment, resources such as capital move to their most highly valued use, which means investors place their capital in the companies that are expected to be the most profitable in the future. If a company's managers do not strive continuously to build its distinctive competencies and competitive advantage, they will ultimately lose out to those companies that have found new ways to pursue their business models successfully over time.

This chapter discusses the corporate-level strategy of diversification, which is a company's decision to enter one or more new industries to take advantage of its existing distinctive competencies and business model. We discuss two different types of diversification, related diversification and unrelated diversification, and we examine the different kinds of distinctive competencies and multibusiness models on which they are based. Then we look at three different methods or strategies that companies can use to implement a diversification strategy: internal new ventures, acquisitions, and joint ventures. By the end of this chapter, you will understand the pros and cons associated with the decision to diversify and enter new markets and industries and the different methods companies can choose from to implement a diversification strategy.

Expanding Beyond a Single Industry

The role of managers in corporate-level strategy is to identify which markets or industries a company should compete in to maximize its long-run profitability. As we discussed in Chapter 9, for many companies, profitable growth and expansion often entail concentrating on a single market or industry. For example, McDonald's focuses on the global fast-food restaurant business and Wal-Mart focuses on global discount retailing. Companies that stay in one industry pursue horizontal integration and strategic outsourcing to strengthen their business models, expand their business, and increase their profitability. Even though vertical integration leads a company to enter industries at adjacent stages of the value chain, the intent is still to strengthen its core business model.

As a result of these strategies, a company's fortunes are tied closely to the profitability of its *original industry*—and this can be dangerous if that industry goes into decline. Moreover, as an industry matures, the opportunities to grow profits often fall. So companies that concentrate on just one industry may miss opportunities to increase their profitability by leveraging their distinctive competencies to make and sell products in *new industries*. There is compelling evidence to suggest that companies that rest on their laurels, do not engage in constant learning, and do not force themselves to stretch can lose out to agile new competitors that come along with superior business models.[4] For these reasons, many argue that companies must *leverage*, that is, find new ways to take advantage of their distinctive competencies and core business model in new markets and industries.

● **A Company as a Portfolio of Distinctive Competencies**

Gary Hamel and C. K. Prahalad have developed a model that can help managers assess how and when they should expand beyond their current market or industry. According to these authors, a fruitful approach to identifying new product market opportunities is to think of a company not as a portfolio of products but as a *portfolio of distinctive competencies*, and then consider how those competencies might be leveraged, that is, used to create more value and profit in new industries.[5]

Recall from Chapter 3 that a distinctive competency is a company-specific resource or capability that gives a company a competitive advantage. Hamel and Prahalad argue that when managers want to identify a profitable opportunity for diversification, they must first define and classify the company's *current* set of distinctive competencies. Then they can use a matrix like the one illustrated in Figure 10.1 to establish an agenda for entering new markets or industries. This matrix distinguishes between existing competencies and new ones that would have to be developed to allow a company to compete in a new industry. It also distinguishes between the existing industries in which a company operates and the new industries in which it might operate in the future. Each quadrant in the matrix has different strategic implications.

FILL IN THE BLANKS   The lower left quadrant of Figure 10.1 represents the company's existing portfolio of competencies and products. The term *fill in the blanks* refers to the opportunity to improve a company's competitive position in its existing industries by sharing its current competencies between divisions. In the 1980s, for example, Canon had distinctive competencies in precision mechanics and fine optics and used them to produce mechanical cameras. Then, it used its competencies in precision mechanics and fine optics, plus an additional competency it had developed in microelectronics, to enter the photocopier industry, so it now competed in two industries: cameras and photocopiers. In the 1990s, Canon realized it could also strengthen its camera business by giving it the microelectronics skills it had developed in its copier business. Thus, Cannon was able to make advanced cameras with electronic features such as autofocusing.

PREMIER PLUS 10   The upper left quadrant in Figure 10.1 is referred to as *premier plus 10*. The term is used to suggest another important question: What *new* distinctive competencies must be developed now to ensure that a company remains a *premier* provider of its existing products in *ten* years' time? To strengthen the business model of its copier business, Canon decided that it needed to build a new competency in digital electronic imaging (the ability to capture and store images in a digital format as opposed to the more traditional chemical-based photographic processes). By developing this new competency, Canon was able to protect its competitive advantage and make advanced products like laser copiers, color copiers, and digital cameras.

WHITE SPACES   The lower right quadrant of Figure 10.1 is referred to as *white spaces* because the issue that managers must address is how the company can fill "white spaces," that is, opportunities to creatively redeploy or recombine its current distinctive competencies to produce new products in new industries. Canon was able to recombine its established competencies in precision mechanics and fine optics and its recently acquired competency in digital imaging to produce fax machines and laser printers, thereby entering the fax and printer industries. In other words, it leveraged its distinctive competencies to take advantage of opportunities in other industries and create valuable new products.

MEGA-OPPORTUNITIES Opportunities represented by the upper right quadrant of Figure 10.1 do not overlap with the company's current industries or its current competencies. Rather, they imply entry into new industries where the company currently has none of the competencies required to succeed. Nevertheless, a company may choose to pursue such opportunities if they are particularly attractive, significant, or relevant to its existing product market activities. For example, in 1979, Monsanto was primarily a manufacturer of chemicals, including fertilizers. However, the company saw enormous opportunities in the emerging biotechnology industry, and the company embarked on a massive investment program to build a world-class competence in biotechnology. This investment, funded by cash flows generated from Monsanto's operations in the chemical industry, paid off in the 1990s, when Monsanto introduced a series of genetically engineered crop seeds that were resistant to many common pests. Roundup®, a Monsanto herbicide that can be used to kill weeds but that will not kill its genetically engineered plants, became the industry leader.[6]

A focus on using or recombining existing competencies or building new competencies to enter new industries helps managers think strategically about how industry boundaries might change over time and how this will affect their current business models. By helping managers think about how to transfer and leverage competencies across industries, Prahalad and Hamel's model can help managers avoid the strategic mistake of entering new markets where their business model will fail to give them a competitive advantage, which has happened to many companies, such as Coca-Cola and Sears, discussed in the last chapter.

Increasing Profitability Through Diversification

Diversification is the process of entering new industries, distinct from a company's core or original industry, to make new kinds of products that can be sold profitably to customers in these new markets. A multibusiness model based on diversification focuses on finding ways to use the company's distinctive competencies to make products that are highly valued by customers in the new industries it has entered. A **diversified company** is one that makes and sells products in two or more industries. In each industry a company enters, it establishes an operating division or business unit, which is essentially a self-contained company that makes and sells products for its particular market. As with the other corporate strategies, to increase profitability, a diversification strategy should enable the company or its individual business units to perform one or more of the value chain functions (1) at a lower cost, (2) in a way that allows for differentiation and gives the company pricing options, or (3) in a way that helps the company to manage industry rivalry better.

The managers of most companies first consider diversification when they are generating **free cash flow**, that is, cash *in excess* of that required to fund investments in the company's existing industry and to meet any debt commitments.[7] In other words, free cash flow is cash in excess of that which can be profitably reinvested in an existing business (*cash* is simply *capital* by another name). When a company is generating free cash flow, managers must decide whether to return that capital to shareholders in the form of higher dividend payouts or invest it in diversification. Technically, any free cash flow belongs to the company's owners—its shareholders. For diversification to make sense, the return on investing free cash flow to pursue diversification opportunities, that is, the return on invested capital (ROIC), *must* exceed the return that stockholders can get by investing that capital in a diversified portfolio of stocks and bonds. If this were not the case, it would be in the best interests of shareholders for the company to return any excess cash to them through higher dividends rather than pursue a diversification strategy. Thus, a diversification strategy is *not* consistent with maximizing returns to shareholders unless the multibusiness model that managers use to justify entry into a new industry will significantly increase the value that a company can create.

Six main justifications for pursuing a multibusiness model based on diversification can be identified. Diversification can increase company profitability when managers (1) transfer competencies between business units in different industries, (2) leverage competencies to create business units in new industries, (3) share resources between business units to realize economies of scope, (4) use product bundling, (5) use diversification to reduce rivalry in one or more industries, and (6) utilize *general* organizational competencies that increase the performance of all the company's business units.

● Transferring Competencies Across Industries

Transferring competencies involves taking a distinctive competency developed by a business unit in one industry and implanting it in a business unit operating in another industry. The second business unit is often one the company has acquired. Companies that base their diversification strategy on transferring competencies believe that they can use one or more of their distinctive competencies in a value chain activity—for example, manufacturing, marketing, materials management, and research and development (R&D)—to significantly strengthen the business model of the acquired business unit or company. For example, over time, Philip Morris developed distinctive competencies in product development, consumer marketing, and brand positioning that had made it a leader in the tobacco industry. Sensing a profitable opportunity, it acquired Miller Brewing, which at the time was a relatively small player in the brewing industry. Then, to create valuable new products in Miller, Philip Morris transferred some of its best marketing experts to Miller, where they applied the skills acquired at Philip Morris to turn around Miller's lackluster brewing business (see Figure 10.2). The result was the creation of Miller Light, the first light beer, and a marketing campaign that helped to push Miller from the number 6 to the number 2 company in the brewing industry in terms of market share.

Companies that base their diversification strategy on transferring competencies tend to acquire new businesses related to their existing business activities because of commonalities between one or more of their value chain functions. A *commonality* is some kind of attribute that, when it is shared or used by two or more business units, will allow them to operate more effectively and efficiently and create more value.

FIGURE 10.2

Transfer of
Competencies at
Philip Morris

For example, Miller Brewing was related to Philip Morris's tobacco business because it was possible to create important marketing commonalities; both beer and tobacco are mass-market consumer goods where brand positioning, advertising, and product development skills are crucial to a new product's success. In general, such competency transfers can increase profitability when they either (1) lower the cost structure of one or more of a diversified company's business units or (2) enable one or more of its business units to better differentiate their products. Both also give that business unit pricing options.

For such a strategy to work, the competencies being transferred must involve value chain activities that will become the source of a specific business unit's competitive advantage in the future. In other words, the distinctive competency being transferred must have real strategic value. All too often, however, companies assume that *any* commonality between their value chains is sufficient for creating value. When they attempt to transfer competencies, they find that the anticipated benefits are not forthcoming because the different business units did not share some important attribute in common. General Motors' acquisition of Hughes Aircraft, made simply because cars and carmaking were "going electronic" and Hughes was an electronics company, demonstrates the folly of overestimating the commonalities among businesses. The acquisition failed to realize any of the anticipated gains for GM, whose competitive position did not improve, and GM subsequently sold Hughes Aircraft.

● Leveraging Competencies

Leveraging competencies involves taking a distinctive competency developed by a business unit in one industry and using it to create a new business unit in a different industry. Once again, the multibusiness model is based on the premise that the set of distinctive competencies that are the source of competitive advantage in one industry might be applied to create a differentiation- or cost-based competitive advantage for a new business unit in a different industry. For example, Canon used its distinctive competencies in precision mechanics, fine optics, and electronic imaging to produce laser printers, which was a new business in a new industry for Canon. Its competitive advantage in laser printers came from the fact that its competencies enabled it to produce high-quality (differentiated) printers that could be manufactured at a low cost.

The difference between leveraging competencies and transferring competencies is that, in the case of leveraging competencies, an entirely *new* business unit is being created, whereas transferring competencies involves a transfer between *existing* business units. This difference is important because each is based on a different multibusiness model. Companies that leverage competencies to establish new businesses tend to be *technology-based* companies that use their R&D competencies to create new business opportunities and units in diverse industries. In contrast, companies that transfer competencies are often industry leaders that enter new industries by acquiring established businesses. They then transfer their strong set of competencies to the acquired businesses to increase their competitive advantage and profitability, as Philip Morris did with Miller Brewing.

A number of companies have based their diversification strategy on leveraging competencies and using them to create new business units in different industries. Microsoft leveraged its skills in software development and marketing to create two business units in new industries: its online network MSN and its Xbox videogame units. Microsoft's managers believed this diversification strategy was in the best interests of shareholders because the company's competencies would enable it to attain a competitive advantage in the online and videogame industries. In fact, the results of this strategy have been mixed. In 2003, when Microsoft first broke its profits down by business unit, it turned out that the software business was generating almost all the profit and most other business units were generating a loss. However, things have improved somewhat because its new Xbox 360 has captured more market share from Sony and its MSN network is breaking even. Nevertheless, realizing that entry into new industries is not a way it can easily increase returns to shareholders, Microsoft decided to give back over $30 billion, or half its $60 billion cash hoard, to shareholders in the form of a dividend in 2004 and has declared more dividends since.

A company that is famous for its ability to leverage competencies to create new businesses in diverse industries is 3M; it leveraged its skills in adhesives to create many new products in new industries (see Strategy in Action 10.1). From a humble

Strategy in Action   10.1

Diversification at 3M: Leveraging Technology

3M is a 100-year-old industrial colossus that in 2005, generated over $21 billion in revenues and $3 billion in net income from a portfolio of more than 50,000 individual products, ranging from sandpaper and sticky tape to medical devices, office supplies, and electronic components. The company has consistently created new businesses by leveraging its scientific knowledge to find new applications for its proprietary technology. Today, the company is composed of fifty-six different business units grouped into six major sectors: Consumer and Office; Display and Graphics; Electro and Communications; Health Care; Industrial and Transportation; and Safety, Security and Protection Services. The company has consistently generated 30% of sales from products introduced within the prior five years and currently operates with the goal to produce 40% of revenues from products introduced within the previous four years.

The process of leveraging technology to create new businesses at 3M can be illustrated by the following quotation from William Coyne, head of R&D at 3M: "It began with sandpaper: mineral and glue on a substrate. After years as an abrasives company, it created a tape business. A researcher left off the mineral, and adapted the glue and substrate to create the first sticky tape. After creating many varieties of sticky tape—consumer, electrical, medical—researchers created the world's first audio and videotapes. In their search to create better tape backings, other researchers happened on multilayer films that, surprise, have remarkable light management qualities. This multiplayer film technology is being used in brightness enhancement films, which

are incorporated in the displays of virtually all laptops and palm computers."

How does 3M do it? First, the company is a science-based enterprise with a strong tradition of innovation and risk taking. Risk taking is encouraged, and failure is not punished but seen as a natural part of the process of creating new products and business. Second, 3M's management is relentlessly focused on the company's customers and the problems they face. Many of 3M's products have come from helping customers solve difficult problems. Third, managers set *stretch goals* that require the company to create new products and businesses at a rapid pace (such as the current goal that 40% of sales should come from products introduced within the last four years). Fourth, employees are given considerable autonomy to pursue their own ideas. An employee can spend 15% of his or her time working on a project of his or her own choosing without management approval. Many products have resulted from this autonomy, including the ubiquitous Post-it Notes. Fifth, while products belong to business units and the business units are responsible for generating profits, the technologies belong to every unit within the company. Anyone at 3M is free to try to develop new applications for a technology developed by its business units. Sixth, 3M has implemented information technology (IT) that promotes the sharing of technological knowledge between business units so that new opportunities can be identified. Also, it hosts many in-house conferences where researchers from different business units are brought together to share the results of their work. Finally, 3M uses numerous mechanisms to recognize and reward those who develop new technologies, products, and businesses, including peer-nominated award programs; a corporate hall of fame; and, of course, monetary rewards.[a]

beginning as a manufacturer of sandpaper, 3M has become one of the most diversified U.S. companies.

● Sharing Resources: Economies of Scope

When two or more business units in different industries share resources and capabilities, they may also be able to realize economies of scope.[8] **Economies of scope arise when one or more of a diversified company's business units are able to realize cost-saving or differentiation advantages because they can more effectively pool, share, and utilize expensive resources or capabilities, such as skilled people, equipment, manufacturing facilities, distribution channels, advertising campaigns, and R&D laboratories.** If business units in different industries can share a common resource or function, they can collectively lower their cost structure.[9] For example, the costs of GE's consumer products advertising, sales, and service activities are spread over a wide range of products, such as small and large appliances, air conditioning, and furnaces, thus reducing unit costs. There are two major sources of these cost reductions.

First, companies that can share resources across business units have to invest proportionately less in the shared resource than companies that cannot share. For example, Procter & Gamble (P&G) makes both disposable diapers and paper towels, paper-based products valued for their ability to absorb liquid without disintegrating. Because both products need the same attribute—absorbency—P&G can share the R&D costs associated with producing an absorbent paper-based product across the two businesses. Similarly, because both products are sold to the same customer group (supermarkets), P&G can use the same sales force to sell both products (see Figure 10.3). In contrast, competitors that make just paper towels or just disposable diapers cannot achieve the same economies and have to invest proportionately more in R&D and in maintaining a sales force. The net result is that, other things being equal, P&G will have lower expenses and can earn a higher ROIC than companies that lack the ability to share resources.

Diversification to attain economies of scope is possible only when there are significant commonalities between one or more of the value chain functions of a company's existing and new business units. Moreover, managers need to be aware that the costs of coordination necessary to achieve economies of scope within a company often outweigh the value that can be created by such a strategy.[10] Consequently, the strategy should be pursued only when sharing is likely to create a

FIGURE 10.3

Sharing Resources at Procter & Gamble

significant competitive advantage in one or more of a company's new or existing business units.

Using Product Bundling

In their search for new ways to differentiate their products, more and more companies are entering into related industries to expand and widen their product lines to be able to satisfy customers' needs for a complete package of related products. This is currently happening in telecommunications, where customers are increasingly seeking a package price for wired phone service, wireless phone service, high-speed access to the Internet, VOIP phone service, television programming, online gaming, video on demand, or any combination of these services. To meet this need, large phone companies have been acquiring other companies that provide one or more of these services, while cable companies such as Comcast Corporation have acquired or formed strategic alliances with companies that allow them to offer their customers phone service, and so on. In 2004, Microsoft announced an alliance with SBC whereby SBC would use its new software to allow it to provide television service and video on demand over DSL phone connections, as well as its other services. Similarly, EchoStar, the satellite broadcaster, formed an alliance with Verizon to offer its television service with Verizon's phone service.

Just as manufacturing companies strive to reduce the number of their component suppliers to reduce costs and increase quality, so the final customer wants to obtain the convenience and reduced price of bundled products. Another example of product bundling comes from the medical equipment industry, where the companies that used to produce different kinds of products, such as operating room equipment, ultrasound devices, magnetic imaging, and x-ray equipment, have been merging to be able to offer hospitals a complete range of medical equipment. This development has been driven by hospitals because they want the convenience of dealing with a single supplier. In addition, because of the increased value of their orders, they also have increased bargaining power with the supplier.

Managing Rivalry: Multipoint Competition

Sometimes a company benefits by diversifying into an industry in order to hold a competitor in check that has either entered its industry or has the potential to do so. For example, if an aggressive company based in another industry enters a company's market and tries to gain market share by cutting prices, the company could respond in kind and diversify into the aggressor's home industry and also cut prices. In this way, the company sends a signal: "If you attack me, I'll respond in kind and make things tough for you." (This is an example of the strategy of tit-for-tat discussed in Chapter 6.) The hope is that such a move will cause the aggressor to pull back from its attack, thus reducing rivalry in the company's home industry and permitting higher prices and profits. Of course, for the tit-for-tat strategy to have its desired effect, the company would then need to pull back from its competitive attack in the aggressor's home market.

An example of diversification to keep a potential competitor in check occurred in the late 1990s, when Microsoft awoke to the fact that Sony might emerge as a rival. Although Sony was in a different industry (consumer electronics as opposed to software), Microsoft realized that the Sony Playstation was in essence nothing more than a specialized computer and, moreover, one that did not use a Microsoft operating system. Microsoft's fear was that Sony might use the Playstation 2, which came equipped with web-browsing potential, as a Trojan horse to gain control of Web browsing and computing from the living room, ultimately taking customers away from PCs with Microsoft operating systems. The desire to keep Sony's ambitions in check was another part of the rationale for Microsoft's diversification into the videogame industry with the launch of the Xbox.

Many diversified companies compete against each other in several different industries. Canon and Kodak compete against each other in photocopiers and digital cameras, for example. Similarly, Unilever and P&G compete against each other in laundry detergents, personal care products, and packaged foods. When companies compete against each other in different industries, we refer to it as **multipoint competition.** Companies that are engaged in multipoint competition might be better able to manage rivalry by signaling that competitive attacks in one industry will be met by retaliatory attacks in another industry. If successful, such signaling might lead to mutual forbearance and thus less intense rivalry and higher profit in each industry in which a company competes. It follows that the desire to manage rivalry better through multipoint competition might be a motive for diversification that increases profitability.

● **Utilizing General Organizational Competencies**

General organizational competencies transcend individual functions or business units and are found at the top or corporate level of the multibusiness company. Typically, these general competencies are the skills of a company's top managers and functional experts, such as those of Tyco's top management team. When these general competencies are present—and many times they are not—they help each business unit within a company perform at a higher level than it could if it operated as an independent company, thus increasing the profitability of the whole corporation.[11] We discuss three kinds of general organizational competencies that can result in superior performance: (1) entrepreneurial capabilities, (2) organizational design capabilities, and (3) strategic capabilities. These managerial skills are often not present because they are rare and difficult to develop and put into action.

ENTREPRENEURIAL CAPABILITIES The example of 3M, profiled in Strategy in Action 10.1, provides many clues as to why entrepreneurial capabilities are important if the process of diversification is to increase profitability. A company may generate considerable excess cash flow, but to take advantage of it, managers must identify new opportunities and act on them to create a stream of new and improved products in both existing and new industries. It appears that some companies are better able to stimulate their managers to act entrepreneurially than are others; examples are 3M, HP, IBM, Toyota, Canon, and Matsushita.[12]

These companies are able to promote entrepreneurship because they have an organizational culture that stimulates managers to act entrepreneurially. Thus, these companies are able to create profitable new business units at a much higher rate than most other companies, which helps promote their diversification. We will highlight some of the systems required to generate profitable new businesses later in this chapter when we discuss internal new ventures. For now, note that the management systems of an entrepreneurial company must (1) encourage managers to take risks, (2) give them the time and resources to pursue novel ideas, (3) not punish managers when a new idea fails, but also (4) make sure the company does not waste resources pursuing too many risky ventures that have a low probability of generating a decent return on investment. Obviously, a difficult organizational balancing act is required here because the company has to simultaneously encourage risk taking while limiting the amount of risk being undertaken.

Companies with entrepreneurial capabilities are able to achieve this balancing act. 3M's corporate goal of generating 40% of revenues from products introduced within the past four years focuses the organization on developing new products and businesses. The company's famous 15% rule, which has been copied by many companies, gives employees the time to pursue novel ideas. Its long-standing commitment to helping customers solve problems helps ensure that ideas for new businesses are customer-focused. The company's celebration of employees who have created successful new businesses helps to reinforce the norm of entrepreneurship and risk taking. Similarly, there is a norm that failure should not be punished but should be viewed as a learning experience.

CAPABILITIES IN ORGANIZATIONAL DESIGN   One of the main sources of entrepreneurial capabilities, as well as an important determinant of whether a company can obtain competencies at the functional level, is organizational design: a company's ability to create a structure, culture, and control systems that motivate and coordinate employees. The degree of autonomy that the structure of an organization provides its managers, the kinds of norms and values present in the organization's culture, and even the design of the buildings of its headquarters to encourage the free flow of ideas are important determinants of a diversified company's ability to reap the gains from its multibusiness model. Effective organizational structure and controls create incentives that encourage business unit (divisional) managers to maximize the efficiency and effectiveness of their units. Moreover, a good organizational design helps prevent the inertia that afflicts so many organizations, when employees become so absorbed in protecting their company's competitive position in existing markets that they lose sight of new or improved ways to do business or changing industry boundaries.

The last three chapters of this book take an in-depth look at these issues. To succeed in diversification, a company must have the structure and culture that enable it to rapidly change the way it motivates and coordinates its resources and capabilities. Companies that seem to be successful at managing their structures and cultures to further the diversification process share a number of features.[13] First, their different business units tend to be placed into self-contained divisions. Second, these business units tend to be managed by senior executives in a decentralized fashion. Rather than get involved in day-to-day operations, they set challenging financial goals for each unit, probe the managers of each unit about their strategies for attaining these goals, monitor their performance, and hold them accountable for that performance. Third, these internal monitoring and control mechanisms are linked with incentive pay systems that reward business unit managers who attain or surpass performance goals. Achieving these three goals, and aligning a company's structure with its strategy, is a complex, never-ending task and only top managers with superior organizational design skills can do it.

SUPERIOR STRATEGIC CAPABILITIES   For diversification to increase profitability, a company's top or corporate managers must have superior strategic capabilities. Specifically, they must have certain intangible governance skills to manage different business units in a way that enables those units to perform better than they would if they were independent companies.[14] Simply put, the business of corporate managers in the diversified company is to manage the managers of its business units or divisions. This is not an easy thing to do well; governance skills are a rare and valuable capability. However, certain senior executives seem to have developed a skill for managing businesses and pushing the heads of business units to achieve superior performance. Examples include Jeffery Immelt at GE, Steve Ballmer at Microsoft, Steve Jobs at Apple, and Larry Ellison at Oracle.

A flair for entrepreneurship and recognizing new business opportunities is often found in top managers who have developed superior strategic capabilities or governance skills. Just as important is a top manager's ability to find ways to enhance the performance of individual managers, functions, and whole business units. Jack Welch, for example, was a master at improving the skills of his managers across the board at GE. He created organizationwide management development programs focusing on change management and created procedures to make middle managers question top management actions. At the functional and business levels, he instituted many of the techniques discussed in Chapter 4 to promote superior efficiency and quality, such as the Six Sigma quality improvement methodology, and he pushed hard to make sure that business unit managers used these techniques to improve the efficiency of their operations. Jeffrey Immelt, GE's current CEO, was one of Welch's protégés.

An especially important governance skill in the diversified company is the ability to diagnose the underlying source of the problems in a poorly performing business unit and understand how to take the appropriate steps to fix those problems, whether by recommending new strategies to the top managers of the unit or by replacing them with a new management team better able to fix the problems. Top managers who have such governance skills tend to be very good at probing business unit managers for information and helping them think through strategic problems.

Related to this skill is the ability of the top managers of a diversified company to identify inefficient and poorly managed companies, and then acquire and restructure them to improve their performance—and thus the profitability of the total corporation. The acquired company does not have to be in the same industry as the acquiring company for the strategy to work; thus, the strategy often leads to diversification. Improvements in the performance of the acquired company can come from a number of sources. First, the acquiring company usually replaces the top managers of the acquired company with a more aggressive management team. Second, the new managers of the acquired business are encouraged to sell off any unproductive assets, such as executive jets and elaborate corporate headquarters, and to reduce staffing levels. Third, the new management team is encouraged to intervene in the operations of the acquired business to discover ways to improve the unit's efficiency, quality, innovation, and customer responsiveness. Fourth, to motivate the new management team and other employees of the acquired unit to undertake such actions, increases in their pay are typically linked to increases in the performance of the acquired unit. Fifth, the acquiring company often establishes performance goals for the acquired company that cannot be met without significant improvements in operating efficiency. It also makes the new top managers aware that failure to achieve performance improvements consistent with these goals within a given amount of time will probably result in their being replaced.

Thus, the system of rewards and sanctions established by the top managers of the acquiring company gives the new managers of the acquired unit strong incentives to look for ways to improve the performance of the unit under their charge. Tyco pursued the strategy of acquiring and restructuring underperforming companies with considerable success in the past; as we discussed earlier, however, its new CEO no longer believes this is the appropriate strategy for the company in the future. We discuss why later in the chapter.

Two Types of Diversification

In the last section, we discussed six principal ways in which companies can use diversification to implant their business models and strategies in other industries to increase their long-run profitability. It is possible to differentiate between two types of diversification based on the ability to realize these benefits: related diversification and unrelated diversification.[15]

● **Related Diversification**

Related diversification is the strategy of establishing a business unit in a new industry that is related to a company's existing business units by some form of linkage or commonality between the value chain functions of the new and existing business units. The goal of this strategy is to obtain the benefits from transferring and leveraging distinctive competencies, sharing resources, and bundling products. The multibusiness model behind related diversification is based on taking advantage of strong technological, manufacturing, marketing, and sales commonalities between new and existing business units that can be successfully tweaked to increase the competitive advantage of one or more business units. Figure 10.4 provides some examples of the different kinds of linkages; the greater the number of linkages that can be formed, the greater the potential for increasing competitive advantage and profitability.

One more potential advantage of related diversification is that it can allow a company to apply any general organizational competencies it possesses to increase overall business unit performance, such as by creating a culture that encourages entrepreneurship across units. 3M, for example, has a set of core technologies that are then shared among different kinds of business units. However, 3M also has a general organizational competency in promoting cross-unit learning. Another example of related diversification is given in Strategy in Action 10.2, which looks at Intel's recent diversification into the communications chip business and the problems surrounding it.

● **Unrelated Diversification**

The multibusiness model underlying **unrelated diversification** aims to enhance profits by implanting general organizational competencies in new business units and perhaps to capture the benefits of multipoint competition. Companies pursuing a strategy of unrelated diversification have *no* intention of transferring or leveraging competencies between business units. Their focus is purely on using general managerial competencies to strengthen the business model of each individual business unit or division. Tyco, which was discussed in the Opening Case, provides a good example

FIGURE 10.4

Commonalities Between the Value Chains of Three Business Units

Strategy in Action 10.2

Related Diversification at Intel

Although Intel has had a small presence in the communications chip business since the 1980s, the company focused most of its attention and resources on the booming business of making microprocessors for personal computers. According to managers at Intel, "feeding the processor monster" was a way to boost profitability, and the company invested all its substantial free cash flows into designing new generations of ever more powerful microprocessors and building the large-scale, and expensive, fabrication facilities necessary to manufacture them efficiently. The decision seemed logical: Intel had the dominant position in the microprocessor market, its primary customers (PC makers like Dell) were growing by leaps and bounds, and demand for its microprocessors was soaring.

This strategy of staying in a single business changed at a contentious strategy meeting of Intel's top executives in 1996. Intel's executives came away from that meeting with two important insights. First, the PC industry would approach market saturation in the early 2000s, which meant that the growth in demand for Intel's microprocessors would slow down. To maintain its profit growth, Intel needed to find a new "growth driver." Second, its executives decided that because of the growing use of the Internet, "communications was going to be the driver for everything in the future, that all computing was connected computing, and that connectivity had as important and strategic a role to play as the microprocessor did." Moreover, it was clear that demand for products of the communications industry such as communications network gear, which needed advanced communications chips, was accelerating rapidly.

Intel's executives decided that they could boost the company's ROIC by diverting some cash flow from new PC chip development and using Intel's competencies to build a new business model in the rapidly growing communications chip industry. This was a different industry: the production technology was different, the customers were different, and the competitors were different. Intel believed, however, that because the communications chip industry was related to the microprocessor industry, it could obtain a competitive advantage by transferring its leading-edge PC microprocessor technology, as well as its manufacturing and marketing capabilities, to the communications chip industry.

Once the decision was made to enter the communications chip industry on a significant scale, Intel had to decide how best to execute the strategy. The company's managers decided that the only way they could get big enough fast enough to gain scale economies and establish a sustainable competitive advantage in this booming market was for the company to buy the required technology, fabrication facilities, and sales force. It could then improve the performance of the acquired businesses by transferring its competencies to them. So Intel went on an acquisitions binge. Between January 1997 and June 2001, it made eighteen major acquisitions of companies in the communications chip industry, for a combined total of $8 billion. As a result of these acquisitions, Intel became the fourth largest global company in the communications chip industry by mid-2001, behind only Lucent, Motorola, and Texas Instruments. Unfortunately, Intel and all these other companies were hard hit by the slump in global demand for telecommunications equipment in the early 2000s.

Then, to make matters worse, Intel's push into communications chips had launched it on the road to designing chips that were faster and faster because speed was seen as the most vital ingredient in communication. By 2003, however, it was clear that what customers wanted was chips that could support high bandwidth and could process vast amounts of information simultaneously. Both these capabilities are needed for high-quality music, movie viewing, and other multimedia applications such as videoconferencing. Intel lacked such a chip, but in the meantime Advanced Micro Devices (AMD), its major competitor, had perceived the need to develop it. Suddenly Intel found itself at a competitive disadvantage. In 2004, it announced plans to abandon its high-speed communications chips to focus on those that could support the bandwidth needed for sophisticated multimedia applications. Intel had made the mistake of not focusing on what PC users and digital content providers needed in next-generation chips. It was so concerned with the need to increase speed that it entered a new industry assuming there was a commonality based on speed, but there was none. Intel should have focused on customer needs, not its own distinctive competencies. It has since refocused its strategy and in 2006, it introduced its new dual-core and quad-core chips that once again have given it the competitive edge.[b]

of a company that pursued a strategy of unrelated diversification successfully in the past, which created a lot of value for its shareholders.

Disadvantages and Limits of Diversification

As we have discussed, many companies, such as 3M, Intel, and GE, have reaped enormous advantages from pursuing a strategy of diversification and have consistently increased their profitability over time. Nevertheless, many companies that have pursued diversification have enjoyed far less success, and for some companies, diversification has actually dissipated or reduced their profitability. As a result, over the last few decades, many companies, such as Tyco, have de-diversified and split apart or sold off their individual business units; each business unit headed by its own top management team then pursues some kind of single-business strategy. Clearly, important disadvantages may result from diversification that can make it an unprofitable strategy to pursue over time. Three main conditions can make diversification disadvantageous: changing industry- and firm-specific conditions, diversification for the wrong reasons, and the increasing bureaucratic costs of extensive diversification.

● **Changing Industry- and Firm-Specific Conditions**

Diversification is a complex strategy to pursue, and top managers must have the entrepreneurial ability to sense profitable new opportunities and the ability to implement the strategies needed to make diversification pay off. Over time, however, a company's top management team changes: sometimes its most able executives leave to join other companies and become their CEOs, and sometimes successful CEOs decide to retire or step down. When they leave, these managers often take their vision with them, and their successors may lack the skills or commitment needed to manage and implement diversification successfully over time. Thus, the multibusiness model loses its ability to create value, and as we discuss below, the cost structure of the diversified company often starts to increase, swallowing up the gains that the strategy produces.

Over time, the environment can also change rapidly and in unpredictable ways. We discussed earlier how blurring industry boundaries can destroy the source of a company's competitive advantage. If this happens in its core business, then clearly benefits from transferring or leveraging distinctive competencies will disappear and a company will now be saddled with a collection of businesses that have all become poor performers in their respective industries. When the computer industry changed, for example, and PCs and servers became the dominant product, IBM was left with unprofitable operations in the mainframe hardware and software industries that almost led to its bankruptcy. Thus, one major problem with diversification is that the future success of this strategy is hard to predict; therefore, if a company is to profit from it over time, managers should be as willing to divest businesses as they are to acquire them. Unfortunately, research suggests that managers do not behave in this way.

● **Diversification for the Wrong Reasons**

As we have discussed, if a company pursues diversification, its managers must have a clear vision of how their entry into new industries will allow them to create more value. Over time, however, as the profitability of their diversification strategy falls for reasons like those just noted, managers, rather than divesting their businesses, often use false or mistaken justifications for keeping their collection of businesses together—or even growing those businesses. There are many famous historical examples of this faulty behavior.

For example, one widely used justification for diversification used to be that diversification could be used to obtain the benefits of risk pooling or risk reduction.

Many CEOs argued that diversification, particularly unrelated diversification into industries that have different business cycles so that their revenues rise and fall in different cycles, would allow them to create a more stable companywide income stream over time—one that avoids the sharp swings up and down that can make the value of a company's stock volatile and unpredictable. An example of risk pooling might be the diversification by U.S. Steel into the oil and gas industry in an attempt to offset the adverse effects of cyclical downturns in the steel industry. According to advocates of risk pooling, a more stable income stream reduces the risk of bankruptcy and is in the best interests of the company's stockholders.

This simple argument ignores two facts. First, stockholders can easily eliminate the risks inherent in holding an individual stock by diversifying their own portfolios, and they can do so at a much lower cost than the company can. Thus, far from being in the best interests of stockholders, attempts to pool risks through diversification represent an unproductive use of resources; instead, profits should be returned to shareholders in the form of increased dividends. Second, research on this topic suggests that corporate diversification is not an effective way to pool risks because the business cycles of different industries are *inherently difficult to predict*, and a diversified company might just find that a general economic downturn hits all its industries simultaneously. If this happens, the company's profitability will plunge.[16]

When the core business is in trouble, another mistaken justification for diversification is that the new industries will rescue it. An example of a company that made this mistake is Kodak. In the 1980s, increased competition from low-cost Japanese competitors like Fuji, combined with the beginnings of the digital revolution, led Kodak's revenues and profits first to plateau and then to fall. Its managers should have done all they could to reduce its cost structure; instead, they took its still huge free cash flow and spent tens of billions of dollars to enter new industries such as health care, biotechnology, and computer hardware in a desperate and mistaken attempt to find ways to increase profitability.

This approach was a disaster because every industry Kodak entered was populated by strong companies such as 3M, Canon, and Xerox, and Kodak's corporate managers lacked any general competencies to give their new business units a competitive advantage. And the more industries they entered, the greater the range of threats they encountered and the more time they had to spend dealing with these threats. As a result, they could spend much less time improving the performance of their core film business, which continued to decline. In reality, Kodak's diversification was just for growth itself, but *growth does not create value*; growth is simply the byproduct, not the objective, of a diversification strategy. However, in desperation, companies diversify for reasons of growth alone rather than to gain any well-thought-out strategic advantage.

A large number of academic studies suggest that extensive diversification tends to reduce rather than improve company profitability.[17] For example, in a study that looked at the diversification of thirty-three major U.S. corporations over thirty-five years, Michael Porter observed that the track record of corporate diversification has been poor.[18] Porter found that most of the companies had divested many more diversified acquisitions than they had kept. He and others have concluded that the corporate diversification strategies pursued by most companies can dissipate value instead of create it.[19]

● **The Bureaucratic Costs of Diversification**

A company diversifies to boost its profitability from higher product differentiation or a lower cost structure, but to achieve this, it has to invest valuable resources. One reason that diversification often fails to boost profitability is that all too often, the bureaucratic costs of diversification exceed the value created by the strategy. As we mentioned in the last chapter, **bureaucratic costs** are the costs associated with solving the transaction difficulties that arise between a company's business units, and between business units and corporate headquarters, as the company attempts to obtain the benefits from transferring, sharing, and leveraging competencies. They also include the costs of using general organizational competencies to solve managerial and functional inefficiencies. The level of bureaucratic costs in a diversified organization is a function of two factors: (1) the number of business units in a company's portfolio and (2) the extent to which coordination is required among these different business units to realize the benefits of diversification.

NUMBER OF BUSINESSES   The greater the number of business units in a company's portfolio, the more difficult it is for corporate managers to remain informed about the complexities of each business. Managers simply do not have the time to assess the business model of each unit. This problem began to occur at GE in the 1970s when its growth-hungry CEO Reg Jones acquired many new businesses. As Jones commented,

> I tried to review each plan [of each business unit] in great detail. This effort took untold hours and placed a tremendous burden on the corporate executive office. After a while I began to realize that no matter how hard we would work, we could not achieve the necessary in-depth understanding of the 40-odd business unit plans.[20]

The inability of top managers in extensively diversified companies to maintain a superior multibusiness model over time may lead them to base important resource allocation decisions on only the most superficial analysis of each business unit's competitive position. For example, a promising business unit may be starved of investment funds, while other business units receive far more cash than they can profitably reinvest in their operations. Furthermore, because they are distant from the day-to-day operations of the business units, corporate managers may find that business unit managers try to hide information on poor performance to save their own jobs. For example, business unit managers might blame poor performance on difficult competitive conditions, even when it is the result of their inability to craft a successful business model. But when inefficiencies such as the suboptimal allocation of capital within the company and a failure by corporate executives to successfully encourage and reward aggressive profit-seeking behavior by business unit managers become extensive, the time and effort top managers must devote to solve such problems cancel the value created by diversification.

COORDINATION AMONG BUSINESSES   The coordination required to realize value from a diversification strategy based on transferring, sharing, or leveraging competencies is a major source of bureaucratic costs. The bureaucratic mechanisms needed to oversee and manage coordination and handoffs between units, such as cross-business-unit teams and management committees, are one source of these costs. A second source is the costs associated with accurately measuring the performance, and therefore the unique profit contribution, of a business unit that is transferring or sharing resources with another. Consider a company that has two business units, one making household products (such as liquid soap and laundry detergent) and another making packaged food products. The products of both units are sold through supermarkets. To lower the costs of value creation, the parent company decides to pool the marketing and sales functions of each business unit using an organizational structure similar to that illustrated in Figure 10.5. The company is organized into three divisions: a household products division, a food products division, and a marketing division.

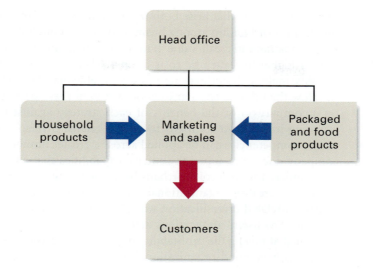

FIGURE 10.5

Coordination Among Related Business Units

Although such an arrangement may result in substantial cost savings, it can also give rise to substantial control problems and hence bureaucratic costs. For example, if the performance of the household products business begins to slip, identifying who is to be held accountable—managers in the household products division or managers in the marketing division—may prove difficult. Indeed, each may blame the other for poor performance. Although these kinds of problems can be resolved if corporate management performs an in-depth audit of both divisions, the bureaucratic costs (managers' time and effort) involved in doing so may once again cancel any value achieved from diversification.

In sum, diversification is the most complex and difficult strategy that a company can pursue. Changing conditions both in the external environment and inside a company can reduce the value creation advantages from pursuing this strategy either because they rob business units of their competitive advantage or because they increase the bureaucratic costs associated with pursuing this strategy, which then also cancel its advantages. Thus, the existence of bureaucratic costs places a limit on the amount of diversification that can profitably be pursued. It makes sense for a company to diversify only as long as the value created by such a strategy exceeds the bureaucratic costs associated with expanding the boundaries of the organization to incorporate additional business activities.

Choosing a Strategy

● **Related Versus Unrelated Diversification**

Because related diversification involves more sharing of competencies, one might think it can boost profitability in more ways than unrelated diversification and so is the better diversification strategy. However, some companies can create as much or more value from pursuing unrelated diversification, so that approach must also have some substantial benefits. An unrelated company does *not* have to achieve coordination among business units, and so it has to cope only with the bureaucratic costs that arise from the number of businesses in its portfolio. In contrast, a related company has to achieve coordination among business units if it is to realize the gains that come from utilizing its distinctive competencies. Consequently, it has to cope with the bureaucratic costs that arise both from the number of business units in its portfolio *and* from coordination among business units. Although it is true that related diversified companies can create value in more ways than unrelated companies, they also have to bear higher bureaucratic costs to do so. These higher costs may cancel the higher benefits, making the strategy no more profitable than one of unrelated diversification.

How then does a company choose between these strategies? The choice depends on a comparison of the benefits of each strategy against the bureaucratic costs of pursuing it. It pays a company to pursue related diversification when (1) the company's competencies can be applied across a greater number of industries and (2) the company does have superior strategic capabilities that allow it to keep bureaucratic costs under close control—perhaps by encouraging entrepreneurship or by developing a value-creating organizational culture. Using the same logic, it pays a company to pursue unrelated diversification when (1) each business unit's functional competencies have few useful applications across industries, but the company's top managers are skilled at raising the profitability of poorly run businesses, and (2) the company's managers have good organizational design skills to build distinctive competencies and keep bureaucratic costs in control and even to reduce them.

● The Web of Corporate-Level Strategy

Finally, it is important to note that while some companies may choose to pursue a strategy of related or unrelated diversification, there is nothing that stops them from pursuing both strategies at the same time—*as well as all the other corporate-level strategies we have discussed.* The purpose of corporate-level strategy is to increase long-term profitability. A company should pursue any and all strategies as long as strategic managers have weighed the advantages and disadvantages of those strategies and arrived at a multibusiness model that justifies them. Figure 10.6 shows how Sony has entered into industries that have led it to pursue various strategies.

First, Sony's core business is its electronic consumer products business, which is well known for its generic distinctive competencies of innovation and marketing

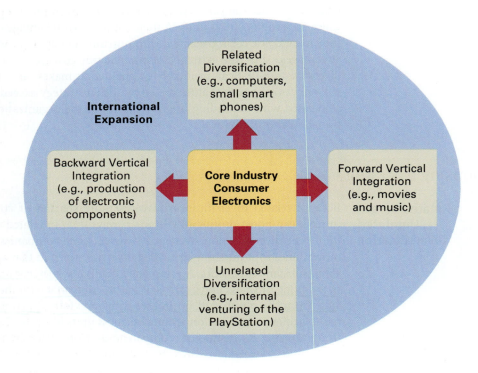

(it has one of the best-known brand names in the world). To protect the quality of its electronic products, Sony manufactures a high percentage of the component parts for its televisions, DVD players, and so on, and in this sense, it has pursued a strategy of backward vertical integration. Sony also engages in forward vertical integration: after having acquired Columbia Pictures and MGM in 2004, it now operates in the movie industry and has opened a chain of Sony stores in exclusive shopping malls. Sony also shared and leveraged its distinctive competencies by developing its own business units that operate in the computer and smart phone industries, a strategy of related diversification. Finally, in deciding to enter the home videogame industry and developing its Playstation to compete with Nintendo, it is also pursuing a strategy of unrelated diversification. Today, this division contributes more to Sony's total profits than its core electronics business.

While Sony has had enormous success pursuing all these strategies in the past, its profitability has fallen in the 2000s. Analysts claim that its multibusiness model, which led it to diversify extensively and focus on innovating high-quality products, led it to neglect its cost structure. They also claim that its strategy of giving each business unit great autonomy has led each unit to pursue its own goals at the expense of the company's multibusiness model. Sony's escalating bureaucratic costs have been draining its profitability and slowing innovation, which has allowed competitors like Samsung to catch up and even overtake it in areas like cell phones and flat-screen LCDs. Sony has been responding to these problems: it has taken major steps to reduce bureaucratic costs, speed innovation, and lower its cost structure, including exiting industries like PDAs and videocassette recorders. The next few years will show whether the company has been able to better implement its corporate strategies to improve its profitability.

Entering New Industries: Internal New Ventures

Having discussed all the corporate-level strategies that managers use to formulate the multibusiness model, we now examine the three main vehicles used to enter new industries: internal new ventures, acquisitions, and joint ventures. In this section, we look at the pros and cons of using internal new ventures. In the following sections, we look at acquisitions and joint ventures.

● The Attractions of Internal New Venturing

Internal new venturing is typically used to implement corporate-level strategies when a company possesses one or more generic distinctive competencies in its core business model that can be leveraged or recombined to enter a new industry. **Internal new venturing** is the process of transferring resources to and creating a new business unit or division in a new industry. As a rule, companies whose business model is based on using their technology to innovate new kinds of products for related markets or industries tend to favor internal new venturing as a way to enter a new market or industry. Thus, technology-based companies that pursue related diversification, like DuPont, which has created new markets with products such as cellophane, nylon, Freon, and Teflon, tend to use internal new venturing. 3M has a near-legendary knack for creating new or improved products from internally generated ideas and then establishing a new business unit to create the business model that enables it to dominate a new market (see Strategy in Action 10.1). Similarly, HP moved into computers and peripherals through internal new venturing.

A company may also use internal venturing to enter a newly emerging or embryonic industry—one in which no company has yet developed the competencies or business model that give it a dominant position in that industry. This was Monsanto's situation in 1979 when it contemplated entering the biotechnology field to produce herbicides and pest-resistant crop seeds. The biotechnology field was young at that time, and there were no incumbent companies focused on applying biotechnology to agricultural products. Monsanto internally ventured a new division to develop the required competencies necessary to enter and establish a strong competitive position in this newly emerging industry.

● **Pitfalls of New Ventures**

Despite the popularity of internal new venturing, there is a high risk of failure. Research suggests that somewhere between 33% and 60% of all new products that reach the marketplace do not generate an adequate economic return,[21] and most of these products were the result of internal new ventures. Three reasons are often put forward to explain the relatively high failure rate of internal new ventures: (1) market entry on too small a scale, (2) poor commercialization of the new-venture product, and (3) poor corporate management of the new-venture division.[22]

SCALE OF ENTRY Research suggests that large-scale entry into a new industry is often a critical precondition for the success of a new venture. This means that in the short run, large-scale entry requires a substantial capital investment to develop the product—and thus the prospect of substantial losses. But in the long run, which can be as long as five to twelve years depending on the industry, such a large investment results in far greater returns than if a company enters on a small scale and limits its investment to reduce its potential losses.[23] Large-scale entrants can more rapidly realize scale economies, build brand loyalty, and gain access to distribution channels, all of which increase the probability of a new venture's success. In contrast, small-scale entrants may find themselves handicapped by high costs due to a lack of scale economies and a lack of market presence that limits their ability to build brand loyalty and gain access to distribution channels. These scale effects are particularly significant when a company is entering an established industry where incumbent companies do possess scale economies, brand loyalty, and access to distribution channels. Now, the new entrant has to make a major investment to succeed.

Figure 10.7 plots the relationship between scale of entry and profitability over time for successful small-scale and large-scale ventures. The figure shows that successful small-scale entry is associated with lower initial losses but that, in the long

Scale of Entry Versus Profitability for Small-Scale and Large-Scale Ventures

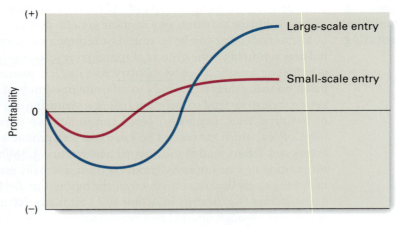

run, large-scale entry generates greater returns. However, because of the costs of large-scale entry and the huge potential losses if the venture fails, many companies make the mistake of choosing a small-scale entry strategy, which often means they fail to build the market share necessary for long-term success.

COMMERCIALIZATION   Many internal new ventures are driven by the use of new or high technology to make better products. But to be commercially successful, the products must be developed with customer requirements in mind. Many internal new ventures fail when a company ignores the needs of customers in a market and instead becomes blinded by the technological possibilities of a new product.[24] Thus, a new venture may fail because it is marketing a product based on a technology for which there is no demand or because the company fails to commercialize or position the product correctly in the market.

For example, consider the desktop computer marketed by NeXT, the company started by the founder of Apple, Steven Jobs. The NeXT system failed to gain market share because the computer incorporated an array of expensive technologies that consumers simply did not want, such as optical disk drives and hi-fidelity sound. The optical disk drives, in particular, turned off customers because they made it tough to switch work from a PC with a floppy drive to a NeXT machine with an optical drive. In other words, NeXT failed because its founder was so dazzled by leading-edge technology that he ignored customer needs. However, Jobs redeemed himself when he successfully commercialized Apple's iPod, which dominates the MP3 player market today.

POOR IMPLEMENTATION   Managing the new-venture process and division raises difficult organizational issues.[25] For example, one common mistake some companies make is to try to increase their chance of making a successful product by establishing many different internal new-venture divisions at the same time. This shotgun approach of spreading the risks among divisions places great demands on a company's cash flow and can result in the best ventures being starved of the cash they need to succeed.[26] Another common mistake is the failure of corporate managers to carefully develop upfront all the aspects of the business model that will be needed for the new venture to succeed—and to include scientists in the model-building process. Taking a team of research scientists and giving them the resources they need to do research in their favorite field may produce novel results, but these results may have little strategic or commercial value. Managers must clarify how and why the project will lead to a product that has a competitive advantage and establish strategic objectives and a timetable to manage the venture until the product reaches the market. Failure to anticipate the time and costs involved in the new-venture process constitutes a further mistake. Many companies have unrealistic expectations regarding the time frame, expecting profits to flow in quickly. Research suggests that some companies operate with a philosophy of killing new businesses if they do not turn a profit by the end of the third year, which is clearly an unrealistic view given that it can take five to twelve years before a venture generates substantial profits.

● **Guidelines for Successful Internal New Venturing**

To avoid the pitfalls discussed above, a company should adopt a well-thought-out, structured approach to manage internal new venturing. New venturing begins with R&D, *exploratory research* (the "R" in R&D) to advance basic science and technology and *development research* (the "D" in R&D) to find and refine the commercial applications for a technology. Companies with a strong track record of internal new venturing excel at both kinds of R&D: they help to advance basic science and

354 PART 3 Strategies

then they find commercial applications for it.[27] To advance basic science, it is important for companies to (1) have strong links with universities, where much of the scientific knowledge that underlies new technologies is discovered, and (2) to make sure that significant research funds are under the control of researchers who can pursue blue-sky projects that might ultimately yield unexpected and commercially valuable technologies and products. For example, 3M has close links with several universities, including the University of Minnesota in its hometown, and funds basic research at those universities. As already mentioned, 3M's researchers spend 15% of their time on projects of their own choosing, many of which are basic research projects.

However, if the pursuit of basic research is all that a company does well, it will probably generate few successful commercial ventures. To translate good science into good products, it is critical that a major proportion of R&D funding be directed toward commercial ventures. Companies can take a number of steps to ensure that this happens. First, many companies place much of the funding for research in the hands of business unit managers who are responsible for narrowing down and then selecting the small number of research projects they believe have the best chance of a significant commercial payoff. Second, to make effective use of its R&D skills, a company's top managers must continually spell out the strategic objectives in its business model and communicate them clearly to scientists and engineers. Research must be in the pursuit of strategic goals.[28] For example, one of the biggest research projects at Microsoft has been language recognition software because a central objective of the company is to make computers easy to use. Researchers reason that if computers can understand spoken language, commands can be input by voice rather than through a keyboard, thus making computers easier to use and strengthening the Windows platform.

A company must also foster close links between R&D and marketing to increase the probability of a new product's commercial success, because this is the best way to ensure that research projects address the needs of the market. Also, a company should foster close links between R&D and manufacturing to ensure that it has the ability to make a proposed new product. Many companies successfully integrate the activities of different functions by creating cross-functional project teams to oversee the development of new products, from their inception to their market introduction. This approach can significantly reduce the time this process takes. For example, while R&D is working on the design, manufacturing is setting up facilities and marketing is developing a campaign to show customers how much the new product will benefit them.

Finally, because large-scale entry often leads to greater long-term profits, a company can promote the success of internal new venturing by thinking big. Well in advance, a company should construct efficient-scale manufacturing facilities and establish a large marketing program to develop a campaign for building a market presence and brand loyalty quickly. Corporate managers should not panic; they should accept that there will be initial losses and realize that, as long as market share is expanding, the product will eventually succeed.

Entering New Industries: Acquisitions

In Chapter 9, we explained that acquisitions are the main vehicle that companies use to implement a horizontal integration strategy. They are also a principal way companies enter new industries to pursue vertical integration and diversification. In the

Opening Case, we saw how Tyco acquired many new businesses to pursue unrelated diversification; now, however, it is de-diversifying, so it is necessary to understand both the benefits and risks associated with using acquisitions to implement a corporate-level strategy.

● **The Attractions of Acquisitions**

Acquisitions are used to pursue vertical integration or diversification when a company lacks the distinctive competencies to compete in a new industry and therefore uses its capital to purchase an established company that has those competencies. A company is particularly likely to use acquisitions when it needs to move fast to establish a presence in an industry. Entering a new industry through internal venturing is a relatively slow process; acquisition is a much quicker way for a company to establish a significant market presence. A company can purchase a leading company with a strong competitive position in months rather than spend years building up a market leadership position through internal venturing. Thus, when speed is important, acquisition is the favored entry mode. Intel, for example, used acquisitions to build its communications chip business because it sensed that the market was developing very quickly and it would take too long to develop the required competencies internally (see Strategy in Action 10.2).

In addition, acquisitions are often perceived as somewhat less risky than internal new ventures primarily because they involve less commercial uncertainty. Because of the risks associated with an internal new venture, it is difficult to predict its future profitability and cash flows. In contrast, when a company makes an acquisition, it is acquiring a company with a reputation whose market share and profitability can be easily evaluated.

Finally, acquisitions are an attractive way to enter an industry that is protected by high barriers to entry. Recall from Chapter 2 that barriers to entry arise from factors associated with product differentiation (brand loyalty), absolute cost advantages, and economies of scale. When these barriers are substantial, a company may find it very difficult to enter an industry through internal new venturing because it will have to construct large-scale manufacturing facilities and invest in a massive advertising campaign to establish brand loyalty—difficult goals that require large capital expenditures. In contrast, if a company acquires an established company in the industry, it can circumvent most entry barriers because it has acquired a market leader that already has substantial scale economies and brand loyalty. In general, the greater the barriers to entry, the more likely it is that acquisitions will be the favored entry mode.

● **Acquisition Pitfalls**

For these reasons, acquisitions have long been a popular vehicle for executing corporate-level strategies. As we mentioned earlier, however, despite this popularity, there is ample evidence that many acquisitions fail to add value for the acquiring company and, indeed, often end up dissipating value. For example, a study by KPMG, an accounting and management consulting company, looked at 700 large acquisitions and found that, although some 30% of these actually created value for the acquiring company, 31% destroyed value, and the remainder had little impact.[29] A wealth of evidence from academic research suggests that many acquisitions fail to realize their anticipated benefits.[30] In a major study of the postacquisition performance of acquired companies, David Ravenscraft and Mike Scherer concluded that the profitability and market shares of acquired companies often declined after acquisition.[31] This evidence suggests that many acquisitions destroy rather than create value.

Acquisitions may fail to create value for four reasons: (1) companies often experience difficulties when trying to integrate different organizational structures and cultures,

(2) companies overestimate the potential economic benefits from an acquisition, (3) acquisitions tend to be very expensive, and (4) companies often do not adequately screen their acquisition targets.

INTEGRATING THE ACQUIRED COMPANY Once an acquisition has been made, the acquiring company has to integrate the acquired company and combine it with its own organizational structure and culture. Integration involves the adoption of common management and financial control systems, the joining together of operations from the acquired and the acquiring company, the establishment of bureaucratic mechanisms to share information and personnel, and the need to create a common culture. Experience has shown that many problems can occur as companies attempt to integrate their activities.

After an acquisition, many acquired companies experience high management turnover because their employees do not like the acquiring company's way of operating—its structure and culture.[32] Research suggests that the loss of management talent and expertise, to say nothing of the damage from constant tension between the businesses, can materially harm the performance of the acquired unit.[33] Strategy in Action 10.3 describes what happened at Boston Co. after it was acquired by Mellon Bank.

OVERESTIMATING ECONOMIC BENEFITS Even when companies find it easy to integrate their activities, they often overestimate the potential for creating value by joining together different businesses. They overestimate the competitive advantages that can be derived from the acquisition and so pay more for the target company than it is worth. Richard Roll has attributed this tendency to hubris on the part of top management. According to Roll, top managers typically overestimate their ability to create value from an acquisition primarily because rising to the top of a corporation has given them an exaggerated sense of their own capabilities.[34] Coca-Cola's acquisition of a number of medium-sized winemaking companies illustrates this situation. Reasoning that a beverage is a beverage, Coca-Cola thought it would be able to use its distinctive competence in marketing to dominate the U.S. wine industry. But after buying three wine companies and enduring seven years of marginal profits, Coca-Cola finally conceded that wine and soft drinks are very different products, with different kinds of appeal, pricing systems, and distribution networks. It subsequently sold the wine operations to Joseph E. Seagram & Sons at a substantial loss when adjusted for inflation.[35]

THE EXPENSE OF ACQUISITIONS Perhaps the most important reason for the failure of acquisitions is that the acquisition of companies whose stock is publicly traded tends to be very expensive—and the expense of the acquisition cancels the prospective value-creating gains from the acquisition described earlier. One reason is that the management of the target company is not likely to agree to an acquisition unless there is a substantial premium over its current market value. Another reason is that the stockholders of the acquired company are unlikely to sell their stock unless they are paid a significant premium over its current market value—and premiums tend to run 25% to 50% over a company's stock price prior to a takeover bid. Therefore, the acquiring company must be able to increase the value of the acquired company after it has been integrated by at least the same amount to make the acquisition pay: a tall order. This is a major reason why acquisitions are frequently unprofitable for the acquiring company.

Strategy in Action

10.3

Postacquisition Problems at Mellon Bank

In the search for a profitable way to expand his company's business, Frank Cahouet, the CEO of Philadelphia-based Mellon Bank, decided to reduce the large swings in Mellon's earnings (caused by changes in interest rates) by diversifying into financial services to gain access to a steady flow of fee-based income from money management operations. As part of this strategy, he acquired Boston Co. for $1.45 billion. Boston Co. is a high-profile money management company that manages investments for major institutional clients, such as state and corporate pension funds. Mellon followed up its Boston Co. acquisition with the acquisition of mutual fund provider Dreyfus Corp. for $1.7 billion. As a result, almost half of Mellon's income was now generated from fee-based financial services.

Problems at Boston Co. began to surface soon after the Mellon acquisition. From the beginning, corporate cultures clashed. At Mellon, many managers arrived at their mundane offices by 7 A.M. and put in twelve-hour days for modest pay by banking industry standards. They were also accustomed to Frank Cahouet's management style, which emphasized cost containment and frugality. Boston Co. managers also put in twelve-hour days, but they expected considerable autonomy, flexible work schedules, high pay, ample perks, and large performance bonuses. In most years, the top twenty executives at Boston Co. earned between $750,000 and $1 million each. Mellon executives who visited the Boston Co. unit were dumbstruck by its country club atmosphere and opulence. In its move to streamline Boston Co., Mellon insisted that Boston Co. cut expenses and introduced new regulations for restricting travel, entertainment, and perks.

Things started to go wrong when the Wisconsin state pension fund complained to Mellon of lower returns on a portfolio run by Boston Co. Mellon was forced to liquidate the portfolio and take a $130 million charge against earnings; it also fired the responsible portfolio manager, claiming that this manager was making "unauthorized trades." At Boston Co., however, many managers saw Mellon's action as violating the guarantees of operating autonomy that it had given Boston Co. at the time of the acquisition. They blamed Mellon for prematurely liquidating a portfolio whose strategy, they claimed, Mellon executives had approved and that, moreover, could still prove a winner if interest rates fell (which they subsequently did).

Infuriated by Mellon's interference, seven of Boston Co.'s asset unit managers, including the unit's CEO, Desmond Heathwood, proposed a management buyout to Mellon. This unit was one of the gems in Boston Co.'s crown, with over $26 billion in assets under management. Heathwood had been openly disdainful of Mellon's bankers, believing that they were out of their league in the investment business. Mellon rejected the buyout proposal, and Heathwood promptly left to start his own investment management company. A few days later, Mellon asked employees at Boston Co. to sign employment contracts that limited their ability to leave and work for Heathwood's competing business. Thirteen senior employees refused to sign and then quit to join Heathwood's new money management operation.

The defection of Heathwood and his colleagues was followed by a series of high-profile client defections. The Arizona State Retirement System, for example, pulled $1 billion out of Mellon and transferred it to Heathwood's firm, and the Fresno County Retirement System transferred $400 million in assets over to Heathwood. As one client stated, "We have a relationship with the Boston Co. that goes back over 30 years, and the people who worked on the account are the people who left—so we left too."

Reflecting on the episode, Frank Cahouet noted, "We've clearly been hurt. . . . But this episode is very manageable. We are not going to lose our momentum." Others were not so sure. In this incident, they saw yet another example of how difficult it can be to merge two divergent corporate cultures and how the management turnover that results from trying such a merger can deal a serious blow to any attempt to create value out of an acquisition. In 2006, Mellon merged with the Bank of New York to create a new financial powerhouse. Only time will tell if this merger results in yet another round of the kind of problems just discussed.[c]

The problem for the acquiring company is that the stock price of the acquisition target gets bid up enormously during the acquisition process. This frequently occurs in the case of a bidding contest where two or more companies simultaneously bid to acquire the target company. In addition, when many acquisitions are happening in a particular sector or industry, the price of *potential* target companies are bid up by investors who speculate that a bid for these companies will be made at some future point, which further increases the cost of making acquisitions. This happened in the telecommunications sector when, to make sure they could meet the needs of customers who were demanding leading-edge equipment, many large companies went on acquisition binges. Cisco Systems, Nortel, Corning, and Lucent all raced each other to buy smaller companies that were developing new telecommunications equipment. The result was that stock prices for these companies got bid up by investors. When the telecommunications boom turned to bust, the acquiring companies found that they had vastly overpaid for their acquisitions and had to take enormous accounting losses.

INADEQUATE PREACQUISITION SCREENING   As the problems of these companies suggest, top managers often do a poor job of preacquisition screening, that is, evaluating the value-creating potential of potential acquisitions. After researching acquisitions made by twenty different companies, a study by Philippe Haspeslagh and David Jemison concluded that one reason for acquisition failure is managers' decision to acquire other firms without thoroughly analyzing the potential benefits and costs.[36] Indeed, in many cases after an acquisition has been completed, many acquiring companies discover that instead of buying a well-run business, they have purchased a troubled organization. Moreover, companies often have to take on an enormous amount of debt to fund these acquisitions, and they frequently are unable to pay it once the weaknesses of the acquired company's business model become clear.

● **Guidelines for Successful Acquisition**

To avoid pitfalls and make successful acquisitions, companies need to take a structured approach to purchasing companies based on four components: (1) target identification and preacquisition screening, (2) bidding strategy, (3) integration, and (4) learning from experience.[37]

IDENTIFICATION AND SCREENING   Thorough preacquisition screening increases a company's knowledge about a potential takeover target and lessens the risk of purchasing a potential problem business—one with a weak business model. It also leads to a more realistic assessment of the problems involved in executing a particular acquisition so that a company can plan how to integrate the new business and blend the organizational structures and cultures. The screening process should begin with a detailed assessment of the strategic rationale for making the acquisition, an identification of the kind of company that would make an ideal acquisition candidate, and a thorough analysis of the strengths and weaknesses of its business model by comparing it to other possible acquisition targets.

Indeed, an acquiring company should scan potential acquisition candidates and evaluate each according to a detailed set of criteria, focusing on (1) its financial position, (2) its distinctive competencies and competitive advantage, (3) the changing industry boundaries, (4) its management capabilities, and (5) its corporate culture. Such an evaluation will help the company identify the strengths and weaknesses of each candidate and the potential economies of scale and scope between the acquiring and the acquired companies. It will also help it to recognize potential integration problems and the problems that might exist when it is necessary to integrate the corporate cultures of the acquiring and the acquired companies. In 2004, for example, Microsoft and SAP, the world's leading provider of enterprise resource planning software, sat down together to discuss a possible acquisition by Microsoft. Both companies decided that even though there was a strong strategic rationale for a merger—together they would dominate the global computing market for most large global companies—the problems of creating an organizational structure that could successfully integrate their hundreds of thousands of employees throughout the world and blend two very different corporate cultures were insurmountable.

Once a company has reduced the list of potential acquisition candidates to the most favored one or two, it needs to contact expert third parties, such as investment bankers like Goldman Sachs and Merrill Lynch, that may be able to provide valuable insights about the attractiveness of the potential acquisition and that will also handle the many issues surrounding the acquisition, such as the process of establishing the bidding strategy for acquiring the company's stock.

BIDDING STRATEGY   The objective of the bidding strategy is to reduce the price that a company must pay for the target company. The most effective way that a company can acquire another is to make a friendly takeover bid, which means the two companies work out an amicable way to merge the two companies that satisfies the needs of stockholders and top managers. A friendly takeover helps prevent speculators from bidding up stock prices. By contrast, in a hostile bid, such as the one between Oracle and PeopleSoft, the price of the target company is often bid up by speculators who expect that the offer price will be raised by the acquirer or that another company, sometimes called a white knight, might come in with a counteroffer more favorable to the management of the target company.

Another essential element of a good bidding strategy is timing. For example, Hanson PLC, one of the most successful companies to pursue unrelated diversification, searched for essentially sound companies suffering from short-term problems due to cyclical industry factors or one underperforming division. Such companies are typically undervalued by the stock market and so can be acquired without the standard 25% to 50% stock premium. With good timing, a company can make a bargain purchase. Tyco also followed this practice; it bought essentially sound companies that were underperforming their peers because of short-term problems and then helped them establish a competitive business model.

INTEGRATION   Despite good screening and bidding, an acquisition will fail unless the acquiring company possesses the essential organizational design skills needed to integrate the acquired company into its operations and so quickly develop a viable multibusiness model. Integration should center on the source of the potential strategic advantages of the acquisition—for instance, opportunities to share marketing, manufacturing, logistics, R&D, financial, or management resources. Integration should also involve steps to eliminate any duplication of facilities or functions. In addition, any unwanted business units of the acquired company should be divested.

LEARNING FROM EXPERIENCE   Research suggests that, although many acquisitions do fail to create value for the acquiring company, companies that acquire many companies over time become expert in this process and so can generate significant value from their acquisitions.[38] One reason may be that they learn from their experience and develop a system of how to execute an acquisition most efficiently and effectively. Tyco, profiled in the Opening Case, did not make hostile acquisitions; it audited the accounts of the target company in detail, acquired companies to help it achieve a critical mass in an industry, moved quickly to realize cost savings after an acquisition, promoted managers one or two layers down to lead the newly acquired entity, and introduced profit-based incentive pay systems in the acquired unit.[39]

Entering New Industries: Joint Ventures

Joint ventures are most commonly used to enter a new industry that is an embryonic or growth industry. Suppose a company is contemplating creating a new venture division in an embryonic industry. Such a move involves substantial risks and costs because the company must establish from scratch the set of value chain activities needed to operate in that new market. On the other hand, an acquisition can be a dangerous proposition because there is no established leader in the emerging industry, and if there is a leading company, it will be extremely expensive to purchase.

In this situation, a joint venture often becomes the most appropriate vehicle because it allows a company to share the risks and costs associated with establishing a new business unit with another company. This is especially true when the companies share complementary skills or distinctive competencies. Now a joint venture with another company may increase the probability of success. Consider the 50/50 equity joint venture formed between UTC and Dow Chemical to build plastic-based composite parts for the aerospace industry. UTC was already involved in the aerospace industry (it builds Sikorsky helicopters), and Dow Chemical had skills in the development and manufacture of plastic-based composites. The alliance called for UTC to contribute its advanced aerospace skills and Dow to contribute its skills in developing and manufacturing plastic-based composites. Through the joint venture, both companies would become involved in new activities and would be able to realize the benefits associated with related diversification without having to merge their activities into one company or bear the costs and risks of developing new products on their own. Thus, both companies would enjoy the value-creating benefits of entering a new market without having to bear the increased bureaucratic costs.

Although in some situations joint ventures can benefit both partner companies, they have three main drawbacks. First, while a joint venture allows companies to share the risks and costs of developing a new business, it also requires that they share in the profits if it succeeds. So, if it turns out later that one partner's skills are more important than the other's, that partner will have to give away profits to the other party because of the 50/50 agreement. This can create conflict and sour the working relationship as time goes on. Second, the joint venture partners may have different business philosophies, time horizons, or investment preferences, and so once again substantial problems can arise. Conflicts over how to run the joint venture can tear it apart and result in business failure.

Third, a company that enters into a joint venture always runs the risk of giving critical know-how away to its partner, which might then take that know-how and use it to compete with the other partner in the future. For example, having gained access to Dow's expertise in plastic-based composites, UTC might have dissolved the alliance and produced these materials on its own. As we discussed in the last chapter, such a risk can be minimized if Dow gets a credible commitment from UTC, which is what it did. UTC had to make an expensive asset-specific investment to make the products that the joint venture was formed to create.

Restructuring

Many companies expand into new markets and industries to increase profitability; however, sometimes they also need to exit markets and industries to achieve the same goal or even split up their existing businesses into separate companies, like Tyco did. **Restructuring** is the process of reorganizing and divesting business units and exiting markets and industries to refocus on core distinctive competencies.[40] Why are so many companies restructuring and how do they do it?

● **Why Restructure?**   One main reason that diversified companies have restructured in recent years is that the stock market has valued their stock at a **diversification discount,** meaning that the stock of highly diversified companies is valued lower, relative to their earnings, than the stock of less diversified enterprises.[41] Investors see highly diversified companies as less attractive investments for four reasons. First, as we discussed earlier, investors often feel these companies, like Tyco, no longer have a multibusiness model that justifies their participation in many different industries. Second, the complexity of the consolidated financial statements of highly diversified enterprises disguises the performance of its individual business units and thus whether the multibusiness model is succeeding. As a result, investors perceive the company as being riskier than companies that operate in one industry and whose competitive advantage and financial statements are more easily understood. Given this situation, restructuring can be seen as an attempt to boost the returns to shareholders by splitting up a multibusiness company like Tyco into separate and independent parts.

The third reason for the diversification discount is that many investors have learned from experience that managers often have a tendency to pursue too much diversification or do it for the wrong reasons; they do not diversify to increase profitability.[42] Some top managers pursue growth for its own sake. They are empire builders who expand the scope of their company to the point where bureaucratic costs exceed the additional value such diversification creates. Restructuring thus becomes a response to declining financial performance brought about by overdiversification.

A final factor leading to restructuring is that innovations in strategic management have diminished the advantages of vertical integration or diversification. For example, a few decades ago, there was little understanding of how long-term cooperative relationships, or strategic alliances, between a company and its suppliers could be a viable alternative to vertical integration. Most companies considered only two alternatives for managing the supply chain: vertical integration or competitive bidding. As we discussed in Chapter 9, in many situations, long-term cooperative relationships can create the most value, especially because they avoid the need to incur bureaucratic costs or dispense with market discipline. As this strategic innovation has spread throughout the business world, the relative advantages of vertical integration have declined.

Summary of Chapter

1. Managers often first consider diversification when their company is generating free cash flow, which are financial resources in excess of those necessary to maintain a competitive advantage in the company's original, or core, business.

2. A diversified company can create value by (a) transferring competencies among existing businesses, (b) leveraging competencies to create new businesses, (c) sharing resources to realize economies of scope, (d) using product bundling, (e) using diversification as a means of managing rivalry in one or more industries, and (f) exploiting general organizational competencies that enhance the performance of all business units within a diversified company. The bureaucratic costs of diversification are a function of the number of independent business units within the company and the extent of the coordination needed among those business units.

3. Diversification motivated by a desire to pool risks or achieve greater growth is often associated with the dissipation of value.

4. Companies use three vehicles to enter new industries: internal new venturing, acquisition, and joint ventures.

5. Internal new venturing is typically used to enter a new industry when a company has a set of valuable competencies in its existing businesses that can be leveraged or recombined to enter the new business or industry.

6. Many internal ventures fail because of entry on too small a scale, poor commercialization, and poor corporate management of the internal venture process. Guarding against failure involves a structured approach toward project selection and management, integration of R&D and marketing to improve commercialization of a venture idea, and entry on a significant scale.

7. Acquisitions are often the best way to enter a new industry when the company lacks the important competencies (resources and capabilities) required to compete in a new market, and it can purchase a company that does have has those competencies at a reasonable price. Acquisitions also tend to be favored when the barriers to entry into the target industry are high and the company is unwilling to accept the time frame, development costs, and risks of internal new venturing.

8. Many acquisitions fail because of poor postacquisition integration, overestimation of the value that can be created from an acquisition, the high cost of acquisition, and poor preacquisition screening. Guarding against acquisition failure requires structured screening, good bidding strategies, positive attempts to integrate the acquired company into the organization of the acquiring one, and learning from experience.

9. Joint ventures are used most often to enter a new industry when (a) the risks and costs associated with setting up a new business unit are more than the company is willing to assume on its own and (b) the company can increase the probability of successfully establishing a new business by teaming up with another company that has skills and assets complementing its own.

10. Restructuring is often a response to (a) an inadequate multibusiness model, (b) the complexity of consolidated financial statements, (c) excessive diversification due to top managers' empire building, and (d) innovations in the strategic management process that have reduced the advantages of vertical integration and diversification.

Discussion Questions

1. When is a company likely to choose related diversification and when is it likely to choose unrelated diversification? Discuss with reference to an electronics manufacturer and an ocean shipping company.

2. Under what circumstances might it be best to enter a new market or industry through acquisition, and under what circumstances might internal new venturing be the preferred entry mode?

3. Imagine that IBM has decided to diversify into the cellular telecommunications provider business. What entry vehicle would you recommend that the company pursue? Why?

4. Look at Honeywell's portfolio of businesses (described in Honeywell's 10-K statements, which can be accessed on the Web at www.honeywell.com). How many different industries is Honeywell involved in? Would you describe Honeywell as a related or unrelated diversification company? How do you think that Honeywell's diversification strategy increases profitability?

Practicing Strategic Management

SMALL-GROUP EXERCISE
Dun & Bradstreet

Break into small groups of three to five, appoint one group member as a spokesperson who will communicate your findings to the class, and then read the following news release from Dun & Bradstreet. On the basis of this information, identify the strategic rationale for the split and evaluate how the split might affect the performance of the three successor companies. If you were a stockholder in the old Dun & Bradstreet Corporation, would you approve of this split? Why?

Dun & Bradstreet CEO Robert E. Weissman today announced a sweeping strategy that will transform the 155-year-old business information giant into three publicly traded, global corporations. "This important action is designed to increase shareholder value by unlocking D&B's substantial underlying franchise strengths," said Weissman.

Building on preeminent Dun & Bradstreet businesses, the reorganization establishes three independent companies focused on high-growth information markets; financial information services; and consumer-product market research.

"Since the 1800s, D&B has grown by effectively managing a portfolio of businesses and gaining economies of scale," stated Weissman. "But the velocity of change in information markets has dramatically altered the rules of business survival. Today, market focus and speed are the primary drivers of competitive advantage. This plan is our blueprint for success in the 21st century," said Weissman.

The plan, approved today at a special meeting of D&B's board of directors, calls for D&B to create three separate companies by spinning off two of its businesses to shareholders. "D&B is the leader in business information," said Weissman. "By freeing our companies to tightly focus on our core vertical markets, we can more rapidly leverage this leadership position into emerging growth areas." The three new companies are:

- Cognizant Corporation, a new high-growth company, including IMS International, the leading global supplier of marketing information to the pharmaceutical and healthcare industries; Nielsen Media Research, the leader in audience measurement for electronic media; and Gartner Group, the premier provider of advisory services to high-tech users, vendors and suppliers, in which Cognizant will hold a majority interest.

- The Dun & Bradstreet Corporation, consisting of Dun & Bradstreet Information Services, the world's largest source of business-to-business marketing and commercial-credit information; Moody's Investors Service, a global leader in rating debt; and Reuben H. Donnelley, a premier provider of Yellow Pages marketing and publishing.

- A. C. Nielsen, the global leader in marketing information for the fast-moving consumer packaged goods industry.

"These three separate companies will tailor their strategies to the unique demands of their markets, determining investments, capital structures and policies that will strengthen their respective global capabilities. This plan also clarifies D&B from an investor's perspective by grouping the businesses into three logical investment categories, each with distinct risk/reward profiles," said Weissman.

The Dun & Bradstreet Corporation is the world's largest marketer of information, software and services for business decision-making, with worldwide revenue of $4.9 billion in 1994.

ARTICLE FILE 10

Find an example of a diversified company that made an acquisition that apparently failed to create any value. Identify and critically evaluate the rationale that top management used to justify the acquisition when it was made. Explain why the acquisition subsequently failed.

STRATEGIC MANAGEMENT PROJECT
Module 10

This module requires you to assess your company's use of acquisitions, internal new ventures, and joint ventures as strategies for entering a new business area or as attempts to restructure its portfolio of businesses.

A. **Your company has entered a new industry during the past decade.**
   1. Pick one new industry that your company has entered during the past ten years.
   2. Identify its rationale for entering this industry.
   3. Identify your company's strategy for entering this industry.
   4. Evaluate the rationale for using this particular entry strategy. Do you think that this was the best entry strategy to use? Justify your answer.

5. Do you think that the addition of this business unit to the company has added or dissipated value? Again, justify your answer.

B. **Your company has restructured its corporate portfolio during the past decade.**

1. Identify your company's rationale for pursuing a restructuring strategy.
2. Pick one industry that your company has exited during the past ten years.
3. Identify your company's strategy for exiting this particular industry. Do you think that this was the best exit strategy to use? Justify your answer.
4. In general, do you think that exiting from this industry has been in the company's best interest?

ETHICS EXERCISE

For the past few years, YCN (Your Communication Network) Inc. had been on a massive buying spree, acquiring companies one after another. To outsiders, YCN looked successful, but those inside the company were beginning to wonder if the company's situation was actually a dangerous one. Scott, who worked in accounting, had just discovered what he thought was a major accounting error. It seemed the company might have illegally recorded $2 billion in capital expenditures, thereby increasing cash flow and profit.

If Scott was correct, YCN had reported the erroneous $2 billion to cover up the company's true net losses. As he understood it, capital expenditures could be deducted over a long period of time, while expenses would be immediately subtracted from revenue. Because of the way the books had been handled, investors had been buying up the company's stock, causing stock prices to rise. If Scott had truly uncovered accounting fraud, many people would be in for a shock.

Scott knew that something had to be done, but it was obvious that this fraud had been perpetrated from within. Because it was an internal matter, Scott didn't know where to turn. What should he do?

1. Define the ethical issue presented in this case.
2. What would you do if you were in Scott's position?
3. If Scott is correct, what can the company do to correct the issue?

CLOSING CASE

United Technologies Has an "ACE in Its Pocket"

United Technologies Corporation (UTC), based in Hartford, Connecticut, is a *conglomerate*, a company that owns a wide variety of other companies that operate in different businesses and industries. Some of the companies in UTC's portfolio are more well known than UTC itself, such as Sikorsky Aircraft Corporation; Pratt & Whitney, the aircraft engine and component maker; Otis Elevator Company; Carrier air conditioning; and Chubb, the security and lock maker that UTC acquired in 2003. Today, investors frown upon companies like UTC that own and operate companies in widely different industries. There is a growing perception that managers can better manage a company's business model when the company operates as an independent or stand-alone entity. How can UTC justify holding all these companies together in a conglomerate? Why would this lead to a greater increase in their long-term profitability than if they operated as separate companies? In the last decade, the boards of directors and CEOs of many conglomerates, such as Greyhound-Dial, ITT Industries, and Textron, have realized that by holding diverse companies together, they were reducing, not increasing, the profitability of their companies. As a result, many conglomerates have been broken up and their companies spun off to allow them to operate as separate, independent entities.

UTC's CEO George David claims that he has created a unique and sophisticated multibusiness model that adds value across UTC's diverse businesses. David joined Otis Elevator as an assistant to its CEO in 1975, but within one year Otis was acquired by UTC, during a decade when "bigger is better" ruled corporate America and mergers and acquisitions, of whatever kind, were seen as the best way to grow profits. UTC sent David to manage its South American operations and later gave him responsibility for its Japanese operations. Otis had formed an alliance with Matsushita to develop an elevator for the Japanese market, and the resulting Elevonic 401, after being installed widely in Japanese buildings, proved to be a disaster. It broke down much more often than elevators made by other Japanese companies, and customers were concerned about its reliability and safety.

Matsushita was extremely embarrassed about the elevator's failure and assigned one of its leading total quality management (TQM) experts, Yuzuru Ito, to head a team of Otis engineers to find out why it performed so poorly. Under Ito's direction, all the employees—managers, designers, and production workers—who had produced the elevator analyzed why the elevators were malfunctioning. This intensive study led to a total redesign of the elevator, and when their new and improved elevator was launched worldwide, it met with great success. Otis's share of the global elevator market increased dramatically, and one result was that David was named president of UTC in 1992. He was given the responsibility to cut costs across the entire corporation, including its important Pratt & Whitney division, and his success in reducing UTC's cost structure and increasing its ROIC led to his appointment as CEO in 1994.

Now responsible for all of UTC's diverse companies, David decided that the best way to increase UTC's profitability, which had been falling, was to find ways to improve efficiency and quality in all its constituent companies. He convinced Ito to move to Hartford and take responsibility for championing the kinds of improvements that had by now transformed the Otis division, and Ito began to develop UTC's TQM system, which is known as Achieving Competitive Excellence (ACE).

ACE is a set of tasks and procedures that are used by employees from the shop floor to top management to analyze all aspects of the way a product is made. The goal is to find ways to improve quality and reliability, to lower the costs of making the product, and especially to find ways to make the next generation of a particular product perform better—in other words, to encourage technological innovation. David makes every employee in every function and at every level take responsibility for achieving the incremental, step-by-step gains that can result in innovative

and efficient products that enable a company to dominate its industry—to push back the value creation frontier.

David calls these techniques process disciplines, and he has used them to increase the performance of all UTC companies. Through these techniques, he has created the extra value for UTC that justifies it owning and operating such a diverse set of businesses. David's success can be seen in the performance that his company has achieved in the decade since he took control: he has quadrupled UTC's earnings per share, and in the first six months of 1994, profit grew by 25% to $1.4 billion, while sales increased by 26% to $18.3 billion. UTC has been in the top three performers of the companies that make up the Dow Jones industrial average for the last three years, and the company has consistently outperformed GE, another huge conglomerate, in its returns to investors.

David and his managers believe that the gains that can be achieved from UTC's process disciplines are never-ending because its own R&D—in which it invests over $2.5 billion a year—is constantly producing product innovations that can help all its businesses. Indeed, recognizing that its skills in creating process improvements are specific to manufacturing companies, UTC's strategy is to acquire only those companies that make products that can benefit from the use of its ACE program—hence, its Chubb acquisition. At the same time, David only invests in companies that have the potential to remain leading companies in their industries and so can charge above-average prices. His acquisitions strengthen the competencies of UTC's existing businesses. For example, he acquired a company called Sunderstrand, a leading aerospace and industrial systems company, and combined it with UTC's Hamilton aerospace division to create Hamilton Sunderstrand, which is now a major supplier to Boeing and makes products that command premium prices.

Case Discussion Questions

1. What kind of corporate-level strategy is UTC pursuing? What is UTC's multibusiness model, and in what ways does it create value?

2. What are the dangers and disadvantages of this business model?

3. Collect some recent information on UTC from sources like Yahoo! Finance. How successful has it been in pursuing its strategy?

Corporate Performance, Governance, and Business Ethics

OPENING CASE

The Rise and Fall of Dennis Kozlowski

Under the leadership of Dennis Kozlowski, who became CEO of Tyco in 1990, the company's revenues expanded from $3.1 billion to almost $40 billion. Most of this growth was due to a series of acquisitions that took Tyco into a diverse range of unrelated businesses. Tyco financed the acquisitions by taking on significant debt commitments, which exceeded $23 billion by 2002. As Tyco expanded, some questioned the company's ability to service its debt commitments and claimed that management was engaging in "accounting tricks" to pad its books and make the company appear more profitable than it actually was. These criticisms, which were ignored for several years, were finally shown to have some validity in 2002 when Kozlowski was forced out by the board and subsequently charged with tax evasion by federal authorities.

Among other charges, authorities claimed that Kozlowski treated Tyco as his personal treasury, drawing on company funds to purchase an expensive Manhattan apartment and a world-class art collection that he obviously thought were befitting of the CEO of a major corporation. Kozlowski even used company funds to help pay for an expensive birthday party for his wife—which included toga-clad women, gladiators, a naked-woman-with-exploding-breasts birthday cake, and a version of Michelangelo's David that peed vodka. Kozlowski was replaced by a company outsider, Edward Breen. In 2003, Tyco took a $1.5 billion charge against earnings for accounting errors made during the Kozlowski era (i.e., Tyco's profits had been overstated by $1.5 billion during Kozlowski's tenure). Breen also set about dismantling parts of the empire that Kozlowski had built and divested several businesses.

After a lengthy criminal trial, in June 2005, Dennis Kozlowski and Mark Swartz, the former chief financial officer of Tyco, were convicted of twenty-three counts of grand larceny, conspiracy, securities fraud, and falsifying business records in connection with what prosecutors described as the systematic looting of millions of dollars from the conglomerate (Kozlowski was found guilty of looting $90 million from Tyco). Both were sentenced to jail for a minimum of eight years. As for Tyco, CEO Ed Breen announced in 2006 that the company would be broken up into three parts, a testament to the strategic incoherence of the conglomerate that Kozlowski built.[1]

The Tyco story detailed in the Opening Case is an important one because it illustrates that not all managers adhere to what should be a cardinal principle of business: that the quest to maximize profitability should be constrained by both the law and ethical obligations. In Chapter 1, we noted that the goal of managers should be to pursue strategies that maximize long-run shareholder value, but we also note that managers must behave in a legal, ethical and socially responsible manner when pursuing this goal. Kozlowski's behavior was both unethical and illegal, and he paid a heavy price for his behavior.

In this chapter, we take a close look at the governance mechanisms that shareholders put in place to make sure that managers are acting in their interests and pursuing strategies that maximize shareholder value. We also discuss how managers need to pay attention to other stakeholders, such as employees, suppliers, and customers. Balancing the needs of different stakeholder groups is in the long-run interests of the company's owners, its shareholders. Good governance mechanisms recognize this truth. In addition, we will spend some time reviewing the ethical implications of strategic decisions, and we will discuss how managers can make sure that their strategic decisions are founded on strong ethical principles.

Stakeholders and Corporate Performance

A company's **stakeholders** are individuals or groups with an interest, claim, or stake in the company, in what it does, and in how well it performs.[2] They include stockholders, creditors, employees, customers, the communities in which the company does business, and the general public. Stakeholders can be divided into internal stakeholders and external stakeholders (see Figure 11.1). **Internal stakeholders** are stockholders and employees, including executive officers, other managers, and board members. **External stakeholders** are all other individuals and groups that have some claim on the company. Typically, this group is comprised of customers, suppliers, creditors (including banks and bondholders), governments, unions, local communities, and the general public.

All stakeholders are in an exchange relationship with the company. Each of the stakeholder groups listed in Figure 11.1 supplies the organization with important resources (or contributions), and in exchange, each expects its interests to be satisfied (by inducements).[3] Stockholders provide the enterprise with risk capital and in exchange expect management to try to maximize the return on their investment. Creditors, and particularly bondholders, also provide the company with capital in the form of debt, and they expect to be repaid on time and with interest. Employees provide labor and skills and in exchange expect commensurate income, job satisfaction, job security, and good working conditions. Customers provide a company with its revenues and in

FIGURE 11.1

Stakeholders and the Enterprise

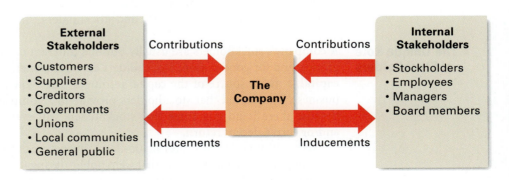

exchange want high-quality reliable products that represent value for money. Suppliers provide a company with inputs and in exchange seek revenues and dependable buyers. Governments provide a company with rules and regulations that govern business practice and maintain fair competition. In exchange, they want companies to adhere to these rules. Unions help to provide a company with productive employees, and in exchange they want benefits for their members in proportion to their contributions to the company. Local communities provide companies with local infrastructure and in exchange want companies that are responsible citizens. The general public provides companies with national infrastructure and in exchange seeks some assurance that the quality of life will be improved as a result of the company's existence.

A company must take these claims into account when formulating its strategies or stakeholders may withdraw their support. For example, stockholders may sell their shares, bondholders may demand higher interest payments on new bonds, employees may leave their jobs, and customers may buy elsewhere. Suppliers may seek more dependable buyers. Unions may engage in disruptive labor disputes. Governments may take civil or criminal action against the company and its top officers, imposing fines and in some cases jail terms. Communities may oppose the company's attempts to locate its facilities in their area, and the general public may form pressure groups, demanding action against companies that impair the quality of life. Any of these reactions can have a damaging impact on an enterprise.

Stakeholder Impact Analysis

A company cannot always satisfy the claims of all stakeholders. The goals of different groups may conflict, and in practice few organizations have the resources to manage all stakeholders.[4] For example, union claims for higher wages can conflict with consumer demands for reasonable prices and stockholder demands for acceptable returns. Often the company must make choices. To do so, it must identify the most important stakeholders and give highest priority to pursuing strategies that satisfy their needs. Stakeholder impact analysis can provide such identification. Typically, stakeholder impact analysis follows these steps:

1. Identify stakeholders.

2. Identify stakeholders' interests and concerns.

3. As a result, identify what claims stakeholders are likely to make on the organization.

4. Identify the stakeholders who are most important from the organization's perspective.

5. Identify the resulting strategic challenges.[5]

Such an analysis enables a company to identify the stakeholders most critical to its survival and to make sure that the satisfaction of their needs is paramount. Most companies that have gone through this process quickly come to the conclusion that three stakeholder groups must be satisfied above all others if a company is to survive and prosper: customers, employees, and stockholders.

The Unique Role of Stockholders

A company's stockholders are usually put in a different class from other stakeholder groups, and for good reason. Stockholders are legal owners and the providers of **risk capital**, a major source of the capital resources that allow a company to operate its business. The capital that stockholders provide to a company is seen as risk capital because there is no guarantee that stockholders will ever recoup their investment and/or earn a decent return.

Recent history demonstrates all too clearly the nature of risk capital. Many investors who bought shares in companies that went public during the late 1990s and early 2000s through an initial public offering (IPO) subsequently saw the value of their holdings decline to zero, or something close to it. For example, in early 2000, Oniva.com, a provider of an online business-to-business marketplace aimed at small businesses, went public. On the first day of trading, the shares hit $25. They fell steadily afterward, and two years later, having lost 99% of their value, they were trading at $0.25, effectively wiping out the investment many made in the company. Of course, there are also some spectacular successes: investors who purchased shares of Dell, Microsoft, or Intel at their IPO have done extraordinarily well. But this is the nature of risk capital: the variance of returns is very high. To reward stockholders for providing the company with risk capital, management is obligated to pursue strategies that maximize the returns that stockholders receive from their investment in the company's stock.

Over the past decade, maximizing returns to stockholders has taken on added importance because more and more employees have themselves become stockholders in the company for which they work through an employee stock ownership plan (ESOP). At Wal-Mart, for example, all employees who have served for more than one year are eligible for the company's ESOP. Under an ESOP, employees are given the opportunity to purchase stock in their company, sometimes at a discount compared to the market value of the stock. The company may also contribute a certain proportion of the purchase price. By making employees stockholders, ESOPs tend to increase the already strong emphasis on maximizing returns to stockholders because they now help to satisfy two key stakeholder groups: stockholders and employees.

● **Profitability, Profit Growth, and Stakeholder Claims**

Because of the unique position assigned to stockholders, managers normally seek to pursue strategies that maximize the returns that stockholders receive from holding shares in the company. As we noted in Chapter 1, stockholders receive a return on their investment in a company's stock in two ways: from dividend payments and from capital appreciation in the market value of a share (that is, by increases in stock market prices). The best way for managers to generate the funds for future dividend payments and to keep the stock price appreciating is for them to pursue strategies that maximize the company's long-run profitability (as measured by the return on invested capital or ROIC) and grow the profits of the company over time.[6]

As we saw in Chapter 3, ROIC is an excellent measure of the profitability of a company. It tells managers how efficiently they are using the capital resources of the company (including the risk capital provided by stockholders) to generate profits. A company that is generating a positive ROIC is covering all of its ongoing expenses and has money left over, which is then added to shareholders' equity, thereby increasing the value of a company and thus the value of a share of stock in the company. The value of each share will increase further if a company can grow its profits over time because then the profit that is attributable to every share (that is, the company's earning per share) will also grow. As we have seen in this book, to grow their profits, companies must be doing one or more of the following: (a) participating in a market that is growing; (b) taking market share from competitors; (c) consolidating the industry through horizontal integration; and (d) developing new markets through international expansion, vertical integration, or diversification.

While managers should strive for profit growth if they are trying to maximize shareholder value, the relationship between profitability and profit growth is a complex one because attaining future profit growth may require investments that reduce the current rate of profitability. The task of managers is to find the right balance between profitability and profit growth.[7] Too much emphasis on current profitability at the expense of future profitability and profit growth can make an enterprise less attractive to shareholders. Too much emphasis on profit growth can reduce the profitability of the enterprise and have the same effect. In an uncertain world where the future is unknowable, finding the right balance between profitability and profit growth is certainly as much art as it is science, but it is something that managers must try to do.

In addition to maximizing returns to stockholders, boosting a company's profitability and profit growth rate is also consistent with satisfying the claims of several other key stakeholder groups. When a company is profitable and its profits are growing, it can pay higher salaries to productive employees and can also afford benefits such as health insurance coverage, all of which help to satisfy employees. In addition, companies with a high level of profitability and profit growth have no problem meeting their debt commitments, which provides creditors, including bondholders, with a measure of security. More profitable companies are also better able to undertake philanthropic investments, which can help to satisfy some of the claims that local communities and the general public place on a company. Pursuing strategies that maximize the long-run profitability and profit growth of the company is therefore generally consistent with satisfying the claims of various stakeholder groups.

There is an important cause-and-effect relationship here. Pursuing strategies to maximize profitability and profit growth helps a company to better satisfy the demands that several stakeholder groups place on it, not the other way around. The company that overpays its employees in the current period, for example, may have very happy employees for a short while, but such action will raise the company's cost structure and limit its ability to attain a competitive advantage in the marketplace, thereby depressing its long-run profitability and hurting its ability to award future pay increases. As far as employees are concerned, the way many companies deal with this situation is to make future pay increases contingent on improvements in labor productivity. If labor productivity goes up, labor costs as a percentage of revenues will fall, profitability will rise, and the company can afford to pay its employees more and offer greater benefits.

Of course, not all stakeholder groups want the company to maximize its long-run profitability and profit growth. Suppliers are more comfortable about selling goods and services to profitable companies because they can be assured that the company will have the funds to pay for those products. Similarly, customers may be more willing to purchase from profitable companies because they can be assured that those companies will be around in the long run to provide after-sales services and support. But neither suppliers nor customers want the company to maximize its profitability at their expense. Rather, they would like to capture some of these profits from the company in the form of higher prices for their goods and services (in the case of suppliers) or lower prices for the products they purchase from the company (in the case of customers). Thus, the company is in a bargaining relationship with some of its stakeholders, which was a phenomenon we discussed in Chapter 2.

Despite the argument that maximizing long-run profitability and profit growth is the best way to satisfy the claims of several key stakeholder groups, it should be noted that a company must do so within the limits set by the law and in a manner consistent with societal expectations. The unfettered pursuit of profit can lead to behaviors that are outlawed by government regulations, are opposed by important public constituencies, or are simply unethical. Governments have enacted a wide range of regulations to govern business behavior, including antitrust laws, environmental laws, and laws pertaining to health and safety in the workplace. It is incumbent on managers to make sure that the company is in compliance with these laws when pursuing strategies.

Unfortunately, there is plenty of evidence that managers can be tempted to cross the line between the legal and illegal in their pursuit of greater profitability and profit growth. For example, in mid-2003, the Air Force stripped Boeing of $1 billion in contracts to launch satellites when it was discovered that Boeing had obtained thousand of pages of proprietary information from rival Lockheed Martin. Boeing had used that information to prepare its winning bid for the satellite contract. This was followed by the revelation that Boeing's CFO, Mike Sears, had offered a government official, Darleen Druyun, a lucrative job at Boeing while Druyun was still involved in evaluating whether Boeing should be awarded a $17 billion contract to build tankers for the Air Force. Boeing won the contract against strong competition from Airbus, and Druyun was hired by Boeing. It was clear that the job offer may have had an impact on the Air Force decision. Boeing fired the CFO and Druyun, and shortly afterward, Boeing CEO Phil Condit resigned in a tacit acknowledgment that he bore responsibility for the ethics violations that had occurred at Boeing during his tenure as leader.[8]In another case, the chief executive of Archer Daniels Midland, one of the world's largest producers of agricultural products, was sent to jail after an FBI investigation revealed that the company had systematically tried to fix the price for lysine by colluding with other manufacturers in the global marketplace. In another example of price fixing, the seventy-six-year-old chair of Sotheby's auction house was sentenced to a jail term and the former CEO to house arrest for fixing prices with rival auction house Christie's over a six-year period (see Strategy in Action 11.1).

Strategy in Action   11.1

Price Fixing at Sotheby's and Christie's

Sotheby's and Christie's are the two largest fine art auction houses in the world. In the mid-1990s, the two companies controlled 90% of the fine art auction market, which at the time was worth some $4 billion a year. Traditionally, auction houses make their profit by the commission they charge on auction sales. In good times, these commissions can range as high as 10% on some items, but in the early 1990s, the auction business was in a slump, with the supply of art for auction drying up. With Sotheby's and Christie's desperate for works of art, sellers played the two houses against each other, driving commissions down to 2% or even lower.

To try to control this situation, Sotheby's CEO, Dede Brooks, met with her counterpart at Christie's, Christopher Davidge, in a series of clandestine meetings held in car parking lots that began in 1993. Brooks claims that she was acting on behalf of her boss, Alfred Taubman, the chair and controlling shareholder of Sotheby's. According to Brooks, Taubman had agreed with the chair of Christie's, Anthony Tennant, to work together in the weak auction market and limit price competition. In their meetings, Brooks and Davidge agreed to a fixed and non-negotiable commission structure. Based on a sliding scale,

the commission structure would range from 10% on a $100,000 item to 2% on a $5 million item. In effect, Brooks and Davidge were agreeing to eliminate price competition between them, thereby guaranteeing both auction houses higher profits. The price-fixing agreement started in 1993 and continued unabated for six years until federal investigators uncovered the arrangement and brought charges against Sotheby's and Christie's.

With the deal out in the open, lawyers filed several class-action lawsuits on behalf of sellers who had been defrauded by Sotheby's and Christie's. Ultimately, some 100,000 sellers joined the class-action lawsuits, which the auction houses settled with a $512 million payment. The auction houses also pleaded guilty to price fixing and paid $45 million in fines to U.S. antitrust authorities. As for the key players, the chair of Christie's, as a British subject, was able to avoid prosecution in the United States (price fixing is not an offense for which someone can be extradited). Christie's CEO, Davidge, struck a deal with prosecutors and in return for amnesty handed over incriminating documents to the authorities. Brooks also cooperated with federal prosecutors and avoided jail (in April 2002, she was sentenced to three years' probation, six months' home detention, 1,000 hours of community service, and a $350,000 fine). Taubman, ultimately isolated by all his former co-conspirators, was sentenced to a year in jail and fined $7.5 million.[a]

Examples such as these beg the question: Why would managers engage in such risky behavior? A body of academic work collectively known as agency theory provides an explanation for why managers might engage in behavior that is either illegal or, at the very least, not in the interests of the company's shareholders.

Agency Theory

Agency theory looks at the problems that can arise in a business relationship when one person delegates decision-making authority to another. It offers a way of understanding why managers do not always act in the best interests of stakeholders and why they might sometimes behave unethically and perhaps also illegally.[9] Although agency theory was originally formulated to capture the relationship between management and stockholders, the basic principles have also been extended to cover the relationship with other key stakeholders, such as employees, as well as relationships between different layers of management within a corporation.[10] While the focus of attention in this section is on the relationship between senior management and stockholders, some of the same language can be applied to the relationship between other stakeholders and top managers and between top management and lower levels of management.

● **Principal-Agent Relationships**

The basic propositions of agency theory are relatively straightforward. First, an agency relationship arises whenever one party delegates decision-making authority or control over resources to another. The principal is the person delegating authority, and the agent is the person to whom authority is delegated. The relationship between stockholders and senior managers is the classic example of an agency relationship. Stockholders, who are the principals, provide the company with risk capital, but they delegate control over that capital to senior managers, and particularly the CEO, who as their agent is expected to use that capital in a manner that is consistent with the best interests of the stockholders. As we have seen, this means using that capital to maximize the company's long-run profitability and profit growth rate.

The agency relationship continues down within the company. For example, in the large, complex, multibusiness company, top managers cannot possibly make all important decisions, so they delegate some decision-making authority and control over capital resources to business unit (divisional) managers. Thus, just as senior managers such as the CEO are the agents of stockholders, business unit managers are the agents of the CEO (and in this context, the CEO is the principal). The CEO trusts business unit managers to use the resources over which they have control in the most effective manner so that they maximize the performance of their units, which helps the CEO to make sure that he or she maximizes the performance of the entire company, thereby discharging agency obligations to stockholders. More generally, whenever managers delegate authority to managers below them in the hierarchy and give them the right to control resources, an agency relation is established.

● **The Agency Problem**

While agency relationships often work well, problems may arise if agents and principals have different goals and if agents take actions that are not in the best interests of their principals. Agents may be able to do this because there is an **information asymmetry** between the principal and the agent: agents almost always have more information about the resources they are managing than the principal does. Unscrupulous agents can take advantage of any information asymmetry to mislead principals and maximize their own interests at the expense of principals.

In the case of stockholders, information asymmetry arises because they delegate decision-making authority to the CEO, their agent, who by virtue of his or her position inside the company is likely to know far more than stockholders do about the company's operations. Indeed, there may be certain information about the company that the CEO is unwilling to share with stockholders because it would also help competitors. In such a case, withholding some information from stockholders may be in their best interests. More generally, the CEO, who is involved in the day-to-day running of the company, is bound to have an information advantage over stockholders, just as the CEO's subordinates may well have an information advantage over the CEO with regard to the resources under their control.

The information asymmetry between principals and agents is not necessarily a bad thing, but it can make it difficult for principals to measure how well an agent is performing and thus hold the agent accountable for how well he or she is using the entrusted resources. There is a certain amount of performance ambiguity inherent in the relationship between a principal and agent: principals cannot know for sure if the agent is acting in his or her best interests. They cannot know for sure if the agent is using the resources to which he or she has been entrusted as effectively and efficiently as possible. To an extent, principals have to trust the agent to do the right thing.

Of course, this trust is not blind: principals do put mechanisms in place whose purpose is to monitor agents, evaluate their performance, and take corrective action if necessary. As we shall see shortly, the board of directors is one such mechanism because in part the board exists to monitor and evaluate senior managers on behalf of stockholders. Other mechanisms serve a similar purpose. In the United States, publicly owned companies must regularly file detailed financial statements with the Securities and Exchange Commission (SEC) that are in accordance with generally accepted accounting principles (GAAP). This requirement exists to give stockholders consistent and detailed information about how well management is using the capital with which it has been entrusted. Similarly, internal control systems within a company help the CEO make sure that subordinates are using the resources with which they have been entrusted as efficiently and effectively as possible.

Despite the existence of governance mechanisms and comprehensive measurement and control systems, a degree of information asymmetry will always remain between principals and agents, and there is always an element of trust involved in the relationship. Unfortunately, not all agents are worthy of this trust. A minority will deliberately mislead principals for personal gain, sometimes behaving unethically or breaking laws in the process. The interests of principals and agents are not always the same; they diverge, and some agents may take advantage of information asymmetries to maximize their own interests at the expense of principals and to engage in behaviors that the principals would never condone.

For example, some authors have argued that, like many other people, senior managers are motivated by desires for status, power, job security, and income.[11] By virtue of their position within the company, certain managers, such as the CEO, can use their authority and control over corporate funds to satisfy these desires at the cost of returns to stockholders. CEOs might use their position to invest corporate funds in various perks that enhance their status—executive jets, lavish offices, and expense-paid trips to exotic locations—rather than investing those funds in ways that increase stockholder returns. Economists have termed such behavior **on-the-job consumption**.[12] Dennis Kozlowski is an example of a CEO who appeared to engage in excessive on-the-job consumption (see the Opening Case).

Besides engaging in on-the-job consumption, CEOs, along with other senior managers, might satisfy their desires for greater income by using their influence or control over the board of directors to get the compensation committee of the board to grant pay increases. Critics of U.S. industry claim that extraordinary pay has now become an endemic problem and that senior managers are enriching themselves at the expense of stockholders and other employees. They point out that CEO pay has been increasing far more rapidly than the pay of average workers primarily because of very liberal stock option grants that enable a CEO to earn huge pay bonuses in a rising stock market, even if the company underperforms in the market and compared to competitors.[13] In 1950, when *Business Week* started its annual survey of CEO pay, the highest-paid executive was General Motors CEO Charles Wilson, whose $652,156 pay packet translated into $4.7 million in inflation-adjusted dollars in 2005. In contrast, the highest-paid executive in 2005, Lee Raymond of Exxon, earned $405 million[14] In 1980, the average CEO in *Business Week*'s survey of CEOs of the largest 500 American companies earned forty-two times what the average blue-collar worker earned. By 1990, this figure had increased to eighty-five times. Today, the average CEO in the survey earns more than three hundred and fifty times the pay of the average blue-collar worker.[15]

What rankles critics is the size of some CEO pay packages and their apparent lack of relationship to company performance.[16] For example, in May 2006, shareholders of Home Depot complained bitterly about the compensation package for CEO Bob Nardelli at the company's annual meeting. Nardelli, who was appointed in 2000, had received $124 million in compensation, despite mediocre financial performance at Home Depot and a 12% decline in the company's stock price since he joined. When unexercised stock options were included, his compensation exceeded $250 million.[17] Another target of complaints was Pfizer CEO, Hank McKinnell, who garnered an $83 million lump sum pension, and $16 million in compensation in 2005, despite a 40-plus percentage point decline in Pfizer's stock price since he took over as CEO.[18] Critics feel that the size of pay awards such as these is out of all proportion to the achievement of the CEOs. If so, this represents a clear example of the agency problem.

A further concern is that in trying to satisfy a desire for status, security, power, and income, a CEO might engage in empire building, or buying many new businesses in an attempt to increase the size of the company through diversification.[19] Although such growth may depress the company's long-run profitability and thus stockholder returns, it increases the size of the empire under the CEO's control and, by extension, the CEO's status, power, security, and income (there is a strong relationship between company size and CEO pay). Instead of trying to maximize stockholder returns by seeking the right balance between profitability and profit growth, some senior managers may trade long-run profitability for greater company growth by buying new businesses. Figure 11.2 graphs long-run profitability against the rate of growth in company revenues. A company that does not grow is probably missing some profitable opportunities.[20] A moderate revenue growth rate of G* allows a company to maximize long-run profitability, generating a return of Π^*. Thus, a growth rate of G1 in Figure 11.2 is not consistent with maximizing profitability ($\Pi1 < \Pi^*$). By the same token, however, attaining growth in excess of G2 requires diversification into areas that the company knows little about. Consequently, it can

FIGURE 11.2

The Tradeoff
Between Profitability
and Revenue
Growth Rates

be achieved only by sacrificing profitability; that is, past G*, the investment required to finance further growth does not produce an adequate return and the company's profitability declines. Yet G2 may be the growth rate favored by an empire-building CEO because it will increase his or her power, status, and income. At this growth rate, profitability is equal only to $\Pi2$. Because $\Pi^* > \Pi2$, a company growing at this rate is clearly not maximizing its long-run profitability or the wealth of its stockholders.

For an example of this kind of excessive growth, consider again the case of Tyco International, profiled in the Opening Case. Tyco's growth through acquisitions under Dennis Kozlowski enabled him to build a corporate empire, which clearly satisfied Kozlowski's ego and financial needs, although it was financially shaky.

Just how serious agency problems can be was emphasized in the early 2000s when a series of scandals swept through the corporate world, many of which could be attributed to self-interest-seeking by senior executives and a failure of corporate governance mechanisms to hold the excess of those executives in check. Between 2001 and 2004, accounting scandals unfolded at a number of major corporations, including Enron, WorldCom, Tyco, Computer Associates, HealthSouth, Adelphia Communications, Dynegy, Royal Dutch Shell, and the major Italian food company, Parmalat. At Enron, some $27 billion in debt was hidden from shareholders, employees, and regulators in special partnerships that were kept off the balance sheet. At Parmalat, managers apparently "invented" some $8 to $12 billion in assets to shore up the company's balance sheet, assets that never existed. In the case of Royal Dutch Shell, senior managers knowingly inflated the value of the company's oil reserves by one-fifth, which amounted to 4 billion barrels of oil that never existed, making the company appear much more valuable than it actually was. At the other companies, earnings were systematically overstated, often by hundreds of millions of dollars, or even billions of dollars in the case of Tyco (see the Opening Case) and WorldCom, which understated its expenses by $3 billion in 2001. Strategy in Action 11.2 discusses accounting fraud at Computer Associates. In all of these cases, the prime motivation seems to have been an effort to present a more favorable view of corporate affairs to shareholders than was actually the case, thereby securing senior executives significantly higher pay packets.[21]

Strategy in Action

11.2

Self-Dealing at Computer Associates

Computer Associates is one of the world's largest software companies. During the 1990s, its stock price appreciated at a rapid rate, driven in large part by surging revenues and a commensurate rise in profits. Because its revenues were growing more rapidly than those of rivals during the late 1990s, investors assumed that the company was gaining market share and that high profitability would follow, so they bid up the price of the company's stock. The senior managers of Computer Associates were major beneficiaries of this process. Under a generous incentive program given to the company's three top managers—Charles Wang, then CEO and chair of the board; Sanjay Kumar, the chief operating officer; and Russell Artzt, the chief technology officer—by the board of directors, they would receive a special incentive stock award amounting to some 20 million shares if the stock price stayed above $53.13 for sixty days. In May 1998, Kumar announced that Computer Associates had "record" revenues and earnings for the quarter. The stock price surged over the $53.13 trigger and stayed there long enough for all three to receive the special incentive stock award, then valued at $1.1 billion.

In late July 1998, after all three had received the award, Kumar announced that the effect of Asian economic turmoil and the year 2000 bug "leads us to believe that our revenue and earnings growth will slow over the next few quarters." The stock price promptly fell from over $55.00 to under $40.00 a share. What followed was a series of class-action lawsuits, undertaken on behalf of stockholders, that claimed that management had misled stockholders to enrich themselves. As a result of the lawsuits, the three top managers were compelled to give back some of their gains, and the size of the award was reduced to 4.5 million shares. Wang stepped down as CEO, although he retained his position as chair of the board, and Kumar became the CEO.

This was not the end of matters, however, because Computer Associates had attracted the attention of both the Justice Department and the SEC, which launched a joint investigation into the company's accounting practices. By 2002, they were reportedly focusing on a little-noticed action the company had taken in May 2000 to reduce its revenues by 10%, or $1.76 billion, below what it had previously reported for the three fiscal years that ended March

2000. The downward revisions, detailed in the company's 10-K filings with the SEC, retroactively took hundreds of millions of dollars away from the top line in the fourteen months preceding the May 1998 stock award to senior managers, including some $513 million for the fiscal year ending March 1998. According to the company, earnings were unaffected by the revision because the lost revenue was offset by a commensurate downward revision of expenses. The downward revision reportedly came at the urging of auditor KPMG, which replaced Ernst & Young as the company's accountant in June 1999.

The implication that some observers were drawing was that Computer Associates deliberately overstated its revenues in the period prior to May 1998 to enrich the three top managers. The losers in this process were stockholders who purchased shares at the inflated price and longer-term shareholders who saw the value of their holdings diluted by the stock awarded to Wang, Kumar, and Artzt. In a statement issued after a report of the ongoing investigation was published in the *Wall Street Journal*, Computer Associates stated that it changed how it classified revenue and expenses at the advice of its auditors. "We continue to believe CA has acted appropriately," the company said. "This change in presentation had no impact on reported earnings, earnings per share, or cash flows."

By 2004, it was clear that Computer Associates had been acting anything but appropriately. According to the SEC investigation, between 1998 and 2000, the company adopted a policy of backdating contracts to boost revenues. For example, in January 2000, Computer Associates negotiated a $300 million contract with a customer but backdated the contract so that the revenues appeared in 1999. Although initially this may have been done to help secure the $1.1 billion special stock award, by 2000, the practice represented an increasingly desperate attempt to meet financial projections that the company was routinely missing. Under increasing pressure, Charles Wang stepped down in 2002 as chair, and in 2004, Kumar was forced to resign as CEO by the board of Computer Associates, which had belatedly come to recognize that the company's financial statements were fraudulent. In late 2004, in a deal with federal regulators, the company admitted to $2.2 billion in fraud. As part of the deal, Kumar was indicted by federal prosecutors on charges of obstruction of justice and securities fraud. In November 2006, Kumar was sentenced to twelve years in jail for his part in the fraud.[b]

It is important to remember that the agency problem is not confined to the relationship between senior managers and stockholders. It can also bedevil the relationship between the CEO and subordinates, and between them and their subordinates. Subordinates might use control over information to distort the true performance of their unit to enhance their pay, increase their job security, or make sure their unit gets more than its fair share of company resources.

Confronted with agency problems, the challenge for principals is to (1) shape the behavior of agents so that they act in accordance with the goals set by principals, (2) reduce the information asymmetry between agents and principals, and (3) develop mechanisms for removing agents who do not act in accordance with the goals of principals and mislead them. Principals try to deal with these challenges through a series of governance mechanisms.

Governance Mechanisms

Governance mechanisms are mechanisms that principals put in place to align incentives between principals and agents and to monitor and control agents. The purpose of governance mechanisms is to reduce the scope and frequency of the agency problem: to help ensure that agents act in a manner that is consistent with the best interests of their principals. In this section, the primary focus is on the governance mechanisms that align the interests of senior managers (as agents) with their principals, stockholders. It should not be forgotten, however, that governance mechanisms also exist to align the interests of business unit managers with those of their superiors, and so on down within the organization.

Here we look at four main types of governance mechanisms for aligning stockholder and management interests: the board of directors, stock-based compensation, financial statements, and the takeover constraint. The section closes with a discussion of governance mechanisms within a company to align the interest of senior and lower-level managers.

● **The Board of Directors**

The board of directors is the centerpiece of the corporate governance system in the United States and the United Kingdom. Board members are directly elected by stockholders, and under corporate law, they represent the stockholders' interests in the company. Hence, the board can be held legally accountable for the company's actions. Its position at the apex of decision making within the company allows it to monitor corporate strategy decisions and ensure that they are consistent with stockholder interests. If the board's sense is that corporate strategies are not in the best interests of stockholders, it can apply sanctions, such as voting against management nominations to the board of directors or submitting its own nominees. In addition, the board has the legal authority to hire, fire, and compensate corporate employees, including, most importantly, the CEO.[22] The board is also responsible for making sure that audited financial statements of the company present a true picture of its financial situation. Thus, the board exists to reduce the information asymmetry between stockholders and managers and to monitor and control management actions on behalf of stockholders.

The typical board of directors is composed of a mix of inside and outside directors. **Inside directors** are senior employees of the company, such as the CEO. They are required on the board because they have valuable information about the company's activities. Without such information, the board cannot adequately perform its monitoring function. But because insiders are full-time employees of the company, their interests tend to be aligned with those of management. Hence, outside directors are needed to bring objectivity to the monitoring and evaluation processes. **Outside directors** are not full-time employees of the company. Many of them are full-time professional directors who hold positions on the boards of several companies. The need to maintain a reputation as competent outside directors gives them an incentive to perform their tasks as objectively and effectively as possible.[23]

There is little doubt that many boards perform their assigned functions admirably. For example, when the board of Sotheby's discovered that the company had been engaged in price fixing with Christie's, board members moved quickly to oust both the CEO and the chair of the company (see Strategy in Action 11.1). But not all boards perform as well as they should. The board of now-bankrupt energy company Enron signed off on that company's audited financial statements, which were later shown to be grossly misleading.

Critics of the existing governance system charge that inside directors often dominate the outsiders on the board. Insiders can use their position within the management hierarchy to exercise control over what kind of company-specific information the board receives. Consequently, they can present information in a way that puts them in a favorable light. In addition, because insiders have intimate knowledge of the company's operations and because superior knowledge and control over information are sources of power, they may be better positioned than outsiders to influence boardroom decision making. The board may become the captive of insiders and merely rubber-stamp management decisions instead of guarding stockholder interests.

Some observers contend that many boards are dominated by the company CEO, particularly when the CEO is also the chair of the board.[24] To support this view, they point out that both inside and outside directors are often the personal nominees of the CEO. The typical inside director is subordinate to the CEO in the company's hierarchy and therefore unlikely to criticize the boss. Because outside directors are frequently the CEO's nominees as well, they can hardly be expected to evaluate the CEO objectively. Thus, the loyalty of the board may be biased toward the CEO, not the stockholders. Moreover, a CEO who is also chair of the board may be able to control the agenda of board discussions to deflect any criticisms of his or her leadership.

In the aftermath of a wave of scandals that hit the corporate world in the early 2000s, there are clear signs that many corporate boards are moving away from merely rubber-stamping top management decisions and are beginning to play a much more active role in corporate governance. In part, they have been prompted by new legislation, such as the 2002 Sarbanes-Oxley Act in the United States, which tightened rules governing corporate reporting and corporate governance. Also important has been a growing trend on the part of the courts to hold directors liable for corporate misstatements. Powerful institutional investors such as pension funds have also been more aggressive in exerting their power, often pushing for more outside representation on the board of directors and for a separation between the roles of chair and CEO, with the chair role going to an outsider. Partly as a result, over 50% of big companies had outside directors in the chair's role by the mid-2000s, up from less than half that amount in 1990. Separating the role of chair and CEO limits the ability of corporate insiders, and particularly of the CEO, to exercise control over the board. Still, when all is said and done, it must be recognized that boards of directors do not work as well as they should in theory, and other mechanisms are need to align the interests of stockholders and managers.

● Stock-Based Compensation

According to agency theory, one of the best ways to reduce the scope of the agency problem is for principals to establish incentives for agents to behave in their best interests through pay-for-performance systems. In the case of stockholders and top managers, stockholders can encourage top managers to pursue strategies that maximize a company's long-run profitability and profit growth, and thus the gains from holding its stock, by linking the pay of those managers to the performance of the stock price.

The most common pay-for-performance system has been to give managers **stock options**: the right to buy the company's shares at a predetermined (strike) price at some point in the future, usually within ten years of the grant date. Typically, the strike price is the price that the stock was trading at when the option was originally granted. The idea behind stock options is to motivate managers to adopt strategies that increase the share price of the company because in doing so, they will also increase the value of their own stock options. Another stock-based pay-for-performance system is to grant managers stock if they attain predetermined performance targets.

Several academic studies suggest that stock-based compensation schemes for executives, such as stock options and stock grants, can align management and stockholder interests. For instance, one study found that managers were more likely to consider the effects of their acquisition decisions on stockholder returns if they themselves were significant shareholders.[25] According to another study, managers who were significant stockholders were less likely to pursue strategies that would maximize the size of the company rather than its profitability.[26] More generally, it is difficult to argue with the proposition that the chance to get rich from exercising stock options is the primary reason for the fourteen-hour days and six-day workweeks that many employees of fast-growing companies put in.

However, the practice of granting stock options has become increasingly controversial. Many top managers often earn huge bonuses from exercising stock options that were granted several years previously. While not denying that these options do motivate managers to improve company performance, critics claim that they are often too generous. A particular cause for concern is that stock options are often granted at such low strike prices that the CEO can hardly fail to make a significant amount of money by exercising them, even if the company underperforms in the stock market by a significant margin. Indeed, a serious example of the agency problem emerged in 2005 and 2006 when the Securities and Exchange Commission started to investigate a number of companies where stock options granted to senior executives had apparently been backdated to a time when the stock price was lower, enabling the executive to earn more money than if those options had simply been dated on the day that they were granted.[27] By late 2006, the SEC was investigating some 130 companies for possible fraud relating to stock option dating. Included in the list were some major corporations, including Apple Computer, Jabil Circuit, United Health, and Home Depot.[28]

Other critics of stock options, including the famous investor Warren Buffett, complain that huge stock option grants increase the outstanding number of shares in a company and therefore dilute the equity of stockholders; accordingly, they should be shown in company accounts as an expense against profits. Under accounting regulations that were in force until 2005, stock options, unlike wages and salaries, were not expensed. However, this has now changed and, as a result, many companies are starting to reduce their use of stock options. At Microsoft, for example, which had long given generous stock option grants to high-performing employees, stock options were replaced with stock grants in 2005.

● Financial Statements and Auditors

Publicly traded companies in the United States are required to file quarterly and annual reports with the SEC that are prepared according to generally accepted accounting principals (GAAP). The purpose of this requirement is to give consistent, detailed, and accurate information about how efficiently and effectively the agents of stockholders—the company's managers—are running the company. To make sure that managers do not misrepresent this financial information, the SEC also requires that the accounts be audited by an independent and accredited accounting firm. Similar regulations exist in most other developed nations. If the system works as intended, stockholders can have a lot of faith that the information contained in financial statements accurately reflects the state of affairs at a company. Among other things, such information can enable a stockholder to calculate the profitability (ROIC) of a company in which he or she invests and to compare its ROIC against that of competitors.

Unfortunately, in the United States at least, this system has not always worked as intended. Although the vast majority of companies do file accurate information in their financial statements and although most auditors do a good job of reviewing that information, there is substantial evidence that a minority of companies have abused the system, aided in part by the compliance of auditors. This was clearly an issue at bankrupt energy trader Enron, where the CFO and others misrepresented the true financial state of the company to investors by creating off-balance-sheet partnerships that hid the true state of Enron's indebtedness from public view. Enron's auditor, Arthur Andersen, also apparently went along with this deception, in direct violation of its fiduciary duty. Arthur Anderson also had lucrative consulting contracts with Enron that it did not want to jeopardize by questioning the accuracy of the company's financial statements. The losers in this mutual deception were shareholders, who had to rely on inaccurate information to make their investment decisions.

There have been numerous examples in recent years of managers' manipulating financial statements to present a distorted picture of their company's finances to investors. The typical motive has been to inflate the earnings or revenues of a company, thereby generating investor enthusiasm and propelling the stock price higher, which gives managers an opportunity to cash in stock option grants for huge personal gain, obviously at the expense of stockholders who have been misled by the reports (see Strategy in Action 11.2 for an example).

The gaming of financial statements by companies such as Enron and Computer Associates raises serious questions about the accuracy of the information contained in audited financial statements. In response, in 2002, the United States passed the Sarbanes-Oxley Act into law; it represents the biggest overhaul of accounting rules and corporate governance procedures since the 1930s. Among other things, Sarbanes-Oxley set up a new oversight board for accounting firms, required CEOs and CFOs to endorse their company's financial statements, and barred companies from hiring the same accounting firm for auditing and consulting services.

● The Takeover Constraint

Given the imperfections in corporate governance mechanisms, it is clear that the agency problem may still exist at some companies. However, stockholders still have some residual power because they can always sell their shares. If they start doing so in large numbers, the price of the company's shares will decline. If the share price falls far enough, the company might be worth less on the stock market than the book value of its assets. At this point, it may become an attractive acquisition target and run the risk of being purchased by another enterprise, against the wishes of the target company's management.

The risk of being acquired by another company is known as the **takeover constraint**. The takeover constraint limits the extent to which managers can pursue strategies and take actions that put their own interests above those of stockholders. If they ignore stockholder interests and the company is acquired, senior managers typically lose their independence and probably their jobs as well. So the threat of takeover can constrain management action and limit the worst excesses of the agency problem.

During the 1980s and early 1990s, the threat of takeover was often enforced by corporate raiders: individuals or corporations that buy up large blocks of shares in companies that they think are pursuing strategies inconsistent with maximizing stockholder wealth. Corporate raiders argue that if these underperforming companies pursued different strategies, they could create more wealth for stockholders. Raiders buy stock in a company either to take over the business and run it more efficiently or to precipitate a change in the top management, replacing the existing team with one more likely to maximize stockholder returns. Raiders are motivated not by altruism but by gain. If they succeed in their takeover bid, they can institute strategies that create value for stockholders, including themselves. Even if a takeover bid fails, raiders can still earn millions because their stockholdings will typically be bought out by the defending company for a hefty premium. Called **greenmail**, this source of gain stirred much controversy and debate about its benefits. While some claim that the threat posed by raiders has had a salutary effect on enterprise performance by pushing corporate management to run their companies better, others claim there is little evidence of this.[29]

Although the incidence of hostile takeover bids has fallen off significantly since the early 1990s, this should not be taken as evidence that the takeover constraint is no longer operating. Unique circumstances exist in the early 2000s that have made it more difficult to execute hostile takeovers. The boom years of the 1990s left many corporations with excessive debt: corporate America entered the new century with record levels of debt on its balance sheets. These debt levels limit the ability of companies to finance acquisitions, especially hostile acquisitions, which are often particularly expensive. In addition, the market valuations of many companies got so out of line with underlying fundamentals during the stock market bubble of the 1990s that even after a substantial fall in certain segments of the stock market, such as the technology sector, valuations are still high relative to historic norms, making the hostile acquisition of even poorly run and unprofitable companies expensive. However, takeovers tend to go in cycles, and it seems likely that once excesses are worked out of the stock market and worked off corporate balance sheets, the takeover constraint will begin to reassert itself. It should be remembered that the takeover constraint is the governance mechanism of last resort and is often invoked only when other governance mechanisms have failed.

● Governance Mechanisms Inside a Company

So far, this section has focused on the governance mechanisms designed to reduce the agency problem that potentially exists between stockholders and managers. Agency relationships also exist within a company, and the agency problem can thus arise between levels of management. In this section, we explore how the agency problem can be reduced within a company by using two complementary governance mechanisms to align the incentives and behavior of employees with those of upper-level management: strategic control systems and incentive systems.

STRATEGIC CONTROL SYSTEMS Strategic control systems are the primary governance mechanisms established within a company to reduce the scope of the agency problem between levels of management. These systems are the formal target setting, measurement, and feedback systems that allow managers to evaluate whether a company is executing the strategies necessary to maximize its long-run profitability and, in particular, whether the company is achieving superior efficiency, quality, innovation, and customer responsiveness. They are discussed in more detail in subsequent chapters.

The purpose of strategic control systems is to (1) establish standards and targets against which performance can be measured, (2) create systems for measuring and monitoring performance on a regular basis, (3) compare actual performance against the established targets, and (4) evaluate results and take corrective action if necessary. In governance terms, the purpose of strategic control systems is to make sure that lower-level managers, as the agents of top managers, are acting in a way that is consistent with top managers' goals, which should be to maximize the wealth of stockholders, subject to legal and ethical constraints.

One increasingly influential model that guides managers through the process of creating the right kind of strategic control systems to enhance organizational performance is the balanced scorecard model.[30] According to the balanced scorecard model, managers have primarily used financial measures of performance, such as return on invested capital, to measure and evaluate organizational performance. Financial information is extremely important, but it is not enough by itself. If managers are to obtain a true picture of organizational performance, financial information must be supplemented with performance measures that indicate how well an organization has been achieving the four building blocks of competitive advantage: efficiency, quality, innovation, and responsiveness to customers. Financial results simply inform strategic managers about the results of decisions they have already taken; the other measures balance this picture of performance by informing managers about how accurately the organization has in place the building blocks that drive future performance.[31]

One version of the way the balanced scorecard operates is presented in Figure 11.3. Strategic managers develop a set of strategies, based on an organization's mission and goals, to build competitive advantage to achieve these goals. They then establish an organizational structure to use resources to obtain a competitive advantage.[32] To evaluate how well the strategy and structure are working, managers develop specific performance measures that assess how well the four building blocks of competitive advantage are being achieved:

- *Efficiency* can be measured by the level of production costs, the productivity of labor (such as the employee hours needed to make a product), the productivity of capital (such as revenues per dollar invested in property, plant, and equipment), and the cost of raw materials.

- *Quality* can be measured by the number of rejects, the number of defective products returned from customers, and the level of product reliability over time.

- *Innovation* can be measured by the number of new products introduced, the percentage of revenues generated from new products in a defined period, the time taken to develop the next generation of new products versus the competition, and the productivity of R&D (how much R&D spending is required to produce a successful product).

FIGURE 11.3

A Balanced Scorecard
Approach

- *Responsiveness to customers* can be measured by the number of repeat customers, customer defection rates, level of on-time delivery to customers, and level of customer service.

As Kaplan and Norton, the developers of this approach, suggest, "Think of the balanced scorecard as the dials and indicators in an airplane cockpit. For the complex task of navigating and flying an airplane, pilots need detailed information about many aspects of the flight. They need information on fuel, air speed, altitude, learning, destination, and other indicators that summarize the current and predicted environment. Reliance on one instrument can be fatal. Similarly, the complexity of managing an organization today requires that managers be able to view performance in several areas simultaneously."[33]

The way in which managers' ability to build a competitive advantage translates into organizational performance is then measured using financial measures such as the return on invested capital, the return on sales, and the capital turnover ratio (see Chapter 3). Based on an evaluation of the complete set of measures in the balanced scorecard, strategic managers are in a good position to reevaluate the company's mission and goals and take corrective action to rectify problems, limit the agency problem, or exploit new opportunities by changing the organization's strategy and structure—which is the purpose of strategic control.

EMPLOYEE INCENTIVES   Control systems alone may not be sufficient to align incentives among stockholders, senior management, and the rest of the organization. To help do this, positive incentive systems are often put into place to motivate employees to work toward goals that are central to maximizing long-run profitability. As already noted, employee stock ownership plans (ESOPs) are one form of positive incentive, as are stock option grants. In the 1990s, ESOPs and stock ownership grants were pushed down deep within many organizations. The logic behind such systems is straightforward: recognizing that the stock price, and therefore their own wealth, is dependent on the profitability of the company, employees will work toward maximizing profitability.

In addition to stock-based compensation systems, employee compensation can also be tied to goals that are linked to the attainment of superior efficiency, quality, innovation, and customer responsiveness. For example, the bonus pay of a manufacturing employee might depend on attaining quality and productivity targets, which, if reached, will lower the costs of the company, increase customer satisfaction, and boost profitability. Similarly, the bonus pay of a salesperson might be dependent on surpassing sales targets, and of an R&D employee, on the success of new products he or she helped develop.

Ethics and Strategy

The term **ethics** refers to accepted principles of right or wrong that govern the conduct of a person, the members of a profession, or the actions of an organization. **Business ethics** are the accepted principles of right or wrong governing the conduct of businesspeople. Ethical decisions are in accordance with those accepted principles, whereas unethical decisions violate accepted principles. This is not as straightforward as it sounds. Managers may be confronted with **ethical dilemmas**, which are situations where there is no agreement over the accepted principles of right and wrong, or where none of the available alternatives seems ethically acceptable.

In our society, many accepted principles of right and wrong are not only universally recognized but also codified into law. In the business arena, there are laws governing product liability (tort laws), contracts and breaches of contract (contract law), the protection of intellectual property (intellectual property law), competitive behavior (antitrust law), and the selling of securities (securities law). Not only is it unethical to break these laws, it is illegal.

In this book, we argue that the preeminent goal of managers in a business should be to pursue strategies that maximize the long-run profitability and profit growth of the enterprise, thereby boosting returns to stockholders. Strategies, of course, must be consistent with the laws that govern business behavior: managers must act legally while seeking to maximize the long-run profitability of the enterprise. As we have already seen in this chapter, there are examples of managers breaking the law. Moreover, managers may take advantage of ambiguities and gray areas in the law, of which there are many in our common law system, to pursue actions that are at best legally suspect and, in any event, clearly unethical. It is important to realize, however, that behaving ethically goes beyond staying within the bounds of the law. For example, see Strategy in Action 11.3, which discusses Nike's use of sweatshop labor in developing nations to make sneakers for consumers in the developed world. While Nike was not breaking any laws by using inexpensive labor (employees who worked long hours for poor pay in poor working conditions), neither were its subcontractors; however, many considered it unethical to use subcontractors who, by western standards, clearly exploited their work force. In this section, we take a closer look at the ethical issues that managers may confront when developing strategy and at the steps managers can take to ensure that strategic decisions are not only legal, but also ethical.

● **Ethical Issues in Strategy**

The ethical issues that strategic managers confront cover a wide range of topics, but most are due to a potential conflict between the goals of the enterprise, or the goals of individual managers, and the fundamental rights of important stakeholders, including stockholders, customers, employees, suppliers, competitors, communities, and the general public. Stakeholders have basic rights that should be respected, and it is unethical to violate those rights.

Strategy in Action

11.3

Nike and the Sweatshop Debate

In many ways, Nike is the quintessential global corporation. Established in 1972 by former University of Oregon track star Phil Knight, Nike is now one of the leading marketers of athletic shoes and apparel in the world. By 2004, the company had more than $12 billion in annual revenues, had a return on invested capital of 17.5%, and sold its products in some 140 countries. Nike does not do any manufacturing. Rather, it designs and markets its products and contracts for their manufacture from a global network of 600 factories owned by subcontractors scattered around the globe that together employ some 550,000 people. This huge corporation has made founder Phil Knight into one of the richest people in America. Nike's marketing phrase, "Just Do It!" has become as recognizable in popular culture as its "swoosh" logo or the faces of its celebrity sponsors, such as Tiger Woods.

For all of its successes, the company has been dogged by repeated and persistent accusations that its products are made in sweatshops where workers, many of them children, slave away in hazardous conditions for wages that are below subsistence levels. Nike's wealth, its detractors claim, has been built on the backs of the world's poor. Many see Nike as a symbol of the evils of globalization: a rich western corporation exploiting the world's poor to provide expensive shoes and apparel to the pampered consumers of the developed world. Nike's Niketown stores have become standard targets for antiglobalization protestors. Several nongovernmental organizations, such as San Francisco–based Global Exchange, a human rights organization dedicated to promoting environmental, political, and social justice around the world, have targeted Nike for repeated criticism and protests. News organizations such as CBS's *48 Hours*, hosted by Dan Rather, have run exposés on working conditions in foreign factories that supply Nike. And students on the campuses of several major U.S. universities with which Nike has lucrative sponsorship deals have protested against those deals, citing Nike's use of sweatshop labor.

Typical of the allegations were those detailed in the CBS news program *48 Hours* in 1996. The report painted a picture of young women at a Vietnamese subcontractor who worked six days a week, in poor working conditions with toxic materials, for only 20 cents an hour. The report also stated that a living wage in Vietnam was at least $3 a day, an income that could not be achieved without working substantial overtime. Nike and its subcontractors were not breaking any laws, but this report and others like it raised questions about the ethics of using sweatshop labor to make what were essentially fashion accessories. It may have been legal, it may have helped the company to increase its profitability, but was it ethical to use subcontractors who, by western standards, clearly exploited their work force? Nike's critics thought not, and the company found itself the focus of a wave of demonstrations and consumer boycotts.

Adding fuel to the fire, in November 1997, Global Exchange obtained and leaked a confidential report by Ernst & Young of an audit that Nike had commissioned of a Vietnam factory owned by a Nike subcontractor. The factory had 9,200 workers and made 400,000 pairs of shoes a month. The Ernst & Young report painted a dismal picture of thousands of young women, most under age twenty-five, laboring ten and a half hours a day, six days a week, in excessive heat and noise and foul air, for slightly more than $10 a week. The report also found that workers with skin or breathing problems had not been transferred to departments free of chemicals. More than half the workers who dealt with dangerous chemicals did not wear protective masks or gloves. The report stated that, in parts of the plant, workers were exposed to carcinogens that exceeded local legal standards by 177 times and that 77% of the employees suffered from respiratory problems.

These exposés surrounding Nike's use of subcontractors forced the company to reexamine its policies. Realizing that its subcontracting policies were perceived as unethical, Nike's management took a number of steps, including establishing a code of conduct for Nike subcontractors and setting up a scheme whereby all subcontractors would be monitored annually by independent auditors. Nike's code of conduct required that all employees at footwear factories be at least eighteen years old and that exposure to potentially toxic materials would not exceed the permissible exposure limits established by the U.S. Occupational Safety and Health Administration (OSHA) for workers in the United States. In short, Nike concluded that behaving ethically required going beyond the requirements of the law. It required the establishment and enforcement of rules that adhere to accepted moral principles of right and wrong.[c]

Stockholders have the right to timely and accurate information about their investment (in accounting statements), and it is unethical to violate that right. Customers have the right to be fully informed about the products and services they purchase, including the right to information about how those products might cause harm to them or others, and it is unethical to restrict their access to such information. Employees have the right to safe working conditions, fair compensation for the work they perform, and just treatment by managers. Suppliers have the right to expect contracts to be respected, and the firm should not take advantage of a power disparity between itself and a supplier to opportunistically rewrite a contract. Competitors have the right to expect that the firm will abide by the rules of competition and not violate the basic principles of antitrust laws. Communities and the general public, including their political representatives in government, have the right to expect that a firm will respect the basic expectations that society places on enterprises: for example, by not dumping toxic pollutants into the environment or not overcharging for work performed on government contracts.

Those who take the stakeholder view of business ethics often argue that it is in the enlightened self-interest of managers to behave in an ethical manner that recognizes and respects the fundamental rights of stakeholders because doing so will ensure the support of stakeholders and thus ultimately benefit the firm and its managers. Others go beyond this instrumental approach to ethics to argue that, in many cases, acting ethically is simply the right thing to do. They argue that businesses need to recognize their *noblesse oblige* and give something back to the society that made their success possible. *Noblesse oblige* is a French term that refers to honorable and benevolent behavior that is considered the responsibility of people of high (noble) birth. In a business setting, it is taken to mean benevolent behavior that is the moral responsibility of successful enterprises.

Unethical behavior often arises in a corporate setting when managers decide to put the attainment of their own personal goals, or the goals of the enterprise, above the fundamental rights of one or more stakeholder groups (in other words, unethical behavior may arise from agency problems). The most common examples of such behavior involve self-dealing, information manipulation, anticompetitive behavior, opportunistic exploitation of other players in the value chain in which the firm is embedded (including suppliers, complement providers, and distributors), the maintenance of substandard working conditions, environmental degradation, and corruption.

Self-dealing occurs when managers find a way to feather their own nests with corporate monies, and we have already discussed several examples in this chapter (such as Tyco and Computer Associates). **Information manipulation** occurs when managers use their control over corporate data to distort or hide information in order to enhance their own financial situation or the competitive position of the firm. As we have seen, many of the recent accounting scandals involved the deliberate manipulation of financial information. Information manipulation can also occur with regard to nonfinancial data. This occurred when managers at the tobacco companies suppressed internal research that linked smoking to health problems, violating the rights of consumers to accurate information about the dangers of smoking. When evidence of this came to light, lawyers brought class-action suits against the tobacco companies, claiming that they had intentionally caused harm to smokers: they had broken tort law by promoting a product that they knew did serious harm to consumers. In 1999, the tobacco companies settled a lawsuit brought by the states who sought to recover health care costs associated with tobacco-related illnesses; the total payout to the states was $260 billion.

Anticompetitive behavior covers a range of actions aimed at harming actual or potential competitors, most often by using monopoly power, and thereby enhancing the long-run prospects of the firm. For example, in the 1990s, the Justice Department claimed that Microsoft used its monopoly in operating systems to force PC makers to bundle Microsoft's Web browser, Internet Explorer, with Windows and to display Internet Explorer prominently on the computer desktop (the screen you see when you start a personal computer). Microsoft reportedly told PC makers that it would not supply them with Windows unless they did this. Since the PC makers had to have Windows to sell their machines, this was a powerful threat. The alleged goal of the action, which is an example of tie-in sales and is illegal under antitrust laws, was to drive a competing browser maker, Netscape, out of business. The courts ruled that Microsoft was indeed abusing its monopoly power in this case, and under a 2001 consent decree, the company agreed to stop the practice.

Putting the legal issues aside, action such as that allegedly undertaken by managers at Microsoft is unethical on at least three counts. First, it violates the rights of end-users by unfairly limiting their choice. Second, it violates the rights of downstream participants in the industry value chain, in this case PC makers, by forcing them to incorporate a particular product in their design, Third, it violates the rights of competitors to free and fair competition.

Opportunistic exploitation of other players in the value chain in which the firm is embedded is another example of unethical behavior. Exploitation of this kind typically occurs when the managers of a firm seek to unilaterally rewrite the terms of a contract with suppliers, buyers, or complement providers in a way that is more favorable to the firm, often using their power to force the revision through. For example, in the late 1990s, Boeing entered into a $2 billion contract with Titanium Metals Corporation to buy certain amounts of titanium annually for ten years. In 2000, after Titanium Metals had already spent $100 million to expand its production capacity to fulfill the contract, Boeing demanded that the contract be renegotiated, asking for lower prices and an end to minimum purchase agreements. As a major purchaser of titanium, managers at Boeing probably thought they had the power to push this contract revision through, and the investment by Titanium meant that they would be unlikely to walk away from the deal. Titanium promptly sued Boeing for breach of contract. The dispute was settled out of court, and under a revised agreement, Boeing agreed to pay monetary damages (reported to be in the $60 million range) to Titanium Metals and entered into an amended contract to purchase titanium.[34] Regardless of the legality of this action, it was arguably unethical because it violated the rights of suppliers to deal with buyers who negotiate with them in a fair and open way.

Substandard working conditions arise when managers underinvest in working conditions or pay employees below-market rates in order to reduce their costs of production. The most extreme examples of such behavior occur when a firm establishes operations in countries that lack the workplace regulations found in developed nations such as the United States. The example of Nike, which was given earlier in Strategy in Action 11.3, falls into this category. In another recent example, the Ohio Art Company ran into an ethical storm when newspaper reports alleged that it had moved production of its popular Etch A Sketch toy from Ohio to a supplier in Shenzhen Province, China, where employees, mostly teenagers, work long hours for 24 cents per hour, below the legal minimum wage of 33 cents an hour in Shenzhen Province. Moreover, production reportedly started at 7:30 A.M. and continued until 10 P.M., with breaks only for lunch and dinner. Saturdays and Sundays are treated as normal workdays. This translates into a workweek of seven twelve-hour days, or eighty-four hours a week, well above the standard forty-hour week set by authorities in Shenzhen. Such working conditions clearly violate the rights of employees in China, as specified by local regulations (which are poorly enforced). Is it ethical for the Ohio Art Company to use such a supplier? Many would say not.[35]

Environmental degradation occurs when the firm takes actions that directly or indirectly result in pollution or other forms of environmental harm. Environmental degradation can violate the rights of local communities and the general public for things such as clean air and water, land that is free from pollution by toxic chemicals, and properly managed forests (because forests absorb rainfall, improper deforestation results in land erosion and floods).

Finally, **corruption** can arise in a business context when managers pay bribes to gain access to lucrative business contracts. For example, it was alleged that Halliburton was part of a consortium that paid some $180 million in bribes to win a lucrative contract to build a natural gas plant in Nigeria.[36] Corruption is clearly unethical because it violates a bundle of rights, including the right of competitors to a level playing field when bidding for contracts and, when government officials are involved, the right of citizens to expect that government officials act in the best interests of the local community or nation and not in response to corrupt payments that feather their own nests.

● The Roots of Unethical Behavior

Why do some managers behave unethically? What motivates them to engage in actions that violate accepted principals of right and wrong, trample on the rights of one or more stakeholder groups, or simply break the law? While there is no simple answer to this question, a few generalizations can be made.[37] First, it is important to recognize that business ethics are not divorced from **personal ethics**, which are the generally accepted principles of right and wrong governing the conduct of individuals. As individuals, we are taught that it is wrong to lie and cheat and that it is right to behave with integrity and honor and to stand up for what we believe to be right and true. The personal ethical code that guides our behavior comes from a number of sources, including our parents, our schools, our religion, and the media. Our personal ethical code exerts a profound influence on the way we behave as businesspeople. An individual with a strong sense of personal ethics is less likely to behave in an unethical manner in a business setting; in particular, he or she is less likely to engage in self-dealing and more likely to behave with integrity.

Second, many studies of unethical behavior in a business setting have come to the conclusion that businesspeople sometimes do not realize that they are behaving unethically, primarily because they simply fail to ask the relevant question: Is this decision or action ethical? Instead, they apply a straightforward business calculus to what they perceive to be a business decision, forgetting that the decision may also have an important ethical dimension.[38] The fault here lies in processes that do not incorporate ethical considerations into business decision making. This may have been the case at Nike when managers originally made subcontracting decisions (see Strategy in Action 11.3). Those decisions were probably made on the basis of good economic logic. Subcontractors were probably chosen on the basis of business variables such as cost, delivery, and product quality, and key managers simply failed to ask, "How does this subcontractor treat its work force?" If they thought about the question at all, they probably reasoned that it was the subcontractor's concern, not theirs.

Unfortunately, the climate in some businesses does not encourage people to think through the ethical consequences of business decisions. This brings us to the third cause of unethical behavior in businesses: an organizational culture that de-emphasizes business ethics and considers all decisions to be purely economic ones. A related fourth cause of unethical behavior may be pressure from top management to meet performance goals that are unrealistic and can be attained only by cutting corners or acting in an unethical manner.

An organizational culture can "legitimize" behavior that society would judge as unethical, particularly when this is mixed with a focus on unrealistic performance goals, such as maximizing short-term economic performance regardless of the costs. In such circumstances, there is a greater-than-average probability that managers will violate their own personal ethics and engage in behavior that is unethical. By the same token, an organizational culture can do just the opposite and reinforce the need for ethical behavior. At Hewlett-Packard, for example, Bill Hewlett and David Packard, the company's founders, propagated a set of values known as "The HP Way." These values, which shape the way business is conducted both within and by the corporation, have an important ethical component. Among other things, they stress the need for confidence in and respect for people, open communication, and concern for the individual employee.

This brings us to a fifth root cause of unethical behavior: *unethical leadership*. Leaders help to establish the culture of an organization, and they set the example that others follow. Other employees in a business often take their cues from business leaders, and if those leaders do not behave in an ethical manner, employees might not either. It is not what leaders say that matters, but what they do. A good example is Ken Lay, the former CEO of the failed energy company Enron. While constantly referring to Enron's code of ethics in public statements, Lay simultaneously engaged in behavior that was ethically suspect. Among other things, he failed to discipline subordinates who had inflated earnings by engaging in corrupt energy trading schemes. Such behavior sent a very clear message to Enron's employees: unethical behavior would be tolerated if it boosted earnings.

● **Philosophical Approaches to Ethics**

In this section, we look at the philosophical underpinnings of business ethics because ultimately it is a philosophy that can provide managers with a moral compass that will help them to navigate their way through difficult ethical issues. We will start with the approach suggested by the Nobel Prize–winning economist Milton Friedman.

THE FRIEDMAN DOCTRINE In 1970, Milton Friedman wrote an article that has since become a classic case that business ethics scholars outline only to then tear down. Friedman's basic position is that the only social responsibility of business is to increase profits, as long as the company stays within the rules of law. He explicitly rejects the idea that businesses should undertake social expenditures beyond those mandated by the law and required for the efficient running of a business. For example, his arguments suggest that improving working conditions beyond the level required by the law and necessary to maximize employee productivity will reduce profits and is therefore not appropriate. His belief is that a firm should maximize its profits because that is the way to maximize the returns that accrue to the owners of the firm, its stockholders. If stockholders then wish to use the proceeds to make social investments, that is their right, according to Friedman, but managers of the firm should not make that decision for them.

Although Friedman is talking about social responsibility rather than business ethics per se, most business ethics scholars equate social responsibility with ethical behavior and thus believe Friedman is also arguing against business ethics. However, the assumption that Friedman is arguing against ethics is not quite true because Friedman does state the following:

> There is one and only one social responsibility of business—to use its resources and engage in activities designed to increase its profits so long as it stays within the rules of the game, which is to say that it engages in open and free competition without deception or fraud.

In other words, Friedman does state that businesses should behave in an ethical manner and not engage in deception and fraud.

Nevertheless, Friedman's arguments break down under closer examination. This is particularly true where the "rules of the game" are not well established, are ambiguous and open to different interpretations, or differ substantially from country to county. Consider again the case of sweatshop labor: using child labor may not be against the law in a developing nation, but it is still immoral to employ children because the practice conflicts with widely held views about what is the right thing to do. Similarly, there may be no rules against pollution in a developed nation, and spending money on pollution control may reduce the profit rate of the firm, but generalized notions of morality hold that it is still unethical to dump toxic pollutants into rivers or foul the air with gas releases. In addition to the local consequences of such pollution, which may have serious health effects for the surrounding population, there is also a global consequence because pollutants degrade those two global environments that we all have a stake in: the atmosphere and the oceans.

UTILITARIAN AND KANTIAN ETHICS Utilitarian and Kantian approaches to business ethics were developed in the eighteenth and nineteenth centuries. Utilitarian approaches to ethics hold that the moral worth of actions or practices is determined by their consequences.[39] An action is judged to be desirable if it leads to the best possible balance of good consequences over bad consequences. **Utilitarianism** is committed to the maximization of good and the minimization of harm. It recognizes that actions have multiple consequences, some of which are good in a social sense and some of which are harmful. As a philosophy for business ethics, it focuses attention on the need to carefully weigh all of the social benefits and costs of a business action and to pursue only those actions where the benefits outweigh the costs. The best decisions, from a utilitarian perspective, are those that produce the greatest good for the greatest number of people.

Many businesses have adopted specific tools, such as cost-benefit analysis and risk assessment, that are firmly rooted in a utilitarian philosophy. Managers often weigh the benefits and costs of a course of action before deciding whether to pursue it. An oil company considering drilling in the Alaskan wildlife preserve must weigh the economic benefits of increased oil production and the creation of jobs against the costs of environmental degradation in a fragile ecosystem.

For all of its appeal, however, the utilitarian philosophy has some serious drawbacks. One problem is measuring the benefits, costs, and risks of a course of action. In the case of an oil company considering drilling in Alaska, how does one measure the potential harm done to the fragile ecosystem of the region? In general, utilitarian philosophers recognize that benefits, costs, and risks often cannot be measured because of limited knowledge.

The second problem with utilitarianism is that the philosophy does not consider justice. The action that produces the greatest good for the greatest number of people may result in the unjustified treatment of a minority. Such action cannot be ethical precisely because it is unjust. For example, suppose that in the interests of keeping down health insurance costs, the government decides to screen people for the HIV virus and deny insurance coverage to those who are HIV positive. By reducing health costs, such action might produce significant benefits for a large number of people, but the action is unjust because it discriminates unfairly against a minority.

Kantian ethics are based on the philosophy of Immanuel Kant (1724–1804), who argued that people should be treated as ends and never purely as means to the ends of others. People are not instruments, like a machine. People have dignity and need to be respected as such. Employing people in sweatshops where they work long hours for low pay in poor work conditions is a violation of ethics according to Kantian philosophy because it treats people as mere cogs in a machine and not as conscious moral beings that have dignity. Although contemporary moral philosophers tend to view Kant's ethical philosophy as incomplete—for example, his system has no place for moral emotions or sentiments such as sympathy or caring—the notion that people should be respected and treated with dignity still resonates in the modern world.

RIGHTS THEORIES Developed in the twentieth century, rights theories recognize that human beings have fundamental rights and privileges. Rights establish a minimum level of morally acceptable behavior. One well-known definition of a fundamental right construes it as something that takes precedence over or "trumps" a collective good.[40] Thus, we might say that the right to free speech is a fundamental right that takes precedence over all but the most compelling collective goals; for example, it overrides the interest of the state in civil harmony or moral consensus. Moral theorists argue that fundamental human rights form the basis for the *moral compass* managers should navigate by when making decisions that have an ethical component. In a business setting, stakeholder theory provides a useful way for managers to frame any discussion of rights. As noted earlier, stakeholders have basic rights that should be respected, and it is unethical to violate those rights.

It is important to note that along with *rights* come *obligations*. Because we have the right to free speech, we are also obligated to make sure that we respect the free speech of others. Within the framework of a theory of rights, certain people or institutions are obligated to provide benefits or services that secure the rights of others. Such obligations also fall upon more than one class of moral agent (a moral agent is any person or institution that is capable of moral action, such as a government or corporation).

For example, in the late 1980s, to escape the high costs of toxic waste disposal in the West, several firms shipped their waste in bulk to African nations, where it was disposed of at a much lower cost. In 1987, five European ships unloaded toxic waste containing dangerous poisons in Nigeria. Workers wearing thongs and shorts unloaded the barrels for $2.50 a day and placed them in a dirt lot in a residential area. They were not told about the contents of the barrels. Who bears the obligation for protecting the safety rights of workers and residents in a case like this? According to rights theorists, the obligation rests not on the shoulders of one moral agent but on the shoulders of all moral agents whose actions might harm, or contribute to the harm of, the workers and residents. Thus, it was the obligation not just of the Nigerian government, but also of the multinational firms that shipped the toxic waste, to make sure that it did no harm to residents and workers. In this case, both the government and the multinationals obviously failed to recognize their basic obligation to protect the fundamental human rights of others.

JUSTICE THEORIES Justice theories focus on the attainment of a just distribution of economic goods and services. A **just distribution** is one that is considered fair and equitable. The most famous theory of justice is attributed to philosopher John Rawls.[41] Rawls argues that all economic goods and services should be distributed equally except when an unequal distribution would work to everyone's advantage.

According to Rawls, valid principles of justice are those with which all persons would agree if they could freely and impartially consider the situation. Impartiality is guaranteed by a conceptual device that Rawls calls the veil of ignorance. Under the veil of ignorance, everyone is imagined to be ignorant of all of his or her particular characteristics, for example, his or her race, sex, intelligence, nationality, family background, and special talents. Rawls then asks: What system would people design under a veil of ignorance? His answer is that, under these conditions, people would unanimously agree on two fundamental principles of justice.

The first principle is that each person should be permitted the maximum amount of basic liberty compatible with a similar liberty for others. Roughly speaking, Rawls takes these liberties to be political liberty (the right to vote), freedom of speech and assembly, liberty of conscience and freedom of thought, the freedom and right to hold personal property, and freedom from arbitrary arrest and seizure. The second principle is that once equal basic liberty is ensured, inequality in basic social goods—such as income, wealth, and opportunities—is to be allowed only if it benefits everyone. Rawls believes that inequalities can be just as long as the system that produces them is to the advantage of everyone. More precisely, he formulates what he calls the *difference principle*, which is that inequalities are justified if they benefit the position of the least advantaged person. So, for example, the wide variations in income and wealth that we see in the United States can be considered "just" if the market-based system that produces this unequal distribution also benefits the least advantaged members of society.

In the context of business ethics, Rawls's theory creates an interesting perspective. Managers can ask themselves whether the policies they adopt would be considered "just" under Rawls's veil of *ignorance*. Is it "just," for example, to pay foreign workers less than workers in the firm's home country? Rawls's second principle would suggest that it is, as long as the inequality benefits the least advantaged members of the global society. Alternatively, it is difficult to imagine that managers operating under a veil of ignorance would design a system where employees are paid subsistence wages to work long hours in sweatshop conditions and be exposed to toxic materials. Such working conditions are clearly unjust in Rawls's framework and therefore it is unethical to adopt them. Similarly, operating under a veil of ignorance, most people would probably design a system that imparts protection from environmental degradation, preserves a free and fair playing field for competition, and prohibits self-dealing. Thus, Rawls's veil of ignorance is a conceptual tool that helps define the moral compass managers can use to navigate through difficult ethical dilemmas.

● Behaving Ethically

What, then, is the best way for managers to ensure that ethical considerations are taken into account? In many cases, there is no easy answer to this question because many of the most vexing ethical problems involve very real dilemmas and suggest no obvious right course of action. Nevertheless, managers can and should do at least seven things to ensure that basic ethical principles are adhered to and that ethical issues are routinely considered when making business decisions. They can (1) favor hiring and promoting people with a well-grounded sense of personal ethics, (2) build an organizational culture that places a high value on ethical behavior, (3) make sure that leaders within the business not only articulate the rhetoric of ethical behavior but also act in a manner that is consistent with that rhetoric, (4) put decision-making processes in place that require people to consider the ethical dimension of business decisions, (5) hire ethics officers, (6) put strong governance processes in place, and (7) act with moral courage.

HIRING AND PROMOTION It seems obvious that businesses should strive to hire people who have a strong sense of personal ethics and would not engage in unethical or illegal behavior. Similarly, you would rightly expect a business not to promote people, and perhaps fire people, whose behavior does not match generally accepted ethical standards. But doing so is actually very difficult. How do you know that someone has a poor sense of personal ethics? In our society, if someone lacks personal ethics, he or she may hide this fact to retain people's trust.

Is there anything that businesses can do to make sure that they do not hire people who turn out to have poor personal ethics, particularly given that people have an incentive to hide this from public view (indeed, unethical people may well lie about their nature)? Businesses can give potential employees psychological tests to try to discern their ethical predisposition, and they can check with prior employees regarding someone's reputation, such as by asking for letters of reference and talking to people who have worked with the prospective employee. The latter approach is certainly not uncommon and does indeed influence the hiring process. As for promoting people who have displayed poor ethics, that should not occur in a company where the organizational culture values ethical behavior and where leaders act accordingly.

ORGANIZATIONAL CULTURE AND LEADERSHIP To foster ethical behavior, businesses need to build an organizational culture that places a high value on ethical behavior. Three actions are particularly important. First, businesses must explicitly articulate values that place a strong emphasis on ethical behavior. Many companies now do this by drafting a **code of ethics**, a formal statement of the ethical priorities a business adheres to. Others have incorporated ethical statements into documents that articulate the values or mission of the business. For example, the food and consumer products giant Unilever has a code of ethics that includes the following points: "We will not use any form of forced, compulsory or child labor" and "No employee may offer, give or receive any gift or payment which is, or may be construed as being, a bribe. Any demand for, or offer of, a bribe must be rejected immediately and reported to management."[42] Unilever's principles send a very clear message to managers and employees within the organization. As you can see from the Running Case, Dell also has a well established code of ethics.

Having articulated values in a code of ethics or some other document, it is important that leaders in the business give life and meaning to those words by repeatedly emphasizing their importance and then acting on them. This means using every relevant opportunity to stress the importance of business ethics and making sure that key business decisions not only make good economic sense but also are ethical. Many companies have gone a step further and hired independent firms to audit them and make sure that they are behaving in a manner consistent with their ethical code. Nike, for example, has hired independent auditors in recent years to make sure that its subcontractors are living up to Nike's code of conduct. Finally, building an organizational culture that places a high value on ethical behavior requires incentive and reward systems, including promotion systems, that reward people who engage in ethical behavior and sanction those who do not.

RUNNING CASE

Dell's Code of Ethics

Michael Dell has long put his name on a comprehensive code of ethics at Dell Computer. The code specifies with great precision what Dell requires of its employees. Dell states that the success of the company is built on "a foundation of personal and professional integrity" and that the company's employees must hold themselves to standards of ethical behavior that "go well beyond legal minimums."

At the center of the code of conduct is a set of values that Michael Dell characterizes as "the Soul of Dell." These values are as follows:

Trust—Our word is good. We keep our commitments to each other and to our stakeholders.

Integrity—We do the right thing without compromise. We avoid even the appearance of impropriety.

Honesty—What we say is true and forthcoming—not just technically correct. We are open and transparent in our communications with each other and about business performance.

Judgment—We think before we act and consider the consequences of our actions.

Respect—We treat people with dignity and value their contributions. We maintain fairness in all relationships.

Courage—We speak up for what is right. We report wrongdoing when we see it.

Responsibility—We accept the consequences of our actions. We admit our mistakes and quickly correct them. We do not retaliate against those who report violations of law or policy.

The code goes beyond these general statements, however, to detail what Dell employees cannot do. For example, with regard to bribes and gifts, the code states that "as a Dell employee you must never accept or give a bribe." The code also prohibits the receipt of any gifts with a nominal value of over $50 that may "compromise your judgment."

Dell has established a global ethics officer, a global ethics council, and regional ethics committees to make sure that the company's ethics policy is enforced. Employees can report ethics violations directly to the officer and associated committees, or via an anonymous ethics hotline.[d]

DECISION-MAKING PROCESSES In addition to establishing the right kind of ethical culture in an organization, businesspeople must be able to think through the ethical implications of decisions in a systematic way. To do this, they need a moral compass, and both rights theories and Rawls's theory of justice help to provide such a compass. Beyond these theories, some experts on ethics have proposed a straightforward practical guide, or ethical algorithm, to determine whether a decision is ethical. A decision is acceptable on ethical grounds if a businessperson can answer yes to each of these questions:

1. Does my decision fall within the accepted values or standards that typically apply in the organizational environment (as articulated in a code of ethics or some other corporate statement)?

2. Am I willing to see the decision communicated to all stakeholders affected by it—for example, by having it reported in newspapers or on television?

3. Would the people with whom I have a significant personal relationship, such as family members, friends, or even managers in other businesses, approve of the decision?

ETHICS OFFICERS To make sure that a business behaves in an ethical manner, a number of firms now have ethics officers. These individuals are responsible for making sure that all employees are trained to be ethically aware, that ethical considerations enter the business decision-making process, and that the company's code of ethics is adhered to. Ethics officers may also be responsible for auditing decisions to make sure that they are consistent with this code. In many businesses, ethics officers act as an internal ombudsperson with responsibility for handling confidential inquiries from employees, investigating complaints from employees or others, reporting findings, and making recommendations for change.

United Technologies, a large aerospace company with worldwide revenues of over $28 billion, has had a formal code of ethics since 1990. There are now some 160 business practice officers (this is the company's name for ethics officers) within United Technologies who are responsible for making sure that the code is adhered to. United Technologies also established an ombudsperson program in 1986 that lets employees inquire anonymously about ethics issues. The program has received some 56,000 inquiries since 1986, and 8,000 cases have been handled by an ombudsperson.[43]

STRONG CORPORATE GOVERNANCE Strong corporate governance procedures are needed to make sure that managers adhere to ethical norms, in particular, that senior managers do not engage in self-dealing or information manipulation. The key to strong corporate governance procedures is an independent board of directors that is willing to hold top managers accountable for self-dealing and is able to question the information provided to them by managers. If companies like Tyco, WorldCom, and Enron had had a strong board of directors, it is unlikely that they would have been racked by accounting scandals or that top managers would have been able to view the funds of these corporations as their own personal treasuries.

There are five cornerstones of strong governance. The first is a board of directors that is composed of a majority of outside directors who have no management responsibilities in the firm, are willing and able to hold top managers accountable, and do not have business ties with important insiders. The outside directors should be individuals of high integrity whose reputation is based on their ability to act independently. The second cornerstone is a board where the positions of CEO and chair are held by separate individuals and the chair is an outside director. When the CEO is also chair of the board of directors, he or she can control the agenda, thereby furthering his or her own personal agenda (which may include self-dealing) or limiting criticism against current corporate policies. The third cornerstone is a compensation committee formed by the board that is composed entirely of outside directors. The compensation committee sets the level of pay for top managers, including stock option grants and the like. By making sure that the compensation committee is independent of managers, one reduces the scope of self-dealing. Fourth, the audit committee of the board, which reviews the financial statements of the firm, should also be composed of outsiders, thereby encouraging vigorous independent questioning of the firm's financial statements. Finally, the board should use outside auditors who are truly independent and do not have a conflict of interest. This was not the case in many recent accounting scandals, where the outside auditors were also consultants to the corporation and therefore less likely to ask hard questions of management for fear that doing so would jeopardize lucrative consulting contracts.

MORAL COURAGE It is important to recognize that sometimes managers and others need significant moral courage. Moral courage enables managers to walk away from a decision that is profitable but unethical, gives employees the strength to say no to superiors who instruct them to behave unethically, and gives employees the integrity to go to the media and blow the whistle on persistent unethical behavior in a company. Moral courage does not come easily; there are well-known cases where individuals have lost their jobs because they blew the whistle on corporate behaviors.

Companies can strengthen the moral courage of employees by committing themselves to not take retribution on employees who exercise moral courage, say no to superiors, or otherwise complain about unethical actions. For example, Unilever's code of ethics includes the following:

> *Any breaches of the Code must be reported in accordance with the procedures specified by the Joint Secretaries. The Board of Unilever will not criticize management for any loss of business resulting from adherence to these principles and other mandatory policies and instructions. The Board of Unilever expects employees to bring to their attention, or to that of senior management, any breach or suspected breach of these principles. Provision has been made for employees to be able to report in confidence and no employee will suffer as a consequence of doing so.*

This statement gives permission to employees to exercise moral courage. Companies can also set up ethics hotlines that allow employees to register a complaint anonymously with a corporate ethics officer.

FINAL WORDS The steps discussed here can help to ensure that, when managers make business decisions, they are fully cognizant of the ethical implications and do not violate basic ethical prescripts. At the same time, not all ethical dilemmas have a clean and obvious solution—that is why they are dilemmas. At the end of the day, there are clearly things that a business should not do, and there are things that they should do, but there are also actions that present managers with true dilemmas. In these cases, a premium is placed on the ability of managers to make sense out of complex, messy situations and to make balanced decisions that are as just as possible.

Summary of Chapter

1. Stakeholders are individuals or groups that have an interest, claim, or stake in the company, in what it does, and in how well it performs.

2. Stakeholders are in an exchange relationship with the company. They supply the organization with important resources (or contributions) and in exchange expect their interests to be satisfied (by inducements).

3. A company cannot always satisfy the claims of all stakeholders. The goals of different groups may conflict. The company must identify the most important stakeholders and give highest priority to pursuing strategies that satisfy their needs.

4. A company's stockholders are its legal owners and the providers of risk capital, a major source of the capital resources that allow a company to operate its business. As such, they have a unique role among stakeholder groups.

5. Maximizing long-run profitability and profit growth is the route to maximizing returns to stockholders, and it is also consistent with satisfying the claims of several other key stakeholder groups.

6. When pursuing strategies that maximize profitability, a company has the obligation to do so within the limits set by the law and in a manner consistent with societal expectations.

7. An agency relationship is held to arise whenever one party delegates decision-making authority or control over resources to another.

8. The essence of the agency problem is that the interests of principals and agents are not always the same, and some agents may take advantage of information asymmetries to maximize their own interests at the expense of principals.

9. A number of governance mechanisms serve to limit the agency problem between stockholders and managers. These include the board of directors, stock-based compensation schemes, financial statements and auditors, and the threat of a takeover.

10. The term *ethics* refers to accepted principles of right or wrong that govern the conduct of a person, the members of a profession, or the actions of an organization. Business ethics are the accepted principles of right or wrong governing the conduct of businesspeople, and an ethical strategy is one that does not violate these accepted principles.

11. Unethical behavior is rooted in poor personal ethics; the inability to recognize that ethical issues are at stake, as when there are psychological and geographical distances between a foreign subsidiary and the home office; failure to incorporate ethical issues into strategic and operational decision making; a dysfunctional culture; and failure of leaders to act in an ethical manner.

12. Philosophies underlying business ethics include the Friedman doctrine, utilitarianism, Kantian ethics, rights theories, and justice theories such as that proposed by Rawls.

13. To make sure that ethical issues are considered in business decisions, managers should (a) favor hiring and promoting people with a well-grounded sense of personal ethics, (b) build an organizational culture that places a high value on ethical behavior, (c) make sure that leaders within the business not only articulate the rhetoric of ethical behavior but also act in a manner that is consistent with that rhetoric, (d) put decision-making processes in place that require people to consider the ethical dimension of business decisions, (e) hire ethics officers, (f) have strong corporate governance procedures, and (g) be morally courageous and encourage others to be the same.

Discussion Questions

1. How prevalent has the agency problem been in corporate America during the last decade? During the late 1990s, there was a boom in initial public offerings of Internet companies (dot.com companies). The boom was supported by sky-high valuations often assigned to Internet start-ups that had no revenues or earnings. The boom came to an abrupt end in 2001 when the NASDAQ stock market collapsed, losing almost 80% of its value. Who do you think benefited most from this boom: investors (stockholders) in those companies, managers, or investment bankers?

2. Why is maximizing return on invested capital consistent with maximizing returns to stockholders?

3. How might a company configure its strategy-making processes to reduce the probability that managers will pursue their own self-interest at the expense of stockholders?

4. In a public corporation, should the CEO of the company also be allowed to be the chair of the board (as allowed for by the current law)? What problems might this give rise to?

5. Under what conditions is it ethically defensible to outsource production to producers in the developing world who have much lower labor costs when such actions involve laying off long-term employees in the firm's home country?

6. Is it ethical for a firm faced with a shortage of labor to employ illegal immigrants as labor?

Practicing Strategic Management

SMALL-GROUP EXERCISE
Evaluating Stakeholder Claims

Break up into groups of three to five, appoint one group member to be a spokesperson who will communicate your findings to the class when called on by the instructor, and discuss the following:

1. Identify the key stakeholders of your educational institution. What claims do they place on the institution?
2. Strategically, how is the institution responding to those claims? Do you think the institution is pursuing the correct strategies in view of those claims? What might it do differently, if anything?
3. Prioritize the stakeholders in order of their importance for the survival and health of the institution. Do the claims of different stakeholder groups conflict with each other? If claims conflict, whose should be tackled first?

ARTICLE FILE 11

Find an example of a company that ran into trouble because it failed to take into account the rights of one of its stakeholder groups when making an important strategic decision.

STRATEGIC MANAGEMENT PROJECT
Module 11

This module deals with the relationships your company has with its major stakeholder groups. With the information you have at your disposal, perform the tasks and answer the questions that follow:

1. Identify the main stakeholder groups in your company. What claims do they place on the company? How is the company trying to satisfy those claims?
2. Evaluate the performance of the CEO of your company from the perspective of (a) stockholders, (b) employees, (c) customers, and (d) suppliers. What does this evaluation tell you about the ability of the CEO and the priorities that he or she is committed to?

3. Try to establish whether the governance mechanisms that operate in your company do a good job of aligning the interests of top managers with those of stockholders.
4. Pick a major strategic decision made by your company in recent years, and try to think through the ethical implications of that decision. In the light of your review, do you think that the company acted correctly?

ETHICS EXERCISE

Sam works for Juice International as an administrative assistant. Although unrelated, he and the CEO of the company share the same last name, and somehow a report destined for the CEO and marked both *confidential* and *urgent* had landed on Sam's desk. Normally Sam would have noticed the mistake and sent the envelope, unopened, straight to the CEO's office, but it had been a busy day and Sam hadn't noticed the error in the name until after he had opened the envelope and read the contents.

Inside the envelope were lab reports. One of Juice International's newest fruit drinks was being marketed to the public under false pretenses. The labels on the containers claimed that the juice was 100% natural, but the lab report suggested that the drink contained only the chemical equivalent of the juice. Should news of this get out, Juice International would lose customers rapidly. To make matters worse, the CEO to whom the information had been headed was known for doing anything to maintain the company's bottom line. Sam feared that by handing the lab reports over to the CEO, the information would never get out and customers would continue to purchase the juice, thinking it was 100% fruit juice. On the other hand, Sam didn't know whom he could trust with the information. He simply didn't know what to do.

1. Define the ethical issues at stake in this case.
2. What would you do if you were in Sam's position?
3. How do you think the company should handle this issue?

CLOSING CASE

Working Conditions At Wal-Mart

When Sam Walton founded Wal-Mart, now the world's largest retailer, one of his core values was that if you treated employees with respect, tied compensation to the performance of the enterprise, trusted the employees with important information and decisions, and provided ample opportunities for advancement, employees would repay the company with dedication and hard work. For years, the formula seemed to work. Employees were called associates to reflect their status within the company. Even the lowest hourly employee was eligible to participate in profit sharing schemes and could use profit sharing bonuses to purchase company stock at a discount compared to its market value. And the company made a virtue of promoting from within (two-thirds of managers at Wal-Mart started as hourly employees). At the same time, Walton and his successors always demanded loyalty and hard work from employees. Managers, for example, were expected to move to a new store on very short notice, and base pay for hourly workers was very low. Still, as long as the upside was there, little grumbling was heard from employees.

In the last ten years, however, the relationship between the company and its employees has been strained by a succession of law suits claiming that Wal-Mart pressures hourly employees to work without compensation, requires overtime without compensating them, systematically discriminates against women, and knowingly uses contractors who hire undocumented immigrant workers to clean its stores and pay them below minimum wage. For example, a class-action law suit in Washington State claims that Wal-Mart routinely (a) pressured hourly employees not to report all their time worked; (b) failed to keep true time records, sometimes shaving hours from employee logs; (c) failed to give employees full rest or meal breaks; (d) threatened to fire or demote employees who would not work off the clock; and (e) required workers to attend unpaid meetings and computer training. Moreover, the suit claims that Wal-Mart has a strict no overtime policy, punishing employees who work more than forty hours a week, but that the company also gives employees more work than can be completed in a forty-hour week. The Washington suit is one of more than thirty lawsuits that have been filed around the nation in recent years.

With regard to discrimination against women, complaints date back to 1996 when an assistant manager in a California store, Stephanie Odle, came across the W2 of a male assistant manager who worked in the same store. The W2 showed that he was paid $10,000 more than Odle. When she asked her boss to explain the disparity, she was told that her coworker had "a wife and kids to support." When Odle, who is a single mother, protested, she was asked to submit a personal household budget. She was then granted a $2,080 raise. Subsequently Odle was fired, she claims for speaking up. In 1998, she filed a discrimination suit against the company. Others began to file suits around the same time, and by 2004, the legal action had evolved into a class-action suit that covered 1.6 million current and former female employees at Wal-Mart. The suit claims that Wal-Mart did not pay female employees the same as their male counterparts, and did not provide them with equal opportunities for promotion.

In the case of both undocumented overtime and discrimination, Wal-Mart admits to no wrongdoing. The company does recognize that with some 1.6 million employees, some problems are bound to arise, but it claims that there is no systematic, companywide effort to get hourly employees to work without pay or to discriminate against women. Indeed, the company claims that this could not be the case because hiring and promotion decisions are made at the store level.

For their part, critics charge that, while the company may have no policies that promote undocumented overtime or discrimination, the hard-driving, cost-containment culture of the company had created an environment where abuses can thrive. Store managers, for example, are expected to meet challenging performance goals, and in an effort to do so, they may be tempted to pressure subordinates to work additional hours without pay. Similarly, company policy requiring managers to move to different stores on short notice unfairly discriminates against women, who lack the flexibility to uproot their families and move them to another state on short notice.

To compound matters, in the early 2000s, Wal-Mart was hit by charges from U.S. Immigration and Customs Enforcement, which claimed that the company hired hundreds of illegal immigrants at low pay to clean floors at sixty stores around the country. Wal-Mart paid an $11 million fine and promised that the practice would stop, but the successful suit was yet another embarrassment for the company.

While the pay and discrimination lawsuits are ongoing and may take years to resolve (there are some forty lawsuits in process at the time of this writing), Wal-Mart has taken steps to change its employment practices. For example, the company has created a director of diversity and a diversity compliance team, and restructured its pay scales to promote equal pay regardless of gender. In 2006, the company also created a panel that has independent outside experts on it, in addition to company insiders.

The panel is charged with developing policies for extending work force diversity at Wal-Mart.[44]

Case Discussion Questions

1. What do you think are the root causes of the problems related to working conditions, discrimination, and the hiring of illegal immigrants at Wal-Mart?

2. How might these problems affect Wal-Mart in the future if they are not fixed?

3. Why do you think that problems related to poor working conditions started to emerge at Wal-Mart in the last ten years? Why didn't they arise when Wal-Mart was a smaller and faster growing enterprise?

4. Has the company done all that it can do deal with these problems? What else could it do?

Implementing Strategy in Companies That Compete in a Single Industry

Strategy Implementation at Dell Computer

Dell Computer was one of the fastest-growing companies of the 1990s, and its stock price increased at the rate of 100% a year, delighting its stockholders. Achieving this high return has been a constant challenge for Michael Dell, and one of his biggest battles has been to manage and change Dell's organizational structure, control systems, and culture as his company grows.

Dell was nineteen when, in 1984, he took $1,000 and spent it on the computer parts he assembled himself into PCs that he then sold over the phone. Increasing demand for his PCs meant that within a few weeks, he needed to hire people to help him, and soon he found himself supervising three employees who worked together around a six-foot table to assemble computers while two more employees took orders over the phone.[1]

By 1993, Dell employed 4,500 workers and was hiring over 100 new workers each week just to keep pace with the demand for the computers. When he found himself working eighteen-hour days managing the company, he realized that he could not lead the company single-handedly. The company's growth had to be managed, and he knew that he had to recruit and hire strategic managers who had experience in managing different functional areas, such as marketing, finance, and manufacturing. He recruited executives from IBM and Compaq and, with their help, created a functional structure, one in which employees are grouped by the common skills they have or tasks they perform, such as sales or manufacturing, to organize the value chain activities necessary to deliver his PCs to customers. As a part of this organizing process, Dell's structure also became taller, with more levels in the management hierarchy, to ensure that he and his managers had sufficient control over the different activities of his growing business. Dell delegated authority to control Dell's functional value chain activities to his managers, which gave him the time he needed to perform his entrepreneurial task of finding new opportunities for the company.

Dell's functional structure worked well and, under its new management team, the company's growth continued to soar. By 1993, the company had sales of over $2 billion, twice as much as in 1992. Moreover, Dell's new structure had given functional managers the control they needed to squeeze out costs, and Dell had become the lowest-cost PC maker. Analysts also reported that Dell had developed a lean organizational culture, meaning that employees had developed norms and values that emphasized the importance of working hard to help each other find innovative new ways of making products to keep costs low and increase their reliability. Indeed, with the fewest customer complaints, Dell rose to the top of the customer satisfaction rankings for PC makers; its employees became known for the excellent customer service they gave to PC buyers who were experiencing problems with setting up their computers.

However, Michael Dell realized that new and different kinds of problems were arising. Dell was now selling huge numbers of computers to different kinds of customers, for example, home, business, and educational customers and the different branches of government. Because customers now demanded computers with very different features or different amounts of computing power, the company's product line broadened rapidly. It started to become more difficult for employees to meet the needs of these different kinds of customers efficiently because each employee needed information about all product features or all of Dell's thousands of different sales offers across its product range.

In 1995, Dell moved to change his company to a market structure and created separate divisions, each geared to the needs of a different group of customers: a consumer division, a business division, and so on. In each division, teams of employees specialize in servicing the needs of one of these customer groups. This move to a more complex structure also allowed each division to develop a unique subculture that suited its tasks, and employees were able to obtain in-depth knowledge about the needs of their market that helped them to respond better to their customers' needs. So successful was this change in structure and culture that by 2000, Dell's revenues were over \$35 billion and its profits were in excess of \$3 billion, a staggering increase from 1984.[2]

Dell continued to alter his company's structure in the 1990s to respond to changing customer needs and to the company's increase in distinctive competencies. For example, Dell realized that he could leverage his company's strengths in materials management, manufacturing, and Internet sales over a wider range of computer hardware products. So he decided to begin assembling servers, workstations, and storage devices to compete with IBM, Sun, and Compaq. The increasing importance of the Internet led him to split the market divisions into thirty-five smaller subunits that focus on more specialized groups of customers, and they all conduct the majority of their business over the Internet. Today, for example, Dell can offer large and small companies and private buyers a complete range of computers, workstations, and storage devices that can be customized to their needs.

To help coordinate its growing activities, Dell is increasingly making use of its corporate intranet and using information technology (IT) to standardize activities across divisions and thus integrate across functions. Dell's hierarchy is shrinking as managers are increasingly delegating everyday decision making to employees who have access, through IT, to the facts they need to provide excellent customer service. To help reduce costs, Dell has also outsourced most of its customer service activities to India.[3] As a result of these moves, Dell's work force has become even more committed to sustaining its low-cost advantage, and its cost-conscious culture has become an important source of competitive advantage that is the envy of its competitors, and one that has been imitated by HP and Gateway.[4]

OVERVIEW   As the story of Dell suggests, organizational structure and culture can have a direct bearing on a company's profits. This chapter examines how managers can best implement their strategies through their organization's structure and culture to achieve a competitive advantage and superior performance. A well-thought-out business model becomes profitable only if it can be implemented successfully. In practice, however, implementing strategy through structure and culture is a difficult, challenging, and never-ending task. Managers cannot just create an organizing framework for a company's value chain activities and then assume it will keep working efficiently and effectively over time, just as they cannot select strategies and assume that these strategies will still work in the future when the competitive environment is changing.

We begin by discussing the main elements of organizational design and the way they work together to create an organizing framework that allows a company to implement its strategy. We also discuss how strategic managers can use structure, control, and culture to pursue functional-level strategies that create and build distinctive competencies. The analysis then moves to the industry level and the issues facing managers in a single industry. The next chapter takes up where this one leaves off and examines strategy implementation across industries and countries—that is, corporate and global strategy. By the end of this chapter and the next, you will understand why the fortunes of a company often rest on its managers' ability to design and manage its structure, control systems, and culture to best implement its business model.

Implementing Strategy Through Organizational Design

Strategy implementation involves the use of **organizational design,** the process of deciding how a company should create, use, and combine organizational structure, control systems, and culture to pursue a business model successfully. **Organizational structure** assigns employees to specific value creation tasks and roles, and specifies how these tasks and roles are to be linked together in a way that increases efficiency, quality, innovation, and responsiveness to customers—the distinctive competencies that build competitive advantage. The purpose of organizational structure is to coordinate and integrate the efforts of employees at all levels—corporate, business, and functional—and across a company's functions and business units so that they work together in the way that will allow it to achieve the specific set of strategies in its business model.

Organizational structure does not, by itself, provide the set of incentives through which people can be motivated to make it work. Hence, there is a need for control systems. The purpose of a **control system** is to provide managers with (*1*) a set of incentives to motivate employees to work toward increasing efficiency, quality, innovation, and responsiveness to customers and (**2**) specific feedback on how well an organization and its members are performing and building competitive advantage so that managers can constantly take action to strengthen a company's business model. Structure provides an organization with a skeleton; control gives it the muscles, sinews, nerves, and sensations that allow managers to regulate and govern its activities.

Organizational culture, the third element of organizational design, is the specific collection of values, norms, beliefs, and attitudes that are shared by people and groups in an organization and that control the way they interact with each other and with stakeholders outside the organization.[5] Organizational culture is a company's way of doing something: it describes the characteristic ways in which members of an organization get the job done, such as the way Nokia uses teams to speed innovation. As we discuss in detail below, top managers, because they can influence which kinds of beliefs and values develop in an organization, are an important determinant of how organizational members will work toward achieving organizational goals.[6]

Figure 12.1 sums up the discussion so far. Organizational structure, control, and culture are the means by which an organization motivates and coordinates its members to work toward achieving the building blocks of competitive advantage.

FIGURE 12.1

Implementing Strategy Through Organizational Design

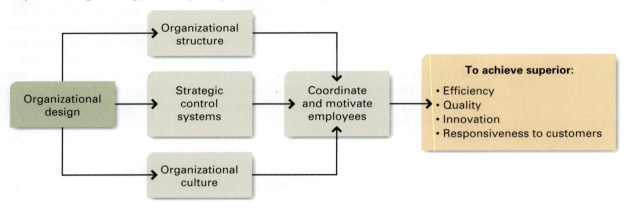

Top managers who wish to find out why it takes a long time for people to make decisions in a company, why there is a lack of cooperation between sales and manufacturing, or why product innovations are few and far between, need to understand how the design of a company's structure and control system and the values and norms in its culture affect employee motivation and behavior. *Organizational structure, control, and culture shape people's behaviors, values, and attitudes and determine how they will implement an organization's business model and strategies.*[7] On the basis of such an analysis, top managers can devise a plan to restructure or change their company's structure, control systems, and culture to improve coordination and motivation. Effective organizational design allows a company to obtain a competitive advantage and achieve above-average profitability.

Building Blocks of Organizational Structure

After formulating a company's business model and strategies, managers must make designing an organizational structure their next priority. The value creation activities of organizational members are meaningless unless some type of structure is used to assign people to tasks and connect the activities of different people and functions.[8] Managers must make three basic choices:

1. How best to group tasks into functions and to group functions into business units or divisions to create distinctive competencies and pursue a particular strategy

2. How to allocate authority and responsibility to these functions and divisions

3. How to increase the level of coordination or integration between functions and divisions as a structure evolves and becomes more complex

We first discuss basic issues and then revisit them when considering appropriate choices of structure at different levels of strategy.

● **Grouping Tasks, Functions, and Divisions**

Because an organization's tasks are, to a large degree, a function of its strategy, the dominant view is that companies choose a form of structure to match their organizational strategy. Perhaps the first person to address this issue formally was the

Harvard business historian Alfred D. Chandler.[9] After studying the organizational problems experienced in large U.S. corporations such as DuPont and GM as they grew in the early decades of the twentieth century, Chandler reached two conclusions: (1) that, in principle, organizational structure follows the range and variety of tasks that the organization chooses to pursue, and (2) that U.S. companies' structures change as their strategy changes in a predictable way over time.[10] In general, this means that most companies first group people and tasks into functions, and then functions into divisions.[11]

As we discussed earlier, a *function* is a collection of people who work together and perform the same types of tasks or hold similar positions in an organization.[12] For example, the salespeople in a car dealership belong to the sales function. Together, car sales, car repair, car parts, and accounting are the set of functions that allow a car dealership to sell and maintain cars.

As organizations grow and produce a wider range of products, the amount and complexity of the *handoffs*, that is, the work exchanges or transfers among people, functions, and subunits, increase. The communications and measurement problems and the managerial inefficiencies surrounding these transfers or handoffs are a major source of *bureaucratic costs*, which we discussed in Chapter 10. Recall that these are the costs associated with monitoring and managing the functional exchanges necessary to add value to a product as it flows along a company's value chain to the final customer.[13] We discuss why bureaucratic costs increase as companies pursue more complex strategies later in the chapter.

For now, it is important to note that managers group tasks into functions and then group functions into a business unit or division to reduce bureaucratic costs. For example, as Dell started to produce different kinds of products, it created separate divisions, each with its own marketing, sales, and accounting functions. A *division* is a way of grouping functions to allow an organization to better produce and transfer its goods and services to customers. In developing an organizational structure, managers must decide how to group an organization's activities by function and division in a way that achieves organizational goals effectively, which is what happened at Dell.[14]

Top managers can choose from among many kinds of structures to group their activities. The choice is made on the basis of the structure's ability to implement the company's business models and strategies successfully.

● **Allocating Authority and Responsibility**

As organizations grow and produce a wider range of goods and services, the size and number of their functions and divisions increase. The number of handoffs or transfers between employees also increases, and to economize on bureaucratic costs and effectively coordinate the activities of people, functions, and divisions, managers must develop a clear and unambiguous **hierarchy of authority,** or chain of command, that defines each manager's relative authority, from the CEO down through the middle managers and first-line managers, to the nonmanagerial employees who actually make goods or provide services.[15] Every manager, at every level of the hierarchy, supervises one or more subordinates. The term **span of control** refers to the number of subordinates who report directly to a manager. When managers know exactly what their authority and responsibility are, information distortion problems that promote managerial inefficiencies are kept to a minimum, and handoffs or transfers can be negotiated and monitored to economize on bureaucratic costs. For example, managers are less likely to risk invading another manager's turf and thus can avoid the costly fights and conflicts that inevitably result from such encroachments.

FIGURE 12.2

Tall and Flat
Structures

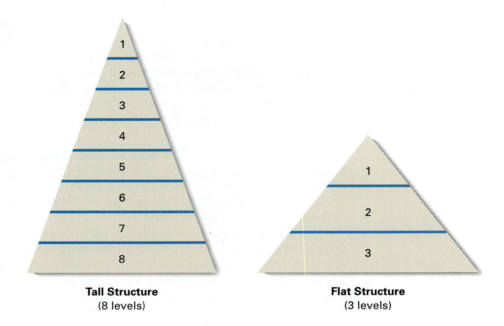

Tall Structure
(8 levels)

Flat Structure
(3 levels)

TALL AND FLAT ORGANIZATIONS Companies choose the number of hierarchical levels they need on the basis of their strategy and the functional tasks necessary to create distinctive competencies.[16] As an organization grows in size or complexity (measured by the number of its employees, functions, and divisions), its hierarchy of authority normally lengthens, making the organizational structure taller. A **tall structure** has many levels of authority relative to company size; a **flat structure** has fewer levels relative to company size (see Figure 12.2). As the hierarchy becomes taller, problems that make the organization's structure less flexible and slow managers' response to changes in the competitive environment may result. It is vital that managers understand how these problems arise so they know how to change a company's structure to respond to them.

First, communication problems may arise. When an organization has many levels in the hierarchy, it can take a long time for the decisions and orders of top managers to reach managers further down in the hierarchy, and it can take a long time for top managers to learn how well their decisions worked out. Feeling out of touch, top managers may want to verify that lower-level managers are following orders and may require written confirmation from them. Lower-level managers, who know they will be held strictly accountable for their actions, start devoting more time to the process of making decisions in order to improve their chances of being right. They might even try to avoid responsibility by making top managers decide what actions to take.

A second communication problem that can result is the distortion of commands and orders as they are transmitted up and down the hierarchy, which causes managers at different levels to interpret what is happening differently. Accidental distortion of orders and messages occurs when different managers interpret messages from their own narrow functional perspectives. Intentional distortion can occur because managers lower in the hierarchy decide to interpret information to increase their own personal advantage.

A third problem with tall hierarchies is that they usually indicate that an organization is employing too many managers, and managers are expensive. Managerial salaries, benefits, offices, and secretaries are a huge expense for organizations. Large companies such as IBM, GM, and Dell pay their managers billions of dollars a year. In the 2000s, hundreds of thousands of middle managers were laid off as dot-coms collapsed and high-tech companies like HP and Lucent attempted to reduce costs by restructuring and downsizing their work forces.

THE MINIMUM CHAIN OF COMMAND   To ward off the problems that result when an organization becomes too tall and employs too many managers, top managers need to ascertain whether they are employing the right number of top, middle, and first-line managers and see whether they can redesign their hierarchies to reduce the number of managers. Top managers might well follow a basic organizing principle: the **principle of the minimum chain of command,** which states that a company should choose the hierarchy with the *fewest* levels of authority necessary to use organizational resources efficiently and effectively.

Effective managers constantly scrutinize their hierarchies to see whether the number of levels can be reduced—for example, by eliminating one level and giving the responsibilities of managers at that level to managers above and empowering employees below. This practice has become increasingly common as companies battle with low-cost overseas competitors and search for ways to reduce costs. One manager who is constantly trying to empower employees and keep the hierarchy flat is Colleen C. Barrett, the number 2 executive of Southwest Airlines.[17] Barrett, the highest-ranking woman in the airline industry, is well known for continually reaffirming Southwest's message that employees should feel free to go above and beyond their prescribed roles to provide better customer service. Her central message is that Southwest values and trusts its employees, who are empowered to take responsibility. Southwest employees are encouraged not to look to their superiors for guidance but rather to take responsibility to find ways to do the job better themselves. As a result, Southwest keeps the number of its middle managers to a minimum.

When companies become too tall and the chain of command too long, strategic managers tend to lose control over the hierarchy, which means that they lose control over their strategies. Disaster often follows because a tall organizational structure decreases, rather than promotes, motivation and coordination between employees and functions, and bureaucratic costs escalate as a result. One important way to overcome such problems, at least partially, and to lessen bureaucratic costs is to decentralize authority—that is, vest authority in the hierarchy's lower levels as well as at the top.

CENTRALIZATION OR DECENTRALIZATION?   Authority is centralized when managers at the upper levels of a company's hierarchy retain the authority to make the most important decisions. When authority is decentralized, it is delegated to divisions, functions, and employees at lower levels in the company. By delegating authority in this fashion, managers can economize on bureaucratic costs and avoid communication and coordination problems because information does not have to be constantly sent to the top of the organization for decisions to be made. There are three advantages to decentralization.

First, when top managers delegate operational decision-making responsibility to middle and first-level managers, they reduce information overload and so are able to spend more time on positioning the company competitively and strengthening its business model. Second, when managers in the bottom layers of the company become responsible for implementing strategies to suit local conditions, their motivation and

Strategy in Action

12.1

Union Pacific Decentralizes to Increase Customer Responsiveness

Union Pacific, one of the biggest rail freight carriers in the United States, was experiencing a crisis in the late 1990s. The U.S. economic boom was causing a record increase in the amount of freight that the railroad had to transport, but at the same time, the railroad was experiencing record delays in moving the freight. Union Pacific's customers were irate and complaining bitterly about the problem, and the delays were costing the company millions of dollars in penalty payments—$150 million annually.

The problem stemmed from Union Pacific's very centralized management approach, devised in its attempt to cut costs. All scheduling and route planning were handled centrally at its headquarters in an attempt to promote operating efficiency. The job of regional managers was largely to ensure the smooth flow of freight through their regions. Now, recognizing that efficiency had to be balanced by the need to be responsive to customers, Union Pacific's CEO, Dick Davidson, announced a sweeping reorganization to the company's customers. Henceforth, regional managers were to be given the authority to make operational decisions at the level at which they were most important: field operations. Regional managers could now alter scheduling and routing to accommodate customer requests even if this raised costs. The goal of the organization was to "return to excellent performance by simplifying our processes and becoming easier to deal with." In making this decision, the company was following the lead of its competitors, most of which had already moved to decentralize their operations. Union Pacific has continued its decentralization approach in the 2000s. In its recent announcement that it was adding a new region, it stated that "the new four-region system will continue the effort to decentralize decision-making into the field, while fostering improved customer responsiveness, operational excellence, and personal accountability."[a]

accountability increase. The result is that decentralization promotes flexibility and reduces bureaucratic costs because lower-level managers are authorized to make on-the-spot decisions; handoffs are not needed. The third advantage is that when lower-level employees are given the right to make important decisions, fewer managers are needed to oversee their activities and tell them what to do—a company can flatten its hierarchy. Strategy in Action 12.1 shows how Union Pacific experienced some of these advantages after it decentralized its operations.

If decentralization is so effective, why don't all companies decentralize decision making and avoid the problems of tall hierarchies? The answer is that centralization has its advantages too. Centralized decision making allows for easier coordination of the organizational activities needed to pursue a company's strategy. If managers at all levels can make their own decisions, overall planning becomes extremely difficult, and the company may lose control of its decision making.

Centralization also means that decisions fit broad organization objectives. When its branch operations were getting out of hand, for example, Merrill Lynch increased centralization by installing more information systems to give corporate managers greater control over branch activities. Similarly, HP centralized research and development (R&D) responsibility at the corporate level to provide a more directed corporate strategy. Furthermore, in times of crisis, centralization of authority permits strong leadership because authority is focused on one person or group. This focus allows for speedy decision making and a concerted response by the whole organization. How to choose the right level of centralization for a particular strategy is discussed later.

Integration and Integrating Mechanisms

Much coordination takes place among people, functions, and divisions through the hierarchy of authority. Often, however, as a structure becomes complex, this is not enough, and top managers need to use various **integrating mechanisms** to increase communication and coordination among functions and divisions. The greater the complexity of an organization's structure, the greater is the need for coordination among people, functions, and divisions to make the organizational structure work efficiently.[18] We discuss three kinds of integrating mechanisms that illustrate the kinds of issues involved.[19] Once again, these mechanisms are employed to economize on the information distortion problems that commonly arise when managing the handoffs or transfers among the ideas and activities of different people, functions, and divisions.

DIRECT CONTACT Direct contact among managers creates a context within which managers from different functions or divisions can work together to solve mutual problems. However, several problems are associated with establishing this contact. Managers from different functions may have different views about what must be done to achieve organizational goals. But if the managers have equal authority (as functional managers typically do), the only manager who can tell them what to do is the CEO. If functional managers cannot reach agreement, no mechanism exists to resolve the conflict apart from the authority of the boss. In fact, one sign of a poorly performing organizational structure is the number of problems sent up the hierarchy for top managers to solve. The need to solve everyday conflicts and solve handoff or transfer problems raises bureaucratic costs. To reduce such conflicts and solve transfer problems, top managers use more complex integrating mechanisms to increase coordination among functions and divisions.

LIAISON ROLES Managers can increase coordination among functions and divisions by establishing liaison roles. When the volume of contacts between two functions increases, one way to improve coordination is to give one manager in each function or division the responsibility for coordinating with the other. These managers may meet daily, weekly, monthly, or as needed to solve handoff issues and transfer problems. The responsibility for coordination is part of the liaison's full-time job, and usually an informal relationship forms between the people involved, greatly easing strains between functions. Furthermore, liaison roles provide a way of transmitting information across an organization, which is important in large organizations where employees may know no one outside their immediate function or division.

TEAMS When more than two functions or divisions share many common problems, direct contact and liaison roles may not provide sufficient coordination. In these cases, a more complex integrating mechanism, the **team,** may be appropriate. One manager from each relevant function or division is assigned to a team that meets to solve a specific mutual problem; team members are responsible for reporting back to their subunits on the issues addressed and the solutions recommended. Teams are increasingly being used at all organizational levels.

Strategic Control Systems

Strategic managers choose the organizational strategies and structure they hope will allow the organization to use its resources most effectively to pursue its business model and create value and profit. Then they create **strategic control systems,** tools that allow them to monitor and evaluate whether, in fact, their strategy and structure are working as intended, how they could be improved, and how they should be changed if they are not working.

Strategic control is not just about monitoring how well an organization and its members are performing currently or about how well the firm is using its existing resources. It is also about how to create the incentives to keep employees motivated and focused on the important problems that may confront an organization in the future so that they work together to find solutions that can help an organization perform better over time.[20] To understand the vital importance of strategic control, consider how it helps managers to obtain superior efficiency, quality, innovation, and responsiveness to customers, the four basic building blocks of competitive advantage:

- *Control and efficiency.* To determine how *efficiently* they are using organizational resources, managers must be able to measure accurately how many units of inputs (raw materials, human resources, and so on) are being used to produce a unit of output. They must also be able to measure the number of units of outputs (goods and services) they produce. A control system contains the measures or yardsticks that allow managers to assess how efficiently they are producing goods and services. Moreover, if managers experiment to find a more efficient way to produce goods and services, these measures tell managers how successful they have been. Without a control system in place, managers have no idea how well their organizations are performing and how they can make it perform better, something that is becoming increasingly important in today's highly competitive environment.[21]

- *Control and quality.* Today, competition often revolves around increasing the *quality* of goods and services. In the car industry, for example, within each price range, cars compete against one another in terms of their features, design, and reliability. So whether a customer buys a Ford 500, a GM Impala, a Chrysler 300, a Toyota Camry, or a Honda Accord depends significantly on the quality of each company's product. Strategic control is important in determining the quality of goods and services because it gives managers feedback on product quality. If managers consistently measure the number of customers' complaints and the number of new cars returned for repairs, they have a good indication of how much quality they have built into their product.

- *Control and innovation.* Strategic control can help to raise the level of *innovation* in an organization. Successful innovation takes place when managers create an organizational setting in which employees feel empowered to be creative and in which authority is decentralized to employees so that they feel free to experiment and take risks, such as at Nokia. Deciding on the appropriate control systems to encourage risk taking is an important management challenge and, as discussed later in the chapter, an organization's culture becomes important in this regard.

- *Control and responsiveness to customers.* Finally, strategic managers can help make their organizations more *responsive to customers* if they develop a control system that allows them to evaluate how well employees with customer contact are performing their jobs. Monitoring employees' behavior can help managers find ways to help increase employees' performance level, perhaps by revealing areas in which skills training can help employees or by finding new procedures that allow employees to perform their jobs better. When employees know their behaviors are being monitored, they may have more incentive to be helpful and consistent in the way they act toward customers.

FIGURE 12.3

Steps in Designing an Effective Strategic Control System

Established standards and targets.

Create measuring and monitoring systems.

Compare actual performance against the established targets.

Evaluate result and take action if necessary.

Strategic control systems are the formal target-setting, measurement, and feedback systems that allow strategic managers to evaluate whether a company is achieving superior efficiency, quality, innovation, and customer responsiveness and implementing its strategy successfully. An effective control system should have three characteristics. It should be *flexible* enough to allow managers to respond as necessary to unexpected events; it should provide *accurate information*, thus giving a true picture of organizational performance; and it should supply managers with the information in a *timely manner* because making decisions on the basis of outdated information is a recipe for failure.[22] As Figure 12.3 shows, designing an effective strategic control system requires four steps: establishing standards and targets, creating measuring and monitoring systems, comparing performance against targets, and evaluating the result.

● **Levels of Strategic Control**

Strategic control systems are developed to measure performance at four levels in a company: corporate, divisional, functional, and individual. Managers at all levels must develop the most appropriate set of measures to evaluate corporate-, business-, and functional-level performance. As the balanced scorecard approach discussed in Chapter 11 suggests, these measures should be tied as closely as possibly to the goals of developing distinctive competencies in efficiency, quality, innovativeness, and responsiveness to customers. Care must be taken, however, to ensure that the standards used at each level do not cause problems at the other levels—for example, that a division's attempts to improve its performance does not conflict with corporate performance. Furthermore, controls at each level should provide the basis on which managers at lower levels design their control systems. Figure 12.4 illustrates these links.

● **Types of Strategic Control Systems**

In Chapter 11, the balanced scorecard approach was discussed as a way to ensure that managers complement the use of ROIC with other kinds of strategic controls to ensure they are pursuing strategies that maximize long-run profitability. Here, we consider three more types of control systems: *personal control, output control,* and *behavior control.*

PERSONAL CONTROL   **Personal control** is the desire to shape and influence the behavior of a person in a *face-to-face interaction* in the pursuit of a company's goals. The

FIGURE 12.4

Levels of Organizational Control

most obvious kind of personal control is direct supervision from a manager further up in the hierarchy. The personal approach is useful because managers can question and probe subordinates about problems or new issues they are facing to get a better understanding of the situation, as well as to ensure that subordinates are performing their work effectively and not hiding any information that could cause problems down the line. Personal control also can come from a group of peers, such as when people work in teams. Once again, personal control at the group level means that there is more possibility for learning to occur and competencies to develop, as well as greater opportunities to prevent free-riding or shirking.

OUTPUT CONTROL **Output control** is a system in which strategic managers estimate or forecast appropriate performance goals for each division, department, and employee and then measure actual performance relative to these goals. Often a company's reward system is linked to performance on these goals, so output control also provides an incentive structure for motivating employees at all levels in the organization. Goals keep managers informed about how well their strategies are creating a competitive advantage and building the distinctive competencies that lead to future success. Goals exist at all levels in an organization.

Divisional goals state corporate managers' expectations for each division concerning performance on dimensions such as efficiency, quality, innovation, and responsiveness to customers. Generally, corporate managers set challenging divisional goals to encourage divisional managers to create more effective strategies and structures in the future. At Dell, for example, each division is given a clear performance goal to achieve, and divisional managers are given considerable autonomy in formulating a strategy to meet this goal.

Output control at the functional and individual levels is a continuation of control at the divisional level. Divisional managers set goals for functional managers that will allow the division to achieve its goals. As at the divisional level, functional goals are established to encourage the development of the generic competencies that provide the company with a competitive advantage, and functional performance is evaluated by how well a function develops a competency. In the sales function, for example, goals related to efficiency (such as cost of sales), quality (such as number of returns), and customer responsiveness (such as the time needed to respond to customer needs) can be established for the whole function.

Finally, functional managers establish goals that individual employees are expected to achieve to allow the function to achieve its goals. Sales personnel, for example, can be given specific goals (related to functional goals) that they are required to achieve. Functions and individuals are then evaluated on the basis of achieving or not achieving their goals, and in sales, compensation is commonly pegged to achievement. The achievement of these goals is a sign that the company's strategy is working and meeting organizational objectives.

The inappropriate use of output control can promote conflict among divisions. In general, setting across-the-board output targets, such as ROIC targets, for divisions can lead to destructive results if divisions single-mindedly try to maximize divisional ROIC at the expense of corporate ROIC. Moreover, to reach output targets, divisions may start to distort the numbers and engage in strategic manipulation of the figures to make their divisions look good—which increases bureaucratic costs.[23]

BEHAVIOR CONTROL **Behavior control** is control through the establishment of a comprehensive system of rules and procedures to direct the actions or behavior of divisions, functions, and individuals.[24] The intent of behavior controls is not to specify the *goals* but to standardize the *way or means* of reaching them. Rules standardize behavior and make outcomes predictable. If employees follow the rules, then actions are performed and decisions are handled the same way time and time again. The result is predictability and accuracy, the aim of all control systems. The main kinds of behavior controls are operating budgets, standardization, and rules and procedures.

Once managers at each level have been given a goal to achieve, they establish operating budgets that regulate how managers and workers are to attain those goals. An **operating budget** is a blueprint that states how managers intend to use organizational resources to achieve organizational goals most efficiently. Most commonly, managers at one level allocate to managers at a lower level a specific amount of resources to use in the production of goods and services. Once they have been given a budget, lower-level managers must decide how they will allocate certain amounts of money for different organizational activities. They are then evaluated on the basis of their ability to stay inside the budget and make the best use of it. For example, managers at GE's washing machine division might have a budget of $50 million to develop and sell a new line of washing machines; they have to decide how much money to allocate to R&D, engineering, sales, and so on, so that the division generates the most revenue and hence makes the biggest profit. Most commonly, large companies treat each division as a stand-alone profit center, and corporate managers evaluate each division's performance by its relative contribution to corporate profitability, something discussed in detail in the next chapter.

Standardization refers to the degree to which a company specifies how decisions are to be made so that employees' behavior becomes predictable.[25] In practice, there are three things an organization can standardize: *inputs, conversion activities,* and *outputs.*

When managers standardize, they screen *inputs* according to preestablished criteria, or standards, that determine which inputs to allow into the organization. If employees are the input in question, for example, then one way of standardizing them is to specify which qualities and skills they must possess and then to select only applicants who possess them. If the inputs in question are raw materials or component parts, the same considerations apply. The Japanese are renowned for the high quality and precise tolerances they demand from component parts to minimize problems with the product at the manufacturing stage. Just-in-time inventory systems also help standardize the flow of inputs.

The aim of standardizing *conversion activities* is to program work activities so that they are done the same way time and time again. The goal is predictability. Behavior controls, such as rules and procedures, are among the chief means by which companies can standardize throughputs. Fast-food restaurants such as McDonald's and Burger King standardize all aspects of their restaurant operations; the result is consistent fast food.

The goal of standardizing *outputs* is to specify what the performance characteristics of the final product or service should be—the dimensions or tolerances the product should conform to, for example. To ensure that their products are standardized, companies apply quality control and use various criteria to measure this standardization. One criterion might be the number of goods returned from customers or the number of customers' complaints. On production lines, periodic sampling of products can indicate whether they are meeting performance characteristics.

As with other kinds of controls, the use of behavior control is accompanied by potential pitfalls that must be managed if the organization is to avoid strategic problems. Top management must be careful to monitor and evaluate the usefulness of behavior controls over time. Rules constrain people and lead to standardized, predictable behavior. However, rules are always easier to establish than to get rid of, and over time the number of rules an organization uses tends to increase. As new developments lead to additional rules, often the old rules are not discarded, and the company becomes overly bureaucratized. Consequently, the organization and the people in it become inflexible and are slow to react to changing or unusual circumstances. Such inflexibility can reduce a company's competitive advantage by lowering the pace of innovation and reducing its responsiveness to customers.

● Using Information Technology

Information technology is playing an increasing role in strategy implementation at all organizational levels. In fact, it is making it much easier for organizations to cost-effectively develop output and behavior controls that give strategic managers much more and much better information to monitor the many aspects of their strategies and to respond appropriately. IT, which provides a way of standardizing behavior through the use of a consistent, often cross-functional software platform, is a form of behavior control. IT is also a form of output control; when all employees or functions use the same software platform to provide up-to-date information on their activities, this codifies and standardizes organizational knowledge and makes it easier to monitor progress toward strategic objectives. IT is also a kind of integrating mechanism because it provides people at all levels in the hierarchy and across all functions with more of the information and knowledge they need to perform their

Strategy in Action   12.2

Control at Cypress Semiconductor

In the fast-moving semiconductor business, a premium is placed on organizational adaptability. At Cypress Semiconductor, CEO T. J. Rodgers was facing a problem: how to control his growing 1,500-employee organization without developing a bureaucratic management hierarchy. Rodgers believed that a tall hierarchy hinders the ability of an organization to adapt to changing conditions. He was committed to maintaining a flat and decentralized organizational structure with a minimum of management layers. At the same time, he needed to control his employees to ensure that they performed in a manner consistent with company goals. The solution that Rodgers adopted was to implement a computer-based information system through which he can manage what every employee and team is doing in the decentralized organization. Each employee maintains a list of ten to fifteen goals, such as "Meet with marketing for new product launch" or "Make sure to check with customer X." Noted next to each goal is when it was agreed on, when it is due to be finished, and whether it has been finished. All of this information is stored on a central computer. Rodgers claims that he can review the goals of all 1,500 employees in about four hours, and he does so each week. He can do this because he manages by exception, looking only for employees who are falling behind. He then calls them—not to scold but to ask whether there is anything he can do to help them get the job done. It takes only about half an hour each week for employees to review and update their lists. This system allows Rodgers to exercise control over his organization without resorting to the expensive layers of a management hierarchy.[b]

roles effectively. For example, today functional-level employees are able to access information easily from other functions using cross-functional software systems that keep them all informed about changes in product design, engineering, manufacturing schedules, and marketing plans that will have an impact on their activities. In this sense, IT overlays the structure of tasks and roles that is normally regarded as the "real" organizational structure. The many ways in which IT affects strategy implementation is discussed in different sections of this and the next chapter. Strategy in Action 12.2 illustrates one way in which IT can help managers monitor and coordinate the effectiveness with which their strategies are being put into action.

● Strategic Reward Systems   Organizations strive to control employees' behavior by linking reward systems to their control systems.[26] Based on the company's strategy (cost leadership or differentiation, for example), strategic managers must decide which behaviors to reward. They then create a control system to measure these behaviors and link the reward structure to them. Determining how to relate rewards to performance is a crucial strategic decision because it determines the incentive structure that affects the way managers and employees at all levels in the organization behave. As Chapter 11 pointed out, top managers can be encouraged to work in shareholders' interests by being rewarded with stock options linked to a company's long-term performance. Companies such as Kodak and GM require managers to buy company stock. When managers become shareholders, they are more motivated to pursue long-term rather than short-term goals. Similarly, in designing a pay system for salespeople, the choice is whether to motivate them through straight salary or salary plus a bonus based on how much they sell. Neiman Marcus, the luxury retailer, pays employees a straight salary because it wants to encourage high-quality service but discourage a hard-sell approach. Thus, there are no incentives based on quantity sold. On the other hand, the pay system for rewarding car salespeople encourages high-pressure selling; it typically contains a large bonus based on the number and price of cars sold.

Organizational Culture

The third element that goes into successful strategy implementation is managing *organizational culture*, the specific collection of values and norms shared by people and groups in an organization.[27] Organizational values are beliefs and ideas about what kinds of goals the members of an organization should pursue and about the appropriate kinds or standards of behavior organizational members should use to achieve these goals. Bill Gates is famous for the set of organizational values that he created for Microsoft: entrepreneurship, ownership, creativity, honesty, frankness, and open communication. By stressing entrepreneurship and ownership, he strives to get his employees to feel that Microsoft is not one big bureaucracy but a collection of smaller and very adaptive companies run by their members. Gates emphasizes giving lower-level managers autonomy and encourages them to take risks—to act like entrepreneurs, not corporate bureaucrats.[28]

From organizational values develop organizational norms, guidelines, or expectations that prescribe appropriate kinds of behavior by employees in particular situations and control the behavior of organizational members toward one another. The norms of behavior for software programmers at Microsoft include working long hours and weekends, wearing whatever clothing is comfortable (but never a suit and tie), consuming junk food, and communicating with other employees by email and the company's state-of-the-art intranet.

Organizational culture functions as a kind of control because strategic managers can influence the kind of values and norms that develop in an organization—values and norms that specify appropriate and inappropriate behaviors and that shape and influence the way its members behave.[29] Strategic managers such as Gates deliberately cultivate values that tell their subordinates how they should perform their roles; at Microsoft and Nokia, innovation and creativity are stressed. These companies establish and support norms that tell employees they should be innovative and entrepreneurial and should experiment even if there is a significant chance of failure.

Other managers might cultivate values that tell employees they should always be conservative and cautious in their dealings with others, consult with their superiors before they make important decisions, and record their actions in writing so they can be held accountable for what happens. Managers of organizations such as chemical and oil companies, financial institutions, and insurance companies—any organization in which great caution is needed—may encourage a conservative, vigilant approach to making decisions.[30] In a bank or mutual fund, for example, the risk of losing investors' money makes a cautious approach to investing highly appropriate. Thus, we might expect that managers of different kinds of organizations will deliberately try to cultivate and develop the organizational values and norms that are best suited to their strategy and structure.

Organizational socialization is the term used to describe how people learn organizational culture. Through socialization, people internalize and learn the norms and values of the culture so that they become organizational members.[31] Control through culture is so powerful that once these values have been internalized, they become part of the individual's values, and the individual follows organizational values without thinking about them.[32] Often the values and norms of an organization's culture are transmitted to its members through the stories, myths, and language that people in the organization use, as well as by other means.

Culture and Strategic Leadership

Organizational culture is created by the strategic leadership provided by an organization's founder and top managers. The organization's founder is particularly important in determining culture because the founder imprints his or her values and management style on the organization. Walt Disney's conservative influence on the company he established continued until well after his death. Managers were afraid to experiment with new forms of entertainment because they were afraid "Walt Disney wouldn't like it." It took the installation of a new management team under Michael Eisner to turn around the company's fortunes and allow it to deal with the realities of the new entertainment industry.

The leadership style established by the founder is transmitted to the company's managers, and as the company grows, it typically attracts new managers and employees who share the same values. Moreover, members of the organization typically recruit and select only those who share their values. Thus, a company's culture becomes more and more distinct as its members become more similar. The virtue of these shared values and common culture is that they *increase integration and improve coordination among organizational members.* For example, the common language that typically emerges in an organization because people share the same beliefs and values facilitates cooperation among managers. Similarly, rules and procedures and direct supervision are less important when shared norms and values control behavior and motivate employees. When organizational members buy into cultural norms and values, they feel a bond with the organization and are more committed to finding new ways to help it succeed. Strategy in Action 12.3 profiles how Ray Kroc built a strong culture at McDonald's.

Strategic leadership also affects organizational culture through the way managers design organizational structure, that is, the way they delegate authority and divide task relationships. Thus, the way an organization designs its structure affects the cultural norms and values that develop within the organization. Managers need to be aware of this fact when implementing their strategies. Michael Dell, for example, has tried to keep his company as flat as possible and has decentralized authority to lower-level managers and employees who are charged with striving to get as close to the customer as they can. As a result, he has created a cost-conscious customer service culture at Dell in which employees strive to provide high-quality customer service.

Traits of Strong and Adaptive Corporate Cultures

Few environments are stable for a prolonged period of time. If an organization is to survive, managers must take actions that enable it to adapt to environmental changes. If they do not take such action, they may find themselves faced with declining demand for their products.

Managers can try to create an **adaptive culture**, one that is innovative and that encourages and rewards middle and lower-level managers for taking the initiative.[33] Managers in organizations with adaptive cultures are able to introduce changes in the way the organization operates, including changes in its strategy and structure that allow it to adapt to changes in the external environment. Organizations with adaptive cultures are more likely to survive in a changing environment and indeed should have higher performance than organizations with inert cultures.

Strategy in Action

How Ray Kroc Established McDonald's Culture

In the restaurant business, maintaining product quality is all-important because the quality of the food and the service varies with the chefs and waiters as they come and go. If a customer gets a bad meal, poor service, or dirty silverware, that customer may not come back, and other potential customers may stay away as negative comments travel by word of mouth. This was the problem that Ray Kroc, the man who pioneered McDonald's growth, faced when McDonald's franchises began to open by the thousands throughout the United States. Kroc solved his problem by developing a sophisticated control system that specified every detail of how each McDonald's restaurant was to be operated and managed. This control system also created a distinct organizational culture.

First, Kroc developed a comprehensive system of rules and procedures for franchise owners and employees to follow in running each restaurant. The most effective way to perform tasks, from cooking burgers to cleaning tables, was worked out in advance, written down in rule books, and then taught to each McDonald's manager and employee through a formal training process. Prospective franchise owners had to attend "Hamburger University," the company's training center in Chicago, where they learned all aspects of a McDonald's operation in an intensive, month-long program. They were then expected to train their work force and make sure that employees thoroughly understood operating procedures. Kroc's goal in establishing this system of rules

and procedures was to build a common culture so that customers would always find the same level of quality in food and service. If customers always get what they expect from a restaurant, the restaurant has developed superior customer responsiveness.

Kroc also developed the McDonald's franchise system to help the company control its structure as it grew. He believed that a manager who is also a franchise owner (and thus receives a large share of the profits) is more motivated to buy into a company's culture than a manager paid on a straight salary. Thus, the McDonald's reward and incentive system allowed it to keep control over its operating structure as it expanded. Moreover, McDonald's was very selective in selling to its franchisees; they had to be people with the skills and capabilities that Kroc believed McDonald's managers should have.

Within each restaurant, franchise owners were instructed to pay particular attention to training their employees and instilling in them McDonald's concepts of efficiency, quality, and customer service. Shared norms, values, and an organizational culture also helped McDonald's standardize employees' behavior so that customers would know how they would be treated in a McDonald's restaurant. Moreover, McDonald's includes customers in its culture: it asks customers to bus their own tables, and it also shows concern for customers' needs by building playgrounds, offering Happy Meals, and organizing birthday parties for children. In creating its family-oriented culture, McDonald's ensures future customer loyalty because satisfied children are likely to become loyal adult customers.[c]

Several scholars in the field have tried to uncover the common traits that strong and adaptive corporate cultures share and to find out whether there is a particular set of values that dominates adaptive cultures that is missing from weak or inert ones. An early but still influential attempt is T. J. Peters and R. H. Waterman's account of the values and norms characteristic of successful organizations and their cultures.[34] They argue that adaptive organizations show three common value sets. First, successful companies have values promoting a *bias for action*. The emphasis is on autonomy and entrepreneurship, and employees are encouraged to take risks—for example, to create new products—even though there is no assurance that these products will be winners. Managers are closely involved in the day-to-day operations of the company and do not simply make strategic decisions isolated in some ivory tower, and employees have a hands-on, value-driven approach.

The second set of values stems from the *nature of the organization's mission*. The company must stick with what it does best and develop a business model focused on its mission. A company can easily get sidetracked into pursuing activities outside its area of expertise just because they seem to promise a quick return. Management should cultivate values so that a company sticks to its knitting, which means strengthening its business model. A company must also establish close relationships with customers as a way of improving its competitive position. After all, who knows more about a company's performance than those who use its products or services? By emphasizing customer-oriented values, organizations are able to learn customers' needs and improve their ability to develop products and services that customers desire. All of these management values are strongly represented in companies such as McDonald's, Wal-Mart, and Toyota, which are sure of their mission and continually take steps to maintain it.

The third set of values bears on *how to operate the organization*. A company should try to establish an organizational design that will motivate employees to do their best. Inherent in this set of values is the belief that productivity is obtained through people and that respect for the individual is the primary means by which a company can create the right atmosphere for productive behavior. An emphasis on entrepreneurship and respect for the employee leads to the establishment of a structure that gives employees the latitude to make decisions and motivates them to succeed. Because a simple structure and a lean staff best fit this situation, the organization should be designed with only the number of managers and hierarchical levels that are necessary to get the job done. The organization should also be sufficiently decentralized to permit employees' participation but centralized enough for management to make sure that the company pursues its strategic mission and that cultural values are followed.

In summary, these three main sets of values are at the heart of an organization's culture, and management transmits and maintains them through strategic leadership. Strategy implementation continues as managers build strategic control systems that help perpetuate a strong adaptive culture, further the development of distinctive competencies, and provide employees with the incentive to build a company's competitive advantage. Finally, organizational structure contributes to the implementation process by providing the framework of tasks and roles that reduces transaction difficulties and allows employees to think and behave in ways that enable a company to achieve superior performance.

Building Distinctive Competencies at the Functional Level

In this section, we turn to the issue of creating specific kinds of structures, control systems, and cultures to implement a company's business model. The first level of strategy to examine is the functional level because, as Chapters 3 and 4 discussed, a company's business model is implemented through the functional strategies managers adopt to develop the distinctive competencies that allow a company to pursue a particular business model.[35] What is the best kind of structure to use to group people and tasks to build competencies? The answer for most companies is to group them by function and create a functional structure.

● **Functional Structure: Grouping by Function**

In the quest to deliver a final product to the customer, two related value chain management problems increase. First, the range of value chain activities that must be performed expands, and it quickly becomes clear that a company lacks the expertise needed to perform them effectively. For example, in a new company, it quickly

FIGURE 12.5

Functional Structure

becomes apparent, as in Dell's case, that the expertise necessary to perform them effectively is lacking. It becomes apparent, perhaps, that the services of a professional accountant, a production manager, or a marketing expert are needed to take control of specialized tasks as sales increase. Second, it also becomes clear that a single person cannot successfully perform more than one value chain activity without becoming overloaded. The new company's founder, for instance, who may have been performing many value chain activities, realizes that he or she can no longer simultaneously make and sell the product. As most entrepreneurs discover, they have to decide how to group new employees to perform the various value chain activities most efficiently. Most choose the functional structure.

Functional structures group people on the basis of their common expertise and experience or because they use the same resources.[36] For example, engineers are grouped in a function because they perform the same tasks and use the same skills or equipment. Figure 12.5 shows a typical functional structure. Each of the rectangles represents a different functional specialization—R&D, sales and marketing, manufacturing, and so on—and each function concentrates on its own specialized task.[37]

Functional structures have several advantages. First, if people who perform similar tasks are grouped together, they can learn from one another and become more specialized and productive at what they do. This can create capabilities and competencies in each function. Second, they can monitor each other to make sure that all are performing their tasks effectively and not shirking their responsibilities. As a result, the work process becomes more efficient, reducing manufacturing costs and increasing operational flexibility. A third important advantage of functional structures is that they give managers greater control of organizational activities. As already noted, many difficulties arise when the number of levels in the hierarchy increases. If people are grouped into different functions, each with their own managers, then *several different hierarchies are created*, and the company can avoid becoming too tall. There will be one hierarchy in manufacturing, for example, and another in accounting and finance. Managing the business is much easier when different groups specialize in different organizational tasks and are managed separately.

● **The Role of Strategic Control**   An important element of strategic control is to design a system that sets ambitious goals and targets for all managers and employees and then develops performance measures that *stretch and encourage managers and employees* to excel in their quest to raise performance. A functional structure promotes this goal because it increases the ability of managers and employees to monitor and make constant improvements to operating procedures. The structure also encourages organizational learning because managers, working closely with subordinates, can mentor them and help develop their technical skills.

Grouping by function also makes it easier to apply output control. Measurement criteria can be developed to suit the needs of each function to encourage members to stretch themselves. Each function knows how well it is contributing to overall performance, and indeed the part it plays in reducing the cost of goods sold or the gross margin. Managers can look closely to see if they are following the principle of the minimum chain of command and whether they need several levels of middle managers. Perhaps, instead of using middle managers, they could practice **management by objectives**, a system in which employees are encouraged to help set their own goals so that managers, like Cypress's Rodgers, *manage by exception*, intervening only when they sense something is not going right. Given this increase in control, a functional structure also makes it possible to institute an effective strategic reward system in which pay can be closely linked to performance and managers can accurately assess the value of each person's contributions.

Developing Culture at the Functional Level

Often functional structures offer the easiest way for managers to build a strong, cohesive culture. We discussed earlier how Ray Kroc, who first developed a functional structure to implement his cost-leadership business model, worked hard to create values and norms that were shared by the members of McDonald's different functions. To see how structure, control, and culture help create distinctive competencies, we consider how they affect the way three functions—manufacturing, R&D, and sales—operate.

MANUFACTURING In manufacturing, functional strategy usually centers on improving efficiency and quality. A company must create an organizational setting in which managers can learn how to economize on costs and lower the cost structure. Many companies today follow the lead of Japanese companies such as Toyota and Honda, which developed strong capabilities in manufacturing by operating total quality management (TQM) and flexible manufacturing systems (see Chapter 4).

With TQM, the inputs and involvement of all employees in the decision-making process are necessary to improve production efficiency and quality. Thus, it becomes necessary to decentralize authority to motivate employees to improve the production process. In TQM, work teams are created, and workers are given the responsibility and authority to discover and implement improved work procedures. Managers assume the role of coach and facilitator, and team members jointly take on the supervisory burdens. Work teams are often given the responsibility to control and discipline their own members and even to decide who should work in their team. Frequently, work teams develop strong norms and values, and work-group culture becomes an important means of control; this type of control matches the new decentralized team approach. Quality control circles are created to exchange information and suggestions about problems and work procedures. A bonus system or employee stock ownership plan (ESOP) is frequently established to motivate workers and to allow them to share in the increased value that TQM often produces.

Nevertheless, to move down the experience curve quickly, most companies still exercise tight control over work activities and create behavior and output controls that standardize the manufacturing process. For example, human inputs are standardized through the recruitment and training of skilled personnel; the work process is programmed, often by computers; and quality control is used to make sure that outputs are being produced correctly. In addition, managers use output controls such as operating budgets to continuously monitor costs and quality. The extensive use of output controls and the continuous measurement of efficiency and quality ensure that the work team's activities meet the goals set for the function by management. Efficiency and quality increase as new and improved work rules and procedures are developed to raise the level of standardization. The aim is to find the match between structure and control and a TQM approach so that manufacturing develops the distinctive competency that leads to superior efficiency and quality.

R&D   The functional strategy for an R&D department is to develop distinctive competencies in innovation and quality as excellence that result in products that fit customers' needs. Consequently, the R&D department's structure, control, and culture should provide the coordination necessary for scientists and engineers to bring high-quality products quickly to market. Moreover, these systems should motivate R&D scientists to develop innovative products.

In practice, R&D departments typically have a flat, decentralized structure that gives their members the freedom and autonomy to experiment and be innovative. Scientists and engineers are also grouped into teams because their performance can typically be judged only over the long term (it may take several years for a project to be completed). Consequently, extensive supervision by managers and the use of behavior control are a waste of managerial time and effort.[38] By letting teams manage their own transfer and handoff issues rather than using managers and the hierarchy of authority to coordinate work activities, managers avoid the information distortion problems that cause bureaucratic costs. Strategic managers take advantage of scientists' ability to work jointly to solve problems and to enhance each other's performance. In small teams, too, the professional values and norms that highly trained employees bring to the situation promote coordination. A culture for innovation frequently emerges to control employees' behavior, as it did at Nokia, Intel, and Microsoft, where the race to be first energizes the R&D teams. To create an innovative culture and speed product development, Intel uses a team structure in its R&D function. Intel has many work teams that operate side by side to develop the next generation of chips. So, when it makes mistakes, as it has recently, it can act quickly to join each team's innovations together to make a state-of-the-art chip that does meet customer needs, such as for multimedia chips. At the same time, to sustain its leading-edge technology, the company creates healthy competition between teams to encourage its scientists and engineers to champion new product innovations that will allow Intel to control the technology of tomorrow.[39]

To spur teams to work effectively, the reward system should be linked to the performance of the team and company. If scientists, individually or in a team, do not share in the profits a company obtains from its new products, they may have little motivation to contribute wholeheartedly to the team. To prevent the departure of their key employees and encourage high motivation, companies such as Merck, Intel, and Microsoft give their researchers stock options, stock, and other rewards that are tied to their individual performance, their team's performance, and the company's performance.

SALES   Salespeople work directly with customers, and when they are dispersed in the field, these employees are especially difficult to monitor. The cost-effective way to monitor their behavior and encourage high responsiveness to customers is usually to develop sophisticated output and behavior controls. Output controls, such as specific sales goals or goals for increasing responsiveness to customers, can be easily established and monitored by sales managers. These controls can then be linked to a bonus reward system to motivate salespeople. Behavior controls, such as detailed reports that salespeople file describing their interactions with customers, can also be used to standardize salespeople's behavior and make it easier for supervisors to review their performance.[40]

Usually, few managers are needed to monitor salespeople's activities, and a sales director and regional sales managers can oversee even large sales forces because outputs and behavior controls are employed. Frequently, however, and especially when salespeople deal with complex products such as pharmaceutical drugs or even luxury clothing, it becomes important to develop shared employee values and norms about the importance of patient safety or high-quality customer service, and managers spend considerable time training and educating employees to create such norms.

Similar considerations apply to the other functions, such as accounting, finance, engineering, and human resource management. Managers must implement functional strategy through the combination of structure, control, and culture to allow each function to create the competencies that lead to superior efficiency, quality, innovation, and responsiveness to customers. Strategic managers must also develop the incentive systems that motivate and align employees' interests with those of their companies.

● Functional Structure and Bureaucratic Costs

No matter how complex their strategies become, most companies always retain a functional orientation because of its many advantages. Whenever different functions work together, however, bureaucratic costs inevitably arise because of information distortions that lead to the communications and measurement problems discussed in Chapter 10. These problems often arise from the transfers or handoffs across different functions that are necessary to deliver the final product to the customer.[41] Indeed, the need to economize on the bureaucratic costs of solving such problems leads managers to adopt new organizational arrangements that reduce the scope of information distortions. Most commonly, companies divide their activities according to a more complex plan to match their business model and strategy in a discriminating way. These more complex structures are discussed later in the chapter. First, we review five areas in which information distortions can arise—communications, measurement, customers, location, and strategy.

COMMUNICATION PROBLEMS   As separate functional hierarchies evolve, functions can grow more remote from one another, and it becomes increasingly difficult to communicate across functions and to coordinate their activities. This communication problem stems from *differences in goal orientations:* the various functions develop distinct outlooks or understandings of the strategic issues facing a company.[42] For example, the pursuit of different competencies can often lead to different time or goal orientations. Some functions, such as manufacturing, have a short time frame and concentrate on achieving short-run goals, such as reducing manufacturing costs. Others, such as R&D, have a long-term point of view; their product development goals may have a time horizon of several years. These factors may cause each function to develop a different view of the strategic issues facing the company. Manufacturing, for example, may see the strategic issue as the need to reduce costs, sales may see it as the need to increase customer responsiveness, and R&D may see it as the need to create new products. These communication and coordination problems among functions increase bureaucratic costs.

MEASUREMENT PROBLEMS Often a company's product range widens as it develops new competencies and enters new market segments, as happened to Nokia. When this happens, a company may find it difficult to gauge or measure the contribution of a product or a group of products to its overall profitability—as we noted in Chapter 10. Consequently, the company may turn out some unprofitable products without realizing it and may also make poor decisions about resource allocation. This means that the company's measurement systems are not complex enough to serve its needs. Dell Computer's explosive growth in the early 1990s, for example, caused it to lose control of its inventory management systems; hence, it could not accurately project supply and demand for the components that go into its personal computers. Problems with its organizational structure plagued Dell, reducing efficiency and quality. As one manager commented, designing its structure to keep pace with its growth was like "building a high-performance car while going around the race track."[43] However, Dell succeeded and today it still maintains its cost advantage over competitors like Gateway and HP.

CUSTOMER PROBLEMS As the range and quality of an organization's goods and services increase, often more, and different kinds of, customers are attracted to its products. Servicing the needs of more customer groups and tailoring products to suit new kinds of customers result in increasing handoff problems among functions. It becomes increasingly difficult to coordinate the activities of value chain functions across the growing product range. Also, functions like production, marketing, and sales have little opportunity to differentiate products and increase value for customers by specializing in the needs of particular customer groups. Instead, they are responsible for servicing the complete product range. Thus, the ability to identify and satisfy customer needs may fall short in a functional structure.

LOCATION PROBLEMS Location factors may hamper coordination and control. If a growing company begins producing or selling in many different regional areas, then a functional structure may not be able to provide the flexibility needed for managers to respond to the different customer needs or preferences in the various regions. A functional structure is simply not the right way to handle regional diversity.

STRATEGIC PROBLEMS Sometimes the combined effect of all these factors is that long-term strategic considerations are ignored because managers are preoccupied with solving communication and coordination problems. As a result, a company may lose direction and fail to take advantage of new opportunities while bureaucratic costs escalate.

Experiencing one or more of these problems is a sign that bureaucratic costs are increasing and that managers must change and adapt their organization's structure, control systems, and culture to economize on bureaucratic costs, build new distinctive competencies, and strengthen the company's business model. These problems indicate that the company has outgrown its structure and that managers need to develop a more complex structure that can meet the needs of their competitive strategy. An alternative, however, is to reduce these problems by adopting the outsourcing option.

● The Outsourcing Option

Rather than move to a more complex, expensive structure, increasingly companies are turning to the outsourcing option (discussed in Chapter 9) and solving the organizational design problem by contracting with other companies to perform specific functional tasks. Obviously, it does not make sense to outsource activities in which a company has a distinctive competency because this would lessen its competitive advantage. But it does make sense to outsource and contract with companies to perform particular value chain activities in which they specialize and therefore have a competitive advantage.

Thus, one way of avoiding the kinds of communication and measurement problems that arise when a company's product line becomes complex is to reduce the number of functional value chain activities it performs. This allows a company to focus on those competencies that are at the heart of its competitive advantage and to economize on bureaucratic costs. Today, responsibility for activities such as a company's marketing, pension and health benefits, materials management, and information systems is being increasingly outsourced to companies that often specialize in the needs of a company in a particular industry. More outsourcing options, such as using a global network structure, are considered in Chapter 13.

Implementing Strategy in a Single Industry

Building capabilities in organizational design that allow a company to develop a competitive advantage starts at the functional level. However, to pursue its business model successfully, managers must find the right combination of structure, control, and culture that *links and combines* the competencies in a company's value chain functions so that it enhances its ability to differentiate products or lower the cost structure. Therefore, it is important to coordinate and integrate across functions and business units or divisions. In organizational design, managers must consider two important issues: one concerns the revenue side of the profit equation and the other concerns the cost side, as Figure 12.6 illustrates.

First, effective organizational design improves the way in which people and groups choose the business-level strategies that lead to increasing differentiation, more value for customers, and the opportunity to charge a premium price. For example, capabilities in

FIGURE 12.6

How Organizational
Design Increases
Profitability

managing its structure and culture allow a company to more rapidly and effectively combine its distinctive competencies or transfer or leverage competencies across business units to create new and improved, differentiated products.

Second, effective organizational design reduces the bureaucratic costs associated with solving the measurement and communications problems that derive from factors such as transferring a product in progress between functions or a lack of cooperation between marketing and manufacturing or between business units. A poorly designed or inappropriate choice of structure or control system or a slow-moving bureaucratic culture (for example, a structure that is too centralized, an incentive system that causes functions to compete instead of cooperate, or a culture whose value and norms have little impact on employees) can cause the motivation, communication, measurement, and coordination problems that lead to high bureaucratic costs.

Effective organizational design often means moving to a more complex structure that economizes on bureaucratic costs. A more complex structure will cost more to operate because additional, experienced, and more highly paid managers will be needed; a more expensive IT system will be required; there may be a need for extra offices and buildings; and so on. However, these are simply costs of doing business, and a company will happily bear this extra expense provided its new structure leads to increased revenues from product differentiation and/or new ways to lower its *overall* cost structure by obtaining economies of scale or scope from its expanded operations.

In the following sections, we first examine the implementation and organizational design issues involved in pursuing a cost-leadership or differentiation business model. Then we describe different kinds of organizational structures that allow companies to pursue business models oriented at (1) managing a wide range of products; (2) being responsive to customers; (3) expanding nationally; (4) competing in a fast-changing, high-tech environment; and (5) focusing on a narrow product line.

● Implementing Cost Leadership

The aim of a company pursuing cost leadership is to become the lowest-cost producer in the industry, and this involves reducing costs across *all* functions in the organization, including R&D and sales and marketing.[44] If a company is pursuing a cost-leadership strategy, its R&D efforts probably focus on product and process development rather than on the more expensive product innovation, which carries no guarantee of success. In other words, the company stresses competencies that improve product characteristics or lower the cost of making existing products. Similarly, a company tries to decrease the cost of sales and marketing by offering a standard product to a mass market rather than different products aimed at different market segments, which is also more expensive.[45]

To implement cost leadership, a company chooses a combination of structure, control, and culture compatible with lowering its cost structure while preserving its ability to attract customers. In practice, the functional structure is the most suitable provided that care is taken to select integrating mechanisms that will reduce communication and measurement problems. For example, a TQM program can be effectively implemented when a functional structure is overlaid with cross-functional teams because now team members can search for ways to improve operating rules and procedures that lower the cost structure or standardize and raise product quality.[46]

Cost leadership also requires that managers continuously monitor their structures and control systems to find ways to restructure or streamline them so that they operate more effectively. For example, managers need to be alert to ways of using IT to standardize operations and lower costs. To reduce costs further, cost leaders use the cheapest and easiest forms of control available: output controls. For each function, a cost leader adopts output controls that allow it to closely monitor and evaluate functional performance. In the manufacturing function, for example, the company imposes tight controls and stresses meeting budgets based on production, cost, or quality targets.[47] In R&D, the emphasis also falls on the bottom line, and to demonstrate their contribution to cost savings, R&D teams focus on improving process technology. Cost leaders are likely to reward employees through generous incentive and bonus plans to encourage high performance. Their culture is often based on values that emphasize the bottom line, such as those of Dell, Wal-Mart, and McDonald's.

● Implementing Differentiation

Effective strategy implementation can improve a company's ability to add value and to differentiate its products. To make its product unique in the eyes of the customer, for example, a differentiated company must design its structure, control, and culture around the *particular source* of its competitive advantage.[48] Specifically, differentiators need to design their structures around the source of their distinctive competencies, the differentiated qualities of their product, and the customer groups they serve. Commonly, in pursuing differentiation, a company starts to produce a wider range of products to serve more market segments, which means it has to customize its products for different groups of customers. These factors make it more difficult to standardize activities and usually increase the bureaucratic costs associated with managing the handoffs or transfers between functions. Integration becomes much more of a problem; communications, measurement, location, and strategic problems increasingly arise; and the demands on functional managers increase.

To respond to these problems, strategic managers develop more sophisticated control systems, increasingly make use of IT, and focus on developing cultural norms and values that overcome problems associated with differences in functional orientations and focus on cross-functional objectives. The control systems used to match the structure should be geared to a company's distinctive competencies. For successful differentiation, it is important that the various functions do not pull in different directions; indeed, cooperation among the functions is vital for cross-functional integration. However, when functions work together, output controls become much harder to use. In general, it is much more difficult to measure the performance of people in different functions when they are engaged in cooperative efforts. Consequently, a differentiator must rely more on behavior controls and shared norms and values.

That is why companies pursuing differentiation often have a markedly different kind of culture from those pursuing cost leadership. Because human resources—good scientists, designers, or marketing employees—are often the source of differentiation, these organizations have a culture based on professionalism or collegiality, one that emphasizes the distinctiveness of the human resources rather than the high pressure of the bottom line.[49] HP, Motorola, and Coca-Cola, all of which emphasize some kind of distinctive competency, exemplify companies with professional cultures.

In practice, the implementation decisions that confront managers who must simultaneously strive for differentiation and a low cost structure are dealt with together as strategic managers move to implement new, more complex kinds of organizational structure. As a company's business model and strategies evolve, strategic managers usually start to *superimpose* a more complex divisional grouping of activities on its functional structure to better coordinate value chain activities. This is especially true of companies seeking to become *broad differentiators*, the companies that have the ability to both increase differentiation and lower their cost structures. These companies are the most profitable in their industry, and they have to be especially adept at organizational design because this is a major source of a differentiation and cost advantage (see

Figure 12.6). No matter what their business model, however, more complex structures cost more to operate than a simple functional structure, but managers are willing to bear this extra cost as long as the new structure makes better use of functional competencies, increases revenues, and lowers the overall cost structure.

● **Product Structure: Implementing a Wide Product Line**

The structure that organizations most commonly adopt to solve the control problems that result from producing many different kinds of products for many different market segments is the *product structure.* The intent is to break up a company's growing product line into a number of smaller, more manageable subunits to reduce bureaucratic costs due to communication, measurement, and other problems. Nokia moved to a product structure as it grew in size; its structure is shown in Figure 12.7.

An organization that chooses a product structure first divides its overall product line into product groups or categories (see Figure 12.7). Each product group focuses on satisfying the needs of a particular customer group and is managed by its own team of managers. Second, to keep costs as low as possible, value chain support functions such as basic R&D, marketing, materials, and finance are centralized at the top of the organization, and the different product groups share their services. Each support function, in turn, is divided into product-oriented teams of functional specialists who focus on the needs of one particular product group. This arrangement allows each team to specialize and become expert in managing the needs of its product group. Because all of the R&D teams belong to the same centralized function, however, they can share knowledge and information with each other and so can build their competence over time.

Strategic control systems can now be developed to measure the performance of each product group separately from the others. Thus, the performance of each product group is easy to monitor and evaluate, and corporate managers at the center can move more quickly to intervene if necessary. Also, the strategic reward system can be linked more closely to the performance of each product group, although top managers can still decide to make rewards based on corporate performance an important part

FIGURE 12.7

Nokia's Product Structure

of the incentive system. Doing so will encourage the different product groups to share ideas and knowledge and promote the development of a corporate culture, as well as the product group culture that naturally develops inside each product group. A product structure is commonly used by food processors, furniture makers, personal and health products companies, and large electronics companies like Nokia.

● **Market Structure: Increasing Responsiveness to Customer Groups**

Suppose the source of competitive advantage in an industry depends on the ability to meet the needs of distinct and important sets of customers or different customer groups. What is the best way of implementing strategy now? Many companies develop a **market structure** that is conceptually quite similar to the product structure except that the focus is on customer groups instead of product groups.

For a company pursuing a strategy based on increasing responsiveness to customers, it is vital that the nature and needs of each different customer group be identified. Then employees and functions are grouped by customer or market segment, and a different set of managers becomes responsible for developing the products that each group of customers wants and tailoring or customizing products to the needs of each particular customer group. In other words, to promote superior responsiveness to customers, companies design a structure around their customers and a market structure is adopted. A typical market structure is shown in Figure 12.8.

A market structure brings customer group managers and employees closer to specific groups of customers. These people can then take their detailed knowledge and feed it back to the support functions, which are kept centralized to reduce costs. For example, information about changes in customers' preferences can be quickly fed back to R&D and product design so that a company can protect its competitive advantage by supplying a constant stream of improved products for its installed customer base. This is especially important when a company serves well-identified customer groups such as *Fortune 500* companies or small businesses. The Opening Case describes how Dell uses a market structure to maximize its responsiveness to important customer groups while at the same time keeping its overall cost structure as low as possible.

● **Geographic Structure: Expanding Nationally**

Suppose a company starts to expand nationally through internal expansion or by engaging in horizontal integration and merging with other companies to expand its geographical reach. A company pursuing this competitive approach frequently moves to a **geographic structure** in which geographic regions become the basis for the grouping of organizational activities (see Figure 12.9). A company may divide its manufacturing operations and establish manufacturing plants in different regions of

FIGURE 12.8

Market Structure

FIGURE 12.9

Geographic Structure

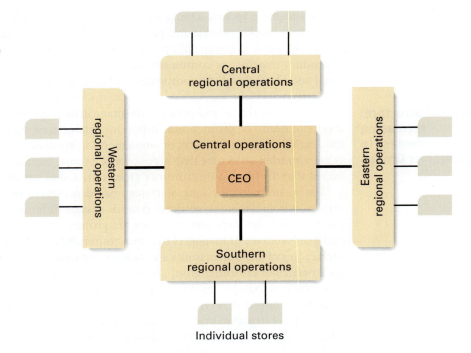

the country, for example. This allows it to be responsive to the needs of regional customers and reduces transportation costs. Similarly, as a service organization such as a store chain or bank expands beyond one geographic area, it may begin to organize sales and marketing activities on a regional level to better serve the needs of customers in different regions.

A geographic structure provides more coordination and control than a functional structure does because several regional hierarchies are created to take over the work, just as in a product structure, where several product group hierarchies are created. A company such as FedEx clearly needs to operate a geographic structure to fulfill its corporate goal: next-day delivery. Large merchandising organizations, such as Neiman Marcus, Dillard's Department Stores, and Wal-Mart, also moved to a geographic structure as they started building stores across the country. With this type of structure, different regional clothing needs (for example, sunwear in the South, down coats in the Midwest) can be handled as required. At the same time, because the information systems, purchasing, distribution, and marketing functions remain centralized, they can leverage their skills across all the regions. Thus, in using a geographic structure, a company can achieve economies of scale in buying, distributing, and selling and lower its cost structure while at the same time being more responsive (differentiated) to customer needs.

Neiman Marcus developed a geographic structure similar to the one shown in Figure 12.9 to manage its nationwide chain of stores. In each region, it established a team of regional buyers to respond to the needs of customers in each geographic area, for example, the western, central, eastern, and southern regions. The regional buyers then fed their information to the central buyers at corporate headquarters, who coordinated their demands to obtain purchasing economies and to ensure that Neiman Marcus's high-quality standards, on which its differentiation advantage depends, were maintained nationally.

● **Matrix and Product-Team Structures: Competing in Fast-Changing, High-Tech Environments**

The communication and measurement problems that lead to bureaucratic costs escalate quickly when technology is rapidly changing and industry boundaries are blurring. Frequently, competitive success depends on fast mobilization of a company's skills and resources, and managers face complex strategy implementation issues. A new grouping of people and resources becomes necessary, often one that is based on fostering a company's distinctive competencies in R&D, and managers need to make structure, control, and culture choices around the R&D function. At the same time, they need to ensure that implementation will result in new products that meet customer needs in a way that is cost-effective and will not result in high-priced products that are so expensive customers will not wish to buy them.

MATRIX STRUCTURE To address these problems, many companies choose a matrix structure.[50] In a **matrix structure,** value chain activities are grouped in two ways (see Figure 12.10). First, activities are grouped vertically by *function* so that there is a familiar differentiation of tasks into functions such as engineering, sales and marketing, and R&D. In addition, superimposed on this vertical pattern is a horizontal pattern based

FIGURE 12.3

Matrix Structure

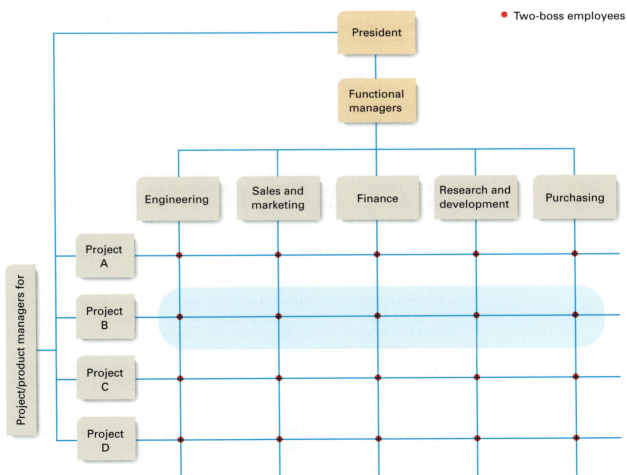

on grouping by *product or project* in which people and resources are grouped to meet ongoing product development needs. The resulting network of reporting relationships among projects and functions is designed to make R&D the focus of attention.

Matrix structures are flat and decentralized, and employees inside a matrix have two bosses: a *functional boss*, who is the head of a function, and a *product or project boss*, who is responsible for managing the individual projects. Employees work on a project team with specialists from other functions and report to the project boss on project matters and the functional boss on matters relating to functional issues. All employees who work in a project team are called **two-boss employees** and are responsible for managing coordination and communication among the functions and projects.

Implementing a matrix structure promotes innovation and speeds product development because this type of structure permits intensive cross-functional integration. Integrating mechanisms such as teams help transfer knowledge among functions and are designed around the R&D function. Sales, marketing, and production targets are geared to R&D goals, marketing devises advertising programs that focus on technological possibilities, and salespeople are evaluated on their understanding of new-product characteristics and their ability to inform potential customers about them.

Matrix structures were first developed by companies in high-technology industries such as aerospace and electronics, for example, TRW and Hughes. These companies were developing radically new products in uncertain, competitive environments, and speed of product development was the crucial consideration. They needed a structure that could respond to this need, but the functional structure was too inflexible to allow the complex role and task interactions that are necessary to meet new-product development requirements. Moreover, employees in these companies tend to be highly qualified and professional and perform best in autonomous, flexible working conditions. The matrix structure provides such conditions.

This structure requires a minimum of direct hierarchical control by supervisors. Team members control their own behavior, and participation in project teams allows them to monitor other team members and to learn from each other. Furthermore, as the project goes through its different phases, different specialists from various functions are required. For example, at the first stage, the services of R&D specialists may be called for, and then, at the next stage, engineers and marketing specialists may be needed to make cost and marketing projections. As the demand for the type of specialist changes, team members can be moved to other projects that require their services. Thus, the matrix structure can make maximum use of employees' skills as existing projects are completed and new ones come into existence. The freedom given by the matrix not only provides the autonomy to motivate employees but also leaves top management free to concentrate on strategic issues because they do not have to become involved in operating matters. On all these counts, the matrix is an excellent tool for creating the flexibility necessary for quick reactions to competitive conditions.

In terms of strategic control and culture, the development of norms and values based on innovation and product excellence is vital if a matrix structure is to work effectively.[51] The constant movement of employees around the matrix means that time and money are spent establishing new team relationships and getting the project off the ground. The two-boss employee's role, balancing as it does the interests of the project with the function, means that cooperation among employees is problematic and conflict between different functions and between functions and projects is possible and must be managed. Furthermore, the changing composition of product teams, the ambiguity arising from having two bosses, and the greater difficulty of monitoring and evaluating the work of teams increase the problems of coordinating task activities. A strong and

FIGURE 12.11

Product-Team
Structure

cohesive culture with unifying norms and values can mitigate these problems, as can a strategic reward system based on a group- and organizational-level reward system.

PRODUCT-TEAM STRUCTURE   A major structural innovation in recent years has been the **product-team structure**. Its advantages are similar to those of a matrix structure, but it is much easier and far less costly to operate because of the way people are organized into permanent cross-functional teams, as Figure 12.11 illustrates. In the product-team structure, as in the matrix structure, tasks are divided along product or project lines. However, instead of being assigned only *temporarily* to different projects, as in the matrix structure, functional specialists become part of a *permanent* cross-functional team that focuses on the development of one particular range of products such as luxury cars or computer workstations. As a result, the problems associated with coordinating cross-functional transfers or handoffs are much lower than in a matrix structure, in which tasks and reporting relationships change rapidly. Moreover, cross-functional teams are formed at the beginning of the product development process so that any difficulties that arise can be ironed out early, before they lead to major redesign problems. When all functions have direct input from the beginning, design costs and subsequent manufacturing costs can be kept low. Moreover, the use of cross-functional teams speeds innovation and customer responsiveness because, when authority is decentralized, team decisions can be made more quickly.

A product-team structure groups tasks by product, and each product group is managed by a cross-functional product team that has all the support services necessary to bring the product to market. This is why it is different from the product structure, where support functions remain centralized. The role of the product team is to protect and enhance a company's differentiation advantage and at the same time coordinate with manufacturing to lower costs.

● **Focusing on a Narrow Product Line**   As Chapter 5 discussed, a focused company concentrates on developing a narrow range of products aimed at one or two market segments, which may be defined by type of customer or location. As a result, a focuser tends to have a higher cost structure than a cost leader or differentiator because output levels are lower, making it harder to obtain substantial scale economies. For this reason, a focused company must exercise cost control. On the other hand, some attribute of its product gives the focuser its distinctive competency—possibly its ability to provide customers with high-quality, personalized service. For both reasons, the structure and control system adopted by a focused company has to be inexpensive to operate but flexible enough to allow a distinctive competency to emerge.

A company using a focus strategy normally adopts a functional structure to meet these needs. This structure is appropriate because it is complex enough to manage the activities necessary to make and sell a narrow range of products for one or a few market segments. At the same time, the handoff problems are likely to be relatively easy to solve because a focuser remains small and specialized. Thus, a functional structure can provide all the integration necessary, provided that the focused firm has a strong, adaptive culture, which is vital to the development of some kind of distinctive competency.[52] Additionally, because such a company's competitive advantage is often based on personalized service, the flexibility of this kind of structure lets the company respond quickly to customers' needs and change its products in response to customers' requests. The way in which Lexmark reorganized itself to focus on the production of office printers, an approach examined in Strategy in Action 12.4, illustrates many of the issues in implementing a focus strategy.

Strategy in Action   12.4

Restructuring at Lexmark

Lexmark, a printer and typewriter manufacturer, was one of IBM's many divisions, but IBM sold it after years of losses brought on by high operating costs and an inability to produce new printers that could compete with those made by HP and Canon. Marvin Mann, an ex-IBM executive, was given the task of finding a way to restructure the company and turn it around. Mann realized at once that the company had to focus on producing a particular kind of printer to lower its out-of-control cost structure.

One of the biggest contributors to its high cost structure was Lexmark's structure and control system, so Mann decided to transform it. Then, he believed, he could begin to focus the company on producing a line of state-of-the-art laser and inkjet office printers. Like the rest of IBM at that time, Lexmark had developed a tall, centralized structure, and all important decision making was made by top managers. This slowed decision making and made it very difficult to communicate across functions because so many managers at different levels and in different functions had to approve new plans. Moving quickly to change this system, Mann streamlined the company's hierarchy, which meant terminating 50% of its managers. This action cut out three levels in the hierarchy. He then decentralized authority to the managers of each of the company's four product lines and told them to develop their own plans and goals. In addition, to continue the process of decentralization, product managers were instructed to develop cross-functional teams comprised of employees from all functions, with the goal of finding new and improved ways of organizing task activities to reduce costs. The teams were to use competitive benchmarking and evaluate their competitors' products in order to establish new performance standards to guide their activities. Finally, as an incentive for employees to work hard at increasing efficiency, innovation, and quality, Mann established a company stock ownership scheme to reward employees for their efforts.

Mann's strategy of restructuring Lexmark to focus on a narrow range of printers was successful. Within two years, the cost of launching new products went down by 50% and its new-product development cycle speeded up by 30%. Focusing on a narrow range of products also improved Lexmark's R&D competence. Lexmark is a technology leader in the laser and inkjet industry and makes the printers sold by Dell—showing that it is a focused cost leader in the printer market. Its stock has performed well as a result, and the company is enjoying considerable success against HP and Japanese competitors.[d]

The message of the preceding sections is clear. Strategic managers must continually monitor the performance of their organization as measured by its ability to increase differentiation, lower costs, and increase profitability. When managers sense declining performance or sense ways to increase performance, they must move quickly to change the way people and activities are organized and controlled. Organizational design, the process of combining and harmonizing structure, control, and culture, is a demanding and difficult task but one that is crucial to promoting and sustaining competitive advantage.

Restructuring and Reengineering

To improve performance, a single business company often employs restructuring and reengineering. **Restructuring** a company involves two steps: (1) streamlining the hierarchy of authority and reducing the number of levels in the hierarchy to a minimum, and then (2) reducing the number of employees to lower operating costs. When Jack Smith took over as head of GM, for example, GM had more than twenty-two levels in the hierarchy and more than 20,000 corporate managers. Describing his organization as a top-heavy bureaucracy, Smith quickly moved to slash costs and restructure the company. Today, GM has only twelve levels in the hierarchy and half as many corporate managers. In 2004, Kodak announced it would lay off 20% of its work force over a three-year period to reduce costs.

Restructuring and downsizing become necessary for many reasons.[53] Sometimes a change in the business environment occurs that could not have been foreseen; perhaps a shift in technology made the company's products obsolete, as happened to Kodak when the use of digital cameras exploded. Sometimes an organization has excess capacity because customers no longer want the goods and services it provides; maybe the goods and services are outdated or offer poor value for the money. Sometimes organizations downsize because they have grown too tall and inflexible and bureaucratic costs have become much too high—as happened to IBM. Sometimes they restructure even when they are in a strong position simply to build and improve their competitive advantage and stay on top—which Dell and Microsoft frequently do.

All too often, however, companies are forced to downsize and lay off employees because they fail to monitor and control their basic business operations and have not made the incremental changes to their strategies and structures over time that allow them to adjust to changing conditions. Advances in management, such as the development of new models for organizing work activities, or advances in information technology offer strategic managers the opportunity to implement their strategies in more effective ways.

One way of helping a company operate more effectively is to use **reengineering**, which involves the "fundamental rethinking and radical redesign of business processes to achieve dramatic improvements in critical, contemporary measures of performance such as cost, quality, service, and speed."[54] As this definition suggests, strategic managers who use reengineering must completely rethink how they organize their value chain activities. Instead of focusing on how a company's *functions* operate, strategic managers make business *processes* the focus of attention.

A **business process** is any activity that is vital to delivering goods and services to customers quickly or that promotes high quality or low costs (such as IT, materials management, or product development) and that is not the responsibility of any one function but *cuts across functions*. Because reengineering focuses on business processes and not on functions, a company that reengineers always has to adopt a different approach to organizing its activities. Companies that take up reengineering deliberately ignore the existing arrangement of tasks, roles, and work activities. They start the reengineering process with the customer (not the product or service) and ask: How can we reorganize the way we do our work, our business processes, to provide the best quality and the lowest-cost goods and services to the customer?

Frequently, when companies ask this question, they realize that there are more effective ways to organize their value chain activities. For example, a business process that encompasses members of ten different functions working sequentially to provide goods and services might be performed by one person or a few people at a fraction of the cost. Often individual jobs become increasingly complex, and people are grouped into cross-functional teams as business processes are reengineered to reduce costs and increase quality.

Hallmark Cards, for example, reengineered its card design process with great success. Before the reengineering effort, artists, writers, and editors worked separately in different functions to produce all kinds of cards. After reengineering, these same artists, writers, and editors were put in cross-functional teams, each of which now works on a specific type of card, such as birthday, Christmas, or Mother's Day. The result is that the time it takes to bring a new card to market dropped from years to months, and Hallmark's performance increased dramatically.

Reengineering and total quality management (TQM), discussed in Chapter 4, are highly interrelated and complementary. After reengineering has taken place and value chain activities have been altered to speed the product to the final customer, TQM takes over, with its focus on how to continue to improve and refine the new process and find better ways of managing task and role relationships. Successful organizations examine both issues simultaneously and continuously attempt to identify new and better processes for meeting the goals of increased efficiency, quality, and customer responsiveness. Thus, they are always seeking to improve their visions of their desired future.

Another example of reengineering is the change program that took place at IBM Credit, a wholly owned division of IBM that manages the financing and leasing of IBM computers, particularly mainframes, to IBM's customers. Before reengineering took place, a financing request arrived at the division's headquarters in Old Greenwich, Connecticut, and went through a five-step approval process that involved the activities of five different functions. First, the IBM salesperson called the credit department, which logged the request and recorded details about the potential customer. Second, this information was taken to the credit-checking department, where a credit check on the potential customer was done. Third, when the credit check was complete, the request was taken to the contracts department, which wrote the contract. Fourth, from the contracts department, it went to the pricing department, which determined the actual financial details of the loan, such as the interest rate and the term of the loan. Finally, the whole package of information was assembled by the dispatching department and delivered to the sales representative, who gave it to the customer.

This series of cross-functional activities took an average of seven days to complete, and sales representatives constantly complained that this delay resulted in a low level of customer responsiveness that reduced customer satisfaction. Also, potential customers were tempted to shop around for financing and even to look at competitors' machines. The delay in closing the deal caused uncertainty for all concerned.

The change process began when two senior IBM credit managers reviewed the finance approval process. They found that the time spent by different specialists in the different functions actually processing a loan application was only ninety minutes. The seven-day approval process was caused by the delay in transmitting information and requests between departments. The managers also learned that the activities taking place in each department were not complex; each department had its own computer system containing its own work procedures, but the work done in each department was pretty routine.

Armed with this information, IBM managers realized that the approval process could be reengineered into one overarching process handled by one person with a computer system containing all the necessary information and work procedures to perform the five loan-processing activities. If the application were complex, a team of experts stood ready to help process it, but IBM found that, after the reengineering effort, a typical application could be done in four hours rather than the previous seven days. A sales representative could go back to the customer the same day to close the deal, and all the uncertainty surrounding the transaction was removed.

As reengineering consultants Hammer and Champy note, this dramatic performance increase was brought about by a radical change to the process as a whole. Change through reengineering requires managers to go back to the basics and pull apart each step in the work process to identify a better way to coordinate and integrate the activities necessary to provide customers with goods and services. As this example makes clear, the introduction of new IT is an integral aspect of reengineering. IT also allows a company to restructure its hierarchy because it provides more and better-quality information. IT today is an integral part of the strategy implementation process.

Summary of Chapter

1. Implementing a company's business model and strategies successfully depends on organizational design, the process of selecting the right combination of organizational structure, control systems, and culture. Companies need to monitor and oversee the organizational design process to achieve superior profitability.

2. Effective organizational design can increase profitability in two ways. First, it economizes on bureaucratic costs and helps a company lower its cost structure. Second, it enhances the ability of a company's value creation functions to achieve superior efficiency, quality, innovativeness, and customer responsiveness and to obtain the advantages of differentiation.

3. The main issues in designing organizational structure are how to group tasks, functions, and divisions; how to allocate authority and responsibility (whether to have a tall or flat organization, or to have a centralized or decentralized structure); and how to use integrating mechanisms to improve coordination between functions (such as direct contacts, liaison roles, and teams).

4. Strategic control provides the monitoring and incentive systems necessary to make an organizational structure work as intended and extends corporate governance down to all levels inside the company. The main kinds of strategic control systems are personal control, output control, and behavior control. Information technology is an aid to output and behavior control, and reward systems are linked to every control system.

5. Organizational culture is the set of values, norms, beliefs, and attitudes that help to energize and motivate employees and control their behavior. Culture is a way of doing something, and a company's founder and top managers help determine which kinds of values emerge in an organization.

6. At the functional level, each function requires a different combination of structure and control system to achieve its functional objectives.

7. To successfully implement a company's business model, structure, control, and culture must be combined in ways that increase the relationships among all functions to build distinctive competencies.

8. Cost leadership and differentiation each require a structure and control system that strengthens the business model that is the source of their competitive advantage. Managers have to use organizational design in a way that balances pressures to increase differentiation against pressures to lower the cost structure.

9. Other specialized kinds of structures include the product, market, geographic, matrix, and product-team structures. Each has a specialized use and is implemented as a company's strategy warrants.

10. Restructuring and reengineering are two ways of implementing a company's business model more effectively.

Discussion Questions

1. What is the relationship among organizational structure, control, and culture? Give some examples of when and under what conditions a mismatch among these components might arise.

2. What kind of structure best describes the way your (a) business school and (b) university operate? Why is the structure appropriate? Would another structure fit better?

3. When would a company choose a matrix structure? What are the problems associated with managing this structure, and why might a product-team structure be preferable?

4. For each of the structures discussed in the chapter, outline the most suitable control systems.

5. What kind of structure, controls, and culture would you be likely to find in (a) a small manufacturing company, (b) a chain store, (c) a high-tech company, and (d) a Big Four accounting firm?

Practicing Strategic Management

SMALL-GROUP EXERCISE
Deciding on an Organizational Structure

Break up into groups of three to five people, and discuss the following scenario. You are a group of managers of a major soft drink company that is going head-to-head with Coca-Cola to increase market share. Your business model is based on increasing your product range to offer a soft drink in every segment of the market to attract customers. Currently you have a functional structure. What you are trying to work out now is how best to implement your business model in order to launch your new products. Should you move to a more complex kind of product structure and, if so, which one? Alternatively, should you establish new-venture divisions and spin off each kind of new soft drink into its own company so that it can focus its resources on its market niche? Thinking strategically, debate the pros and cons of the possible organizational structures, and decide which structure you will implement.

ARTICLE FILE 12

Find an example of a company that competes in one industry and has recently changed the way it implements its business model and strategies. What changes did it make? Why did it make these changes? What effect did these changes have on the behavior of people and functions?

STRATEGIC MANAGEMENT PROJECT
Module 12

This module asks you to identify how your company implements its business model and strategy. For this part of your project, you need to obtain information about your company's structure, control systems, and culture. This information may be hard to obtain unless you can interview managers directly. But you can make many inferences about the company's structure from the nature of its activities, and if you write to the company, it may provide you with an organizational chart and other information. Also, published information, such as compensation for top management, is available in the company's annual reports or 10-K reports. If your company is well known, magazines such as *Fortune* and *Business Week* frequently report on corporate culture or control issues. Nevertheless, you may be forced to make some bold assumptions to complete this part of the project.

1. How large is the company as measured by the number of its employees? How many levels in the hierarchy

does it have from the top to the bottom? Based on these two measures and any other information you may have, would you say your company operates with a relatively tall or flat structure? Does your company have a centralized or decentralized approach to decision making?

2. What changes (if any) would you make to the way the company allocates authority and responsibility?

3. Draw an organizational chart showing the main way in which your company groups its activities. Based on this chart, decide what kind of structure (functional, product, or divisional) your company is using.

4. Why did your company choose this structure? In what ways is it appropriate for its business model? In what ways is it not?

5. What kind of integration or integration mechanisms does your company use?

6. What are the main kinds of control systems your company is using? What kinds of behaviors is the organization trying to (a) shape and (b) motivate through the use of these control systems?

7. What role does the top management team play in creating the culture of your organization? Can you identify the characteristic norms and values that describe the way people behave in your organization? How does the design of the organization's structure affect its culture?

8. What are the sources of your company's distinctive competencies? Which functions are most important to it? How does your company design its structure, control, and culture to enhance its (a) efficiency, (b) quality, (c) innovativeness, and (d) responsiveness to customers?

9. How does it design its structure and control systems to strengthen its business model? For example, what steps does it take to further cross-functional integration? Does it have a functional, product, or matrix structure?

10. How does your company's culture support its business model? Can you determine any ways in which its top management team influences its culture?

11. Based on this analysis, would you say your company is coordinating and motivating its people and subunits effectively? Why or why not? What changes (if any) would you make to the way your company's structure operates? What use could it make of restructuring or reengineering?

ETHICS EXERCISE

Rose checked and rechecked the petty cash log. No matter how many times she calculated the amount, the log always ended up $100 short. Only Rose, Jason, and their boss David had access to the petty cash account. A month ago, the account had been short $150, and the month before that, $75 had been missing. On both occasions, Jason figured out where the money had gone. Rose called him now. "Jason, do you know anything about a missing $100 in the petty cash account? I can't find a $100 expense anywhere in the log and we're definitely missing money." Jason told Rose he would be right down.

Jason finally arrived at Rose's desk a half an hour later. "No problem, Rose," he said. "David doesn't have the receipt anymore, but he used the money to take care of dinner with a client."

Rose paused; the same excuse had been offered on previous occasions. "Jason, we can't keep logging expenses without receipts. Accounting is going to question our records sooner or later."

Jason glanced around and said quietly, "Trust me, Rose. This is what we have to do—just do it." Then he walked away.

Rose knew something was wrong. She was worried that Jason was somehow stealing from petty cash. Finally she decided to tell David, their boss. When she arrived for her 1:00 appointment in David's office, she was surprised to see Jason already there. He wouldn't meet her eyes, and she assumed that David had already discovered his stealing. Before she could speak, David said, in a voice that Rose had never heard before, "It seems that I have to let you in on a little secret, Rose. From time to time, I need a little extra from petty cash. For a corporation this size, $100 here, $200 there is nothing. I've already had a few chats with Jason here, who needs to keep his job to help his mother. It seems to me that you need your job, too—kids at home, right? Well, if either of you mentions these little 'expenses' of mine to anyone, you'll be fired instantly. Who will they believe, you two peons, or me—with 25 years of loyal service to the company? All I have to do is tell them that you've been the ones robbing petty cash!"

1. Define the ethical dilemmas addressed in this case.

2. What should the company do to ensure that employees feel safe reporting wrongdoing?

3. What would you do if you were in Rose's situation?

CLOSING CASE

Nokia's New Product Structure

Nokia is the largest cellular or mobile phone maker in the world, with sales of over $45 billion in 2006. The company was a pioneer of cell phone technology, and throughout the 1990s, its sales surged every year; however, business has not been as good in the 2000s. Like Motorola, another cell phone pioneer, Nokia's profits have fallen because it has run into tough competition from companies like Samsung, Sony, and hand-held makers like Palm that have been rushing to offer their customers new and improved varieties of hand-held devices or smart phones. In the Opening Case to Chapter 5, we saw how Samsung was the first company to realize that customers wanted a color screen so that they could play games on their phones, and Samsung was also one of the first to realize the potential of integrating digital cameras into phones. The market is growing for game-playing phones, Internet-connected phones, and smart phones that include functions such as an MP3 player, record keeping software, and applications software for PowerPoint presentations and word processing. Also growing rapidly is the market for wireless technology that can securely link smart phones used in the field to the company's central databases and the PCs in employees' offices or homes, especially now that broadband communication is becoming the norm.

Analysts claim that Nokia was slow to sense these emerging trends partly because of its organizational structure and culture. Nokia's way of operating was to push down or decentralize decision making to lower levels, where teams of employees were responsible for developing innovative new cell phone software and hardware. Bureaucracy was kept to a minimum, and team members normally discussed product development in informal meetings. In addition, Nokia's culture was based on Finnish values and norms that emphasized democratic, shared, and informal work relationships rather than the use of formal authority.

This way of implementing strategy had led to superior innovation and a successful business model, but as Nokia grew bigger, problems emerged. While the cell phone market was changing rapidly, Nokia's team structure resulted in slow decision making. It was taking more and more time for Nokia to create new products and bring them to market. Higher-level managers had to wait longer to find out what the teams below them were doing, and then top managers from all parts of the organization had to meet in so-called company committees to decide which products should be given the most funding and the highest priority. Another problem was that Nokia's top managers, headquartered in Espoo, Finland, were remote from global customers, and its marketing and engineering managers were slow to pick up on developing wireless trends, such as customers' desire for digital cameras. In particular, they did not appreciate how fast the global market was fragmenting into customers in rich countries like Japan and the United States who wanted sophisticated, broadband-capable smart phones and were prepared to pay high prices for them, and customers in developing countries such as China, India, and those in South America who needed an inexpensive cell phone infrastructure and service, as well as inexpensive cell phones.

In the early 2000s, when the company's sales started to fall and its Japanese competitors took the lead, Nokia's managers realized they needed to change the way the company operated to quicken Nokia's response to the changing marketplace. Nokia's CEO, Jorma Ollila, announced that in 2004, Nokia would split its activities into four separate product divisions, each of which would focus on developing cell phone software and hardware for a particular market segment. Three of these were new divisions: (1) the *mobile phone* division, which would primarily design and sell low-cost, low-priced handsets mostly for voice calls; (2) the *multimedia* division, which would design and sell advanced smart phones with features such as gaming and picture taking and which would pursue differentiation and, Nokia managers hoped, premium pricing; and (3) the *networks* division, which would sell the technology necessary to build mobile phone networks and create wireless infrastructure in regions and countries around the globe. Finally, Nokia announced it would greatly expand the activities of its *enterprise solutions* division, which was responsible for developing hardware and software products for corporate customers in search of a wireless corporate intranet. Here, it was competing directly against companies like Microsoft, IBM, and HP.[55]

The plan was that each product division would be under the control of its own team of top executives and that each team would build the business model necessary to compete successfully in its market segment. By decentralizing control to each division, Nokia hoped to speed up team decision making, reasoning that managers would be in much closer contact with these teams and could intervene quickly as the need arises. Nokia hoped the new structure would allow it to innovate new models of cell phones at a faster rate and at a lower cost and thus combat the threat from Samsung. In addition, to get closer to its customers, Nokia announced that it would expand its overseas operations—for example, by outsourcing more manufacturing to Asia and establishing more local sales offices. It would also create a U.S. headquarters for its new enterprise solutions division, and it hired a former HP executive, Mary McDowell, to head the division and spearhead its push into this large and profitable corporate networking market. Only time will tell if Nokia's new structure will be successful, but the company has introduced many new products in the last few years and its sales are once again on the upward path, which has hurt competitors like Motorola and Samsung.[56]

Case Discussion Questions

1. Why and how did Nokia move to a product structure to better implement its business model?

2. What organizational design lessons could other companies learn from Nokia's example?

3. Go to the Internet and try to discover any recent changes Nokia has made to its structure.

Implementing Strategy in Companies That Compete Across Industries and Countries

Ford Has a New CEO and a New Global Structure

Designing a global business organization to operate in many countries is a critical issue for multinational companies. Ford is a good example of a company that has experienced these types of problems. Ford realized early that there was a major opportunity to increase profitability by taking its skills in carmaking to countries abroad. Over time, it established carmaking business units in different countries in Europe, Asia, and Australia. Decision-making authority was decentralized to each unit, which controlled its own activities and developed cars suited to its local market. The result was that each unit came to operate independently from the Ford parent company in the United States. Ford of Europe, for example, became the largest and most profitable carmaker in Europe.

Ford remained a highly profitable enterprise until Japanese carmakers began to flood the world with their small, reliable, low-priced cars in the 1970s and 1980s. When car buyers began buying these imports in large numbers, Ford tried to draw on the skills of its European unit to help build smaller, more fuel-efficient cars for the U.S. market. But it had never before tried to get its U.S. and European design and manufacturing units to cooperate, and this proved very difficult to achieve because of the nature of its global organizational structure. In the 1990s, Ford embarked on a massive project to create a new global matrix structure for the company that would solve the decentralized task and authority problems that were preventing it from utilizing its resources effectively. In its Ford 2000 plan, for example, it laid out a timetable of how all its global carmaking units would learn to cooperate with one set of global support functions such as design, purchasing, and so on. However, huge political problems arose with its new structure; the redesign went through one change after another; and by the mid 2000s, Ford was still operating as a collection of different "empires." Its U.S., European, and Asia/Pacific units were operating almost autonomously.

So Ford decided to restructure itself. It moved to a so-called world structure in which one set of managers was given authority over the whole of a specific global operation such as manufacturing or car design. Then it began to design cars for the global market. Its new structure never worked to quicken car design and production, even though it constantly changed global lines of authority and the locations in which it operated to increase profitability. Ford went through multiple reorganizations to try to meet the Japanese challenge but nothing worked. By 2006, it was in deep trouble. Losing billions of dollars, Ford announced in September 2006 a revamped "Way Forward" plan to turn around its U.S. and global operations, a plan that called for cutting 44,000 jobs; closing sixteen plants; and freshening 70% of the company's Ford, Mercury, and Lincoln car lineup.

But in October 2006, Ford also appointed a new president and CEO, Alan Mulally, an expert in organizational design, to help turn around its operations. Mulally, a former Boeing executive, had led that company's global reorganization effort. Now he began to work out how to change Ford's global structure to reduce costs and speed product development. In the structure Mulally inherited, Ford's Americas unit reported to the CEO, but its other global and functional operations reported to the next two most senior executives, Mark Fields, president of Ford's Americas operation, and Mark Schulz, president of international operations. Mulally decided that Ford's downsizing should be accompanied by a major reorganization of its hierarchy, and he decided to flatten Ford's structure and recentralize control. At the same time, however, he put the focus on teamwork and adopted a cross-functional approach to handling the enormous value chain challenges that still confronted the organization.

The position of president of international operations was eliminated and Mark Fields continues to report to Mulally, but so too do the heads of the other two world regions—Lewis Booth, head of Ford of Europe, and John Parker, head of Ford of Asia Pacific and Africa, and Mazda. Two levels in the hierarchy are now gone, and Mulally's new organizational design clearly defines each global executive's role in the company's hierarchy so Ford can begin acting like one company instead of separate global units, each with their own interests.[1] In addition, the heads of its global value chain functions also now report directly to Mulally, not to Fields; these heads include Tony Brown, global head of purchasing; Nick Smither, head of information technology (IT); Richard Parry-Jones, chief technical officer; and Bennie Fowler, head of quality and advanced manufacturing engineering. Mulally's goal is to provide a centralized focus on using the company's global functional assets to better support its carmaking business units.

At the same time, Mulally also took a major restructuring step when he announced the creation of a new position, global product development chief, who is responsible for overseeing the development of Ford's entire global lines of vehicles. He appointed Derrick Kuzak, head of product development in the Americas, to head Ford's new global engineering design effort, and he also reports directly to Mulally. Kuzak oversees efforts to streamline product development and engineering systems around the world. As Mulally commented, "An integrated, global product development team supporting our automotive business units will enable us to make the best use of our global assets and capabilities and accelerate development of the new vehicles our customers prefer, and do so more efficiently."[2]

So Mulally's goal is to force a cross-functional approach on all his top managers—one that he will personally oversee—to standardize its global carmaking and allow functional units to continuously improve quality, productivity, and the speed at which new products can be introduced. But beyond streamlining and standardizing its approach, its new-product development group must also ensure that its new vehicles—vehicles that it intends to introduce at a rapid rate in the rest of the 2000s—are customized to better meet the needs of regional customers All Ford's executives understand the company's very survival is at stake; they must work together to accelerate efforts to reduce costs and catch up to more efficient competitors such as Toyota. If Mulally's new global design cannot achieve this goal, it is likely that Ford will be taken over by a competitor in the next decade.

OVERVIEW   The story of Ford's efforts to develop a competitive global business model to compete effectively in car markets around the world suggests how complex strategic thinking can become at the corporate level. Companies have to continually examine how to improve the way they implement their business and multibusiness models to increase their long-run profitability and grow their profits. This chapter takes off where the last one ends and examines how to implement strategy when a company decides to enter and compete in new industries, or in new countries when it expands globally, and when it chooses strategies such as merger or outsourcing to strengthen its business model. The strategy implementation issue remains the same: how to use organizational design and combine organizational structure, control, and culture to allow a company to pursue its business model and strategies successfully. Once a company decides to compete across industries and countries, however, it confronts a new set of problems, some of them continuations of problems discussed in Chapter 12 and some of them a direct consequence of its decision to enter and compete in overseas markets and new industries. As a result, it has to make a new series of organizational design decisions to successfully implement its new global and multibusiness model. By the end of the chapter, you will appreciate the many complex issues and choices confronting managers of multibusiness and global companies and the reasons that strategy implementation is an integral part of achieving superior performance.

Managing Corporate Strategy Through the Multidivisional Structure

As Chapter 10 discussed, corporate-level strategies such as vertical integration or diversification can be used in many ways to strengthen a company's business model to improve its competitive position. However, substantial implementation problems also arise, many of them due to the increasing bureaucratic costs associated with managing a larger collection of companies that operate in different industries. These costs are especially high when a company is seeking to gain the differentiation and low-cost advantages of transferring, sharing, or leveraging its distinctive competencies across its business units in different industries. For companies pursuing a multibusiness model, the problems and costs of managing the handoffs or transfers between value chain functions across industries to obtain these benefits rise sharply. The need to economize on these costs propels strategic managers to search for improved ways of implementing the corporate-level strategies necessary to pursue a multibusiness model.

As a company begins to enter new industries and produce completely different kinds of products such as cars, fast food, and computers, the structures described in Chapter 12, like the functional and product structures, are not up to the task. They cannot provide sufficient coordination between functions and motivation to employees that implementing a multibusiness model requires. As a result, the control problems that give rise to bureaucratic costs, such as those related to measurement, customers, location, or strategy, escalate. Experiencing these problems is a sign that the company has outgrown its structure. Strategic managers need to invest more resources to develop a more complex structure—one that can meet the needs of its multibusiness model and strategies. The answer for most large, complex companies is to move to a multidivisional structure, design a cross-industry control system, and fashion a corporate culture to reduce these problems and economize on bureaucratic costs.

The multidivisional structure possesses two main innovations over a functional or product structure, and these innovations allow a company to grow and diversify while reducing the coordination and control problems inherent in entering and competing in new industries. First, in each industry in which a company operates, strategic managers organize its business units or companies in that industry into one or more *divisions.* Sometimes each division contains a full set of all the value chain functions it needs to pursue its business model; in this case, it is called a *self-contained division.* For example, GE competes in over 150 different industries, and in each industry, all of its divisions are self-sufficient and perform all the value creation functions. Sometimes, however, divisions in *different* industries share value chain functions to obtain cost savings and to benefit from leveraging competencies across divisions, as discussed in detail below. For example, PepsiCo has two major divisions in the soft drink and snack foods industries; each has its own research and development (R&D) and manufacturing functions, but they share the marketing and distribution functions to lower operating costs and achieve the gains from differentiation.

Second, the office of *corporate headquarters staff* is created to monitor divisional activities and to exercise financial control over each of the divisions.[3] This staff contains the corporate-level managers who oversee the activities of divisional managers. Hence, the organizational hierarchy is taller in a multidivisional structure than in a product or functional structure. The role of the new level of corporate management is to develop strategic control systems that lower a company's overall cost structure, including finding ways to economize on the costs of controlling the handoffs and transfers between divisions. The extra cost of these corporate managers is more than justified if their actions can lower the cost structure of the operating divisions or increase the divisions' ability to differentiate their product—both of which boost a company's return on invested capital (ROIC).

In the multidivisional structure, the day-to-day operations of each division are the responsibility of divisional management; that is, divisional management has *operating responsibility.* The corporate headquarters, which includes top executives as well as their support staff, is responsible for overseeing the company's long-term multibusiness model and for providing guidance for interdivisional projects. These executives have *strategic responsibility.* Such a combination of self-contained divisions with a centralized corporate management provides the extra coordination and control necessary to manage entry into new industries.

Figure 13.1 illustrates a typical multidivisional structure found in a large chemical company such as DuPont. Although this company might easily have twenty different divisions, only three—the oil, pharmaceuticals, and plastics divisions—are represented here. Each division possesses some combination of the value chain functions it needs to pursue its own business model. Each is also normally treated by the corporate center as a profit center, and strategic control measures such as ROIC are used to monitor and evaluate each division's performance.[4] The use of this kind of output control makes it easier for corporate managers to identify high-performing and underperforming divisions and to take corrective action as necessary.

Because they have been separated into subunits by industry, each division is also able to develop the structure (for example, a product, matrix, or market structure) and culture that best suit its particular business model. As a result, implementing a multidivisional structure allows a multibusiness company to let each separate division adopt the structure and control systems necessary to implement its business model and strategies effectively.

Figure 13.1 shows that the oil division has a functional structure because it is pursuing cost leadership. The pharmaceuticals division has a product-team structure to encourage speedy development of new drugs, and the plastics division has a matrix structure to allow it to quickly develop new kinds of customized plastic products to suit the changing needs of its customers. These divisions are pursuing differentiation

FIGURE 13.1

Multidivisional Structure

Typical Chemical Company

Oil division
(functional structure)

Pharmaceuticals division
(product-team structure)

Plastics division
(matrix structure)

based on a distinctive competence in innovation. Sometimes the size of its operations alone is enough to compel a company to use a multidivisional structure. For example, inside one industry, the car industry, Ford operates the whole corporation through a multidivisional structure, and each of its main car brands—Ford, Jaguar, Mercury, Mazda, Lincoln, and so on—is organized as a separate division. In addition, as we discussed in the Opening Case, Ford has an overseas division in each country in which it assembles cars abroad.

In fact, the executive most famous for employing the multidivisional structure in this way was also the CEO of a car company, Alfred Sloan, former CEO of GM. He implemented its multidivisional structure in 1921, noting that GM "needs to find a principle for coordination without losing the advantages of decentralization." Sloan placed each of GM's different car brands in a self-contained division with support services like sales, production, engineering, and finance. Each division became a profit center and was evaluated on its return on investment. Sloan was quite clear about the main advantage of linking decentralization to return on investment: it raised the visibility of each division's performance. And, Sloan observed, it (1) "increases the morale of the organization by placing each operation on its own foundation, . . . assuming its own responsibility and contributing its share to the final result"; (2) "develops statistics correctly reflecting . . . the true measure of efficiency"; and (3) "enables the corporation to direct the placing of additional capital where it will result in the greatest benefit to the corporation as a whole."[5]

Sloan recommended that exchanges or handoffs between divisions be set by a *transfer-pricing scheme* based on cost plus some predetermined rate of return. To avoid protecting a high-cost internal supplier, however, he also recommended a number of steps involving analysis of the operations of outside competitors to determine the fair price. Sloan established a strong, professional, centralized headquarters management staff to perform such calculations. Corporate management's primary role was to audit divisional performance and plan strategy for the total organization. Divisional managers were to be responsible for all product-related decisions.

As the Opening Case related, fierce competition from efficient Japanese competitors has resulted in Ford CEO Mulally reorganizing the way Ford's multidivisional structure operated, both domestically and globally. The duplication of R&D and engineering between divisions at home and abroad, and the purchasing of components by each global division independently, was costing the company billions of extra dollars. Globally, Ford's goal is to streamline the number of cars in its product range and the number of different plants in which its cars are made. As Ford's experience suggests, operating a multidivisional structure is a *continuing* challenge for managers. Because the multidivisional structure is so widely used, it is necessary to look closely at its advantages and disadvantages.

● **Advantages of a Multidivisional Structure**

When managed effectively at both the corporate and the divisional levels, a multidivisional structure offers several advantages. Together, they can raise corporate profitability to a new peak because they allow a company to more effectively implement its multibusiness model and strategies at all levels.

ENHANCED CORPORATE FINANCIAL CONTROL   The profitability of different business divisions is clearly visible in the multidivisional structure.[6] Because each division is its own profit center, financial controls can be applied to each business on the basis of profitability criteria such as ROIC. Typically, these controls cover establishing targets, monitoring performance on a regular basis, and selectively intervening when problems arise. Corporate headquarters is also in a better position to allocate corporate financial resources among competing divisions. The visibility of divisional performance means that corporate headquarters can identify the divisions in which investment of funds will yield the greatest long-term ROIC. In a sense, the corporate office is in a position to act as the investor or banker in an internal capital market, channeling funds to high-yield uses.

ENHANCED STRATEGIC CONTROL   The multidivisional structure frees corporate managers from business-level responsibilities. Corporate managers have the time and scope for contemplating wider strategic issues and for developing responses to environmental changes, such as quickly changing industry boundaries. The multidivisional structure also enables corporate headquarters to obtain the proper information to perform long-run strategic and scenario planning for the entire corporation, including decisions about which businesses to expand and which to exit.

GROWTH   The multidivisional structure lets the company overcome an organizational limit to its growth. Because information overload at the center is reduced, corporate managers can consider emerging opportunities for further growth and diversification. Communication problems are reduced because the same set of standardized accounting and financial output controls can be used for all divisions. Also, from a behavior control perspective, corporate managers can implement a policy of management by exception, which means that they intervene only when problems arise.

STRONGER PURSUIT OF INTERNAL EFFICIENCY   As a company grows, it often becomes difficult for managers to accurately assess the profit contribution of each functional activity because their activities are so interdependent. This means that it is often more difficult for top managers to evaluate how well their company is performing relative to others in its industry. As a result, inside one company, considerable degrees of organizational slack—that is, the unproductive use of functional resources—can go undetected. For example, the head of the finance function might employ a larger staff than is required for efficiency to reduce work pressures inside the department and to bring the manager higher status. In a multidivisional structure, however, corporate managers can compare the performance of one division against another in terms of its cost structure or the profit it generates. The corporate office is thus in a better position to identify the managerial inefficiencies that result in bureaucratic costs, and divisional managers have no alibis for poor performance.

● **Problems in Implementing a Multidivisional Structure**

Although research suggests that large companies that adopt a multidivisional structure outperform those that retain the functional structure, this structure has its disadvantages as well.[7] Good management can eliminate some of them, but others are inherent in the way the structure operates and require constant managerial attention, as Ford's problems suggest.

ESTABLISHING THE DIVISIONAL-CORPORATE AUTHORITY RELATIONSHIP The authority relationship between corporate headquarters and the divisions must be correctly established. The multidivisional structure introduces a new level in the hierarchy: the corporate level. The problem lies in deciding how much authority and control to delegate to the operating divisions and how much authority to retain at corporate headquarters to increase long-run profitability. This was the problem Sloan encountered when he implemented GM's multidivisional structure.[8] Sloan found that when headquarters retained too much power and authority, the operating divisions lacked sufficient autonomy to develop the business model and strategies that best met their needs. On the other hand, when too much power was delegated to the divisions, they pursued divisional objectives, with little heed to the needs of the whole corporation. As a result, not all the potential gains from using this structure could be achieved. At Ford, Mulally has recentralized control at the global level to force carmaking and functional divisions to cooperate and improve efficiency and effectiveness.

Thus, the central issue in managing the multidivisional structure is how much authority should be *centralized* at corporate headquarters and how much should be *decentralized* to the divisions. This issue must be decided by each company in reference to the nature of its business- and corporate-level strategies. There are no easy answers, and as the environment changes or the company alters its multibusiness model strategies over time, the balance between corporate and divisional control will also change.

DISTORTION OF INFORMATION If corporate headquarters places too much emphasis on each division's individual profitability—for instance, by setting very high and stringent ROIC targets—divisional managers may choose to distort the information they supply to top management and paint a rosy picture at the expense of future profitability. Bureaucratic costs now increase as divisions may attempt to make ROIC look better by cutting product development, new investments, or marketing expenditures. Although such actions might boost short-run ROIC, they do so at the cost of cutting back on the investments and expenditures that are necessary to maintain the long-term profitability of the company. The problem stems from too tight financial control. GM suffered from this problem in recent years as declining performance prompted divisional managers to try to make their divisions look good to corporate headquarters and thus secure greater funds for future investment. Managing the corporate-divisional interface requires coping with subtle power issues.

COMPETITION FOR RESOURCES The third problem of managing a multidivisional structure is that the divisions themselves may compete for resources, and this rivalry can make it difficult or impossible to obtain the gains from transferring, sharing, or leveraging distinctive competencies across business units. For example, the amount of capital for investment that corporate managers have to distribute to the divisions is fixed. Generally, the divisions that can demonstrate the highest ROIC get the lion's share of the money. Because that large share strengthens them in the next time period, the strong divisions grow stronger. Consequently, divisions may actively compete for resources and thereby reduce interdivisional coordination. As a result, the potential gains from pursuing a multibusiness model will be lost.

TRANSFER PRICING Divisional competition may lead to battles over **transfer pricing,** that is, conflicts over establishing the fair or "competitive" price of a resource or skill developed in one division that is to be transferred and sold to other divisions that require it. As we discussed in Chapter 9, one of the origins of the problems of handoffs or transfers between divisions, and thus a major source of bureaucratic costs, is the problem of setting prices for resource transfers to obtain the benefits of the multibusiness models when pursuing a vertical integration or related diversification strategy.

Rivalry among divisions is common in the transfer pricing process because each supplying division has the incentive to set the highest price for its resources or skills to maximize its own revenues and profits. However, purchasing divisions view attempts to charge high prices as undermining their own profitability—hence the problem. Such competition can completely undermine the corporate culture and turn the company into a battleground. If such battles go unresolved, the benefits of the multibusiness model will not be achieved. Hence, there is a need for the sensitive design of incentive and control systems to make the multidivisional structure work.

SHORT-TERM R&D FOCUS If corporate headquarters sets extremely high and rigid ROIC targets, there is a danger that the divisions will cut back on R&D expenditures to improve their financial performance. Although this inflates divisional performance in the short term, it undermines a division's ability to develop new products and leads to a fall in the stream of long-term profits. Hence, corporate headquarters personnel must carefully control their interactions with the divisions to ensure that both the short- and long-term goals of the business are being achieved.

DUPLICATION OF FUNCTIONAL RESOURCES Because each division often possesses its own set of value chain functions, multidivisional structures are expensive to run and manage. R&D is an especially costly activity, and so some companies centralize such functions at the corporate level to serve all divisions. The duplication of specialist services is not a problem if the cost and differentiation gains from having separate specialist functions are substantial, however. Corporate managers decide whether duplication is financially justified and, if so, which functions to centralize or decentralize to optimize short- and long-run profitability.

In sum, the advantages of divisional structures must be balanced against the problems of implementing them, but an observant, professional management team that is aware of the issues involved can manage these problems. The increasing use of information technology is also making implementation easier. We discuss information technology after we describe the use of structure, control, and culture for different kinds of multibusiness models.

● **Structure, Control, Culture, and Corporate-Level Strategy**

Once strategic managers select a multidivisional structure, they must then make choices about what kind of integrating mechanisms and control systems to use to make the structure work efficiently. Such choices depend on whether a company chooses to pursue a multibusiness model based on a strategy of unrelated diversification, vertical integration, or related diversification.

As discussed in Chapter 9, many possible differentiation and cost advantages derive from vertical integration. A company can coordinate resource-scheduling decisions among divisions operating in adjacent industries to reduce manufacturing costs and improve quality, for example.[9] This might mean locating a rolling mill next to a steel furnace to save the costs of reheating steel ingots and make it easier to control the quality of the final product.

The principal benefits from related diversification also come from transferring, sharing, or leveraging functional resources or skills across divisions, such as sharing distribution and sales networks to increase differentiation or lower the overall cost structure. With both strategies, the benefits to the company come from some *exchange of distinctive competencies* among divisions. To secure these benefits, the company must coordinate activities among divisions. Consequently, structure and control must be designed to manage the handoffs or transfers among divisions.

In the case of unrelated diversification, the multibusiness model is based on using general managerial capabilities in entrepreneurship, organizational design, or strategy—for example, through top managers' ability to create a culture that supports entrepreneurial behavior that leads to rapid product development; or from restructuring an underperforming company and establishing an efficient internal capital market that allows corporate managers to make superior capital allocation decisions than would be possible using the external capital market. With this strategy, there are no exchanges among divisions, each operates separately and independently, and the exchanges that need to be coordinated take place between divisions and corporate headquarters. Structure and control must therefore be designed to allow each division to operate independently while giving corporate managers easy ability to monitor and to intervene if necessary.

The choice of structure and control mechanisms depends on the degree to which a company using a multidivisional structure needs to control the handoffs and interactions among divisions. The more interdependent the divisions—that is, the more they depend on each other for skills, resources, and competencies—the greater are the bureaucratic costs associated with obtaining the potential benefits from a particular strategy.[10] Table 13.1 indicates what forms of structure and control companies should adopt to economize on the bureaucratic costs associated with the three corporate strategies of unrelated diversification, vertical integration, and related diversification.[11] We examine these strategies in detail in the next sections.

UNRELATED DIVERSIFICATION   Because there are *no exchanges or linkages* among divisions, unrelated diversification is the easiest and cheapest strategy to manage; it is associated with the lowest level of bureaucratic costs. The main advantage of the structure and control system is that it allows corporate managers to evaluate divisional performance easily and accurately. Thus, companies use a multidivisional

TABLE 13.1

Corporate Strategy and Structure and Control

Corporate Strategy	Appropriate Structure	Need for Integration	Type of Control		
			Financial Control	Behavior Control	Organizational Culture
Unrelated Diversification	Multidivisional	Low (no exchanges between divisions)	Great use (e.g., ROIC)	Some use (e.g., budgets)	Little use
Vertical Integration	Multidivisional	Medium (scheduling resource transfers)	Great use (e.g., ROIC, transfer pricing)	Great use (e.g., standardization, budgets)	Some use (e.g., shared norms and values)
Related Diversification	Multidivisional	High (achieving synergies between divisions by integrating roles)	Little use	Great use (e.g., rules, budgets)	Great use (e.g., norms, values, common language)

structure, and each division is evaluated by output controls such as return on invested capital. A company also applies sophisticated accounting controls to obtain information quickly from the divisions so that corporate managers can readily compare divisions on several dimensions. UTC, Tyco, Textron, and Dover are good examples of companies that use sophisticated computer networks and accounting controls to manage their structures, which allow them almost daily access to divisional performance.

Divisions usually have considerable autonomy *unless* they fail to reach their ROIC goals. Generally, corporate headquarters will not intervene in the operations of a division unless there are problems. If problems arise, corporate headquarters may step in to take corrective action, perhaps replacing managers or providing additional financial resources, depending on the reason for the problem. If they see no possibility of a turnaround, they may decide to divest the division. The multidivisional structure allows the unrelated company to operate its businesses as a portfolio of investments that can be bought and sold as business conditions change. Often managers in the various divisions do not know one another; they may not even know what other companies are in the corporate portfolio. Hence, the idea of a corporate culture is meaningless.

The use of financial controls to manage a company means that no integration among divisions is necessary. This is why the bureaucratic costs of managing an unrelated company are low. The biggest problem facing corporate personnel is determining capital allocations to the various divisions so that the overall profitability of the portfolio is maximized. They also have to oversee divisional managers and make sure that divisions are achieving ROIC targets.

Alco Standard, based in Valley Forge, Pennsylvania, demonstrates how to operate a successful strategy of unrelated diversification. Alco is one of the largest office supply companies in the United States, distributing office and paper supplies and materials through a nationwide network of wholly owned distribution companies. The policy of Alco's top management is that authority and control should be completely decentralized to the managers in each of the company's fifty divisions. Each division is left alone to make its own manufacturing or purchasing decisions even though some potential benefits, in the form of corporatewide purchasing or marketing, are being lost. Top management pursues this nonintervention policy because it believes that the gains from allowing its managers to act as independent entrepreneurs exceed any potential cost savings that might result from coordinating interdivisional activities. It believes that a decentralized operating system allows a big company to act in a way that is similar to a small company, avoiding the problem of growing bureaucracy and organizational inertia.

At Alco, top management interprets its role as relieving the divisions of administrative chores, such as bookkeeping and accounting, and collecting market information on competitive pricing and products, which allows divisional managers to improve their business-level strategy. Centralizing these information activities reduces each division's cost structure and provides the standardization that lets top management make better decisions about resource allocation. Alco's division heads are regarded as partners in the corporate enterprise and are rewarded through stock options linked to the performance of their divisions. So far, Alco has been very successful with its decentralized operating structure and has achieved a compound growth rate of 19% a year.

VERTICAL INTEGRATION Vertical integration is a more expensive strategy to manage than unrelated diversification because *sequential resource flows* from one division to the next must be coordinated. Once again, the multidivisional structure economizes on the bureaucratic costs associated with achieving such coordination. This structure provides the centralized control necessary for the vertically integrated company to achieve benefits from the control of resource transfers. Corporate personnel assume the responsibility for devising financial output and behavior controls that solve the problems of transferring resources from one division to the next; for example, they are involved in solving transfer pricing problems. Also, complex rules and procedures are instituted that specify how exchanges are to be made to solve potential transaction problems. As previously noted, complex resource exchanges can lead to conflict among divisions, and corporate managers must try to minimize divisional conflicts. Centralizing authority at corporate headquarters must be done with care in vertically related companies. It carries the risk of involving corporate managers in operating issues at the business level to the point that the divisions lose their autonomy and motivation. These companies must strike the right balance of centralized control at corporate headquarters and decentralized control at the divisional level if they are to implement this strategy successfully.

Because their interests are at stake, divisions need to have input into scheduling and decisions regarding resource transfer. For example, the plastics division in a chemical company has a vital interest in the activities of the oil division because the quality of the products it gets from the oil division determines the quality of its own products. Divisional integrating mechanisms can bring about direct coordination and information transfers among divisions.[12] To handle communication among divisions, a company sets up teams for that purpose; it can also use **integrating roles** whereby an experienced senior manager assumes responsibility for managing complex transfers between two or more divisions. The use of integrating roles to coordinate divisions is common in high-tech and chemical companies, for example.

Thus, a strategy of vertical integration is managed through a combination of corporate and divisional controls. As a result, the organizational structure and control systems used for managing this strategy to economize on bureaucratic costs are more complex and more difficult to implement than those used for unrelated diversification. However, as long as the benefits that derive from vertical integration are realized, the extra expense in implementing this strategy can be justified.

RELATED DIVERSIFICATION   In the case of related diversification, the gains from pursuing this multibusiness model derive from the transfer, sharing, or leveraging of R&D knowledge, industry information, customer bases, and so on, across divisions. Also, with this structure, the high level of resource sharing and joint production by divisions makes it hard for corporate managers to measure the performance of each individual division.[13] Thus, bureaucratic costs are substantial. The multidivisional structure helps to economize on these costs because it provides some of the extra coordination and control that is required. However, if a related company is to obtain the potential benefits from using its competencies efficiently and effectively, it has to adopt more complicated forms of integration and control at the divisional level to make the structure work.

First, output control is difficult to use because divisions share resources, so it is not easy to measure the performance of an individual division. Therefore, a company needs to develop a corporate culture that stresses cooperation among divisions and corporate rather than purely divisional goals. Second, corporate managers must establish sophisticated integrating devices to ensure coordination among divisions. Integrating roles and even integrating teams of managers are often essential because they provide the context in which managers from different divisions can meet and develop a common vision of corporate goals. This is Mulally's intention at Ford, where he is trying to essentially create a high-level integrating team composed of its top operating and functional managers to coordinate its global strategy.

An organization with a multidivisional structure must have the right mix of incentives and rewards for cooperation if it is to achieve gains from sharing skills and resources among divisions.[14] With unrelated diversification, divisions operate autonomously, and the company can quite easily reward managers on their division's individual performance. With related diversification, however, rewarding divisions is more difficult because they are engaged in so many shared activities, and strategic managers must be sensitive and alert to achieve equity in rewards among divisions. The aim always is to design structure and control systems so that they can maximize the benefits from pursuing the strategy while economizing on bureaucratic costs.

● **The Role of Information Technology**   The expanding use of IT is increasing the advantages and reducing the problems associated with implementing a multibusiness model effectively because it facilitates output control, behavior control, and integration between divisions and between divisions and corporate headquarters.

On the advantage side, IT provides a common software platform that can make it much less problematic for divisions to share information and knowledge and to obtain the benefits from leveraging their competencies. IT also facilitates output and financial control, making it easier for corporate headquarters to monitor divisional performance and decide when to intervene selectively. It also helps corporate managers better use their strategic and implementation skills because they can react more quickly given that they possess higher-quality, more timely information from the use of a sophisticated cross-organizational IT infrastructure.

In a similar fashion, IT makes it easier to manage the problems that occur when implementing a multidivisional structure. Because it provides both corporate and divisional managers with more and better information, it makes it easier for corporate managers to decentralize control to divisional managers and yet react quickly if the need arises. IT can also make it more difficult to distort information and hide bad news because divisional managers must provide standardized information that can be compared across divisions. Finally, IT eases the transfer pricing problem because divisional managers have access to detailed up-to-date information about how much a certain resource or skill would cost to buy in the external marketplace. Thus, a fair transfer price is easier to determine. The way in which SAP's enterprise resources planning (ERP) software helps to integrate the activities of divisions in a multidivisional structure is discussed in Strategy in Action 13.1.

Strategy in Action   13.1

SAP's ERP Systems

SAP is the world's leading supplier of enterprise resources planning (ERP) software; it introduced the world's first ERP system in 1973. So great was the demand for its software that it had to train thousands of IT consultants from companies like IBM, HP, Accenture, and Cap Gemini to install and customize it to meet the needs of companies around the globe. SAP's ERP system is popular because it manages functional activities at all stages of a company's value chain, as well as resource transfers between a company's different divisions.

First, SAP's software has modules specifically designed to manage each core functional activity. Each module contains the set of best practices that SAP's IT engineers have found works in building competencies in efficiency, quality, innovation, and responsiveness to customers. Each function inputs its data into its functional module in the way specified by SAP. For example, sales inputs all the information about customer needs required by SAP's sales module, and materials management inputs information about the product specifications it requires from suppliers into SAP's materials-management module. Each SAP module functions as an *expert system* that can reason through the information that functional managers put into it. It then provides managers with real-time feedback about the current state of vital functional operations—and gives recommendations that allow managers to improve them. However, the magic of

ERP does not stop there. SAP's ERP software then connects across functions inside each division. This means that managers in all functions of a division have access to other functions' expert systems, and SAP's software is designed to alert managers when their functional operations are affected by changes taking place in another function. *Thus, SAP's ERP software allows managers throughout a division to better coordinate their activities,* which is a major source of competitive advantage.

Moreover, SAP software, running on corporate mainframe computers, takes the information from all the different expert systems in the divisions and creates a companywide ERP system that provides corporate managers with an overview of the operations of all a company's divisions. In essence, SAP's ERP system creates a sophisticated corporate-level expert system that can reason through the huge volume of information being provided by all its divisions and functions. The ERP system can then recognize and diagnose common issues and problems and recommend organizationwide solutions, such as by suggesting new ways to leverage, transfer, and share competencies and resources. Top managers, armed with the knowledge that their ERP software provides, can also use it to adjust their business model with the changing environment. The result, SAP claims, is that when a multidivisional company implements its corporatewide ERP software, it can achieve productivity gains of 30 to 50%, which amounts to billions of dollars of savings for large multinational companies like Nestlé and Exxon.[a]

Implementing Strategy Across Countries

Global strategy can play a crucial role in strengthening the business model of both single-business and multibusiness companies. Indeed, few large companies that have expanded into new industries have not already expanded globally and replicated their business model in new countries to grow their profits. Companies can use four basic strategies as they begin to market their products and establish production facilities abroad:

- A *localization strategy* is oriented toward local responsiveness, and a company decentralizes control to subsidiaries and divisions in each country in which it operates to produce and customize products to local markets.

- An *international strategy* is based on R&D and marketing being centralized at home and all the other value creation functions being decentralized to national units.

- A *global standardization strategy* is oriented toward cost reduction, with all the principal value creation functions centralized at the optimal global location.

- A *transnational strategy* is focused so that it can achieve local responsiveness and cost reduction. Some functions are centralized and others are decentralized at the global location best suited to achieving these objectives.

The need to coordinate and integrate global value chain activities increases as a company moves from a localization to an international, to a global standardization, and then to a transnational strategy. To obtain the benefits of pursuing a transnational strategy, a company must transfer its distinctive competencies to the global location where they can create the most value and establish a global network to coordinate its divisions at home and abroad. The objective of such coordination is to obtain the benefits from transferring or leveraging competencies across a company's global business units. Thus, the bureaucratic costs associated with solving the communication and measurement problems that arise in managing handoffs or transfers across countries are much higher for companies pursuing a transnational strategy than it is for those pursuing the other strategies. The localization strategy does not require coordinating activities on a global level because value creation activities are handled locally, by country or world region. The international and global standardization strategies fit between the other two strategies: although products have to be sold and marketed globally, and hence global product transfers must be managed, there is less need to coordinate skill and resource transfers when using an international strategy than there is when using a transnational strategy.

The implication is that, as companies change from a localization to an international, global standardization, or transnational strategy, they require a more complex structure, control system, and culture to coordinate the value creation activities associated with implementing that strategy. More complex structures economize on bureaucratic costs. In general, the choice of structure and control systems for managing a global business is a function of three factors:

1. The decision about how to distribute and allocate responsibility and authority between managers at home and abroad so that effective control over a company's global operations is maintained

2. The selection of the organizational structure that groups divisions both at home and abroad in a way that allows the best use of resources and serves the needs of foreign customers most effectively

3. The selection of the right kinds of integration and control mechanisms and organizational culture to make the overall global structure function effectively

TABLE 13.2

Global Strategy/Structure Relationships

	Localization Strategy	International Strategy	Global Standardization Strategy	Transnational Strategy
	Low ←——————————— Need for Coordination ————————→ High			
	Low ←——————————— Bureaucratic Costs ————————→ High			
Centralization of Authority	Decentralized to national unit	Core competencies centralized; others decentralized to national units	Centralized at optimal global location	Simultaneously centralized and decentralized
Horizontal Differentiation	Global-area structure	Global-division structure	Global product-group structure	Global-matrix structure, matrix-in-the-mind
Need for Complex Integrating Mechanisms	Low	Medium	High	Very high
Organizational Culture	Not important	Quite important	Important	Very important

Table 13.2 summarizes the appropriate design choices for companies pursuing each of these strategies.

● **Implementing a Localization Strategy**

When a company pursues a localization strategy, it generally operates with a global-area structure (see Figure 13.2). When using this structure, a company duplicates all value creation activities and establishes an overseas division in every country or world area in which it operates. Authority is decentralized to managers in each overseas division, who devise the appropriate strategy for responding to the needs of the local environment. Managers at global headquarters use market and output controls, such as ROIC, growth in market share, and operation costs, to evaluate the performance of overseas divisions. On the basis of such global comparisons, they can make decisions about capital allocation and orchestrate the transfer of new knowledge among divisions.

A company that makes and sells the same products in many different countries often groups its overseas divisions into world regions to simplify the coordination of

FIGURE 13.2

Global-Area Structure

products across countries. Europe might be one region, the Pacific Rim another, and the Middle East a third. Grouping allows the same set of output and behavior controls to be applied across all divisions inside a region. Thus, global companies can reduce communications and transfer problems because information can be transmitted more easily across countries with broadly similar cultures. For example, consumers' preferences regarding product design and marketing are likely to be more similar among countries in one world region than among countries in different world regions.

Because the overseas divisions themselves have little or no contact with others in different regions, no integrating mechanisms are needed. Nor does a global organizational culture develop because there are no transfers of skills or resources or transfer of managerial personnel among the various world regions. Historically, car companies such as DaimlerChrysler, GM, and Ford used global-area structures to manage their overseas operations. Ford of Europe, for example, had little or no contact with its U.S. parent; capital was the principal resource exchanged.

One problem with a global-area structure and a localization strategy is that the duplication of specialist activities across countries raises a company's overall cost structure. Moreover, the company is not taking advantage of opportunities to transfer, share, or leverage its competencies and capabilities on a global basis; for example, it cannot apply the low-cost manufacturing expertise that it has developed in one world region to another. Thus, localization companies lose the many benefits of operating globally. As Chapter 8 discussed, the popularity of this strategic orientation has decreased.

Implementing an International Strategy

A company pursuing an international strategy adopts a different route to global expansion. Normally, the company shifts to this strategy when it decides to sell domestically made products in markets abroad. Until the 1990s, for example, companies such as Mercedes-Benz and Jaguar made no attempt to produce in a foreign market; instead, they distributed and sold their domestically produced cars internationally. Such companies usually just add a *foreign sales organization* to their existing structure and continue to use the same control system. If a company is using a functional structure, this department has to coordinate manufacturing, sales, and R&D activities with the needs of the foreign market. Efforts at customization are minimal. In overseas countries, a company usually establishes a subsidiary to handle local sales and distribution. For example, the Mercedes-Benz overseas subsidiaries allocate dealerships; organize supplies of spare parts; and, of course, sell cars. A system of behavior controls is then established to keep the home office informed of changes in sales, spare parts requirements, and so on.

A company with many different products or businesses operating from a multidivisional structure has the challenging problem of coordinating the flow of different products across different countries. To manage these transfers, many companies create a *global division*, which they add to their existing divisional structure (see Figure 13.3).[15] Global operations are managed as a separate divisional business, with managers given the authority and responsibility for coordinating domestic product divisions with overseas markets. The global division also monitors and controls the overseas subsidiaries that market the products and decides how much authority to delegate to managers in these countries.

This arrangement of tasks and roles reduces the transaction of managing handoffs across countries and world regions. However, managers abroad are essentially under the control of managers in the global division, and if domestic and overseas managers compete for control of strategy making, conflict and lack of cooperation

FIGURE 13.3

Global Division
Structure

may result. Many companies such as IBM, Citibank, and DaimlerChrysler have experienced this problem. Very often, significant strategic control has been decentralized to overseas divisions. When cost pressures force corporate managers to reassess their strategy and they decide to intervene, such intervention frequently provokes resistance, much of it due to differences in culture—not just corporate but also country differences.

● **Implementing
a Global
Standardization
Strategy**

When a company embarks on a global standardization strategy today, it locates its manufacturing and other value chain activities at the global location that will allow it to increase efficiency, quality, and innovation. In doing so, it has to solve the problems of coordinating and integrating its global value chain activities. It has to find a structure that lowers the bureaucratic costs associated with resource transfers between corporate headquarters and its overseas divisions and provides the centralized control that a global standardization strategy requires. The answer for many companies is a *global product-group structure* (see Figure 13.4).

In this structure, a product-group headquarters is created to coordinate the activities of a company's home and overseas operations. The managers at each product

FIGURE 13.4

Global Product-Group
Structure

group's headquarters decide where to locate the different functions at the optimal global location for performing that activity. For example, Phillips has one product group responsible for global R&D, manufacturing, marketing, and sales of its light bulbs; another for medical equipment; and so on. The headquarters of the medical division and its R&D is located in Bothell, Washington; manufacturing is done in Taiwan; and the products are sold by sales subsidiaries in each local market.

The product-group structure allows managers to decide how best to pursue a global standardization strategy—for example, to decide which value chain activities, such as manufacturing or product design, should be performed in which country to increase efficiency. Increasingly, U.S. and Japanese companies are moving manufacturing to low-cost countries such as China but establishing product design centers in Europe or the United States to take advantage of foreign skills and capabilities and thus obtain the benefits from this strategy.

 Implementing a Transnational Strategy

The main failing of the global product-group structure is that, although it allows a company to achieve superior efficiency and quality, it is weak when it comes to responsiveness to customers because the focus is still on centralized control to reduce costs. Moreover, this structure makes it difficult for the different product divisions to trade information and knowledge and to obtain the benefits from transferring, sharing, and leveraging their competencies. Sometimes the potential gains from sharing product, marketing, or R&D knowledge among product groups are high, but so too are the bureaucratic costs associated with achieving these gains. Is there a structure that can simultaneously economize on these costs and provide the coordination necessary to obtain these benefits?

In the 1990s, many companies implemented a *global-matrix structure* to simultaneously lower their global cost structures *and* differentiate their activities through superior innovation and responsiveness to customers globally. Figure 13.5 shows such a structure that might be used by a company like Ford, HP, SAP, or Nestlé. On the vertical axis, instead of functions are the company's product *groups*. These groups provide specialist services such as R&D, product design, and marketing information

FIGURE 13.5

Global-Matrix Structure

● Individual operating companies

Strategy in Action

Using IT to Make Nestlé's Global Structure Work

Nestlé, based in Vevey, Switzerland, is the world's biggest food company, with global sales in excess of $65 billion in 2004. The company has been pursuing an ambitious program of global expansion by acquiring many famous companies—for instance, Perrier, the French mineral water producer, and Rowntree, the British candy maker. In the United States, Nestlé bought the giant Carnation Company, Stouffer Foods, Contadina, Ralston Purina, and Dreyer's Grand Ice Cream.

Traditionally, Nestlé pursued a localization strategy and managed its operating companies through a global-area structure. In each country, each individual division (such as its Carnation division) was responsible for managing all aspects of its business-level strategy: in other words, companies were free to control their own product development and marketing and to manage all local operations. Nestlé's corporate executives at the Vevey headquarters made acquisitions, expansions, and corporate resource decisions such as capital investment. Because all important decisions were made centrally, the size of the corporate staff increased dramatically.

In the 1990s, Nestlé realized it had major problems. Corporate managers had become remote from the difficulties experienced by the individual operating divisions or companies, and the centralized structure slowed decision making and made it difficult for Nestlé to respond quickly to the changing environment. Moreover, the company was forfeiting all the possible benefits from sharing and leveraging its distinctive competencies in food product development and marketing, both between divisions in a product group and between product groups and world regions. Because each product group operated separately, corporate executives could not integrate product-group activities around the world. To raise corporate performance, Nestlé's managers sought to find a new way of organizing its activities.

Its CEO at the time, Helmut Maucher, started restructuring Nestlé from the top down. He stripped away the power of corporate managers by decentralizing authority to the managers of seven global product groups that he created to oversee the company's major product lines (for example, coffee, milk, and candy). Each global product group was to integrate the activities of all the operating divisions in its group to transfer and leverage distinctive competencies to create value. After the change, managers in the candy product group, for instance, began orchestrating the marketing and sale of Rowntree candy products, such as After Eight Mints and Smarties, throughout Europe and the United States, and sales climbed by 60%.

Maucher then grouped all divisions within a country or world region into one national or regional strategic business unit (SBU) and created a team of SBU managers to link, coordinate, and oversee their activities. When the different divisions started to share joint purchasing, marketing, and sales activities, major cost savings resulted. In the United States, the SBU management team reduced the number of sales officers nationwide from 115 to twenty-two and decreased the number of suppliers of packaging from forty-three to three.

Finally, Maucher decided to use a matrix structure to integrate the activities of the seven global-product groups with the operations of Nestlé's country-based SBUs. The goal of this matrix structure is to have the company pursue a transnational strategy that allows it to obtain the gains from both differentiation through global learning and cost reduction. For example, regional SBU managers now spend considerable time in Vevey with product-group executives discussing ways of exploiting and sharing the resources of the company on a global basis.

Although the new decentralized matrix structure improved Nestlé's ability to coordinate its structure, by 1998, it was clear that it still was not providing enough integration and coordination. Although more coordination was taking place between product groups *inside* a region such as the United States, little coordination was taking place across world regions. Nestlé's top managers searched for ways to improve integration on a global scale. Their conclusion was that more output and behavior control was needed so that different product groups and regional SBUs could learn from and understand what everyone else was doing—for example, what their product development plans were or how each product group handled its global supply chain.

Nestlé's solution was to sign a $300 million contract with SAP in 2002 to install and maintain a companywide ERP system to integrate across *all* its global operations.

Top managers hoped this system would give them the information they needed to exert centralized control over operations, which the matrix structure apparently did not provide. In essence, Nestlé began to use SAP's value chain management software as a *substitute* for the matrix structure. With this IT, they would no longer need to rely on divisional managers to transfer information but henceforth could obtain it from their ERP system. They would then be able to intervene at a global level as necessary.

Nestlé's Globe Project to create uniform business processes and computer systems around the world has led to major successes. Nestlé was able to shut down 15% of its global operating structure by 2005, which has saved billions of dollars and lowered its cost structure. At the same time, it has been able to leverage the competencies of its product groups around the world by creating new kinds of food and candy products. However, its ROIC is still significantly lower than that of competitors like Hershey and Cadbury Schweppes because, some analysts claim, the company's global food empire is simply too big to manage—no global structure can make it operate profitably. What Nestlé should do is sell off many of its businesses, reduce the number of its product groups, exit countries where its profits are marginal, and in this way shrink until it can increase its ROIC and profits to match those of its competitors.[b]

to its overseas divisions, which are often grouped by world region. These might be the petroleum, plastics, pharmaceuticals, or fertilizer product groups. On the horizontal axis are the company's *overseas divisions* in the various countries or world regions in which it operates. Managers at the regional or country level control local operations. Through a system of output and behavior controls, they then report to managers in product-group headquarters in the United States and ultimately to the CEO. Managers for world regions or countries are also responsible for working with U.S. product-group managers to develop the control and reward systems that will promote transfer, sharing, or leveraging of competencies.

Implementing a matrix structure thus decentralizes control to overseas managers and provides them with considerable flexibility for managing local issues, but it can still give product-group and top corporate executives in the United States the centralized control they need to coordinate company activities on a global level. The matrix structure can allow knowledge and experience to be transferred among divisions in both product groups and geographic regions because it offers many opportunities for face-to-face contact between managers at home and abroad. The matrix also facilitates the transmission of a company's norms and values and, hence, the development of a global corporate culture. This is especially important for a company with far-flung global operations for which lines of communication are longer. Club Med, for instance, uses a matrix to standardize high-quality customer service across its global vacation villages. Nestlé's experience with the global-matrix structure is profiled in Strategy in Action 13.2.

Nestlé is not the only company to find the task of integrating and controlling a global-matrix structure a difficult task. Some, like ABB and Motorola, and Ford discussed in the Opening Case, have dismantled their matrix structures and moved to a simplified global product-group approach using IT to integrate across countries. If a matrix is chosen, however, other possible ways of making it work effectively include developing a strong cross-country organizational culture to facilitate communication and coordination among managers. For example, many companies are increasingly transferring managers between their domestic and overseas operations so they can implant the domestic culture in the new location and also learn by studying how their structure and systems work in the foreign country.

Toyota has made great efforts to understand how to manage car plants in overseas locations and how to transplant its culture into those plants. When it decided to enter and make cars in the United States, it first formed a joint venture with GM, and the companies combined their expertise in this carmaking venture, which was known as NUMMI. Toyota was responsible for implanting its knowledge of lean production in this plant; all the workers were cross-trained and taught how to monitor and benchmark their own performance and how to work in quality teams to improve it. Toyota then took all its learning from this venture and transferred it to its wholly owned car plant in Georgetown, Kentucky, where it turns out cars with as good a reliability record as those produced in its Japanese plants.

Every Toyota plant is under the control of Japanese managers, however, and managers from Toyota's Japanese headquarters are constantly monitoring its plants' performance and transferring and implanting Toyota's R&D innovations into its next car models. Toyota used a similar implementation strategy when it established car component and assembly operations in south Wales to serve the European Union market. Indeed, it chose south Wales and Virginia as locations for its plants because both regions have a strong local culture based on family and tradition that closely parallels Japan's culture. Toyota's managers felt that a similar local culture would enable them to better implement Toyota's highly efficient work processes and procedures.

As the example of Toyota suggests, forming global networks of managers who can move to and work in other countries so they can turn to each other for help is an important aspect of helping a company realize the benefits from its global operations. When managers can hold a *matrix-in-the-mind*—that is, learn to think about how they could transfer competencies around the company to create value—they can work to develop an information network that lets a company capitalize globally on the skills and capabilities of its employees.[16] To foster the development of the matrix-in-the-mind concept and promote cooperation, companies are increasingly making use of IT's integrating capability by using online teleconferencing, email, and global intranets among the parts of their global operations. For example, Hitachi coordinates its nineteen Japanese laboratories by means of an online teleconferencing system. Both Microsoft and HP make extensive use of global intranets to integrate their activities, and Nestlé still hopes its Globe Project will accomplish the same goal.

Entry Mode and Implementation

As we discussed in Chapter 10, many organizations today are altering their business models and strategies and restructuring their organizations to find new ways to use their resources and capabilities to create value. This section focuses on the implementation issues that arise when companies use the three different modes of entry into new industries: internal new venturing, joint ventures, and mergers and acquisitions.

● **Internal New Venturing**

Chapter 10 discussed how companies can enter new industries by using internal new venturing and by transferring and leveraging their existing resources to create the set of value chain activities necessary to compete effectively in a new industry. How can managers create a setting in which employees are to be encouraged to act in ways that allow them to see how their functional competencies or products can be used in other industries? Specifically, how can structure, control, and culture be used to increase the success of the new-venturing process?

At the heart of the issue is that corporate managers must treat the internal new-venturing process as a form of entrepreneurship and the people who are to pioneer and lead new ventures as **intrapreneurs** (inside or internal entrepreneurs). This means that organizational structure, control, and culture must be designed to encourage creativity and give new-venture managers autonomy and freedom to develop and champion new products. At the same time, corporate managers want to make sure that the investment in new markets will be profitable and that a fit does exist between the new industry and the old one so that benefits can in fact be leveraged.[17] As we discussed in Chapter 10, 3M is one company that carefully uses structure, control, and culture to create a formal organizationwide new-venturing process that is one of the best known for promoting product innovation. 3M's goal is that at least 30% of its growth in sales each year should be attributed to new products developed within the past five years. To achieve this challenging goal, 3M has developed an implementation formula to ensure that its employees are provided with the freedom and motivation to experiment and take risks.

On the structure side, 3M recognized early the increasing importance of linking and coordinating the efforts of people in different functions to speed product development. As noted in the previous chapter, people in different functions tend to develop different subunit orientations and to focus their efforts on their own tasks to the exclusion of the needs of other functions. The danger of such tendencies is that each function will develop norms and values that suit its own needs but do little to promote organizational coordination and integration.

To avoid this problem, 3M established a system of cross-functional teams composed of members of product development, process development, marketing, manufacturing, packaging, and other functions to create organizationwide norms and values of innovation. So that all groups have a common focus, the teams work closely with customers; customers' needs become the platform on which the different functions can then apply their skills and capabilities.[18] For example, one of 3M's cross-functional teams worked closely with disposable diaper manufacturers to develop the right kind of sticky tape for their needs. To promote integration in the team and foster cooperative norms and values, each team is headed by a so-called product champion who takes responsibility for building cohesive team relationships and developing a team culture. In addition, one of 3M's senior managers becomes a management sponsor whose job is to help the team get resources and to provide support when the going gets tough. After all, product development is a highly risky process; many projects do not succeed.

3M is also careful to use integrating mechanisms such as high-level product development committees to screen new ideas. Proven entrepreneurs and experienced managers from the other divisions and from R&D, marketing, sales, and manufacturing serve on this committee to screen the new ideas. New-product champions defend their products and projects before this committee to secure the resources for developing them. (Chapter 4 described this development funnel.) On the control side, 3M copied HP and developed a companywide norm that researchers should use 15% of their time on their own projects, which helps create new products such as Post-it Notes. In addition, 3M is careful to establish career ladders for its scientists in order to gain their long-term commitment, and it rewards successful product innovators. For example, it established the Golden Step program that gives employees substantial monetary bonuses to honor and reward the launch of successful new products and to develop norms and values that support and reward the sharing of information among scientists and people in different functions.

3M's structure and control systems have created an atmosphere in which employees know it is better to take a chance and risk making a mistake than to do nothing at all. Managers understand that their job is to encourage creativity in their employees and teams and to foster a culture of innovation. However, the regular work of the organization goes on side by side with all this intrapreneurial activity.

The other main approach to internal new venturing has been championed by those who believe that the best way to encourage new-product development is to separate this effort from the rest of the organization. To provide new-venture managers with the autonomy to experiment and take risks, the company sets up a **new-venture division**, separate and independent from its other divisions, for the development of a new product. The logic behind this is that if a new-product team works from within a company's existing structure, its members will never have the freedom or autonomy to pursue radical new-product ideas. Away from the day-to-day scrutiny of top managers, new-venture managers will be able to pursue the creation of a new product and develop a new business model as though they were external entrepreneurs.

The new-venture division is controlled in a way that reinforces the entrepreneurial spirit. Thus, strict output controls are regarded as inappropriate because they can promote short-term thinking and inhibit risk taking. Instead, stock options are often used to reinforce a culture for entrepreneurship. Another issue with output controls is to keep top managers at bay. The thinking is that the upfront R&D costs of new venturing are high and its success is uncertain. After spending millions of dollars, corporate managers might become concerned about the new-venture division's performance and might try to introduce tight output controls or strong budgets to increase accountability, measures that hurt the entrepreneurial culture.[19] Corporate managers may believe it is important to institute behavior and output controls that put some limits on freedom of action; otherwise, costly mistakes may be made and resources wasted on frivolous ideas.

Recently, there have been some indications that 3M's internal approach may be superior to the use of external new-venture divisions. It appears that many new-venture divisions have failed to get successful new products to market. And even if they do, usually the new-venture division eventually begins to operate like any other division, and a company's cost structure rises because of the duplication of value chain activities.

Another issue is that scientists are often not the best people to develop successful business models because they lack formal training. Just as many medical doctors are earning MBAs today to understand the many strategic issues confronting their profession, so scientists need to be able to think strategically, and these skills may be lacking in a new-venture division.

HP illustrates many of these issues. Early in its history, HP used the new-venturing approach. As soon as a new self-supporting product was developed in one of HP's operating divisions, a new-venture division was spun off to develop and market the product. In this fashion, HP's goal was to keep its divisions small and entrepreneurial. Soon HP had over twenty-eight different divisions, each with its own value chain functions. At first, the value these divisions created exceeded their operating costs, but then problems emerged because of changing technological conditions. Because they were operated separately, the divisions could not learn from each other, and because they all had separate R&D departments, sales forces, and so on, they began to compete for resources. For example, when one HP scientist pioneered what was to become biotechnology, the managers of other divisions could not see how it related to HP's existing activities and would not fund it. HP became saddled with high operating costs and missed product opportunities. To solve the problem, it merged some divisions and brought their technologies and product lines together. It also sold off divisions to other companies to focus its activities and thus make it easier to transfer resources between its divisions.

● Joint Venturing

Internal new venturing is one important way in which large, established companies can maintain their momentum and grow from within.[20] One alternative is for two companies to establish a joint venture and to collaborate on the development of a new business model to compete in a new market or industry. Often in joint venturing, two or more companies agree to pool specific resources and capabilities that they believe will create more value for both companies, and they appoint managers from both companies to oversee the new operation. In this case, no separate entity is set up. Sometimes companies do establish a separate company and agree to share ownership of the new company, often 50/50 ownership, but sometimes one company insists on having a 51% or more stake to give it the controlling interest. The companies then transfer to the new company whatever resources and capabilities they have agreed on to help it pursue the business model that will promote both companies' interests. From an implementation perspective, important issues concern the way the venture is structured and controlled and the problems that frequently emerge in managing differences between the cultures of companies in a joint venture.

Allocating authority and responsibility is the first major implementation issue companies have to decide on. Both companies need to be able to monitor the progress of the joint venture so that they can learn from its activities and benefit from their investment in it. Some companies prefer to establish a new company and obtain a 51% ownership of it because then they can solve the problem of which company will have the ultimate authority and control over the new venture. As discussed in Chapter 8, a company also risks losing control of its core technology or competence when it enters into a strategic alliance. Because the future is unknown, it is unclear which company will benefit the most from whatever innovations the new company might develop.[21] A joint venture can also be dangerous not only because the partners may take whatever they learn and then go it alone, but also because the other party might be acquired by a competitor. For example, Compaq shared its technical knowledge with a company in the computer storage industry to promote joint product development, only to watch helplessly as that company was acquired by Sun Microsystems, which consequently obtained Compaq's knowledge.

The implementation issues are strongly dependent on whether the purpose of the joint venture is to share and develop technology, jointly distribute and market products and brands, or share access to customers. Sometimes companies can simply realize the joint benefits from collaboration without having to form a new company. For example, Nestlé and Coca-Cola announced a ten-year joint venture, to be called Beverage Partners Worldwide, through which Coca-Cola will distribute and sell Nestlé's Nestea iced tea, Nescafé, and other brands throughout the globe.[22] Similarly, Starbuck's Frappuccino is distributed by Pepsi. In this kind of joint venture, both companies can gain from sharing and pooling different competencies so that both realize value that would not otherwise be possible. In these cases, issues of ownership are less important, although the issue of allocating responsibility and monitoring performance remains.

Once the ownership issue has been settled, one company appoints the CEO, who is responsible for creating a cohesive top management team from the ranks of managers who have been transferred from the parent companies. The job of the top management team is to develop a successful business model. These managers then need to choose an organizational structure, such as the functional or product team, that will make the best use of the resources and skills transferred from the parent. The need to provide a framework that combines their activities and integrates people and functions is of paramount importance. So is the need to build a new company culture that can unite the members of the hitherto different cultures. In essence, top managers need to solve all the implementation problems discussed in the previous chapter.

Because solving these issues is expensive and time-consuming, it is not surprising that, if a lot is at stake and the future possibilities are unknown, many companies decide that they would be better off by acquiring the other company and integrating it into their operations. This has been Microsoft's favored strategy in recent years as it enters new industries in the computer sector. Normally, it takes a 51% stake in an emerging company that gives it the right to buy out the company and integrate it into Microsoft should it have technology that proves vital to Microsoft's future interests. Then, Microsoft shares its resources and expertise with the new company to spur its research and development. If the stakes are less, however, and the future is easier to forecast, as in the venture between Coca-Cola and Nestlé, then it makes sense to establish a new entity that can manage the transfers of complementary resources and skills between companies.

● Mergers and Acquisitions

Mergers and acquisitions are the third and most widely used vehicle that companies can use to enter new industries or countries.[23] How to implement structure, control systems, and culture to manage a new acquisition is important because many acquisitions are unsuccessful. And one of the main reasons acquisitions perform poorly is that many companies do not anticipate the difficulties associated with merging or integrating new companies into their existing operations.[24]

At the level of structure, managers of both the acquiring and acquired companies have to confront the problem of how to establish new lines of authority and responsibility that will allow them to make the best use of both companies' competencies. The massive merger between HP and Compaq illustrates the issues. Before the merger, the top management teams of both companies spent thousands of hours analyzing the range of both companies' activities and performing a value chain analysis to determine how cost and differentiation advantages might be achieved. Based on this analysis, they merged all of both company's divisions into four main product groups.

Imagine the problems deciding who would control which group and which operating division and to whom these managers would report! To counter fears that infighting would prevent the benefits of the merger from being realized, the companies' top executives were careful to announce in press releases that the process of merging divisions was going smoothly and that battles over responsibilities and control of resources were being resolved. One problem with a mishandled merger is that skilled managers who feel they have been demoted will leave the company, and if many do leave, this also may prevent the benefits of the merger from being realized.

Once the issue of lines of authority has been addressed, the merged companies must decide how to coordinate and streamline operations to reduce costs and leverage competencies. For large companies, as for HP, the answer is the multidivisional structure, but important control issues have to be resolved. In general, the more similar or related are the acquired companies' products and markets, the easier it is to integrate their operations. If the acquiring company has an efficient control system, it can be adapted to the new company to standardize the way its activities are monitored and measured. Or managers can work hard to combine the best elements of each company's control systems and cultures or introduce a new IT system.

If managers make unrelated acquisitions, however, and then try to interfere with a company's strategy in an industry they know little about or apply inappropriate structure and controls to manage the new business, then major strategy implementation problems can arise. For example, if managers try to integrate unrelated companies with related ones in the search for some elusive benefits, apply the wrong kinds of controls at the divisional level, or interfere in business-level strategy, corporate performance can suffer as bureaucratic costs skyrocket. These mistakes explain why related acquisitions are sometimes more successful than unrelated ones.[25]

Even in the case of related diversification, the business processes of each company frequently are different, and their computer systems may be incompatible, as in the Nestlé case. The issue facing the merged company is how to use output and behavior controls to standardize business processes and reduce the cost of handing off and transferring resources. While installing the SAP software, for example, managers in charge of the U.S. effort discovered that each of Nestlé's 150 different U.S. divisions was buying its own supply of vanilla from the same set of suppliers. However, the divisions were not sharing information about these purchases, and vanilla suppliers, dealing with each Nestlé division separately, tried to charge each division as much as they could, with the result that each division paid a different price for the same input![26] Each division at Nestlé used a different code for its independent purchase, and managers at U.S. headquarters did not have the information to discover this. SAP's software provides such information.

Finally, even when acquiring a company in a closely related industry, managers must realize that each company has a unique culture, or way of doing things. Such idiosyncrasies must be understood in order to manage the merged company effectively. Indeed, such idiosyncrasies are likely to be especially important when companies from different countries merge. Over time, top managers can change the culture and alter the internal workings of the company, but this is a difficult implementation task.

In sum, managers' capabilities in organizational design are vital in ensuring the success of a merger or acquisition. Their ability to integrate and connect divisions to leverage competencies ultimately determines how well the new merged company will perform.[27] The path to merger and acquisition is fraught with danger, which is why some companies claim that internal new venturing is the safest path and that it is best to grow organically from within. Yet with industry boundaries blurring and new global competitors emerging, companies often do not have the time or resources to go it alone. How to enter a new industry or country is a complex implementation issue that requires thorough strategic analysis.

Information Technology, the Internet, and Outsourcing

The many ways in which advances in information technology (IT) affect strategy implementation is an important issue today. Evidence that managerial capabilities in managing IT can be a source of competitive advantage is growing; companies that do not adopt leading-edge information systems are likely to be at a competitive disadvantage. IT includes the many different varieties of computer software platforms and databases and the computer hardware on which they run, such as mainframes and servers. IT also encompasses a broad array of communication media and devices that link people, including voice mail, email, voice conferencing, videoconferencing, the Internet, groupware and corporate intranets, cell phones, fax machines, personal digital assistants (PDAs), smart phones, and so on.[28]

● **Information Technology and Strategy Implementation**

At the level of organizational structure, control, and culture, IT has given strategic managers many new options in implementing their strategies. IT is instrumental in both shaping and integrating resources and capabilities—capabilities that can be difficult to imitate because they are often embedded in firm-specific IT skills. Wal-Mart, for example, legally protected what it regards as a core competency in IT by blocking the movement of some of its key programmers to dot-coms like Amazon.com. A company's ability to pursue a cost-leadership or differentiation business model depends on its possession of distinctive competencies in efficiency, quality, innovation, and customer responsiveness, and IT has a major impact on these sources of competitive advantage.[29]

Information technology enables companies to integrate knowledge and expertise across functional groups so that they can deliver new differentiated goods and services to customers. The way in which Citibank implemented an organizationwide IT system to increase responsiveness to customers is instructive. In the 2000s, Citibank set a goal to be the premier global international financial company. After studying its business model, managers found that the main customer complaint was the amount of time customers had to wait for a response to their request, so Citibank managers set out to solve this problem. Teams of managers examined the way Citibank's current IT system worked and then redesigned it to empower employees and reduce the handoffs between people and functions. Employees were then given extensive training in operating the new IT system. Citibank has been able to document significant time and cost savings, as well as an increase in the level of personalized service it is able to offer its clients, which has led to a significant increase in the number of global customers.[30]

Indeed, IT has important effects on a company's ability to innovate. It improves the base of knowledge that employees draw on when they engage in problem solving and decision making and provides a mechanism for promoting collaboration and information sharing both inside and across functions and business units. However, knowledge or information availability alone will not lead to innovation; the ability to use knowledge creatively is the key to promoting innovation and creating competitive advantage. One argument is that the absolute level of knowledge a firm possesses does not lead to competitive advantage, but the speed or velocity with which it is circulated in the firm does.[31]

IT transfers knowledge where it can add the highest value to the organization. The project-based work that is characteristic of matrix structures provides a vivid example of this process. As a project progresses, the need for particular team members waxes and wanes. Some employees will be part of a project from beginning to end, and others will be asked to participate only at key times when their expertise is required. IT provides managers with the real-time capability to monitor project progress and needs, to allocate resources accordingly, and thus to increase the value added of each employee. Traditionally, product design has involved sequential processing across functions, with handoffs as each stage of the process is completed (see Chapter 4). This linear process is being replaced by parallel, concurrent engineering made possible through the application of IT that allows employees to work simultaneously with continual interaction through electronic communication. All of this can promote innovation.

IT has major effects on other aspects of a company's structure and control systems. The increasing use of IT has been associated with a flattening of the organizational hierarchy and a move toward greater decentralization and increased integration within organizations. By providing managers with high-quality, timely, and relatively complete electronic information, IT has reduced the need for a management hierarchy to coordinate organizational activities. Email systems and the development of organizationwide corporate intranets are breaking down the barriers that have traditionally separated departments, and the result has been improved performance.[32] To facilitate the use of IT and to make organizational structure work, however, a company must create a control and incentive structure to motivate people and subunits, as Strategy in Action 13.3 suggests.

Some companies are taking full advantage of IT's ability to help them integrate their activities to respond better to customer needs. These companies make the most

Strategy in Action   13.3

Oracle's New Approach to Control

As we discussed in Chapter 9, Oracle is the second largest independent software company after Microsoft. Like Bill Gates, Microsoft's chair, Oracle's cofounder and chair, Larry Ellison, recognized in 1999 that his company had a major problem: it was not using the software it had developed to control its own activities, even though its customers were using the software to control theirs! As a result, Oracle was having a difficult time understanding its customers' needs, and internally it was not experiencing the cost savings that could result from implementing its own database and financial control software. Ellison moved quickly to change Oracle's control systems so that they were Internet-based.

One of the main advantages of Internet-based control software is that it permits the centralized management of a company's widespread operations. Corporate managers can easily compare and contrast the performance of different divisions spread throughout the globe in real time and can quickly identify problems and take corrective action. However, to his embarrassment, Ellison discovered that Oracle's financial and human resource information was located on over seventy different computing systems across the world. It took a lot of time and effort to track basic details such as the size of the company's work force and the sales of its leading products. As a result, it took a long time to take corrective action, and many opportunities were being missed.

Recognizing the irony of the situation, Ellison ordered his managers to change the way the company controlled— that is, monitored and evaluated—its activities and to implement its new Internet-based control systems as quickly as possible. His goal was to have all of Oracle's sales, cost, profit, and human resource information systems consolidated in two locations and to make this information available to managers throughout the company with one click of a mouse. In addition, he instructed managers to investigate which kinds of activities were being monitored and controlled by people and, wherever possible, to substitute Internet-based control. For example, previously Oracle had over 300 people responsible for monitoring and managing tasks such as paper-based travel planning and expense report systems. These tasks were automated into software systems and put online, and employees were made responsible for filing their own reports. These 300 people were then transferred into sales and consulting positions. The savings was over $1 billion a year.

By using Internet-based software control systems, Oracle's managers are also able to get closer to their customers. Oracle gave all its salespeople new customer relationship management software and instructed them to enter into the system detailed information about customers' purchases, future plans, Web orders, and service requests. As a result, headquarters managers can now track sales orders easily, and if they see problems such as lost sales or multiple service requests, they can quickly contact customers to solve those problems. This speed builds better customer relations.

So amazed was Ellison at the result of implementing Internet software systems that he radically rethought Oracle's control systems. He now believes that, because of the advances of modern computer information systems, Oracle's employees should be doing only one of three tasks: building its products, servicing its products, or selling its products. All other activities should be automated by developing new information control systems, and it should be the manager's job to use control only to facilitate one of these three front-line activities.[c]

cost-effective use of their employees' skills by using a virtual organizational structure. The **virtual organization** is composed of people who are linked by computers, fax machines, computer-aided design systems, and video teleconferencing and who may rarely, if ever, see one another face to face. People come and go as their services are needed, much as in a matrix structure.

Accenture, the global management consulting company, is becoming just such a virtual organization. Consultants are connected by laptops to an organization's **knowledge management system**, its company-specific information system that systematizes the knowledge of its employees and provides them with access to other employees who have the expertise to solve the problems that they encounter as they perform their jobs. The consultants pool their knowledge in a massive internal database that they can access easily through computer and the company's intranet. The company's 40,000 consultants often work from their homes, traveling to meet the company's clients throughout the world and only rarely stopping at one of Accenture's branch offices to meet their superiors and colleagues. CEO George Shaheen says that the company's headquarters are wherever he happens to be at the time. (He spends 80% of his time traveling.)[33]

● Strategic Outsourcing and Network Structure

Information technology has also affected a company's ability to pursue strategic outsourcing to strengthen its business model. As Chapter 9 discussed, the use of strategic outsourcing is increasing rapidly because organizations recognize the many opportunities it offers to promote differentiation, reduce costs, and increase flexibility. Recall that outsourcing occurs as companies use short- and long-term contracts, joint ventures, and strategic alliances to form relationships with other companies. IT increases the efficiency of such relationships. For example, it allows for the more efficient movement of raw materials and component parts between a company and its suppliers and distributors. It also promotes the transfer, sharing, and leveraging of competencies between companies, which can lead to design and engineering improvements that increase differentiation and lower costs.

As a consequence, there has been growing interest in electronic **business-to-business (B2B)** networks in which most or all of the companies in an industry (for example, carmakers) use the same software platform to link to each other and establish industry specifications and standards. Then these companies jointly list the quantity and specifications of the inputs they require and invite bids from the thousands of potential suppliers around the world. Because suppliers use the same software platform, electronic bidding, auctions, and transactions are possible between buyers and sellers around the world. The idea is that high-volume standardized transactions can help drive down costs and raise quality at the industry level. The role Li & Fung plays in managing the global supply chain for companies in Southeast Asia is instructive in this regard, as Strategy in Action 13.4 shows.

Cross-company global electronic networks reduce the costs associated with finding and monitoring competing suppliers and make global strategic alliances and joint ventures more attractive than vertical integration. In addition, companies that use electronic networks not only reduce costs because they increase the pool of potential suppliers, they also reduce the bargaining power of suppliers. Beyond using IT to link backward with suppliers, companies can also use IT to link forward in the value chain to connect its operations with those of customers, something that reduces their costs and creates a disincentive for customers to seek other suppliers.

To implement outsourcing effectively, strategic managers must decide what organizational arrangements to adopt. Increasingly, a **network structure**—the set of strategic

Strategy in Action

13.4

Li & Fung's Global Supply-Chain Management

Finding the overseas suppliers that offer the lowest-priced and highest-quality products is an important task facing the managers of global organizations. These suppliers are located in thousands of cities in many countries around the world, so finding them is difficult. Often global companies use the services of foreign intermediaries or brokers, located near these suppliers, to find the one that best meets their input requirements. Li & Fung, now run by brothers Victor and William Fung, is one of these brokers that have helped hundreds of global companies locate suitable foreign suppliers, especially suppliers in mainland China.

In the 2000s, managing global companies' supply chains became an even more complicated task because overseas suppliers were increasingly specializing in just one part of the task of producing a product in their search for ways to reduce costs. In the past, a company such as Target might have negotiated with a supplier to manufacture 1 million units of a shirt at a certain cost per unit. But with specialization, Target might find it can reduce the costs of producing the shirt even further by splitting the operations involved in producing the shirt and having different suppliers, often in different countries, perform each operation. For example, to get the lowest cost per unit, Target might first negotiate with a yarn manufacturer in Vietnam to make the yarn, then ship the yarn to a Chinese supplier to weave it into cloth, and then ship the cloth to several different factories in Malaysia and the Philippines to cut the cloth and sew the shirts. Another company might take responsibility for packaging and shipping the shirts to wherever in the world they are required. Because a company like Target has thousands of different clothing products under production and these products change all the time, the problems of managing such a supply chain to get the full cost savings from global expansion are clear.

This is the opportunity that Li & Fung has capitalized on. Realizing that many global companies do not have the time or expertise to find such specialized low-price suppliers, they moved quickly to provide such a service. Li & Fung employs 3,600 agents who travel across thirty-seven countries to find new suppliers and inspect existing suppliers to find new ways to help their clients, global companies, get lower prices or higher-quality products. Global companies are happy to outsource their supply-chain management to Li & Fung because they realize significant cost savings. And although they pay a hefty fee to Li & Fung, they avoid the costs of employing their own agents. As the complexity of supply-chain management continues to increase, more and more companies like Li & Fung will be appearing.[d]

alliances that an organization creates with suppliers, manufacturers, and distributors to produce and market a product—is becoming the structure of choice to implement outsourcing. An example of a network structure is the series of strategic alliances that Japanese carmakers such as Toyota and Honda, and now Ford and GM, have formed with their suppliers of inputs, such as car axles, gearboxes, and air conditioning systems. Members of the network work together on a long-term basis to find new ways to reduce costs and increase the quality of their products. Moreover, developing a network structure allows an organization to avoid the high bureaucratic costs of operating a complex organizational structure. Finally, a network structure allows a company to form strategic alliances with foreign suppliers, which gives managers access to low-cost foreign sources of inputs. The way Nike uses a global network structure to produce and market its sports, casual, and dress shoes is instructive.

Nike, located in Beaverton, Oregon, is the largest and most profitable sports shoe manufacturer in the world. The key to Nike's success is the network structure that Philip Knight, its founder and CEO, created to allow his company to produce and market shoes. The most successful companies today simultaneously pursue a low-cost and a differentiation strategy. Knight realized this early and created an organizational structure to allow his company to achieve this goal.

By far, the largest function at Nike's headquarters in Beaverton is the design function, which is staffed by talented designers who pioneer innovations in sports shoe design such as the air pump and Air Jordans that Nike introduced so successfully. Designers use computer-aided design (CAD) to design their shoes, and all new-product information, including manufacturing instructions, is stored electronically. When the designers have done their work, they relay the blueprints for the new products electronically to a network of suppliers and manufacturers throughout Southeast Asia with which Nike has formed strategic alliances. Instructions for the design of a new sole, for example, may be sent to a supplier in Taiwan, and instructions for the leather uppers may be sent to a supplier in Malaysia. These suppliers produce the shoe parts, which are then sent for final assembly to a manufacturer in China with which Nike has established an alliance. From China, these shoes are shipped to distributors throughout the world. Of the 99 million pairs of shoes Nike makes each year, 99% are made in Southeast Asia.

There are three main advantages to this network structure for Nike. First, Nike can lower its cost structure because wages in Southeast Asia are a fraction of what they are in the United States. Second, Nike can respond to changes in sports shoe fashion very quickly. Using its global computer system, it can, literally overnight, change the instructions it gives to each of its suppliers so that, within a few weeks, its foreign manufacturers are producing new kinds of shoes. Any alliance partners that fail to meet Nike's standards are replaced with new partners, so Nike has great control over its network structure. In fact, the company works closely with its suppliers to take advantage of any new developments in technology that can help it reduce costs and increase quality. Third, the ability to outsource all its manufacturing abroad allows Nike to keep its U.S. structure fluid and flexible. Nike uses a functional structure to organize its activities and decentralizes control of the design process to teams that are assigned to develop each of the new kinds of sports shoes for which Nike is known.

In conclusion, the implications of IT for strategy implementation are still evolving and will continue to do so as new software and hardware reshape a company's business model and its strategies. IT is changing the nature of value chain activities both inside and between organizations, affecting all four building blocks of competitive advantage. For the multibusiness company, as for the single-business company, the need to be alert to such changes to strengthen its position in its core business has become vital, and the success of companies like Dell and Wal-Mart compared to the failure of others like Gateway and Kmart can be traced, in part, to their success in developing the IT capabilities that lead to sustained competitive advantage.

Summary of Chapter

1. A company uses organizational design to combine structure, control systems, and culture in ways that allow it to implement its multibusiness model successfully.

2. As a company grows and diversifies, it adopts a multidivisional structure. Although this structure costs more to operate than a functional or product structure,

it economizes on the bureaucratic costs associated with operating through a functional structure and enables a company to handle its value creation activities more effectively.

3. As companies change their corporate strategies over time, they must change their structures because different strategies are managed in different ways. In

particular, the move from unrelated diversification to vertical integration to related diversification increases the bureaucratic costs associated with managing a multibusiness model. Each requires a different combination of structure, control, and culture to economize on those costs.

4. As a company moves from a localization to an international, global standardization, and transnational strategy, it also needs to switch to a more complex structure that allows it to coordinate increasingly complex resource transfers. Similarly, it needs to adopt a more complex integration and control system that facilitates resource sharing and the leveraging of competencies around the globe. When the gains are substantial, companies frequently adopt a global-matrix structure to share knowledge and expertise or to implement their control systems and culture.

5. To encourage internal new venturing, companies must design an internal venturing process that gives new-venture managers the autonomy they need to develop new products. Corporate managers need to provide the oversight that keeps new-venture managers motivated and on track.

6. The profitability of mergers and acquisitions depends on the structure and control systems that companies adopt to manage them and the way a company integrates them into its existing businesses.

7. IT is having increasingly important effects on the way multibusiness companies implement their strategies. Not only does IT help improve the efficiency with which the multidivisional structure operates, it also allows for the better control of complex value chain activities. The growth of outsourcing has also been promoted by IT, and some companies have developed network structures to coordinate their global value chain activities.

Discussion Questions

1. When would a company decide to change from a functional to a multidivisional structure?
2. If a related company begins to buy unrelated businesses, in what ways should it change its structure or control mechanisms to manage the acquisitions?
3. What prompts a company to change from a global standardization to a transnational strategy, and what new implementation problems arise as it does so?
4. How would you design a structure and control system to encourage entrepreneurship in a large, established corporation?
5. What are the problems associated with implementing a strategy of related diversification through acquisitions?

Practicing Strategic Management

SMALL-GROUP EXERCISE
Deciding on an Organizational Structure

This small-group exercise is a continuation of the small-group exercise in Chapter 12. Break into the same groups that you used in Chapter 12, reread the scenario in that chapter, and recall your group's debate about the appropriate organizational structure for your soft drink company. Because it is your intention to compete with Coca-Cola for market share worldwide, your strategy should also have a global dimension, and you must consider the best structure globally as well as domestically. Debate the pros and cons of the types of global structures, and decide which is most appropriate and will best fit your domestic structure.

ARTICLE FILE 13

Find an example of a company pursuing a multibusiness model that has changed its structure and control systems to manage its strategy better. What were the problems with the way it formerly implemented its strategy? What changes did it make to its structure and control systems? What effects does it expect these changes to have on performance?

STRATEGIC MANAGEMENT PROJECT
Module 13

Take the information that you collected in the strategic management project from Chapter 12 on strategy implementation and link it to the multibusiness model. You should collect information to determine if your company competes across industries or countries and also to see what role IT plays in allowing it to implement its business model. If your company *does* operate across countries or industries, answer the following questions:

1. Does your company use a multidivisional structure? Why or why not? What crucial implementation problems must your company manage to implement its strategy effectively? For example, what kind of integration mechanisms does it employ?

2. What are your company's corporate-level strategies? How do they affect the way it uses organizational structure, control, and culture?

3. What kind of international strategy does your company pursue? How does it control its global activities? What kind of structure does it use? Why?

4. Can you suggest ways of altering the company's structure or control systems to strengthen its business model? Would these changes increase or decrease bureaucratic costs?

5. Does your company have a particular entry mode that it has used to implement its strategy?

6. In what ways does your company use IT to coordinate its value chain activities?

7. Assess how well your company has implemented its multibusiness (or business) model.

ETHICS EXERCISE

Becky had been working at Cool Clothing Inc. for twelve years. Her early years with the company, then small, had been happy, stress-free ones. As the company grew and grew, however, rumors began to surface regarding practices that were less than ethical. Now, Becky was beginning to suspect that some of these rumors were in fact true.

Cool Clothing Inc. had followed the trend of using overseas workers to assemble its clothes, always maintaining that it was one of the companies adhering to strict standards regarding the treatment of its workers. The company claimed to be offering a fair wage and reasonable working hours and conditions. Regardless of its claims, rumors of mistreatment had been swirling for some time now. Some of the sources of these rumors were fairly reliable, and Becky was concerned. She had taken the matter to her supervisor, only to be dismissed. She had then requested appointments with her supervisor's boss and finally the president and CEO of the company, but her requests had been inexplicably denied.

Becky did not feel that she could continue to work for a company that would mistreat its workers, but if she quit her job, nothing would change and she would be out of a paycheck. She needed to figure out a way to stay with the company while at the same time fighting for the rights of these workers.

1. Define the ethical dilemma presented in this case.
2. What would you do if you were in Becky's position?
3. What might Becky do to verify the rumors once and for all?
4. Who could help Becky find assistance for the mistreated workers?

CLOSING CASE

GM Searches for the Right Global Structure

In the past, GM, like the other major U.S. carmakers, decentralized control of its overseas car operations to the managers who controlled its global car divisions in countries such as the United Kingdom, Germany, Australia, and Sweden. Each of GM's global car divisions was responsible for designing cars that suited local customer tastes, and each global division had its own design, component parts, manufacturing, and sales functions. Today, GM has to rethink the way its global structure operates. Although it is the world's biggest carmaker in terms of sales volume, it is one of the least profitable. GM currently makes only about 1% profit margin on the cars it sells in the United States, and it loses money on its sales overseas. The problem facing GM is finding ways to make its global structure operate more efficiently and effectively to implement its global business model.

The major reason for GM's low profit margins is its high cost structure, which is largely due to the way it has allowed its global divisions to operate autonomously in a decentralized fashion. Over time, this mode of operating led its divisions to become fiercely independent to protect their own interests, and this independence resulted in a massive duplication of functional activities. For example, when GM asked its Saab division to work on building a small car based on the Vectra platform developed by its German division as a way to share resources, Saab managers proceeded to give the car a whole new electrical system and engine mounting, expensive modifications that eroded all the potential cost savings from sharing resources.

To reduce its global cost structure, GM decided to place all authority over important car design and production decisions with top managers at its U.S. corporate headquarters. Now its top executives tell its global divisions what they must do to keep costs down, such as which global component suppliers to buy from. To show how this approach can reduce costs, GM's global divisions bought 270 different kinds of radios from global suppliers in the past. They set and achieved a goal of reducing this number to fifty by 2006, which slashed 40% off the cost of its global radio purchases.

Another goal of GM's policy of recentralizing control of decision making is to better coordinate the activities of its global engineering and design groups to speed the development of new car models. GM now tells its global divisions how they should work together and share their expertise to design cars that can be sold anywhere in the world. It currently takes GM about five years to design a new car model, whereas it takes Toyota only three—a tremendous advantage. Now a global council in Detroit makes the key model development decisions. Although this activity involves a $7 billion yearly investment in new car design, it also prevents global car divisions from pursuing their own goals. In fact, after the Saab debacle, GM basically took away all authority from Saab's engineering department and its engineers now work according to GM's master plan. Similarly, GM's Daewoo division in Korea decided it didn't want to use an existing GM SUV platform and modify it to fit the Korean market; instead, it wanted to create a new one from scratch. GM squashed the resistance and took the steps necessary to make its Daewoo division toe the line. Although GM wants cars to be customized to the needs of each market, CEO Rich Waggoner says he wants "all these variations to be 'plug and play,'" meaning that they do not involve costly redesigns that can adds hundreds of millions of dollars to the new car design budget.

Despite its cost problems, GM, like other U.S. carmakers, has been rapidly catching up with the quality of Japanese carmakers and has closed the gap substantially. So on the differentiation side of the equation, it must facilitate communication among its global car divisions to take advantage of the enormous pool of talent that it has throughout the world. If it can use its new, more centralized global product-group structure to design cars that better satisfy customer needs more quickly, it will be able to compete effectively against companies such as Toyota and Honda in the future.

Case Discussion Questions

1. What kind of global multibusiness model is GM pursuing?

2. How has GM been changing its global structure to allow it to coordinate the production and sale of its products most effectively around the world?

Notes

Chapter 1

1. *Sources:* D. Hunter, "How Dell Keeps from Stumbling," *Business Week,* May 14, 2001, pp. 38–40; "Enter the Eco-System: From Supply Chain to Network," *Economist,* November 11, 2000; "Dell's Direct Initiative," *Country Monitor,* June 7, 2000, p. 5; D. G. Jacobs, "Anatomy of a Supply Chain," *Transportation and Distribution,* June 2003, pp. 60–61; S. Scherreik, "How Efficient Is That Company," *Business Week,* December 23, 2003, pp. 94–95; Dell Computer Corporation 10K, March 2006; A. Serwer, "Dell's Midlife Crisis," *Fortune,* November 28, 2005, pp. 147–151; L. Lee, "Dell: Facing up to Past Mistakes," *Business Week,* June 19, 2006, p. 35; K. Allison, "Can Dell Succeed in Getting Its Mojo Back?" *Financial Times,* June 29, 2006, p. 19; David Kirkpatrick, "Dell in the Penalty Box," *Fortune,* September 18, 2006, pp. 70–74.

2. There are several different ratios for measuring profitability, such as return on invested capital, return on assets, and return on equity. Although these different measures are highly correlated with each other, finance theorists argue that the return on invested capital is the most accurate measure of profitability. See Tom Copeland, Tim Koller, and Jack Murrin, *Valuation: Measuring and Managing the Value of Companies* (New York: Wiley, 1996).

3. Trying to estimate the relative importance of industry effects and firm strategy on firm profitability has been one of the most important areas of research in the strategy literature during the past decade. See Y. E. Spanos and S. Lioukas, "An Examination of the Causal Logic of Rent Generation," *Strategic Management* 22:10 (October 2001): 907–934; and R. P. Rumelt, "How Much Does Industry Matter?" *Strategic Management* 12 (1991): 167–185. See also A. J. Mauri and M. P. Michaels, "Firm and Industry Effects Within Strategic Management: An Empirical Examination," *Strategic Management* 19 (1998): 211–219.

4. This view is known as "agency theory." See M. C. Jensen and W. H. Meckling, "Theory of the Firm: Managerial Behavior, Agency Costs and Ownership Structure," *Journal of Financial Economics* 3 (1976): 305–360; and E. F. Fama, "Agency Problems and the Theory of the Firm," *Journal of Political Economy* 88 (1980): 375–390.

5. K. R. Andrews, *The Concept of Corporate Strategy* (Homewood, Ill.: Dow Jones Irwin, 1971); H. I. Ansoff, *Corporate Strategy* (New York: McGraw-Hill, 1965); C. W. Hofer and D. Schendel, *Strategy Formulation: Analytical Concepts* (St. Paul, Minn.: West, 1978). See also P. J. Brews and M. R. Hunt, "Learning to Plan and Planning to Learn," *Strategic Management* 20 (1999): 889–913; and R. W. Grant, "Planning in a Turbulent Environment," *Strategic Management* 24 (2003): 491–517.

6. www.kodak.com/US/en/corp/careers/why/valuesmission.jhtml.

7. www.ford.com/en/company/about/overview.htm.

8. These three questions were first proposed by P. F. Drucker, *Management—Tasks, Responsibilities, Practices* (New York: Harper & Row, 1974), pp. 74–94.

9. Derek F. Abell, *Defining the Business: The Starting Point of Strategic Planning* (Englewood Cliffs, N.J.: Prentice-Hall, 1980).

10. P. A. Kidwell and P. E. Ceruzzi, *Landmarks in Digital Computing* (Washington, D.C.: Smithsonian Institute, 1994).

11. J. C. Collins and J. I. Porras, "Building Your Company's Vision," *Harvard Business Review* (September–October 1996): 65–77.

12. www.nucor.com/.

13. See J. P. Kotter and J. L. Heskett, *Corporate Culture and Performance* (New York: Free Press, 1992). For similar work, see Collins and Porras, "Building Your Company's Vision."

14. E. Freeman, *Strategic Management: A Stakeholder Approach* (Boston: Pitman Press, 1984).

15. See J. P. Kotter and J. L. Heskett, *Corporate Culture and Performance* (New York: Free Press, 1992).

16. M. D. Richards, *Setting Strategic Goals and Objectives* (St. Paul, Minn.: West, 1986).

17. E. A. Locke, G. P. Latham, and M. Erez, "The Determinants of Goal Commitment," *Academy of Management Review* 13 (1988): 23–39.

18. R. E. Hoskisson, M. A. Hitt, and C. W. L. Hill, "Managerial Incentives and Investment in R&D in Large Multiproduct Firms," *Organization Science* 3 (1993): 325–341.

19. Robert H. Hayes and William J. Abernathy, "Managing Our Way to Economic Decline," *Harvard Business Review* (July–August 1980): 67–77.

20. Andrews, *Concept of Corporate Strategy;* Ansoff, *Corporate Strategy;* Hofer and Schendel, *Strategy Formulation.*

21. For details, see R. A. Burgelman, "Intraorganizational Ecology of Strategy Making and Organizational Adaptation: Theory and Field Research," *Organization Science* 2 (1991): 239–262; H. Mintzberg, "Patterns in Strategy Formulation," *Management Science* 24 (1978): 934–948; S. L. Hart, "An Integrative Framework for Strategy Making Processes," *Academy of Management Review* 17 (1992): 327–351; G. Hamel, "Strategy as Revolution," *Harvard Business Review* 74 (July–August 1996): 69–83; and R. W. Grant, "Planning in a Turbulent Environment," *Strategic Management Journal* 24 (2003): 491–517. See also G. Gavetti, D. Levinthal and J. W. Rivkin, "Strategy Making in Novel and Complex Worlds: The Power of Analogy," *Strategic Management Journal,* 26 (2005): 691–712.

22. This is the premise of those who advocate that complexity and chaos theory should be applied to strategic management. See S. Brown and K. M. Eisenhardt, "The Art of Continuous Change: Linking Complexity Theory and Time Based Evolution in Relentlessly Shifting Organizations," *Administrative Science Quarterly* 29 (1997): 1–34; and R. Stacey and D. Parker, *Chaos, Management and Economics* (London: Institute for Economic Affairs, 1994). See also H. Courtney, J. Kirkland, and P. Viguerie, "Strategy Under Uncertainty," *Harvard Business Review* 75 (November–December 1997): 66–79.

23. Hart, "Integrative Framework"; Hamel, "Strategy as Revolution."

24. See Burgelman, "Intraorganizational Ecology," and Mintzberg, "Patterns in Strategy Formulation."

25. R. A. Burgelman and A. S. Grove, "Strategic Dissonance," *California Management Review* (Winter 1996): 8–28.

26. C. W. L. Hill and F. T. Rothaermel, "The Performance of Incumbent Firms in the Face of Radical Technological Innovation," *Academy of Management Review* 28 (2003): 257–274.

27. This story was related to the author by George Rathmann, who at one time was head of 3M's research activities.

28. Richard T. Pascale, "Perspectives on Strategy: The Real Story Behind Honda's Success," *California Management Review* 26 (1984): 47–72.

29. This viewpoint is strongly emphasized by Burgelman and Grove, "Strategic Dissonance."

30. C. C. Miller and L. B. Cardinal, "Strategic Planning and Firm Performance: A Synthesis of More Than Two Decades of Research," *Academy of Management Journal* 37 (1994): 1649–1665. Also see P. R. Rogers, A. Miller, and W. Q. Judge, "Using Information Processing Theory to Understand Planning/Performance Relationships in the Context of Strategy," *Strategic Management* 20 (1999): 567–577.

31. P. J. Brews and M. R. Hunt, "Learning to Plan and Planning to Learn," *Strategic Management Journal* (1999) 20: 889–913.

32. P. Cornelius, A. Van de Putte, and M. Romani, "Three Decades of Scenario Planning at Shell," *California Management Review,* 48 (2005): 92–110.

33. H. Courtney, J. Kirkland, and P. Viguerie, "Strategy Under Uncertainty," *Harvard Business Review,* November–December 1997, 75, 66–79.

34. P. J. H. Schoemaker, "Multiple Scenario Development: Its Conceptual and Behavioral Foundation," *Strategic Management Journal,* 14, 1993, 193–213.

35. P. Schoemaker, P. J. H. van der Heijden, and A. J. M. Cornelius, "Integrating Scenarios into Strategic Planning at Royal Dutch Shell," *Planning Review,* 1992, 20(3), pp. 41–47; I. Wylie, "There is no alternative to . . . ." *Fast Company,* July 2002, pp. 106–111.

36. "The Next Big Surprise: Scenario Planning," *The Economist,* October 13, 2001, p. 71.

37. C. Kim and R. Mauborgne, "Procedural Justice, Strategic Decision Making, and the Knowledge Economy," *Strategic Management* 19 (1998): 323–338; W. C. Kim and R. Mauborgne, "Fair Process: Managing in the Knowledge Economy," *Harvard Business Review* 75 (July–August 1997): 65–76.

38. G. Hamel and C. K. Prahalad, *Competing for the Future* (New York: Free Press, 1994).

39. See G. Hamel and C. K. Prahalad, "Strategic Intent," *Harvard Business Review* (May–June 1989): 64.

40. See C. R. Schwenk, "Cognitive Simplification Processes in Strategic Decision Making," *Strategic Management* 5 (1984): 111–128; and K. M. Eisenhardt and M. Zbaracki, "Strategic Decision Making," *Strategic Management* 13 (Special Issue, 1992): 17–37.

41. H. Simon, *Administrative Behavior* (New York: McGraw-Hill, 1957).

42. The original statement of this phenomenon was made by A. Tversky and D. Kahneman, "Judgment Under Uncertainty: Heuristics and Biases," *Science* 185 (1974): 1124–1131. See also D. Lovallo and D. Kahneman, "Delusions of Success: How Optimism Undermines Executives' Decisions," *Harvard Business Review* 81 (July 2003): 56–67; and J. S. Hammond, R. L. Keeny, and H. Raiffa, "The Hidden Traps in Decision Making," *Harvard Business Review* 76 (September–October 1998): 25–34.

43. Schwenk, "Cognitive Simplification Processes," pp. 111–128.

44. B. M. Staw, "The Escalation of Commitment to a Course of Action," *Academy of Management Review* 6 (1981): 577–587.

45. R. Roll, "The Hubris Hypotheses of Corporate Takeovers," *Journal of Business* 59 (1986): 197–216.

46. Irvin L. Janis, *Victims of Groupthink,* 2nd ed. (Boston: Houghton Mifflin, 1982). For an alternative view, see S. R. Fuller and R. J. Aldag, "Organizational Tonypandy: Lessons from a Quarter Century of the Groupthink Phenomenon," *Organizational Behavior and Human Decision Processes* 73 (1998): 163–184.

47. See R. O. Mason, "A Dialectic Approach to Strategic Planning," *Management Science* 13 (1969): 403–414; R. A. Cosier and J. C. Aplin, "A Critical View of Dialectic Inquiry in Strategic Planning," *Strategic Management* 1 (1980): 343–356; and I. I. Mintroff and R. O. Mason, "Structuring III—Structured Policy Issues: Further Explorations in a Methodology for Messy Problems," *Strategic Management* 1 (1980): 331–342.

48. Mason, "A Dialectic Approach," pp. 403–414.

49. Lovallo and Kahneman, "Delusions of Success."

50. For a summary of research on strategic leadership, see D. C. Hambrick, "Putting Top Managers Back into the Picture," *Strategic Management* 10 (Special Issue, 1989): 5–15. See also D. Goldman, "What Makes a Leader?" *Harvard Business Review* (November–December 1998): 92–105; H. Mintzberg, "Covert Leadership," *Harvard Business Review* (November–December 1998): 140–148; and R. S. Tedlow, "What Titans Can Teach Us," *Harvard Business Review* (December 2001): 70–79.

51. N. M. Tichy and D. O. Ulrich, "The Leadership Challenge: A Call for the Transformational Leader," *Sloan Management Review* (Fall 1984): 59–68; F. Westley and H. Mintzberg, "Visionary Leadership and Strategic Management," *Strategic Management* 10 (Special Issue, 1989): 17–32.

52. Comments were made by Jim Donald at a presentation to University of Washington MBA students.

53. B. McConnell and J. Huba. *Creating Customer Evangelists* (Chicago: Dearborn Trade Publishing, 2003).

54. E. Wrapp, "Good Managers Don't Make Policy Decisions," *Harvard Business Review* (September–October 1967): 91–99.

55. J. Pfeffer, *Managing with Power* (Boston: Harvard Business School Press, 1992).

56. D. Goldman, "What Makes a Leader?" *Harvard Business Review* (November–December 1998): 92–105.

57. M. Maynard and N. Bunkley, "A Reversal of Fortune at Chrysler Too," *New York Times,* September 20, 2006, p. C1; Gail Edmondson and K. Kerwin, "Stalled: Is the Daimler Chrysler Deal a Mistake?" *Business Week,* September 29, 2003, pp. 55–56; N. Boudette and S. Power, "Gearing Down: Chrysler Turnaround Falters as Unsold Gas Guzzlers Fill Lots," *Wall Street Journal,* September 20, 2006, p. A1.

58. *Sources:* C. Y. Baldwin, *Fundamental Enterprise Valuation: Return on Invested Capital,* Harvard Business School Note 9-801-125, July 3, 2004; T. Copeland et al., *Valuation: Measuring and Managing the Value of Companies* (New York: Wiley, 2000).

Chapter 2

1. *Sources:* S. Theodore, "Brewers Take the Good with the Bad," *Beverage Industry* 97 (April 2006): 17–23. V. Tremblay, N. Iwasaki, and C. Tremblay, "The Dynamics of Industry Concentration for U.S. Micro and Macro Brewers," *Review of Industrial Organization* 26 (2005): 307–324; J. P. Nelson, "Beer Advertising and Marketing Update: Structure, Conduct and Social Costs," *Review of Industrial Organization* 26 (2005): 269–306; Beer Institute, *Brewers Almanac, 2006,* (Washington D.C.: Beer Institute, 2006).

2. M. E. Porter, *Competitive Strategy* (New York: Free Press, 1980).

3. J. E. Bain, *Barriers to New Competition* (Cambridge, Mass.: Harvard University Press, 1956). For a review of the modern literature on barriers to entry, see R. J. Gilbert, "Mobility Barriers and the Value of Incumbency," in R. Schmalensee and R. D. Willig (eds.), *Handbook of Industrial Organization,* Vol. 1 (Amsterdam: North-Holland, 1989). See also R. P. McAfee, H. M. Mialon, and M. A. Williams, "What Is a Barrier to Entry?" *American Economic Review* 94 (May 2004): 461–468.

4. A detailed discussion of switching costs and lock-in can be found in C. Shapiro and H. R. Varian, *Information Rules: A*

Strategic Guide to the Network Economy (Boston: Harvard Business School Press, 1999).

5. Most of this information on barriers to entry can be found in the industrial organization economics literature. See especially the following works: Bain, *Barriers to New Competition*; M. Mann, "Seller Concentration, Barriers to Entry and Rates of Return in 30 Industries," *Review of Economics and Statistics* 48 (1966): 296–307; W. S. Comanor and T. A. Wilson, "Advertising, Market Structure and Performance," *Review of Economics and Statistics* 49 (1967): 423–440; Gilbert, "Mobility Barriers"; and K. Cool, L. H. Roller, and B. Leleux, "The Relative Impact of Actual and Potential Rivalry on Firm Profitability in the Pharmaceutical Industry," *Strategic Management* 20 (1999): 1–14.

6. For a discussion of tacit agreements, see T. C. Schelling, *The Strategy of Conflict* (Cambridge, Mass.: Harvard University Press, 1960).

7. M. Busse, "Firm Financial Condition and Airline Price Wars," *Rand Journal of Economics* 33 (2002): 298–318.

8. For a review, see F. Karakaya, "Market Exit and Barriers to Exit: Theory and Practice," *Psychology and Marketing* 17 (2000): 651–668.

9. P. Ghemawat, *Commitment: The Dynamics of Strategy* (Boston: Harvard Business School Press, 1991).

10. A. S. Grove, *Only the Paranoid Survive* (New York: Doubleday, 1996).

11. In standard microeconomic theory, the concept used for assessing the strength of substitutes and complements is the cross elasticity of demand.

12. For details and further references, see Charles W. L. Hill, "Establishing a Standard: Competitive Strategy and Technology Standards in Winner Take All Industries," *Academy of Management Executive* 11 (1997): 7–25; and Shapiro and Varian, *Information Rules*.

13. The development of strategic group theory has been a strong theme in the strategy literature. Important contributions include the following: R. E. Caves and Michael E. Porter, "From Entry Barriers to Mobility Barriers," *Quarterly Journal of Economics* (May 1977): 241–262; K. R. Harrigan, "An Application of Clustering for Strategic Group Analysis," *Strategic Management Journal* 6 (1985): 55–73; K. J. Hatten and D. E. Schendel, "Heterogeneity Within an Industry: Firm Conduct in the U.S. Brewing Industry, 1952–71," *Journal of Industrial Economics* 26 (1977): 97–113; Michael E. Porter, "The Structure Within Industries and Companies' Performance," *Review of Economics and Statistics* 61 (1979): 214–227. See also K. Cool and D. Schendel, "Performance Differences Among Strategic Group Members," *Strategic Management* 9 (1988): 207–233; A. Nair and S. Kotha, "Does Group Membership Matter? Evidence from the Japanese Steel Industry," *Strategic Management* 20 (2001): 221–235; and G. McNamara, D. L. Deephouse, and R. A. Luce, "Competitive Positioning Within and Across a Strategic Group Structure," *Strategic Management* 24 (2003): 161–180.

14. For details on the strategic group structure in the pharmaceutical industry, see K. Cool and I. Dierickx, "Rivalry, Strategic Groups, and Firm Profitability," *Strategic Management* 14 (1993): 47–59.

15. Charles W. Hofer argued that life cycle considerations may be the most important contingency when formulating business strategy. See Hofer, "Towards a Contingency Theory of Business Strategy," *Academy of Management* 18 (1975): 784–810. There is empirical evidence to support this view. See C. R. Anderson and C. P. Zeithaml, "Stages of the Product Life Cycle, Business Strategy, and Business Performance," *Academy of Management* 27 (1984): 5–24; and D. C. Hambrick and D. Lei, "Towards an Empirical Prioritization of Contingency Variables for Business Strategy," *Academy of Management* 28 (1985): 763–788. See also G. Miles, C. C. Snow, and M. P. Sharfman, "Industry Variety and Performance," *Strategic Management* 14 (1993): 163–177; G. K. Deans, F. Kroeger, and S. Zeisel, "The Consolidation Curve," *Harvard Business Review* (December 2002): 2–3. Vol. 80(6).

16. The characteristics of declining industries have been summarized by K. R. Harrigan, "Strategy Formulation in Declining Industries," *Academy of Management Review* 5 (1980): 599–604. See also J. Anand and H. Singh, "Asset Redeployment, Acquisitions and Corporate Strategy in Declining Industries," *Strategic Management* 18 (1997): 99–118.

17. This perspective is associated with the Austrian school of economics, which goes back to Schumpeter. For a summary of this school and its implications for strategy, see R. Jacobson, "The Austrian School of Strategy," *Academy of Management Review* 17 (1992): 782–807; and C. W. L. Hill and D. Deeds, "The Importance of Industry Structure for the Determination of Industry Profitability: A Neo-Austrian Approach," *Journal of Management Studies* 33 (1996): 429–451.

18. "A Tricky Business," *Economist*, June 30, 2001, pp. 55–56.

19. D. F. Barnett and R. W. Crandall, *Up from the Ashes* (Washington, D.C.: Brookings Institution, 1986).

20. M. E. Porter, *The Competitive Advantage of Nations* (New York: Free Press, 1990).

21. The term *punctuated equilibrium* is borrowed from evolutionary biology. For a detailed explanation of the concept, see M. L. Tushman, W. H. Newman, and E. Romanelli, "Convergence and Upheaval: Managing the Unsteady Pace of Organizational Evolution," *California Management Review* 29:1 (1985): 29–44; C. J. G. Gersick, "Revolutionary Change Theories: A Multilevel Exploration of the Punctuated Equilibrium Paradigm," *Academy of Management Review* 16 (1991): 10–36; and R. Adner and D. A. Levinthal, "The Emergence of Emerging Technologies," *California Management Review* 45 (Fall 2002): 50–65.

22. A. J. Slywotzky, *Value Migration: How to Think Several Moves Ahead of the Competition* (Boston: Harvard Business School Press, 1996).

23. R. D'Avani, *Hypercompetition* (New York: Free Press, 1994).

24. G. McNamara, P. M. Vaaler, and C. Devers, "Same as It Ever Was: The Search for Evidence of Increasing Hypercompetition," *Strategic Management* 24 (2003): 261–278.

25. Hill and Deeds, "Importance of Industry Structure."

26. R. P. Rumelt, "How Much Does Industry Matter?" *Strategic Management* 12 (1991): 167–185. See also A. J. Mauri and M. P. Michaels, "Firm and Industry Effects Within Strategic Management: An Empirical Examination," *Strategic Management* 19 (1998): 211–219.

27. See R. Schmalensee, "Inter-Industry Studies of Structure and Performance," in Schmalensee and Willig (eds.), *Handbook of Industrial Organization*. Similar results were found by A. N. McGahan and M. E. Porter, "How Much Does Industry Matter, Really?" *Strategic Management* 18 (1997): 15–30.

28. For example, see K. Cool and D. Schendel, "Strategic Group Formation and Performance: The Case of the U.S. Pharmaceutical Industry, 1932–1992," *Management Science* (September 1987): 1102–1124.

29. See M. Gort and J. Klepper, "Time Paths in the Diffusion of Product Innovations," *Economic Journal* (September 1982): 630–653. Looking at the history of forty-six products, Gort and

Klepper found that the length of time before other companies entered the markets created by a few inventive companies declined from an average of 14.4 years for products introduced before 1930 to 4.9 years for those introduced after 1949.

30. The phrase was originally coined by J. Schumpeter, *Capitalism, Socialism and Democracy* (London: Macmillan, 1950), p. 68.

31. M. E. Porter, "Strategy and the Internet," *Harvard Business Review* (March 2001): 62–79.

32. U.S. Dept. of Labor, Bureau of Labor Statistics.

33. *Economist, The Economist Book of Vital World Statistics* (New York: Random House, 1990).

34. For a detailed discussion of the importance of the structure of law as a factor explaining economic change and growth, see D. C. North, *Institutions, Institutional Change, and Economic Performance* (Cambridge: Cambridge University Press, 1990).

35. *Sources:* Staff Reporter, "Pharm Exec 50," *Pharmaceutical Executive,* May 2004, pp. 61–68; J. A. DiMasi, R. W. Hansen, and H. G. Grabowski, "The Price of Innovation: New Estimates of Drug Development Costs," *Journal of Health Economics* 22 (March 2003): 151–170; "Where the Money Is: The Drug Industry," *Economist,* April 26, 2003, pp. 64–65; Value Line Investment Survey, various issues; "Heartburn: Pharmaceuticals," *Economist,* August 19, 2006, p. 57; P. B. Ginsberg et al., "Tracking Health Care Costs," *Health Affairs,* October 3, 2006, www.healthaffairs.org (accessed October 10, 2006).

Chapter 3

1. M. Brelis, "Simple Strategy Makes Southwest a Model for Success," *Boston Globe,* November 5, 2000, p. F1; M. Trottman, "At Southwest, New CEO Sits in the Hot Seat," *Wall Street Journal,* July 19, 2004, p. B1; J. Helyar, "Southwest Finds Trouble in the Air," *Fortune,* August 9, 2004, p. 38; Southwest Airlines 10-K 2005; United Airlines 10-K 2005; Bureau of Transportation Statistics at http://www.transtats.bts.gov/ (accessed March 11, 2007).

2. M. Cusumano, *The Japanese Automobile Industry* (Cambridge, Mass.: Harvard University Press, 1989); S. Spear and H. K. Bowen, "Decoding the DNA of the Toyota Production System," *Harvard Business Review* (September–October 1999): 96–108.

3. The material in this section relies on the resource-based view of the company. For summaries of this perspective, see J. B. Barney, "Company Resources and Sustained Competitive Advantage," *Journal of Management* 17 (1991): 99–120; J. T. Mahoney and J. R. Pandian, "The Resource-Based View Within the Conversation of Strategic Management," *Strategic Management* 13 (1992): 63–380; R. Amit and P. J. H. Schoemaker, "Strategic Assets and Organizational Rent," *Strategic Management* 14 (1993): 33–46; M. A. Peteraf, "The Cornerstones of Competitive Advantage: A Resource-Based View," *Strategic Management* 14 (1993): 179–191; B. Wernerfelt, "A Resource Based View of the Company," *Strategic Management* 15 (1994): 171–180; and K. M. Eisenhardt and J. A. Martin, "Dynamic Capabilities: What Are They?" *Strategic Management* 21 (2000): 1105–1121.

4. J. B. Barney, "Company Resources and Sustained Competitive Advantage," *Journal of Management* 17 (1991): 99–120.

5. For a discussion of organizational capabilities, see R. R. Nelson and S. Winter, *An Evolutionary Theory of Economic Change* (Cambridge, Mass.: Belknap Press, 1982).

6. W. Chan Kim and R. Mauborgne, "Value Innovation: The Strategic Logic of High Growth," *Harvard Business Review* (January–February 1997): 102–115.

7. The concept of consumer surplus is an important one in economics. For a more detailed exposition, see D. Besanko, D. Dranove, and M. Shanley, *Economics of Strategy* (New York: Wiley, 1996).

8. However, $P = U$ only in the special case when the company has a perfect monopoly and it can charge each customer a unique price that reflects the utility of the product to that customer (i.e., where perfect price discrimination is possible). More generally, except in the limiting case of perfect price discrimination, even a monopolist will see most customers capture some of the utility of a product in the form of a consumer surplus.

9. This point is central to the work of Michael Porter. See M. E. Porter, *Competitive Advantage* (New York: Free Press, 1985). See also P. Ghemawat, *Commitment: The Dynamic of Strategy* (New York: Free Press, 1991), chap. 4.

10. Harbour Consulting, "Productivity Gap Among North American Auto Makers Narrows in Harbour Report 2006," Harbour Consulting Press Release, July 1, 2006.

11. Porter, *Competitive Advantage.*

12. Ibid.

13. This approach goes back to the pioneering work by K. Lancaster, *Consumer Demand, a New Approach* (New York: 1971).

14. D. Garvin, "Competing on the Eight Dimensions of Quality," *Harvard Business Review* (November–December 1987): 101–119; P. Kotler, *Marketing Management* (Millennium ed.) (Upper Saddle River, N.J.: Prentice-Hall, 2000).

15. "Proton Bomb," *Economist* (May 8, 2004): p. 77.

16. C. K. Prahalad and M. S. Krishnan, "The New Meaning of Quality in the Information Age," *Harvard Business Review* (September–October 1999): 109–118.

17. See D. Garvin, "What Does Product Quality Really Mean?" *Sloan Management Review* 26 (Fall 1984): 25–44; P. B. Crosby, *Quality Is Free* (New York: Mentor, 1980); and A. Gabor, *The Man Who Discovered Quality* (New York: Times Books, 1990).

18. M. Cusumano, *The Japanese Automobile Industry* (Cambridge, Mass.: Harvard University Press, 1989); S. Spear and H. K. Bowen, "Decoding the DNA of the Toyota Production System," *Harvard Business Review* (September–October 1999): 96–108.

19. Kim and Mauborgne, "Value Innovation."

20. G. Stalk and T. M. Hout, *Competing Against Time* (New York: Free Press, 1990).

21. Ibid.

22. Tom Copeland, Tim Koller, and Jack Murrin, *Valuation: Measuring and Managing the Value of Companies* (New York: Wiley, 1996). See also S. F. Jablonsky and N. P. Barsky, *The Manager's Guide to Financial Statement Analysis* (New York: Wiley, 2001).

23. Copeland, Koller, and Murrin, *Valuation.*

24. This is done as follows: signifying net profit by π, invested capital by K, and revenues by R, then ROIC $= \pi/K$. If we multiply through by revenues, R, this becomes $R \times (\pi/K) = (\pi \times R)/(K \times R)$, which can be rearranged as $\pi/R \times R/K$. π/R is the return on sales and R/K capital turnover.

25. Note that Figure 3.9 is a simplification and ignores some other important items that enter the calculation, such as depreciation/sales (a determinant of ROS) and other assets/sales (a determinant of capital turnover).

26. This is the nature of the competitive process. For more detail, see C. W. L. Hill and D. Deeds, "The Importance of Industry Structure for the Determination of Company Profitability: A Neo-Austrian Perspective," *Journal of Management Studies* 33 (1996): 429–451.

27. As with resources and capabilities, so the concept of barriers to imitation is also grounded in the resource-based view of the

company. For details, see R. Reed and R. J. DeFillippi, "Causal Ambiguity, Barriers to Imitation, and Sustainable Competitive Advantage," *Academy of Management Review* 15 (1990): 88–102.

28. E. Mansfield, "How Economists See R&D," *Harvard Business Review* (November–December 1981): 98–106.

29. S. L. Berman, J. Down, and C. W. L. Hill, "Tacit Knowledge as a Source of Competitive Advantage in the National Basketball Association," *Academy of Management Journal* (2002): 13–33, Vol. 45.

30. P. Ghemawat, *Commitment: The Dynamic of Strategy* (New York: Free Press, 1991).

31. W. M. Cohen and D. A. Levinthal, "Absorptive Capacity: A New Perspective on Learning and Innovation," *Administrative Science Quarterly* 35 (1990): 128–152.

32. M. T. Hannah and J. Freeman, "Structural Inertia and Organizational Change," *American Sociological Review* 49 (1984): 149–164.

33. See "IBM Corporation," Harvard Business School Case #180-034.

34. Ghemawat, *Commitment*.

35. D. Miller, *The Icarus Paradox* (New York: HarperBusiness, 1990).

36. P. M. Senge, *The Fifth Discipline: The Art and Practice of the Learning Organization* (New York: Doubleday, 1990).

37. D. Kearns, "Leadership Through Quality," *Academy of Management Executive* 4 (1990): 86–89.

38. The classic statement of this position was made by A. A. Alchain, "Uncertainty, Evolution, and Economic Theory," *Journal of Political Economy* 84 (1950): 488–500.

39. *Sources:* Starbucks 10-K, various years; C. McLean, "Starbucks Set to Invade Coffee-Loving Continent," *Seattle Times,* October 4, 2000, p. E1; J. Ordonez, "Starbucks to Start Major Expansion in Overseas Market," *Wall Street Journal,* October 27, 2000, p. B10; S. Homes and D. Bennett, "Planet Starbucks," *Business Week,* September 9, 2002, pp 99–110; J. Batsell, "A Bean Counters Dream," *Seattle Times,* March 28, 2004, p. E1; "Boss Talk: It's a Grande Latte World," *Wall Street Journal,* December 15, 2003, p. B1; C. Harris, "Starbucks Beats Estimates, Outlines Expansion Plans," *Seattle Post Intelligencer,* October 5, 2006, p. C1.

Chapter 4

1. K. Hall, "No One Does Lean Like the Japanese," *Business Week* (July 10, 2006): 40–41; I. Rowley and H. Tashiro, "Lessons from Matsushita's Playbook," *Business Week* (March 21, 2005): 32; K. Hall, "Matsushita's Transformer Steps Down," *Business Week Online,* June 30, 2006.

2. G. J. Miller, *Managerial Dilemmas: The Political Economy of Hierarchy* (Cambridge: Cambridge University Press, 1992).

3. H. Luft, J. Bunker, and A. Enthoven, "Should Operations Be Regionalized?" *New England Journal of Medicine* 301 (1979): 1364–1369.

4. S. Chambers and R. Johnston, "Experience Curves in Services," *International Journal of Operations and Production Management* 20 (2000): 842–860.

5. G. Hall and S. Howell, "The Experience Curve from an Economist's Perspective," *Strategic Management Journal* 6 (1985): 197–212; M. Lieberman, "The Learning Curve and Pricing in the Chemical Processing Industries," *RAND Journal of Economics* 15 (1984): 213–228; R. A. Thornton and P. Thompson, "Learning from Experience and Learning from Others," *American Economic Review* 91 (2001): 1350–1369.

6. Boston Consulting Group, *Perspectives on Experience* (Boston: Boston Consulting Group, 1972); Hall and Howell, "The

Experience Curve," pp. 197–212; W. B. Hirschmann, "Profit from the Learning Curve," *Harvard Business Review* (January–February 1964): 125–139.

7. A. A. Alchian, "Reliability of Progress Curves in Airframe Production," *Econometrica* 31 (1963): 679–693.

8. M. Borrus, L. A. Tyson, and J. Zysman, "Creating Advantage: How Government Policies Create Trade in the Semi-Conductor Industry," in P. R. Krugman (ed.), *Strategic Trade Policy and the New International Economics* (Cambridge, Mass.: MIT Press, 1986); S. Ghoshal and C. A. Bartlett, "Matsushita Electrical Industrial (MEI) in 1987," Harvard Business School Case #388-144 (1988).

9. W. Abernathy and K. Wayne, "Limits of the Learning Curve," *Harvard Business Review* 52 (September–October 1974): 59–69.

10. D. F. Barnett and R. W. Crandall, *Up from the Ashes: The Rise of the Steel Minimill in the United States* (Washington, D.C.: Brookings Institution, 1986).

11. See P. Nemetz and L. Fry, "Flexible Manufacturing Organizations: Implications for Strategy Formulation," *Academy of Management Review* 13 (1988): 627–638; N. Greenwood, *Implementing Flexible Manufacturing Systems* (New York: Halstead Press, 1986); J. P. Womack, D. T. Jones, and D. Roos, *The Machine That Changed the World* (New York: Rawson Associates, 1990); and R. Parthasarthy and S. P. Seith, "The Impact of Flexible Automation on Business Strategy and Organizational Structure," *Academy of Management Review* 17 (1992): 86–111.

12. B. J. Pine, *Mass Customization: The New Frontier in Business Competition* (Boston: Harvard Business School Press, 1993); S. Kotha, "Mass Customization: Implementing the Emerging Paradigm for Competitive Advantage," *Strategic Management Journal* 16 (1995): 21–42; J. H. Gilmore and B. J. Pine II, "The Four Faces of Mass Customization," *Harvard Business Review* (January–February 1997): 91–101.

13. P. Waurzyniak, "Ford's Flexible Push," *Manufacturing Engineering* (September 2003): 47–50.

14. F. F. Reichheld and W. E. Sasser, "Zero Defections: Quality Comes to Service," *Harvard Business Review* (September–October 1990): 105–111.

15. The example comes from Reichheld and Sasser, op. cit.

16. Ibid.

17. R. Narasimhan and J. R. Carter, "Organization, Communication and Coordination of International Sourcing," *International Marketing Review* 7 (1990): 6–20.

18. H. F. Busch, "Integrated Materials Management," *IJDP & MM* 18 (1990): 28–39.

19. G. Stalk and T. M. Hout, *Competing Against Time* (New York: Free Press, 1990).

20. See Peter Bamberger and Ilan Meshoulam, *Human Resource Strategy: Formulation, Implementation, and Impact* (Thousand Oaks, Calif.: Sage, 2000); P. M. Wright and S. Snell, "Towards a Unifying Framework for Exploring Fit and Flexibility in Human Resource Management," *Academy of Management Review* 23 (October 1998): 756–772.

21. A. Sorge and M. Warner, "Manpower Training, Manufacturing Organization, and Work Place Relations in Great Britain and West Germany," *British Journal of Industrial Relations* 18 (1980): 318–333; R. Jaikumar, "Postindustrial Manufacturing," *Harvard Business Review* (November–December 1986): 72–83.

22. J. Hoerr, "The Payoff from Teamwork," *Business Week* (July 10, 1989): 56–62.

23. "The Trouble with Teams," *Economist* (January 14, 1995): 61.

24. T. C. Powell and A. Dent-Micallef, "Information Technology as Competitive Advantage: The Role of Human, Business, and

Technology Resource," *Strategic Management Journal* 18 (1997): 375–405; B. Gates, *Business @ the Speed of Thought* (New York: Warner Books, 1999).

25. "Cisco@speed," *Economist* (June 26, 1999): 12; S. Tully, "How Cisco Mastered the Net," *Fortune* (August 17, 1997): 207–210; C. Kano, "The Real King of the Internet," *Fortune,* (September 7, 1998): 82–93.

26. B. Gates, *Business @ the Speed of Thought* (New York: Warner Books, 1999); Anonymous, "Enter the Eco-System: From Supply Chain to Network," *The Economist* (November 11, 2000); Anonymous, "Dell's Direct Initiative," *Country Monitor* (June 7, 2000): 5; Michael Dell, *Direct from Dell: Strategies that Revolutionized an Industry* (New York: Harper Business, 1999), quote from p. 91; Staff reporter, "Survey: Shining Examples," *The Economist* (June 17, 2006): 4–5.

27. See the articles published in the special issue of the *Academy of Management Review on Total Quality Management* 19:3 (1994). The following article provides a good overview of many of the issues involved from an academic perspective: J. W. Dean and D. E. Bowen, "Management Theory and Total Quality," *Academy of Management Review* 19 (1994): 392–418. See also T. C. Powell, "Total Quality Management as Competitive Advantage," *Strategic Management Journal* 16 (1995): 15–37.

28. For general background information, see "How to Build Quality," *Economist* (September 23, 1989): 91–92; A. Gabor, *The Man Who Discovered Quality* (New York: Penguin, 1990); and P. B. Crosby, *Quality Is Free* (New York: Mentor, 1980).

29. W. E. Deming, "Improvement of Quality and Productivity Through Action by Management," *National Productivity Review* 1 (Winter 1981–1982): 12–22.

30. J. Bowles, "Is American Management Really Committed to Quality?" *Management Review* (April 1992): 42–46.

31. O. Port and G. Smith, "Quality," *Business Week* (November 30, 1992): 66–75. See also "The Straining of Quality," *Economist* (January 14, 1995): 55–56.

32. Bowles, "Is American Management Really Committed to Quality?" pp. 42–46; "The Straining of Quality," pp. 55–56.

33. Gabor, *The Man Who Discovered Quality.*

34. W. E. Deming, *Out of the Crisis* (Cambridge, Mass.: MIT Center for Advanced Engineering Study, 1986).

35. Deming, "Improvement of Quality and Productivity," pp. 12–22.

36. A. Ries and J. Trout, *Positioning: The Battle for Your Mind* (New York: Warner Books, 1982).

37. R. G. Cooper, *Product Leadership* (Reading, Mass.: Perseus Books, 1999).

38. E. Mansfield, "How Economists See R&D," *Harvard Business Review* (November–December 1981): 98–106.

39. Ibid.

40. G. A. Stevens and J. Burley, "Piloting the Rocket of Radical Innovation," *Research Technology Management* 46 (2003): 16–26.

41. Ibid.; see also S. L. Brown and K. M. Eisenhardt, "Product Development: Past Research, Present Findings, and Future Directions," *Academy of Management Review* 20 (1995): 343–378; M. B. Lieberman and D. B. Montgomery, "First Mover Advantages," *Strategic Management Journal* 9 (Special Issue, Summer 1988): 41–58; D. J. Teece, "Profiting from Technological Innovation: Implications for Integration, Collaboration, Licensing and Public Policy," *Research Policy* 15 (1987): 285–305; and G. J. Tellis and P. N. Golder, "First to Market, First to Fail?" *Sloan Management Review* (Winter 1996): 65–75.

42. Stalk and Hout, *Competing Against Time.*

43. K. B. Clark and S. C. Wheelwright, *Managing New Product and Process Development* (New York: Free Press, 1993); M. A. Schilling and C. W. L. Hill, "Managing the New Product Development Process," *Academy of Management Executive* 12:3 (August 1998): 67–81.

44. Clark and Wheelwright, *Managing New Product and Process Development.*

45. P. Sellers, "Getting Customers to Love You," *Fortune* (March 13, 1989): 38–42.

46. O. Port, "Moving Past the Assembly Line," *Business Week* (Special Issue, Reinventing America, 1992): 177–180.

47. G. P. Pisano and S. C. Wheelwright, "The New Logic of High Tech R&D," *Harvard Business Review* (September–October 1995): 93–105.

48. K. B. Clark and T. Fujimoto, "The Power of Product Integrity," *Harvard Business Review* (November–December 1990): 107–118; Clark and Wheelwright, *Managing New Product and Process Development*; Brown and Eisenhardt, "Product Development"; Stalk and Hout, *Competing Against Time.*

49. C. Christensen, "Quantum Corporation—Business and Product Teams," Harvard Business School Case #9-692-023.

50. E. Biyalogorsky, W. Boulding, and R. Starlin, "Stuck in the Past: Why Managers Persist with New Product Failures," *Journal of Marketing,* 70(2) (2006): 1–15.

51. H. Petroski, *Success through Failure: The Paradox of Design* (Princeton, NJ: Princeton University Press, 2006). See also A. C. Edmondson, "Learning from Mistakes Is Easier Said Than Done," *Journal of Applied Behavioral Science,* 40 (2004): 66–91.

52. P. Sellers, "Getting Customers to Love you", Fortune, March 13, 1989, pp. 38–45.

53. Sellers, "Getting Customers to Love You."

54. S. Caminiti, "A Mail Order Romance: Lands' End Courts Unseen Customers," *Fortune* (March 13, 1989): 43–44.

55. Stalk and Hout, *Competing Against Time.*

56. *Sources:* A. Latour and C. Nuzum, "Verizon Profit Soars Fivefold on Wireless Growth," *Wall Street Journal* (July 28, 2004): A3; S. Wooley, "Do You Fear Me Now?" *Forbes* (November 10, 2003): 78–80; A. Z. Cuneo, "Call Verizon Victorious," *Advertising Age* (March 24, 2004): 3–5; M. Alleven, "Wheels of Churn," *Wireless Week* (September 1, 2006), published online at www.wirelessweek.com.

Chapter 5

1. www.etrade.com, 2007; www.bankofamerica.com, 2006; www.etrade.com, 2006 (accessed 2007).

2. Derek F. Abell, *Defining the Business: The Starting Point of Strategic Planning* (Englewood Cliffs, N.J.: Prentice-Hall, 1980), p. 169.

3. R. Kotler, *Marketing Management,* 5th ed. (Englewood Cliffs, N.J.: Prentice-Hall, 1984); M. R. Darby and E. Karni, "Free Competition and the Optimal Amount of Fraud," *Journal of Law and Economics* 16 (1973): 67–86.

4. Abell, *Defining the Business,* p. 8.

5. Some of the theoretical underpinnings for this approach can be found in G. R. Jones and J. Butler, "Costs, Revenues, and Business Level Strategy," *Academy of Management Review* 13 (1988): 202–213; and C. W. L. Hill, "Differentiation Versus Low Cost or Differentiation and Low Cost: A Contingency Framework," *Academy of Management Review* 13 (1988): 401–412.

6. This section and the material on the business model draw heavily on C. W. L. Hill and G. R. Jones, "The Dynamics of Business-Level Strategy" (unpublished paper, 2002).

7. Many authors have discussed cost leadership and differentiation as basic competitive approaches—for example, F. Scherer, *Industrial Market Structure and Economic Performance*, 10th ed. (Boston: Houghton Mifflin, 2000). The basic cost-leadership/differentiation dimension has received substantial empirical support; see, for example, D. C. Hambrick, "High Profit Strategies in Mature Capital Goods Industries: A Contingency Approach," *Academy of Management Journal* 26 (1983): 687–707.

8. Michael E. Porter, *Competitive Advantage: Creating and Sustaining Superior Performance* (New York: Free Press, 1985), p. 37.

9. Ibid., pp. 13–14.

10. www.walmart.com (2007) (accessed January 2007).

11. D. Miller, "Configurations of Strategy and Structure: Towards a Synthesis," *Strategic Management Journal 7* (1986): 217–231.

12. J. Guyon, "Can the Savoy Cut Costs and Be the Savoy?" Wall Street Journal, October 25, 1994, p. B1.

13. Michael E. Porter, *Competitive Strategy: Techniques for Analyzing Industries and Competitors* (New York: Free Press, 1980), p. 46.

14. Peter F. Drucker, *The Practice of Management* (New York: Harper, 1954).

15. Charles W. Hofer and D. Schendel, *Strategy Formulation: Analytical Concepts* (St. Paul, Minn.: West, 1978).

16. W. K. Hall, "Survival Strategies in a Hostile Environment," *Harvard Business Review* 58 (1980): 75–85; Hambrick, "High Profit Strategies," pp. 687–707.

17. J. Guyon, "Can the Savoy Cut Costs and Be the Savoy?" *Wall Street Journal* (October 25, 1994): B1; www.savoy.com, 2007 (accessed January 2007).

18. The development of strategic-group theory has been a strong theme in the strategy literature. Important contributions include R. E. Caves and Michael Porter, "From Entry Barriers to Mobility Barriers," *Quarterly Journal of Economics* (May 1977): 241–262; K. R. Harrigan, "An Application of Clustering for Strategic Group Analysis," *Strategic Management Journal* 6 (1985): 55–73; K. J. Hatten and D. E. Schendel, "Heterogeneity Within an Industry: Company Conduct in the U.S. Brewing Industry, 1952–1971," *Journal of Industrial Economics, (1985)*, 26: 97–113; and Michael E. Porter, "The Structure Within Industries and Companies Performance," *Review of Economics and Statistics* 61 (1979): 214–227.

19. G. Hamel and C. K. Prahalad, *Competing for the Future* (Boston: Harvard Business School Press, 1994).

20. www.samsung.com (accessed 2007).

21. R. Foroohar and J. Lee, "Masters of the Digital Age," *Newsweek* (October 18, 2004): E10–E13.

Chapter 6

1. www.mattel.com. 2006.0 (accessed 2007).

2. "Doll Wars," *Business Life* (May 2005): 40–42.

3. www.mattel.com (accessed 2006).

4. M. Porter, *Competitive Strategy: Techniques for Analyzing Industries and Competitors* (New York: Free Press, 1980), pp. 191–200.

5. S. A. Shane, "Hybrid Organizational Arrangements and Their Implications for Firm Growth and Survival: A Study of New Franchisors," *Academy of Management Journal* 1 (1996): 216–234.

6. Microsoft is often accused of not being an innovator, but the fact is that Gates and Allen wrote the first commercial software program for the first commercially available personal computer. Microsoft was the first mover in their industry. See P. Freiberger and M. Swaine, *Fire in the Valley* (New York: McGraw-Hill, 2000).

7. J. M. Utterback, *Mastering the Dynamics of Innovation* (Boston: Harvard Business School Press, 1994).

8. See Freiberger and Swaine, *Fire in the Valley*.

9. G. A. Moore, *Crossing the Chasm* (New York: HarperCollins, 1991).

10. Utterback, *Mastering the Dynamics of Innovation*.

11. Everett Rogers, *Diffusion of Innovations* (New York: Free Press, 1995).

12. Charles W. Hofer and D. Schendel, *Strategy Formulation: Analytical Concepts* (St. Paul, Minn.: West, 1978).

13. Ibid.

14. Ibid.

15. Ibid.

16. J. Brander and J. Eaton, "Product Line Rivalry," *American Economic Review* 74 (1985): 323–334.

17. Ibid.

18. Porter, *Competitive Strategy*, pp. 76–86.

19. O. Heil and T. S. Robertson, "Towards a Theory of Competitive Market Signaling: A Research Agenda," *Strategic Management Journal* 12 (1991): 403–418.

20. Robert Axelrod, *The Evolution of Cooperation* (New York: Basic Books, 1984).

21. F. Scherer, *Industrial Market Structure and Economic Performance*, 10th ed. (Boston: Houghton Mifflin, 2000), chap. 8.

22. The model differs from Ansoff's model for this reason.

23. H. Igor Ansoff, *Corporate Strategy* (London: Penguin Books, 1984), pp. 97–100.

24. Robert D. Buzzell, Bradley T. Gale, and Ralph G. M. Sultan, "Market Share—A Key to Profitability," *Harvard Business Review* (January–February 1975): 97–103; Robert Jacobson and David A. Aaker, "Is Market Share All That It's Cracked Up to Be?" *Journal of Marketing* 49 (1985): 11–22.

25. Ansoff, *Corporate Strategy*, pp. 98–99.

26. The next section draws heavily on Marvin B. Lieberman, "Strategies for Capacity Expansion," *Sloan Management Review* 8 (1987): 19–27; and Porter, *Competitive Strategy*, pp. 324–338.

27. For a basic introduction to game theory, see A. K. Dixit and B. J. Nalebuff, *Thinking Strategically* (London: W.W. Norton, 1991). See also A. M. Brandenburger and B. J. Nalebuff, "The Right Game: Using Game Theory to Shape Strategy," *Harvard Business Review* (July–August 1995): 59–71; and D. M. Kreps, *Game Theory and Economic Modeling* (Oxford: Oxford University Press, 1990).

28. www.nike.com (accessed 2006).

29. www.nike.com (accessed 2004), press release; "The New Nike," yahoo.com (accessed September 12, 2004).

30. A. Wong, "Nike: Just Don't Do It," *Newsweek* (November 1, 2004): 84.

31. www.nike (accessed 2006).

Chapter 7

1. *The Economist*, "Singin the Blus; Standard Wars" (November 5, 2005): 87; Andrew Park, "HD-DVD vs Blu-ray," *Business Week* (October 30, 2006): 110; B. Dipert, "Subpar Wars: High Resolution Disc Formats Fight Each Other, Consumers Push Back," *EDN* (March 2, 2006): 40–48; B. S. Bulik, "Marketing War Looms for Dueling DVD Formats," *Advertising Age* (April 10, 2006): 20.

2. Data from Bureau of Economic Analysis, *Survey of United States Current Business, 2006*. Available online at http://www.bea.gov/ (accessed November 18, 2006).

3. J. M. Utterback, *Mastering the Dynamics of Innovation* (Boston: Harvard Business School Press, 1994); C. Shapiro and H. R. Varian,

Information Rules: A Strategic Guide to the Network Economy (Boston: Harvard Business School Press, 1999).

4. The layout is not universal, although it is widespread. The French, for example, use a different layout.

5. For details, see Charles W. L. Hill, "Establishing a Standard: Competitive Strategy and Technology Standards in Winner Take All Industries," *Academy of Management Executive* 11 (1997): 7–25; Shapiro and Varian, *Information Rules*; B. Arthur, "Increasing Returns and the New World of Business," *Harvard Business Review* (July–August 1996): 100–109; G. Gowrisankaran and J. Stavins, "Network Externalities and Technology Adoption: Lessons from Electronic Payments," *Rand Journal of Economics* 35 (2004): 260–277; and V. Shankar and B. L. Bayus, "Network Effects and Competition: An Empirical Analysis of the Home Video Game Industry," *Strategic Management Journal* 24 (2003): 375–394. R Casadesus-Masanell and P. Ghemawat, "Dynamic Mixed Duopoly: A Model Motivated by Linux vs Windows," *Management Science*, 52 (2006): 1072–1085.

6. See Shapiro and Varian, *Information Rules*; Hill, "Establishing a Standard"; and M. A. Schilling, "Technological Lockout: An Integrative Model of the Economic and Strategic Factors Driving Technology Success and Failure," *Academy of Management Review* 23:2 (1998): 267–285.

7. Microsoft does not disclose the per-unit licensing fee that it gets from original equipment manufacturers, although media reports speculate it is around $50 a copy.

8. P. M. Romer, "The Origins of Endogenous Growth," *Journal of Economic Perspectives* 8:1 (1994): 3–22.

9. Data from www.btechnews.com (accessed November 18, 2006).

10. Shapiro and Varian, *Information Rules*.

11. International Federation of the Phonographic Industry, *The Commercial Music Industry Global Piracy Report, 2005*, accessed at www.ifpi.org (accessed November 18, 2006).

12. Business Software Alliance, "Third Annual BSA and IDC Global Software Piracy Study," May 2006, www.bsa.org (accessed 2006).

13. Ibid.

14. Charles W. L. Hill, "Digital Piracy: Causes, Consequences and Strategic Responses," *Asian Pacific Journal of Management*, forthcoming 2007.

15. Much of this section is based on Charles W. L. Hill, Michael Heeley, and Jane Sakson, "Strategies for Profiting from Innovation," in *Advances in Global High Technology Management* (Greenwich, Conn.: JAI Press, 1993) 3: 79–95.

16. M. Lieberman and D. Montgomery, "First Mover Advantages," *Strategic Management Journal* 9 (Special Issue, Summer 1988): 41–58.

17. W. Boulding and M. Christen, "Sustainable Pioneering Advantage? Profit Implications of Market Entry Order," *Marketing Science* 22 (2003): 371–386; C. Markides and P. Geroski, "Teaching Elephants to Dance and Other Silly Ideas," *Business Strategy Review* 13 (2003): 49–61.

18. J. Borzo, "Aging Gracefully," *Wall Street Journal* (October 15, 2001): R22.

19. The importance of complementary assets was first noted by D. J. Teece. See D. J. Teece, "Profiting from Technological Innovation," in D. J. Teece (ed.), *The Competitive Challenge* (New York: Harper & Row, 1986), pp. 26–54.

20. M. J. Chen and D. C. Hambrick, "Speed, Stealth, and Selective Attack: How Small Firms Differ from Large Firms in Competitive Behavior," *Academy of Management Journal* 38 (1995): 453–482.

21. E. Mansfield, M. Schwartz, and S. Wagner, "Imitation Costs and Patents: An Empirical Study," *Economic Journal* 91 (1981): 907–918.

22. E. Mansfield, "How Rapidly Does New Industrial Technology Leak Out?" *Journal of Industrial Economics* 34 (1985): 217–223.

23. This argument has been made in the game theory literature. See R. Caves, H. Cookell, and P. J. Killing, "The Imperfect Market for Technology Licenses," *Oxford Bulletin of Economics and Statistics* 45 (1983): 249–267; N. T. Gallini, "Deterrence by Market Sharing: A Strategic Incentive for Licensing," *American Economic Review* 74 (1984): 931–941; and C. Shapiro, "Patent Licensing and R&D Rivalry," *American Economic Review* 75 (1985): 25–30.

24. M. Christensen, *The Innovator's Dilemma* (Boston: Harvard Business School Press, 1997); R. N. Foster, *Innovation: The Attacker's Advantage* (New York: Summit Books, 1986).

25. Foster, *Innovation*.

26. Ray Kurzweil, *The Age of the Spiritual Machines* (New York: Penguin Books, 1999).

27. See Christensen, *The Innovator's Dilemma*; and C. M. Christensen and M. Overdorf, "Meeting the Challenge of Disruptive Change," *Harvard Business Review* (March–April 2000): 66–77.

28. Charles W. L. Hill and Frank T. Rothaermel, "The Performance of Incumbent Firms in the Face of Radical Technological Innovation," *Academy of Management Review* 28 (2003): 257–274; F. T. Rothaermel and Charles W. L. Hill, "Technological Discontinuities and Complementary Assets: A Longitudinal Study of Industry and Firm Performance," *Organization Science* 16(1), (2005): 52–70.

29. *Sources*: Gary Rivlin, "Wallflower at the Web Party," *New York Times*, Business Section (October 15, 2006): 1, 9; V. Vara, "Friendster Patent on Linking Web Friends Could Hurt Rivals," *Wall Street Journal* (July 27, 2006): B1; V. Vara and R. Buckman, "Friendster Gets $10 Million Infusion for Revival Bid," *Wall Street Journal* (August 21, 2006): C4.

Chapter 8

1. *Sources*: M. Gunther, "MTV's Passage to India," *Fortune* (August 9, 2004): 117–122; B. Pulley and A. Tanzer, "Sumner's Gemstone," *Forbes* (February 21, 2000): 107–11; K. Hoffman, "Youth TV's Old Hand Prepares for the Digital Challenge," *Financial Times* (February 18, 2000): 8; presentation by Sumner M. Redstone, chair and CEO, Viacom Inc., delivered to Salomon Smith Barney 11th Annual Global Entertainment Media, Telecommunications Conference, Scottsdale, AZ, January 8, 2001, archived at www.viacom.com (accessed November 30, 2006); and Viacom 10K Statement, 2005.

2. K. Santana, "MTV Goes to Asia," Global Policy Forum, August 12, 2003, available at www.globalpolicy.org (accessed November 30, 2006).

3. World Trade Organization, *International Trade Trends and Statistics, 2005* (Geneva: WTO, 2006), and WTO press release, "World Trade for 2005: Prospects for 2006," April 11, 2006, available at www.wto.org (accessed 2006).

4. World Trade Organization, *International Trade Statistics, 2005* (Geneva: WTO, 2005), and United Nations, *World Investment Report, 2005*.

5. P. Dicken, *Global Shift* (New York: Guilford Press, 1992).

6. D. Pritchard, "Are Federal Tax Laws and State Subsidies for Boeing 7E7 Selling America Short?" *Aviation Week* (April 12, 2004): 74–75.

7. T. Levitt, "The Globalization of Markets," *Harvard Business Review* (May–June 1983): 92–102.

8. M. E. Porter, *The Competitive Advantage of Nations* (New York: Free Press, 1990). See also R. Grant, "Porter's Competitive Advantage of Nations: An Assessment," *Strategic Management Journal* 7 (1991): 535–548.

9. Porter, *Competitive Advantage of Nations*.

10. Example is disguised; it comes from interviews by Charles Hill.

11. See J. Birkinshaw and N. Hood, "Multinational Subsidiary Evolution: Capability and Charter Change in Foreign Owned Subsidiary Companies," *Academy of Management Review* 23 (October 1998): 773–795; A. K. Gupta and V. J. Govindarajan, "Knowledge Flows Within Multinational Corporations," *Strategic Management Journal* 21 (2000): 473–496; V. J. Govindarajan and A. K. Gupta, *The Quest for Global Dominance* (San Francisco: Jossey-Bass, 2001); T. S. Frost, J. M. Birkinshaw, and P. C. Ensign, "Centers of Excellence in Multinational Corporations," *Strategic Management Journal* 23 (2002): 997–1018; and U. Andersson, M. Forsgren, and U. Holm, "The Strategic Impact of External Networks," *Strategic Management Journal* 23 (2002): 979–996.

12. S. Leung, "Armchairs, TVs and Espresso: Is It McDonald's?" *Wall Street Journal* (August 30, 2002): A1, A6.

13. C. K. Prahalad and Yves L. Doz, *The Multinational Mission: Balancing Local Demands and Global Vision* (New York: Free Press, 1987). See also J. Birkinshaw, A. Morrison, and J. Hulland, "Structural and Competitive Determinants of a Global Integration Strategy," *Strategic Management Journal* 16 (1995): 637–655.

14. J. E. Garten, "Wal-Mart Gives Globalization a Bad Name," *Business Week* (March 8, 2004): 24.

15. Prahalad and Doz, *Multinational Mission*. Prahalad and Doz actually talk about local responsiveness rather than local customization.

16. Levitt, "Globalization of Markets."

17. C. A. Bartlett and S. Ghoshal, *Managing Across Borders* (Boston: Harvard Business School Press, 1989).

18. W. W. Lewis; *The Power of Productivity* (Chicago, University of Chicago Press, 2004).

19. C. J. Chipello, "Local Presence Is Key to European Deals," *Wall Street Journal* (June 30, 1998): A15.

20. Bartlett and Ghoshal, *Managing Across Borders*.

21. Ibid.

22. T. Hout, M. E. Porter, and E. Rudden, "How Global Companies Win Out," *Harvard Business Review* (September–October 1982): 98–108.

23. See Charles W. L. Hill, *International Business: Competing in the Global Marketplace* (New York: McGraw-Hill, 2000).

24. This can be reconceptualized as the resource base of the entrant, relative to indigenous competitors. For work that focuses on this issue, see W. C. Bogenr, H. Thomas, and J. McGee, "A Longitudinal Study of the Competitive Positions and Entry Paths of European Firms in the U.S. Pharmaceutical Market," *Strategic Management Journal* 17 (1996): 85–107; D. Collis, "A Resource Based Analysis of Global Competition," *Strategic Management Journal* 12 (1991): 49–68; and S. Tallman, "Strategic Management Models and Resource Based Strategies Among MNEs in a Host Market," *Strategic Management Journal* 12 (1991): 69–82.

25. For a discussion of first-mover advantages, see M. Liberman and D. Montgomery, "First Mover Advantages," *Strategic Management Journal* 9 (Special Issue, Summer 1988): 41–58.

26. J. M. Shaver, W. Mitchell, and B. Yeung, "The Effect of Own Company and Other Company Experience on Foreign Direct Investment Survival in the U.S., 1987–92," *Strategic Management Journal* 18 (1997): 811–824.

27. S. Zaheer and E. Mosakowski, "The Dynamics of the Liability of Foreignness: A Global Study of Survival in the Financial Services Industry," *Strategic Management Journal* 18 (1997): 439–464.

28. Shaver, Mitchell, and Yeung, "The Effect of Own Company and Other Company Experience."

29. P. Ghemawat, *Commitment: The Dynamics of Strategy* (New York: Free Press, 1991).

30. This section draws on numerous studies, including: C. W. L. Hill, P. Hwang, and W. C. Kim, "An Eclectic Theory of the Choice of International Entry Mode," *Strategic Management Journal* 11 (1990): 117–28; C. W. L. Hill and W. C. Kim, "Searching for a Dynamic Theory of the Multinational Enterprise: A Transaction Cost Model," *Strategic Management Journal* 9 (Special Issue on Strategy Content, 1988): pp. 93–104; E. Anderson and H. Gatignon, "Modes of Foreign Entry: A Transaction Cost Analysis and Propositions," *Journal of International Business Studies* 17 (1986): 1–26; F. R. Root, *Entry Strategies for International Markets* (Lexington, MA: D. C. Heath, 1980); A. Madhok, "Cost, Value and Foreign Market Entry: The Transaction and the Firm," *Strategic Management Journal* 18 (1997): 39–61; K. D. Brouthers and L. B. Brouthers, "Acquisition or Greenfield Start-Up?" *Strategic Management Journal* 21:1 (2000): 89–97; X. Martin and R. Salmon, "Knowledge Transfer Capacity and Its Implications for the Theory of the Multinational Enterprise," *Journal of International Business Studies* (July 2003): 356; and A. Verbeke, "The Evolutionary View of the MNE and the Future of Internalization Theory," *Journal of International Business Studies* (November 2003): 498–515.

31. F. J. Contractor, "The Role of Licensing in International Strategy," *Columbia Journal of World Business* (Winter 1982): 73–83.

32. O. E. Williamson, *The Economic Institutions of Capitalism* (New York: Free Press, 1985).

33. Andrew E. Serwer, "McDonald's Conquers the World," *Fortune* (October 17, 1994): 103–116.

34. For an excellent review of the basic theoretical literature of joint ventures, see B. Kogut, "Joint Ventures: Theoretical and Empirical Perspectives," *Strategic Management Journal* 9 (1988): 319–332. More recent studies include: T. Chi, "Option to Acquire or Divest a Joint Venture," *Strategic Management Journal* 21:6 (2000): 665–688; H. Merchant and D. Schendel, "How Do International Joint Ventures Create Shareholder Value?" *Strategic Management Journal* 21:7 (2000): 723–737; H. K. Steensma and M. A. Lyles, "Explaining IJV Survival in a Transitional Economy Through Social Exchange and Knowledge Based Perspectives," *Strategic Management Journal* 21:8 (2000): 831–851; and J. F. Hennart and M. Zeng, "Cross Cultural Differences and Joint Venture Longevity," *Journal of International Business Studies* (December 2002): 699–717.

35. J. A. Robins, S. Tallman, and K. Fladmoe-Lindquist, "Autonomy and Dependence of International Cooperative Ventures," *Strategic Management Journal* (October 2002): 881–902.

36. C. W. L. Hill, "Strategies for Exploiting Technological Innovations," *Organization Science* 3 (1992): 428–441.

37. See K. Ohmae, "The Global Logic of Strategic Alliances," *Harvard Business Review* (March–April 1989): 143–154; G. Hamel, Y. L. Doz, and C. K. Prahalad, "Collaborate with Your Competitors and Win!" *Harvard Business Review* (January–February 1989): 133–139; W. Burgers, C. W. L. Hill, and W. C. Kim, "Alliances in the Global Auto Industry," *Strategic Management Journal* 14 (1993): 419–432; and P. Kale, H. Singh, and H. Perlmutter, "Learning and Protection of Proprietary Assets in Strategic Alliances: Building Relational Capital," *Strategic Management Journal* 21 (2000): 217–237.

38. L. T. Chang, "China Eases Foreign Film Rules," *Wall Street Journal* (October 15, 2004): B2.

39. B. L. Simonin, "Transfer of Marketing Knowhow in International Strategic Alliances," *Journal of International Business Studies* (1999): 463–491: and J. W. Spencer, "Firms' Knowledge Sharing

Strategies in the Global Innovation System," *Strategic Management Journal* 24 (2003): 217–233.

40. C. Souza, "Microsoft Teams with MIPS, Toshiba," *EBN* (February 10, 2003): 4.

41. M. Frankel, "Now Sony Is Giving Palm a Hand," *BusinessWeek* (November 29, 2000): 50.

42. Kale, Singh, and Perlmutter, "Learning and Protection of Proprietary Assets."

43. R. B. Reich and E. D. Mankin, "Joint Ventures with Japan Give Away Our Future," *Harvard Business Review* (March–April 1986): 78–90.

44. J. Bleeke and D. Ernst, "The Way to Win in Cross-Border Alliances," *Harvard Business Review* (November–December 1991): 127–135.

45. E. Booker and C. Krol, "IBM Finds Strength in Alliances," *B to B* (February 10, 2003): 3, 27.

46. W. Roehl and J. F. Truitt, "Stormy Open Marriages Are Better," *Columbia Journal of World Business* (Summer 1987): 87–95.

47. See T. Khanna, R. Gulati, and N. Nohria, "The Dynamics of Learning Alliances: Competition, Cooperation, and Relative Scope," *Strategic Management Journal* 19 (1998): 193–210: P. Kale, H. Singh, H. Perlmutter, "Learning and Protection of Proprietary Assets in Strategic Alliances: Building Relational Capital," *Strategic Management Journal* 21 (2000): 217–237.

48. Kale, Singh, and Perlmutter, "Learning and Protection of Proprietary Assets."

49. Hamel, Doz, and Prahalad, "Collaborate with Competitors"; Khanna, Gulati, and Nohria, "The Dynamics of Learning Alliances: Competition, Cooperation, and Relative Scope"; and E. W. K. Tang, "Acquiring Knowledge by Foreign Partners from International Joint Ventures in a Transition Economy: Learning by Doing and Learning Myopia," *Strategic Management Journal* 23 (2002): 835–854.

50. Hamel, Doz, and Prahalad, "Collaborate with Competitors."

51. B. Wysocki, "Cross Border Alliances Become Favorite Way to Crack New Markets," *Wall Street Journal* (March 4, 1990): A1.

52. *Sources*: J. Neff, "P&G Outpacing Unilever in Five-Year Battle," *Advertising Age* (November 3, 2003): 1–3; G. Strauss, "Firm Restructuring into Truly Global Company," *USA Today* (September 10, 1999): B2; Procter & Gamble 10K Report, 2006; M. Kolbasuk McGee, "P&G Jump-Starts Corporate Change," *Information Week* (November 1, 1999): 30–34; J. Birchall, "P&G's Strong Sales Growth Beats Forecasts," *Financial Times* (August 3, 2006): 22.

Chapter 9

1. www.sap.com (2006).

2. www.oracle.com (2006).

3. United Nations, *World Investment Report 2001* (New York: United Nations, November 2001).

4. Y .J. Dreazen, G. Ip, and N. Kulish, "Why the Sudden Rise in the Urge to Merge and Create Oligopolies?" *Wall Street Journal*, February 25, 2002, p. A1.

5. For evidence on acquisitions and performance, see R. E. Caves, "Mergers, Takeovers, and Economic Efficiency," *International Journal of Industrial Organization* 7 (1989): 151–174; M. C. Jensen and R. S. Ruback, "The Market for Corporate Control: The Scientific Evidence," *Journal of Financial Economics* 11 (1983): 5–50; R. Roll, "Empirical Evidence on Takeover Activity and Shareholder Wealth," in J. C. Coffee, L. Lowenstein, and S. Rose (eds.), *Knights, Raiders and Targets* (Oxford: Oxford University Press, 1989); A. Schleifer and R. W. Vishny, "Takeovers in the 60s and 80s: Evidence

and Implications," *Strategic Management Journal* 12 (Special Issue, Winter 1991): 51–60; and T. H. Brush, "Predicted Changes in Operational Synergy and Post Acquisition Performance of Acquired Businesses," *Strategic Management Journal* 17 (1996): 1–24.

6. "Few Takeovers Pay Off for Big Buyers," *Investors Business Daily* (May 25, 2001): 1.

7. K. R. Harrian, "Formulating Vertical Integration Strategies," *Academy of Management Review* 9 (1984): 638–652.

8. This is the essence of Chandler's argument. See Alfred D. Chandler, *Strategy and Structure* (Cambridge, Mass.: MIT Press, 1962). The same argument is also made by Jeffrey Pfeffer and Gerald R. Salancik, *The External Control of Organizations* (New York: Harper & Row, 1978). See also K. R. Harrigan, *Strategic Flexibility* (Lexington, Mass.: Lexington Books, 1985); K. R. Harrigan, "Vertical Integration and Corporate Strategy," *Academy of Management Journal* 28 (1985): 397–425; and F. M. Scherer, *Industrial Market Structure and Economic Performance* (Chicago: Rand McNally, 1981).

9. Oliver E. Williamson, *The Economic Institutions of Capitalism.* (New York: The Free Press, 1985). For recent empirical work that uses this framework, see L. Poppo and T. Zenger, "Testing Alternative Theories of the Firm: Transaction Cost, Knowledge Based, and Measurement Explanations for Make or Buy Decisions in Information Services," *Strategic Management Journal* 19 (1998): 853–878.

10. Williamson, *Economic Institutions of Capitalism.*

11. A. D. Chandler, *The Visible Hand* (Cambridge, Mass.: Harvard University Press, 1977).

12. Julia Pitta, "Score One for Vertical Integration," *Forbes* (January 18, 1993): 88–89.

13. Joseph White and Neal Templin, "Harsh Regimen: A Swollen GM Finds It Hard to Stick with Its Crash Diet," *Wall Street Journal* (September 9, 1992): A1.

14. Harrigan, *Strategic Flexibility*, pp. 67–87. See also Allan Afuah, "Dynamic Boundaries of the Firm: Are Firms Better Off Being Vertically Integrated in the Face of a Technological Change?" *Academy of Management Journal* 44 (2001): 1121–1228.

15. Kevin Kelly, Zachary Schiller, and James Treece, "Cut Costs or Else," *Business Week* (March 22, 1993): 28–29.

16. X. Martin, W. Mitchell, and A. Swaminathan, "Recreating and Extending Japanese Automobile Buyer-Supplier Links in North America," *Strategic Management Journal* 16 (1995): 589–619; C. W. L. Hill, "National Institutional Structures, Transaction Cost Economizing, and Competitive Advantage," *Organization Science* 6 (1995): 119–131.

17. *Standard & Poor's Industry Survey, Autos—Auto Parts*, June 24, 1993.

18. See James Womack, Daniel Jones, and Daniel Roos, *The Machine That Changed the World* (New York: Rawson Associates, 1990); and James Richardson, "Parallel Sourcing and Supplier Performance in the Japanese Automobile Industry," *Strategic Management Journal* 14 (1993): 339–350.

19. R. Mudambi and S. Helper, "The Close but Adversarial Model of Supplier Relations in the U.S. Auto Industry," *Strategic Management Journal* 19 (1998): 775–792.

20. Williamson, *Economic Institutions of Capitalism.* See also J. H. Dyer, "Effective Inter-Firm Collaboration: How Firms Minimize Transaction Costs and Maximize Transaction Value," *Strategic Management Journal* 18 (1997): 535–556.

21. Richardson, "Parallel Sourcing and Supplier Performance in the Japanese Automobile Industry."

22. W. H. Davidow and M. S. Malone, *The Virtual Corporation* (New York: Harper & Row, 1992).

23. A. M. Porter, "Outsourcing Gains Popularity," *Purchasing* (March 11, 1999): 22–24.

24. D. Garr, "Inside Outsourcing," *Fortune* 142:1 (2001): 85–92.

25. J. Krane, "American Express Hires IBM for $4 billion," *Columbian* (February 26, 2002): E2; www.ibm.com (2006).

26. www.ibm.com (2006).

27. Davidow and Malone, *The Virtual Corporation*.

28. Davidow and Malone, *The Virtual Corporation*; H. W. Chesbrough and D. J. Teece, "When Is Virtual Virtuous? Organizing for Innovation," *Harvard Business Review* (January–February 1996): 65–74; J. B. Quinn, "Strategic Outsourcing: Leveraging Knowledge Capabilities," *Sloan Management Review* (Summer 1999): 9–21.

Chapter 10

1. J. R. Laing, "Tyco's Titan," *Barron's* (April 12, 1999): 27–32; M. Maremont, "How Is Tyco Accounting for Cash Flow?"; *Wall Street Journal* (March 5, 2002): C1; J. R. Laing, "Doubting Tyco," *Barron's* (January 28, 2002): 19–20.

2. "Tyco Shares Up on Report Mulling Breakup," www.yahoo.com (accessed January 9, 2006).

3. www.tyco.com (2006), press release.

4. G. Hamel and C. K. Prahalad, *Competing for the Future* (Boston: Harvard Business School Press, 1994).

5. Ibid.

6. D. Leonard Barton and G. Pisano, "Monsanto's March into Biotechnology," Harvard Business School Case #690-009 (1990). See Monsanto's homepage for details about its genetically engineered seed products at http://www.monsanto.com.

7. This resource-based view of diversification can be traced to Edith Penrose's seminal book, *The Theory of the Growth of the Firm* (Oxford: Oxford University Press, 1959).

8. D. J. Teece, "Economies of Scope and the Scope of the Enterprise," *Journal of Economic Behavior and Organization* 3 (1980): 223–247. For recent empirical work on this topic, see C. H. St. John and J. S. Harrison, "Manufacturing Based Relatedness, Synergy and Coordination," *Strategic Management Journal* 20 (1999): 129–145.

9. Teece, "Economies of Scope." For recent empirical work on this topic, see St. John and Harrison, "Manufacturing Based Relatedness, Synergy and Coordination."

10. For a detailed discussion, see C. W. L. Hill and R. E. Hoskisson, "Strategy and Structure in the Multiproduct Firm," *Academy of Management Review* 12 (1987): 331–341.

11. See, for example, G. R. Jones and C. W. L. Hill, "A Transaction Cost Analysis of Strategy Structure Choice," *Strategic Management Journal* (1988): 159–172; and Oliver E. Williamson, *Markets and Hierarchies: Analysis and Antitrust Implications* (New York: Free Press, 1975), pp. 132–175.

12. R. Buderi, *Engines of Tomorrow* (New York: Simon & Schuster, 2000).

13. C. W. L. Hill, "The Role of Headquarters in the Multidivisional Firm," in R. Rumelt, D. J. Teece, and D. Schendel (eds.), *Fundamental Issues in Strategy Research* (Cambridge, Mass.: Harvard Business School Press, 1994), pp. 297–321.

14. See, for example, Jones and Hill, "A Transaction Cost Analysis"; Williamson, *Markets and Hierarchies*; and Hill, "The Role of Headquarters in the Multidivisional Firm."

15. The distinction goes back to R. P. Rumelt, *Strategy, Structure and Economic Performance* (Cambridge, Mass.: Harvard Business School Press, 1974).

16. For evidence, see C. W. L. Hill, "Conglomerate Performance over the Economic Cycle," *Journal of Industrial Economics* 32 (1983): 197–212; and D. T. C. Mueller, "The Effects of Conglomerate Mergers," *Journal of Banking and Finance* 1 (1977): 315–347.

17. For reviews of the evidence, see V. Ramanujam and P. Varadarajan, "Research on Corporate Diversification: A Synthesis," *Strategic Management Journal* 10 (1989): 523–551; G. Dess, J. F. Hennart, C. W. L. Hill, and A. Gupta, "Research Issues in Strategic Management," *Journal of Management* 21 (1995): 357–392; and David C. Hyland and J. David Diltz, "Why Companies Diversify: An Empirical Examination," *Financial Management* 31 (Spring 2002): 51–81.

18. M. E. Porter, "From Competitive Advantage to Corporate Strategy," *Harvard Business Review* (May–June 1987): 43–59.

19. For reviews of the evidence, see Ramanujam and Varadarajan, "Research on Corporate Diversification"; Dess, Hennart, Hill, and Gupta, "Research Issues in Strategic Management"; and Hyland and Diltz, "Why Companies Diversify."

20. C. R. Christensen et al., *Business Policy Text and Cases* (Homewood, Ill.: Irwin, 1987), p. 778.

21. See Booz, Allen, and Hamilton, "New Products Management for the 1980's" (privately published, 1982); A. L. Page, "PDMA's New Product Development Practices Survey: Performance and Best Practices" (presented at the PDMA Fifteenth Annual International Conference, Boston, October 16, 1991); and E. Mansfield, "How Economists See R&D," *Harvard Business Review* (November–December 1981): 98–106.

22. See R. Biggadike, "The Risky Business of Diversification," *Harvard Business Review* (May–June 1979): 103–111; R. A. Burgelman, "A Process Model of Internal Corporate Venturing in the Diversified Major Firm," *Administrative Science Quarterly* 28 (1983): 223–244; and Z. Block and I. C. MacMillan, *Corporate Venturing* (Boston: Harvard Business School Press, 1993).

23. Biggadike, "The Risky Business of Diversification"; Block and Macmillan, *Corporate Venturing*.

24. Buderi, *Engines of Tomorrow*.

25. I. C. MacMillan and R. George, "Corporate Venturing: Challenges for Senior Managers," *Journal of Business Strategy* 5 (1985): 34–43.

26. See R. A. Burgelman, M. M. Maidique, and S. C. Wheelwright, *Strategic Management of Technology and Innovation* (Chicago: Irwin, 1996), pp. 493–507. Also see Buderi, *Engines of Tomorrow*.

27. Buderi, *Engines of Tomorrow*.

28. Buderi, *Engines of Tomorrow*.

29. For evidence on acquisitions and performance, see R. E. Caves, "Mergers, Takeovers, and Economic Efficiency," *International Journal of Industrial Organization* 7 (1989): 151–174; M. C. Jensen and R. S. Ruback, "The Market for Corporate Control: The Scientific Evidence," *Journal of Financial Economics* 11 (1983): 5–50; R. Roll, "Empirical Evidence on Takeover Activity and Shareholder Wealth," in J. C. Coffee, L. Lowenstein, and S. Rose (eds.), *Knights, Raiders and Targets* (Oxford: Oxford University Press, 1989); A. Schleifer and R. W. Vishny, "Takeovers in the 60s and 80s: Evidence and Implications," *Strategic Management Journal* 12 (Special Issue, Winter 1991): 51–60; T. H. Brush, "Predicted Changes in Operational Synergy and Post Acquisition Performance of Acquired Businesses," *Strategic Management Journal* 17 (1996): 1–24; and T. Loughran and A. M. Vijh, "Do Long Term Shareholders Benefit from Corporate Acquisitions?" *Journal of Finance* 5 (1997): 1765–1787.

30. For evidence on acquisitions and performance, see R. E. Caves, "Mergers, Takeovers, and Economic Efficiency," *International Journal of Industrial Organization* 7 (1989): 151–174; M. C. Jensen and R. S. Ruback, "The Market for Corporate Control: The Scientific Evidence," *Journal of Financial Economics* 11 (1983): 5–50; R. Roll, "Empirical Evidence on Takeover Activity

and Shareholder Wealth," in J. C. Coffee, L. Lowenstein, and S. Rose (eds.), *Knights, Raiders and Targets* (Oxford: Oxford University Press, 1989); A. Schleifer and R. W. Vishny, "Takeovers in the 60s and 80s: Evidence and Implications," *Strategic Management Journal* 12 (Special Issue, Winter 1991): 51–60; T. H. Brush, "Predicted Changes in Operational Synergy and Post Acquisition Performance of Acquired Businesses," *Strategic Management Journal* 17 (1996): 1–24; and T. Loughran and A. M. Vijh, "Do Long Term Shareholders Benefit from Corporate Acquisitions?" *Journal of Finance* 5 (1997): 1765–1787.

31. D. J. Ravenscraft and F. M. Scherer, *Mergers, Sell-offs, and Economic Efficiency* (Washington, D.C.: Brookings Institution, 1987).

32. See J. P. Walsh, "Top Management Turnover Following Mergers and Acquisitions," *Strategic Management Journal* 9 (1988): 173–183.

33. See A. A. Cannella and D. C. Hambrick, "Executive Departure and Acquisition Performance," *Strategic Management Journal* 14 (1993): 137–152.

34. R. Roll, "The Hubris Hypothesis of Corporate Takeovers," *Journal of Business* 59 (1986): 197–216.

35. "Coca-Cola: A Sobering Lesson from Its Journey into Wine," *Business Week* (June 3, 1985): 96–98.

36. P. Haspeslagh and D. Jemison, *Managing Acquisitions* (New York: Free Press, 1991).

37. For views on this issue, see L. L. Fray, D. H. Gaylin, and J. W. Down, "Successful Acquisition Planning," *Journal of Business Strategy* 5 (1984): 46–55; C. W. L. Hill, "Profile of a Conglomerate Takeover: BTR and Thomas Tilling," *Journal of General Management* 10 (1984): 34–50; D. R. Willensky, "Making It Happen: How to Execute an Acquisition," *Business Horizons* (March–April 1985): 38–45; Haspeslagh and Jemison, *Managing Acquisitions;* and P. L. Anslinger and T. E. Copeland, "Growth Through Acquisition: A Fresh Look," *Harvard Business Review* (January–February 1996): 126–135.

38. M. L. A. Hayward, "When Do Firms Learn from Their Acquisition Experience? Evidence from 1990–1995," *Strategic Management Journal* 23 (2002): 21–39; K. G. Ahuja, "Technological Acquisitions and the Innovation Performance of Acquiring Firms: A Longitudinal Study," *Strategic Management Journal* 23 (2001): 197–220; H. G. Barkema and F. Vermeulen, "International Expansion Through Startup or Acquisition," *Academy of Management Journal* 41 (1998): 7–26.

39. Hayward, "When Do Firms Learn from Their Acquisition Experience?"

40. For a review of the evidence and some contrary empirical evidence, see D. E. Hatfield, J. P. Liebskind, and T. C. Opler, "The Effects of Corporate Restructuring on Aggregate Industry Specialization," *Strategic Management Journal* 17 (1996): 55–72.

41. A. Lamont and C. Polk, "The Diversification Discount: Cash Flows Versus Returns," *Journal of Finance* 56 (October 2001): 1693–1721; R. Raju, H. Servaes, and L. Zingales, "The Cost of Diversity: The Diversification Discount and Inefficient Investment," *Journal of Finance* 55 (February 2000): 35–80.

42. For example, see Schleifer and Vishny, "Takeovers in the 60s and 80s."

Chapter 11

1. *Sources:* "Money Well Spent: Corporate Parties," *Economist* (November 1, 2003): 79; "Tyco Pair Sentencing Expected on September 19th," *Wall Street Journal* (August 2, 2005): 1: "Off to Jail: Corporate Crime in America," *Economist,* (June 25, 2005): 81; N. Varchaver, "What's Ed Breen Thinking?" *Fortune* (March 20, 2006): 135–139.

2. E. Freeman, *Strategic Management: A Stakeholder Approach* (Boston: Pitman Press, 1984).

3. C. W. L. Hill and T. M. Jones, "Stakeholder-Agency Theory," *Journal of Management Studies* 29 (1992): 131–154; J. G. March and H. A. Simon, *Organizations* (New York: Wiley, 1958).

4. Hill and Jones, "Stakeholder-Agency Theory"; C. Eesley and M. J. Lenox, "Firm Responses to Secondary Stakeholder Action," *Strategic Management Journal* 27 (2006): 13–24.

5. I. C. Macmillan and P. E. Jones, *Strategy Formulation: Power and Politics* (St. Paul, Minn.: West, 1986).

6. Tom Copeland, Tim Koller, and Jack Murrin, *Valuation: Measuring and Managing the Value of Companies* (New York: Wiley, 1996).

7. R. S. Kaplan and D. P. Norton, *Strategy Maps* (Boston: Harvard Business School Press, 2004).

8. A. L. Velocci, D. A. Fulghum, and R. Wall, "Damage Control," *Aviation Week* (December 1, 2003): 26–27.

9. M. C. Jensen and W. H. Meckling, "Theory of the Firm: Managerial Behavior, Agency Costs and Ownership Structure," *Journal of Financial Economics* 3 (1976): 305–360; E. F. Fama, "Agency Problems and the Theory of the Firm," *Journal of Political Economy* 88 (1980): 375–390.

10. Hill and Jones, "Stakeholder-Agency Theory."

11. For example, see R. Marris, *The Economic Theory of Managerial Capitalism* (London: Macmillan, 1964); and J. K. Galbraith, *The New Industrial State* (Boston: Houghton Mifflin, 1970).

12. Fama, "Agency Problems and the Theory of the Firm."

13. A. Rappaport, "New Thinking on How to Link Executive Pay with Performance," *Harvard Business Review* (March–April 1999): 91–105.

14. R. Kirkland, "The Real CEO Pay Problem," *Fortune* (July 10, 2006): 78–82.

15. D Henry and D. Stead, "Worker vs CEO: Room to Run," *Business Week* (October 30, 2006): 13.

16. For academic studies that look at the determinants of CEO pay, see M. C. Jensen and K. J. Murphy, "Performance Pay and Top Management Incentives," *Journal of Political Economy* 98 (1990): 225–264; Charles W. L. Hill and Phillip Phan, "CEO Tenure as a Determinant of CEO Pay," *Academy of Management Journal* 34 (1991): 707–717; H. L. Tosi and L. R. Gomez-Mejia, "CEO Compensation Monitoring and Firm Performance," *Academy of Management Journal* 37 (1994): 1002–1016; and Joseph F. Porac, James B. Wade, and Timothy G. Pollock, "Industry Categories and the Politics of the Comparable Firm in CEO Compensation," *Administrative Science Quarterly* 44 (1999): 112–144.

17. Andrew Ward, "Home Depot Investors Stage a Revolt," *Financial Times* (May 26, 2006): 20.

18. R. Kirklad, "The Real CEO Pay Problem," *Fortune* (July 10, 2006): 78–82.

19. For research on this issue, see Peter J. Lane, A. A. Cannella, and M. H. Lubatkin, "Agency Problems as Antecedents to Unrelated Mergers and Diversification: Amihud and Lev Reconsidered," *Strategic Management Journal* 19 (1998): 555–578.

20. E. T. Penrose, *The Theory of the Growth of the Firm* (London: Macmillan, 1958).

21. G. Edmondson and L. Cohn, "How Parmalat Went Sour," *Business Week* (January 12, 2004): 46–50; "Another Enron? Royal Dutch Shell," *Economist* (March 13, 2004): 71.

22. O. E. Williamson, *The Economic Institutions of Capitalism* (New York: Free Press, 1985).

23. Fama, "Agency Problems and the Theory of the Firm."

24. S. Finkelstein and R. D'Aveni, "CEO Duality as a Double Edged Sword," *Academy of Management Journal* 37 (1994): 1079–1108;

B. Ram Baliga and R. C. Moyer, "CEO Duality and Firm Performance," *Strategic Management Journal* 17 (1996): 41–53; M. L. Mace, *Directors: Myth and Reality* (Cambridge, Mass.: Harvard University Press, 1971); S. C. Vance, *Corporate Leadership: Boards of Directors and Strategy* (New York: McGraw-Hill, 1983).

25. W. G. Lewellen, C. Eoderer, and A. Rosenfeld, "Merger Decisions and Executive Stock Ownership in Acquiring Firms," *Journal of Accounting and Economics* 7 (1985): 209–231.

26. C. W. L. Hill and S. A. Snell, "External Control, Corporate Strategy, and Firm Performance," *Strategic Management Journal* 9 (1988): 577–590.

27. The phenomenon of back dating stock options was uncovered by academic research and then picked up by the SEC. See Erik Lie, "On the Timing of CEO Stock Option Awards," *Management Science* 51 (2005): 802–812.

28. G. Colvin, "A Study in CEO Greed," *Fortune* (June 12, 2006): 53–55.

29. J. P. Walsh and R. D. Kosnik, "Corporate Raiders and Their Disciplinary Role in the Market for Corporate Control," *Academy of Management Journal* 36 (1993): 671–700.

30. R. S. Kaplan and D. P. Norton, "The Balanced Scorecard—Measures That Drive Performance," *Harvard Business Review* (January–February 1992): 71–79; R. S. Kaplan and D. P. Norton, *Strategy Maps* (Boston: Harvard Business School Press, 2004).

31. R. S. Kaplan and D. P. Norton, "Using the Balanced Scorecard as a Strategic Management System," *Harvard Business Review* (January–February 1996): 75–85; Kaplan and Norton, *Strategy Maps.*

32. R. S. Kaplan and D. P. Norton, "Putting the Balanced Scorecard to Work," *Harvard Business Review* (September–October 1993): 134–147; Kaplan and Norton, *Strategy Maps.*

33. Kaplan and Norton, "The Balanced Scorecard," p. 72.

34. Timet, "Boeing Settle Lawsuit," *Metal Center News* 41 (June 2001): 38–39.

35. Joseph Kahn. "Ruse in Toyland: Chinese Workers' Hidden Woe," *New York Times* (December 7, 2003): A1, A8.

36. See N. King, "Halliburton Tells the Pentagon Workers Took Iraq Deal Kickbacks," *Wall Street Journal* (January 23, 2004): A1; "Whistleblowers Say Company Routinely Overcharged," Reuters, February 12, 2004; R. Gold and J. R. Wilke; "Data Sought in Halliburton Inquiry," *Wall Street Journal* (February 5, 2004): A6.

37. Saul W. Gellerman, "Why Good Managers Make Bad Ethical Choices," *Ethics in Practice: Managing the Moral Corporation,* ed. Kenneth R. Andrews (Cambridge, Mass.: Harvard Business School Press, 1989).

38. Ibid.

39. See Tom L. Beauchamp and Norman E. Bowie, *Ethical Theory and Business,* 7th ed. (New York: Pearson, Prentice Hall, 2001), 17–23.

40. Thomas Donaldson, *The Ethics of International Business* (Oxford: Oxford University Press, 1989).

41. John Rawles, *A Theory of Justice,* rev. ed. (Cambridge, Mass.: Belknap Press, 1999, original edition 1971).

42. Can be found on Unilever's website at http://www.unilever.com/company/ourprinciples/ (accessed 2006).

43. From United Technologies website www.utc.com (accessed December 15, 2006).

44. *Sources:* S. Holt, "Wal-Mart Workers Suit Wins Class Action Status," *Seattle Times* (October 9, 2004): E1, E4; C. Daniels, "Women v Wal-Mart," *Fortune* (July 21, 2003): 79–82; C. R. Gentry, "Off the Clock," *Chain Store Age* (February 2003): 33–36; M. Grimm, "Wal-Mart Uber Alles," *American Demographic* (October 2003): 38–42; "Wal-Mart Takes Steps to Address Diversity Criticism," *Financial Wire* (April 25, 2006): 1; Andy Serwer, "Bruised in Bentonville," *Fortune* (April 18, 2005): 84–88.

Chapter 12

1. www.dell.com (2004).

2. G. McWilliams, "Dell Looks for Ways to Rekindle the Fire It Had as an Upstart," *Wall Street Journal* (August 31, 2000): A.1, A.8; "Dell Hopes to Lead Firm out of Desert," *Houston Chronicle* (September, 3, 2000): 4D.

3. www.dell.com (2006).

4. G. Rivlin, "He Naps. He Sings. And He Isn't Michael Dell," *New York Times* (September 11, 2005): 31.

5. L. Smircich, "Concepts of Culture and Organizational Analysis," *Administrative Science Quarterly* 28 (1983): 339–358.

6. G. R. Jones and J. M. George, "The Experience and Evolution of Trust: Implications for Cooperation and Teamwork," *Academy of Management Review* 3 (1998): 531–546.

7. Ibid.

8. J. R. Galbraith, *Designing Complex Organizations* (Reading, Mass.: Addison-Wesley, 1973).

9. Alfred D. Chandler, *Strategy and Structure* (Cambridge, Mass.: MIT Press, 1962).

10. The discussion draws heavily on Chandler, *Strategy and Structure* and B. R. Scott, *Stages of Corporate Development* (Cambridge, Mass.: Intercollegiate Clearing House, Harvard Business School, 1971).

11. R. L. Daft, *Organizational Theory and Design,* 3rd ed. (St. Paul, Minn.: West, 1986), p. 215.

12. J. Child, *Organization, A Guide for Managers and Administrators* (New York: Harper & Row, 1977), pp. 52–70.

13. G. R. Jones and J. Butler, "Costs, Revenues, and Business Level Strategy," *Academy of Management Review* 13 (1988): 202–213; G. R. Jones and C. W. L. Hill, "Transaction Cost Analysis of Strategy-Structure Choice," *Strategic Management Journal* 9 (1988): 159–172.

14. G. R. Jones, *Organizational Theory, Design, and Change: Text and Cases* (Englewood Cliffs, N.J.: Prentice-Hall, 2005).

15. P. Blau, "A Formal Theory of Differentiation in Organizations," *American Sociological Review* 35 (1970): 684–695.

16. G. R. Jones, "Organization-Client Transactions and Organizational Governance Structures," *Academy of Management Journal* 30 (1987): 197–218.

17. S. McCartney, "Airline Industry's Top-Ranked Woman Keeps Southwest's Small-Fry Spirit Alive," *Wall Street Journal* (November 30, 1995): B1; www.southwest.com (2005).

18. P. R. Lawrence and J. Lorsch, *Organization and Environment* (Boston: Division of Research, Harvard Business School, 1967), pp. 50–55.

19. Galbraith, *Designing Complex Organizations,* Chapter 1; J. R. Galbraith and R. K. Kazanjian, *Strategy Implementation: Structure System and Process,* 2nd ed. (St. Paul, Minn.: West, 1986), Chapter 7.

20. R. Simmons, "Strategic Orientation and Top Management Attention to Control Systems," *Strategic Management Journal* 12 (1991): 49–62.

21. R. Simmons, "How New Top Managers Use Control Systems as Levers of Strategic Renewal," *Strategic Management Journal* 15 (1994): 169–189.

22. W. G. Ouchi, "The Transmission of Control Through Organizational Hierarchy," *Academy of Management Journal* 21 (1978): 173–192; W. H. Newman, *Constructive Control* (Englewood Cliffs, N.J.: Prentice-Hall, 1975).

23. E. Flamholtz, "Organizational Control Systems as a Managerial Tool," *California Management Review* (Winter 1979): 50–58.

24. O. E. Williamson, *Markets and Hierarchies: Analysis and Antitrust Implications* (New York: Free Press, 1975); W. G. Ouchi, "Markets, Bureaucracies, and Clans," *Administrative Science Quarterly* 25 (1980): 129–141.

25. H. Mintzberg, *The Structuring of Organizations* (Englewood Cliffs, N.J.: Prentice-Hall, 1979), pp. 5–9.

26. E. E. Lawler III, *Motivation in Work Organizations* (Monterey, Calif.: Brooks/Cole, 1973); Galbraith and Kazanjian, *Strategy Implementation*, Chapter 6.

27. Smircich, "Concepts of Culture and Organizational Analysis."

28. General Electric, Harvard Business School Case #9-385-315 (1984).

29. Ouchi, "Markets, Bureaucracies, and Clans," p. 130.

30. Jones, *Organizational Theory, Design, and Change.*

31. J. Van Maanen and E. H. Schein, "Towards a Theory of Organizational Socialization," in B. M. Staw (ed.), *Research in Organizational Behavior* (Greenwich, Conn.: JAI Press, 1979), pp. 1, 209–264.

32. G. R. Jones, "Socialization Tactics, Self-Efficacy, and Newcomers' Adjustments to Organizations," *Academy of Management Journal* 29 (1986): 262–279.

33. J. P. Kotter and J. L. Heskett, *Corporate Culture and Performance.*

34. T. J. Peters and R. H. Waterman, *In Search of Excellence: Lessons from America's Best-Run Companies* (New York: Harper & Row, 1982).

35. G. Hamel and C. K. Prahalad, "Strategic Intent," *Harvard Business Review* (May–June 1989): 64.

36. Galbraith and Kazanjian, *Strategy Implementation*; Child, *Organization*; R. Duncan, "What Is the Right Organization Structure?" *Organizational Dynamics* (Winter 1979): 59–80.

37. J. Pettet, "Wal-Mart Yesterday and Today," *Discount Merchandiser* (December 1995): 66–67; M. Reid, "Stores of Value," *Economist* (March 4, 1995): ss5–ss7; M. Troy, "The Culture Remains the Constant," *Discount Store News* (June 8, 1998): 95–98; www.walmart.com (accessed 2007).

38. W. G. Ouchi, "The Relationship Between Organizational Structure and Organizational Control," *Administrative Science Quarterly* 22 (1977): 95–113.

39. R. Bunderi, "Intel Researchers Aim to Think Big While Staying Close to Development," *Research-Technology Management* (March–April 1998): 3–4.

40. K. M. Eisenhardt, "Control: Organizational and Economic Approaches," *Management Science* 16 (1985): 134–148.

41. Williamson, *Markets and Hierarchies.*

42. P. R. Lawrence and J. W. Lorsch, *Organization and Environment* (Boston: Graduate School of Business Administration, Harvard University, 1967).

43. K. Pope, "Dell Refocuses on Groundwork to Cope with Rocketing Sales," *Wall Street Journal* (June 18, 1987): 7–32.

44. Michael E. Porter, *Competitive Strategy: Techniques for Analyzing Industries and Competitors* (New York: Free Press, 1980); D. Miller, "Configurations of Strategy and Structure," *Strategic Management Journal* 7 (1986): 233–249.

45. D. Miller and P. H. Freisen, *Organizations: A Quantum View* (Englewood Cliffs, N.J.: Prentice-Hall, 1984).

46. J. Woodward, *Industrial Organization: Theory and Practice* (London: Oxford University Press, 1965); Lawrence and Lorsch, *Organization and Environment.*

47. R. E. White, "Generic Business Strategies, Organizational Context and Performance: An Empirical Investigation," *Strategic Management Journal* 7 (1986): 217–231.

48. Porter, *Competitive Strategy*; Miller, "Configurations of Strategy and Structure."

49. E. Deal and A. A. Kennedy, *Corporate Cultures* (Reading, Mass.: Addison-Wesley, 1985); "Corporate Culture," *Business Week* (October 27, 1980): 148–160.

50. S. M. Davis and R. R. Lawrence, *Matrix* (Reading, Mass.: Addison-Wesley, 1977); J. R. Galbraith, "Matrix Organization Designs: How to Combine Functional and Project Forms," *Business Horizons* 14 (1971): 29–40.

51. Duncan, "What Is the Right Organizational Structure?"; Davis and Lawrence, *Matrix.*

52. D. Miller, "Configurations of Strategy and Structure," in R. E. Miles and C. C. Snow (eds.), *Organizational Strategy, Structure, and Process* (New York: McGraw-Hill, 1978).

53. G. D. Bruton, J. K. Keels, and C. L. Shook, "Downsizing the Firm: Answering the Strategic Questions," *Academy of Management Executive* (May 1996): 38–45.

54. M. Hammer and J. Champy, *Reengineering the Corporation* (New York: HarperCollins, 1993).

55. A. Reinhardt, "Can Nokia Capture Mobile Workers?" *Business Week* (February 9, 2004): 80; D. Pringle, "Nokia Unveils a Major Shake-Up," *Wall Street Journal* (September 29, 2003): B6.

56. www.nokia.com (2006).

Chapter 13

1. B. Koenig, "Ford Reorganizes Executives Under New Chief Mulally," www.bloomberg.com (accessed December 14, 2006).

2. www.ford.com (2006).

3. Alfred D. Chandler, *Strategy and Structure* (Cambridge, Mass.: MIT Press, 1962); O. E. Williamson, *Markets and Hierarchies* (New York: Free Press, 1975); L. Wrigley, "Divisional Autonomy and Diversification" (Ph.D. Diss., Harvard Business School, 1970).

4. R. P. Rumelt, *Strategy, Structure, and Economic Performance* (Boston: Division of Research, Harvard Business School, 1974); B. R. Scott, *Stages of Corporate Development* (Cambridge, Mass.: Intercollegiate Clearing House, Harvard Business School, 1971); Williamson, *Markets and Hierarchies.*

5. A. P. Sloan, *My Years at General Motors* (Garden City, N.Y.: Doubleday, 1946); A. Taylor III, "Can GM Remodel Itself?" *Fortune* (January 13, 1992): 26–34; W. Hampton and J. Norman, "General Motors: What Went Wrong?" *Business Week* (March 16, 1987): 102–110; www.gm.com (2002). The quotations are on pp. 46 and 50 in Sloan, *My Years at General Motors.*

6. The discussion draws on each of the sources cited in endnotes 20–27 and on G. R. Jones and C. W. L. Hill, "Transaction Cost Analysis of Strategy-Structure Choice," *Strategic Management Journal* 9 (1988): 159–172.

7. H. O. Armour and D. J. Teece, "Organizational Structure and Economic Performance: A Test of the Multidivisional Hypothesis," *Bell Journal of Economics* 9 (1978): 106–122.

8. Sloan, *My Years at General Motors.*

9. Jones and Hill, "Transaction Cost Analysis of Strategy-Structure Choice," *Strategic Management Journal* 9 (1988): 159–172.

10. Ibid.

11. R. A. D'Aveni and D. J. Ravenscraft, "Economies of Integration Versus Bureaucracy Costs: Does Vertical Integration Improve Performance?" *Academy of Management Journal* 5 (1994): 1167–1206.

12. P. R. Lawrence and J. Lorsch, *Organization and Environment* (Boston: Division of Research, Harvard Business School, 1967); J. R. Galbraith, *Designing Complex Organizations* (Reading, Mass.:

Addison-Wesley, 1973); Michael Porter, *Competitive Advantage: Creating and Sustaining Superior Performance* (New York: Free Press, 1985).

13. P. R. Nayyar, "Performance Effects of Information Asymmetry and Economies of Scope in Diversified Service Firm," *Academy of Management Journal* 36 (1993): 28–57.

14. L. R. Gomez-Mejia, "Structure and Process of Diversification, Compensation Strategy, and Performance," *Strategic Management Journal* 13 (1992): 381–397.

15. J. Stopford and L. Wells, *Managing the Multinational Enterprise* (London: Longman, 1972).

16. C. A. Bartlett and S. Ghoshal, *Managing Across Borders: The Transnational Solution* (Cambridge, Mass.: Harvard Business School, 1991).

17. R. A. Burgelman, "Managing the New Venture Division: Research Findings and the Implications for Strategic Management," *Strategic Management Journal* 6 (1985): 39–54.

18. G. Imperato, "3M Expert Tells How to Run Meetings That Really Work," *Fast Company* (May 23, 1999): 18.

19. Burgelman, "Managing the New Venture Division."

20. R. A. Burgelman, "Corporate Entrepreneurship and Strategic Management: Insights from a Process Study," *Management Science* 29 (1983): 1349–1364.

21. G. R. Jones, "Towards a Positive Interpretation of Transaction Cost Theory: The Central Role of Entrepreneurship and Trust,"

in M. Hitt, R. E. Freeman, and J. S. Harrison (eds.), *Handbook of Strategic Management* (London: Blackwell, 2001), pp. 208–228.

22. M. Prendergast, "Is Coke Turning into a Mickey Mouse Outfit?" *Wall Street Journal* (March 5, 2001): A. 22.

23. M. S. Salter and W. A. Weinhold, *Diversification Through Acquisition* (New York: Free Press, 1979).

24. F. T. Paine and D. J. Power, "Merger Strategy: An Examination of Drucker's Five Rules for Successful Acquisitions," *Strategic Management Journal* 5 (1984): 99–110.

25. H. Singh and C. A. Montgomery, "Corporate Acquisitions and Economic Performance," unpublished manuscript, 1984.

26. B. Worthen, "Nestlé's ERP Odyssey," *CIO* (May 15, 2002): 1–5.

27. G. D. Bruton, B. M. Oviatt, and M. A. White, "Performance of Acquisitions of Distressed Firms," *Academy of Management Journal* 4 (1994): 972–989.

28. T. Dewett and G. R. Jones, "The Role of Information Technology in the Organization: A Review, Model, and Assessment," *Journal of Management* 27 (2001): 313–346.

29. M. E. Porter, *Competitive Strategy* (New York: Free Press, 1980).

30. M. Hammer and J. Champy, *Reengineering the Corporation*, (New York: Harper Collins, 1993).

31. G. Hamel and C.K. Prahalad, "*Competing for the Future* (Boston:Harvard Business Scool press, 1994).

32. Ibid.

33. "Andersen's Androids," *Economist* (May 4, 1996): 72.

Box Source Notes

Chapter 1

a. *Sources:* A. Van Duyn, "Time Inc revamp to include sale of 18 titles," *Financial Times*, September 13, 2006, page 24. M. Karnitsching, "Time Inc. Makes New Bid to be Big Web Player," *Wall Street Journal*, March 29, 2006, page B1. M. Flamm, "Time tries the web again," *Crain's New York Business*, January 16, 2006, page 3.

b. S. Gray and E. Smith. "Coffee and Music Create a Potent Mix at Starbucks," *Wall Street Journal*, July 19, 2005, p. A1.

c. John Kador, *Charles Schwab: How One Company Beat Wall Street and Reinvented the Brokerage Industry*, John Wiley & Sons, New York, 2002; Erick Schonfeld, "Schwab Puts It All Online," *Fortune*, December 7, 1998, pp. 94–99.

d. *Sources:* D. Priest and D. Linzer, "Panel Condemns Iraq Prewar Intelligence," *Washington Post*, July 10, 2004, p. A1; D. Jehl, "Senators Assail CIA Judgments of Iraq's Arms as Deeply Flawed," *New York Times*, July 10, 2004, p. A1. M. Isikoff, "The Dots Never Existed," *Newsweek*, July 19, 2004, pp. 36–40.

Chapter 2

a. *Sources:* A. Kaplan, "Cott Corporation," *Beverage World*, June 15, 2004, p. 32; J. Popp, "2004 Soft Drink Report," *Beverage Industry*, March 2004, pp. 13–18L. Sparks, "From Coca-Colinization to Copy Catting: The Cott Corporation and Retailers Brand Soft Drinks in the UK and US," *Agribusiness*, March 1997, pp. 153–127, Vol. 13, Issue 2; E. Cherney, "After Flat Sales, Cott Challenges Pepsi, Coca-Cola," *Wall Street Journal*, January 8, 2003, pp. B1, B8. Anonymous, "Cott Corporation: Company Profile," *Just Drinks*, August 2006, pp. 19–22.

b. G. Morgenson, "Denial in Battle Creek," *Forbes*, October 7, 1996, p. 44; J. Muller, "Thinking out of the Cereal Box," *Business Week*, January 15, 2001, p. 54; A. Merrill, "General Mills Increases Prices," *Star Tribune*, June 5, 2001, p. 1D; S. Reyes, "Big G, Kellogg Attempt to Berry Each Other," *Brandweek*, October 7, 2002, p. 8.

c. "How Big Can It Grow?—Wal-Mart," *Economist*, April 17, 2004, pp. 74–76; H. Gilman, "The Most Underrated CEO Ever," *Fortune*, April 5, 2004, pp. 242–247; K. Schaffner, "Psst! Want to Sell to Wal-Mart?" *Apparel Industry Magazine*, August 1996, pp. 18–20.

d. *Standard & Poor's Industry Surveys*, Computers: Hardware, "Global Demand for PCs Accelerates," December 8, 2005; M. Dickerson, "Plain PCs Sitting Pretty," *Los Angeles Times*, December 11, 2005, p. C1; IDC Press Release, "Long Term PC Outlook Improves," September 14, 2006.

Chapter 3

a. Quotes from S. Beatty. "Bass Talk: Plotting Plaid's Future," *Wall Street Journal*, September 9, 2004, p. B1. Also see C. M. Moore and G. Birtwistle, "The Burberry Business Model," *International Journal of Retail and Distribution Management* 32 (2004), pp. 412–422. M. Dickson, "Bravo's Legacy in Transforming Burberry," *Financial Times*, October 6, 2005, p. 22.

b. "Shining Examples," *The Economist: A Survey of Logistics*, June 17, 2006, pp. 4–6; K. Capell et al., "Fashion Conquistador," *Business Week*, September 4, 2006, pp. 38–39; K. Ferdows et al., "Rapid Fire Fulfillment," *Harvard Business Review* 82 (November 2004), pp. 101–107.

c. *Source:* Data drawn from 2005 10K Reports for Hewlett-Packard and Dell Computer.

d. *Sources:* D. Miller, *The Icarus Paradox* (New York: HarperBusiness, 1990); P. D. Llosa, "We Must Know What We Are Doing," *Fortune*, November 14, 1994, p. 68.

e. Stephen Manes and Paul Andrews, *Gates* (New York: Simon & Schuster, 1993).

Chapter 4

a. G. P. Pisano, R. M. J. Bohmer, A. C. Edmondson, "Organizational Differences in Rates of Learning: Evidence from the Adoption of Minimally Invasive Cardiac Surgery," *Management Science*, 47 (2001), pp. 752–768.

b. *Sources:* J. Schlosser, "Cashing in on the New World of Me," *Fortune* (December 13, 2004): 244–249; V. S. Borland, "Global Technology in the Twenty First Century," *Textile World* (January 2003): 42–56; www.Landsend.com (accessed March 11, 2007).

c. Gates, op. cit.

d. *Sources*: C. H. Deutsch, "Six-Sigma Enlightenment," *New York Times* (December 7, 1998): 1; J. J. Barshay, "The Six-Sigma Story," *Star Tribune* (June 14, 1999): 1; D. D. Bak, "Rethinking Industrial Drives," *Electrical/Electronics Technology* (November 30, 1998): 58.

e. *Sources:* I. R. Lazarus and K. Butler, "The Promise of Six-Sigma," *Managed Healthcare Executive* (October 2001): 22–26; D. Scalise, "Six-Sigma, the Quest for Quality," *Hospitals and Health Networks* (December 2001): 41–44; S. F.Gale, "Building Frameworks for Six Sigma Success," *Workforce* (May 2003): 64–69; J. Goedert, "Crunching Data: The Key to Six Sigma Success," *Health Data Management* (April 2004): 44–48; M. Hagland, "Six Sigma: It's Real, It's Data Driven, and It's Here," *Health Care Strategic Management*, 23 (December 2005): 1–6.

f. V. Govindarajan and C. Trimble, "How Forgetting Leads to Innovation," *Chief Executive* (March 2006): 46–50; J. McGregor, "How Failure Breeds Success," *Business Week* (July 10, 2006): 42–52.

Chapter 5

a. *Sources*: D. McGinn, "Is This Any Way to Run an Airline?" *Newsweek* (October 4, 2004): E14–E19; E. Torbenson, "Budget Carriers Rule the European Skies," *Dallas Morning News* (September 22, 2004): D1; www.ryanair.com, 2006 (accessed January 2007).

b. *Sources*: www.llbean.com (accessed 2004); D. McGinn, "Swimming Upstream, *Newsweek* (October 1, 2004): E10–E12; www.llbean.com (accessed 2006).

c. *Sources*: www.zara.com (accessed 2006); C. Vitzthum, "Just-in-Time-Fashion," *Wall Street Journal* (May 18, 2001): B1, B4; www.zara.com (accessed 2007).

d. *Source:* www.toyota.com (accessed 2006).

e. *Sources:* "The Holiday Inns Trip; A Breeze for Decades, Bumpy Ride in the 1980s," *Wall Street Journal* (February 11, 1987): 1; Holiday Inns, Annual Report (1985); U.S. Bureau of Labor Statistics, U.S. Industrial Output (Washington, D.C.: U.S. Government Printing Office, 1986); Mark Gleason and Alan Salomon, "Fallon's Challenge: Make Holiday Inn More 'In,'" *Advertising Age* (September 2, 1996): 14; Julie Miller, "Amenities Range from

Snacks to Technology," *Hotel and Motel Management* (July 3, 1996): 38–40; www.sixcontinenthotels.com (accessed 2005).

Chapter 6

a. www.clearchannel.com (accessed 2006); A. W. Mathews, "From a Distance: A Giant Chain Is Perfecting the Art of Seeming Local," *Wall Street Journal* (February 25, 2002): A1, A4.

b. www.AOLTimeWarner.com (accessed 2002, 2004); Kara Swisher, *aol.com* (New York: Random House, 1998); www.aol.com (accessed 2006).

c. www.toysrus.com (accessed 2004); M. Maremont and G. Bowens, "Brawls in Toyland," *Business Week* (December 21, 1992): 36–37; S. Eads, "The Toys 'R' Us Empire Strikes Back," *Business Week* (June 7, 1999): 55–59; www.toysrus.co (accessed 2002); amazon.com (accessed 2002).

d. www.cocacola.com (accessed 2006); www.pepsico.com (accessed 2006).

e. P. Haynes, "Western Electric Redux," *Forbes* (January 26, 1998): 46–47; www.westrexcorp.com (accessed 2006).

Chapter 7

a. *Sources:* M. Snider, "Ray Dolby, Audio Inventor," *USA Today* (December 28, 2000): D3; D. Dritas, "Dealerscope Hall of Fame: Ray Dolby," *Dealerscope* (January 2002): 74–76; J. Pinkerton, "At Dolby Laboratories: A Clean Audio Pipe," *Dealerscope* (December 2000): 33–34; Company history archived at www.dolby.com (accessed November 18, 2006); L. Himelstein, "Dolby Gets Ready to Make a Big Noise," *Business Week* (February 9, 2004): 78; D. Pomerantz, "Seeing in Dolby," *Forbes* (January 30, 2006): 56.

b. *Source:* Interviews by Charles W. L. Hill.

c. *Sources:* S. Yoon, "The Mod Squad," *East Asian Economic Review* (November 7, 2002): 34–36; R. Cunningham, "Controversy as Sony Loses Mod-Chip Verdict," *Managing Intellectual Property* (September 2002): 15–18; A. Pham, "Video Game Losses Nearly $2 Billion," *Los Angeles Times* (February 18, 2002): C8; Andy Holloway, "License to Plunder," *Canadian Business* (November 10, 2003): 95; R. Grover et al., "Game Wars," *Business Week* (February 28, 2005): 60–66.

d. *Source:* Christensen, *The Innovator's Dilemma* (Boston: Harvard Business School Press, 1997).

Chapter 8

a. *Sources:* "Lessons from the Frozen North," *Economist* (October 8, 1994): 76–77; "A Finnish Fable," *Economist* (October 14, 2000); D. O'Shea and K. Fitchard, "The First 3 Billion Is Always the Hardest," *Wireless Review,* 22 (September 2005): 25–31: P. Taylor, "Big Names Dominate in Mobile Phones," *Financial Times* (September 29, 2006): 26; and Nokia website at www.nokia.com (accessed 2006).

b. *Sources:* K. Capell, A. Sains, C. Lindblad, and A. T. Palmer, "IKEA," *Business Week* (November 14, 2005): 96–101: K. Capell et al., "What a Sweetheart of a Love Seat," *Business Week* (November 14, 2005): 101: P. M. Miller, "IKEA with Chinese Characteristics," *Chinese Business Review* (July/August 2004): 36–69: C. Daniels, "Create IKEA, Make Billions, Take Bus," *Fortune* (May 3, 2004): 44.

c. *Sources:* Dell Corporation 2006 10K; Staff Reporter, "Dell Inc: Call Center in India to Expand to 2,500 Workers from 800," *Wall Street Journal* (October 6, 2006): A6.

d. *Sources:* "Fujitsu, Cisco Systems to Develop High-End Routers for Web Traffic," *Knight Ridder Tribune Business News* (December 6, 2004): 1: "Fujitsu and Cisco Introduce New High Performance Routers for IP Next Generation Networks," *JCN Newswire*, May 25, 2006 (accessed November 30, 2006).

Chapter 9

a. *Sources:* www.hp.com (2006); www.dell.com (2006); P. Burrows and A. Park, "Compaq and HP: What's an Investor to Do?" *Business Week* (March 18, 2002): 62–64; "Carly v Walter," *Economist* (January 26, 2002); "Sheltering from the Storm," *Economist* (September 8, 2001): 21–22.

b. Y. J. Dreazen, G. Ip, and N. Kulish, "Why the Sudden Rise?"; L. Kowalczyk, "A Matter of Style," *Boston Globe* (February 22, 2002): C1.

c. *Source:* J-F. Hennart, "Upstream Vertical Integration in the Aluminum and Tin Industries," *Journal of Economic Behavior and Organization* 9 (1988): 281–299.

d. *Sources:* www.chrysler.com (2004, 2006); J. H. Dyer, "How Chrysler Created an American Keiretsu," *Harvard Business Review* (July–August 1996): 42–56.

Chapter 10

a. *Sources:* www.3M.com, (2005 and 2006); W. E. Coyne, "How 3M Innovates for Long-Term Growth," *Research Technology Management* (March–April 2001): 21–24; 3M's 2004 10-K form; Ibid.

b. *Sources:* R. Arensman, "Intel's Second Try," *Electronic Business* (March 2001): 62–70; Intel 10-K Report, 2001; www.amd.com (2006); www.intel.com (2006).

c. *Sources:* M. Murray and J. Rebelled, "Mellon Bank Corp: One Big Unhappy Family," *Wall Street Journal* (April 28, 1995): B1, B4; K. Holland, "A Bank Eat Bank World—with Indigestion," *Business Week* (October 30, 1995): 130; www.mellon.com (2006).

Chapter 11

a. *Sources:* S. Tully, "A House Divided," *Fortune* (December 18, 2000): 264–275; J. Chaffin, "Sotheby's Ex CEO Spared Jail Sentence," *Financial Times* (April 30, 2002): 10; T. Thorncroft, "A Courtroom Battle of the Vanities," *Financial Times* (November 3, 2001): 3.

b. *Sources:* J. Guidera, "Probe of Computer Associates Centers on Firm's Revenues," *Wall Street Journal* (May 20, 2002): A3, A15; Ronna Abramson, "Computer Associates Probe Focus on 1998, 1999 Revenue," *The Street.Com* (accessed May 20, 2002); C. Forelle, M. Maremont, and G. Fields, "U.S. Indicts Sanjay Kumar for Fraud, Lies," *Wall Street Journal* (September 23, 2004): A1; N. Varchaver, "Long Island Confidential," *Fortune* (November 27, 2006): 172–178.

c. *Sources:* "Boycott Nike," CBS News *48 Hours*, October 17, 1996; D. Jones, "Critics Tie Sweatshop Sneakers to 'Air Jordan,'" *USA Today* (June 6, 1996): 1B; "Global Exchange Special Report: Nike Just Don't Do It," available at http://www.globalexchange.org/education/publications/newsltr6.97p2.html#nike (accessed 2003); S. Greenhouse, "Nike Shoeplant in Vietnam Is Called Unsafe for Workers," *New York Times* (November 8, 1997); V. Dobnik, "Chinese Workers Abused Making Nikes, Reeboks," *Seattle Times* (September 21, 1997): A4.

d. *Source:* Dell Computer, "Code of Conduct: Winning with Integrity,"www.dell.com (accessed September 7, 2006).

Chapter 12

a. www.unionpacific.com (accessed 2007).
b. www.cypress.com, press release (1998); www.cypress.com, press release, (2006).
c. www.mcdonalds.com (2006).
d. www.lexmark.com (2006).

Chapter 13

a. www.sap.com (2005 and 2006).
b. A. Edgecliffe-Johnson, "Nestlé and Pillsbury Forge Ice Cream Alliance in U.S.," *Financial Times* (August 20, 1999): 2; B. Worthen, "Nestlé's ERP Odyssey," *CIO* (May 15, 2002): 1–5; www.nestle.com (2006).
c. M. Moeller, "Oracle: Practicing What It Preaches," *Business Week* (August 16, 1999): 1–5; www.oracle.com (2006).
d. Business Link in the Global Chain," *Economist* (June 2, 2001): 62–63; www.li&fung.com (2006).

Appendix:
Analyzing a Case Study and Writing a Case Study Analysis

What Is Case Study Analysis?

Case study analysis is an integral part of a course in strategic management. The purpose of a case study is to provide students with experience of the strategic management problems that actual organizations face. A case study presents an account of what happened to a business or industry over a number of years. It chronicles the events that managers had to deal with, such as changes in the competitive environment, and charts the managers' response, which usually involved changing the business- or corporate-level strategy. The cases in this book cover a wide range of issues and problems that managers have had to confront. Some cases are about finding the right business-level strategy to compete in changing conditions. Some are about companies that grew by acquisition, with little concern for the rationale behind their growth, and how growth by acquisition affected their future profitability. Each case is different because each organization is different. The underlying thread in all cases, however, is the use of strategic management techniques to solve business problems.

Cases prove valuable in a strategic management course for several reasons. First, cases provide you, the student, with experience of organizational problems that you probably have not had the opportunity to experience firsthand. In a relatively short period of time, you will have the chance to appreciate and analyze the problems faced by many different companies and to understand how managers tried to deal with them.

Second, cases illustrate the theory and content of strategic management. The meaning and implications of this information are made clearer when they are applied to case studies. The theory and concepts help reveal what is going on in the companies studied and allow you to evaluate the solutions that specific companies adopted to deal with their problems. Consequently, when you analyze cases, you will be like a detective who, with a set of conceptual tools, probes what happened and what or who was responsible and then marshals the evidence that provides the solution. Top managers enjoy the thrill of testing their problem-solving abilities in the real world. It is important to remember that no one knows what the right answer is. All that managers can do is to make the best guess. In fact, managers say repeatedly that they are happy if they are right only half the time in solving strategic problems. Strategic management is an uncertain game, and using cases to see how theory can be put into practice is one way of improving your skills of diagnostic investigation.

Third, case studies provide you with the opportunity to participate in class and to gain experience in presenting your ideas to others. Instructors may sometimes call on students as a group to identify what is going on in a case, and through classroom discussion the issues in and solutions to the case problem will reveal themselves. In such a situation, you will have to organize your views and conclusions so that you can present them to the class. Your classmates may have analyzed the issues differently from you, and they will want you to argue your points before they will accept your conclusions, so be prepared for debate. This mode of discussion is an example of the dialectical approach to decision making. This is how decisions are made in the actual business world.

Instructors also may assign an individual, but more commonly a group, to analyze the case before the whole class. The individual or group probably will be responsible for a thirty- to forty-minute presentation of the case to the class. That presentation must cover the issues posed, the problems facing the company, and a series of recommendations for resolving the problems. The discussion then will be thrown open to the class, and you will have to defend your ideas. Through such discussions and presentations, you will experience how to convey your ideas effectively to others. Remember that a great deal of managers' time is spent in these kinds of situations: presenting their ideas and engaging in discussion with other managers who have their own views about what is going on. Thus, you will experience in the classroom the actual process of strategic management, and this will serve you well in your future career.

If you work in groups to analyze case studies, you also will learn about the group process involved in working as a team. When people work in groups, it is often difficult to schedule time and allocate responsibility for the case analysis. There are always group members who shirk their responsibilities and group members who are so sure of their own ideas that they try to dominate the group's analysis. Most of the strategic management takes place in groups, however, and it is best if you learn about these problems now.

Analyzing a Case Study

The purpose of the case study is to let you apply the concepts of strategic management when you analyze the issues facing a specific company. To analyze a case study, therefore, you must examine closely the issues confronting the company. Most often you will need to read the case several times—once to grasp the overall picture of what is happening to the company and then several times more to discover and grasp the specific problems.

Generally, detailed analysis of a case study should include eight areas:

1. The history, development, and growth of the company over time

2. The identification of the company's internal strengths and weaknesses

3. The nature of the external environment surrounding the company

4. A SWOT analysis

5. The kind of corporate-level strategy that the company is pursuing

6. The nature of the company's business-level strategy

7. The company's structure and control systems and how they match its strategy

8. Recommendations

To analyze a case, you need to apply the concepts taught in this course to each of these areas. To help you further, we next offer a summary of the steps you can take to analyze the case material for each of the eight points we just noted:

1. *Analyze the company's history, development, and growth.* A convenient way to investigate how a company's past strategy and structure affect it in the present

is to chart the critical incidents in its history—that is, the events that were the most unusual or the most essential for its development into the company it is today. Some of the events have to do with its founding, its initial products, how it makes new-product market decisions, and how it developed and chose functional competencies to pursue. Its entry into new businesses and shifts in its main lines of business are also important milestones to consider.

2. *Identify the company's internal strengths and weaknesses.* Once the historical profile is completed, you can begin the SWOT analysis. Use all the incidents you have charted to develop an account of the company's strengths and weaknesses as they have emerged historically. Examine each of the value creation functions of the company, and identify the functions in which the company is currently strong and currently weak. Some companies might be weak in marketing; some might be strong in research and development. Make lists of these strengths and weaknesses. The SWOT Checklist (Table 1) gives examples of what might go in these lists.

3. *Analyze the external environment.* To identify environmental opportunities and threats, apply all the concepts on industry and macroenvironments to analyze the environment the company is confronting. Of particular importance at the industry level are Porter's five forces model and the stage of the life cycle model. Which factors in the macroenvironment will appear salient depends on the specific company being analyzed. Use each factor in turn (for instance, demographic factors) to see whether it is relevant for the company in question.

   Having done this analysis, you will have generated both an analysis of the company's environment and a list of opportunities and threats. The SWOT Checklist table also lists some common environmental opportunities and threats that you may look for, but the list you generate will be specific to your company.

4. *Evaluate the SWOT analysis.* Having identified the company's external opportunities and threats as well as its internal strengths and weaknesses, consider what your findings mean. You need to balance strengths and weaknesses against opportunities and threats. Is the company in an overall strong competitive position? Can it continue to pursue its current business- or corporate-level strategy profitably? What can the company do to turn weaknesses into strengths and threats into opportunities? Can it develop new functional, business, or corporate strategies to accomplish this change? *Never merely generate the SWOT analysis and then put it aside.* Because it provides a succinct summary of the company's condition, a good SWOT analysis is the key to all the analyses that follow.

5. *Analyze corporate-level strategy.* To analyze corporate-level strategy, you first need to define the company's mission and goals. Sometimes the mission and goals are stated explicitly in the case; at other times, you will have to infer them from available information. The information you need to collect to find out the company's corporate strategy includes such factors as its lines of business and the nature of its subsidiaries and acquisitions. It is important to analyze the relationship among the company's businesses. Do they trade or exchange resources? Are there gains to be achieved from synergy? Alternatively, is the company just running a portfolio of investments? This analysis should enable you to define the corporate strategy that the company is pursuing

TABLE 1

A SWOT Checklist

Potential internal strengths	Potential internal weaknesses
Many product lines?	Obsolete, narrow product lines?
Broad market coverage?	Rising manufacturing costs?
Manufacturing competence?	Decline in R&D innovations?
Good marketing skills?	Poor marketing plan?
Good materials management systems?	Poor material management systems?
R&D skills and leadership?	Loss of customer good will?
Information system competencies?	Inadequate human resources?
Human resource competencies?	Inadequate information systems?
Brand name reputation?	Loss of brand name capital?
Portfolio management skills?	Growth without direction?
Cost of differentiation advantage?	Bad portfolio management?
New-venture management expertise?	Loss of corporate direction?
Appropriate management style?	Infighting among divisions?
Appropriate organizational structure?	Loss of corporate control?
Appropriate control systems?	Inappropriate organizational
Ability to manage strategic change?	structure and control systems?
Well-developed corporate strategy?	High conflict and politics?
Good financial management?	Poor financial management?
Others?	Others?

Potential environmental opportunities	Potential environmental threats
Expand core business(es)?	Attacks on core business(es)?
Exploit new market segments?	Increases in domestic competition?
Widen product range?	Increase in foreign competition?
Extend cost or differentiation advantage?	Change in consumer tastes?
Diversify into new growth businesses?	Fall in barriers to entry?
Expand into foreign markets?	Rise in new or substitute products?
Apply R&D skills in new areas?	Increase in industry rivalry?
Enter new related businesses?	New forms of industry competition?
Vertically integrate forward?	Potential for takeover?
Vertically integrate backward?	Existence of corporate raiders?
Enlarge corporate portfolio?	Increase in regional competition?
Overcome barriers to entry?	Changes in demographic factors?
Reduce rivalry among competitors?	Changes in economic factors?
Make profitable new acquisitions?	Downturn in economy?
Apply brand name capital in new areas?	Rising labor costs?
Seek fast market growth?	Slower market growth?
Others?	Others?

(for example, related or unrelated diversification, or a combination of both) and to conclude whether the company operates in just one core business. Then, using your SWOT analysis, debate the merits of this strategy. Is it appropriate given the environment the company is in? Could a change in corporate strategy provide the company with new opportunities or transform a weakness into a strength? For example, should the company diversify from its core business into new businesses?

Other issues should be considered as well. How and why has the company's strategy changed over time? What is the claimed rationale for any changes? Often, it is a good idea to analyze the company's businesses or products to assess its situation and identify which divisions contribute the most to or detract from its competitive advantage. It is also useful to explore how the company has built its portfolio over time. Did it acquire new businesses, or did it internally venture its own? All of these factors provide clues about the company and indicate ways of improving its future performance.

6. *Analyze business-level strategy.* Once you know the company's corporate-level strategy and have done the SWOT analysis, the next step is to identify the company's business-level strategy. If the company is a single-business company, its business-level strategy is identical to its corporate-level strategy. If the company is in many businesses, each business will have its own business-level strategy. You will need to identify the company's generic competitive strategy—differentiation, low-cost, or focus—and its investment strategy, given its relative competitive position and the stage of the life cycle. The company also may market different products using different business-level strategies. For example, it may offer a low-cost product range and a line of differentiated products. Be sure to give a full account of a company's business-level strategy to show how it competes.

Identifying the functional strategies that a company pursues to build competitive advantage through superior efficiency, quality, innovation, and customer responsiveness and to achieve its business-level strategy is very important. The SWOT analysis will have provided you with information on the company's functional competencies. You should investigate its production, marketing, or research and development strategy further to gain a picture of where the company is going. For example, pursuing a low-cost or a differentiation strategy successfully requires very different sets of competencies. Has the company developed the right ones? If it has, how can it exploit them further? Can it pursue both a low-cost and a differentiation strategy simultaneously?

The SWOT analysis is especially important at this point if the industry analysis, particularly Porter's model, has revealed threats to the company from the environment. Can the company deal with these threats? How should it change its business-level strategy to counter them? To evaluate the potential of a company's business-level strategy, you must first perform a thorough SWOT analysis that captures the essence of its problems.

Once you complete this analysis, you will have a full picture of the way the company is operating and be in a position to evaluate the potential of its strategy. Thus, you will be able to make recommendations concerning the pattern of its future actions. However, first you need to consider strategy implementation, or the way the company tries to achieve its strategy.

7. *Analyze structure and control systems.* The aim of this analysis is to identify what structure and control systems the company is using to implement its strategy and to evaluate whether that structure is the appropriate one for the company. Different corporate and business strategies require different structures. You need to determine the *degree of fit between the company's strategy and structure.* For example, does the company have the right level of vertical differentiation (e.g., does it have the appropriate number of levels in the hierarchy or decentralized control?) or horizontal differentiation (does it use a functional structure when it should be using a product structure?)? Similarly, is the company using the right integration or control systems to manage its operations? Are managers being appropriately rewarded? Are the right rewards in

place for encouraging cooperation among divisions? These are all issues to consider.

In some cases, there will be little information on these issues, whereas in others there will be a lot. In analyzing each case, you should gear the analysis toward its most salient issues. For example, organizational conflict, power, and politics will be important issues for some companies. Try to analyze why problems in these areas are occurring. Do they occur because of bad strategy formulation or because of bad strategy implementation?

Organizational change is an issue in many cases because the companies are attempting to alter their strategies or structures to solve strategic problems. Thus, as part of the analysis, you might suggest an action plan that the company in question could use to achieve its goals. For example, you might list in a logical sequence the steps the company would need to follow to alter its business-level strategy from differentiation to focus.

8. *Make recommendations.* The quality of your recommendations is a direct result of the thoroughness with which you prepared the case analysis. Recommendations are directed at solving whatever strategic problem the company is facing and increasing its future profitability. Your recommendations should be in line with your analysis; that is, they should follow logically from the previous discussion. For example, your recommendation generally will center on the specific ways of changing functional, business, and corporate strategies and organizational structure and control to improve business performance. The set of recommendations will be specific to each case, and so it is difficult to discuss these recommendations here. Such recommendations might include an increase in spending on specific research and development projects, the divesting of certain businesses, a change from a strategy of unrelated to related diversification, an increase in the level of integration among divisions by using task forces and teams, or a move to a different kind of structure to implement a new business-level strategy. Make sure your recommendations are mutually consistent and written in the form of an action plan. The plan might contain a timetable that sequences the actions for changing the company's strategy and a description of how changes at the corporate level will necessitate changes at the business level and subsequently at the functional level.

After following all these stages, you will have performed a thorough analysis of the case and will be in a position to join in class discussion or present your ideas to the class, depending on the format used by your professor. Remember that you must tailor your analysis to suit the specific issue discussed in your case. In some cases, you might completely omit one of the steps in the analysis because it is not relevant to the situation you are considering. You must be sensitive to the needs of the case and not apply the framework we have discussed in this section blindly. The framework is meant only as a guide, not as an outline.

Writing a Case Study Analysis

Often, as part of your course requirements, you will need to present a written case analysis. This may be an individual or a group report. Whatever the situation, there are certain guidelines to follow in writing a case analysis that will improve the evaluation your work will receive from your instructor. Before we discuss these guidelines and before you use them, make sure that they do not conflict with any directions your instructor has given you.

The structure of your written report is critical. Generally, if you follow the steps for analysis discussed in the previous section, *you already will have a good structure for your written discussion*. All reports begin with an *introduction* to the case. In it, outline briefly what the company does, how it developed historically, what problems it is experiencing, and how you are going to approach the issues in the case write-up. Do this sequentially by writing, for example, "First, we discuss the environment of Company X. . . . Third, we discuss Company X's business-level strategy. . . . Last, we provide recommendations for turning around Company X's business."

In the second part of the case write-up, the *strategic analysis* section, do the SWOT analysis, analyze and discuss the nature and problems of the company's business-level and corporate strategies, and then analyze its structure and control systems. Make sure you use plenty of headings and subheadings to structure your analysis. For example, have separate sections on any important conceptual tool you use. Thus, you might have a section on Porter's five forces model as part of your analysis of the environment. You might offer a separate section on portfolio techniques when analyzing a company's corporate strategy. Tailor the sections and subsections to the specific issues of importance in the case.

In the third part of the case write-up, present your *solutions and recommendations*. Be comprehensive, and make sure they are in line with the previous analysis so that the recommendations fit together and move logically from one to the next. The recommendations section is very revealing because your instructor will have a good idea of how much work you put into the case from the quality of your recommendations.

Following this framework will provide a good structure for most written reports, though it must be shaped to fit the individual case being considered. Some cases are about excellent companies experiencing no problems. In such instances, it is hard to write recommendations. Instead, you can focus on analyzing why the company is doing so well, using that analysis to structure the discussion. Following are some minor suggestions that can help make a good analysis even better:

1. Do not repeat in summary form large pieces of factual information from the case. The instructor has read the case and knows what is going on. Rather, use the information in the case to illustrate your statements, defend your arguments, or make salient points. Beyond the brief introduction to the company, you must avoid being *descriptive*; instead, you must be *analytical*.

2. Make sure the sections and subsections of your discussion flow logically and smoothly from one to the next. That is, try to build on what has gone before so that the analysis of the case study moves toward a climax. This is particularly important for group analysis, because there is a tendency for people in a group to split up the work and say, "I'll do the beginning, you take the middle, and I'll do the end." The result is a choppy, stilted analysis; the parts do not flow from one to the next, and it is obvious to the instructor that no real group work has been done.

3. Avoid grammatical and spelling errors. They make your work look sloppy.

4. In some instances, cases dealing with well-known companies end in 1998 or 1999 because no later information was available when the case was written. If possible, do a search for more information on what has happened to the company in subsequent years.

Many libraries now have comprehensive web-based electronic data search facilities that offer such sources as *ABI/Inform, The Wall Street Journal Index,* the *F&S Index,* and the *Nexis-Lexis* databases. These enable you to identify any article that has been written in the business press on the company of your choice within the past few years. A number of nonelectronic data sources are also useful. For example, *F&S Predicasts* publishes an annual list of articles relating to major companies that appeared in the national and international business press. *S&P Industry Surveys* is a great source for basic industry data, and *Value Line Ratings and Reports* can contain good summaries of a firm's financial position and future prospects. You will also want to collect full financial information on the company. Again, this can be accessed from web-based electronic databases such as the *Edgar* database, which archives all forms that publicly quoted companies have to file with the Securities and Exchange Commission (SEC; e.g., 10-K filings can be accessed from the SEC's *Edgar* database). Most SEC forms for public companies can now be accessed from Internet-based financial sites, such as Yahoo's finance site (http://finance.yahoo.com/).

5. Sometimes instructors hand out questions for each case to help you in your analysis. Use these as a guide for writing the case analysis. They often illuminate the important issues that have to be covered in the discussion.

If you follow the guidelines in this section, you should be able to write a thorough and effective evaluation.

The Role of Financial Analysis in Case Study Analysis

An important aspect of analyzing a case study and writing a case study analysis is the role and use of financial information. A careful analysis of the company's financial condition immensely improves a case write-up. After all, financial data represent the concrete results of the company's strategy and structure. Although analyzing financial statements can be quite complex, a general idea of a company's financial position can be determined through the use of ratio analysis. Financial performance ratios can be calculated from the balance sheet and income statement. These ratios can be classified into five subgroups: profit ratios, liquidity ratios, activity ratios, leverage ratios, and shareholder-return ratios. These ratios should be compared with the industry average or the company's prior years of performance. It should be noted, however, that deviation from the average is not necessarily bad; it simply warrants further investigation. For example, young companies will have purchased assets at a different price and will likely have a different capital structure than older companies do. In addition to ratio analysis, a company's cash flow position is of critical importance and should be assessed. Cash flow shows how much actual cash a company possesses.

● **Profit Ratios**   Profit ratios measure the efficiency with which the company uses its resources. The more efficient the company, the greater is its profitability. It is useful to compare a company's profitability against that of its major competitors in its industry to determine whether the company is operating more or less efficiently than its rivals. In addition, the change in a company's profit ratios over time tells whether its performance is improving or declining.

A number of different profit ratios can be used, and each of them measures a different aspect of a company's performance. Here, we look at the most commonly used profit ratios.

● **Return on Invested Capital**   This ratio measures the profit earned on the capital invested in the company. It is defined as follows:

$$\text{Return on invested capital (ROIC)} = \frac{\text{Net profit}}{\text{Invested capital}}$$

Net profit is calculated by subtracting the total costs of operating the company away from its total revenues (total revenues – total costs). Total costs are the (1) costs of goods sold, (2) sales, general, and administrative expenses, (3) R&D expenses, and (4) other expenses. Net profit can be calculated before or after taxes, although many financial analysts prefer the before-tax figure. Invested capital is the amount that is invested in the operations of a company—that is, in property, plant, equipment, inventories, and other assets. Invested capital comes from two main sources: interest-bearing debt and shareholders' equity. Interest-bearing debt is money the company borrows from banks and from those who purchase its bonds. Shareholders' equity is the money raised from selling shares to the public, *plus* earnings that have been retained by the company in prior years and are available to fund current investments. ROIC measures the effectiveness with which a company is using the capital funds that it has available for investment. As such, it is recognized to be an excellent measure of the value a company is creating.[1] Remember that a company's ROIC can be decomposed into its constituent parts.

● **Return on Total Assets (ROA)**   This ratio measures the profit earned on the employment of assets. It is defined as follows:

$$\text{Return on total assests} = \frac{\text{Net profit}}{\text{Total assets}}$$

● **Return on Stockholders' Equity (ROE)**   This ratio measures the percentage of profit earned on common stockholders' investment in the company. It is defined as follows:

$$\text{Return on stockholders' equity} = \frac{\text{Net profit}}{\text{Stockholders' equity}}$$

If a company has no debt, this will be the same as ROIC.

● **Liquidity Ratios**   A company's liquidity is a measure of its ability to meet short-term obligations. An asset is deemed liquid if it can be readily converted into cash. Liquid assets are current assets such as cash, marketable securities, accounts receivable, and so on. Two liquidity ratios are commonly used.

● **Current Ratio**   The current ratio measures the extent to which the claims of short-term creditors are covered by assets that can be quickly converted into cash. Most companies should have a ratio of at least 1, because failure to meet these commitments can lead to bankruptcy. The ratio is defined as follows:

$$\text{Current ratio} = \frac{\text{Current assets}}{\text{Current liabilities}}$$

● **Quick Ratio**   The quick ratio measures a company's ability to pay off the claims of short-term creditors without relying on selling its inventories. This is a valuable

[1] Tom Copeland, Tim Koller, and Jack Murrin, *Valuation: Measuring and Managing the Value of Companies* (New York: Wiley, 1996).

measure since in practice the sale of inventories is often difficult. It is defined as follows:

$$\text{Quick ratio} = \frac{\text{Current assets} - \text{inventory}}{\text{Current liabilities}}$$

● **Activity Ratios**   Activity ratios indicate how effectively a company is managing its assets. Two ratios are particularly useful.

● **Inventory Turnover**   This measures the number of times inventory is turned over. It is useful in determining whether a firm is carrying excess stock in inventory. It is defined as follows:

$$\text{Inventory turnover} = \frac{\text{Cost of goods sold}}{\text{Inventory}}$$

Cost of goods sold is a better measure of turnover than sales because it is the cost of the inventory items. Inventory is taken at the balance sheet date. Some companies choose to compute an average inventory, beginning inventory, and ending inventory, but for simplicity, use the inventory at the balance sheet date.

● **Days Sales Outstanding (DSO) or Average Collection Period**   This ratio is the average time a company has to wait to receive its cash after making a sale. It measures how effective the company's credit, billing, and collection procedures are. It is defined as follows:

$$\text{DSO} = \frac{\text{Accounts receivable}}{\text{Total sales}/360}$$

Accounts receivable is divided by average daily sales. The use of 360 is the standard number of days for most financial analysis.

● **Leverage Ratios**   A company is said to be highly leveraged if it uses more debt than equity, including stock and retained earnings. The balance between debt and equity is called the *capital structure.* The optimal capital structure is determined by the individual company. Debt has a lower cost because creditors take less risk; they know they will get their interest and principal. However, debt can be risky to the firm because if enough profit is not made to cover the interest and principal payments, bankruptcy can result. Three leverage ratios are commonly used.

● **Debt-to-Assets Ratio**   The debt-to-assets ratio is the most direct measure of the extent to which borrowed funds have been used to finance a company's investments. It is defined as follows:

$$\text{Debt-to-assets ratio} = \frac{\text{Total debt}}{\text{Total assets}}$$

Total debt is the sum of a company's current liabilities and its long-term debt, and total assets are the sum of fixed assets and current assets.

● **Debt-to-Equity Ratio**   The debt-to-equity ratio indicates the balance between debt and equity in a company's capital structure. This is perhaps the most widely used measure of a company's leverage. It is defined as follows:

$$\text{Debt-to-equity ratio} = \frac{\text{Total debt}}{\text{Total equity}}$$

● **Times-Covered Ratio**   The times-covered ratio measures the extent to which a company's gross profit covers its annual interest payments. If this ratio declines to less than 1, the company is unable to meet its interest costs and is technically insolvent. The ratio is defined as follows:

$$\text{Times-covered ratio} = \frac{\text{Profit before interest and tax}}{\text{Total interest charges}}$$

● **Shareholder-Return Ratios**   Shareholder-return ratios measure the return that shareholders earn from holding stock in the company. Given the goal of maximizing stockholders' wealth, providing shareholders with an adequate rate of return is a primary objective of most companies. As with profit ratios, it can be helpful to compare a company's shareholder returns against those of similar companies as a yardstick for determining how well the company is satisfying the demands of this particularly important group of organizational constituents. Four ratios are commonly used.

● **Total Shareholder Returns**   Total shareholder returns measure the returns earned by time $t + 1$ on an investment in a company's stock made at time t. (Time t is the time at which the initial investment is made.) Total shareholder returns include both dividend payments and appreciation in the value of the stock (adjusted for stock splits) and are defined as follows:

$$\text{Total shareholder returns} = \frac{\begin{array}{c}\text{Stock price } (t+1) - \text{stock price } (t)\\ + \text{ sum of annual dividends per share}\end{array}}{\text{Stock price } (t)}$$

If a shareholder invests \$2 at time t and at time $t + 1$ the share is worth \$3, while the sum of annual dividends for the period t to $t + 1$ has amounted to \$0.20, total shareholder returns are equal to $(3 - 2 + 0.2)/2 = 0.6$, which is a 60 percent return on an initial investment of \$2 made at time t.

● **Price-Earnings Ratio**   The price-earnings ratio measures the amount investors are willing to pay per dollar of profit. It is defined as follows:

$$\text{Price-earnings ratio} = \frac{\text{Market price per share}}{\text{Earnings per share}}$$

● **Market-to-Book Value**   Market-to-book value measures a company's expected future growth prospects. It is defined as follows:

$$\text{Market-to-book value} = \frac{\text{Market price per share}}{\text{Earnings per share}}$$

● **Dividend Yield**   The dividend yield measures the return to shareholders received in the form of dividends. It is defined as follows:

$$\text{Dividend yield} = \frac{\text{Dividend per share}}{\text{Market price per share}}$$

Market price per share can be calculated for the first of the year, in which case the dividend yield refers to the return on an investment made at the beginning of the year. Alternatively, the average share price over the year may be used. A company must decide how much of its profits to pay to stockholders and how much to reinvest in the company. Companies with strong growth prospects should have a lower dividend payout ratio than mature companies. The rationale is that shareholders can invest the money elsewhere if the company is not growing. The optimal ratio depends on the individual firm, but the key decider is whether the company can produce better returns than the investor can earn elsewhere.

● **Cash Flow** Cash flow position is cash received minus cash distributed. The net cash flow can be taken from a company's statement of cash flows. Cash flow is important for what it reveals about a company's financing needs. A strong positive cash flow enables a company to fund future investments without having to borrow money from bankers or investors. This is desirable because the company avoids paying out interest or dividends. A weak or negative cash flow means that a company has to turn to external sources to fund future investments. Generally, companies in strong-growth industries often find themselves in a poor cash flow position (because their investment needs are substantial), whereas successful companies based in mature industries generally find themselves in a strong cash flow position.

A company's internally generated cash flow is calculated by adding back its depreciation provision to profits after interest, taxes, and dividend payments. If this figure is insufficient to cover proposed new investments, the company has little choice but to borrow funds to make up the shortfall or to curtail investments. If this figure exceeds proposed new investments, the company can use the excess to build up its liquidity (that is, through investments in financial assets) or repay existing loans ahead of schedule.

Conclusion

When evaluating a case, it is important to be *systematic*. Analyze the case in a logical fashion, beginning with the identification of operating and financial strengths and weaknesses and environmental opportunities and threats. Move on to assess the value of a company's current strategies only when you are fully conversant with the SWOT analysis of the company. Ask yourself whether the company's current strategies make sense given its SWOT analysis. If they do not, what changes need to be made? What are your recommendations? Above all, link any strategic recommendations you may make to the SWOT analysis. State explicitly how the strategies you identify take advantage of the company's strengths to exploit environmental opportunities, how they rectify the company's weaknesses, and how they counter environmental threats. Also, do not forget to outline what needs to be done to implement your recommendations.

Index